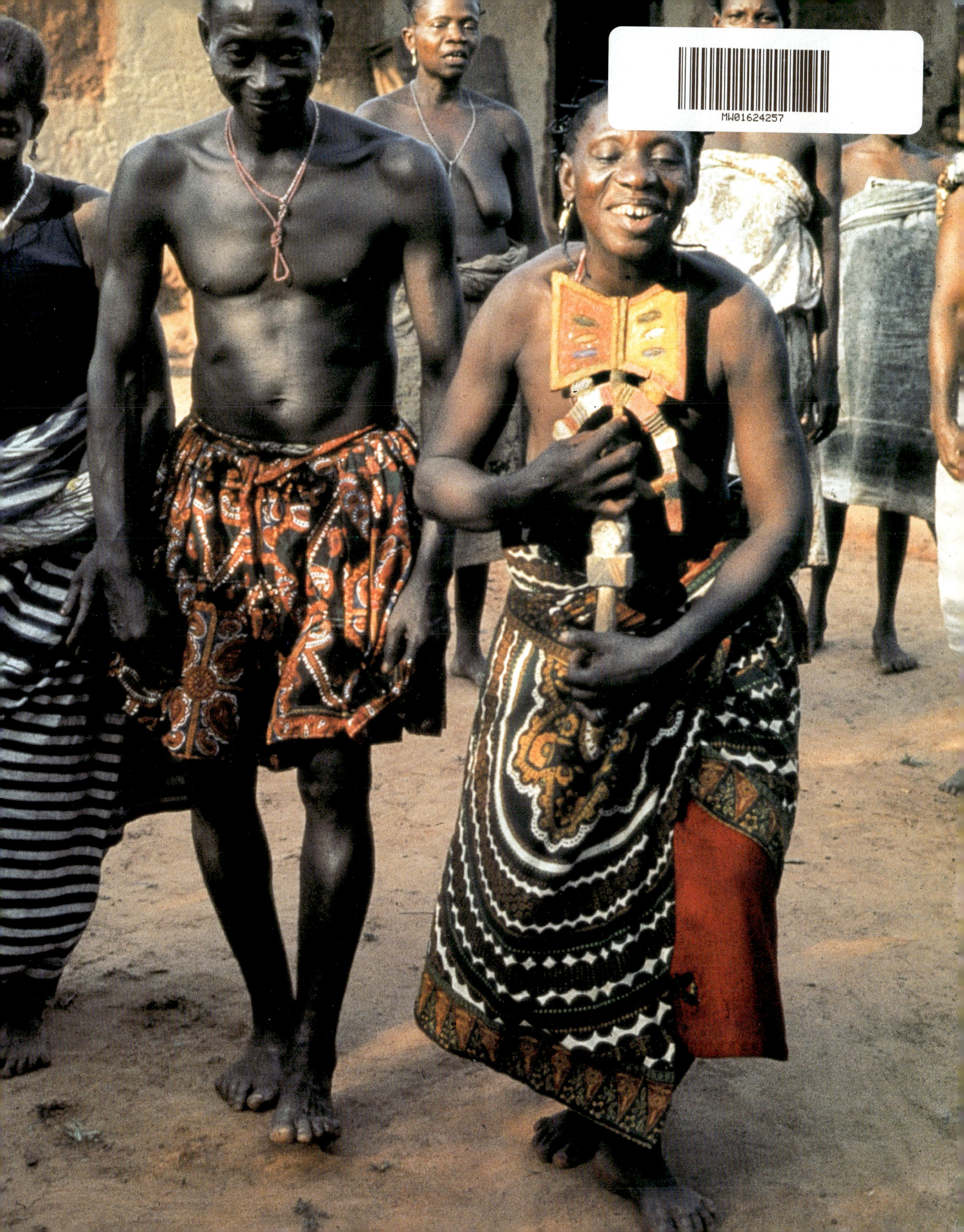

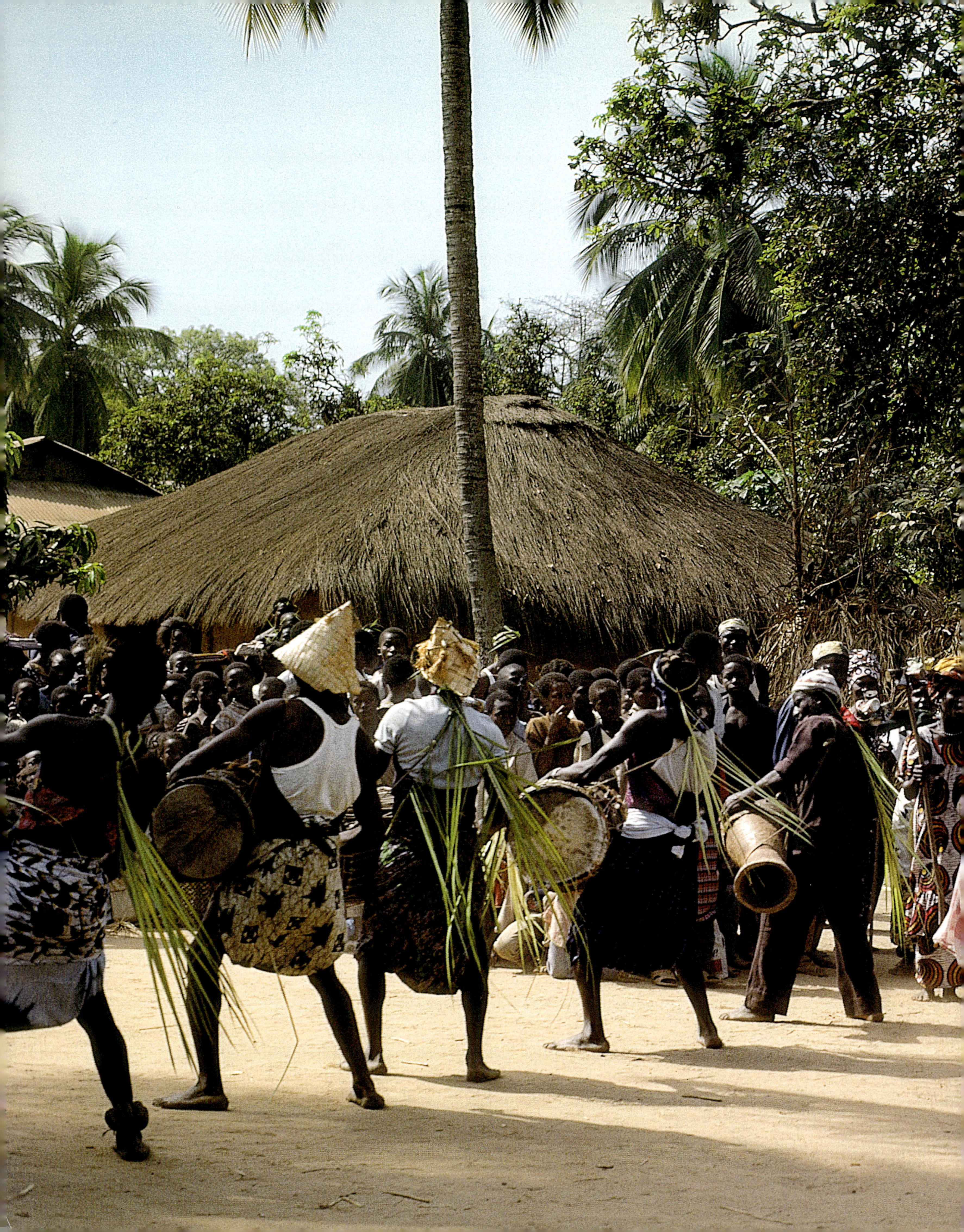

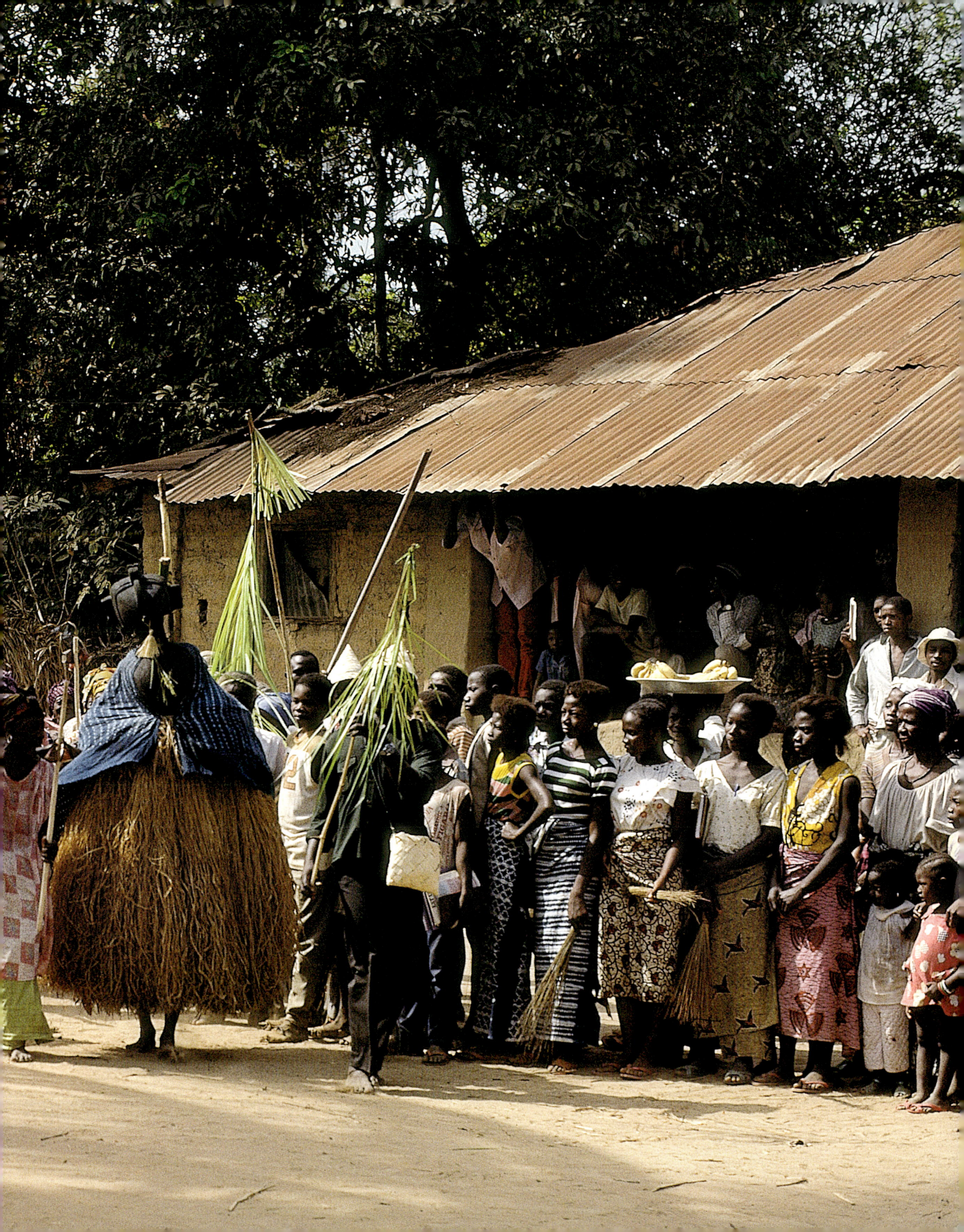

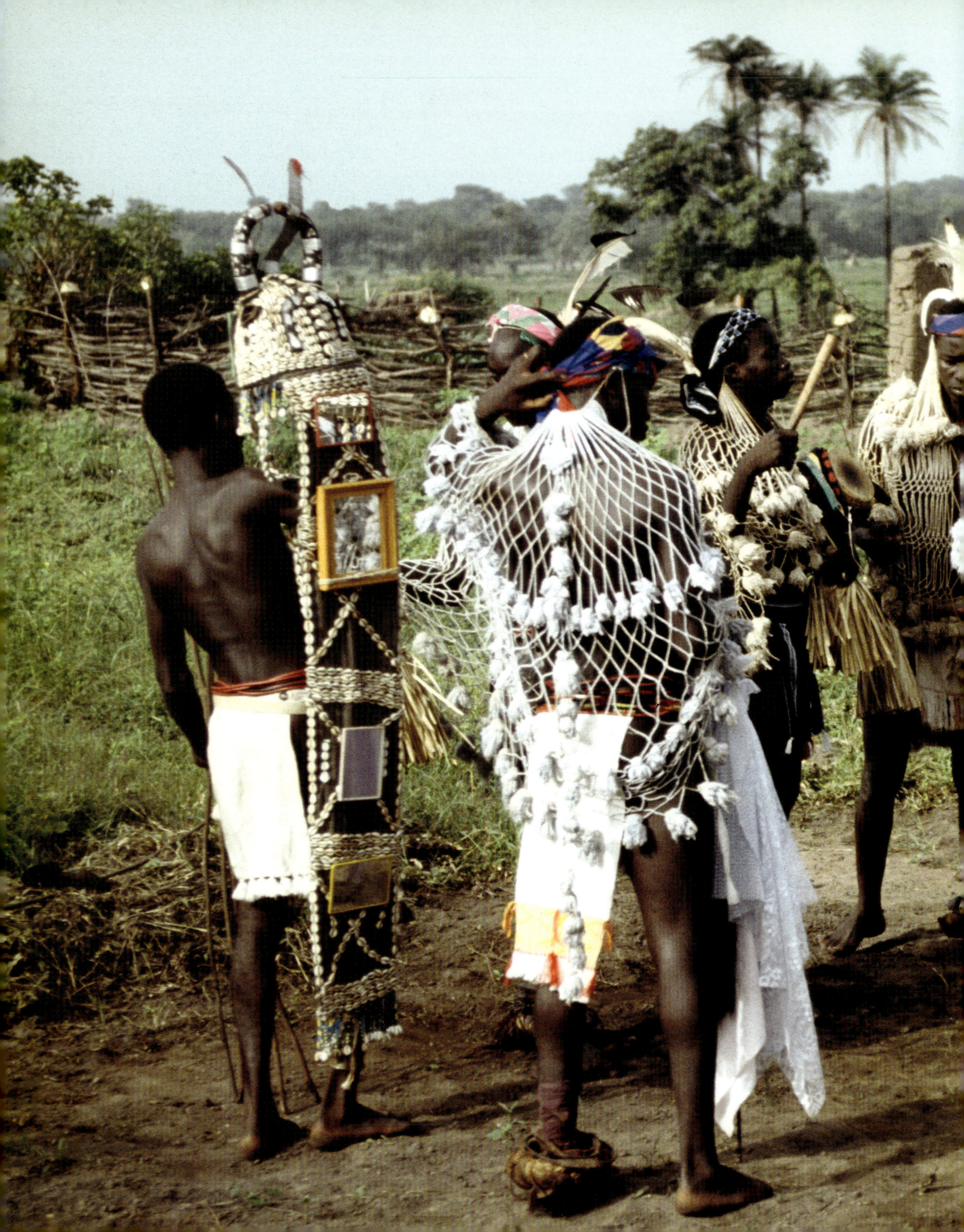

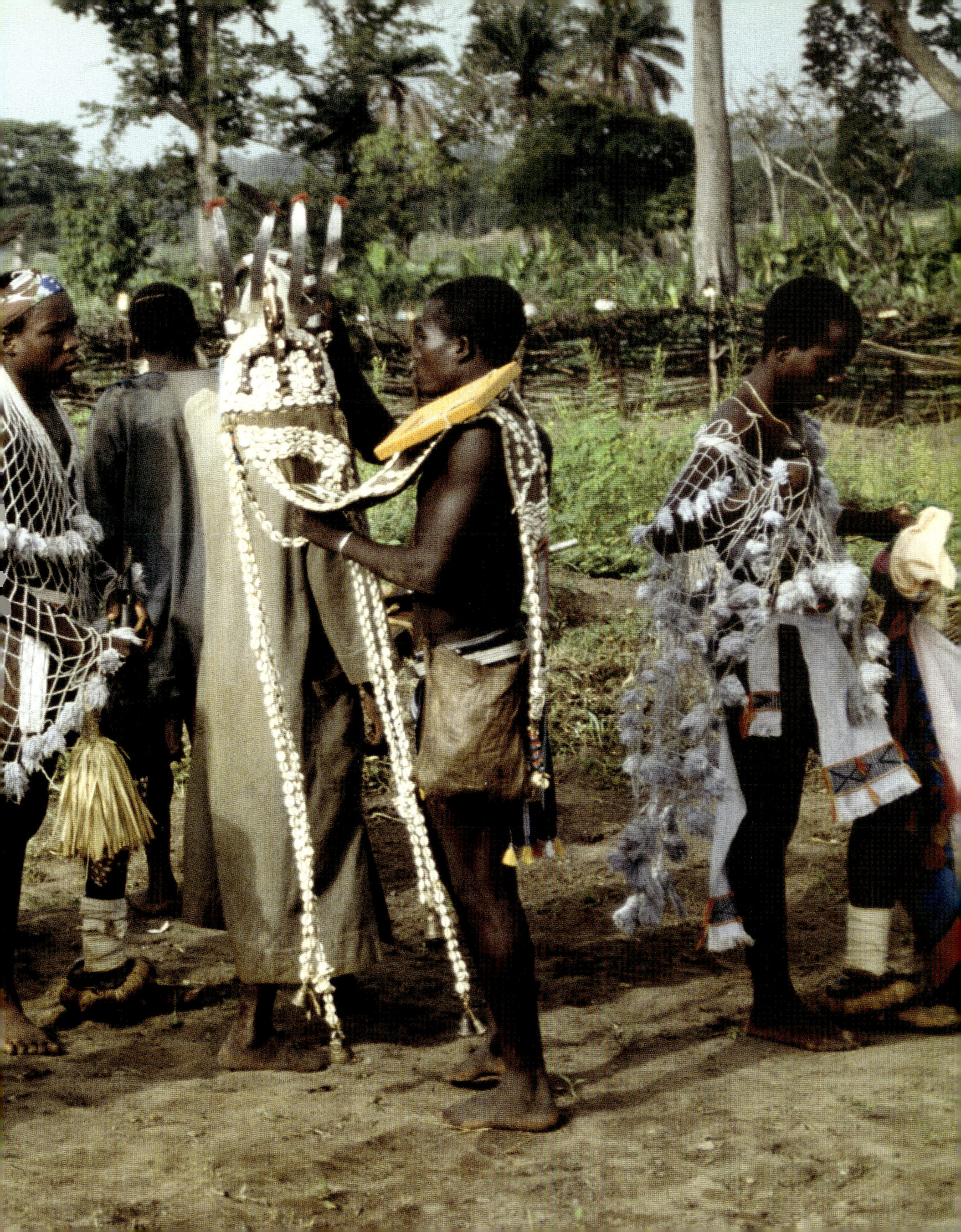

SEE THE MUSIC

HEAR THE DANCE

Rethinking African Art at The Baltimore Museum of Art

Edited by Frederick John Lamp

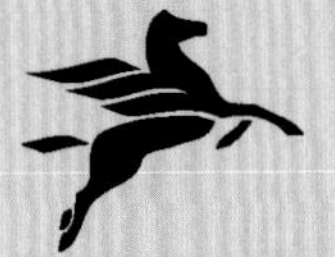

Prestel Munich · Berlin · London · New York

FOREWORD

This publication coincides with the ninetieth anniversary of the founding of The Baltimore Museum of Art and the fiftieth anniversary of the donation of the African art collection of Janet and Alan Wurtzburger, Baltimoreans whose prescient taste and infectious enthusiasm assured a significant place for this field within a growing institution. Their gift marked the beginning of a permanent display of African art at the Museum.

The Wurtzburger gift confirmed a direction already suggested by the Museum's exhibition program. In 1936 the BMA presented an exhibition circulated by the Museum of Modern Art, entitled *African Negro Art*, which drew largely from European collections, and ten years later, the BMA organized *An Exhibition of African Art*, one of the earliest exhibitions of African art from American collections in an American museum of art.

Even before the Wurtzburger's gift, ancient Egyptian and Coptic objects had been given by Florence Levy (1926) and Blanche Adler (1929-31), and this trend continued, with gifts from Saidie A. May (1951), Robert Garrett (1956), and Fulton Lesser (1961). Significant numbers of Coptic textiles were donated by Saidie A. May (1945) and Claribel and Etta Cone (1950), as well as more recently by Dena S. Katzenberg (1985), Kenneth S. Battye (1986), and Dirk Holger (1989). In 1947, a collector, Irene Gulck, donated the first fifteen objects of African art south of the Sahara, mostly simple tools and utilitarian items.

A room in the apartment of Claribel and Etta Cone. Baltimore, *c.* 1930s

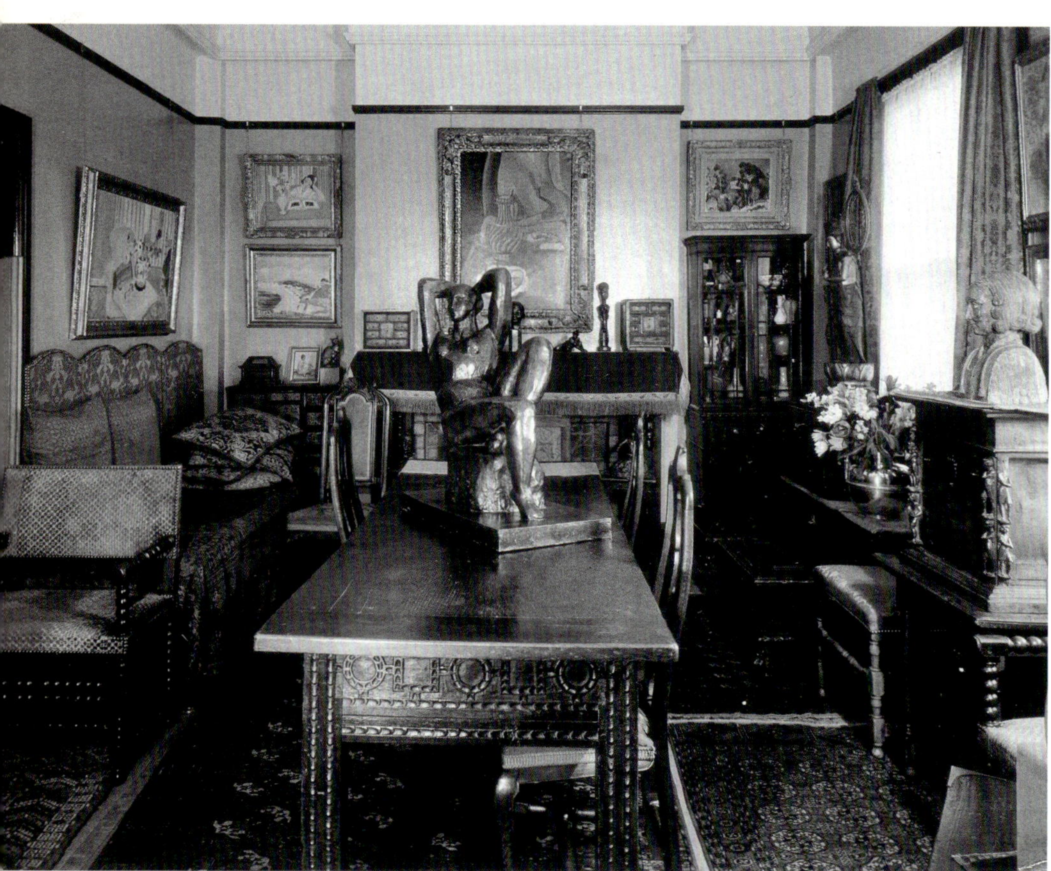

Like other scholars and collectors of their period, the Wurtzburgers entered the world of African art through the aesthetic of modern art, which valued its "primitive" qualities. So, too, did Claribel and Etta Cone, who formed a renowned collection of French nineteenth- and twentieth-century art, its highlight works by Henri Matisse. They added African objects to their holdings, presented in 1950, possibly through some excellent contacts in Paris, among them Gertrude Stein, Henri Matisse, and Pablo Picasso. In 1951 Saidie A. May, an extremely eclectic collector with a particular affection for the School of Paris, donated two items of African art, one obtained from the dealer, Pierre Matisse, Henri's son.

Donors from the city, the region, and the nation have contributed to the BMA collection. Baltimoreans Mr. and Mrs. A. Harvey Schreter, passionate world travelers, donated numerous objects, beginning thirty years ago. In the 1980s, many gifts were received from Dr. Robert Cumming and his wife Mary, a BMA docent for several years and a staff member from 1985 to 1992. In the 1980s and 1990s, Robert and Nancy Nooter of Washington D.C.; Dr. Barry and Toby T. Hecht of Bethesda, Maryland; and Nance Asher of Denton, Maryland, gave a significant groups of objects. Allen Davis, a former U.S. ambassador to a number of African countries, and his sons, made important additions to the collection. A generous collector who has shown a longtime commitment to the Museum is Bernice Barth, of Los Angeles, whose husband Arthur, was a well-known dealer.

A number of thoughtful donations have filled gaps and built particular strengths in the collection. Helen McElhiney, who lived in Ghana as the U.S. ambassador's wife from 1968 to 1971, donated 750 Akan brass miniatures. Dr. Caroline Popper presented sixty-nine objects of South African beadwork. Conrad Turner Bussell, who worked for the government of Liberia during the 1920s, and his wife Pauline received some fabulous gifts, among them the forty-one objects their son, Bruce, and his wife, Catherine, donated to the Museum in 1998. These are some of the people who created the African art collection at The Baltimore Museum of Art and who gave it the definition it exhibits today.

As principal author, Dr. Frederick John Lamp selected the featured objects from as broad a spectrum of geography and media as possible, including ritual and utilitarian art from throughout the continent—ceramics, textiles, costume, metalwork, beadwork, and leatherwork, as well as masks, headdresses, and figures. He chose the examples for their high aesthetic quality as well as for their ability to address the book's theme: the story of the collecting of art from Africa and the need to acknowledge the original larger artistic form.

The book's central focus is the performance of the objects in the context from which they originated. In his opening essay, Dr. Lamp challenges the customary museum presentation of the isolated object, stripped of many important artistic elements as it changed hands, from its African setting to the museum gallery. The chapter headings and succeeding essays on specific performances will help the reader understand that the museum object is

Male Figure
Bembe, Congo (Kinshasa)
c. Late 19th century
Wood, porcelain, H. 17.2 cm
The Cone Collection
BMA 1950.387
(possibly purchased from Gertrude Stein in Paris
in July 1925)

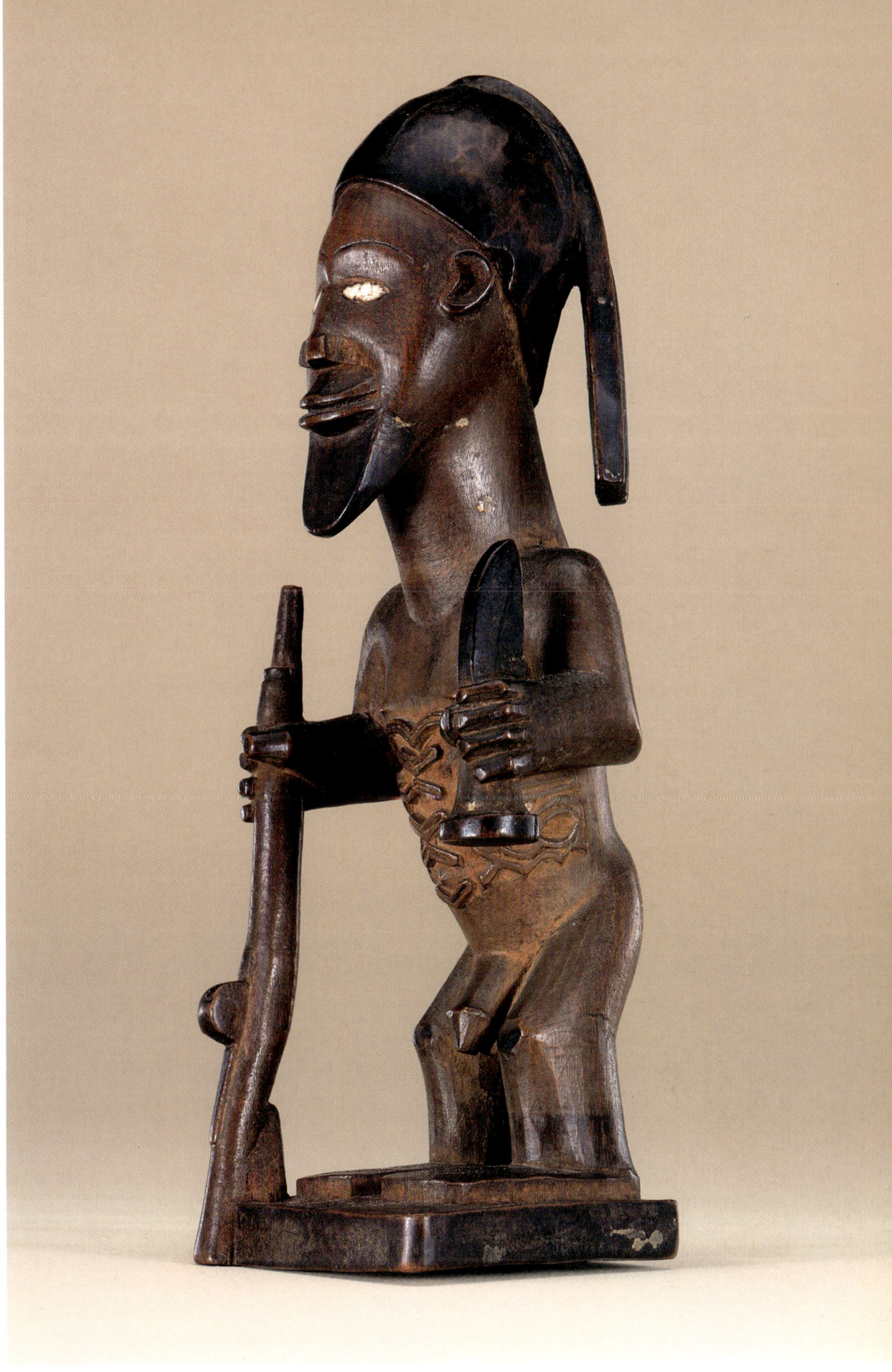

but a fragment of the original art form as conceived by its African community. To understand these art works, we must consider the other elements of the whole art form, such as movement, dance, theater, oral narrative, and costume. As Dr. Lamp argues in his essay, "It is time to show African art in its complexity, in time and space." We present this work as a contribution to the field of African art and to the enterprise of museums to show the best of the creative spirit of mankind in all its complexity. Above all, we wish for the reader and the Museum visitor the enjoyment of an art that has done so much to enrich our world.

We are grateful to all the contributors, but especially to Dr. Lamp, who has worked tirelessly to build and interpret the African art in the Museum's collection. This publication is a fitting culmination of his twenty-two years of curatorial work at the BMA, where he served as Curator of African Art, and Curatorial Department Head, Arts of Africa, Asia, the Americas & Oceania. It appears just as he assumes a new post as The Frances and Benjamin Benenson Curator of African Art at the Yale University Art Gallery.

Finally, we are able to make this great collection and fine scholarship accessible in this ambitious format through the generosity of The St. Paul Companies, Inc. and the National Endowment for the Arts, a federal agency, which has provided funding to underwrite this publication.

Doreen Bolger
Director
The Baltimore Museum of Art

ACKNOWLEDGEMENTS

The concept of the "fragment" to describe African art in museums can be traced to the preparation for a course I gave at The Baltimore Museum of Art many years ago, and benefited from the insights of students and colleagues as it grew into a small, preliminary manuscript, and then a paper presented at The Metropolitan Museum of Art, New York, for the Annual Meeting of the College Art Association in 2000. A director of an art museum might normally be reluctant to produce a book that focuses on what is not in the museum's possession, rather than a standard catalogue that celebrates objects. But immediately, upon her selection as Director of the BMA, Doreen Bolger envisioned the celebration of a fuller art form, and acted to put the production of the book in motion. I am grateful for her courage and foresight.

Many people along my path from graduate studies till today have planted the notions that have coalesced into the text presented here. In the formal study of dance, I owe deep gratitude to the late Shirley Wimmer for my introduction to African dance studies, and the late Irmgard Bartenieff for guiding me to look carefully at all parts of the body. Robert Farris Thompson, a giant in African movement studies, inspired many thoughts here, beginning with his groundbreaking exhibition *African Art in Motion*, and in our seminars on such things as mambo, script, and shrines in trans-Atlantic context, and he has continued to move me. In the course of my personal life I've been influenced by dancers Diane Frank, with whom I shared ten years, and Douglas Dunn, Merce Cunningham, Kevin Kortan, Olufunmilayo, the Baga dance master, Vincent Bangoura, and many others of whose artistic excellence and intellectual intensity I am in awe. Many conversations over the years with the late Arnold Rubin, Susan Vogel, Simon Ottenberg, Paula Girshick, Mary Jo Arnoldi, the late Roy Sieber, and many others too numerous to mention, in the study of African art, have helped me to formulate some of these ideas.

I would sincerely like to thank several leading scholars in particular fields for diligently reading through my entire set of introductory texts and providing helpful suggestions on issues and on the organization of the book. Herbert M. Cole thoroughly combed through the manuscript and, in his direct and no-nonsense way, was able to help me clear out the obstructions to readability, and to force me to rethink issues. Adrienne Kaeppler, who has worked with dance analysis and notation in the Pacific islands, helpfully guided my work throughout, and particularly my introductory remarks on movement. Frances Harding examined the work through the lens of theater and performance theory, and offered many helpful suggestions. Their guidance has been invaluable in the crafting of arguments made here, and any failure of the work reflects only on the author.

Many other scholars in the field of African studies have read parts of the manuscript, and have made suggestions. I would like to thank David Conrad for reading the Bamana texts and correcting translations as well as providing insights into Bamana thought. Patrick McNaughton contributed his guidance on Manding *Kòmò* society masking. Henry Drewal provided helpful information on Gelede headdresses, and on smells in Yoruba art performance that have been included in the text. Arthur Bourgeois assisted in sorting out the complexities of masking in southwestern Congo (Kinshasa). Doran Ross helped with sections dealing with the Akan. Betsy Bryan, Egyptologist at The Johns Hopkins University, and Regine Schulz, Curator of Ancient Art at the Walters Art Museum, provided guidance on the inclusion of Egyptian art in the book. Critical input has come also from David Binkley, Linda Giles, Barry Hecht, Christine Kreamer, David Morris, Robert and Nancy Nooter, Allen Roberts, Raymond Silverman, Barbara Thompson, and Robert Farris Thompson.

At The Baltimore Museum of Art, numerous staff members have work together to make the book possible. Michelle Boardman, Manager of Creative Services, worked fearlessly to negotiate with publishers, set production schedules, guide the physical assembly of the manuscript and illustrations, and to provide liaison between the author and administrative offices of the Museum. For the beauty and magnitude of this book, I am grateful for her persistence. Matthew Bender came on board to take charge of the mechanics of putting the book together, including the very daunting assembly of the visual aspects, e-mailing the far reaches of the globe to pursue precious illustrations and reproduction rights. In-house, the manuscript was read and critiqued at various stages by Michelle Boardman, Allison Perkins, Katherine Fernstrom, and Doreen Bolger. Viola Holmes, Administrative Assistant for the Department of the Arts of Africa, Asia, the Americas & Oceania, has helped over the years with many clerical aspects of the production. I would also like to thank Cecilia Meisner for her skills in producing the successful grant proposal that made this book possible. A number of interns, research assistants, and volunteers have helped with the search for data on African performance with respect to the Museum collection, including Lillian Maria Burgunder, Mary Cumming, Susan Elizabeth Gagliardi, Pawel Kozielski, and Louise MacDonald.

BMA photographer, Jose Sanchez, has been several years photographing the African collection for the book. I am indebted to him for his discerning eye, and for his patience for my always complicated demands. Beth Ryan, Coordinator of Rights & Reproductions, was instrumental in facilitating this monumental project.

Many, many people and institutions generously provided their field photography for inclusion in the book. These are too numerous to list here, but their names are attached to each illustration. This book is about the senses, and they have provided a feast for the eyes.

Thirty-five writers have contributed essays on particular performance contexts throughout Africa. Their names are listed with each essay, and a short biography of each is included at the end of the book. These writers worked hard to fulfill the mission of the book, searching back through their field notes and photography, some going back several decades, and producing original material that will be a lasting contribution to the fields of art history, dance ethnography, performance studies, folklore, and others. I am extremely grateful for their collaboration in this effort.

To the publishers at Prestel, I give my thanks for encouraging us to make this book all that it is, to foreground the performance aspects of African art and to celebrate this with visual magnificence. They have once again excelled in their wonderful design. I am grateful to Peter Stepan for his oversight of the project, Christopher Wynne, the final copy editor, and Petra Lüer who designed the layout.

Finally, the book could not have been produced without the subvension of the National Endowment for the Arts (NEA). Their generous grant, and patience over the years, has enabled us to greatly expand the concept of this publication. We are most grateful for their continuing support.

Frederick John Lamp

Praise singers playing the balaphone. Susu, northern Sierra Leone
Photo: Frederick John Lamp, 1976

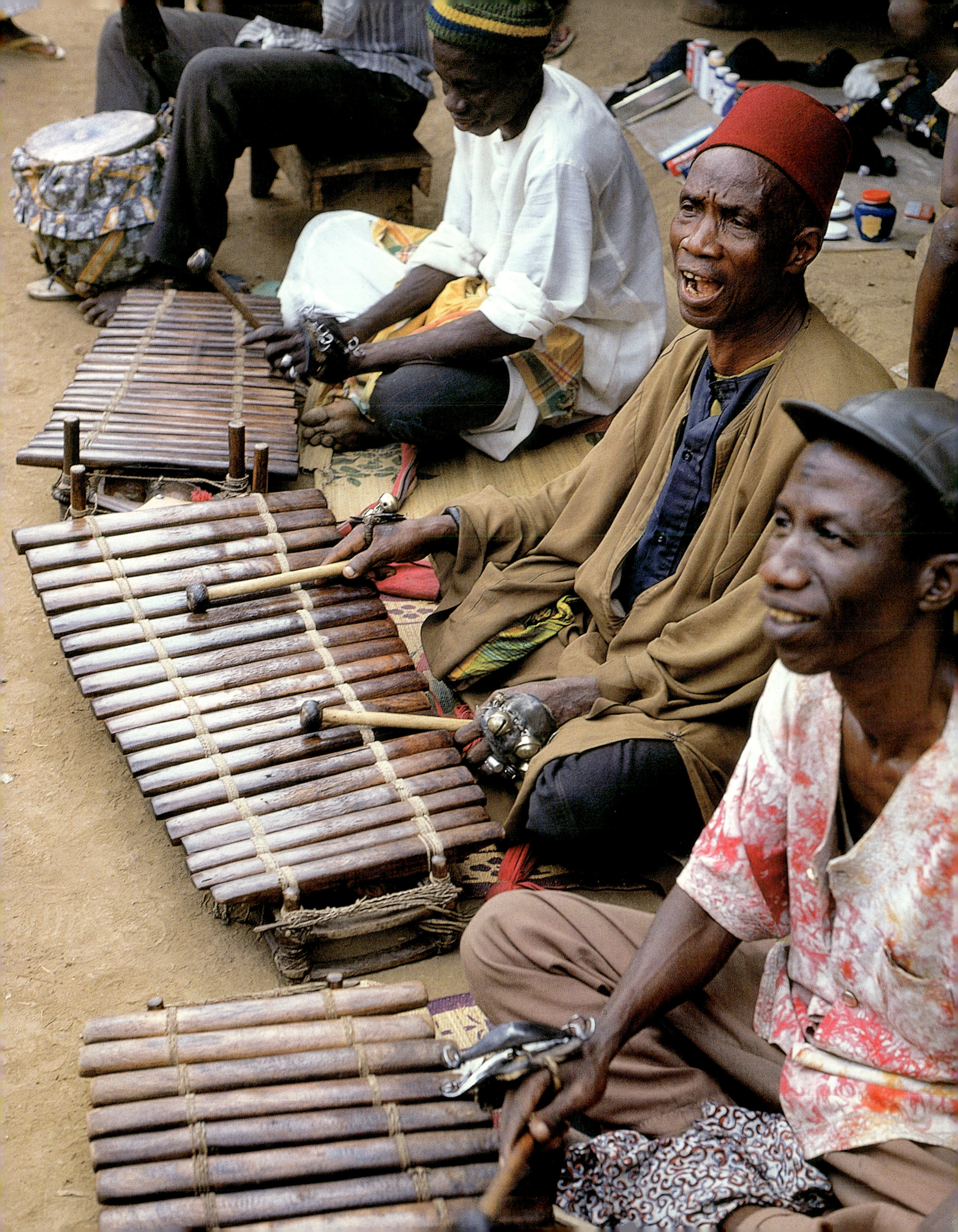

PROLOGUE

This is a book about performance art and ritual in Africa—focusing on human acts and creative processes rather than material products. Based upon selected objects from the African collection of material arts (often called "visual arts")[1] in The Baltimore Museum of Art, it recognizes that these objects are but fragments of a larger, integrated form of art as it is generally seen in Africa. This art involves not only the visual, and the sense of sight, but also the senses of hearing, smell, taste, and touch.

Performance and ritual are studied and presented today in a wide theoretical spectrum, for symbolism and meaning on the one hand, and individual creativity and departure from convention on the other. Many voices and views have been included here with no goal of absolute truth. Ritual may be traditional,[2] that is, "handed down," sometimes from indeterminate sources, but it is the variable acts of real people, with unique intentions, that give it life in performance and captivate the viewer. Some of these actors live in isolated societies cherishing ancestral ways and cultural codes while others enthusiastically embrace and adapt the contemporary and global culture of video, TV, and hip-hop.

As springboards for the essays in this study, a selection of the most significant objects from the BMA's collection of African art has been made. In celebrating these objects, we also confront the fact of their isolation in a museum exhibition, stripped of original artistic context through the changing of hands in the journey from Africa to the West.[3] Both the introductory essays and the individual essays on specific performances are designed to help the reader understand that the museum object is but one element of an original art form as conceived by its African community. Our goal here is to restore a sense of the whole art form, including such elements as movement, sound, theater, oral narrative, and costume.

African art is represented here in the broadest terms of media, style, function, cultural background, chronology, and geography. Essays have been written by scholars in their respective areas of expertise, and are presented here thematically. Included in this cultural survey of Africa is ancient Egypt, as a participant in the culture of black Africa from its earliest history,[4] the border of the Sahara, as it relates to black Africa, and the Northeast, the East, and southern Africa, regions often neglected in museum displays and in catalogues. These areas, together with West and Central Africa, offer a wide variety of ritual and utilitarian art throughout the continent—ceramics, textiles, costume, metalwork, beadwork, and leatherwork, as well as masks, headdresses, and figures.

The book does not attempt to represent an art history of Africa to the current period, but deals rather with historical periods corresponding to the BMA collection. The objects illustrated here are largely from the nineteenth and early twentieth centuries, and, in a few cases, antiquity. Several shifts are required to bring us to the present. First, the respective essays are based largely on performance data from field research conducted during the past four decades as well as historical sources, with some warp and tension inherent. The photography from this field research already represents another era, most taken two or three decades ago. Second, today we are at a further remove even from the time of much of this field research. Many rituals represented here are no longer practiced at all; others continue, but they often respond today to new circumstances in both form and meaning. Furthermore, from the last third of the twentieth century onward, African artists have begun to address the world at large, often identifying more with the international community of artists than with regional sets of patronage and concern. Contemporary Africa has, to a large degree, reinvented itself, and in many cases, moved beyond the sculptural and utilitarian traditions represented by this collection, drawing as much, or more, upon global culture.

In the "Overture" and supporting performance essays we examine the nature of African art collecting and how this, in very significant ways, has inadvertently misled the Western public about African art. The American artist, Fred Wilson, recently expressed this deception in a work displayed at the Museum for African Art, New York, in the form of a mask blindfolded and gagged with strips of the Union Jack (see below). Traditional art has been muted by its removal from Africa, and the viewer misses the context of the work. We explore here how

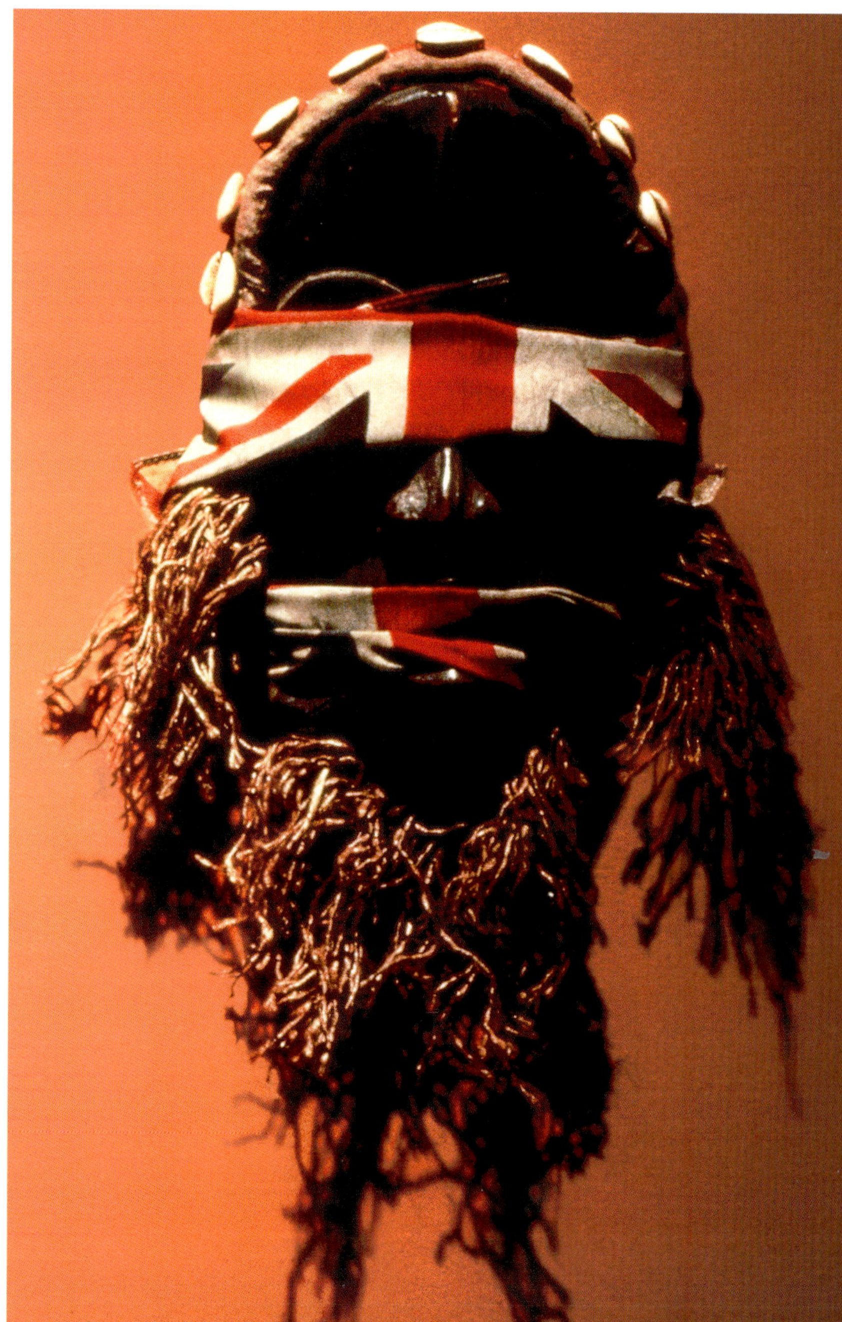

Dan Mask, assemblage by Fred Wilson, *c.* 1990
Courtesy Metro Pictures, New York

such a deception, naively unintended, might be redressed. We have understood for decades that African art is an integration of the arts, not imply isolated sculpture meant for the pedestal or vitrine, but few art museums have acted upon this knowledge in reinstalling their collections and reinterpreting them for their audiences. The BMA hopes that this publication will serve as an intellectual underpinning for future exhibition strategies both here and throughout the museum world and for accompanying educational and interpretive efforts. We also hope it will move the academic community more in the direction of interdisciplinary collaboration and a reconsideration of the primacy of sculpture in a holistic art.

The complexity of African art in its context of performance and installation, movement, and placement, and the extravaganza of the total involvement of viewer and performer is what we strive to present in this publication. Herbert Cole and Chike Aniakor (1984:111) have said of Igbo masquerades in Nigeria, "Masking clearly must be visualized from many perspectives to reach any real understanding, a point well-made in the proverb, 'You cannot be at one spot to watch a masquerade.'" Within these pages we set forth a series of contextual elements—audience, timing, light, serendipity, costuming, dance, movement, gesture, music, narrative, associated objects, staging, smells, taste, and touch—which enliven the material object in its original artistic context. Along with considerations of how the object may have been altered on its path from African creator to museum visitor, the discussion here offers a point of departure for the re-presentation of African art to the public.

Above all, we attempt to show that the elements of African performance are fluid and integrated, and must be experienced in the body to be fully understood. We breathe, regard, feel, listen to, and grasp African art. The elements of performance are so closely intertwined, as suggested by a former director of the Ghana Dance Ensemble, A. M. Ipoku (in Hampton 1982), as to be almost indistinguishable: one must "see the music and hear the dance."

Frederick John Lamp

1 I use the term "material arts" rather than "visual arts," not because material is necessarily central to sculpture, painting, ceramics, etc., above visual appreciation, intellect and process, but because it distinguishes these arts from other arts, which are not dependent upon material other than architecture. Dance, theater, and even music, are also "visual arts." The term "plastic arts" expresses somewhat the same distinction, although it is ambiguous and is not often used today. "Material culture" encompasses material arts as well as any material fabrication by human beings.

2 By the term "traditional" I assume foundation upon a shared memory, or an "encompassing memory" (Pemberton & Afolayan 1996:10), which implies either conscious or unconscious repetition and fidelity to what is known, but also accommodation to contingencies, dependent upon changing perceptions and the vagaries of memory.

3 The terms "West" and "Westerners" refer here to cultures and societies of European descent, whether in Europe itself or elsewhere, for example, the Americas, Australia, or white South Africa.

4 The decision to include Egypt in the rubric of African culture is based upon a current consensus between many established Egyptologists and Africanists that ancient Egypt, though a Mediterranean civilization in part, should be considered as African antiquity, just as ancient Greece, also a Mediterranean civilization, is commonly considered the antiquity and heritage of all Europe. Most Egyptologists now acknowledge that ancient Egypt was a crossroads between black Africa and the Near East. Nubians moved northward as the "Asiatics" moved southward, resulting in a wide physiological range. While the ancient Egyptians from Lower and Upper Egypt distinguished themselves in their art clearly from both the Asiatics and the Nubians, Egyptologists agree that the physical variation of the ancients from north to south corresponds closely to that of the modern Egyptians, who have little Arabic genetic input, in contrast to the rest of North Africa (Betsy Bryan, personal communication, 2002). That is to say that the ancient Egyptians, like their modern counterparts, were of medium-dark skin, black-haired often with a nap, fitting a common, contemporary definition of "black". Cranial studies have shown that the predynastic Upper Egyptians (those of the upper reaches of the Nile) resembled more closely their southern neighbors, the Nubians, than they did the Lower Egyptians in the North (Keita 1996). Egyptian populations, from royalty on down, are now assumed—with some support from DNA studies (Ehret 1996)—also to have had Nubian blood throughout much of ancient Egyptian history. Culturally, ancient Egypt was little influenced by the Near East. The ancient Egyptian language was closely related to Kushitic, of Nubia, as well as Berber, Omotic, and Chadic, and less to Near Eastern Semitic (Ehret 1996). In each of the three great periods of ancient Egyptian history—the Old Kingdom, the Middle Kingdom, and the New Kingdom—Nubia, in part or in whole, formed part of the Egyptian Unified Kingdoms, and Nubians were found in abundance living throughout Egypt (forming portions of the military and artisan classes, for example). One of the most important art-producing dynasties, the 25th, was Nubian, and these black pharaohs took responsibility for continuing Egyptian and Kushite traditions and religion, while their Egyptian subjects accepted them not as conquerors but as a legitimate new dynasty from within. Precedents to dynastic Egyptian culture have been suggested in Nubian culture, and affinities with Egyptian cultural forms are plentiful throughout contemporary and historical Africa, although these are areas of study only now developing.

Map of Africa with peoples to whom works in this volume are attributed

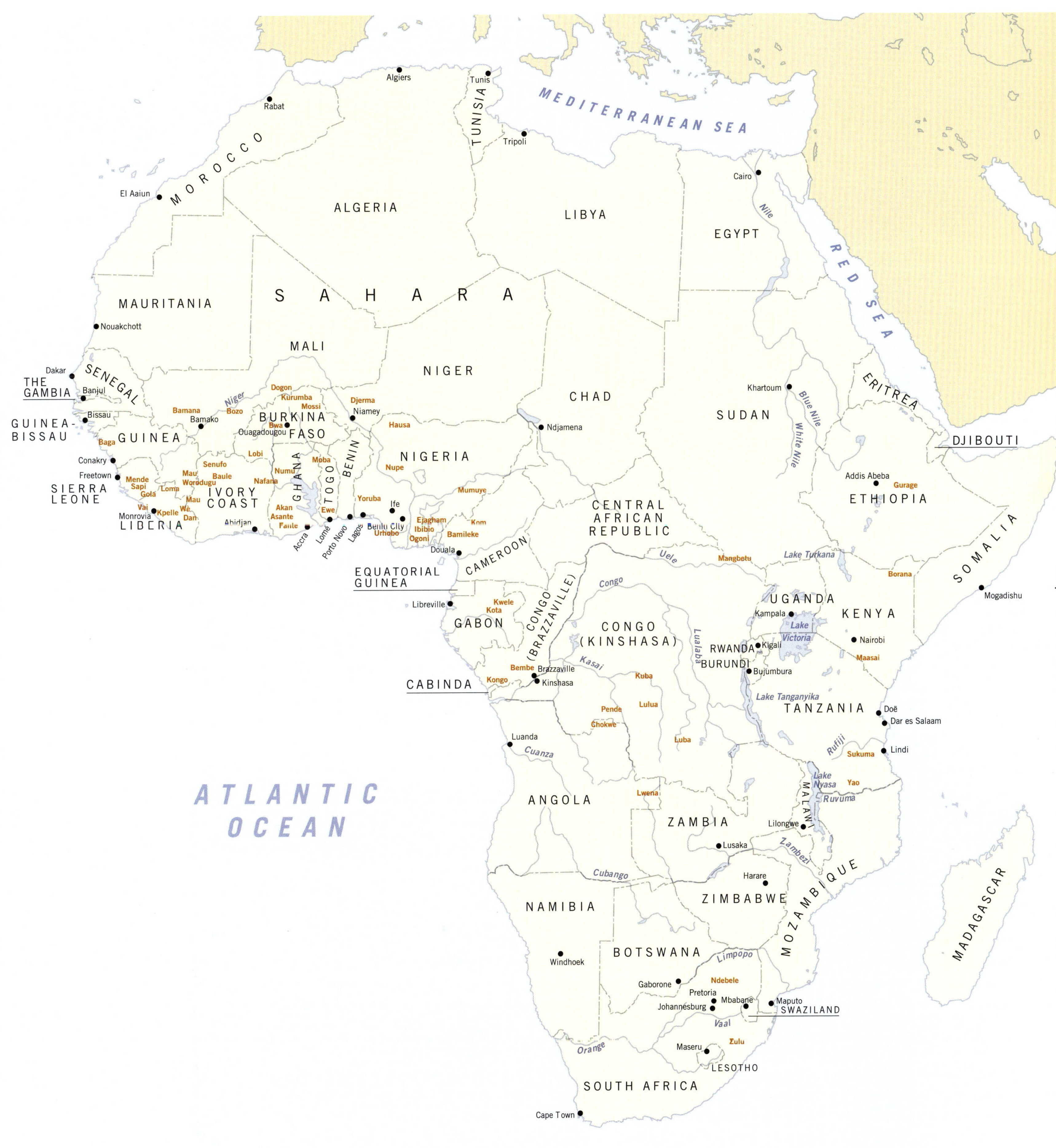
MEDITERRANEAN SEA
RED SEA
ATLANTIC OCEAN
SAHARA
MOROCCO
ALGERIA
TUNISIA
LIBYA
EGYPT
MAURITANIA
MALI
NIGER
CHAD
SUDAN
ERITREA
DJIBOUTI
ETHIOPIA
SOMALIA
SENEGAL
THE GAMBIA
GUINEA-BISSAU
GUINEA
SIERRA LEONE
LIBERIA
IVORY COAST
BURKINA FASO
GHANA
TOGO
BENIN
NIGERIA
CAMEROON
CENTRAL AFRICAN REPUBLIC
EQUATORIAL GUINEA
GABON
CONGO (BRAZZAVILLE)
CONGO (KINSHASA)
CABINDA
UGANDA
KENYA
RWANDA
BURUNDI
TANZANIA
ANGOLA
ZAMBIA
MALAWI
MOZAMBIQUE
ZIMBABWE
NAMIBIA
BOTSWANA
SWAZILAND
LESOTHO
SOUTH AFRICA
MADAGASCAR
Algiers
Tunis
Rabat
Tripoli
Cairo
El Aaiun
Nouakchott
Dakar
Banjul
Bissau
Bamako
Conakry
Freetown
Monrovia
Abidjan
Ouagadougou
Niamey
Accra
Lomé
Porto Novo
Lagos
Ife
Benin City
Ndjamena
Khartoum
Addis Abeba
Mogadishu
Douala
Libreville
Brazzaville
Kinshasa
Kampala
Kigali
Bujumbura
Nairobi
Doë
Dar es Salaam
Lindi
Luanda
Lilongwe
Lusaka
Harare
Windhoek
Gaborone
Pretoria
Johannesburg
Mbabane
Maputo
Maseru
Cape Town
Nile
Blue Nile
White Nile
Niger
Uele
Congo
Lualaba
Kasai
Cuanza
Lake Turkana
Lake Victoria
Lake Tanganyika
Rufiji
Lake Nyasa
Ruvuma
Zambezi
Cubango
Limpopo
Vaal
Orange
Dogon
Kurumba
Mossi
Djerma
Bamana
Bozo
Bwa
Hausa
Baga
Lobi
Senufo
Moba
Mende
Sapi
Gola
Mau
Baule
Worodugu
Numu
Nafana
Nupe
Loma
Mau
Vai
Kpelle
We
Dan
Akan
Asante
Fante
Ewe
Yoruba
Ejagham
Ibibio
Urhobo
Ogoni
Bamileke
Kom
Mumuye
Mangbetu
Borana
Gurage
Kwele
Kota
Bembe
Kongo
Kuba
Lulua
Pende
Chokwe
Luba
Maasai
Sukuma
Yao
Lwena
Ndebele
Zulu

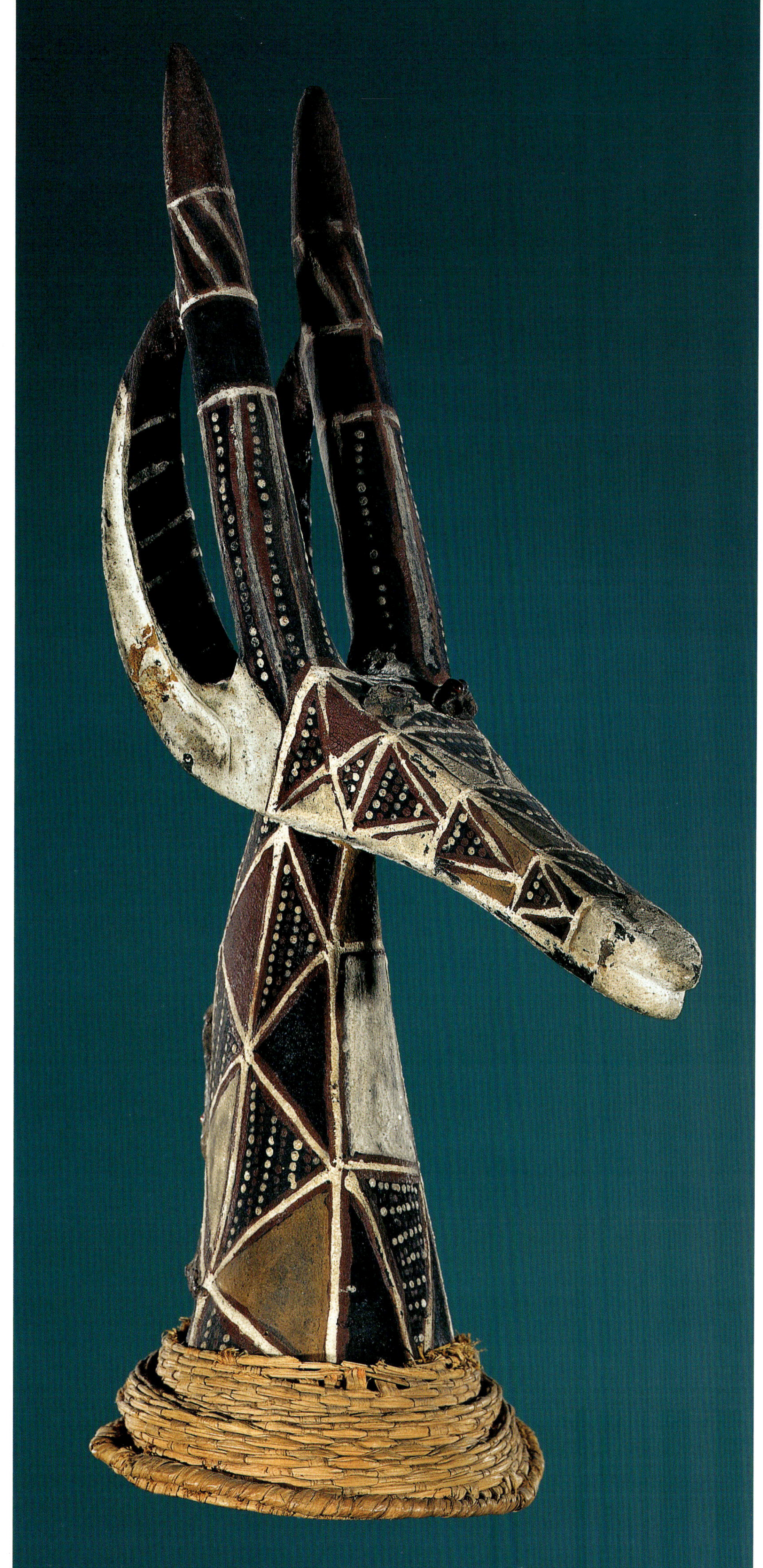

OVERTURE: A CONSIDERATION OF THE FRAGMENT

Antelope Headdress
Kurumba, Burkina Faso
c. Early 20th century
Wood, clay, reeds, seeds, polychrome, H. 45.5 cm
Gift of Alan Wurtzburger
BMA 1954.145.9

Today, we are searching for ways to express how African art is experienced in Africa—how it is conceived by the African artist, how it appears to the African public, and what expectations that public has of the art form. In this opening essay, we explore the specific ways in which the art form has been silenced, how the viewer has been misled, and how such a misrepresentation might be redressed. We focus on the whole form, including all its artistic components—of which the museum object is but a fragment.

In the museum, we regard African objects placed on walls or pedestals in quiet contemplation. Yet when we see the same objects in their original contexts, in videos, films, and photographs, we realize that a museum display is often quite antithetical to their original nature. There are no easy solutions to the problem of showing complex, time-based performance art in a static museum context (p. 20). The incongruity of African art in the gallery was the subject of a major exhibition, *ART/artifact: African Art in Anthropology Collections*, in 1989, at The Center for African Art in New York. In the introduction to the catalogue, Susan Vogel, wrote:

> An examination of how we view African objects (both literally and metaphorically) is important because unless we realize the extent to which our vision is conditioned by our own culture—unless we realize that the image of African art we have made a place for in our world has been shaped by us as much as by Africans—we may be misled into believing that we see African art for what it is.... Most visitors are unaware of the degree to which their experience of any art in a museum is conditioned by the way it is installed (*ART* 1989:11).

In reaction to the decontextualizing of the isolated African object in a museum gallery, a concept has arisen of the "ensemble" in African art, as emphasized again in a 1985 exhibition and publication by Vogel with George Preston. Though we have always understood that African art functions within a cultural context—and that has been well explored—we have paid little attention to the fact that the objects we call African art function within a larger art form that is extremely complex and crosses the lines of the various arts as they are conceived in Western society. These arts would be effectively studied in a collaboration between art historians and anthropologists, who comprise the bulk of African art scholars today, together with ethnomusicologists, architectural historians, dance historians and ethnologists, folklorists, and scholars of performance studies. Holistic studies would draw these disciplines together in a way consistent with the nature of the art of Africa. Clearly, we can little understand African art if we study primarily the material forms that exist in collections as the art form.

We began this book with a foreword offering a brief history of how African art objects entered the collection of The Baltimore Museum of Art. Here we attempt to trace the customary path that African art objects take from their origins in African communities to the walls and pedestals of museums in the West, by which the original art forms become stripped to mere fragments.

From the African Context to an American Museum

> After time and storms have passed, we catch the flotsams on the surface of our memory just as at the bank of our emotions, we collect the jetsams. Time destroys. Time alters. We accept these destructions, these alterations of time, integrating them eventually into our set of aesthetic values, even preferring in some instances the way they are to the way they were.
> Arman, American artist (1980)

> We now declare that the trademark [of the Ivory Coast] will be the mask, for it is representative of this country, rather pleasing to the eye, and enshrouded with an air of mystery.
> Duon Sadia, Minister of Tourism, Ivory Coast, 1982
> (Steiner 1994:95)

The tour that an African art object often takes—from the time it leaves its home in an African community to its placement on a pedestal in an American museum—is a long and reductive one. Along the way, the object becomes "processed" for consumption by an audience that does not share the fundamental assumptions under which the art was created. We now follow that path from Africa to America (or elsewhere out of context), and discuss the ways in which the form of the art changes and, ultimately, the way that the history of African art becomes distorted.

We begin in the African community, through the agency of a person called, for better or worse, "the runner." The runner is an African trader or purchaser who is the initial contact with the original owner of the African art object. The profession is almost exclusively male-dominated.[1] He is generally not a member of the ethnic group from which the object originates, and often a member of a group that has been Islamized (generally the case in West Africa).

Until several decades ago, the work of the runner was confined almost completely to the continent of Africa, and, indeed, to a relatively small region.[2]

In West Africa, runners are most frequently members of either the Malinke or Wolof ethnic groups, from Senegal to the Ivory Coast, or of the Hausa ethnic group, further east, from the Ivory Coast through Cameroon. The Hausa, Wolof, and Malinke have been Islamized for many centuries—the Islamic factor is especially important because of the specific interdiction by Islam of the carving of images. None of these groups produces sculpture for indigenous ritual on the scale of their surrounding neighbors, although some exceptions are featured in this book (pp. 64, 233). One particular Hausa runner/trader by the name of Malam Yaaro revealed his ambivalence about the trade to Christopher Steiner (1994:53):

> "I had left home to earn money, but I had no more job. I saw people making good money selling art. I knew God didn't approve of this kind of work.... When you have nothing and you need to eat you sometimes have to do things that God doesn't like."

Another of Steiner's consultants was more direct (p. 88):

> To these people the masks were fetishes. For those of us who sell masks, however, we can touch them all we want. We don't give a damn. Even if they tell me that there's a certain kind of mask that prevents you from sleeping at night, I could take it home with me and use it as a pillow. Because I don't believe in these things.

The runner, then, often has a certain disdain for the art-producing groups, which he considers retrograde in cultural development. At the same time, he is quite familiar with these ethnic groups, spends time with them, and sometimes even lives among them in their villages, gaining a bit of additional income through the sale of Islamic amulets and his religious expertise. The runner is able, therefore, to make a fairly complete inventory of the art objects that are used in a particular community and of human contacts who will eventually be able to act as agents in the traffic of objects from that community.[3]

The runner often canvasses a large territory, traveling from village to village, getting to know the chief persons in charge in every corner of the region. It is for this reason that this person is called a runner. He may travel from two to four hundred kilometers into the interior of the country to obtain the objects of his trade, on a very arduous, time-consuming, and exhausting journey. Transport is extremely difficult; the runner rarely has his own vehicle and is at the mercy of public transportation in the form, generally, of covered pickup trucks or buses. A journey of sixty or seventy kilometers may take an entire day. Often the passengers are required to sleep overnight by the side of the road. Many times in the year, the roads are virtually unpassable. Many areas cannot be reached by motor vehicle at all and require the runner to travel long distances by foot over mountains and through swamps, fording rivers, and facing a great many hazards.

The installation of African art. Wurtzburger Gallery
The Baltimore Museum of Art, 1996. ©Mark Lee Photo, Inc.

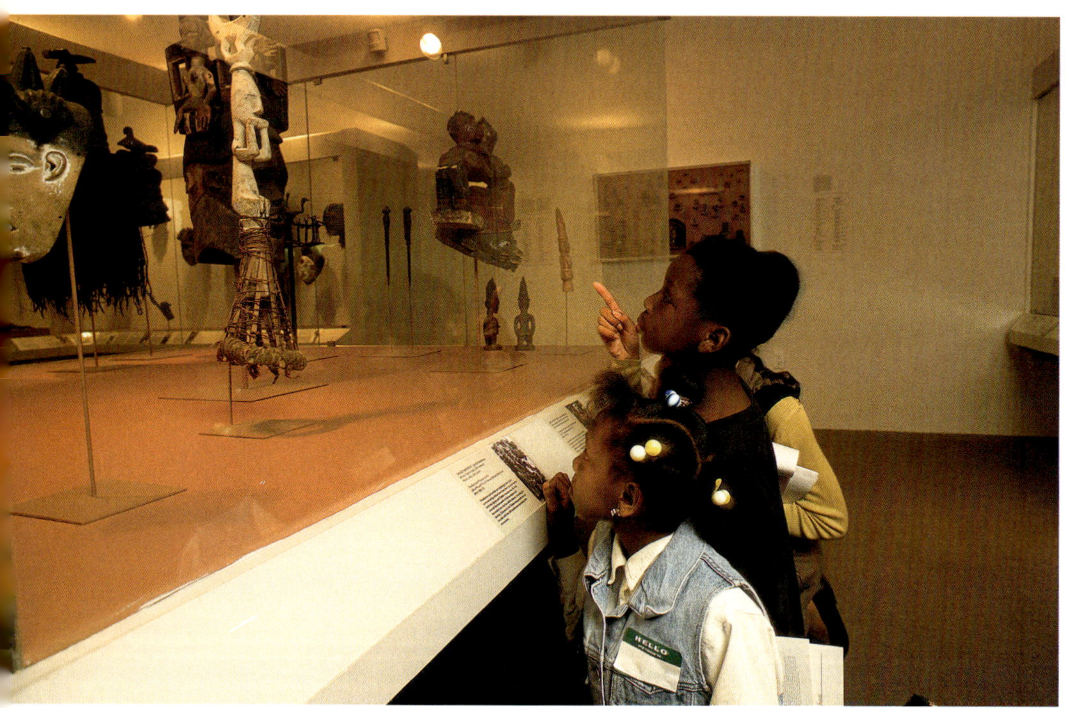

The runner prefers not to carry a lot of baggage, yet, of course, carrying baggage is central to his occupation. His solution is to lighten his load as much as he can, and this often involves stripping away some of the bulkier, less portable, and less marketable elements of the object that he is to carry over a long distance. If the object is an immense costume that includes a carved wooden mask and perhaps a large mantle of raffia and cloth, the runner is likely to detach the raffia mantle or at least to reduce it. If there are a great many cumbersome attachments to the costume itself, he may discard some of these, although more savvy runners today recognize their increasing market value. One can be sure in almost any case that the runner, at least through the 1980s, would arrive at his destination with an object greatly reduced from its original form.

There may also be a second reason why the runner reduces the material volume. Material things contain information, and some things might indicate origin. Steiner (1994:77) has found that a runner's sources upcountry in the villages are closely guarded. Secrecy is an important market strategy. As one of Steiner's consultants noted, "If everyone knew the same thing, then there would be no market." By stripping the object to its minimum, it loses context in a number of senses. It can no longer be traced so easily by those who might have seen it in a performance.

A further consideration, possibly even more important than marketing secrecy, would be along the lines of a fundamental argument on the nature of African art. Runners, though they may be intelligent and even cunning, do not usually share the cutting edge with current scholarship on postmodern thought. By stripping the art form down to the most essential (and essentialist), anonymous, ethnic, sterile, and pristine form, they are erasing its personal identity. Now the object is not, say, the mask with the personal name, "Beast of the Sound of Thunder," that belonged to the *Pòrò* elders of a village named Gbignamou, once danced by an individual by the name of Soriba Vorkpor, but it is simply "Kpelle mask."

The runner's client is often the African "trader," a name used to distinguish them from the itinerant runner and also from the more respectable "dealer." In fact, there is little boundary between the two, as many traders, with market stalls in the capital city, also travel upcountry in search of art (pp. 21, 22). The African trader usually lives in a great port city (sea or air), for example, Monrovia, Liberia (until the civil war).[4] To these great centers, most African art sold to foreigners has filtered down from the surrounding area in each respective country as well as from neighboring countries further inland that do not have a large tourist trade. The African trader is likely to be less in touch with the communities of origin than the runner (unless they are one in the same) and less knowledgeable about the context of the art objects and their meaning, but he is more in touch with the world of collecting outside of Africa—the culture of his clientele.

The African trader has a shop generally in the central area of the city, and he stores a great many objects for months and years and sometimes decades before he finds a client who wants to buy them. He is usually tied to a large storehouse, which most buyers never see. Other traders may operate out of a market stall, surrounded by onions, tomatoes, used television parts, and cow horns. Others set up roadside stands, or travel with display boxes to lay out their wares in front of hotels or on beaches, and go door-to-door to the homes of expatriates (Steiner 1994:19–33, 46). The trader is very much in touch with what the foreign collector wants, and responds to this not only with his selection of purchases from the runner, but also in what he will proffer, to which clients, and what will be the condition of the objects before they reach the clients. The trader's clientele consists of the usual tourist, the more knowledgeable field researcher, and the very savvy art dealer from Europe and America.[5]

The ordinary tourist, as well as some of the European or American residents working in Africa who are carrying or shipping objects home from Africa, would rather not ship a great deal of bulk. The category of "suitcase-sized" art has, therefore, arisen in Africa. The European or American dealer, as well, does not want to carry, and pay for, a great weight in the form of attachments and ritual accoutrements, although he or she will be interested in large objects of sculpture in wood, bronze, or clay. In this way, the complex object as it was used in ritual, becomes stripped down even more.

The African trader may remove what is left of the costume, if any, and sometimes separately sell attachments to the headdress, the main figure, or a set, such as miniature figures once forming part of the contents of a Chokwe divination container (p. 23). Other, less marketable parts, such as medicine bottles attached to a Dan mask (pp. 40, 99) might simply be discarded. In some cases, more horrendous reduction has taken place, such as the cutting of a sculpture into parts for easier resale, especially in cases of multiple figural sculpture or utilitarian objects that include figural embellishment. Decorative figures have been cut from Chokwe chairs and figural groups, and individualized figures forming part of a complex composite in a Cameroon door frame have been removed (pp. 24, 25). The African trader is aware that his clientele often values a more reduced, streamlined, simple version of the art form. He may, in some extreme cases, even alter the surface of an object or reconfigure it to make it more palatable to Western eyes. This may include dulling the surface of painted objects, recarving certain portions, or adding portions that did not originally exist.

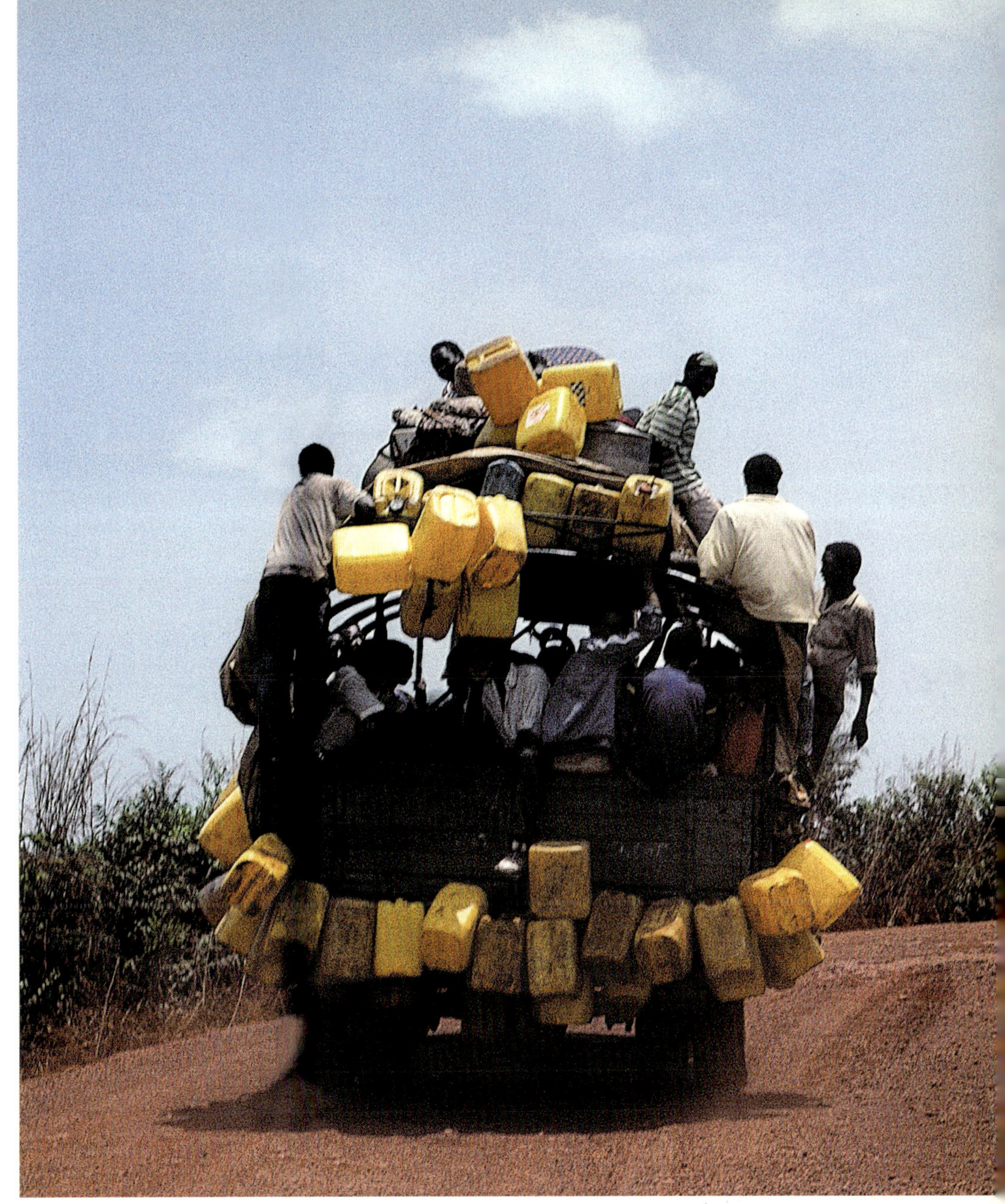

Public transportation in the interior. Guinea
Photo: Frederick John Lamp, 1990

Steiner (1994:143–151) found that African traders have become aware that their European and American clients prefer nude Baule figures (p. 139) over those carved with a loincloth or other clothes, assuming that nude figures predate those with clothes. Figures fully clothed, which the Baule themselves often commissioned for ritual use, to signal success or high status, could not even be given away (before "colon" figures—carved in the colonial period representing Europeans or Africans and European dress—became trendy). "Traders have responded to this preference among collectors by systematically removing, with the use of a chisel or knife, the wooden loincloths which cover the Baule figures ... The unstained wood which is left as a result of this process is restained with an appropriate dye, and an old piece of fabric is tied around the figure's waist to cover the damage."

We and the object now move to the third step in the emigration process, that is, to the European or American dealers. These dealers rarely search for objects in the villages of origin (there are notable exceptions, especially Belgian dealers), but negotiate with the African trader who has amassed a great number of objects from which the dealers can choose. In the past, these have been much more savvy about the desires of the European and American clientele than either the African traders or runners, although with global trade and easier communications, this is changing. Dealers know that collectors generally disdain objects that look fresh and new, but prefer objects that look worn, used, and old. So they are likely to favor purchasing objects from the trader that have these characteristics. This does not necessarily mean that the objects they purchase *are* old and used and worn, but only that they *appear* to fit this category. Consequently, they might choose objects that look eroded and dull rather than fresh and shiny, objects whose natural pigments are faded, rather than objects painted in commercial paints. A classic example of this is found in an account by the Danish art hunter, Kjersmeier (1932:198–199) of his encounter with the Baga in Guinea:

> We found two old, beautiful pieces with their original painted surfaces. The remaining bird masks we saw, we didn't take with

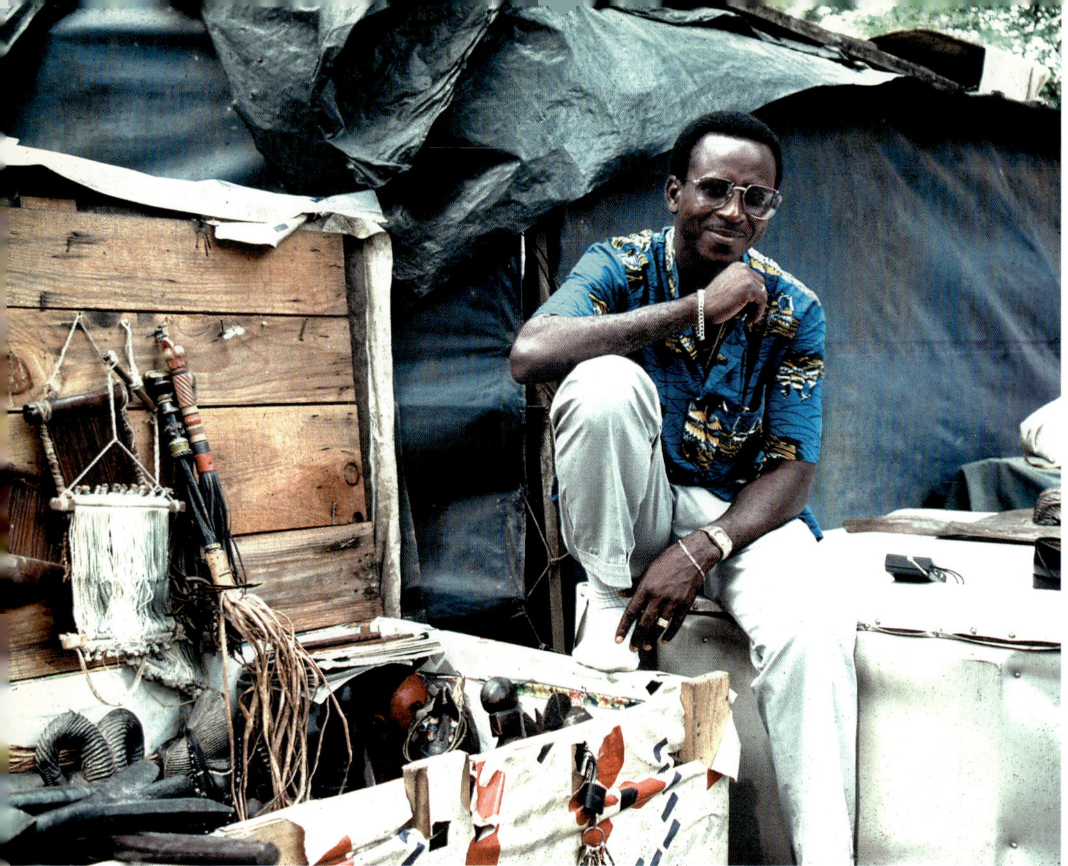

Hausa trader with wooden trunk in the back section of the Plateau Market. Abidjan, Ivory Coast. Photo: Christopher Steiner, 1988

> us. The Baga have a very bad habit of painting their masks every time they use them. In the last year they have begun to use Aniline colors and have entirely spoiled these beautiful sculptures, which otherwise would have been a delight for any lover of black art.

Although some interest has been generated recently in so-called "transitional" pieces,[6] dealers are still happier to purchase those objects that are completely in a "classic, non-influenced, standard" form rather than those that exhibit Western influences such as the depiction of Western clothing, motorcycles, cars, Western hairstyles, and so forth. Dealers also know that their clients are likely to display an object in the home on a shelving unit or to hang it on limited wall space, and the client does not have a need or desire for great bulk. Much is removed, but at least one New York dealer keeps a closet full of blackened raffia dresses taken from Sande masks (p. 174) from Sierra Leone, kept handy for that odd customer who may want a more complete item.[7]

The transformation of the African object often continues in the hands of the private collector. The private collector has a specific decorating scheme to complete that may mean the alteration of some design elements such as works of African art. In the past, collectors have been known to scrub down the surfaces of objects that did not please them, but collectors today, especially those operating in the very upper levels of the market, are much more sophisticated and less likely to significantly alter their purchases at high prices. Besides, the dealers, traders, and runners have already done that.

It is also in the selections collectors make that the history of African art becomes distorted. In the past (and to some extent today), sculpture, especially in wood, was given the highest privilege. The purchaser was more likely to choose wooden, carved objects, often of pristine beauty, rather than complicated, multimedia objects (for example see pp. 86, 102) unwieldy to handle and awkward to display. Many areas of the African arts were de-selected, including primarily arts produced by women, such as weaving, pottery, and basketry.[8] To some extent, the indigenous use of objects also affected collectability: for example, ritual objects that figured in exchange systems or that became obsolete through religious change might more easily have entered the foreign art market than utilitarian objects that were in everyday use, as has been shown elsewhere in the case of Pacific art (Kaeppler 1992). But from the receiving end of the market, the collector is the principal determiner of this taste, or lack of it, and the selection against these so-called "crafts" has already been made all along the line by the dealer, the African trader, and at the outset, by the African runner.

The question of why collectors make the choices they do, and de-select as they do, is a complex one, and outside our purview here, but has been explored recently by many writers (Clifford 1988, Errington 1998, Price 1989, and Steiner 1994, among others), probably too cynically. There are as many motivations for collecting as there are collectors. Some collectors are sensitive to scholarly issues in the field, including artistic and cultural context, African aesthetics, preservation, postcolonialism, and globalization. Obviously, most Western collectors follow their own aesthetic. Much of this has to do with economics.

For some collectors, it may also have to do with a certain thrill of "exploration," which requires a terrain that is either undeveloped or destroyed. Some of the choices suggest a fascination with vanished cultures, vanquished civilizations, and the spoils of conquest, notions of hegemony, possession and dispossession, as suggested by a recent advertisement for the sale of a large Senufo figure at auction, with the bold title, "Who will possess it next?"[9] Arman (1980), the American contemporary artist, expresses a kind of sad excitement about the collector's role in accepting the stewardship of African art from the Africans:

> In the clash of cultures and civilizations, the slow strangulation of African identity became permanent and irreversible, and it is a miracle that it has not been completely obliterated. But to the extent that it was not destroyed and that it has survived, it was changed and altered in such a way as to prevent the exercise of all the prerogatives of the original culture.... In accepting these phases, we recognize the classical period in African art as the reflection of an almost vanished culture.... [In African art we find] the almost disappearing images of an almost disappeared culture which is trying with persistence to pass on to you, like an exhausted relay runner passes the baton, the message of human questions and answers.

The "burden" implied here is reminiscent of arguments for colonialism and pessimistically portrays Africans as "a passive people of origin who are too deprived, bereft, damaged to make their own decisions—just the kind of image of Africa you are challenging [in this book]." (As written by Francis Harding [personal communication, 2003].)

Other collectors develop an intense interest in the cultures underlying the objects they buy, and a rich engagement with the original purpose of the objects and with the intentions of their African sources:

Basket with Ritual Items
Chokwe, Congo (Kinshasa)/Angola/Zambia
c. Late 19th–early 20th century
Basketry, wood, hide, seed pods, gourd, talons/claws, metal, fiber cloth, ceramic tile, shell, horsehair, miscellaneous materials
D. 30.4 cm
Gift of Aaron and Joanie Young, Baltimore
BMA 1997.231

We began collecting African art ... after a friend suggested that an African mask might enhance the decor of our new home.... At first, we collected art from across west and central Africa but we gradually changed our emphasis and now collect art solely from eastern Nigeria. The decision to restrict our collecting was influenced ... by attending such shows as Cole and Aniankor's *Igbo Arts: Community and Cosmos*.... [This] has permitted us to gain more in-depth knowledge of the area and therefore to make more informed choices in our acquisitions.... This might include information about the construction and care of an object, such as the technique of skin covered mask production and the types of woods and colors that are appropriate for a specific object.
Barry Hecht (personal communication, 1993)

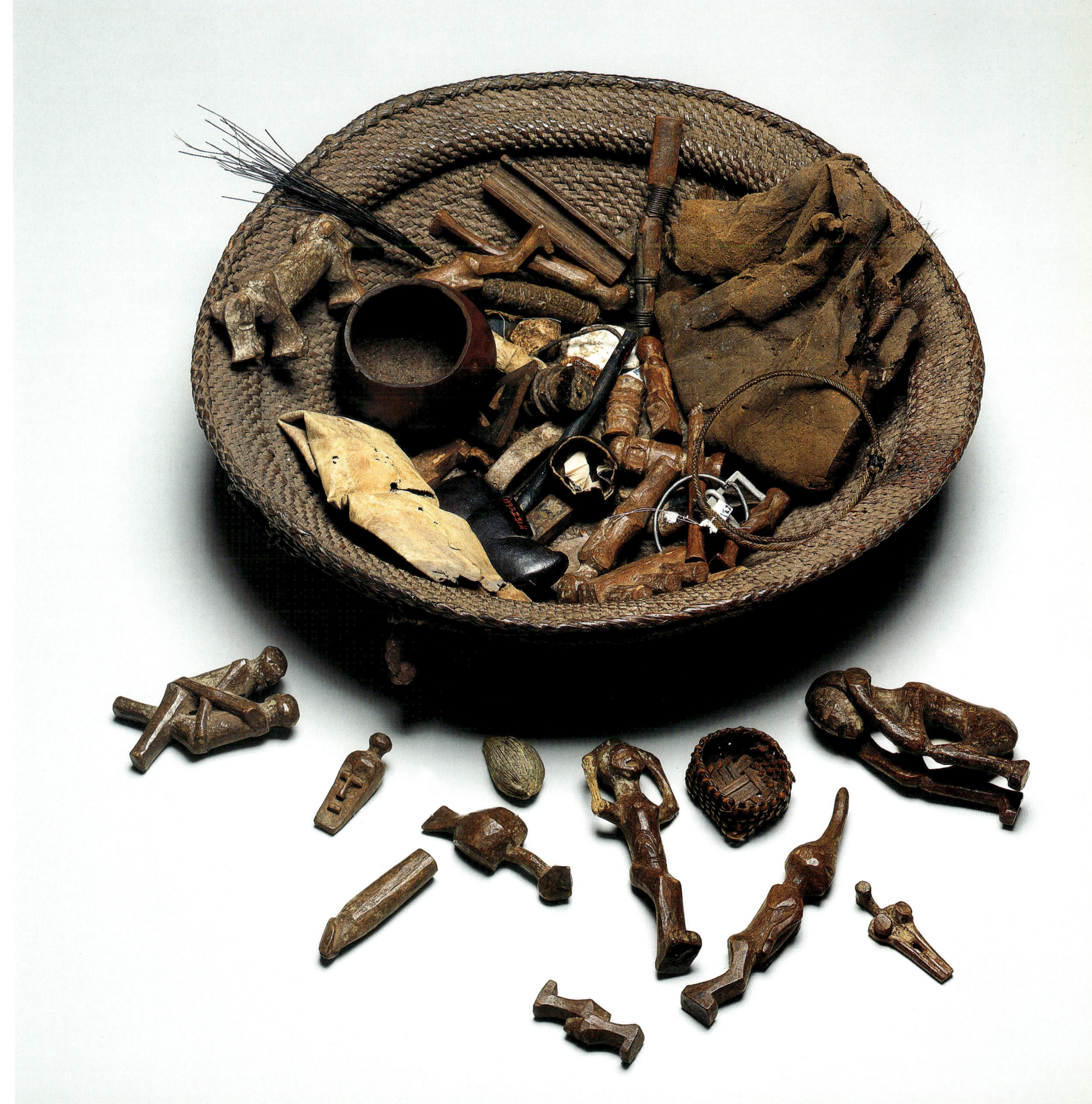

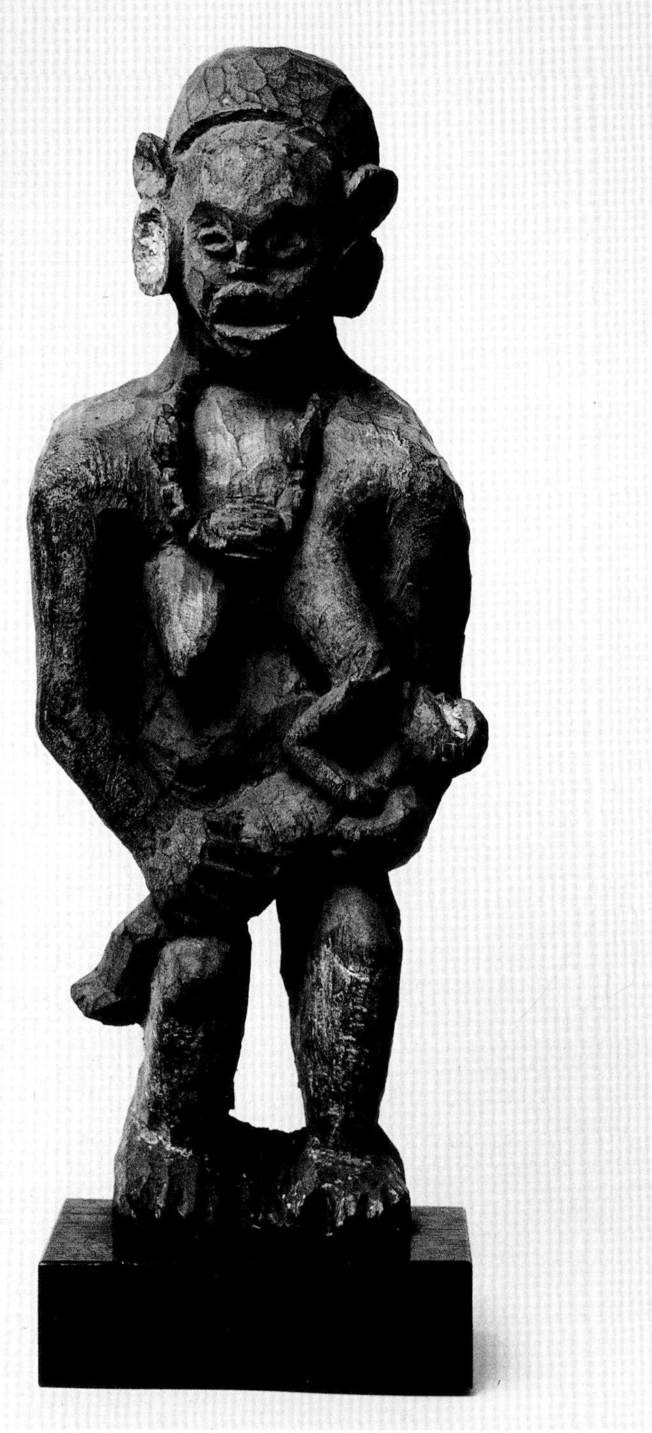

Nursing Female Figure. Bamileke, Cameroon
Deaccessioned from The Baltimore Museum of Art and traded to Murray Frum, Toronto, in 1982

Pokam, King of Baham, in front of his door frame (now in the collection of Murray Frum, Toronto), with the ex-BMA Frum nursing female figure intact (right center), Bamileke, Cameroon. Photo: Father Christol, 1925

Arguments that somehow our collecting will help Africa, as Armand implies, seem gratuitous. Yet collecting, and the ultimate display in museums, has resulted outside the continent in an awareness of Africa and its cultures that could not have been achieved through any other means. Many of us in the study of African art were first drawn to the field by an object in a collection, or its illustration. The collectors, Robert and Nancy Nooter, commented on their first encounter (personal communication, 1993):

> We knew just enough about it to recognize that it was one of the unique cultural traditions there and worth our serious attention. Thus began a lifetime interest that has enriched both of our lives.... we believe that [our] mutually cooperative relationship is an example of how museums, scholars, and collectors interact for the benefit of all parties concerned, helping to create an interchange of knowledge and information and to enhance an appreciation and respect for African art by the public at large.

African Art as Modern Art

> The art of Negro Africa is a sculptor's art. As a sculptural tradition in the last century it has no rival. It is as sculpture we should approach it.
>
> James Johnson Sweeney (1935:11)

The next and ultimate disposition of the object may be the museum. Museums often choose to display African objects as many collectors do, in privileging those objects of sculpture, and especially objects of a classic, "respectable" form, following the general hierarchy in the history of art which prioritizes painting and sculpture higher than utilitarian arts. Textiles frequently have been slighted in exhibition not only for this reason but because they often take a great amount of gallery space, they are light-sensitive and must be rotated off display after a few months. Pottery and basketry are often slighted as well, disdained also for their utilitarianism, and because, often being spherical, they too require a large amount of space. Objects with full costumes and regalia have often been left hanging among the reserves for similar reasons, although this is changing with a more recent demand for contextualization.

Because of the selection of African art by Westerners with their own predilections, privileges, and disdains, the museum collection, like the private collection, is formed by agendas outside Africa. The powerful hand the collectors have had in structuring not only museum collections and exhibitions, but also research agendas, catalogues, and textbooks has been explored in detail by Christopher Steiner (2002). The museum display, therefore, so dependent upon, and representing a legacy of, the collector's choices and interpretations, cannot be seen as representing a history of African art. Too much is missing, distorted, and revised. It is, rather, always a history of the *collecting* of African art.

What has been said here of collectors applies also to curators and directors of museums, who have had their own acquisition priorities. The origin of art museum collections in the United States is revealing in the orientation of its engineers as well as its benefactors.

Modernism, and all that it represents, has been at the foundation of the introduction of African art in the Western museum. One of the best-known objects of African art at the BMA is the headdress known as Nimba in the trade, and as D'mba (p. 223) to the Baga people. As one of the largest headdresses or masks in Africa carved from a single piece of wood, it has gotten quite a bit of press since the early 20th century. Among the several objects of African art with instant visual recognition internationally—such as the ankh-like Asante Akua'ba (p. 156), the Bamana Chi Wara antelope (p. 169), or the brass-faced Kota reliquary

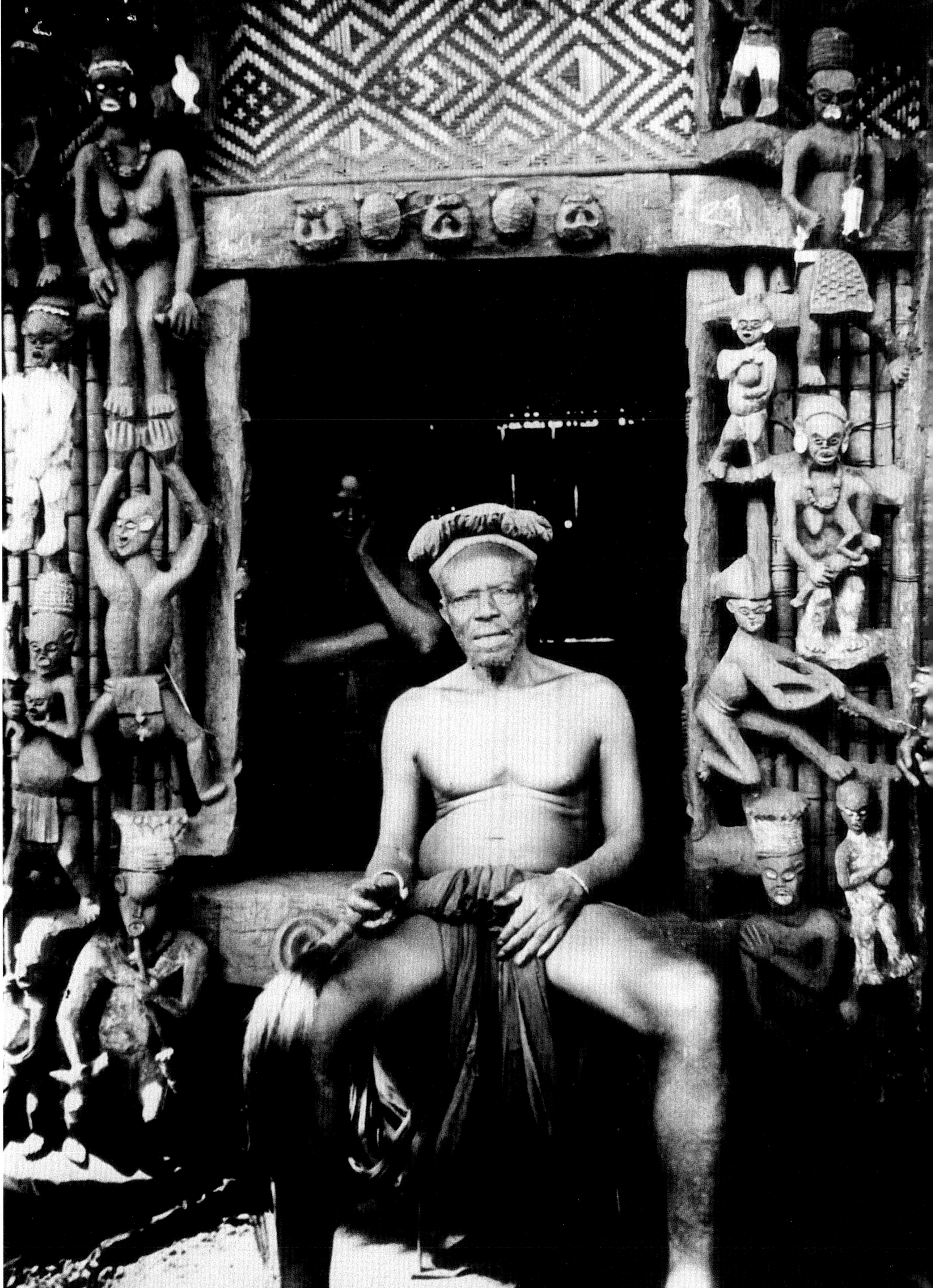

figure (p. 60)—the Baga D'mba is prominent. The D'mba headdress was sketched by Alberto Giacometti, copied and adapted by Pablo Picasso, owned by Picasso and Henri Matisse, and represented in the art of a number of other modern artists (Krauss 1987:521; W. Rubin 1987:325). Because of its appearance of abstraction, as a huge head placed directly on four legs, the D'mba headdress has become emblematic of a common perception: African art as modern art.

African art came into the art museum, just as it came into the academic art history program, largely by way of modern art. Paul Wingert, at Columbia University, and Robert Goldwater, at New York University, both professors of modern art, introduced the first courses on African art in the 1950s. Neither had ever visited Africa, they did not have available the ethnographic data that we have now, and both wrote books on African art, pursuing their predominate interest in pure form. Around the same time, three sets of collectors in Baltimore began to donate African art to the BMA. Claribel and Etta Cone, Sadie A. May, and Alan and Janet Wurtzburger were best known for important collections of modern art which they also donated to the Museum.

African art entered the art museum because it could look and act much like modern art (p. 11). In the forward to the catalogue of the BMA's Wurtzburger collection, Director Adelyn Breeskin wrote extensively of the existing BMA collection of modern art, concluding, "Keeping these facts in mind, an African Negro sculpture collection such as the one now on exhibition attains special importance for our Museum ... as a gift to our Museum in the near future.... It will then take its rightful place in our over-all picture of the background of modern art ... " (Wurtzburger [1954] 1958:4–5)

The prevailing view at the time was that of the art historian, Carl Einstein, who held that African art and all other non-Western arts must be appreciated purely for their aesthetics, and that the knowledge of the content or the social background of the art form could even be an impediment to the aesthetic experience.[10] In the catalogue for the 1935 exhibition at The Museum of Modern Art, James Johnson Sweeney established the view of African art as modern art, and specifically as sculpture, in his quote given above. Art museums and galleries are still heavily invested in this viewpoint. As this book goes to press in 2003, an exhibition goes on view in Munich entitled *Kunst der Lega: Minimalismus einer Waldkultur (Art of the Lega: Minimalism of a Forest Culture).* "African art speaks," as Ladislas Segy used to say—in this case, speaking to a kind of modernist cachet. African art came into the art museums under a pretext of pure form, and the museum world was comfortable. Now we call for a recognition of the fuller art form in the African context, of which our museum objects are simply fragments. One might question whether African art can be as comfortable in the art museum under a new guise. I believe it can.

Integrating the Senses, Restoring the Whole

Labor is blossoming or dancing where
The body is not bruised to pleasure soul,
Nor beauty born out of its own despair,
Nor blear-eyed wisdom out of midnight oil.
O chestnut tree, great rooted blossomer,
Are you the leaf, the blossom or the bole?
O body swayed to music, O brightening glance,
How can we know the dancer from the dance?

William Butler Yeats, "Among School Children"

Contextualization of the African art collection in this book has to do not so much with a social or cultural context, which has its own importance frequently addressed in anthropology museums, but with a context more central to the function of an art museum: the larger, fuller, more integrated art form. The task here is to accept the challenge of presenting the art form as it was conceived by the African artists and viewed by its African audience. The problem of translation in the museum gallery is paramount. African performance may require the space of the entire village, incorporating the architecture, the plazas, the walkways and streets, as well as the hot sun of mid-day or the dim gray of dusk, hundreds of viewer-participants, the cacophony of competing groups of dancers, polyphonic singers, and multiple-meter drummers, the billowing dust from under stamping feet, and five or six hours of duration. Obviously, all this cannot be brought literally into the museum gallery —and should not, for the risk of exoticizing and trivializing something of deep significance. But it should be acknowledged, suggested, and in some ways represented in museum interpretation.

It has been a quarter of a century now since Robert Farris Thompson produced his landmark exhibition and catalogue, *African Art in Motion* (1974), which taught us that we can never look at the object in the same way again. African art, Thompson says, always implies action; art objects exist within both a cognitive (and articulated) and a proprioceptive (understood within the body structure) context of movement and gesture. Herbert Cole, around the same time (1975), introduced the schematic mapping of procession choreography, the spatial relationship between elements of a procession, and the relative effort and intensity of public display and ritual, with a detailed synopsis of the events and their specific timing. He also showed how personal ornamentation becomes the performance of objects in which the human body is an art expressing deep cultural significance (1974). Earlier, he had established the notion of "Art as a Verb" in Africa (1969, III, 1), and the process of the material construction of sacred houses as "a dance" (1969, II, 4). The complexity of specific masquerades[11] has been explored by a number of scholars, in which elements other than the material are given substantial weight.[12] Ottenberg (1969, II, 4), in particular provided detailed play-by-play description of the acts, the scenes, songs, ground plans, steps, and gestures of each performance in a way that had never been done before. More recently, Lawal (1996) emphasized the "spectacle" of narrative and music, and the complexities of costume. Even the stationary shrine has been made to come alive in studies by Robert Thompson (1993) and Susan Vogel (1997).

Still, in museums and in college classrooms, many continue to present the mask or the figure as an isolated art object, in our slides, in the textbooks, on the pedestal, and in our analyses. A search through the literature for data on music, dance, the use of space, and a number of other contributory forms of art reveals overwhelmingly a lack of such data even in the most recent literature. In almost any recent publication on an African art form, the essential component of movement, for example, is dismissed in a few sentences. In African art history we need to develop vocabulary for describing movement and other essential components of traditional African art, such as music, theater, and narrative. A new vocabulary would free us from the constraints of the compartmentalization which obscures our view of the integrated arts.

African art no longer has to feel uncomfortable in the museum setting. Western contemporary art itself is changing, and the museum is changing with it. The art museum is now growing accustomed to the exhibition of multi-media works, installation pieces, performance pieces, kinetic art, and moving images. African art is all of this. We no longer need to prove that African art, too, can fit on a pedestal just as any Western sculpture. It is time to show African art in its complexity, in time and space.

Our task here, then, lies in attempting to find some traces of the form from which the museum object has been taken. Each object was situated in a distinct process-related context which would have differed from any other of its own kind. Nevertheless, it is useful to examine the pieces and snatches of artistic context that relate to the object at hand in the general area of origin. This is a context of ritual process, even in the case of most utilitarian art, as well as masks and shrine figures, and a context of creative performance. Looking at individual works, the general outlines of the original performance art have been reconstituted, based upon the sources that exist, and the material fragment in the museum returned to the company of familiar surroundings.

To present the artistic context in Africa within the pages of this book, we begin with the fragment and reassemble the components lost in the object's voyage from Africa to the museum. Our contention is that the study of the history of art in Africa requires equal attention to a large range of artistic elements that constitute the form, of which the simple material object is only one. In existing studies of African art, ample attention has been paid to the form and style of the material fragment, and a great volume of literature addresses social and cultural contexts; our list of references serves as a guide. Our essays focus on the art form itself, and we begin at the material surface and move outward.

To restore the artistic entirety, we have identified fourteen elements to consider. These elements involve notions of community and of person, the five human senses, the various "arts" that we compartmentalize in the West, and the technical aspects of theater production. They are drawn from interdisciplinary concerns, in order to encourage researchers to think and explore beyond their own training. In some way, in the following essays, one or another writer has dealt with each one of these elements. Ideally, when analyzing a performance comprehensively and exhaustively, we would investigate all of the elements of performance. Furthermore, we would use all our senses to perceive each element. We would "see the music and hear the dance."

The holistic form is presented here, inasmuch as the data exist, dealing with such aspects as costume and ornamentation, and the refurbishing of the sculptural object. Sound is important in respect to singing, musical instruments, body sounds, melody, rhythm, and lyrics. Movement is ubiquitous, involving steps, gestures, choreography, and the displacement of the body, whether in masquerade or in the manipulation and construction of the stationary shrine. Audience participation includes singing, dancing, providing rhythm, giving instructions, critiquing, and identifying space. Staging, as a theatrical element, entails the setting of village and wilderness, sacred and quotidian structures and space, and the spatial relationships among objects and sites in the performance. Timing is important in the scheduling of events, entrances and exits, and the duration. Lighting is a theatrical effect that is a function of the availability of sun and shadow, the significance of such phenomena as high noon and the dry season, the use of fire and electric lights, and the desired visibility or invisibility of the image and the dancer. Olfactory elements are inherent in the costumes, people, environment, libations, and sacrifices. Tastes of sacrificial foods, libations, and other substances can be incorporated into the drama. Often the artistic context involves a complex of other sculptural forms and auxiliary objects, suggesting relationships and polarities, with juxtapositions that provide situational meaning. And it is important to consider improvisation in response to serendipity and in the exercising of human agency, creativity, and intention.

In order to emphasize each specific performance element, the individual essays on performance and objects are organized by the fourteen chapters that follow, highlighting a salient element that each addresses, in the integration of the whole. We begin with the surface of the object, which as mentioned earlier may have been distressed, modified, or embellished by its new owners out of the original context, thus obscuring the original intent.

1 Steiner (1994:41–42) has found that occasionally women occupy specific functions in the trade.

2 Today, these runners travel around the world, to New York, Baltimore, and wherever collectors of African art might be found, arriving in vans usually chauffeured by a relative, and they are still called "runners," a fact which Christopher Steiner (1994:9) has highlighted as definitively ironic and contemptuous.

3 The runner's contacts in the community may be ritual specialists who are in charge of the objects in question, or they may simply be children of the family responsible for the objects, particularly students who need money in order to finance their education. Sometimes these agents are somewhat skeptical of the practices of their own community. In other cases, they are fully immersed in the ritual tradition, but it is, perhaps, a tradition somewhat in decline, in which the objects no longer function in the way that they did in the past. Sometimes the community has simply given up the ritual in question and feels no further need for its objects and accoutrements. In other cases, the issue is more delicate, as there may not be a consensus in the community that the objects are no longer useful, but those who have access to them are often "progressive" and of the opinion that the community need not continue to maintain them. In other cases, the objects were never intended to be maintained, but were intended for specific rituals, and once performed, are no longer necessary. So there are many reasons, from the negative to the positive, why objects leave their communities and are conveyed by these runners.

4 Other important markets were found in Dakar (Senegal), Abidjan (the Ivory Coast), Lagos (Nigeria), Duala (Cameroon), Kinshasa (Congo), Nairobi (Kenya), and, most recently, Johannesburg (South Africa).

5 This trade has been explored in several publications (Steiner 1994, Kasfir 1996, Crowley 1983).

6 The terms "traditional" and "transitional" are used frequently in the trade and in scholarship in varying ways. Dealers and collectors usually use the latter term to designate objects displaying western motifs, while scholars might not see a clear division between the two, arguing for a less static view of tradition.

7 The collectors, Robert and Nancy Nooter (personal communication, 2002), recounted an incident of serendipity in their collecting of a four-sided Igbo helmet mask. After buying the mask in New York, they accidentally came across the French dealer who had brought it out of Africa. In the course of their conversation, the dealer mentioned that the mask originally had a figure on top which he had removed because, as he said, "I thought it looked better." Fortunately, he still had the fragment, which the Nooters were able to acquire and to restore to the mask.

8 This division by gender is not consistent throughout Africa. Exhibitions such as Arnold Rubin's Accumulative African Sculpture, at Pace Gallery in 1974, and Roy Sieber's African Textiles and Decorative Arts, at The Museum of Modern Art in 1972, effected a shift in collectors' preferences, but still, through the 1980s, these arts occupied a decidedly second place on the market, and still do not rank often in the "upper end."

9 The advertisement, for Christie's, New York, appeared in *The New York Times*, May 1, 1995: C18. Christie's has refused permission to reproduce this very impressive, and probably, in retrospect, somewhat embarrassing ad not only for its hegemonic implications but also its overtly sexist tone.

10 For more on the development of African art vis-à-vis modern, see Gerbrands 1990; Ben-Amos 1989; Adams 1989; and Errington 1998:92–98.

11 The term "masquerade" is used here to indicate an event or performance in which a mask is worn. A "mask" refers to a covering that substantially obscures the face. Otherwise, if the covering rests on the head but does not substantially cover the face, it is labeled a "headdress." In some cases, a headdress might be fitted with a mask of cloth or fiber. The term "masking" is used to indicate the practice of wearing a mask, as in "a masking event," equivalent to "a masquerade." The wearer of a mask is sometimes called "a masker" or "a masked dancer/performer."

12 Some of the most focused on performance include René Bravmann (1974), Simon Ottenberg (1975), Anita Glaze (1981), Sidney Kasfir (1988), Jean Borgatti (in Kasfir 1988), Henry and Margaret Drewal (1983), Arnoldi (1995), and Babatunde Lawal (1996).

THE SURFACE: RENEWAL AND IDENTITY

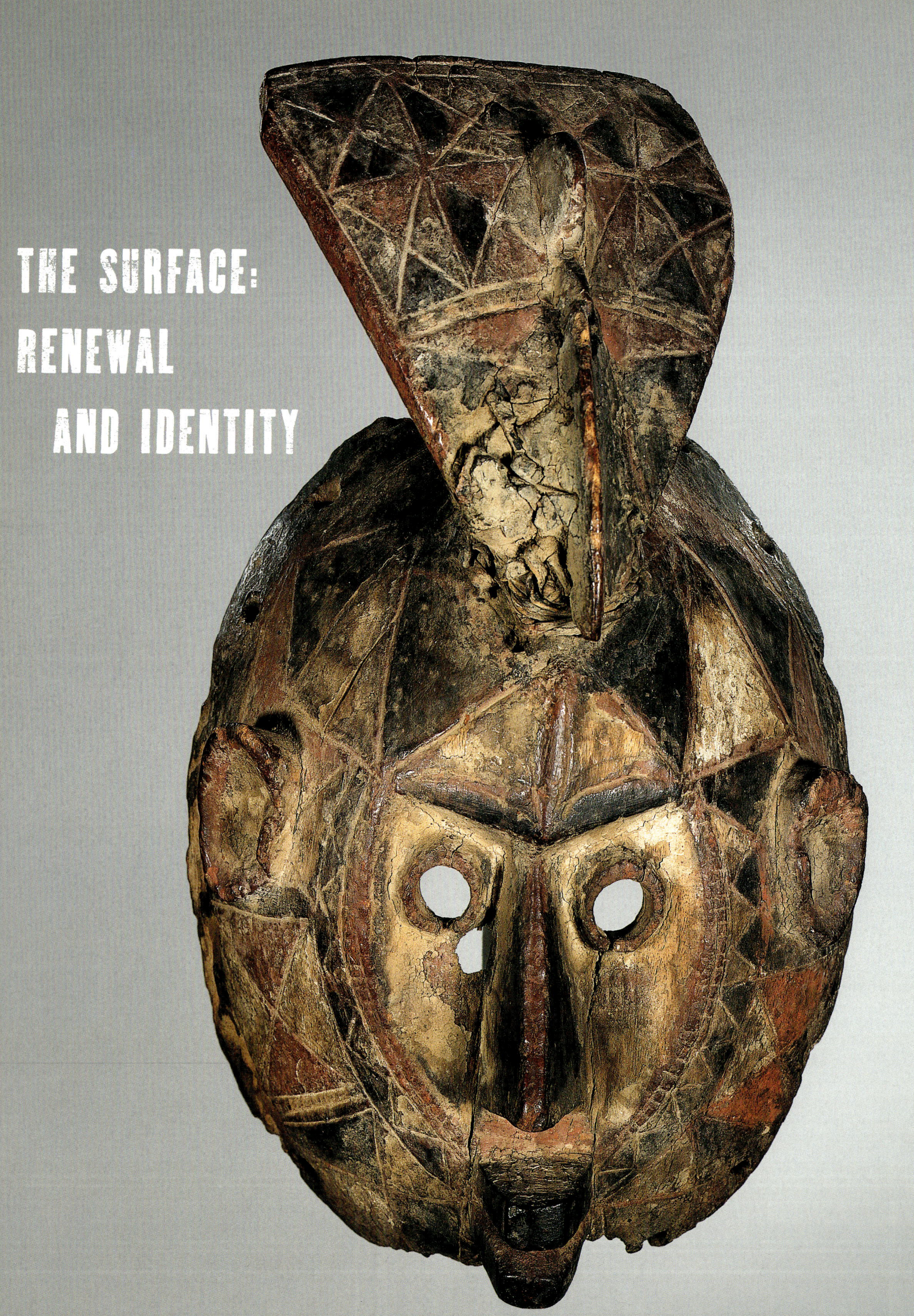

The first step in our reconstruction of the original art form, would be a restoration of the surface condition of the object as it appeared in African performance, ritual, or other artistic contexts. Occasionally visitors to the gallery of African art at the BMA exclaim, "Why is there no color in African art?" "Why is everything so dull/so subdued/so dark/so old looking?"

In fact, there are a few objects in the display that are wildly colorful, and it is precisely their fullness that helps to explain the void.

The male mask of the Wè of Liberia and the Ivory Coast is a good example (p. 43). This was painted in commercial European oil paints applied from cans purchased in the market. These colors have longer staying power than the natural pigments often used in Africa in the past, so they maintain their brilliance indefinitely. In the BMA gallery, the colorful Wè mask seems to be almost an anomaly; but in fact it is, in this sense, more representative of African art. The expressive quality of bright color is often essential to the meaning of the mask in Africa. The Wè mask, in short, refers to the wild, temperamental nature of forest spirits that needs to be channeled and directed by the people through the medium of ritual in which these masks appear. But the Wè mask on the African art market may not command as high a value as many other forms that are of more muted color. One tends to think of the muted or the dark as the older, more traditional, less Western influenced. This sometimes results in the de-selection of masks of brilliant color.

It may be through such selection that we find another mask in the African gallery, that of the Mossi people of Burkina Faso (opposite page). In the muted light of the gallery, one might not notice that the mask is painted in black, red, and white. The original natural colors are now severely faded. In context, the Mossi mask would be refurbished for each new performance with fresh pigments, always viewed as a very colorful object. A muted Mossi Wan-Balinga mask would probably not be considered suitable for appearance by the Mossi, but if two Mossi masks should come up at public auction, it is almost inevitable that the mask of more degenerated color and eroded surface will bring the higher bid.

Although the failure of brilliant objects to come into the museum is often the result of their rejection in the marketplace, there have been documented cases of collectors and dealers actually altering the surface of objects by sanding, brushing, or repainting (documented by Christopher Steiner [1994:115]):

> Not only does Scanzi carefully attempt to construct a pre-colonial past for the African slingshots which he now sells, but when he started his collection he refused to purchase slingshots that had been painted. As a result, slingshots with paint were sanded down and restained with potassium permanganate before being presented for sale at his home.

The BMA Gelede mask from the Yoruba is painted with commercial paints (p. 115). It was given in January 1954, separately from the bulk of over one hundred objects given by the Wurtzburgers in March 1954. On the Museum receipt, the gift is designated "For the Education Department: use" and a note is made that "paint is recent." In other words, the mask was deemed not appropriate for the curatorial collection of fine art, but okay to be handled by children to the point of destruction. Nor was it included in the 1954 catalogue raisonné of the collection, although there were many lesser objects listed and illustrated. Henry Drewal (personal communications, 1992 and 2003) wrote of Gelede masks made by Fagbite and finished by his son, Falola (Drewal & Drewal 1983: Plate 81), that he filmed in 1970 being danced at Idahin: "These masks are now in a New York collection, but their wonderfully painted surfaces were altered badly." "Interestingly, they were blackened, probably by a dealer (whether African or non-African) to remove the polychrome surface to accord more with 'western' taste."

Female Mask (*Wan-Balinga*)
Mossi, Burkina Faso
c. Late 19th century
Wood, rawhide, black and red pigment, H. 28.6 cm
Friends of Art Fund
BMA 1974.38

Many African figures and masks are coated with kaolin, a fine white clay that is obtained from river banks. The Ogoni face mask (p. 32) is an example; the freshness of its white kaolin intact. Often, masks that were meant to be painted white arrive on the marketplace denuded, showing only the surface of the wood and a small trace of the kaolin that once covered them.

Color and its absence is often absolutely critical to understanding the significance of a work of African art (see Turner 1967:59–92, for example). It is often iconic. The Sande mask (p. 175) is black because of a complex symbology relating to coolness, depth, the female, the real, and the beautiful (with some ambiguity: cf. Boone 1986:160, 236–238; Lamp 1985:30). Whiteness, among the Temne of Sierra Leone, is associated with spirits and human beings closest to the spiritual world. The semantic value of color is an extremely complex issue, and one that requires looking beyond obvious analogical resemblance. White and black symbolism often defies the customary usage familiar to European observers, and the white/black dichotomy has resulted in some unfortunate views of Africa and some misreading of African metaphor. Color symbolism may vary widely from one group to another.

Other masks are meant to be seen covered with a great deal of encrustation rather than paint. This often consists of some combination of earth, clay, dung, soot, blood, or oil (pp. 159, 233, 261, 266). Encrustation on an object is often evidence of the additive process in African art in which an object, through decades of use, acquires a surface containing the residue of many sacrifices and ritual annointings that enhance its value to its African audience. To some collectors, however, its appearance is unpleasant. More collectors than one would care to imagine, especially novice buyers, have been known to scrub off encrustation with a toothbrush and soapy water.

In the essays that follow, the authors examine many aspects of individual performance contexts, and touch poignantly on changes to surface aspects of the material elements. Till Förster examines the funerary context of the Senufo figure, emphasizing that criticism of form by the Senufo audience requires diligent restoration in situ. Keith Nicklin associated the fresh, white faces of Ogoni masks with the youthfulness of benevolent spirits. By the surface qualities of ancient Egyptian stone reliefs, Thomas Kittredge has been able to identify the possible original architectural context of a relatively small fragment. By contrast, the essay on the Djerma vessel emphasizes more fleeting surface qualities that call for constant renewal, relating to values widely found south of the Sahara.

Many questions arise on the subject of the significance of surface qualities, some of which are addressed here, and some which are left to ponder. When the surface of the object is altered, what information do we miss, what emotions are not invoked, what intellectual arguments are not made, what personal identification is lost? What history of use and process is obscured? What understanding of African values do we lose? And how do we diminish our own opportunity for enrichment, to engage with other cultural and aesthetic priorities and challenge our own?

1 Weathering, Restoration, and Formal Criticism: a Senufo Figure (*Pòròpya*)

Female Ancestral Figure (*Pòròpya*)
Senufo, Ivory Coast
***Pòrò* Association**
c. Late 19th–early 20th century
Wood, H. 128.3 cm
Purchase with exchange fund from Alan Wurtzburger
BMA 1960.58 (purchased from Henri Kamer, Paris)

Until the 1960s and 1970s, every village initiation center of the Pòrò society in the central Senufo area owned one or several pairs of anthropomorphic figures that were known by the name of Pòròpya (rendered as *Pombia* in Glaze 1981), literally "child of Pòrò". As a rule, these figures were carved from hardwood, and were therefore replaced only rarely. The work of carvers specializing in this type of figure was correspondingly small. Although the societies preferred to commission from regionally-known carvers, these rarely produced more than ten pairs of figures in their lifetime.

Iconographically, Pòròpya figures are highly uniform. Occasionally, at least in the 1970s and 1980s, the figures were ornamented with bead necklaces. Distinctions, however, can be seen in the hairstyles, which come in various forms. Here, in the BMA example, the hairstyle reproduced was documented in the 1930s and, in some places, was worn until the 1950s. This probably represents a bird with its head and beak hanging down from the woman's forehead.

Although the Senufo rarely offer remarks about the aesthetics, style, and artistic execution of the figures, Pòrò members and ordinary Senufo frequently make comments about the appropriateness of the form and iconography of the figures, and the expectations may vary from one local Pòrò organization to the other.

Female and male figures overlooking the log shelter, *kpaala*, in the central square, at the funeral for an elder. The initiates are resting under the trees (upper left). Senufo, Kufulo subgroup, Ivory Coast. Photo: Anita Glaze, 1970

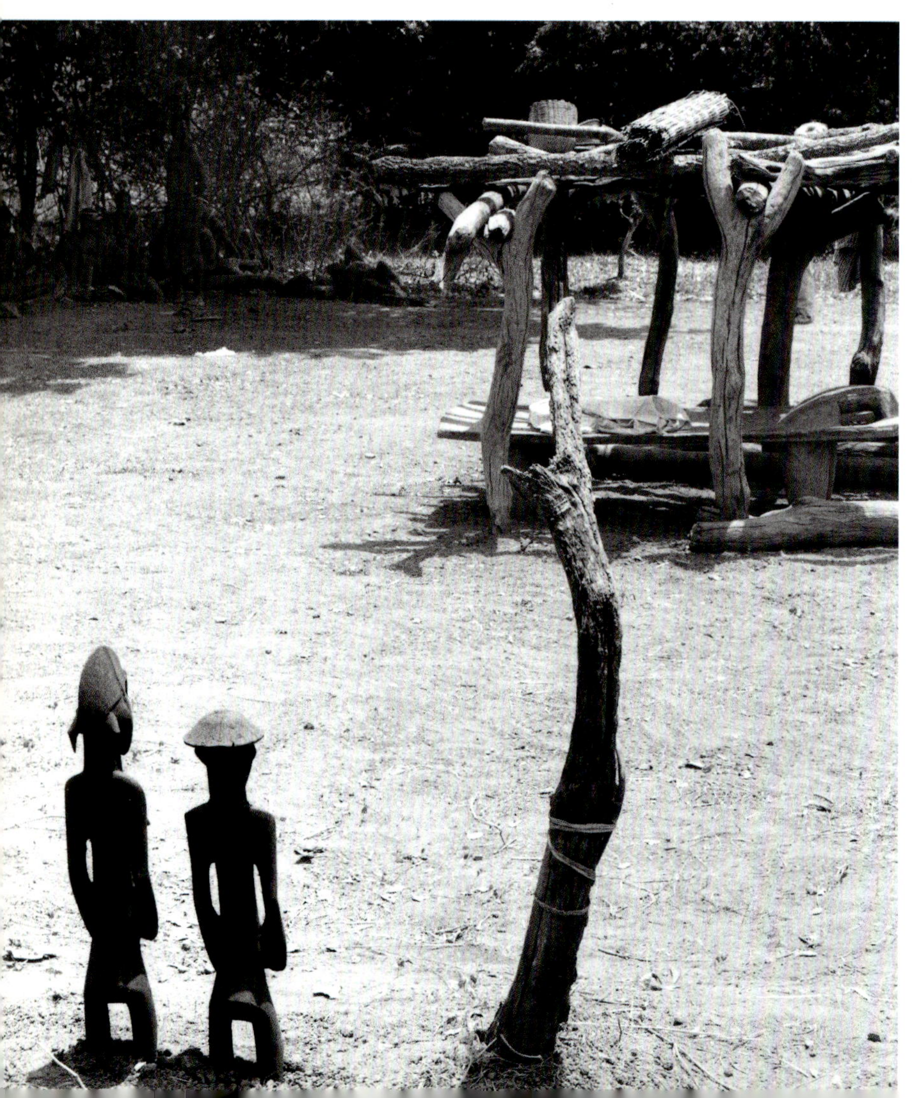

Aesthetic judgments, however are sometimes heard among elder Pòrò members and often among sculptors. Each group within Senufo society has a specific vocabulary on aesthetics which is based on metaphors that mainly refer to the act of sculpting and the hard work associated with it (from observations made in the late 1970s and early 1980s).

For use in ritual, the figures were elaborately prepared and maintained throughout the duration of the events. Almost always, the surface was newly rubbed with shea butter to give it a deep shiny hue. If the figures were blackened, lighter parts were sometimes retouched and subsequently the complete figure oiled again. If they had not been used for a long time and were damaged, attempts were made to fix the damage in such a way that it was no longer noticeable. It was possible to replace smaller wooden parts, and sometimes even whole limbs, and carefully match them to the existing wooden body. Since the figures were stored and displayed standing up, the bases and the lower parts of the legs were particularly liable to weathering. The moment to replace a figure had usually arrived if it was damaged to such an extent that it could no longer stand upright. In the BMA example the legs are badly weathered, and the feet and base no longer exist. Perhaps because of its hairstyle and the advanced weathering of the lower parts, this object was abandoned by a Pòrò society, presumably in the 1950s.

The village Pòrò societies of the Senufo used Pòròpya figures such as this on the occasion of the initiation of new members and, above all, during the elaborate burial ceremonies for older members. During the mourning rituals—often lasting four or five days—the young initiates of the local society were assigned to keep watch at the *kpaala*, a shelter made of coarse thick boards and belonging to the village society. In front of this shelter was an open square where a fire was kept burning for the duration of the mourning rituals, and at all times of the day and night several initiates of Pòrò had to watch over this square. The burial ceremonies included several highlights that were celebrated. First, on the day of the interment, late in the afternoon, the masks of the society appeared in front of the shelter to beat their drums in order to separate the body and the "shadow" (comparable to the soul) of the deceased. A second highlight occurred in the dead of night. Then, the old and the young members of the society danced to the sound of the big, barrel-shaped drums and sang about their initiation. Their voices were distorted by reed pipes held in front of their mouths for this purpose. A third highlight was finally reached when, one or two days after the actual interment, the complete ritual was performed once more with a stick wrapped in cloths in place of the corpse.

From the standpoint of the older as well as the younger members of the society, these days and nights were a time of profound exhaustion for all those who had to keep watch in the square in front of the shelter. Older initiates, already freed from this duty, often visited the younger ones to demonstrate their support.

In order to show continuity and to give support from the ancestors, an anthropomorphic couple was introduced into the funeral ritual. This was the Pòròpya pair, male and female (only the Celibele, a very small subgroup of the Senufo, used two female figures). The figures were required to be in place before the ritual acts began. This was normally carried out by the initiates after the death had been announced by rifle shots in the village. However, the sculpted pair were not the object of public ritual acts. They were placed principally to point out to the young initiates that their labor—since the Senufo call any ritual act labor—was to be carried out in the name of the whole society and, in the end, of the whole village community. The figures showed that the young men's watch merely continued what other generations before them had done to perform common mourning rituals for the benefit of all.

The figures were placed at the edge of the square in a small shelter built of branches and brushwood specially for their display. Their faces were turned towards the square where the young initiates of the society had to keep watch. Thus they were well visible to anyone. The figures were placed not in relationship to the cadaver, but in relationship to the *kpaala*, the Pòrò-society hangar in the village. Throughout the duration of the ritual events, a young and able initiate was assigned to stay with the figures. Even though this meant more than five days on the hard wooden benches of the kpaala, he was prohibited from falling asleep, at least in principle. All members had to assemble at the kpaala during the ritual, and it was there, too, that the most important parts of the ritual took place. It seems as if the figures were official visitors and witnesses to all ritual acts, representing a generalized audience of living as well as deceased members of the Pòrò, but the elders seldom comment on this.

Once the mourning rituals had been concluded, the figures were removed and taken to a secret storage place. Until the end of the 1950s or the beginning of the 1960s, most of the groves had a small hut where these and other ritual objects of the Pòrò society were hidden. Later, the old men of the society started to hide the figures together with the masks of the society in their houses in the village, due to increasing theft.

Thieves were known, especially during the 1960s and 1970s, to invade the groves maintained by every Pòrò society at the edge of the village, where the initiation centers were located, when they were unattended. But the more audacious thieves even stole figures directly from their shelters in the plaza during the mourning ceremonies, making their move in the obscurity of night while ritual acts were being conducted, with the distraction provided by the gathering crowds. Already in the 1960s, thefts had become so numerous that replacing the figures became a serious financial problem for many societies. Towards the end of the 1970s, this expenditure seemed no longer acceptable for many village societies. Increasingly, inexperienced carvers living close by were commissioned who used soft and less durable wood.

Other forces contributed to the demise of this tradition. During the colonial period, elders say, they sometimes sold used figures. In the 1940s and 1950s, the indigenous Christian Massa evangelical movement in the Ivory Coast was instrumental in forcing Pòrò societies to give up their figures and masks, although many later commissioned new ones. By the mid-1980s, the figures had largely disappeared from the ritual sequences of the burial feasts. Some were still kept in the private huts of old members of the society but the village public were hardly aware of their existence.

Till Förster

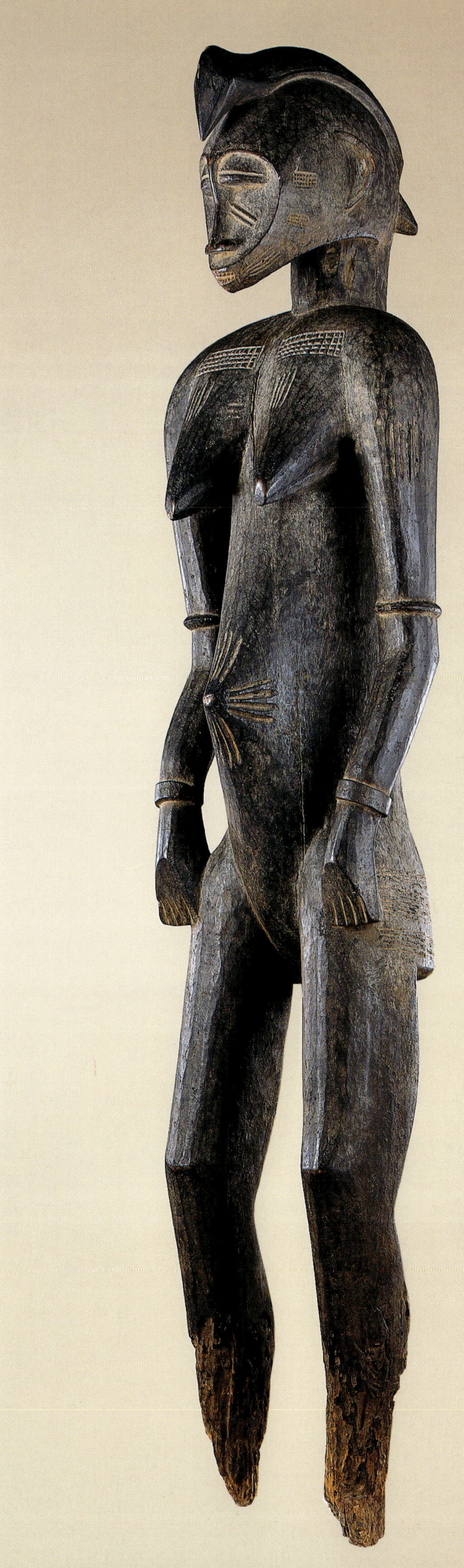

Youthful Faces: an Ogoni Mask (*Elu*)

Mask (*Elu*)
Ogoni, Nigeria
c. Mid-20th century
Wood, polychrome, reeds, H. 20.9 cm
Gift of Robert and Emily Miller Rody, Baltimore
BMA 1975.7

The Ogoni, who number approximately 500,000, live and farm on a fertile plain to the northeast of the Niger Delta. In the 1990s, conflicts with the government of Nigeria and Shell International over oil rights and environmental and health problems resulted in the widespread destruction of Ogoni villages and the execution of their leaders, including the writer, Ken Saro-Wiwa.

Ogoni art is extremely rich and varied. Whilst they share some artistic expressions with their neighbors, most of their masquerades and mask forms are unique to the Ogoni, as is the case of this particular mask style which has the generic name of elu (spirit).

It is typical of the small, delicately-carved oval face masks which can be used for a variety of performances throughout the region. K.C. Murray photographed masks of this type in the 1930s being used in a play called *anuwe*, which was performed on top of a cloth screen or booth of the type used in the *amanikpo* puppet play. Mostly the masks are associated with age grade celebrations and in the 1990s could be seen at Christmas and the time of the New Yam festival where, worn by young men who danced and ran through the villages and farmland, they entertained large audiences of local people. These small masks can be either male or female, portrayed as youthful, and the spirits they represent are beneficent, in contrast to the many forms of malevolent spirits represented by other, more aggressive, larger styles of mask.

These mask forms are characterized by pert, retroussé noses, pouting or smiling mouths, and eyes which are either depicted as thin slits or large circles. Many such masks have hinged jaws, as in this case, which when opened reveal two rows of long, thin teeth made from cane or bamboo *agakorgoo* (teeth bamboo). The effect of the masqueraders being able to "talk" by manipulating the hinged jaws is impressive and animates the face. Often such masks are painted with light colored paints and some are surmounted by hairstyles fashionable at the time of carving, along with smaller faces, figures, or emblems such as birds, chieftaincy stools, or canoes which relate to specific societies.

The masks are so small that they do not cover the face of the wearer completely but perch on the front of the face. They are held in place by a woven raffia, leaf, or textile head covering and by the clenching of the wearer's teeth on a wooden stick inside the mask at mouth level. Costumes also vary from brightly colored cloth to extravagant grass or raffia, depending on the occasion.

Keith Nicklin

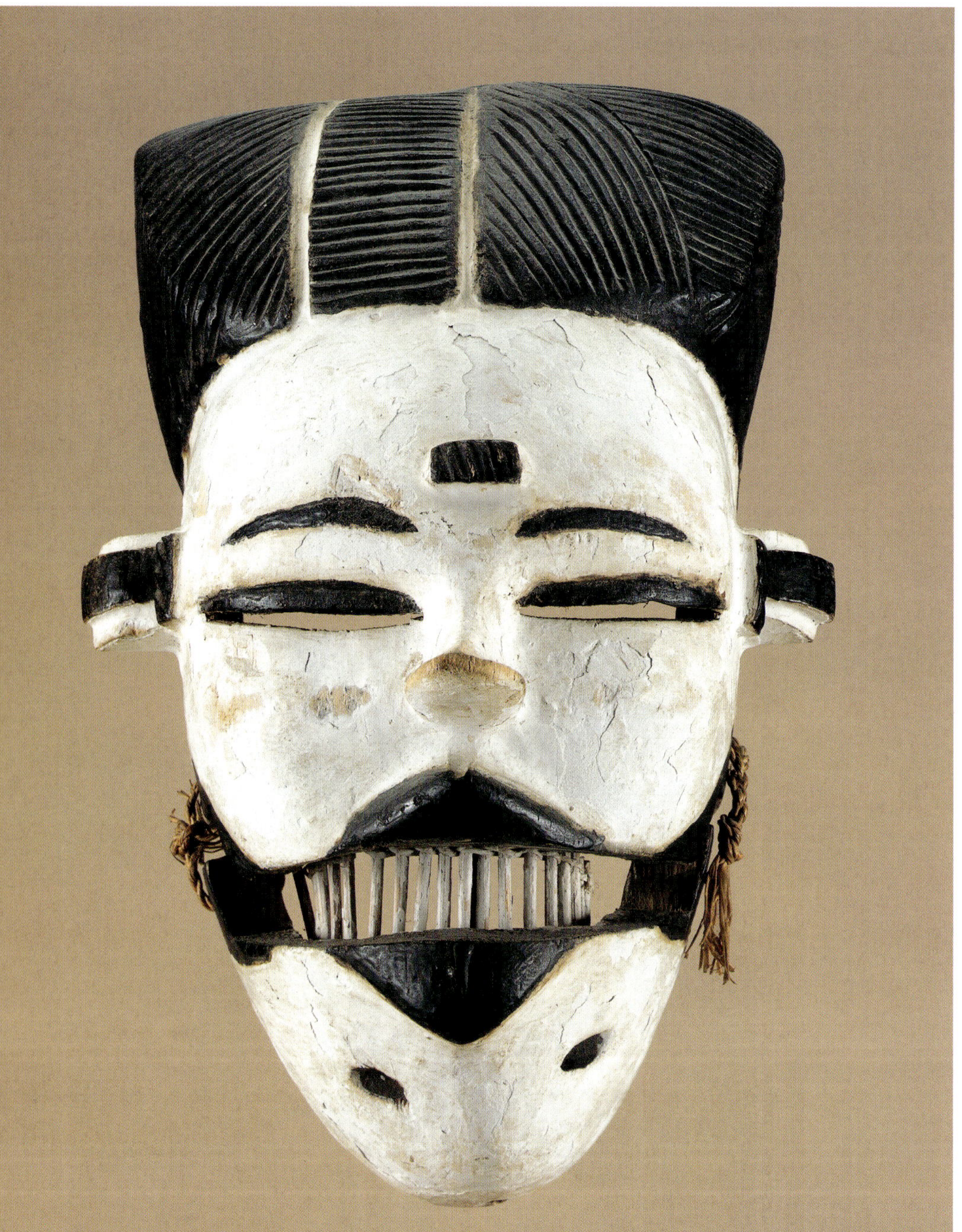

***Elu* mask worn for New Yam Festival. Ogoni, Tai, Nigeria**
Photo: Jill Salmons, 1992

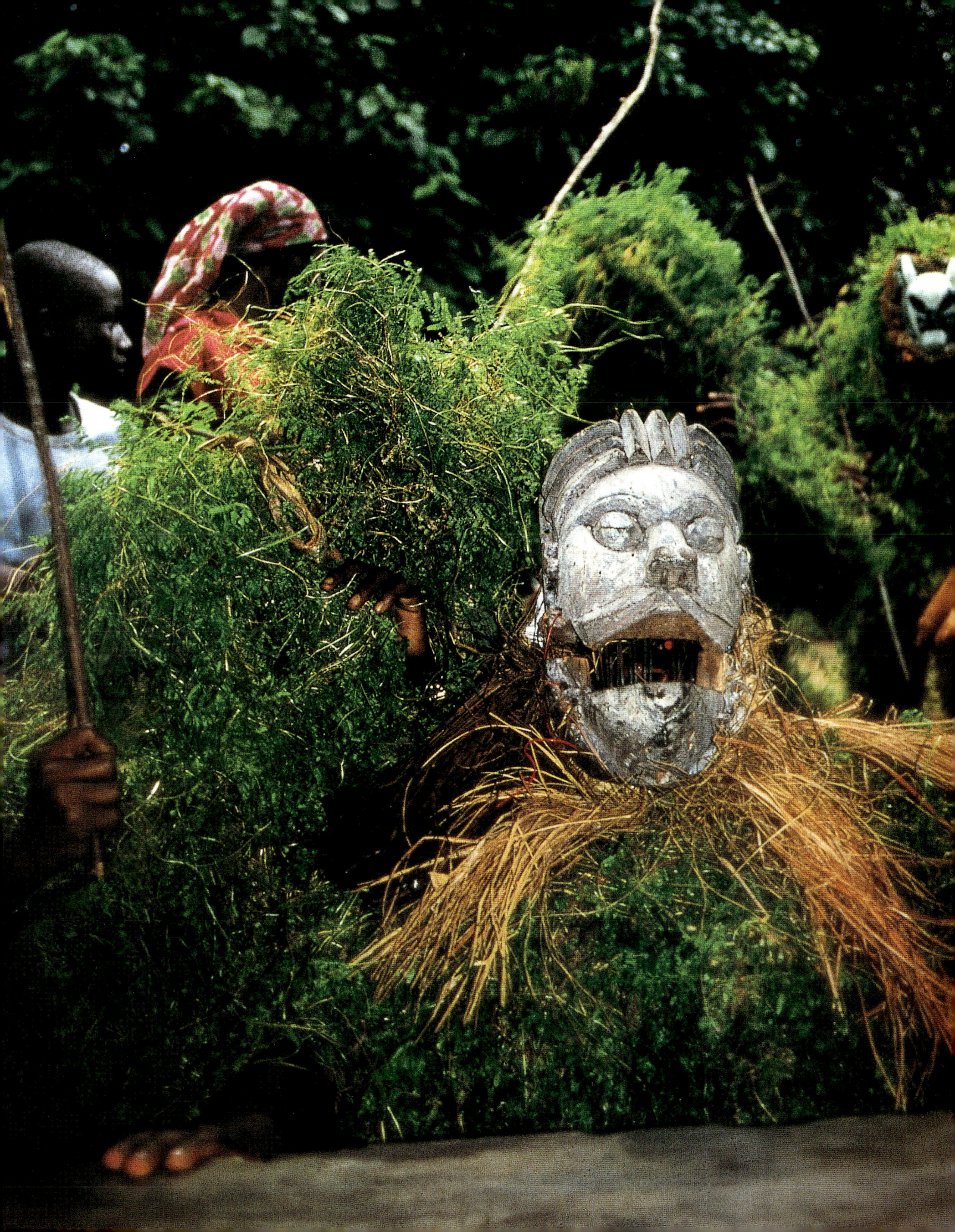

3

Renewable Art of Containment: a Djerma Vessel

Vessel
Djerma, Niger
c. Mid-20th century
Clay, pigment, H. 70 cm
Gift of Dawn M. Liberi, Washington, D.C.
BMA 1999.579a

The Djerma (Zarma) live at the edge of the Sahara Desert, the Sahel, in Niger, in the vicinity of the capital, Niamey, in an extremely arid and sandy environment. They and many of their neighbors produce large vessels such as this to hold milk, water, and grain. The rounded bottoms, which might be seen as an oversight in a Western context, are an obvious solution here, well suited to sit in the sand. They also sit well in a circular porting pad on top of the head.

The decoration of the vessel is made using natural pigments such as kaolin, red clay, soft yellow stone, ground charcoal, and ochre. With a matrix of either water or peanut oil, the colors are applied using a brush for the broad bands, and a knife for the linear designs. As the decorations on the vessel are not fired, but painted, they are not durable, and must be renewed from time to time, an endeavor that keeps them fresh and keeps women artists occupied (Gardi 1969:112). The periodic renewal of surfaces is deeply embedded into the culture of the Sahel. Entire buildings, mosques, residences, and granaries made of earth are annually resurfaced with fresh mud and decorative pigments in a communal effort that is socially binding for the people as well as structurally beneficial. The choice to paint, requiring restoration, rather than to fire in shades of slip, may reflect a common preference for the evidence of use, the observance of change, and the activity of renewal.

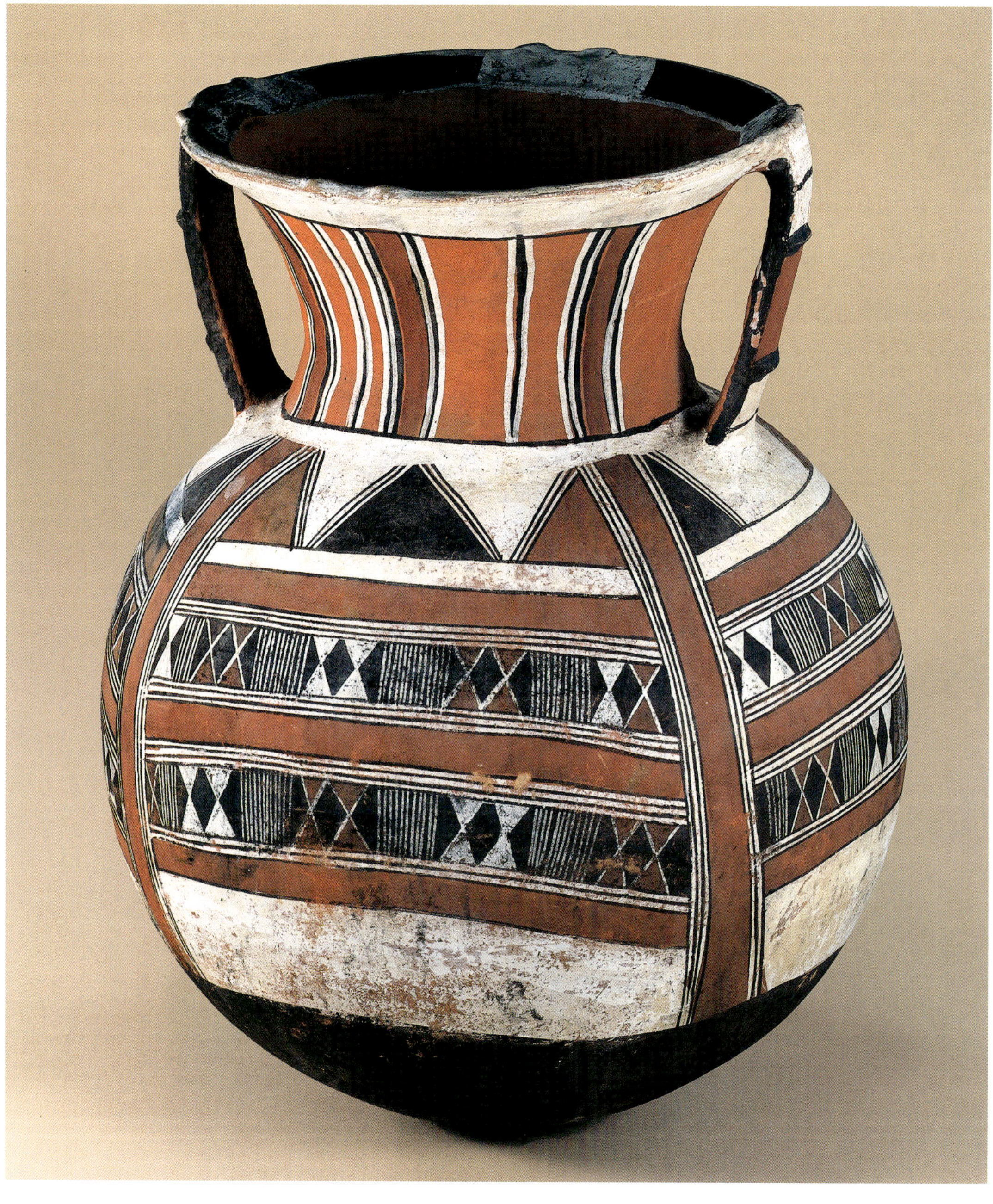

Djerma woman balancing a vessel on her head. Niger
Photo: Eliot Elisofon, 1970. Courtesy of the Eliot Elisofon Photographic Archive, National Museum of African Art, Smithsonian Institution

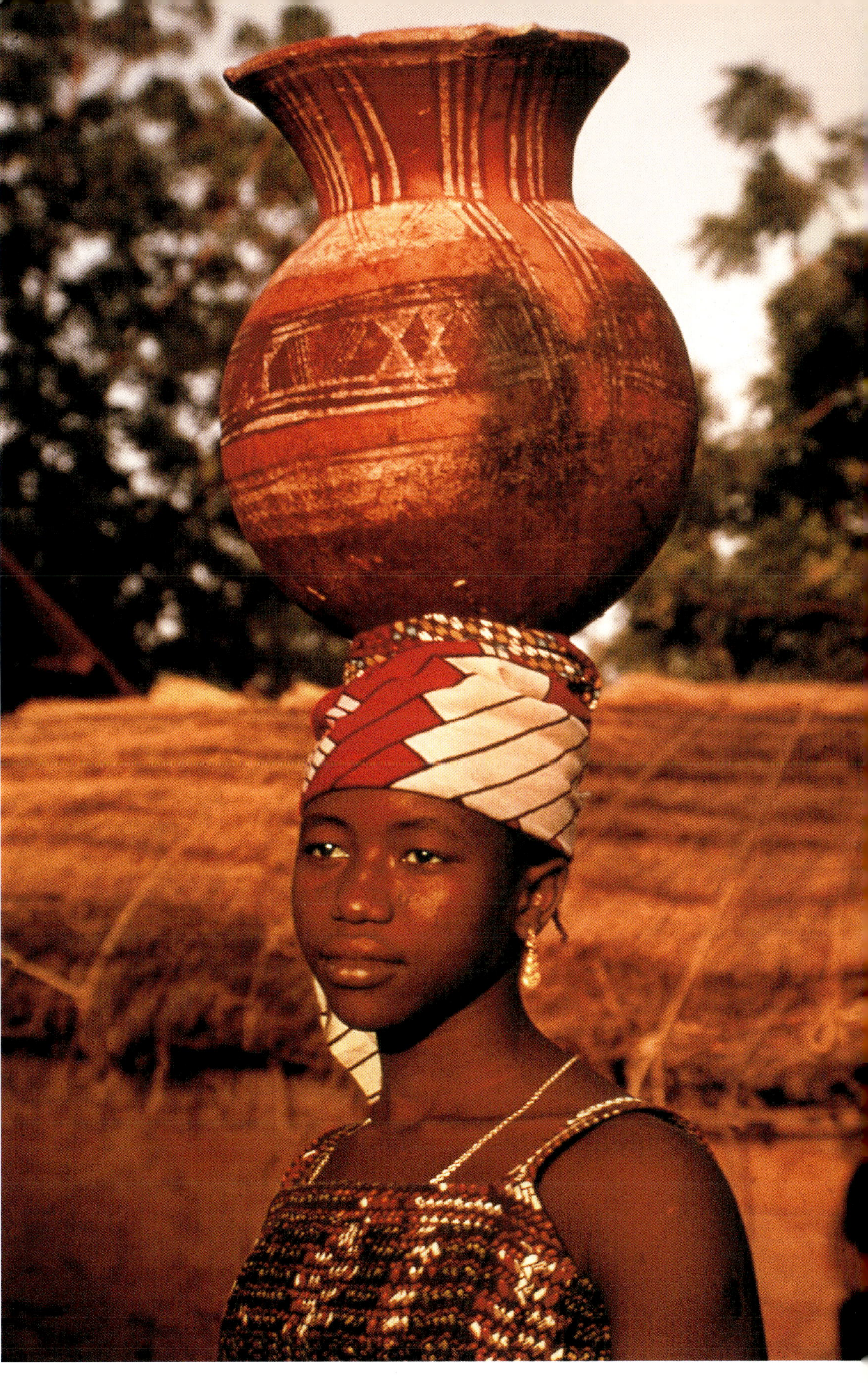

Large decorated vessels in this style have been used for thousands of years in the Sahara region. A painted image on the rocks in the region of Tassili-n-Ajjer, at the junction of Algeria, Libya, and Niger, predating dynastic Egypt, depicts vessels very similar to this one in shape and decoration (Scheel 1978: Fig. 10). The scene includes a habitation site filled with people, with herds of goats, sheep, and cattle, as well as a few dogs and other animals. At three different locations, a large, decorated vessel appears. A man places one vessel on the ground, stooping, and holding it with two hands. In another scene, a person, probably a woman, appears to put her hand in the vessel. And in a third scene, two men kneeling at either side of a vessel seem to hold a straw into it, through which one of the men sips.

F. J. L.

4

Surface as Key to Identity and Place: an Egyptian Relief

Relief Fragment of Ramesses II
Egypt, probably from the Nile Delta (Lower Egypt)
New Kingdom, Dynasty XIX, reign of Ramesses II, *c.* 1279–1213 BC
Rose granite, H. 73.7 cm
Gift of Blanche Adler
BMA 1931.4.1 (Purchased from Joseph Brummer in 1931; ex-coll. Maurice Nahman)

Few pharaohs evoke the grandeur of ancient Egypt as well as Ramesses II, who is often referred to today as simply "Ramesses the Great." His reign was long and stable, longer than any other pharaoh save that of Pepi II of the Old Kingdom (*c.* 2278–2184 BC). This longevity allowed him to undertake an impressive building program, which also extended south of Egypt into Nubia (from Aswan, Egypt, southward through Khartoum in modern-day Sudan), on a scale matched only by that of the 18th Dynasty Pharaoh Amenhotep III (*c.* 1390–1352 BC). Depictions of Ramesses II, which include this fragment, can be found in both two and three dimensions, and in a variety of media.

This fragment depicts the torso of a royal male figure, facing to the left, the left arm extended in a gesture of offering. The right arm is missing. This is no doubt a royal image, because he is shown wearing a serpent emblem on his brow, as well as a divine beard, attached by means of a chin strap, as it is false. In addition, above and behind him is part of a wing of a bird—probably a vulture, the manifestation of the goddess Nekhbet, who was the protector goddess of Upper (Southern) Egypt. Scenes of the king performing activities, whether of a cultic or military nature, often include an image of this bird, which provided the king with protection, hovering behind him.

Hypostyle hall (exterior), north wall, Karnak, Egypt. Battle scenes with Seti I, Dynasty XIX, appearing in three scenes. At lower left, his protector vulture-goddess hovers behind his head
Photo: Felice A. Beato, *c.* Mid–late 19th century (English, born Italy, *c.* 1830–1903), Albumen print, Sheet: 20.4 x 20.6 cm. Gift of Heru Ra Walmsley, Ferndale, Maryland, from the Estate of his Father, Harry R. Walmsley. BMA 1988.154.25

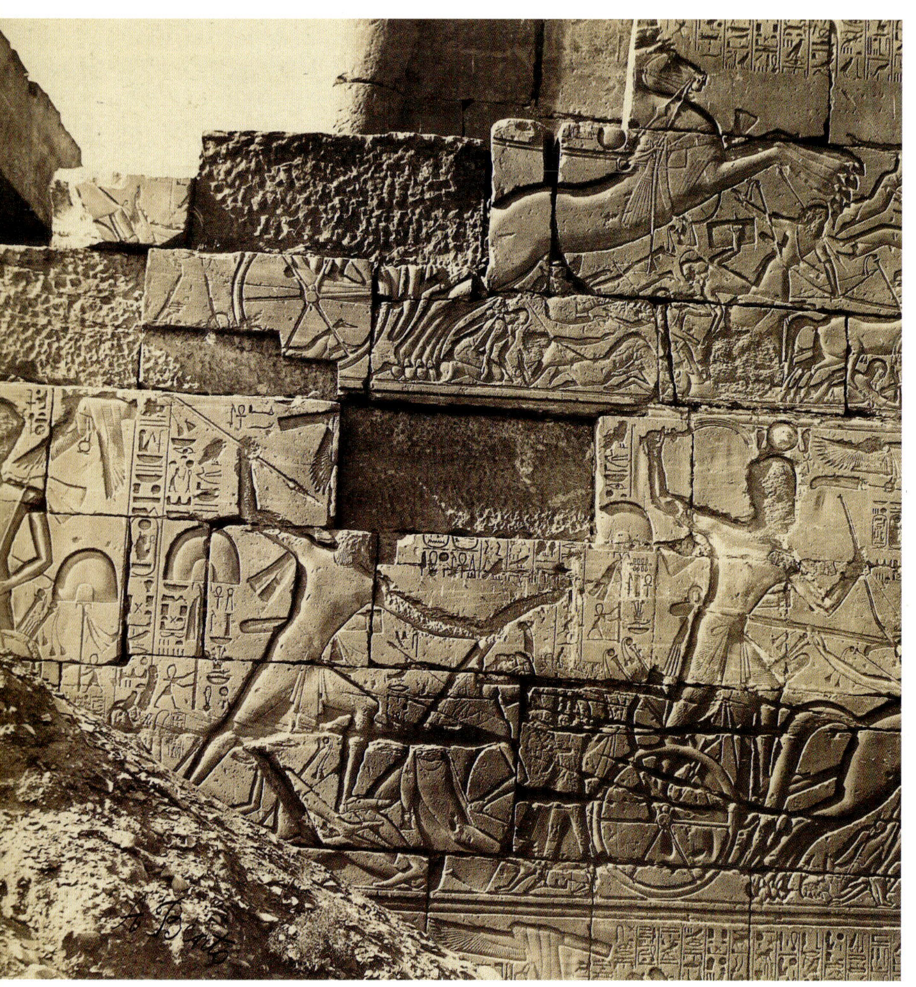

Despite a lack of any accompanying inscription that would serve to identify this king, it is clear that this is an image of Ramesses II, based on certain characteristics that are common to his sculptural representations. It is nearly impossible to assign a more specific date, as these same features do not change appreciably during the course of his reign. They include the soft, rounded cheek, the pursed lips, and the slightly aquiline nose (Robins 1997:169). However, while these are features that are characteristic of images of Ramesses II, it would be incorrect to consider this a true "portrait." Ramesses II, like almost all other Egyptian pharaohs, was consistently depicted in an idealized, youthful manner, even though he reached an advanced age during his long reign. The motivation for the idealization of royal images was at least partially propagandistic, serving to emphasize the king's power, virility, and semi-divine nature.

Ramesses also wears a short wig, which covers his ears and consists of columns of short rectangular curls. This is complemented by a headband that goes around the king's forehead, and is tied at the back of the head. He also wears a series of collars around his neck.

One enigmatic feature of this piece is the incision of two parallel vertical lines, connected by parallel horizontal lines. These are located slightly to the right of the divine beard, and extend from the piece of stone left over between the neck and the divine beard, passing over Ramesses' collars, and ending at the bottom of his left elbow. These probably define part of a scarf-like garment known from other relief depictions of Ramesses II, which consists of alternating tall and short rectangles, terminating at either end in two rows of three *ankh*-hieroglyphs. The possible purpose of this accessory was to heighten the festive character of a scene where the king meets a god (Schoske and Wildung 1985:83). However, it is curious that on this fragment the scarf is not depicted on both sides of the figure's neck. It is possible that it was originally intended to be added to this relief, but was later abandoned, and perhaps the sculptor made a partial attempt to remove it.

All four sides of this piece have been broken off, making it impossible to determine what Ramesses was offering, or to which deity he was presenting this offering. The king, by virtue of his role as intermediary between the divine and earthly spheres, was the only person capable of performing certain cultic activities, such as presenting offerings to the gods.

The ancient Egyptians carved in two different techniques: raised relief and sunk relief. This piece was created using sunk relief; the desired image was cut back within its outline, leaving the surrounding surface higher than the image. In raised relief, the background surrounding the desired image was cut away, leaving the image standing out above the surface. In both techniques, the images were then modeled within their outlines. Traditionally, sunk relief was used on exterior walls, where the sunlight would enhance the carving through the creation of interesting effects of shadow. Raised relief was reserved for interior walls, as the sun's rays tended to diminish its effect, making it appear flatter (Robins 1997:25). Another important difference between the two techniques was that sunk relief was considerably less labor-intensive than raised relief. To help achieve his ambitious building goals, Ramesses II used sunk relief extensively, even in interior areas, and raised relief was almost never carved after the first few years of his reign (Shaw 2000:301).

This fragment was probably originally part of a gateway because of the subject matter and the choice of rose granite as the material. As the figure in this fragment is shown facing left, it probably came from the right side of a gateway. Ramesses faced a deity who would have presumably occupied the more prominent, central position, appearing to emerge from the gateway. It is not possible to tell what kind of structure this gateway belonged to, but access to it would have been restricted to a small, elite group; a temple is one strong possibility. The rear surface of this fragment was left in a roughly chiseled state, but its fresh appearance when compared to the front indicates that the chiseling was probably done in the more recent past.

It is not possible to determine exactly the original site of this fragment. The best possibility is the Ramesside capital of Pi-Ramesses ("The House of Ramesses") in the eastern Delta, which was established by Ramesses II. However, very few of this site's monuments are preserved today, as they were usurped by the pharaohs of the 21st and 22nd Dynasties, who moved them a short distance to their new royal cities at Tanis and Bubastis. These latter two sites are known to have contained large numbers of monuments of Ramesses II, especially those in rose granite.

Thomas Kittredge

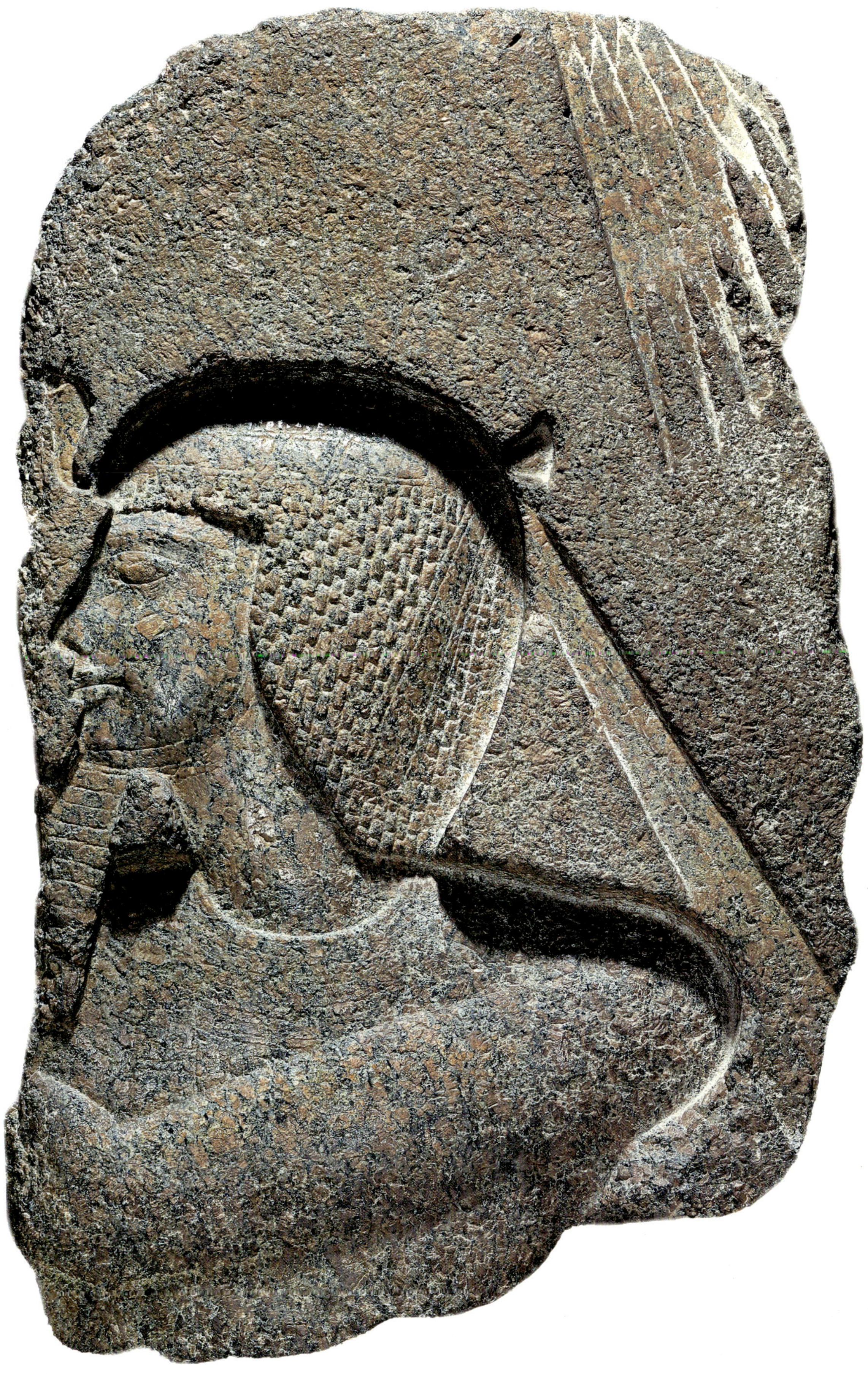

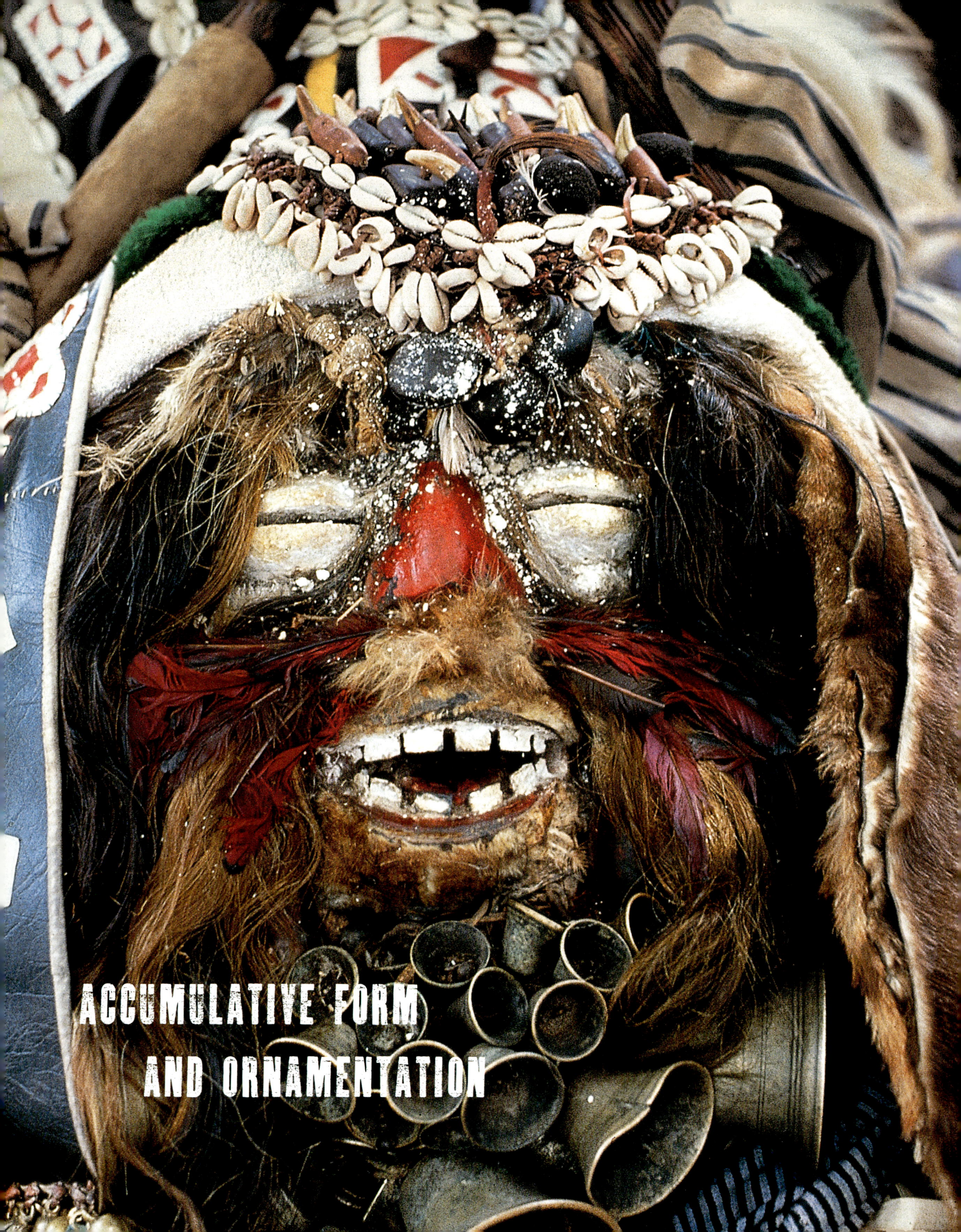

ACCUMULATIVE FORM AND ORNAMENTATION

Continuing our process of reconstruction, we encounter rich "accumulations" (A. Rubin 1974) or accoutrements that often form an important part of a mask or ritual figure. This configuration of elements or "ornamentation" originally applied may consist of seashells, metal ornaments, small glass bottles, large and small horns, hair, fur, cloth, bones, or other miniature carved items. In many cases, this material accumulation is essential to the meaning and function of the object. Generally, such additions are prescribed by a traditional healer or diviner, and the configuration "works" because of the "prescription."

Two examples of face masks from the Dan of Liberia and the Ivory Coast illustrate the way that African masks have been stripped of their accoutrements and, thus, their power. The first is a mask donated by Saidie A. May in 1951 (p. 99). The mask has a pristine and beautiful form in itself as it hangs on the museum wall, but something is missing. Around the periphery of the forehead and the chin is a series of large holes obviously meant for attaching something.

If we compare it with another Dan mask in the collection (p. 40), we begin to get a sense of what has been lost. Surrounding the forehead of this latter mask is a rolled band of padded cloth decorated with cowrie shells. Attached to the chin is a fringe of plaited fibers probably representing a beard, even though the mask may be assigned a feminine role in ritual. Suspended on a cord from the mask's right side is a glass bottle containing what appears to be some earth or sand and the carcass of an insect. Also attached is a miniature whisk of the stumps of feather quills bound with netted fiber at the base. Suspended from the mask's left hand side is a large bag of locally woven cloth containing a small, glazed, ceramic jar half filled with a hard, unidentified soil mixture, eight mussel shells, a short twig or fiber with thread wound around it, and six cowrie shells sanded flat and filled with the same soil mixture. Suspended above this sack are the horn of a small deer, two semicircular iron rattles, another small sack of the same locally made cloth (unopened) containing an unidentified object, and a third sack made of oiled imported linen of which the bottom is entirely decayed and the contents of the sack presumably lost. Behind the mask is a panache of rust-colored feathers backed by a brown imported cloth. Remaining on the mask's left eyebrow is a copper strip, and on the cheek the metal end of a bullet casing with the stamp "Remington Express." In and around the eyes the remains of a red encrustation (probably mashed kola nut) can be found.

This mask was bought directly from a chief in 1967 by the donor, Ray Thompson, and comes with the information that the chief was wearing it over his shoulder in a ceremony meant to honor the American visitor. While it was no longer meant to be worn on the face (its interior is entirely packed with a mixture composed apparently of earth and soot), it is, nevertheless, an excellent example of the kind of ensemble of objects that was essential to the ritual functioning and artistic viability of such masks. The accumulations are often termed "medicine" in many African languages, and are considered capable of effecting change. By containing them in bottles and jars their power may be highlighted and concentrated. Deer horns and bird feathers may invoke the particular spiritual or physical qualities of those animals. Indigenous textile or even imported cloth may bring to bear power relationships and cosmological forces inherent in the act of weaving. A good example of a powerful attachment is that described in this volume for the Mossi "Red Mask" (see p. 86) at the top of which there is a swinging spiritual bundle. Special bundles often adorn the top of the head, as in the Luba Kifwebe mask (p. 285) and the Mau mask (p. 236), or are attached to fiber costumes such as that of the Mende Sande mask (p. 175). Such medicine would be uniquely prescribed by the ritual practitioner

Mask of Wisdom (*Baya Seibli Gnon*)
Sub-district of Fakobly, Wè, Ivory Coast
Photo: Marie-Noël Verger-Fèvre, 1983

to effect the desired changes in an individual or in the community. The embellishment of objects applies as often to shrine figures as it does to masks. Figures taken from the shrine are often stripped by their buyers of what are seen as unnecessary encumbrances to a pristinely beautiful abstract form contributing no value to the object at market.

However, the production of the carved mask alone may be one of the least labor-intensive aspects of the total art form, and one of the least costly items in its preparation. An interesting investigation into the monetary cost of the preparation for a masquerade was made by Jean Borgatti (1983) when she commissioned an Anogiri mask and costume for UCLA from the Okpella people of Nigeria in 1973. She found, first of all, that the mask itself was rather dispensable and could be replaced often. After the carver delivers the mask:

> Tradition dictates that the owner of the mask, not the carver, applies the decorative elements. Using beeswax (*erhue*), he impresses the abrus seeds (*epu*), cowrie shells, and mirrors into the desired patterns on the face.... The owner must also buy the cloth for the costume and bring it to a tailor.... However, no Anogiri is complete without bells, and for these the owner contacts a smith, providing him with all materials: four kerosene tins and a spool of native thread (handspun cotton on a spindle). Kerosene tins ... were available only in Benin City, necessitating a round-trip of 140 miles....
>
> By this time, $10.00 had been invested in the mask (labor, materials [including decorative seeds, shells, and mirrors], refreshments) and about $23.00 in the costume (suit and bells). In terms of resources, then, the mask cost somewhat less than half the price of the costume.... [This] still does not accurately reflect the actual cost borne by an Okpella family when inaugurating a masquerade.... [The "no-frills" UCLA mask] has no props and no *ebe* cloth. There were no medicines linked to consecration which would have involved at least the cost of a cock, ... [and] ritual medication to make the character more powerful. In terms of costume and consecration, the cost depends on what the owner is willing or able to spend, while the price of the wooden mask remains fixed.

The carved wooden mask may also be one of the elements least valued by the owners of the ritual. In some cases the accoutrements are stripped from the object by the original owner and seller, because it is not the basic carved wooden form—no matter how beautiful or intriguing it may seem—that contains the most ritual power, but rather the prescription items that have been attached and empowered by a ritual practitioner. The head of a local Bondo society once brought out a shrine figure and offered it to me for sale, but she insisted upon removing the cloth costume she had made for the female figure before releasing the figure. Packets containing meicinally and spiritually powerful substances, as found on the forehead of Bamana Komo mask (p. 41), are often stripped off the objects before they are released from the ritual owner's care. The carved wooden object is often considered as little more than a nicely crafted product made by an artisan and used to act as the armature for an assemblage of items of ritual power.

Particular elements of the ensemble may take preeminence in the service of one or another artistic or functional goal during a shrine installation or masquerade. Some elements, like bells, rattles, or wooden pendants may be important to the sound of the performance (pp. 175, 279). Shiny mirrors, porcelain, metal tacks, and nails are important to the concept of lighting or staging, attracting spiritual power in the case of the Kongo nail figure, signifying position in the cycle of life in other Kongo figures (P. 259), or expressing intellectual and cultural brilliance, referencing the noonday sun, in the case of the Baga D'mba headdress (p. 223). Hair, fiber, or cloth may be instrumental to the movement of the figure or mask (pp. 57, 175). For Pende masks (p. 88), Strother (in Pemberton 2000:10–103) notes the importance of heavy ruffs of raffia worn by masked diviners around the shoulders, consisting of eight separate belts of raffia, made to fly out during the dance by rolling the shoulders vigorously:

Mask
Bamana, Mali, Kono association
c. 20th century
Wood, string. H 104.1 cm
Purchase with exchange funds from Gift of Alan Wurtzburger
BMA 1960.66

> Of all the attributes for the mask, Muyaga Gangambi (*Les masques pende de Gatundo*, 1974) has stressed the importance of the ruff: ... Nganga Ngombo does not dance lifting its feet so as to sound the foot rattles; all its dance is in the ruff at the neck, whether [the dancer performs] standing or on his knees on the ground".... Muyaga notes that at the climax of Nganga Ngombo's dance the ruff will fly up, even covering the performer's face at times...., [the dancer] rolling his shoulders backward and gently pumping his arms up-and-down.... The ruff both signals the religious associations of the event and highlights the distinctive motions of the initiation dance.

Pierre Harter (1993:199) describes the alienation of the simple wood mask from its context of paraphernalia among the Wè people of the Ivory Coast as follows (p. 43):

> The trappings consist of a group of objects which indicate a mask's category. These include the wooden face mask, or *gla yö wa*, which is mistakenly given the maximum value by collectors of African art. In fact, when this mask is stripped of its paraphernalia it almost invariably loses all identity. Indeed when it is naked, shelved, exposed in a showcase or hung on a wall it becomes extremely difficult, if not impossible, to determine its category. To a society member it has become a dead object, mummified, with neither value nor meaning. It is like a skin shed by a molting snake; all of the personality and power have been transferred to the new mask which has replaced it. This happens after the sweat of the previous wearer has been "washed" and carried to the inside of the new mask, and after the old mask's human teeth have been pulled and implanted in the new one.

In this section, Marie-Noël Verger-Fèvre analyzes the bristling accumulative forces of the Wè Gbona Gla mask in terms of the insecurity of isolation in a heavily forested area. In an ancient Egyptian amulet described by Thomas Kittredge, we see the importance of the individual ornament to the human body. The adornment of living Ndebele women is shown to function as a personal identification, and makes proclamations about status and desire.

In our analysis of the material aspects of African art, we might want to pay more attention to ephemeral elements, such as feathers, fibers, leaves, organic concoctions, and tied-on packets. How is the complex iconography of a mask or figure effaced when so many message-bearing articles are eliminated?

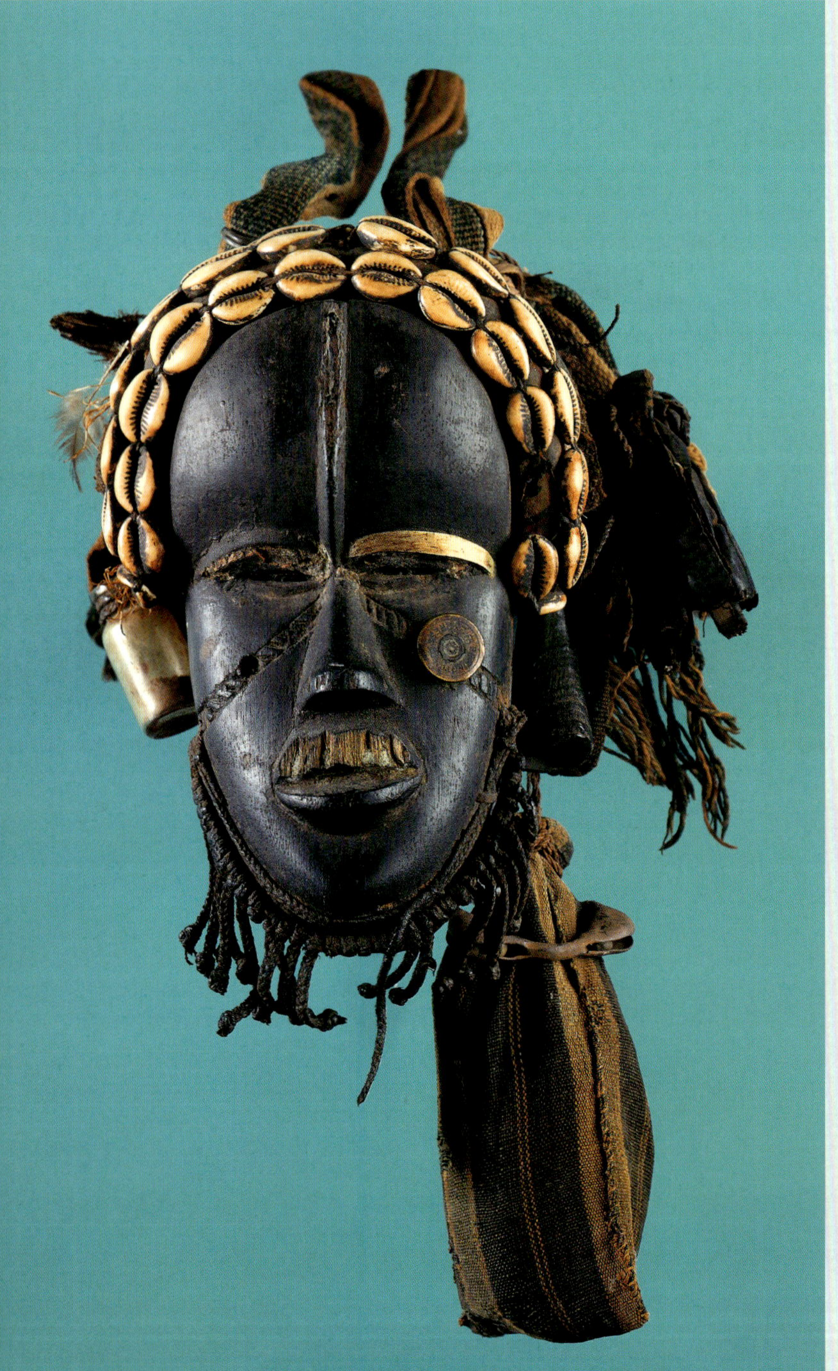

Pendant Mask. Dan, Liberia, *c.* Early 20th century
Wood, metal, cowrie shells, cloth, glass, herbs, horns, feathers, mussel shells, ceramics. H. 22 cm
Gift of Ray Thompson
BMA 1977.34.2

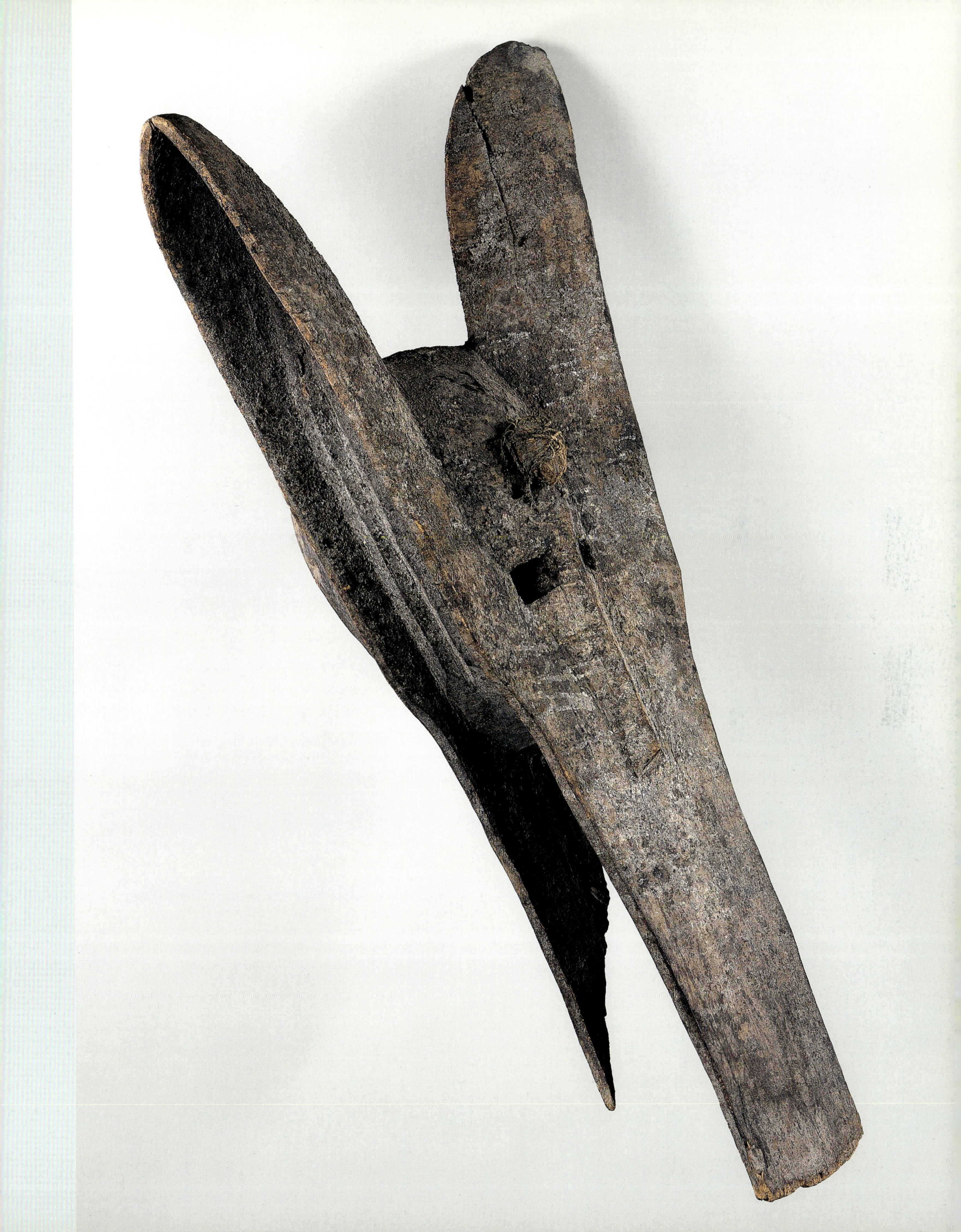

5

Mask of Wisdom: a Wè Mask (*Gbona Gla*)

Mask (*Gbona Gla*)
Wè (Guéré, Wobé, Niabwa, Békoué, Oubi, Krahn and Tchien subgroups), Ivory Coast/Liberia
c. Mid-20th century
Wood, paint, cloth, bush cat skin, beads, human hair, vegetable fiber
H. 45.7 cm
Gift of Dr. and Mrs. Bernard Berk and Mr. and Mrs. Leonard Whitehouse
BMA 1969.11

Because of the large size of this mask, the use of the color white, the numerous tusks, and the ornaments in the form of leopard teeth, the Wè people would characterize it as a "great mask." It is commonly known as Gbona Gla, "mask of wisdom," which can sometimes be glossed as "mother mask," referring not specifically to femininity but, rather, to its antiquity. The visual force of the mask, in the wildly contrasting rhythms of this mask—with its jutting forehead, bold hooked nose, framed by two pairs of protruding eyes, and wide open mouth—connotes masculinity for the Wè. In field research, however, questions whether a specific mask is feminine or masculine often brought on laughter from the people: the mask is neither one or the other because it is not human—it is a spirit.

The Wè country, covering a region extending from southwestern Ivory Coast to eastern Liberia, straddling the Cavally River, is largely covered with primary forest. Here warrior societies (*bloa-dru*), some older than others, are held together by lineage relationships (Schwartz 1971). These societies are isolated one from another by the forest environment, resulting in some feeling of insecurity. They have attempted to ameliorate their vulnerability somewhat through alliances with close neighbors and through the reinforcement of lineage cohesion. But this insecurity has also stimulated the quest for supernatural protection capable of warding off hostile forces of not only the opposing warriors but also the malevolent spiritual beings of the forest. Therefore the manifestation of fantastic creatures, such as is represented by Gbona Gla, continues from an ancient time unknown to traditional genealogists of the Wè.

The Wè are fundamentally devotees of *kwi*, a powerful spiritual force, invisible to non-members, and not represented with a mask. Kwi, by extension, represents a religious culture that extends through the neighboring peoples to the south. It is in the context of this culture that specific masks are created by individual members in the attempt to obtain spiritual force. The mask (*gla*) is visible to the public. The Wè celebrations in honor of their masks, held in the village center, are a seductive spectacle.

Among the different masks that animate Wè ceremonies, the most venerated is the Gbona Gla, the "mask of wisdom." This mask is the property of a family, and often is in its possession for a long time, considered to be the most ancient of the masks of the region, the great peacemaker, the guarantor of the maintenance of social order. "He is not only a mask," explained the guide, referring to a particular mask named Dibaou, "he is also a dancer, policeman, and singer." In sum, he is "polyvalent," as one finds frequently in Wè country masking. The mask is the supreme judge in the case of litigation grave enough to threaten the stability of the village community. In the sacred enclosure of *kpan* (or *kman*—Tierou 1975:73), the mask pronounces a verdict which may not be appealed, imposing a heavy fine on the culpable: an ox, or a sheep, according to the gravity of the transgression, in order to compensate, through the sacrificial offering, for the breach of customary law. The animal is slain, prepared, and offered to the participants in a banquet of reconciliation.

Gbona Gla, inaugurated with the highest dignity in the Gla (mask) society, is brought out in public only in very specific circumstances. Some do not come out from their *kpan* except every ten or fifteen years, or on the occasion of a funeral of a member of the association. It was for such a ceremony that the grand mask, Nang Ného, appeared at Bangolo, in the Guéré region, in February 1984. The name, *nang* (or *nann*—Harter 1993:214) signifying "ancestor," is borne by the most highly venerated masks; it recalls the ties that unite the mask, representing the ancestral spirit, with the members of the lineage.

Nang Ného was accompanied by a number of acolytes all dressed in traditional cloths, carrying the insignia of their ranks. He was preceded by his herald mask, Bao Gla; the masked dancers, Vonhontéhé and Ténédjié; the warrior mask, Bonhoua; and the drum beaters of his slit gong, *glohé*. Nang Neho then followed, bending, leaning on his high cane, and advanced with great deliberation; the act of crossing the neighborhood square that he visits lasted close to one hour.

Nang Ného's face was entirely whitened with kaolin, his huge cotton hood was white, as was his headdress, *kihi van*, bristling with a bundle of tall, predominantly white feathers from the fisher eagle. The color white is the sign of the sacred, of wisdom, of great age, commanding respect. Only the great mask may wear the *kihi van*, and only he may authorize a "younger" mask to add the eagle feathers to its own headdress.

At Fakobly, in the Wobé region, in April 1983, the great mask of the village of Kouibli was accompanied by dignitaries. One of them carried a lance and the other an olifant (elephant-tusk trumpet), the prerogative of the great mask. With the mask covered with a beard of ox tails and the hides of wild animals, the only visible forms of the face were the eyes in the form of crotal bells, whitened with kaolin, reddened nose, and large teeth. The enormous headdress of feathers, accented with ornaments of cowrie shells, added to the mass of the sculpted face, all of this resting on a voluminous fiber skirt, giving the appearance of a misshapen being, the evocation of a totally unhuman bush spirit.

The mask's name was Baya Seiblignon, translated as "he who is responsible for the last bride-price," and suggesting the character of this mask as a peacemaker. When a married woman dies in her husband's village, her parents hold the widower and his lineage group responsible for their inability to save her. It is then necessary for him to offer the deceased's parents "the last bride-price," compensation for the loss of their daughter. The widower can offer the grieving family an ox, or a sheep, according to his means. If the widower at this moment finds himself incapable of supporting such an obligation, the mask of wisdom, "the guarantor of the last bride-price," offers the compensatory animal himself, precluding any litigation. At a future time, the "loan" would be repaid with an animal given to the great mask by the defaulting family, accompanied by numerous "gifts" in gratitude for the service rendered.

Traditionally, in the Wè region, masked dance is the work of men, as in most African areas where masks are utilized. However, in April 1986, at Béouhé-Zabiao (in Bangolo sub-district in the Guéré region), I had the chance to attend a periodic ceremony in honor of the great mask, Dibaou. Dibaou, in a long speech,

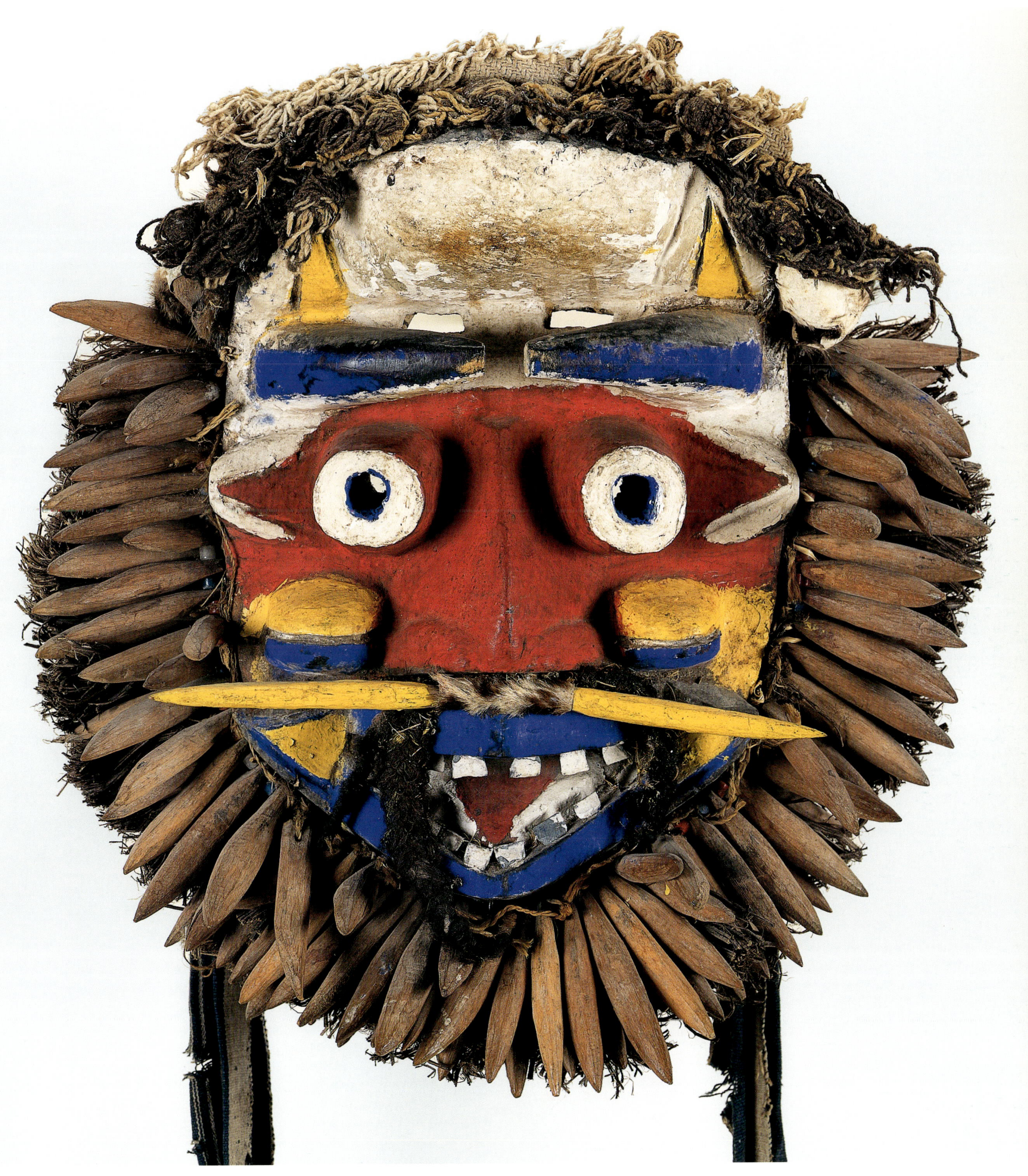

recalled the great deeds marking the history of the lineage, and praised those who, over the course of time, had succeeded one another in its service. The transmission of the oral tradition is one of his most important roles. His words were repeated, phrase by phrase, by his interpreter, as is customary with the great masks, since the voice is always distorted by the obstruction of the sculpted face. His numerous dignitaries surrounded him.

One aspect of this performance was anomalous, though there was nothing to arouse suspicion: the wearer of the mask, invisible under the costume, was a woman. My guide in Bangolo, himself a *gla zo*, in charge of a mask, gave me an explanation: this woman had inherited the mask from her paternal grandfather. She had felt "called," so she went to consult the diviner, who advised her to take on the mask so that her affairs would prosper. "Her relatives did what is necessary" for her then to be accepted by the Gla society of masks. These rare exceptions are admissible in certain villages of the Guéré and the Wobé, but elsewhere in Wè country, only a man may wear a mask.

The mask as it comes from the sculptor's workshop is still nothing more than an inanimate object. The head of the society that has commissioned it will submit it to a series of rituals before the official investiture. The dancer, himself, will have undergone particular initiation tests. The mask will be adorned with facial hair, a feathered headdress, horns, tusks, and leopard teeth (carved by the sculptor of the mask). The dancer will then be enveloped by an ample skirt of fibers.

At the death of the owner of a mask, where no decision has been made concerning its transmission, a ritual is necessary to designate a new wearer. This ceremony follows immediately after the funeral of the former dancer, because it is critical that the mask immediately resume its life: the mask does not die. The following is the procedure that took place after the death of the wearer of the great mask, Zé, in May 1988, as described to me by a *gla zo* from Bangolo, a high dignitary in the society of Gla:

At midnight, after the departure of the multitude of guests, only the initiated men were authorized to remain. The remains of the deceased lay in a coffin in front of his house, and all the masks of the region came to call the deceased by his name. Then the coffin was carried out to the kpan, the sacred grove, where it was placed on a mat together with the mask of the deceased, with its headdress and all its accoutrements. Here all members of Gla were gathered: the dancers, their accompanists, musicians, singers, griots, and trumpet blowers. Two elderly women, "servants" of the mask, were also admitted, although the sacred enclosure is prohibited to all other woman. The eldest made an offering to the deceased, in a calabash of water, of four kola nuts, two white and two red, cracked in half, which she tossed on the ground, asking the deceased to authorize the transmission of the powers of the mask to him who would prove capable of taking it up. The agreement of the deceased was given by the position of the kolas on the ground (if it is unfavorable, the procedure is repeated several times).

Following this, the herald (the "son") of the great mask, who had always accompanied him in every public appearance, danced in the manner of his "father." Now, for several hours, the male members of the lineage—brothers, sons, cousins of the deceased—came to dance within a circle, each in his turn, imitating the behavior and gestures of the mask. The best dancers, i.e. the best imitators, were selected by a jury composed of the accompanyists of the great mask, who know exactly how it should act in public. Each of them was invited to repeat his

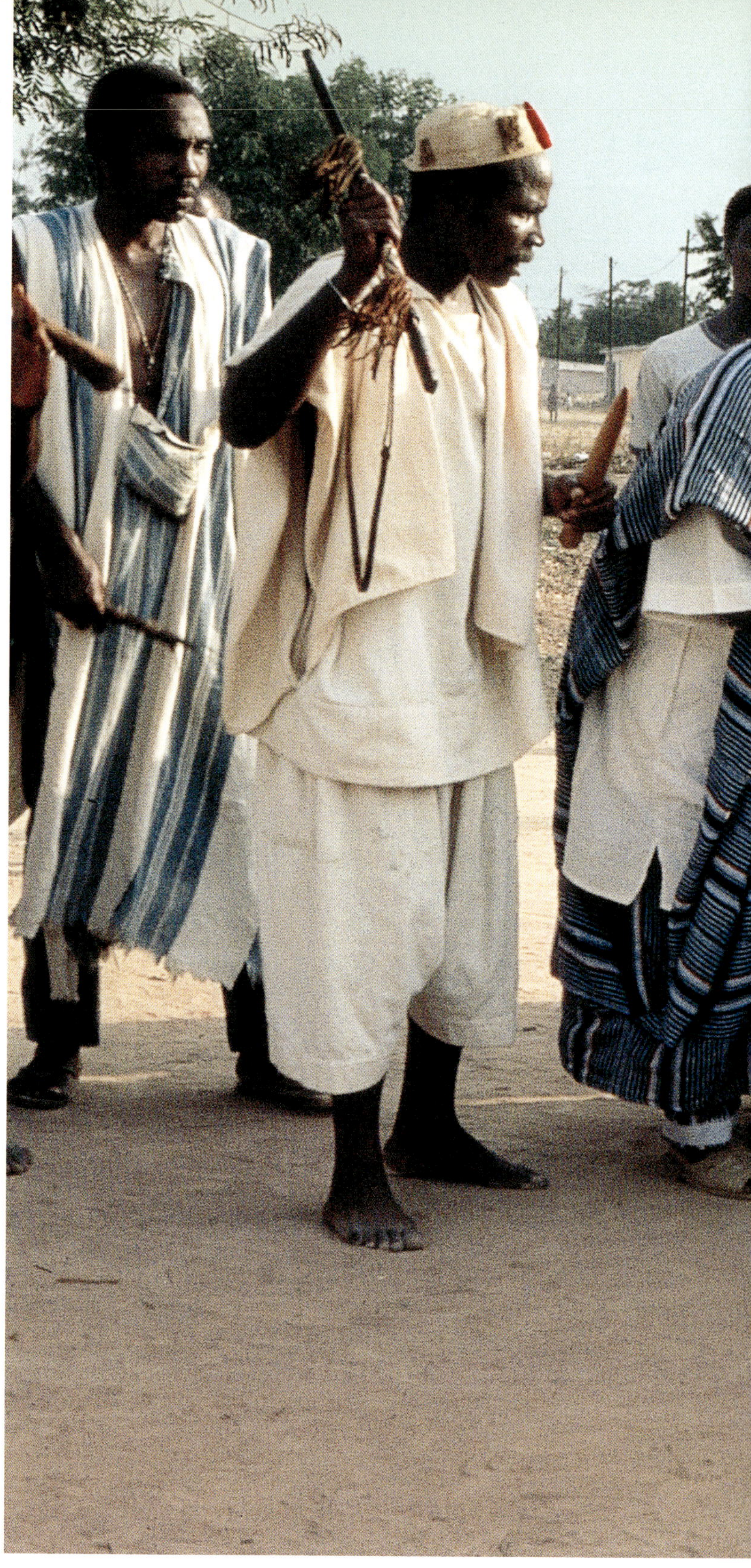

performance, perhaps three or four times, critiqued good-naturedly by those present and by the mocking tones of the trumpet blowers.

Finally the one elected was dressed for the first time in a white cloth by the most important mask of the region, who solemnly declared: "Zé has come again, here he is, come and salute him! His raffia, which had fallen, is renewed, his drum, which had had a trembling voice, trembles no more, and his staff, which had lain on the ground, is taken up!" The new wearer was then saluted by everyone, and given gifts such as cloths, money, and kolas.

When not in dance, the mask must stay in the *dihi*, the house reserved for the mask in the *kpan*, together with the costume

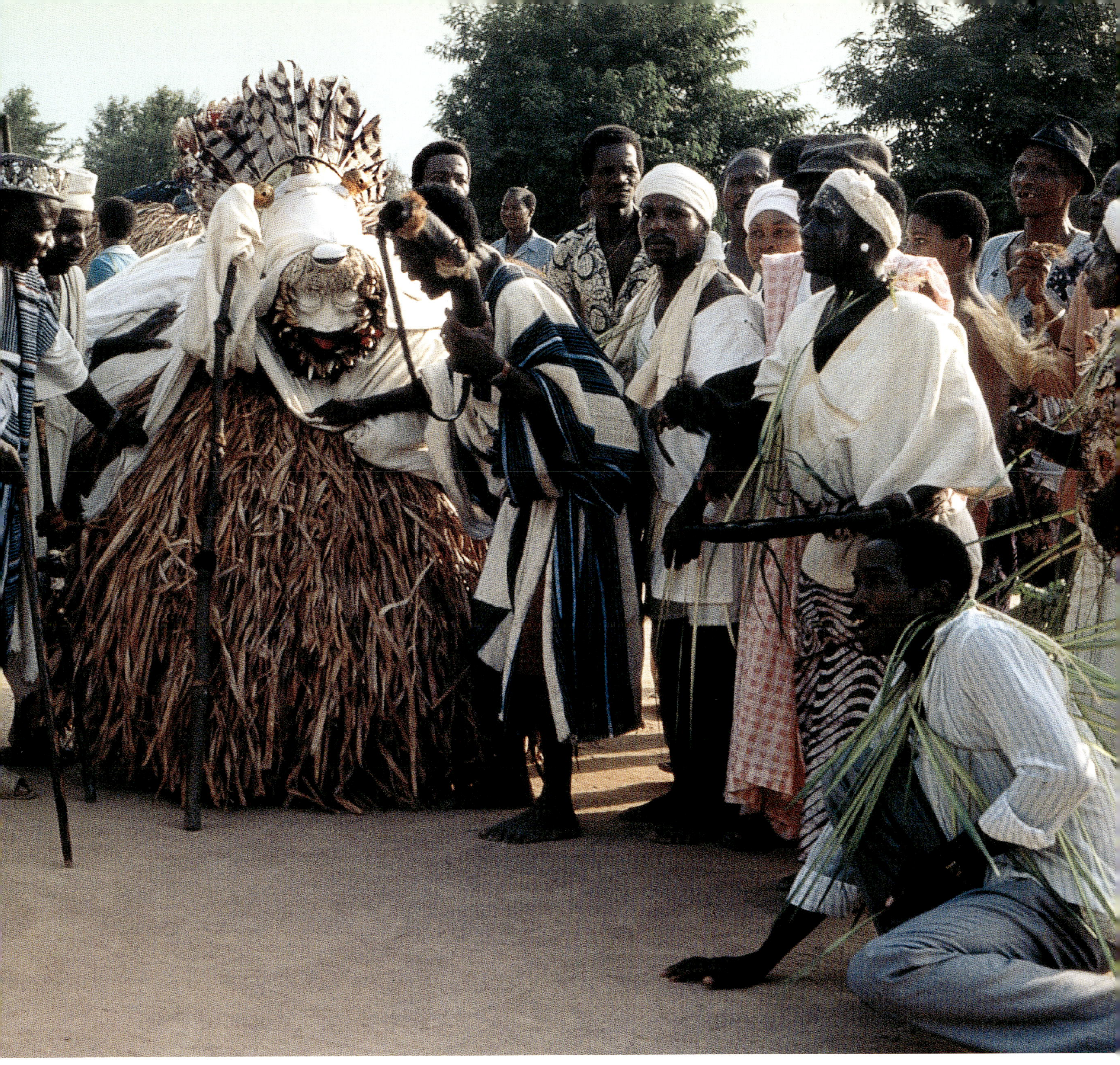

Mask of Wisdom, *Nang Ného*. Sub-district of Bangolo, Wè, Ivory Coast
Photo: Marie-Noël Verger-Fèvre, 1984

and all the effects such as the staff, headdress, and sack of "medicines". The wearer of the mask may return to the *kpan* occasionally to establish himself, and to prepare for the various appearances he will have to make: the anniversary of his succession four years later, and then every eight years (in the case of the mask, Zé—some great masks appear only every ten or fifteen years), and for special occasions such as funerals of the members of the Gla association, or the reception of a VIP. During his initiation, he spends his time learning the immutable discourse of the mask, taking note of the historic events that mark the life of the village since its first appearance, and announcing the succession of chosen interpreters and principal accompanyists. In this way, the transmission of lineage history to new generations is assured and the memory of great deeds performed by their ancestors is preserved.

Marie-Noël Verger-Fèvre

6

Implements of Temple Ritual: an Egyptian Amulet

One of the basic instruments of ancient Egyptian religious practice, throughout all social strata, was the amulet. Usually, this was a small, light object worn on the body, and was believed to possess apotropaic powers, thus providing the bearer with health and other benefits (*Lexikon* I:232; Pinch 1994:107). Amulets were worn by the living, and were represented as pendants in statuary and relief sculpture (*Lexikon* I:233). Amulets could also accompany their owner into the tomb after their death, as part of the mummy's ornamentation (Robins 1997:200). Their existence at Egyptian domestic sites implies that amulets were considered a necessity of life, even by the poorest members of ancient Egyptian society (Pinch 1994:105–6).

The amulet's power was derived from its various characteristics, such as its shape, the texts and representations it carried, its color, and its material (*Lexikon* I:232; Pinch 1994:107). This piece was made of hematite, a black opaque iron oxide with a metallic luster that occurs plentifully in Egypt. In addition to amulets, it was used by the ancient Egyptians for beads, *kohl* sticks (cosmetic applicators), and small ornaments, and was employed as early as the Predynastic Period (Andrews 1994:104; Lucas 1989:395). Its black color, resembling that of the rich Nile silt brought forth by the inundation each season, was symbolic of regeneration and rebirth.

Amulets could be manufactured in the shape of deities, demons, animals, plants, parts of the human body, furniture, tools, or ritual objects (Pinch 1994:108). This particular amulet is in the form of a falcon-headed god. Most amulets that represented deities were worn in order to be placed under that deity's protection and patronage, or to assimilate oneself with the deity represented and thus gain access to his or her particular powers or characteristics (Andrews 1994:13). This god is shown as a mummy, albeit one squatting on a roughly trapezoidal base. Its body barely begins to emerge from the wrappings that he wears, rendered here as a continuous shroud-like garment, with no breaks or folds.

This figure also wears a long wig, whose lappets cover part of its chest, and whose rear surface is incised with concentric oval arcs. One curious feature that this piece possesses is a rectangular nub-like feature on the top of its head. This nub is most likely a remnant of a tenon, designed to fit into a headdress or a crown of a different material (Frederick John Lamp, personal communication).

Based on the presence of this tenon fragment, as well as its squatting, mummiform appearance, this amulet probably represents Sokar, a funerary god associated with the Memphite necropolis (*Lexikon* V:1056), or Horus of Nekhen, a local form of the god Horus belonging to the Upper (Southern) Egyptian Predynastic capital. These two gods were associated with each other at some point in Egyptian history (Betsy Bryan, personal communication; Geoff Graham, personal communication). It is also possible, that this amulet represents Kebehsenuef, one of the four sons of Horus (see pp. 180, 181; Geoffrey Graham, personal communication). The lack of any inscription on this piece makes it impossible to determine its identity definitively.

Many possibilities exist for the headdress that this amulet originally wore. Sokar was known to have worn a number of different ones: a white crown with double ostrich feathers, a double crown, a sun-disk with the royal serpent emblem (*Lexikon* V:1062), the *atef*-crown, which was a composite crown consisting of a papyrus bundle, ram's horns, double ostrich feathers, and a white crown (*Lexikon* V:814; Graindorge II:27 pl. XL), or the *tatjenen*-crown, another composite crown formed from ram's horns, double plumes, and a sun-disk (Geoff Graham, personal communication; *Lexikon* V:1063). If this amulet instead represents Horus of Nekhen, this headdress could have been a double crown (like Sokar), a white crown, or a sun disk with double ostrich plumes (*Lexikon* III:37).

While many amulets could be worn, this piece, surprisingly, was probably not intended for such a use, as it lacks any trace of a loop through which a cord could be passed. It is also unusually large for an amulet. This makes it unlikely that it was of the type placed between each layer of linen wrapped around a mummified body, brushed over with melted resins (El Mahdy 1991:68), and subject to a spell

Amulet of a Falcon-Headed God
Egypt
Third Intermediate Period–Late Period, Dynasties XXI–XXX,
c. 1069–332 BC
Black hematite, H. 3.5 cm
Gift of Robert Garrett
BMA 1956.131

Tomb painting of a mummy being prepared by the jackal god, Anubis, during which amulets would be enclosed within the wrapping; underneath are the four viscera jars, the left jar representing the falcon god, Kebehsenuef. Tomb of Twosret, Left Bank, Luxor
Photo: Frederick John Lamp, 2001

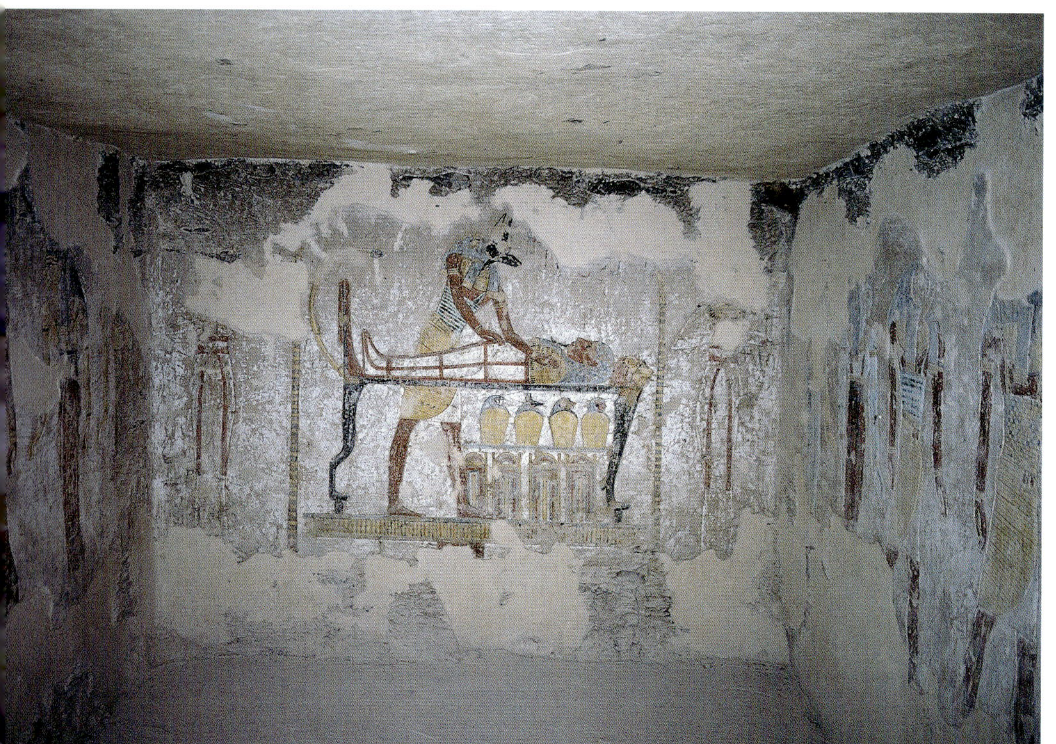

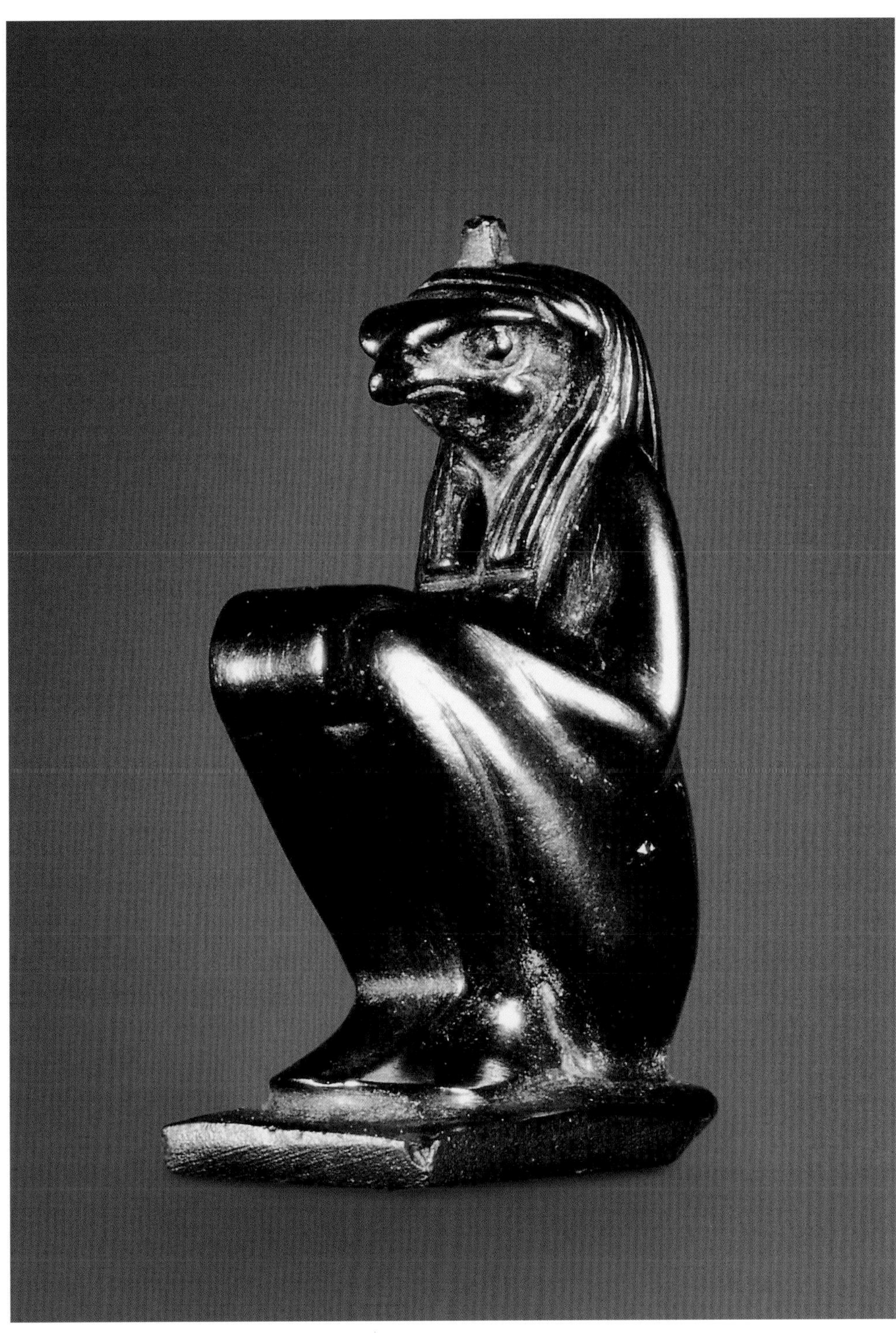

(*Lexikon* I:233). Instead, this piece may have been utilized by a priest as an implement in a temple ritual. Kebehsenuef amulets were known to have been used in rites connected with Osiris, the Egyptian god of the underworld (Cauville 1997:2.108).

Amulets occurred throughout ancient Egyptian history, from the Predynastic until the Christian Period (*Lexikon* I:233), with the first amulets of animal-headed deities occurring during the Old Kingdom (Andrews 1994:10). From the end of the New Kingdom until the Roman Period, amulets of gods were the most numerous and diverse of any group of amulets (Andrews 1994:12; Lise 1988:121–2). They played an increasing role in funerary religion during the first millennium BC (Pinch 1994:118), serving as an important component among the meager assemblages at most burials during the Third Intermediate Period (Shaw 2000:363), and witnessing a proliferation during Dynasty 26 (Andrews 1994:12).

Thomas Kittredge

1

The Body as Billboard: Ndebele Beadwork

In the final decades of the infamous period of apartheid in South Africa, a great number of dissident, white South Africans fled the country for the safety of the United States and Europe, often carrying with them large quantities of beadwork produced by the Ndebele people of South Africa, which had become readily available through dealers and tourist showplaces such as "the Ndebele Village." At the same time, a great many publications about Ndebele art accompanied its exodus (Becker 1982; Courtney-Clarke 1986; Jeffery & Magubane 1986; Knight & Priebatsch 1983; Schneider 1986). The BMA has been the recipient of over fifty articles of Ndebele beadwork, including the four addressed here.

The *itshogolo* is a formal garment worn only for ceremonial occasions by a married woman. At marriage, the husband would give his bride the goatskin panel without beaded decoration, and this is how it was worn for several months. Later it was beaded by the bride's mother-in-law. Married women might also later have beaded their own itshogolo. Itshogolo with miniature side pendant flaps may indicate that the wearer was not the husband's first wife.

By the 1940s, beaded, wool "Middelburg blankets" were worn by brides and married women as a mantle, replacing the earlier sheepskin cape. The strips of beadwork were woven separately and then applied to commercial blankets produced by mills in Middelburg, a town east of Pretoria and Johannesburg. Heavily decorated blankets may weigh up to ten pounds.

Beaded female figures emphasize the encircling of the female body in beaded hoops. Made by the young women upon their initiation into adulthood, or made for them by older women, they were used first in the initiation, and later by the women themselves during the first years of marriage. The figures functioned in role play. They were given personal names, and were assigned a relationship to the owner, such as a girlfriend or mother. Some figures were given to young women by male suitors as a marriage proposal. After the birth of a woman's third child, the figure was discarded.

In a sense, Ndebele art is an art of protest, even if motifs seem innocuous. Though some form of beadwork and wall design has long been characteristic of the Ndebele, the elaborate styles that evolved towards the mid-twentieth century seem to be an ever-intensifying expression of ethnic pride, among a scattered and disenfranchised people, saying in unity to the world: "We are the Ndebele." Why the Ndebele chose such an ostentatious ornamental declaration seems closely bound to the history of their oppression (Schneider 1986:219–220).

Since the late nineteenth century, the Ndebele have been battered by the appropriation of their land and their political prerogative by a succession of European-African governments. In 1882–83, at the apogee of power and prosperity under the chief Nyabela, they were invaded and defeated in a long war by the Boer settlers (of Dutch and French Huguenot descent).

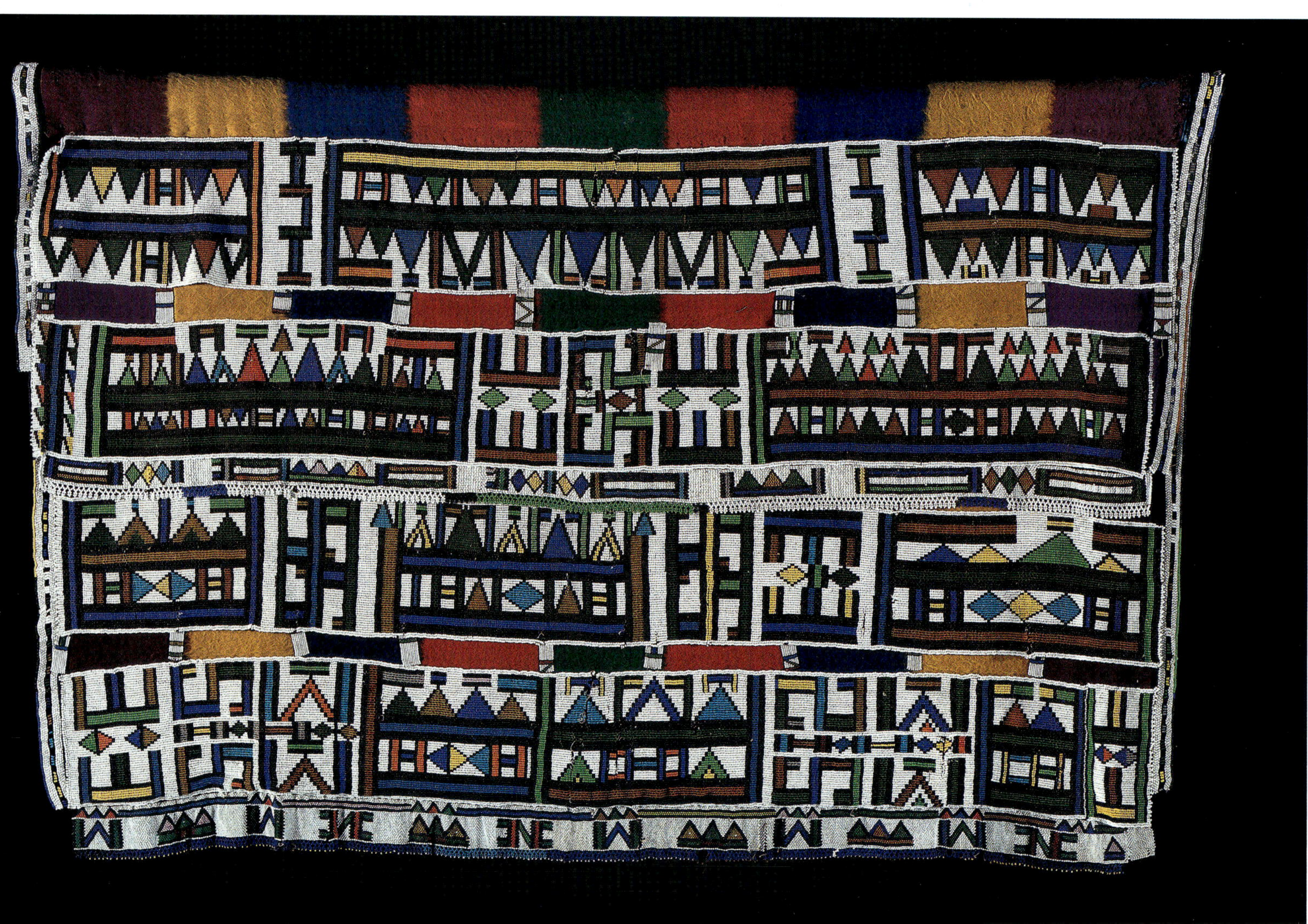

Beaded Blanket
Ndebele, South Africa
c. Mid-20th century
Middelburg wool blanket, beads, string, L. 160 cm
Gift of Aaron and Joanie Young, Baltimore
BMA 2002.631

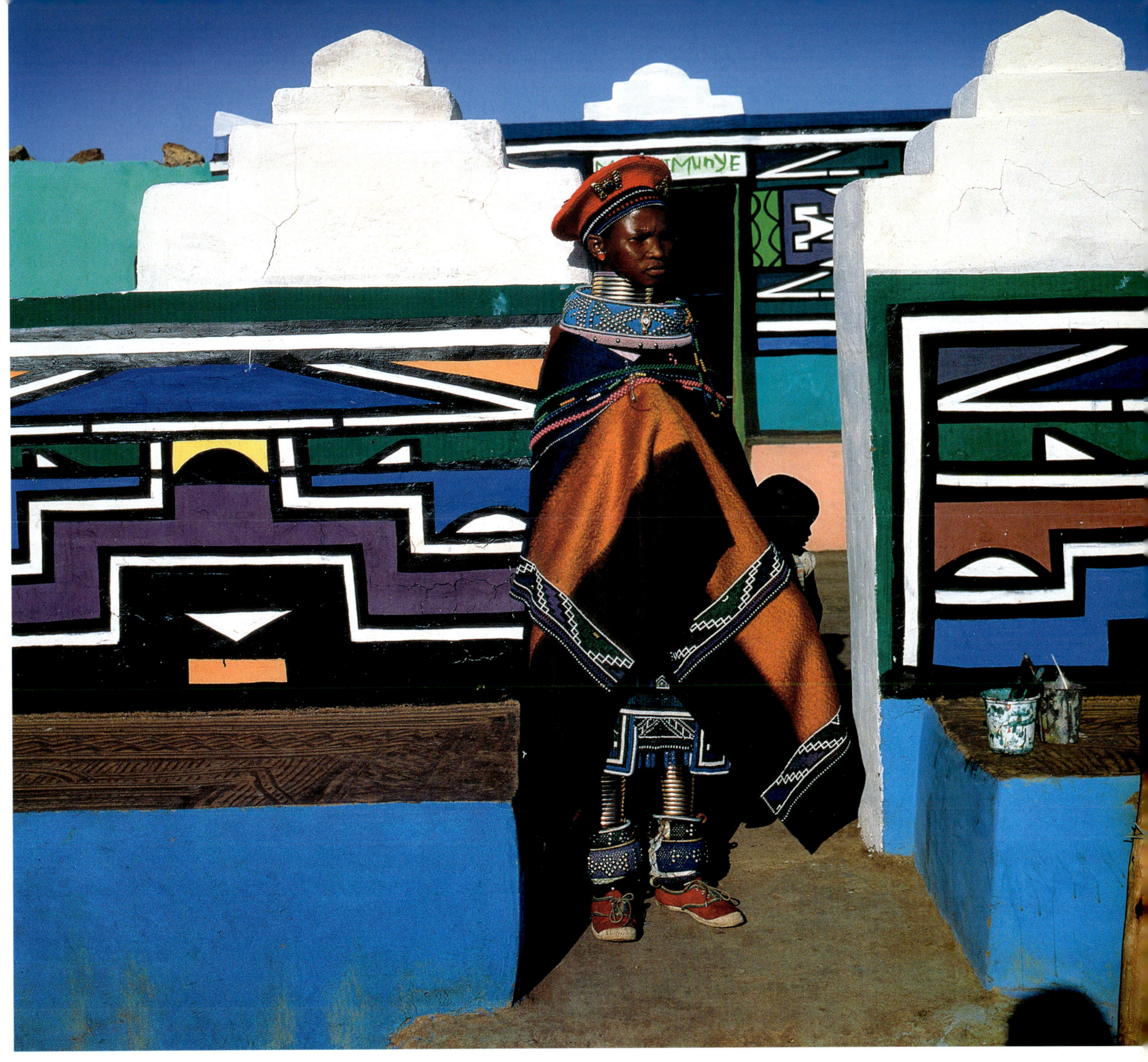

Sara Mthimunye wearing a front waist garment. Ndebele, South Africa
Photo: ©Margaret Courtney-Clarke, 1986

The Ndebele were dispersed and forced to accept the humiliating status of indentured laborers on Boer farms. Under the Afrikaner-dominated government of the twentieth century, with the system of separate racial development, apartheid, legalized in 1948, the Ndebele, like other indigenous groups, were further ostracized. By 1975, the South African government began to create, out of largely barren land, the separate "homeland" of KwaNdebele. Several thousand Ndebele arrived there, having been evicted from their farms, "endorsed out" of cities, dispossessed from "Black spots" in "White" areas, or simply harassed by official complications. Still, for many, their survival necessitated a grueling daily journey back to jobs in the European-African cities, farms, mines, and industries. This official ostracization ended with the election of President Nelson Mandela in 1994.

Ironically, Ndebele art was strongly promoted by the white South African government as a means of magnifying the cultural gap and justifying racial separation. The viewpoint was manifest in patronizing re-creations of Ndebele village life in tourist villages built as a showplace for apartheid, and ultimately in the artificially created "homeland" of KwaNdebele. Since the 1980s, the wearing of such elaborate beaded ornamentation has become rare.

Women in Ndebele society were the producers of beadwork. They were also the principal consumers. Though men fashioned the foundation garment of goatskin or sheepskin, the weaving and stitching of beadwork ornamentation on the garments has always been the work of the women. Men normally did not wear elaborate beadwork except at the end of their ceremonies of initiation into manhood and for special occasions such as a wedding. Young women ending their period of initiation were literally covered from head to foot with headbands, necklaces, and large hoops from the neck to the ankles, together with the stiff front waist panel called *isipepetu*, and the goatskin backskirt called *isithimba*. Married woman wore an elaborate assortment of beadwork even for daily routines; for special occasions the ensemble grew even richer. Only at the death of a husband did the woman remove her beadwork, and there is some evidence that women were ultimately buried with their beadwork.

What do we make of Ndebele apparel that is obviously not meant for comfort, that is not, basically, utilitarian? Young women's front waist garments are not skirts, they are plaques. Married women's garments hang like banners before their bodies. Large hoops on the torso, neck, legs, and arms seriously impede movement. An ensemble of beadwork worn by a married woman may weigh forty to fifty pounds. If there is a function apart from the purely aesthetic, it would be to communicate social status and concern. Front waist garments indicate marital status. Long, narrow, pendant "tears" worn hanging from a woman's head signal that she awaits the return of her son from initiation into adulthood, with is held away from the village. Sometimes, even

Married Woman's Ceremonial Front Waist Garment (*itshogolo*)
Ndebele, South Africa
c. Mid-20th century
Goatskin, glass beads, cotton thread, H. 73 cm
Gift of Caroline Popper, Baltimore
BMA 1991.365 (collected by the donor in South Africa in the early 1980s)

Figure (*umdwana*)
Ndebele, South Africa
c. Mid–late 20th century
Glass beads, grass, cloth, cotton thread, plastic, H. 26.5 cm
Gift of Natalie Fitz-Gerald, New York
BMA 1991.348

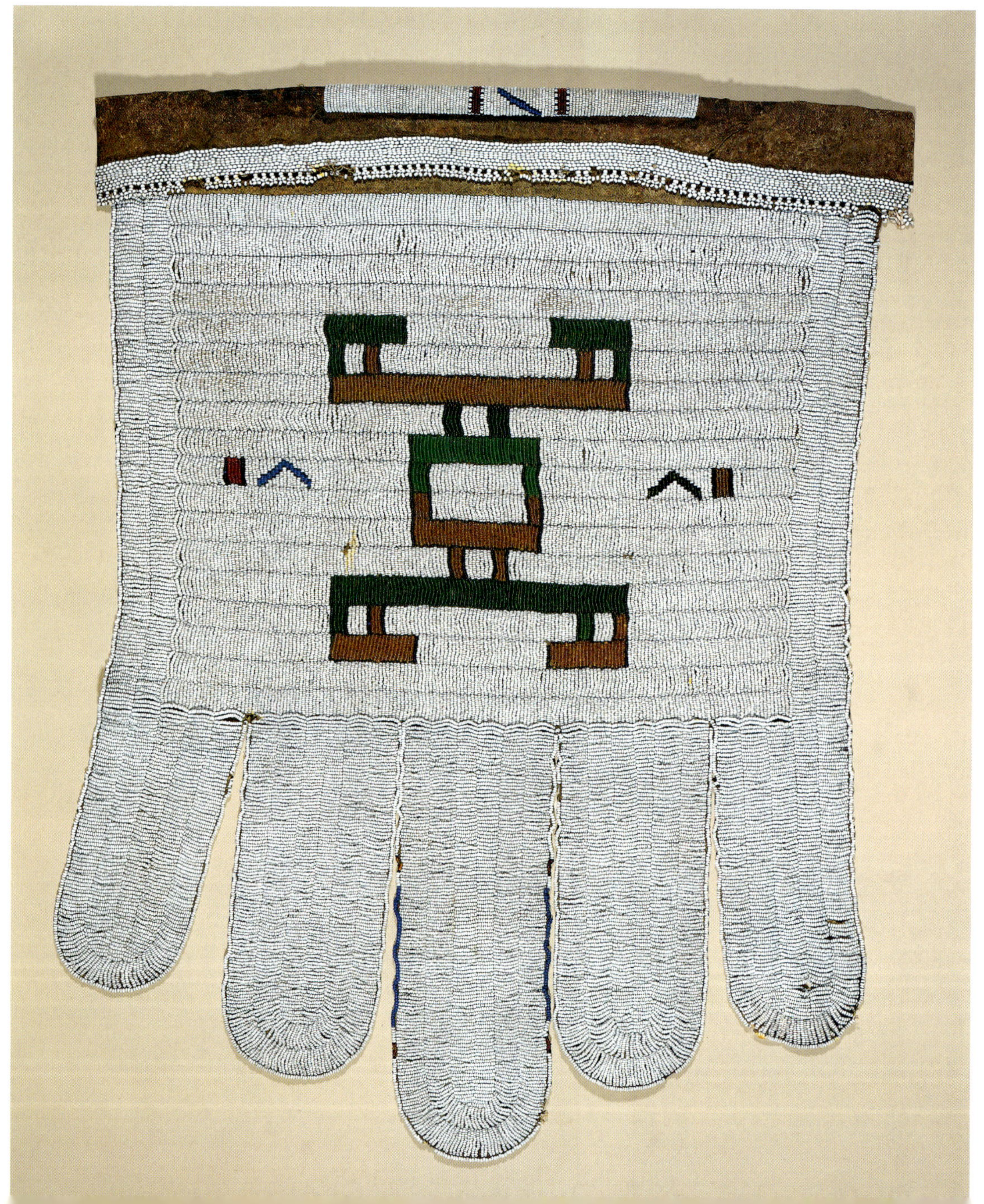

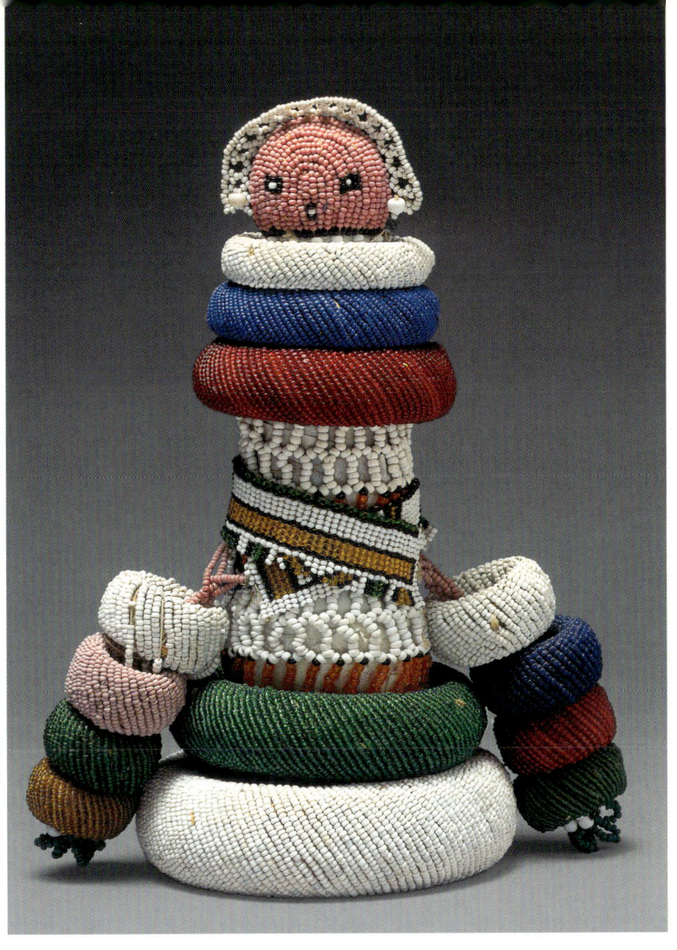

hand-printed paper signs are worn interchangeably with necklaces and pendants to publicly express a particular concern of the wearer. But neither the design motifs nor the colors bear any ritual message or symbolic meaning. The images are used simply to delight the maker and the wearer.

Essentially the Ndebele body is considered a surface to be decorated like the walls of a home or a veranda. In fact, beadwork designs are frequently translated into wall painting designs, and vice versa. Apparel is strongly and symbolically associated with a ritual of display. This concept continues even when the wearing of beadwork does not. For example, when a young man emerges from his initiation into adulthood, the gifts of clothing (a suit, tie, shoes, etc.) from his family are sometimes displayed on a mat in public ceremonies to show the young man's new status (Jeffery & Magubane 1986:282). Ndebele art seems to arise out of a concern for social statement, an extraordinary passion for design, and a deeply valued sense of aesthetic exhibition.

F. J. L.

Girls at their "coming out". Ndebele, South Africa. Photo: Aubrey Elliot, Courtesy of the McGregor Museum, Kimberley, South Africa

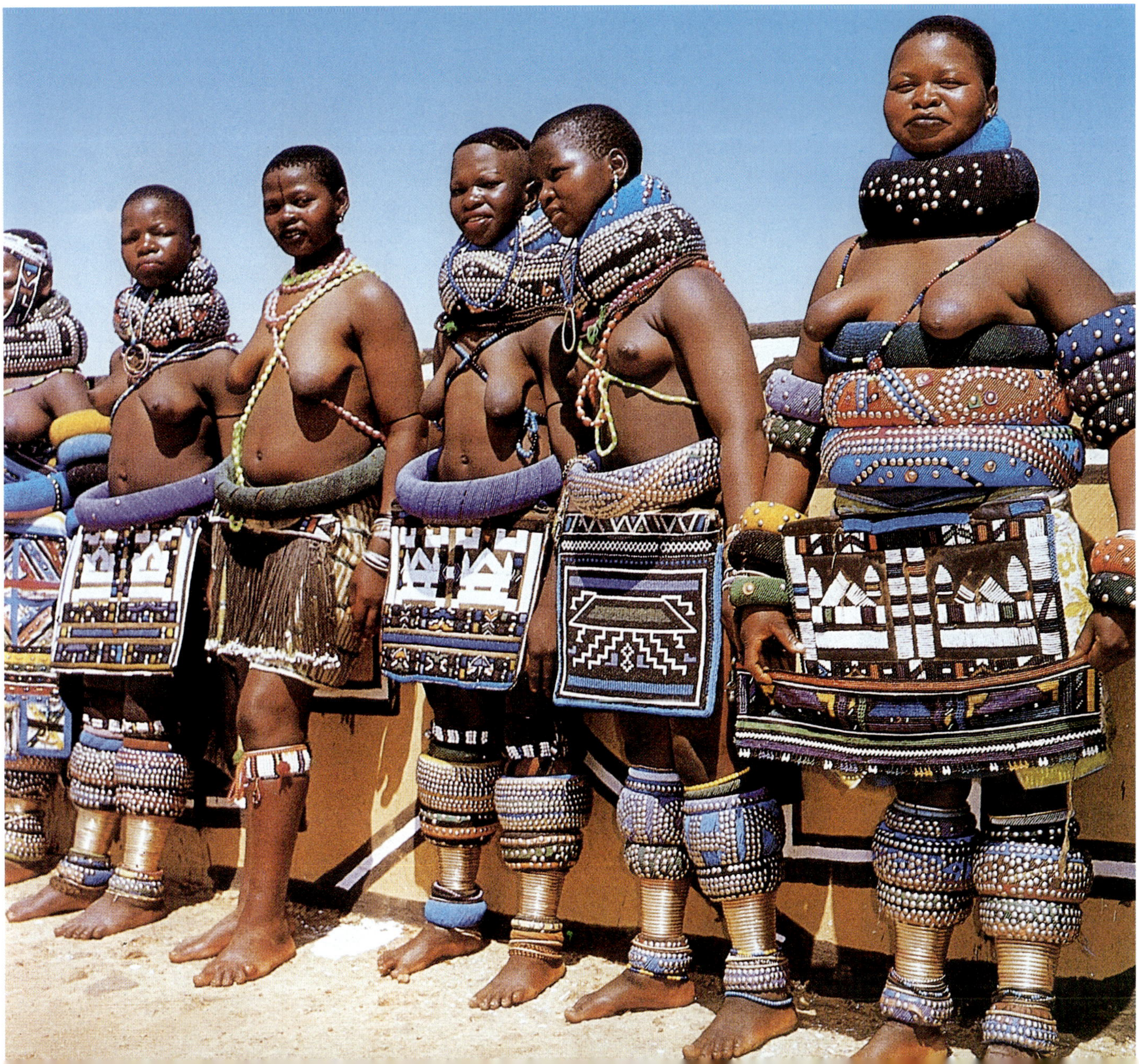

COSTUMING, CONCEALMENT, AND REVELATION

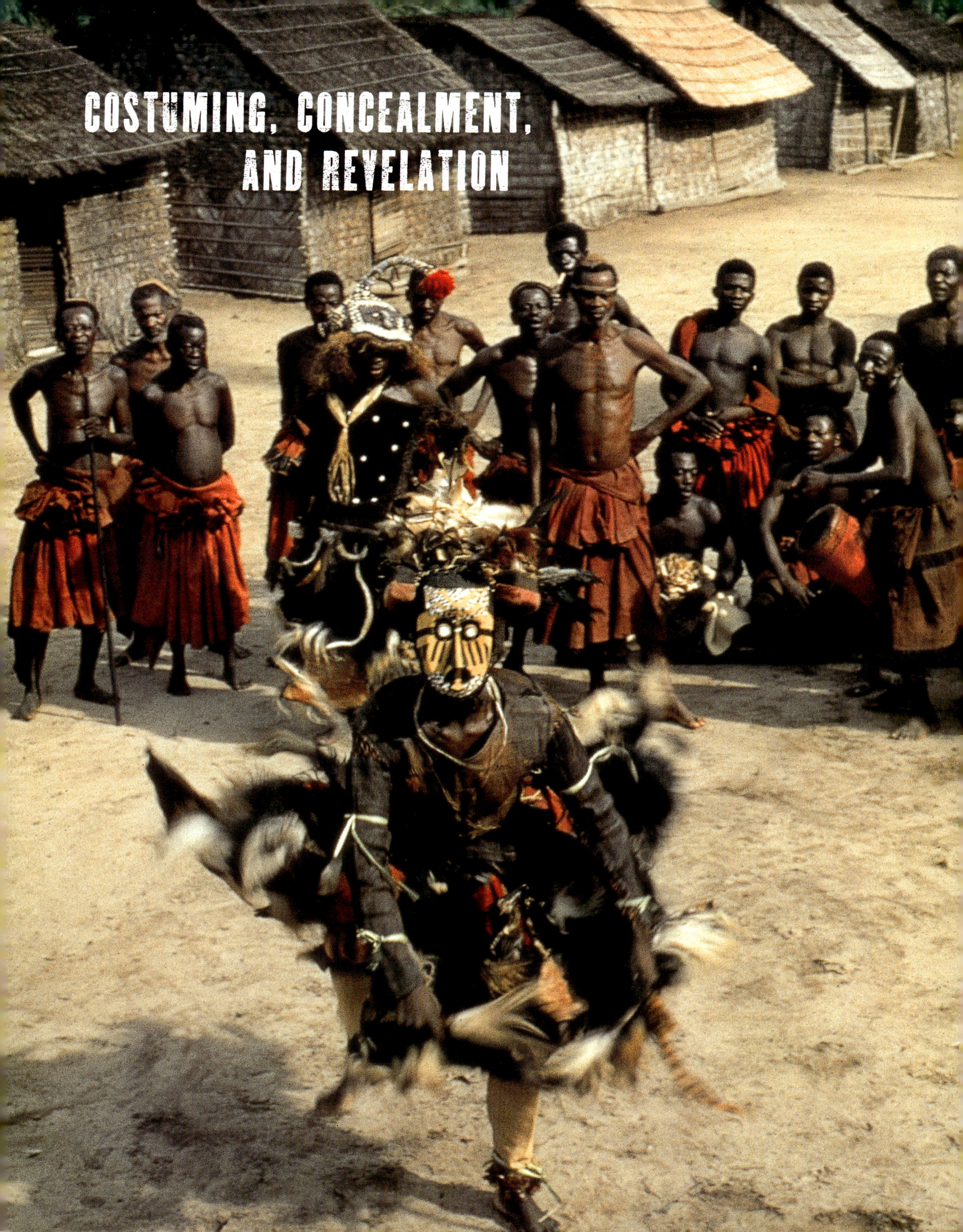

Although face masks and headdresses without attachments can be seen used in dances (pp. 164, 165, for example), face masks are usually part of a larger costume which might have been comprised of raffia, cloth, leather, hide, or other material. Costumes are also often part of the display of sculpture used in shrines. In many cases, the mask or figure is considered only one of many components of a material art form and sometimes even an insignificant element of the entire ensemble of mixed media. Some writers speak of "the figure" when they refer to a manifestation in mask and costume. Other writers, refer to the entire ensemble of mask, costume, and accoutrements, which, taken together, "mask" the wearer's identity. Many examples of masquerade exist in which the costume is the mask, without any separate, carved, wooden face covering.

The isolated object shown in the museum, identifiable as a form to African art enthusiasts in the West, may seem unfamiliar to Africans who have seen it in context. Occasionally, visitors from Africa come to the BMA to view the African objects, and often, they do not recognize those objects produced in their own societies of origin. There may be many reasons for this, among them the fact that many contemporary Africans are unaware of their own artistic heritage, and actually have not seen the artistic products made by their forbears. But it also seems plausible that a person from Africa, having witnessed an event in which objects are moving and full of many components, would not recognize that small fragment, stripped from its original ensemble. A caption from an illustration in an African newspaper supports this view (see below). In Western catalogues of African art, an illustration of a Baga D'mba (or Nimba) mask in a collection (p. 223) would be identified simply as "D'mba," and an illustration of the mask with a costume would probably note something on the order of "D'mba mask with costume" as "D'mba" is recognized by the Western audience as simply the mask. In the African newspaper illustration, the caption for the illustration of the mask alone carries the qualifier, "D'mba, undressed." There it is the full costume that is understood as "D'mba," and the illustration of the mask alone needs a special explanation.

The effect of the costumed D'mba is radically different from the effect of the D'mba on a pedestal. In its indigenous context, the D'mba mask does exist without its costume when it is in storage between performances, but then it is seen only by its ritual guardians. In public performance, however, the D'mba wooden sculpture is carried on top of the dancer's head lodged inside the hollow formed between the four pedestal legs. A wooden hoop is attached at the base of these legs, tightly strapped using natural fiber. Suspended from this hoop, and reaching to the ground, is a long skirt made from the stripped leaves of the raffia palm that had been bleached dry to the color of straw. Over this raffia skirt, a large dark cloth is thrown over the wooden sculpture's shoulders, worn as a shawl, the upper ends tied in a knot just under the tip of the wooden breasts. In performance, D'mba does not appear as an abstract form, but as a towering and elegant, fully dressed, female figure, resembling a mature woman with only her breasts exposed above the line of the shawl.

Significantly, the carved sculpture and its costume often form a conceptual whole. To use the word "costume" in its usual sense is to suggest something superfluous. But in many ritual art forms it is anything but. Among the Temne, the wooden mask of Nòwo (p. 175) forms a bond with its black raffia dress (Lamp 1985:43). The mask is a solid form, with iconography suggesting cultivation, planting, and sprouting. The owner of the mask claims that it was not made by human hands, but, rather, that she went under the water to retrieve it from the spiritual world. Thus the bottom part of the mask, carved with rings, suggests the concentric ripples formed when drawing the mask out of the water. And the gently swaying black raffia may suggest the deep, dark, flowing water from which it comes (Boone 1986:238). Philippe Jespers (p. 233) analyzed the conjunction of the *Kòmò* mask (p. 233) and its costume among the Minianka, as the convergence of a land beast and a creature of the air, in which up and down are reversed in the mask of the hyena and the costume of the vulture. The feathered costume never leaves the earth, while the beast mask gazes skyward in a cosmic construction-performance signifying the extreme tension in the mediating between the "earth of the village" and the "sky of God." Jespers describes this use of the mask and costume in dance as "corporeal writing."

Nearly all the essays in this book cover costuming and attachments to the mask or figure. In this section, special attention is given by Christian K. Højbjerg to the significant profusion of added materials, obscuring lines between spirit, man, and beast, but with the unexpected twist that it is the miniature edition, without costume, that is considered the base, the referent, the "real" mask. The case of the Kota Mbulu Ngulu examined in this section is only one of many examples that might be cited of shrine figures that appear in an almost theatrical context. In the essay by Anita Jones, we examine a costume itself for its iconographic power. The intent to deceive, one of the functions of costuming, is seen as a fundamental power of artistry among the

Pwoom Itok (Ishyeen Imaalu) masked dancer (see p. 93). Kuba, Muentshi, Congo (Kinshasa). Photo: Eliot Elisofon, 1972. Courtesy of the Eliot Elisofon Photographic Archive, National Museum of African Art, Smithsonian Institution

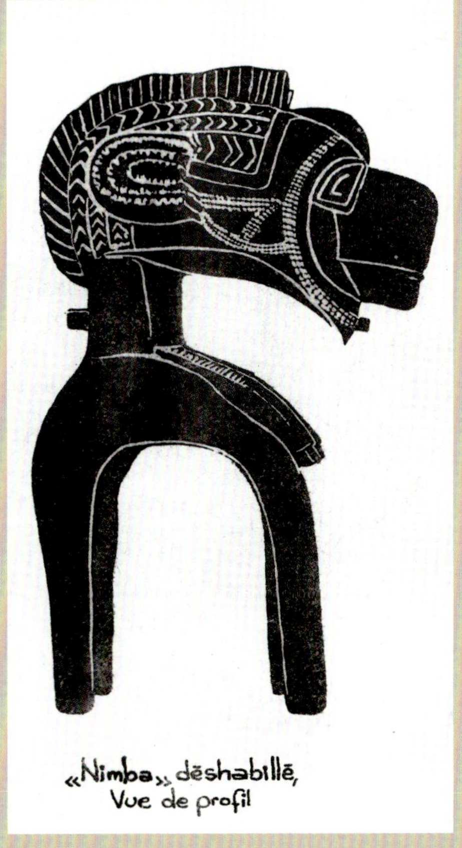

Illustration of a D'mba (Nimba) mask from a collection published in a Guinean newspaper with the caption "Nimba, undressed". In *Horoya*, Saturday, March 2, 1985, supplement, p. 5. Ink drawing: Karamoko Oury Wann

Hausa by Alice R. Burmeister. Sidney Littlefield Kasfir analyzes a conceptual relationship between the warrior and woman embodied in a headdress from the Igede/Ogoja region of Nigeria, and argues that the incongruity between headdress and costume constitutes an essential disjuncture and ambiguity.

Costuming, in masquerade, presents issues of its own. Is it constructed in a way that inhibits movement, facilitates it, or perhaps extends and exaggerates it? Is the costume, itself, "danced" and "played," i.e., does it contribute its own movement and sound, as swaying fabric, rustling grasses, tinkling bells, or floating feathers? What messages does costume convey? Are its messages harmonious with those given by the other media within the same work of art and the same performance, or do the various elements sometimes give conflicting messages, or simply work on their own?

What are the theoretical implications of costume in the context of masquerade, particularly in those societies where men and women, by contrast, normally wear very little, or nothing at all? What does costume accomplish? To what extent is the costume a "mask." Does it cover the whole body? Can it be taken off in public? Does it obscure or does it reveal? John Picton (1990) has identified many complex notions of what masking does, all of which revolve around the concept of metaphysical transformation. In one category, the intent is simply drama, with the focus on the actor as himself, masked to distance himself from the audience. Some masks and costumes are mere adornment. In another category, the actor is a medium, selected to bear a sacred object. In some cases, the body is covered but the identity of the wearer is completely known. In my work among the Baga of Guinea, I found that most masked dancers did not obscure their identity, and, in fact, would frequently raise the masks above their heads acrobatically, revealing their faces (p. 75). In yet another category identified by Picton, probably most commonly portrayed in the literature on African masking, the intent is just the opposite: the actor doesn't exist, there is no human agency, but only the appearance of a spiritual "other." Some masks and costumes are carefully devised to hide the entire body, including the fingers and toes (for example, in the case of the Mende Sande mask, p. 175), and the claim is made that the costume contains no human being at all, but only a spirit. This raises the question, too complex to be examined here, of whether the costume wearer, if one exists, aims to deceive, or whether his or her costume exposes something metaphysical which renders any underlying physical body irrelevant.

Dance of Tumbu. Baga Sitem, Guinea. The Tumbu dancer's face could be seen, as the mask was worn across his upper back. Some Baga masks are lifted up and twirled in the air, revealing the identity of the dancer. Other Baga masks and costumes completely conceal the dancer's body, and in one case the concealment is so strictly observed that the costume is said to be empty, dancing on its own power. Photo: Frederick John Lamp, 1987

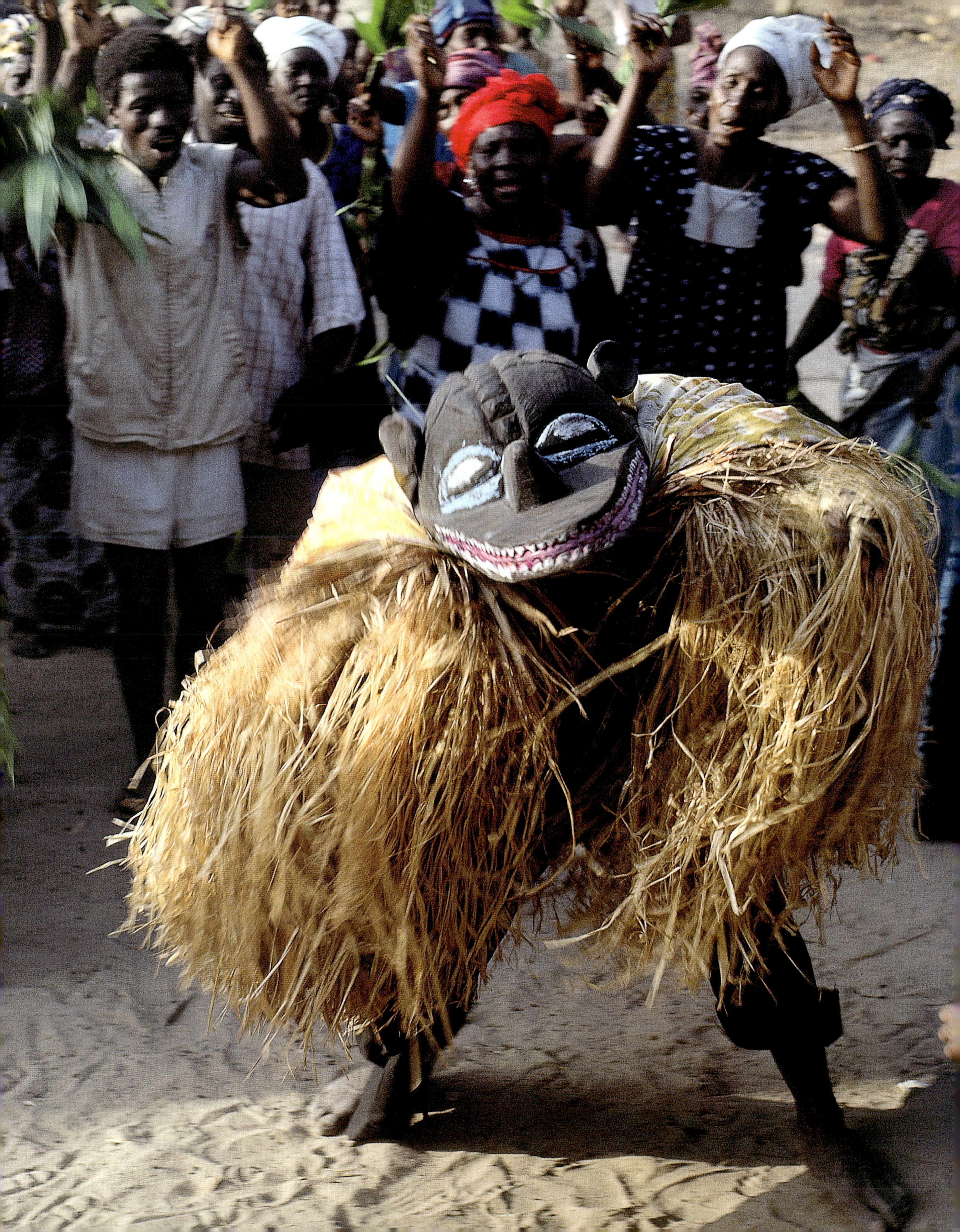

8

The Ambiguity of Gender: a Loma Mask (*Angbaï*) and Cow-Tail Switch

Mask (*Angbaï*) and Cow-Tail Switch
Loma, Liberia/Guinea
Pòrò Association
c. Early 20th century
Mask: Wood, encrustation, string, cowrie shells, H. 48 cm
Switch: cow tail, encrustation, cowrie shells, leopard teeth, metal, string
Gift of Elizabeth and Olivia Cumming, Baltimore
BMA 1985.276.1 & .2

The Loma refer to their masks either as "big things," or as *afuiti*, after the great bush spirit Afui by which neophytes are said to be devoured and given rebirth during male initiation in order to become full members of the society. Angbaï, the three-horned mask with a stern expression, is a local mask style characterized by its oblong, horizontal wooden form that incorporates both zoomorphic and anthropomorphic features. The nose and eyes are among the more discernible physical, human aspects of the masks, whereas the horns, jaws, and costume of most masks point to their animalistic nature. Angbaï is representative of the widespread, semi-secret male societies found in this culture area. During a masked performance, one may instead hear the mask addressed as the 'Old Man' (*Kawalai*), or more frequently as the 'Nephew of the Afuiti.'

Compared to many masks still in use, the BMA's Angbaï is a particularly fine example resembling the one also found on the Guinean twenty-five-franc note. Within a living Loma mask tradition it is now rare to encounter such well-formed symmetrical horns and carved vertical and horizontal ornamentation as found on the rounded forehead and the sides of the BMA piece. Most contemporary Angbaï masks are ornamented instead with a symmetrical patterned facial decoration made of blank metal strips. The metal ornamentation is, however, not a recent introduction, as can be confirmed from a comparison with an older photographic documentation of a Gbande Angbaï (Eberl-Elber 1936:344).

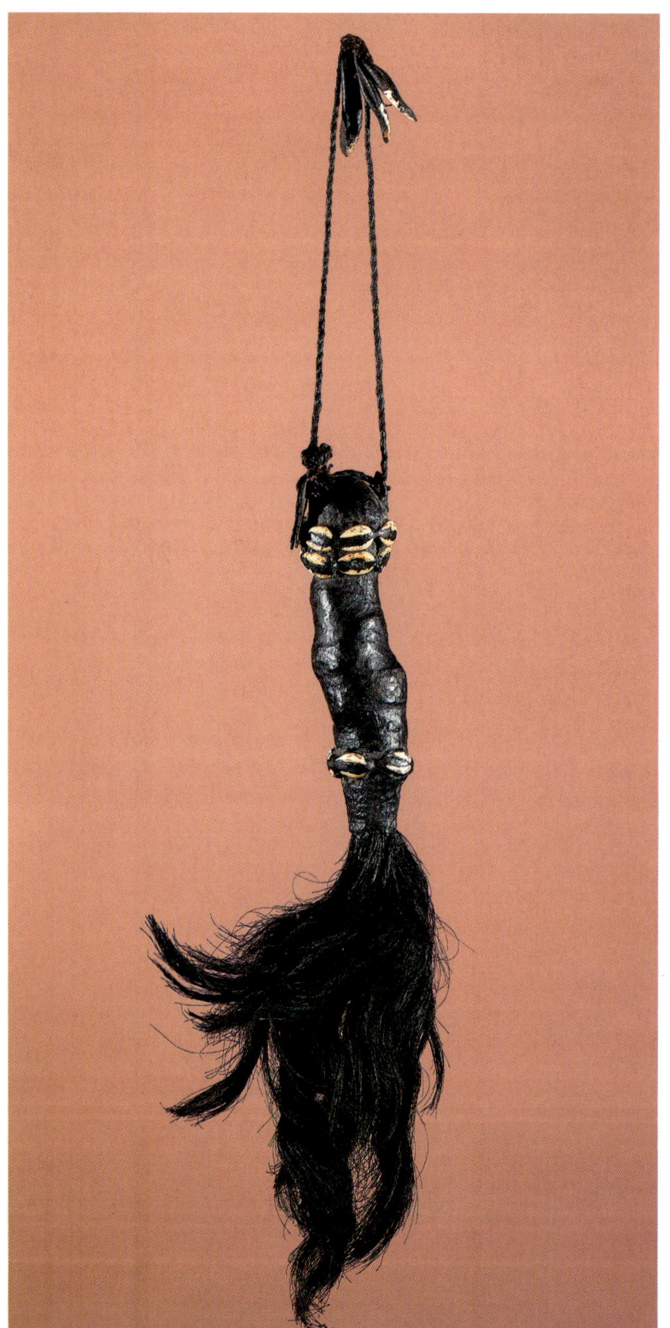

The BMA Angbaï has been stripped of all the paraphernalia worn during public performance. On the other hand, the wooden artifact appears to have been preserved in its original form except for a few of the triple-rowed carved ornamentations that have broken off the side of the mask. The bundle placed on top of the mask round the forked middle horn is a "medicine" (*sale*) having once served as an essential protective and power-providing vehicle of the mask. On the long, flat, dark surface of the mask are encrustations from blood sacrifices and offerings of masticated cola nut spewed onto the object.

Even though the present example is displayed without its dress of animal skins, colorful cotton and raffia skirt, its condition parallels that of masks that on certain occasions are erected as a shrine used for blood offerings in return for wishes fulfilled. Angbaï may thus be viewed both as a mask used in public performance and as a receptacle for offerings and words addressed in secretly performed sacrificial rituals. As an object of worship in this context, the mask is reduced to its wooden sculptured form and treated in the same way as the miniature "replicas" (often called "passport masks" or "insignia masks") owned by most of the members of local Angbaï societies. In fact, the Loma seem to consider the miniature masks as the "real" ones and the big masks as existing mainly for public use. A mask wearer never fails to carry his miniature Angbaï under his left arm while performing with the larger version.

During a dance, a conspicuous physical feature of the Angbaï is the animal skins that envelope the wearer's entire body except for the legs and feet that are covered by a pair of dark trousers and plaited raffia socks. Underneath the skins, and hardly perceptible, the mask also wears a short raffia skirt. Early observers described the Angbaï garment as consisting mainly of leopard skins with a braiding of white monkey fur, or a combination of skins from these two animal species (Eberl-Elber 1936:354; Gaisseau 1953:54; Germann 1933:57). These skins, and the three horns carved on top of the mask, lend the mask its zoomorphic character, especially set in motion when the mask performs. No specific animal, however, is implied by the masquerade. Angbaï belongs instead to a larger class of supernatural beings that are held to originate in natural surroundings and appear in public or concealed cultural space by the means of human intermediaries. More recent observations have shown that in addition to the skins already mentioned, the ones used to costume Angbaï stem from a much

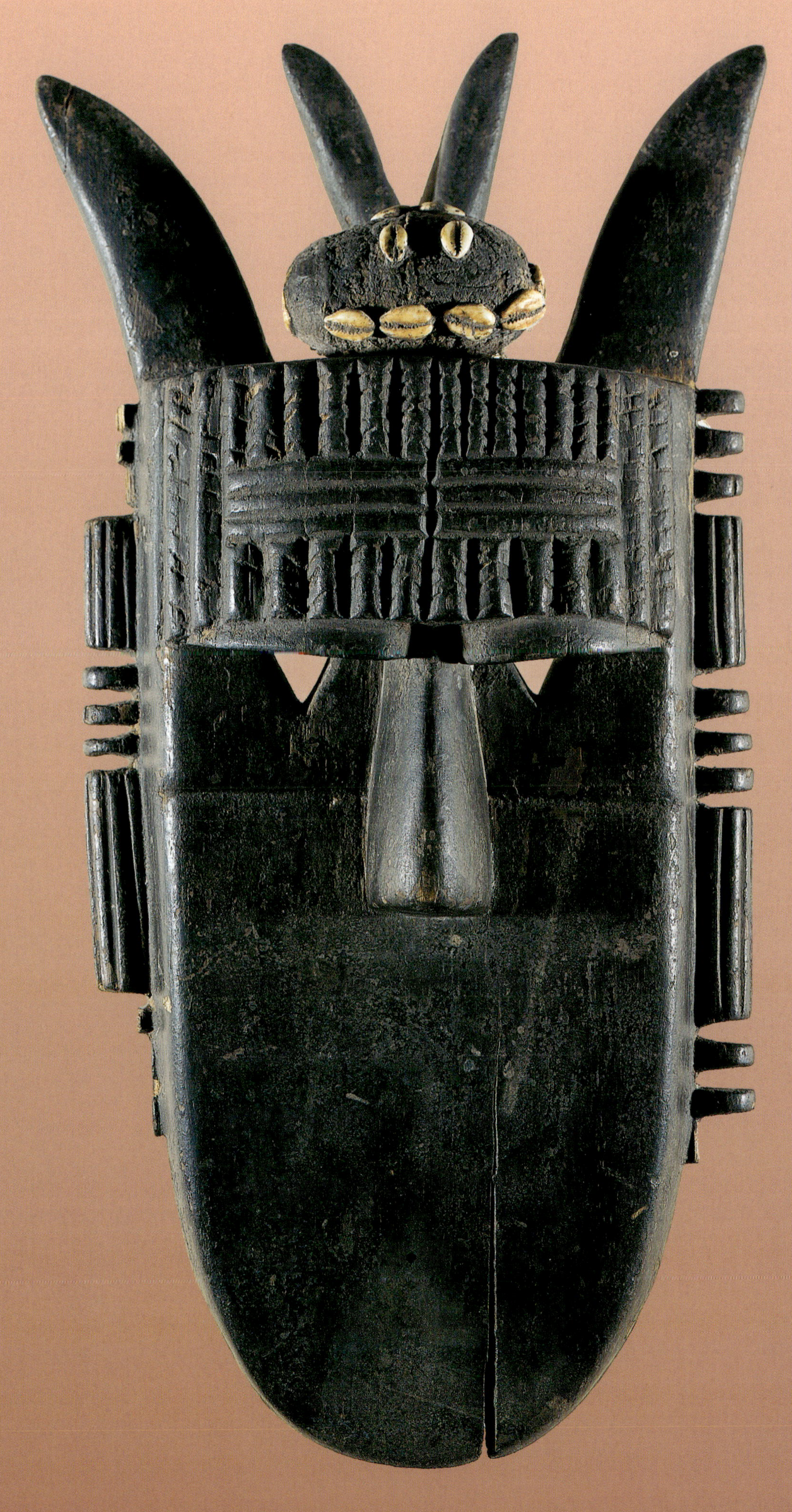

more varied selection of wild animals, such as civet, genet, otter, and mongoose. The variety of skins used nowadays may be explained by the fact that leopard skin has become rare, for the species is threatened by extinction in this part of Africa.

In some cases, the Angbaï has an ornament around its neck locally known as *thoghagi*. This is a large, colorfully patterned, ornamental garment, comprised of four radiating panels joined around the hidden neck of the mask and worn over the dress of skins, decorating the wearer on all sides. It is a part of the costume that the mask owner has purchased the ritual right to wear. According to informants, traditional *thoghagi* are made of animal skins. As with the leopard skins, true *thoghagi* are becoming rare and tend to be replaced by others similar in colour but made of a red, black, and white painted piece of cloth. This gradual change of costume is accompanied by a disappearence of the ritual prescriptions, including value exchange, associated with the thoghagi of hide.

Angbaï Mask Dancing. Loma, Guinea. Photo: Christian Højbjerg, 1991

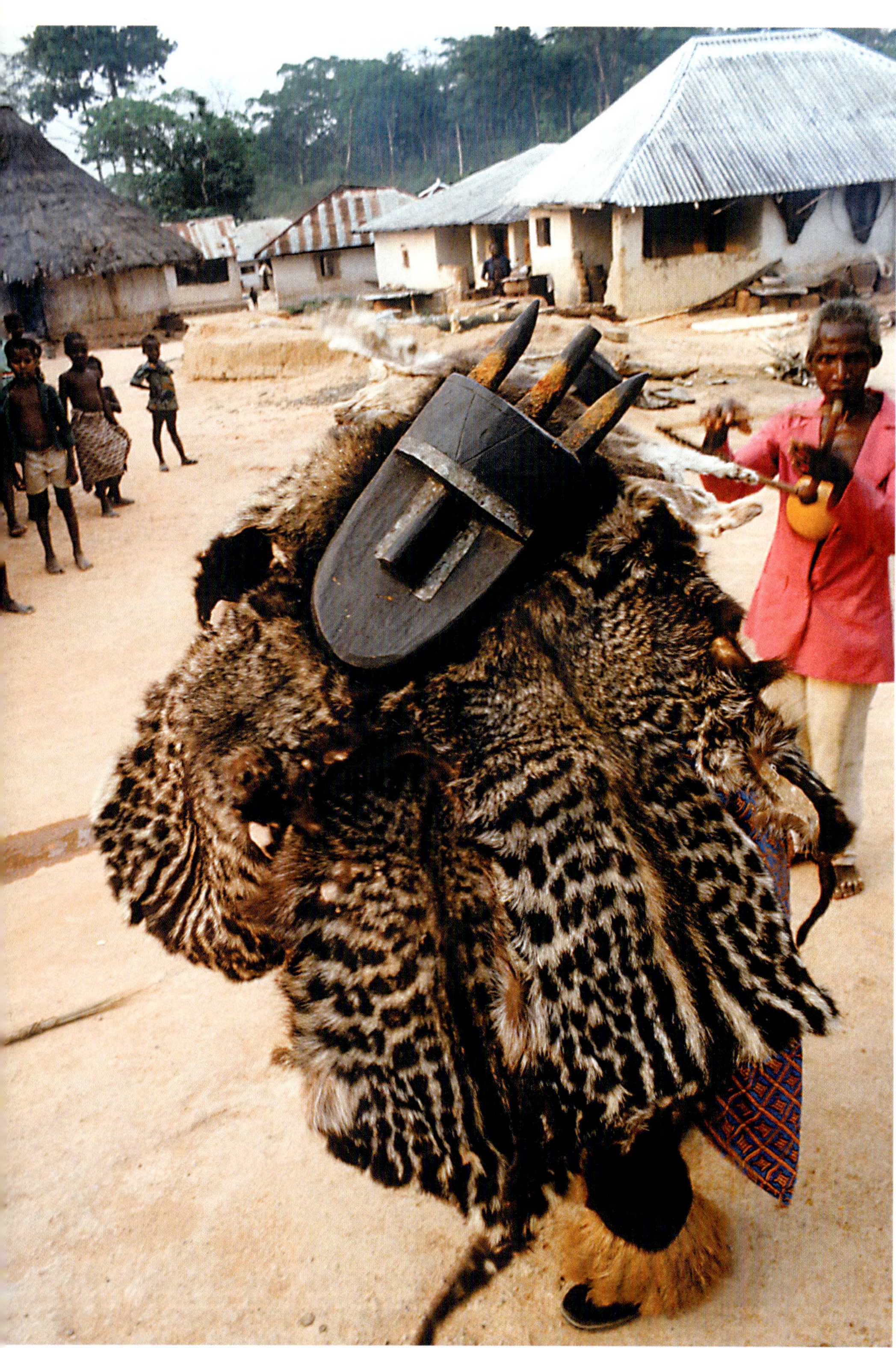

The Angbaï mask can be seen performing with the cow-tail switch in the photo by Eberl (1936); both the male and female Kpakologi (see p. 79) and Loma maskers are generally known to carry it. One may compare the masquerader's use of the tail with the use of one or other oblong object (knife, sword, umbrella, stick, etc.) by the speaker at Loma ceremonies (especially at funerals) and in judicial contexts. In these cases, the object denotes the speaker, and is subsequently handed over to the following speaker. While addressing the audience, the speaker gesticulates with the object to emphasize the tone of his speech and the choice of specific words. I have only once observed the use of the cow-tail in such situations. This was at the return of a group of female singers who had attended a funerary ritual in a neighboring village. The lead singer held the cow-tail switch in her right hand while reporting about the event in a song of praise, and she waved it each time the choir was expected to repeat her words.

During public performance Angbaï is worn horizontally and the wearer advances with small steps leaning forward, waving the body sideways so as to give the impression of a slowly moving animal creature. The mask now and then takes up an immobile, often seated position while accompanying society members carry out oratory performances in accordance with the purpose of the event. Rituals that involve masked performance include the funeral of a deceased society member, occasional thanksgiving sacrifices using animals, or other collective ceremonies, which are carried out in daytime either in the village space or at sacred natural sites. On such occasions, the mask may join the dance of the participating society members. Likewise, children are sometimes reported to join in the dance and to chant along with the mask.

The sound of the mask is a chant that communicates in a distorted yet distinguishable Loma dialect. In addition to plain speech, Angbaï emits a characteristic hollow grunting that is accompanied by one or two pounding sounds coming from inside the mask. Despite such attributes associated with the wilderness, the mask does not invoke fear, as is evident from its popularity among children following in its path. The Angbaï's tender nature is also reflected in the soft and partly monotonous sound of the lyre (*konégi*) that accompanies it in performance. More exceptionally, an elongated iron gong (*koli*) may form the acoustic accompaniment.

There are a dozen Loma mask types, and they each display distinct physical features. A number of norms and functions associated with Angbaï, however, suggests that this particular mask is ascribed a status that sets it apart from other existing masks. For instance, Angbaï is known occasionally to divine, and it is sometimes also referred to as the "Big Thing Nephew" (*Dabeaniwolai*); that is, the sister's son (*daabe*) of all the other masks. A nephew's or sister's son obeys a number of prescribed ritual roles and carries out other functions as intermediaries in Loma society. As in other Upper Guinea forest societies, Loma culture and society is pervaded by a matrilateral ideology comprising all levels from the general political structure to the practice of preferred marriage between mother's-brother's daughter and sister's son, as well as prescribed joking-relationships. Transposed to the world of masks, Angbaï thus occupies the position of nephew called upon to act as broker in conflicts over religious issues involving persons from different mask cults. Likewise, Angbaï is allowed to joke about other masks and may be heard to comment on the simultaneous appearance of the *Kpakologi*, saying, for instance, that the villagers do not have to sweep the ground, implying that the Kpakologi's long raffia skirt will do the job.

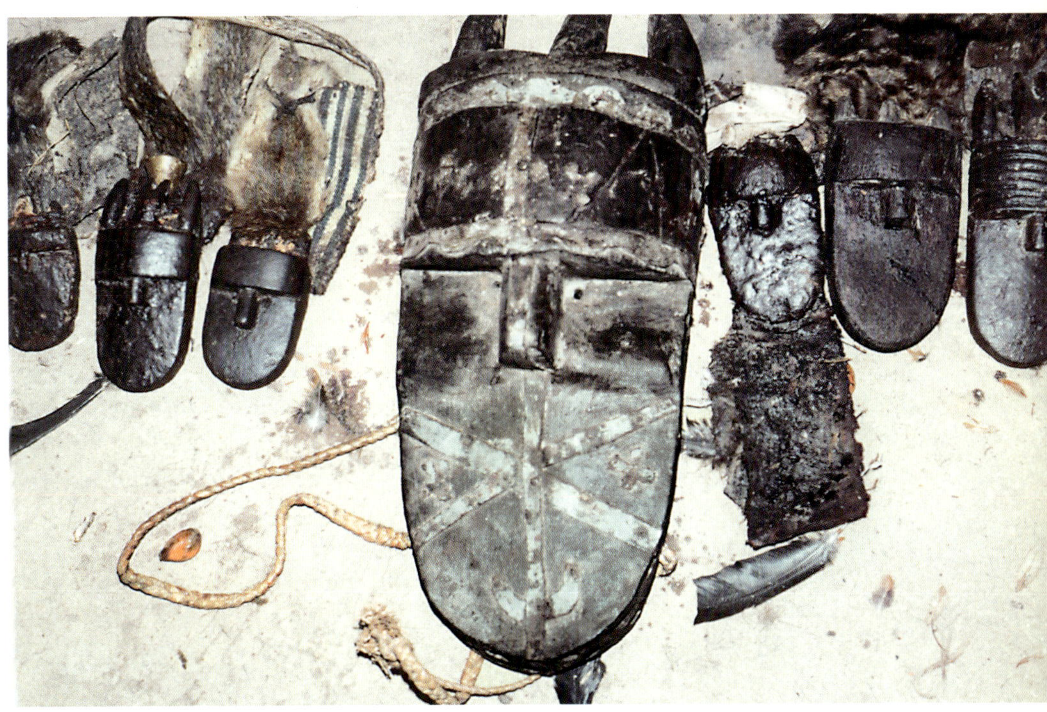

Angbaï mask with miniature masks, which are considered the "real" masks. Loma, Guinea
Photo: Christian Højbjerg, 1999

Angbaï has sometimes been registered as a female mask (Eberl-Elber 1936:353–54; Lamp 1992; Ndiaye 1994:84–85; Phillips 1996:368). What female means is a complex question. The Loma do not refer explicitly to the mask as a female entity and, in consciously expressed Loma religious thought about the Angbaï, one finds no reference whatsoever to gender even though other Loma masks, such as the Kpakologi, are expressly gendered. The gender of Angbaï is ambiguous. There are, in fact, some significant male indications, as the mask is representative of the male *Pòrò* association. It is usually called "the nephew of Afui" (the principal Pòrò mask) and it is also referred to as "the old man." On the other hand, the mask does have certain female associations. Women are held to have discovered Angbaï as well as other masks in the bush and to have brought them home to their husbands. Only Angbaï, among all the Loma masks owned and performed by the men, attends the opening and closing ceremony of the girls' initiation (*zadégi*). In some cases a female coiffure is carved at the top of the mask (such as those displayed at the Musée de l'Homme, Paris, and The Metropolitan Museum of Art, New York, where it replaces the horns). Perhaps most significantly, Angbaï is associated with the symbolic number three, a frequently displayed female symbol among the Loma and neighboring ethnic groups, as opposed to four for the male.

The breaking of this usage in a recent mask performance may serve to illustrate the analogous importance of the number three for Angbaï. At the funeral of a deceased leader of a local Angbaï society, the mask and its adherents appeared in the part of the village where the ceremony was taking place. Preceded by the new society leaders, Angbaï and the rest of the group were going to pay a visit to their deceased and yet-unburied fellow member. Before entering the house of the dead, they danced in large circles in the courtyard. Kinfolk and other villagers, including the local head of the men's secret Pòrò association, were seated and quietly watched the mask performance. However, suddenly the elder Pòrò leader jumped from his chair and loudly scolded the Angbaï performers for ignoring the ritual rules of their own society. The violation? Instead of entering the house of the dead person after three turns, the dancing society members and the mask had continued with a fourth turn.

Clearly, three is the number associated with Angbaï. The mask has three horns and when seen with four, it is always a split middle horn. In sacrifice to the miniature masks and the big mask stripped of its garment, the sacrificer carries the sacrificial victim three times toward the masks before placing it on top of them, and only then immolating the animal. Similarly, some sacrificers let the knife used for immolation move three times around the throat and neck of the sacrificial animal. Such display of the 'female' number three is frequent in Angbaï performance and is part of the general mask representation and form. Yet the incorporation of Loma female symbolism does not necessarily signify Angbaï as a female mask.

Christian K. Højbjerg

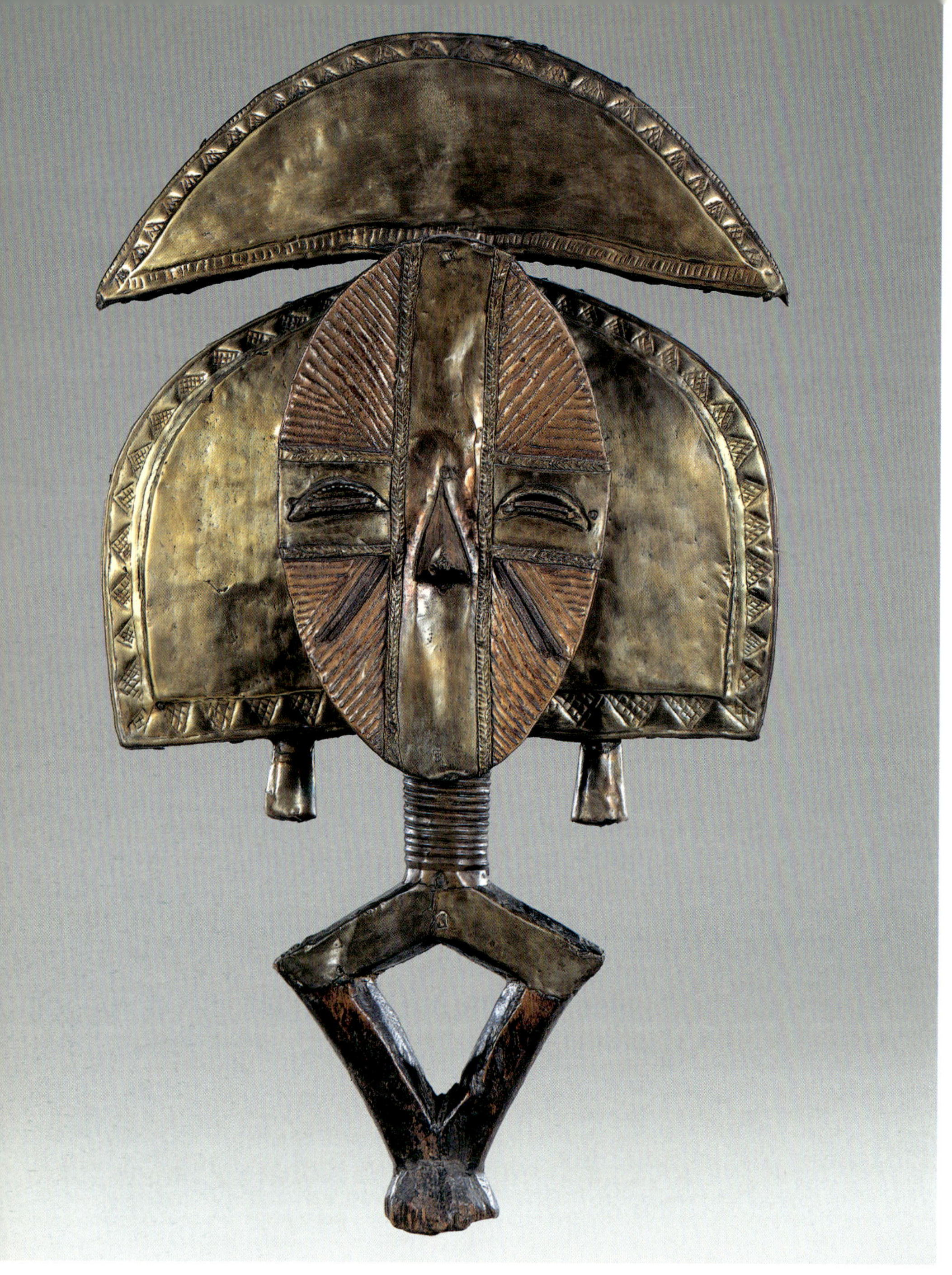

Reliquary Figure (*Mbulu-Ngulu*)
Kota (Obamba), Gabon
c. Early 20th century
Wood, brass, copper, H. 58.4 cm
Gift of Alan Wurtzburger
BMA 1954.145.64

9 Embodying the Ancestors: a Kota Reliquary Figure (*Mbulu-Ngulu*)

In the past, Kota religious belief and ritual were centered on the veneration of the bones of their ancestors. Associated with this belief was the most renowned of their art forms: a highly stylized and abstracted, sculpted, funerary reliquary figure. In antiquity, only Kota clan chiefs were interred; other corpses were left in the forest in a spot far removed from the village. In time, the practice of placing the bones of clan chiefs and other important individuals in basket or box-like bark ossuaries with attached sculpted guardian figures became the norm. The semi-nomadic lifestyle of the Kota dictated that these reliquaries had to be portable, as the dead could not be left behind (Andersson 1953:336; Chaffin n/d:16, 25; Fernández 1992:29; Perrois 1968:32, 36; 1970:22; 1977:75; 1979:126–128, 151; 1981:201; Sieber and Kan 1995:110; Siroto 1968:22–23, 27).

In 1876–1877, Savorgnan de Brazza observed the consultation of the reliquaries:

> The chief took the rattle used to awaken the spirits, and asked the skulls of the ancestors for advice. Their response, following the offering of a basket of bananas, was favorable. Then the young people cut off a lock of their hair, and one nail from each foot and each hand, and bowed before their father [the chief], who wrapped the hair cuttings and nail clippings in a packet that he placed with great pomp in the idol's hut. (de Brazza 1887:331)

The veneration of ancestral relics continued until the Colonial period at the end of the turn of the twentieth century, at which time it began to disappear as the Kota adopted other more common burial beliefs and practices (Chaffin n/d:8, 13, 16; Perrois 1968:36; 1979:151). However spectacular the Kota reliquary figures may appear to the Western eye, the Kota themselves attributed far greater value and power to the attached ossuaries and their contents. There are two types of reliquaries: the northern Kota-Mahongwé box-like bark container, and the southern Kota-Obamba woven raffia basket. These receptacles, whether of bark or raffia, contained the skulls of the most revered ancestors, and some of the smaller bones of lesser forbearers, in addition to potent medicines and objects. In order to augment their power, selected skulls and other bones were painted white or red, or embellished with inlay made from cowrie shells, metal tacks, and pieces of mirror (Chaffin n/d:16; Fernández 1992:29; Perrois 1968:36; 1977:60, 96; 1979:119, 126, 128, 151; 1981:199, 201; Siroto 1968:23, 27).

There is a difference of opinion as to whether or not the reliquary figures represented an actual person. Some scholars believe that among the Kota-Obamba, the decorative motifs of individual reliquary figures may have been intended to help identify them as portrayals of the ancestors whose names they bore. However, many hold to the belief that, in spite of the use of proper names, the carved figures inserted into these ossuaries were merely the sentinels that guarded the precious relics contained therein. In ceremonies involving the reliquaries and their guardian figures, the latter were handled almost carelessly while great reverence was shown when touching or lifting the containers themselves. This helps to explain why the Kota, when Western collectors expressed an interest in the figures while at the same time disdaining the attached sacred containers, were not adverse to parting with the guardian figures. Ironically, the interest of Western collectors in the figures, as well as the negative reaction that these same figures elicited from Christian missionaries actually served to raise their importance in the eyes of their Kota creators (Andersson 1953:336;

Chaffin n/d:16, 19–23, 28; Fernández 1992:30–32; Perrois 1968:36–37; 1977:3, 5, 96; 1979:126–128, 151, 157; Sieber and Kan 1995:110; Siroto 1968:27).

The reliquary figures and attached ossuary containers generally, it would appear, were left in the forest at some distance from the village either out in the open or in a specially constructed communal structure that had a roof and one to three walls. They may also have been stored in a dark corner of the men's communal structure, safe from the prying eyes of women and children (de Brazza 1887:329; 1888:50; Fernández 1992:31; Perrois 1979:151; 1981:201; 1985:47; Sieber and Kan 1995:110; Siroto 1968:27).

Two nineteenth-century sketches give a clearer idea of the appearance of the communal sanctuary and the placement of the reliquaries therein. The first drawing (de Brazza 1887:329) shows four reliquary baskets with attached figures, and two other baskets without figures resting on a shelf built against the back wall of a shelter that is open on three sides; the entire structure has a palm fiber roof. The reliquary figures appear to be variants of the Kota-Obamba style. A dead chicken, conceivably an offering, lies on the ground next to an ordinary open basket. The second drawing of a reliquary shelter in the village of Pongo (de Brazza 1888:50) is a close-up view of the inside of the structure showing three Kota-Obamba figures with their attached ossuary baskets. The reliquaries and three additional figureless covered containers, that may be bark boxes, rest on a slatted wooden shelf along with an instrument resembling a rattle.

What these illustrations demonstrate so clearly is that costuming here, as in so much of African figural art, is an essential component. The reliquary figure is another example of a highly abstract sculpture that is admired by art lovers for its seemingly fantastic forms. Many modern artists have owned examples, and Pablo Picasso is suspected to have borrowed its forms for his *Les Demoiselles d'Avignon*. The sketches show that the reliquary figure of wood and brass is only a fragment of the image intended. With the bottom of the figure inserted into a bag made of hide, the image is complete. The hide bag becomes a costume, to which fiber may be attached as a skirt. In their completed state, the reliquaries resemble more clearly the human form fully dressed, and they house the bones within the "body" of the art form. Also noteworthy in the 1888 sketch are the several containers that are not supplied with wood and brass figures, suggesting that the essential elements in this composition were the containers and their contents. Is the wood and brass figure an essential element? Obviously not to the ritual functioning of the reliquary. But it is essential in completing an image, making it a form of art.

The reliquaries were the focus of ritual action. In times past, before any major event in the life of a family or a village, the initiated male elders consulted with, and made offerings to the spirits of the ancestors whose bones were enshrined in the reliquaries, not only to honor them, but also to assure the fertility, health, success, and welfare of family members, as well as of the community at large. The reliquaries of all the families in the village were often honored in communal ceremonies that were accompanied by "feasting, dancing, and the making of medicines" (Siroto 1968:86; Chaffin n/d:16; de Brazza 1887:331; 1888:50; Fernández 1992:29–31; Perrois 1968:32, 36; 1977:96; 1979:126, 151; Siroto 1968:27, 86).

Evidence exists that the northern Kota-Mahongwé reliquary figures were not only consulted by the elders, but at times brought out into the dazzling sunlight and used in dance, to musical accompaniments. The reflection of light off of the brass surface of the concave face may have served to further enhance the dramatic effects of the scene (Siroto 1968:27, 88–89). Siroto was given testimony to the practice:

> Both the MaHongwé and the BuSamai told me that during the great communal Biwiti rites, their fathers danced with the "face of Biwiti". Whoever spoke of this clenched his hand and made passes back and forth with his arm, as if to show how the image was handled.... Some told me that raffia cloth was used, others said unwoven raffia fibers served to embellish the dance, or perhaps only the image, if the two were not in some way united in a form of disguise....
>
> My tentative interpretation of these accounts is based upon the use of raffia and carved wooden heads in the dances of peoples who live not far from the Mahongwé... peoples of the Middle Alima River ... [who] still perform a dance in which the masker holds a carved wooden head at arm's length above the head; he is completely concealed by a tubular garment made of raffia cloth that descends to the ground from the neck of the image. The effect is that of a very tall, sinuous being (Siroto 1968:88)....

Fernández provides a comparison from another group, the Fang, who have close cultural and geographic ties to the Kota, and who also buried the bones of their ancestors in reliquaries surmounted by guardian figures (very different in appearance to those of the Kota) that were danced "like puppets" (Fernández 1992:29).

As further support for his theory that the Kota-Mahongwé reliquary figures were danced, Siroto observes that the shape of the base may have been designed to act as a handle. He suggests that the diamond-shaped base of the head and lozenge figure (Kota-Obamba), on the other hand, would be less easily manipulated (Siroto 1968:88–89). We find it physically feasible, however, in the case of the BMA figure. Furthermore, the diamond-shaped wooden base of the Museum's Mbulu-Ngulu has a heavy patina that shows signs of smooth wear on the front, possibly caused by frequent handling.

L. M. B. & F. J. L.

Shrine with reliquary figures. Kota, village of Pongo, Gabon. Drawing based upon a description by J. de Brazza. From S. de Brazza, 1888

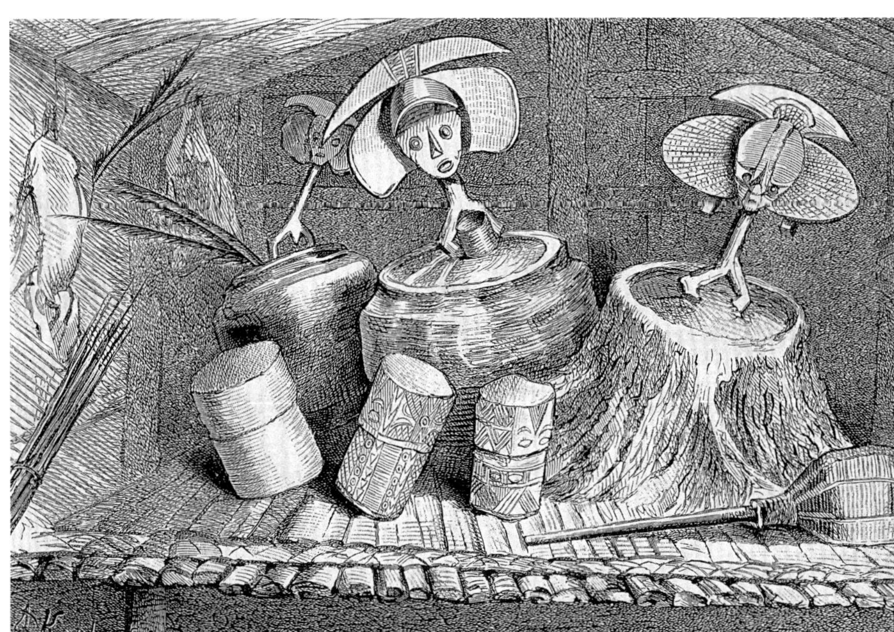

10

Countering the Evil Eye: an Egyptian Child's Tunic

Child's Tunic
Egypt, Coptic Period
c. 5th–10th century
Linen, wool, H. 54.0 cm
Gift of Dena S. Katzenberg, Baltimore
BMA 1985.251

Among the BMA's collection is a group of fragmentary textiles that fall into the general category of late antique, more commonly known as "Coptic." The word "Copt" is believed to have derived from the Greek word for Egypt, *aigyptos* as pronounced in Arabic. In its broadest sense, Coptic textiles are those made for and used by people who lived in Egypt during the early centuries of the Christian Era (Carroll 1988:2; Gonosova 1989:72), generally recognized to span the third century to the Middle Ages. The early limit represents the time when the practice of mummification was being replaced by the custom of burying the dead clothed and wrapped in layers of fabric. This date is significant because those Coptic textiles that have survived have been excavated from gravesites. The terminal date is a matter of conjecture and controversy, ranging from the tenth through the thirteenth century, well beyond the date when Egypt passed into Arab rule in 641 AD (Gonosova 1989:65; Carroll 1988:65; Du Bourguet "Cashiers" June 1960 No. 1 cited in Berliner 1962:6; Baginski and Tidhar 1980:7).

In Coptic textiles dating from the late fifth or early sixth century or earlier, the decoration is often in a "monochrome silhouette style," the color of the ornamentation being purple or a variant of that hue (Carroll 1988:32–33). Garments ornamented with essentially dark monochromatic figures remained popular from the fourth through the first half of the seventh century (Baginski and Tidhar 1980:8). But, from the sixth century onward more colors were often used. The child's tunic in the BMA collection is an example of a polychrome garment, though its patterning seems unusual.

Like the larger early tunics bearing clavi and other ornaments, this small child's tunic was woven in one piece including the sleeves then folded over and sewn up the sides. Unlike most early tunics which were woven lengthwise hem to hem, starting with the sleeve end first (Gonosova 1989:68; Carroll 1988:39–41), this tunic was positioned vertically on the loom, the hemline of the back or front woven first, the sleeve area in the middle. The remaining sides beneath the sleeve area appear to be selvages, which would seem to indicate that the tunic was woven to shape; however, since these areas are somewhat degraded, it is possible that the sides were indeed cut to shape from a rectangular piece of cloth and seamed (see Erikson 1997:92–93 for an example made in this way). By the early fifth century larger tunics were woven vertically in a rectangular shape with the sleeves woven separately and attached afterwards (Carroll 1988:41).

The tunic is decorated with tapestry ornaments, but instead of the clavi, squares, and roundels characteristic of larger garments, a carefully arranged pattern of circlets or ovals, some small (3/8" wide) and composed of red and white or natural yarns, and some larger (5/8") multicolored wool ovals of blue, gold, natural, red, and white. The larger ovals are arranged in an X pattern across the upper portion of the tunic. Considering the "eye-like" design and strategic position over the center of the body, these designs might also be interpreted as a protective design—a defense counteracting harmful glances of others or the "evil eye" (Carroll 1988:54–55). The smaller ovals are arranged in a V shape at the front of the neck, across the shoulders, and downward in a V by the sleeves with the addition of a small irregularly shaped design at the front in the center. Another line of red ornaments crosses the lower back of the garment. This design was probably found on the front as well.

The neck opening was probably cut into the tunic and stitched. The edges are not visible since the neck opening, like the sleeve ends, are covered on the front with a narrow blue tapestry-woven band with a woven design in undyed linen yarn.

The original length of the tunic is not known since the lower portion of the garment has deteriorated. A similar tunic in the Röhss Museum of Applied Art and Design in Gothenburg, Sweden appears to have roughly the same relationship of length to width as the BMA tunic which may indicate that both were only short tops—a convenient length to prevent soiling of the child's clothes. Another child's tunic, which is likewise trimmed with a narrow, figured, tapestry band similar to that used on the BMA example, is in the Victoria and Albert Museum, London (Kendrick 1921:24, #340, pl. XIV). This example, unlike the Baltimore and Gothenburg tunics, appears to be full length, though the lower portion shows significantly more damage than the upper portion, possibly indicating that all three tunics were full length but suffered severe deterioration resulting in complete loss in two instances.

The care and effort involved in the making of this highly decorated garment for an infant child, who would presumably wear the little tunic for only a brief time before growing too large for it, bears witness to a great affection for a child whose life was cut tragically short, and to a belief, nevertheless, in the power of textile to shield from harm.

Anita Jones

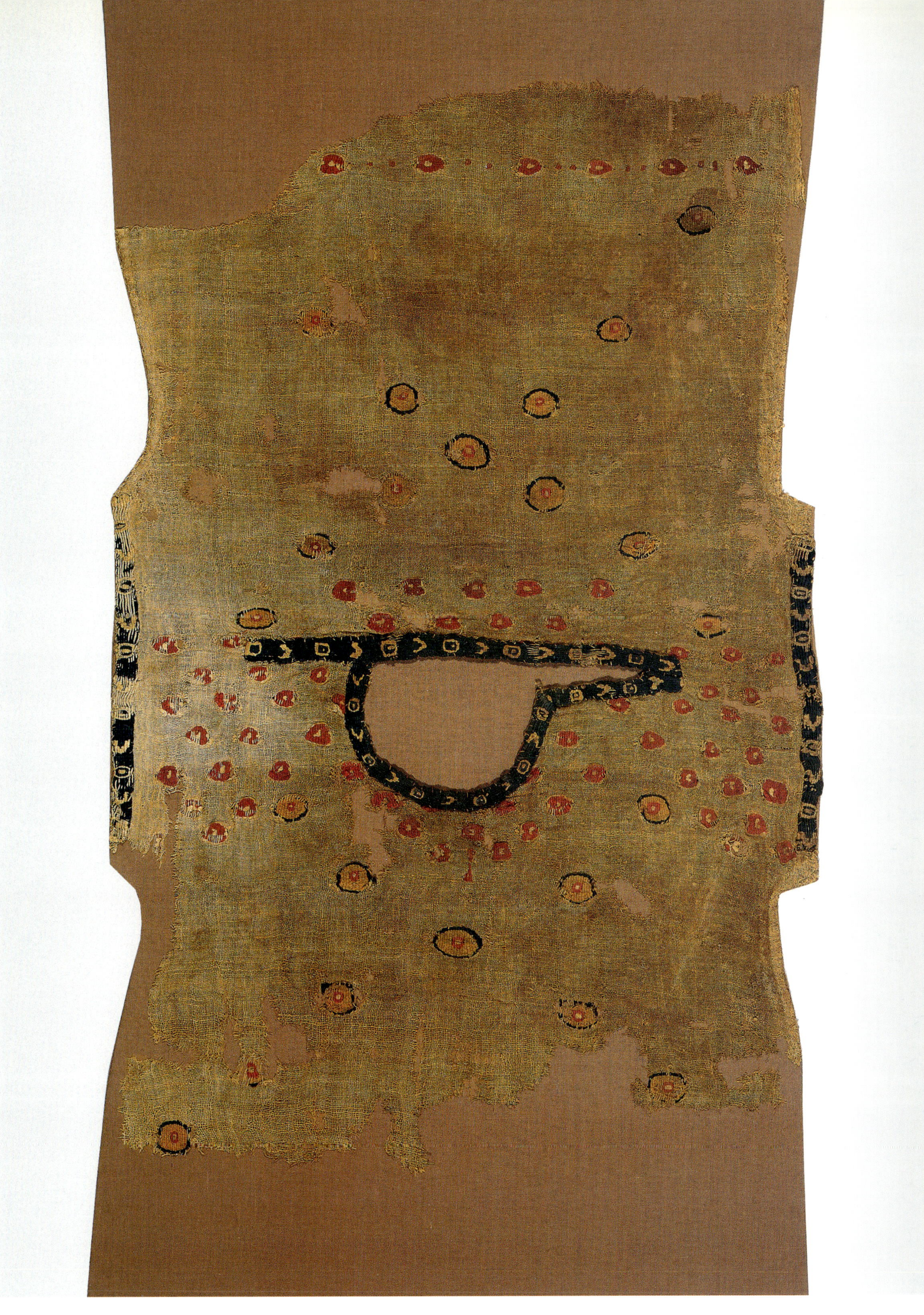

11

The Bird Is Faraway Meat: a Hausa Hunter's Headdress

With a population of over fifty million people, the Hausa are one of the largest ethnic groups in West Africa, best known for their striking architectural façades, though little known for sculpture. The bird decoy stands out for its ability to transcend utilitarian use via performance, costume, music, and cultural significance as a dynamic vehicle of artistic expression.

The bird decoy, *burtu*, is made from the skull of a Ground Hornbill bird attached to a carved wooden neck. The entire decoy is covered with dark-colored goat leather, with cowrie shells or plastic beads used for eyes, and red abrus seeds used for decoration on some areas of the decoy's head or neck. A cord and headband holds the decoy in place. Special herbal medicines, believed to render the hunter's prey helpless, are placed inside the decoy's skull. Hunters in the act of hunting, and actors representing hunters in ritual performance, are the only ones permitted to wear the decoys because of their strong spiritual powers, and hunting practices are usually passed from father to son. Hausa hunters trace the use of decoys back only a century or so (the only extensive prior source on the tradition was published by Mariko [1981]).

Hunter's Bird Decoy Headdress (*Burtu*)
Hausa, Nigeria/Niger
c. Early 20th century
Wood, bird skull and beak, hide, glass, feathers, abrus seeds, H. 30.5 cm
Gift of Alan Wurtzburger
BMA 1954.145.107

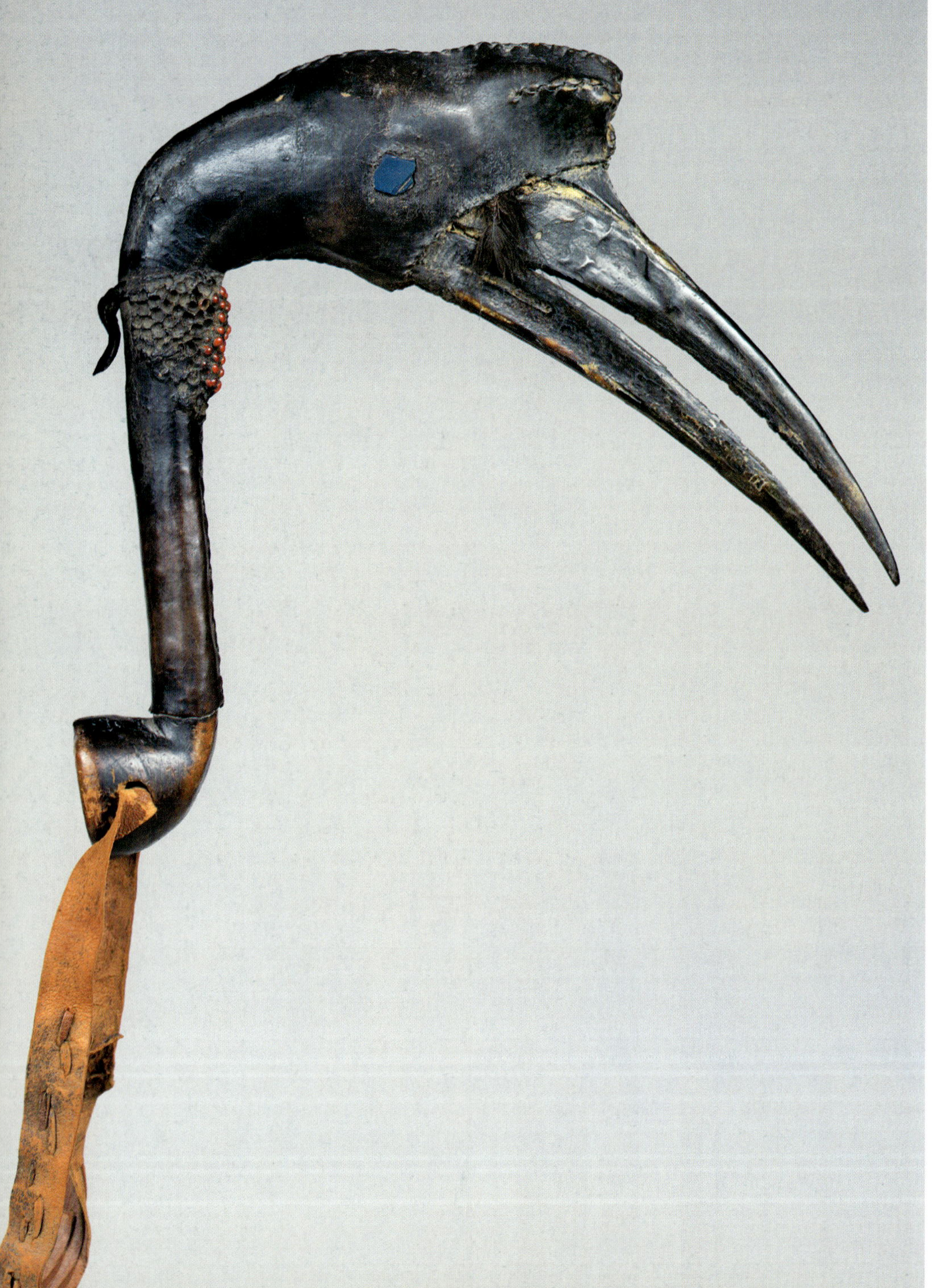

The decoy is worn on the hunter's forehead as part of a larger disguise to help him approach other animals and birds undetected. Placing the decoy on his forehead, a hunter directly addresses the decoy to activate its spiritual power by saying:

> Wake up from your sleep!
> So that the bird [I am hunting] will not have the force to fly away.
> It is not the salt that makes the sauce, the bird is faraway meat.
> The lady of the house should not fill the children's stomachs with desire, but rather with meat (Burmeister 2000).

The hunter's costume consists of dark-colored pants and a matching short-sleeved tunic. Originally the outfits were made of strip-woven cloth dyed a dark indigo color, but today black imported cloth is the most popular choice. The aim is to resemble the actual Ground Hornbill, a large terrestrial bird with dark brown plumage. They also wear special leather-covered amulets on their upper arms and around their waists to protect them from dangerous spirits and hostile animals sometimes found in the bush. Hunting equipment—nets, bow, and a quiver of poisonous arrows, or, today, flint-lock rifles—is carried on the back.

The bird-like appearance of the hunter continues in his physical movements, for in the course of hunting, he remains low to the ground, on his hands and knees, moving his head and body to imitate the movements of real birds. Often hunters perform their bird movements in the shadow of nearby shrubbery, making it almost impossible to detect that they are human. The pecking, head twitching, and other bobbing motions transform the hunter into a living work of art that is extremely convincing, especially from a distance. Indeed, the ability to disguise oneself as a bird—in particular, to move realistically in a bird-like fashion—is considered one of the most important skills of a hunter, often described as *iyawa,* an ideological concept that conveys a person's capacity for artistic and spiritual mastery. In performing these movements, hunters claim to become the birds, attesting to the power of this experience.

Other events in which decoys are worn include hunters' festivals, celebrating the cultural legacy of

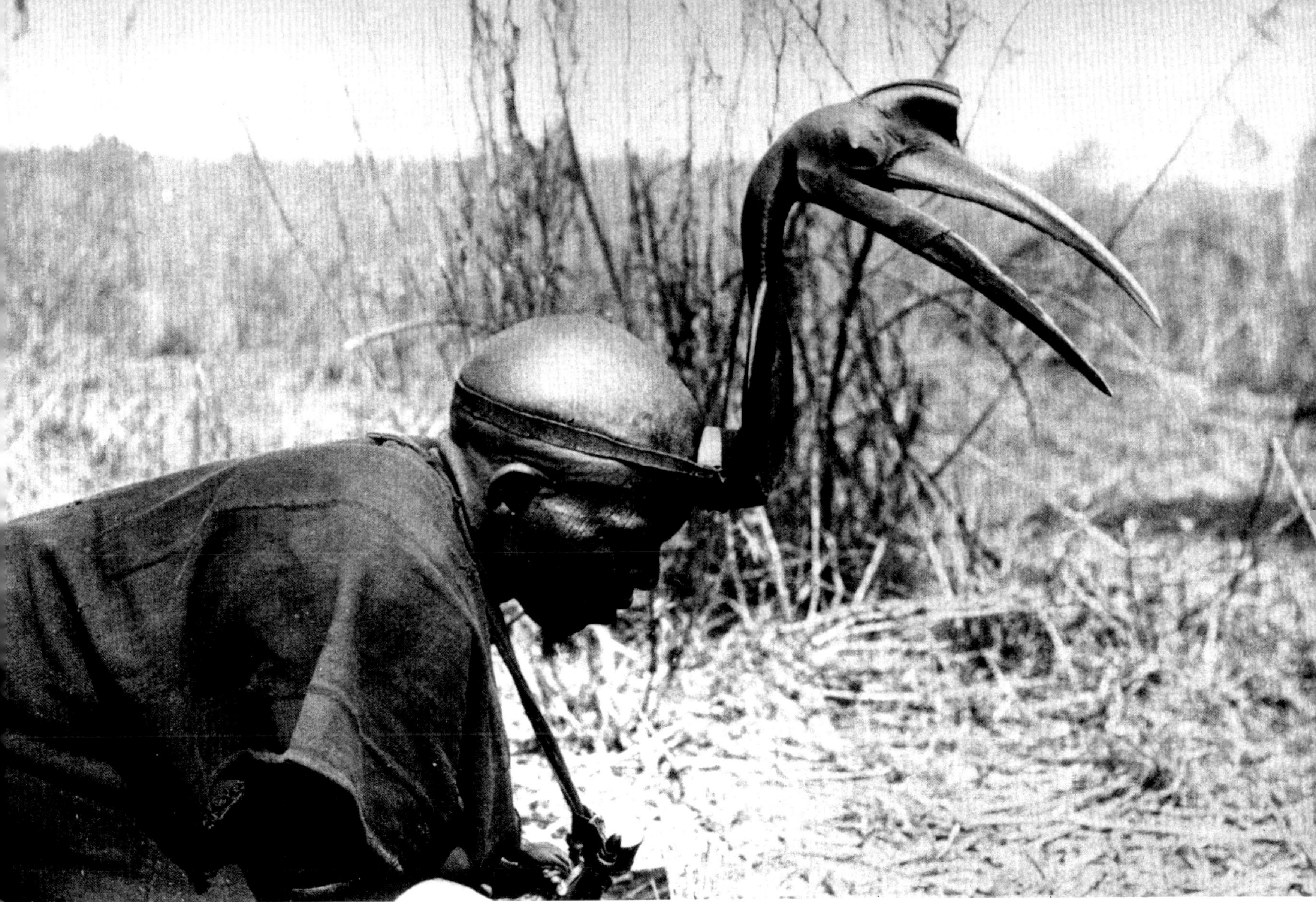

Hunter wearing a bird decoy headdress. Nupe, Nigeria
Photo: ©abm—archives barbier-mueller

hunters and their accomplishments. They are also worn in public performances of hunter folktales, and many public events, such as political rallies and Muslim religious holidays, such as at the end of Ramadan. For many Hausa, the appearance of decoys during public events transforms their status from a simple utilitarian object into a symbol of beauty and moral goodness, representing distinctive Hausa values and cultural pride.

During the public performances of these decoys, special hunters' music and songs of praise accompany the performers. Hunters often play the music themselves, using a special instrument made from a hollowed-out gourd attached to a wooden neck containing metal jingles. They also wear tall crested hats covered with cowrie shells to help distinguish themselves from other performers. The hunter-musicians perform songs praising the accomplishments of famous hunters from the past, as well as special spirits exclusively associated with hunters. The lyrics are frequently improvised, designed to meet the requirements of a specific event or audience. Hausa musicians are considered particularly artful when they demonstrate the ability to stimulate the intellectual and emotional responses of their audiences through the manipulation of lyrics (Ames 1989:145).

Hausa hunters' music has become especially popular in Niger during the past twenty years. The hunters' folktale called *Mai Dawa*, which includes hunters' songs of praise, and actors who dance and sing with decoys on their foreheads, traveled internationally during the 1980s, and postage stamps in Niger commemorate it. A pop song was written to immortalize the famous hunter. At his campaign rallies during the elections in the mid-1990s, President Ibrahim Mainasara Bare employed Hausa hunters, who adapted their music to laud his achievements and bolster his legitimacy as president.

Hausa hunters' bird decoys are thus elevated from being mere objects of utilitarian value to dynamic vehicles for cultural, popular, and even political meaning. The element of performance serves to activate the decoy in essential ways, both spiritually and physically, and helps their users to demonstrate key concepts in Hausa culture.

Alice R. Burmeister

Masking, Dancing, Fighting: Celebrating Male Aggression: an Igede/Ogoja Headdress

This strikingly realistic carved head with traces of its cranial structure under the prominent forehead and mouth, keloid scars on the temples and a tufted coiffure, is a fine example of an Idoma-region prototype but is paired with a feminine hairstyle more commonly associated with the Ogoja-Middle Cross River region (cf. Neyt 1985:125, Ill.41). This layering of mutually unfamiliar characteristics is very common in the Igede and Ogoja regions which lie directly south of the core Idoma districts and is due partly to the latitude given to both sculptors and the masked performers themselves in bringing material objects to life, and partly to the mixing of local practices to create an essentially regional genre.

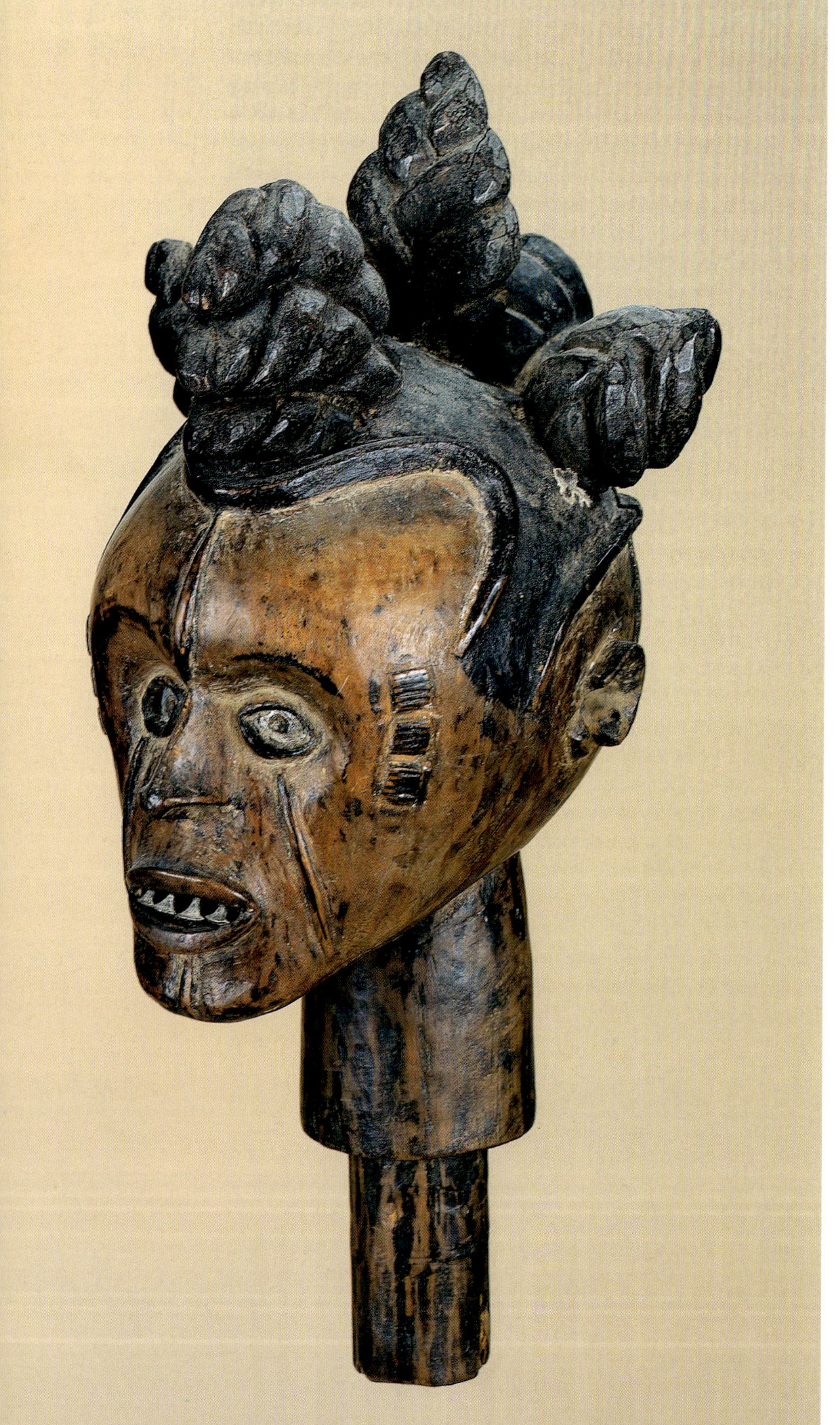

Dance Headdress
Igede/Ogoja region, Nigeria
c. Early 20th century
Wood, metal, H. 37.5 cm
Purchased as the gift of Helen and Howard Benedict, Tiburon, California, in memory of Alan and Janet Wurtzburger
BMA 1982.65 (purchased from Issaka Zango, I. Z. Timbe, Inc., New York; ex Klejman Gallery, New York)

The elimination of the costume for the BMA headdress denies another very crucial aspect of layering in its performance: in the seemingly incongruous use of a woman's coiffure with a warrior's body costume and a warrior's comportment. I will argue in what follows that this is neither a mistake nor the performer's creativity gone awry. It is a mirror of the character's two embodiments, warrior and woman.

Usually identified with the Oglinye society (also written Ogrinye in some districts), this masking genre entered Idomaland sometime in the late-nineteenth or early-twentieth century from the Middle Cross River by way of Ogoja. Early in the twentieth century, Oglinye was very active in large sections of the very broad region between the Benue and Cross Rivers (Kasfir 1988, Nicklin 1979). It is now mainly a memory in the minds of old men, though performed occasionally.

At the time of the earliest British military patrols in 1908–10, the region which is now southeastern Nigeria and the adjacent parts of Cameroon was made up of a highly diverse group of political formations. In all of them warriorhood was a central feature which, in the absence of other male coming-of-age ritual was the principal theater of transition into adulthood. These cohorts of young unmarried men (in Idoma, the *ai-uta*, literally "sons of the law") formed associations which also enforced the laws within their own communities on behalf of the traditional councils of titled elders (the *igabo*), old men too feeble to enforce the law themselves. The Aiuta would recite the laws while dancing: "If anyone slashes another with a knife let him pay the fine of three goats! If anyone steals let them reveal his secret!" But they were also guilty of transgressions such as tunneling into a compound at night to steal animals themselves (Abraham 1967:196). They were, in different contexts, fighters, policemen, dancers, athletes, and exuberant youth.

Embedded in this idea of law enforcement was also a strong belief in the power of spectacle which linked the concepts of fighting, masking, and dance performance to the demonstration of masculine prowess, virility, and often, hubris. In such a situation, the dance performances (some in masquerade and others without) became tests of athletic skill and a proof of fearlessness for the young men who participated. The best known of these associations among the Idoma were Oglinye and Icahoho, both of whom danced with carved masks, though Oglinye used a fully sculpted head, while Icahoho was represented by a white face mask with frontal projections.

The unusual placement of a head sculpted in the round atop a dancer's head, which is in turn made invisible by either a tight knitted or loose cloth costume which hides the dancer's face, raises an issue of aesthetic logic—why not the more usual face mask over the real face, especially in a region where they are so very common? The explanation lies in the style of warfare before the pax Britannica. In the 1920's when the British colonial government developed a passion for the reportage of "customs" by its newly–founded Department of Anthropology within the Colonial Service, Oglinye (banned in 1917 for its headhunting associations) was formally inscribed in colonial officers' reports (e.g., Smith 1919, Brooke 1922, Macleod 1925). But to understand how the template of warfare came to determine the mask's actual form of embodiment one must go to the early writers on Cross River warriors' associations, Partridge (1905) and Talbot (1926). Talbot wrote:

> The most westward of the head-hunting societies appears to be the Ogaranya... of the Asia, Ndokki and Southern Ngwa Ibo, where it is openly confessed to be composed of those who possess the skulls of persons slain by them.... the Ogirinia, or a similar club composed of those who possess the skulls of enemies killed by them, also flourished among the neighbouring Semi-Bantu [Cross River language groups]. The members are the chief warriors, and always lead their town forces in battle.... In most of the plays, especially among the Semi-Bantu, head-dresses are worn consisting either of *real skulls, or of wooden imitations*, sometimes covered with human skin (1926: III, 788–789).

Earlier Partridge (1905:209–210) spoke of the use of human skulls as masks by the Ekpo society at Nko in the Cross River area. The skull was worn on top of the head with false hair and a knitted suit in very much the same way that carved Oglinye heads were still being worn in the late 1970s in Idomaland. Skin covering, on the other hand, appears not to have diffused northward into Igede and Idoma, though it can be seen on a number of Boki masks from Ogoja. Nonetheless, extreme realism, one of the objectives of skin covering, continued to be highly valued.

There is strong evidence that the carved head replaced the defeated enemy's cranium originally held atop the warrior's own head before headhunting was outlawed by the colonial administration. So why, as the mask is regionalized, and warriorhood itself has become diminished, is the head transformed into that of a woman? Women did not fight here. But women nonetheless were the ultimate judges of a warrior's status. No woman would marry a warrior who had not proven his manhood by taking an enemy's life. Men who were afraid to kill therefore became social outcasts and objects of shame. In an Oglinye performance, women honor the masked warrior by entering the arena and approaching him. They are the mirror of his virility, those who accept his manhood.

Yet the masquerade as a total distillation is still very masculine, from its aggressive, athletic dance movements to its tightly fitting knitted suit which emphasizes the masker's muscular, youthful body. At his waist is a civet cat pelt, a totemic animal for some Idoma lineages and a constant reminder of his association with the forest. One is left with the unresolved ambiguity of male/female, warrior/woman. Rather than trying to smooth this over with an elegant structural equivalence, let me leave it as a problem for us to consider: that the total ensemble of mask, dancer, dance, musicians, and audience will and perhaps should contain disjuncture and ambiguity.

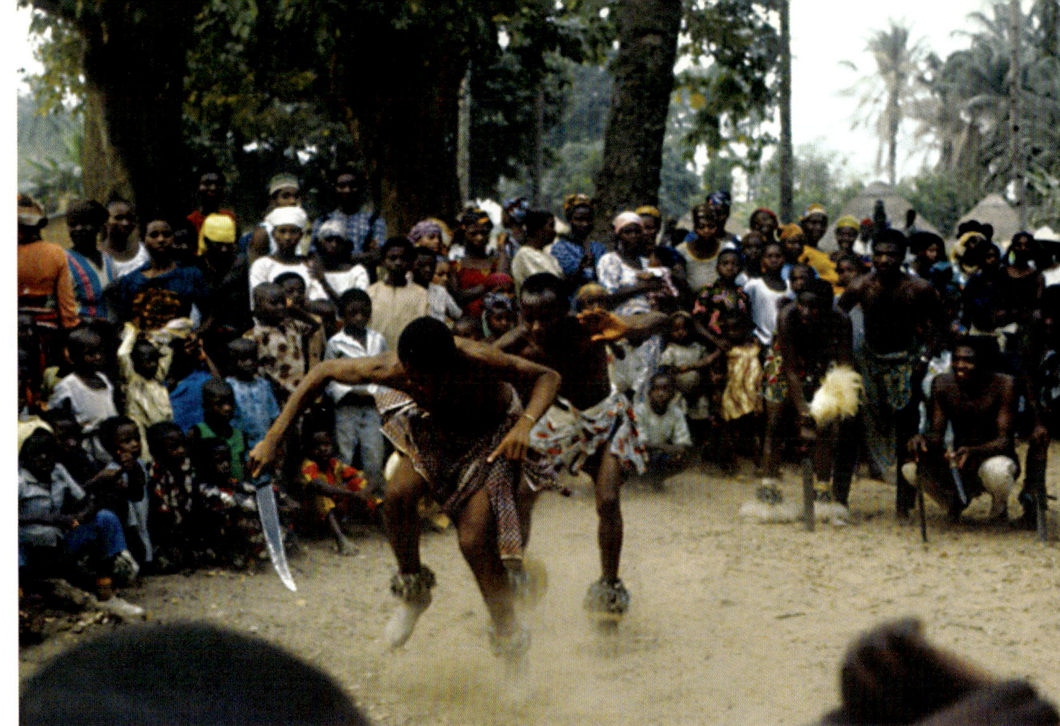

Performing the "Igede" war dance. Idoma, Ejor village, Akpa district, Nigeria
Photo: Sidney Littlefield Kasfir, 1986

The main action in the Oglinye dance performance I filmed in 1977 involved a mock fight with machetes in which a warrior "challenged" an older man with a reputation as a headwinner, symbolized by his right to wear the red *uloko* feather. From start to finish the dance exploited the intimate relationship between aggression and virility in Idoma masculine behavior. The masquerader, summoned by music from a special orchestra of side-blown flutes and drums and running at top speed, burst into the performance space from a bush path, coming to a sudden halt in front of the slit drum, the instrument most closely associated with the celebration of war victories throughout the region. The challenge issued, first to the war drum and then to another dancer, consisted of a series of very rapid ground-stamping steps. Everything—running, challenging, dancing, and running again—happened very quickly in a blur of movements meant to cause a rush of emotion, excitement bordering on fear. Barely five minutes later, Oglinye sprinted away down the same bush path, a reminder that warriors are figures at the margins, both social and spatial, of the stable world of village and farm.

Sidney Littlefield Kasfir

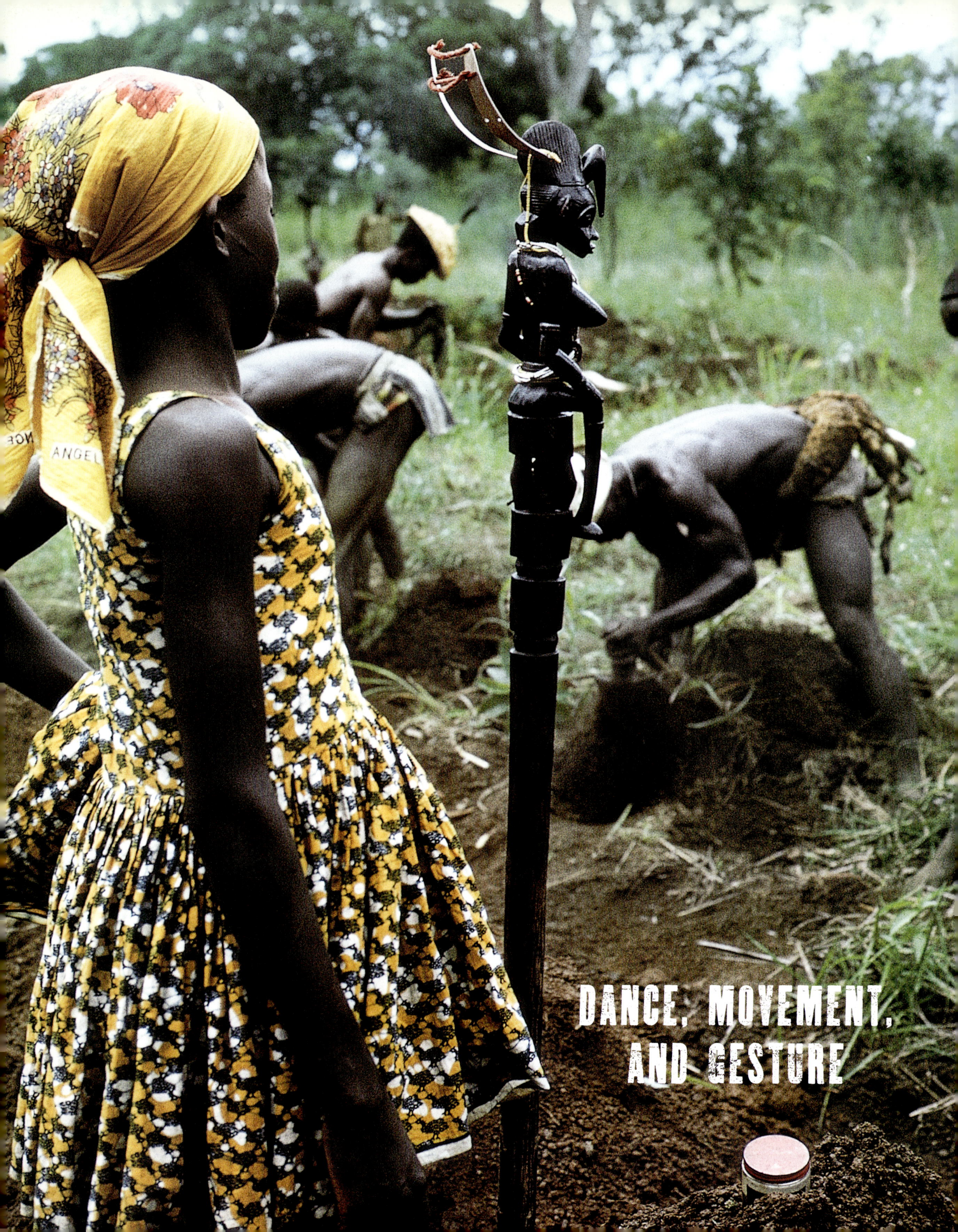

DANCE, MOVEMENT, AND GESTURE

Although sources on African masquerade throughout the twentieth century and into the twenty-first frequently make reference to dance, there is rarely a description of movement. Apart from Robert Farris Thompson's (1974) thorough analysis of African gesture, little else has been published on this subject since. Most scholars in this field, trained in art history and anthropology, have not had exposure to movement studies and its vocabulary. Nevertheless, the desire is there, and we have come a long way since R. E. Bradbury (1973:194) who referred extensively to dances in the kingdom of Benin, but noted: "There would be no point in describing the movements of the dance here." Georgiana Gore (1994), an anthropologist specializing in West African dance, gives a sound historiography of primary and secondary sources, but notes that written documentation is rare. "This can be explained not only by the 'orality' of the societies in question but also by the fact that dance has generally been overlooked by those who have written about West African traditional cultures. This applies equally to indigenous and foreign writers ... " (p. 62–63).

A common Western conception of African dance even today is that it is performed spontaneously, improvisationally, as the natural act of a community of free spirits. While such unstructured dance does occur in Africa, as elsewhere, ceremonial dances, especially those using costume and art objects, almost always follow a choreography, prepared either by a known contemporary member of the community, or by an ancestor, often now anonymous. This has been documented in the recent creation of spirit manifestation and dance by contemporary artists (Lamp 1996: 249–250). Dance, structured movement, the use of space, patterns of steps and gesture of the hands, arms, head, and other body parts such as the tongue are designed specifically, just as is music, for particular artistic events.

The very identification of a mask sometimes depends not upon the physical style and form of the mask itself but upon its use in performance. Masks of the Dan (p. 99), carved as a simple face, though divided into eleven generic categories by Fischer (1984), are extremely similar through four different categories. But each performance situation defines the identity of the mask, and even the same mask may undergo transformations in function through time and new situations (p. 9). In this volume, Strother explains, in her essay on the Pende Forehead Mask (p. 88) that it is sometimes impossible to identify by name a mask in a museum or private collection because its identity is found within the dance. In fact, for a new performance, a dancer may simply use an existing mask and adapt it with a new essence created by the costume and the movement.

Monuments, stationary displays, and shrines may also be centers of movement. They may, in fact—thinking in terms of process—be conceived as "a dance," in the words of Herbert Cole (1969, II, 4). He has described the construction of a sacrificial monument, with molded figures, to honor a particular deity, in which "the spirit workers will eat, work, and live" for a number of years until completion:

> Activity and process, as used here, precede and supersede the modeling and painting of mud. They include the formalized life of the workers, the prayers, sacrifices, games, songs, and all other activities, as well as actual construction, which lead to the unveiling of a completed *mbari* house. All these ritually sanctioned acts are, in the nature of ritual behavior, highly stylized, not to say choreographed. As an Owerri Ibo man said, "*Mbari* is a dance for our God."
>
> ... As one man said: "We dance *mbari*. We sing *mbari*. In the morning we make ourselves beautiful by washing and rubbing camwood on our bodies. We eat sacrificial animals. We have drums too, which we beat, and we dance. *Mbari* is a thing of good heart...." "*Mbari* is life."

Female "champion-cultivator" staff carved by Zana Soro of Poundia, presented during the hoeing contest. Senufo, Kufulo subgroup, Kurufu dialect, Ivory Coast
Photo: Anita Glaze, 1970

Objects seemingly motionless on a shrine might, themselves, be seen by their African owners to be quite mobile and energized, constantly changing and shifting. The objects, including masks, and other instruments, belonging to the Manding or Minianka Kòmò association (p. 233), are thought of as a great organism, constantly revivified by sacrificial blood:

> These "things of *Kòmò*," they say, are alive; they "talk among themselves", and it isn't unusual that little signs [of change] ... —the appearance of cracks, coagulated blood, the slipping of parts—the interpreted as the realization of the "utterances of *Kòmò*". The initiates think of this group of "things" in terms of living bodies, a sort of permanent protective presence near the village (Jespers 1995:44).

The fact that African art must be seen as a form in motion was established in the groundbreaking exhibition curated by Robert Farris Thompson at the National Gallery of Art and the University of California, Los Angeles, in 1974, entitled *African Art in Motion*. In the first few words of the catalogue, he defined a fundamental quality of African art (1974:xii):

> The Tiv people of Nigeria use a basic verb which means "to dance." This word, *vine*, unites the dance with further worlds of artistic happening. Thus a person can sometimes "dance" a top, setting the toy in motion, or "dance" a cutlass, twirling the blade artistically, causing it to glitter before the metal bites into the wood. This broad conception of the dance is widely shared in subsaharan Africa, viz, that dance is not restricted to the moving human body, but can combine in certain contexts with things and objects, granting them autonomy in art, intensifying the aliveness an image must embody to function as a work of art.

The enormous Bedu masks of the Nafana of the Ivory Coast are excellent examples of how movement can belie the apparent weight and mass of an object, and they also are an example of the discrepancy between obvious visual importance and spiritual or artistic significance. The male mask is smaller and more open than the large, solid female mask, which might lead one to believe that the female is the more powerful. But the male mask is designed to be lighter to accommodate the dance movements which are much stronger and have more variety, including traveling leaps, turns, and fast knee falls. "Power, to the Nafana, is determined and judged by the amount of activity and movement present. The male force is considered to be much greater than the female force and the male mask is considered to be more powerful as well" (Williams 1968:72):

Art objects function as a pivotal point within a context of movement, in which the tension between movement and stasis is critical. Figurative staffs produced by the Senufo people of the Ivory Coast contain a finial at the top in the form of a seated female figure (p. 68). Its ritual employment is in the context of farming. On the farm where the young men are busy cultivating the land, the staff is held in an upright position by a boy until the young men have completed their work. The representation of the young woman with firm breasts seated at the top of the shaft is an obvious reference to the aspirations of the young men: "the figure promises a beautiful fiancée, increase for the kinship unit, abundant harvests, and many children," according to Anita Glaze (in Vogel 1981:48). Hard at work, the young men compete through their strength and skill for the position of "champion cultivator." The image of the silent female staff and the proud young men furiously working in the fields is striking in its reference to energy and desires that form a part of agricultural work imbued with spiritual power. "The calm repose of the seated figure is a sign of honor," Glaze says, "and is intended as a deliberate contrast to the bending, striving gestures of the laboring youths." Digging in the fields would seem to be a mundane kind of enterprise, but its situation within a milieu of ritual sculpture and music, performed with ritualized movement

A vast field of information is missing from our understanding of African art if we do not carefully record and analyze the movement, as the same data may not be available in the other performance elements. Cole & Aniakor (1984:219–220) have shown that movement characterizes relative spiritual strengths in masquerade that would not be obvious otherwise:

> Masquerades danced by younger men shows centrifugal characteristics.... Nature and the spirits are present in characters and masking materials—birds/animal/human combinations and fresh palm leaves. Their actual power is rather weak, however.... This theater is bright, showy, and for the most part peaceful. Senior masked spirits are contrastingly centripetal, with more restricted, secretive concentrations of energy focused inward: at selected elders' funerals, shrines, and other weighty situations when spiritually loaded ensembles and ideas are called for.

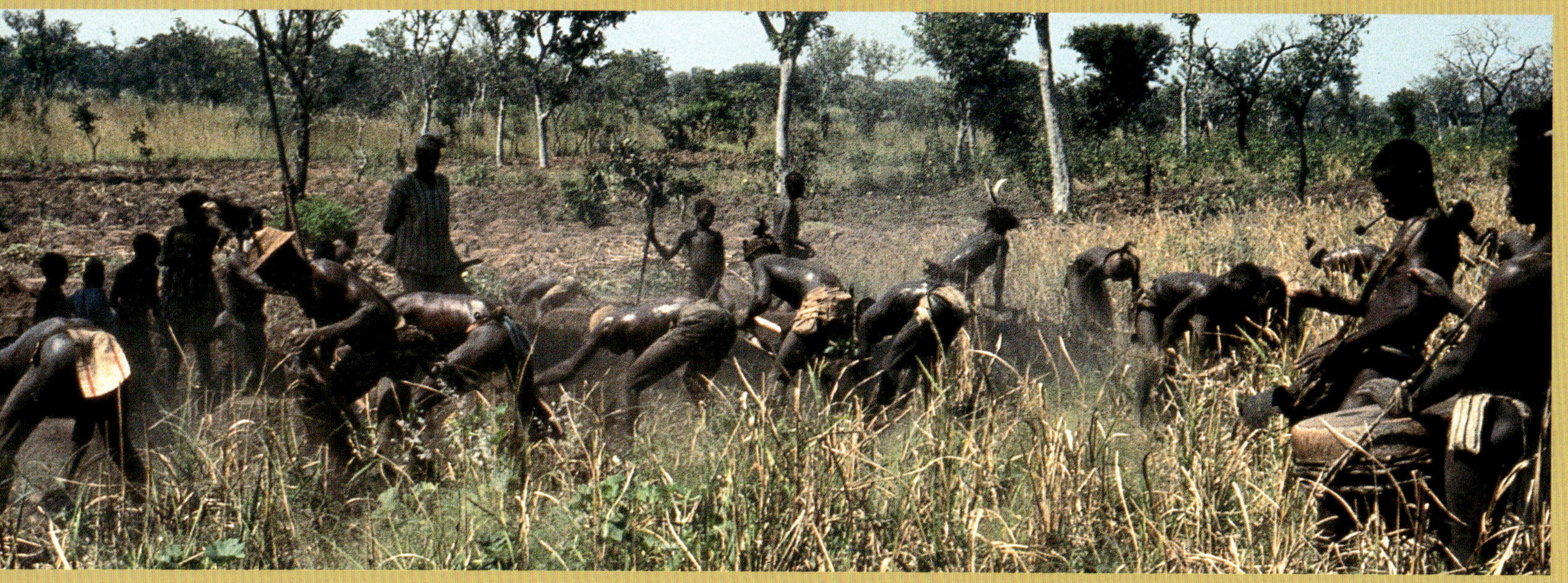

Hoeing contest between matrilineal teams. Senufo, Kufulo subgroup, Kurufu dialect, Ivory Coast. Photo: Anita Glaze, 1970

separates it from the ordinary. The whole event becomes an art form, and the silence of the staff and the sense of anticipation forms a counterpart to the busy activity taking place around it. Glaze argues: "Through the use of sculpture, orchestra, song, and dance, hoeing contests transform grinding labor into ritual." What is the figurative staff without the energy of the event of cultivation?

Dance, movement, and gesture are inalienable elements of art just as they are tightly woven with the texture of sound. John Miller Chernoff (1979:111) in his pioneering study of drumming among the Dagomba in Ghana, recorded the comments of a master drummer, Ibrahim Abdulai, on the oneness between the musician and the dancer, in which one could not exist without the other. In a graphic description, he compared the interaction to sexual maneuvering and intercourse:

> ... she will give you some movement. By all means you have to give her a reply.... And if she does not become active, that means you have to do it coolly.... So it is the same thing with drumming. Immediately a dancer runs in, you give him different styles. If it is a new dancer, you change until you give him his type of beat, and then you continue with that beat.

The thought processes behind the production of a mask or figure used in performance may overlap with those underlying movement in the same performance, but there might be some variance, as well, providing a multi-textured character to the performance. A performance, with multiple elements of music, movement, costume, etc., is therefore composed of several artistic languages, each with their own premises, information systems, structure, and capabilities. The vocabulary of one artistic element may not be translatable into the vocabulary of another.

Understanding of the dance is especially dependent upon the somatic: the body understanding, the comprehension through body experience. Diedre Sklar (2001:4) writes that "all our actions in the world are at the same time interpretations of the world," and that we need to study interpretations through proprioception, the feeling sense:

> I postulated that if ways of moving are also ways of thinking, then it would be possible to look for answers to my large questions in the movement.... If spiritual knowledge is as much somatic as it is textual, then clues to faith, belief, and community would be embedded in the postures and gestures of the fiesta. How does one move here, through what kinds of spaces, constrained by what boundaries? What does the fiesta taste and smell like? What are its sounds? In what rhythms do people move together? My learning, I knew, would begin with my body.

In research on masking in Africa, not a single performance has been notated, although non-masked dance has (for example, by Odette Blum [1973] in Ghana and Peggy Harper [1970] in Nigeria). Notation requires technical training, and there is some disagreement among specialists on which notation system applies best to African movement. Systems used successfully outside of Africa include Labanotation (documenting change within space), Benesh (change in body part relationships), and Stepanov (change in the angle of joints—(Marion 1997). Notation systems use a staff to chart movement through time and space.

The system invented by Rudolf Laban in 1928, and developed further by Irmgard Bartenieff and others, conceives of the body space as a "kinesphere." It is based upon analysis that focuses on the effort and shape of movements of different parts of the body within this sphere, classifying four different motion factors of space, time, weight, and flow. The system was designed initially to analyze pedestrian movement, which Laban felt could describe human personality and cultural values, expressing a cultural system (Laban 1975, Bartenieff 1980):

> In certain epochs, in definite parts of the world ... some attitudes of the body are preferred and more frequently used than others.... Communities seem to regard a certain uniformity of movement behavior as indispensable ... a common ideal of beauty, very often connected with a utilitarian value.... The subconscious evaluation of people's movement is practiced by almost everybody" (Laban, in Bartenieff 1980:165).

It has been argued that although Labanotation is useful as a script to record structural and qualitative movement, it cannot show intent and it focuses more on bodily positions than the movement between them, in the manner of still frames. In this sense, its assumptions are seen by some as fundamentally Western (Williams 1999, Farnell 1999, Marion 1997). Nevertheless, Labanotation and analysis provide a useful vocabulary to analyze basic units and motifs.

For the researcher who is not a dance specialist and has not studied notation, observation as well as participation can still be important, and description should nevertheless be attempted, even in pedestrian terms. Following the concerns of Laban and Bartenieff, what are the dynamics of movement and even of such attitudes as relaxation or an "upright posture?" What is the space around the mover, what are its qualities, what is its shape, and how does the shape change? What kind of effort and impulse can be determined—expanding, condensing, resisting, indulging? Is it light, sustained, and free, or is it strong, sudden, and bound? How does the whole body move, what is its posture, what are the steps, and how are body parts articulated in gesture (Bartenieff 1980)? The recording of African dance in images is as old as rock art in the San or Khoesan area of southern Africa dating to 26,000 BP (Williams 2000:185), and today's observers can use the still camera, video, or film. At the same time, description and notation are important as analysis serving in themselves, as ethnography, and can be aided by still and moving images (Farnell 1999:155).

Just as movement can define and be defined by culture, it is also tied to other divisions such as gender, class, and rank. In African dance generally, there is a distinction between men's and women's movement, even within the same performance. Men and women may mimic each other's styles. "Men's evaluations of women's dancing and their imitation and parody of women in the theater demand a practical knowledge of women's dance forms. For a masked dancer to successfully embellish women's dance movements, sometimes giving them a bawdy or comic interpretation, he must have mastered the original dance being parodied" (Arnoldi 1995:118). Movements are associated with class within a society. Arnoldi notes for the Bamana: "More emotive license in terms of exaggerated gestures and dance movements is the birthright of members of blacksmith, bard, and leatherworking groups, as well as descendants of former slaves." In some performances, she found, "differences between farmer's and fishermen's performance styles were openly acknowledged and celebrated in the event itself" (p. 140). There are particular dance steps for young male initiates, and others which only the most respected elders may perform.

Most importantly, because movement is cultural, as is language, it does not interpret easily. A single gesture may mean vastly different things across cultures. For example, pursing the lips and tilting the head by a West African might be misinterpreted as something sensual by an American observer, and the outstretching of an arm and the index finger by an American would signal nothing but a high offense for a West African, but the two gestures achieve the same thing: pointing (cf. Brenda Farnell in Williams 1999:34, on Native American gesture). So too, participation in a dance does not necessarily lead to understanding. Human movements express cultural values, beliefs, and intentions, and the feeling that an insider might experience through a particular movement may be felt differently by the outsider, "necessarily filtered through the semantics and structure of the bodily language(s) one already knows, one's general cultural and linguistic background, and one's imagination" (Farnell 1999:148). Farnell (pp. 146–147) described the pitfalls she encountered in the Niger Delta attempting to interpret and make judgments about Igbo body movements, which should give caution and guidance to all movement researchers:

> Without being able to talk to the villagers in their language, I could not possibly know what it all meant from their perspective. What were the steps and movements called in their language, if anything? What choreographic rules did they employ for combining movements one with another? What sorts of gender relations existed between these men and women who danced? What did those actions symbolize in their society and how did they conceive of space/time and the body itself?

Most of the writers in this book have addressed movement in one way or another. In this section there is particular emphasis on movement and gesture, with some specific insights. Robert Farris Thompson shows how linear gesture describes space among the Kongo. My discussion of the Baga Banda mask shows how deceptive a still mask on display can be, appearing monumental and extremely heavy. But in dance it seems to be weightless, whirling at a dizzying speed. Christian K. Højbjerg's essay on Loma masking reveals the impression of movement upon the audience in a regional divergence of movement. A discussion of the neckrest maintaining Luba men's and women's elaborate hair styles contrasts its static mundane utilization with a context of movement in spiritual manipulation. The maneuvering of textile and body together, and the imagery of movement, is the subject of the essay on Fante flags by Doran Ross. Christopher Roy describes aggressive colors and movement of the Mossi. Z. S. Strother shows how the Pende equate life with heat and energetic movement, and that just as movement produces sound, sound produces movement. And David Binkley shows how masked movement in Kuba masquerades hinges upon specific sound and presence.

Gestures of Healing: a Kongo Fly Whisk Finial (*Nsesa*)

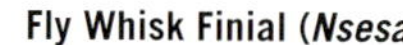

Fly Whisk Finial (*Nsesa*)
Kongo, Mayombe District, Congo (Kinshasa)/Congo (Brazzaville)/Cabinda
c. Late 19th–early 20th century
Wood, H. 26.5 cm
Gift of Howard and Jane Cohen, Baltimore
BMA 1995.151

Flywhisks in action are weapons of ideal protection and punishment. They are critical instruments of good government. They come into sharp focus in ceremonies dealing with serious political issues (*mambu*).

Before the ruler makes his entrance at such a mambu, he dips the filaments of his whisk into a pot filled with medicine (*kinzu nkisi*). When he comes out into the plaza where the issue is to be decided, those spatially close to him take note of gleaming wet droplets glistening on the horsehair and know what it means—the instrument has been activated with powers to heal (*niakisa* or *buka*), block evil (*kandika*), and effect moral punishment (*tumba* or *zemba*).

After the ruler has finished speaking, when the appropriate time comes, he will thrust the flywhisk to his left, then in front of his body, then to the right of his body and finally over his shoulder to the area behind him. He does this in silence. No words need be uttered. The community instantly knows what is happening: he is calling for healing upon all persons who abide by the law and causing to crumble those who do not. So doing, he will hold the flywhisk laterally, more or less parallel to the ground (*simba nsesa mu nkambakani*), or he will hold it at an oblique angle (*evo simba nsesa mu mbaamba*). He does not, normally, hold the figurated emblem upside-down for that is the vantage point of the other world. The reason for this ritual avoidance is summed up in a phrase: "He does not wish to see God's face" (*kadi dazolele mona zizi kia Mpungu-Tulendo ko*).

The splendid little kneeling figure of an important woman who adorns the handle of the flywhisk is meant to suggest and augment the inherent powers of the flywhisk. Her chiefly bonnet (*mpu*) is a *tambala*, i.e., a sign of protection of the power of the king. She covers her head as well to manifest a state of ritual purity and formal observance (*nlongo*). Her closed eyes suggest she is meditating, thinking of issues that relate to two worlds, and double copper bracelets about both arms emphasize her rank and distinction.

When Kongo women wish to voice important blessings, they kneel and cup both breasts with their hands. The gesture used here is symbolic of *nsesa* itself as a life-bearing instrument.

Robert Farris Thompson

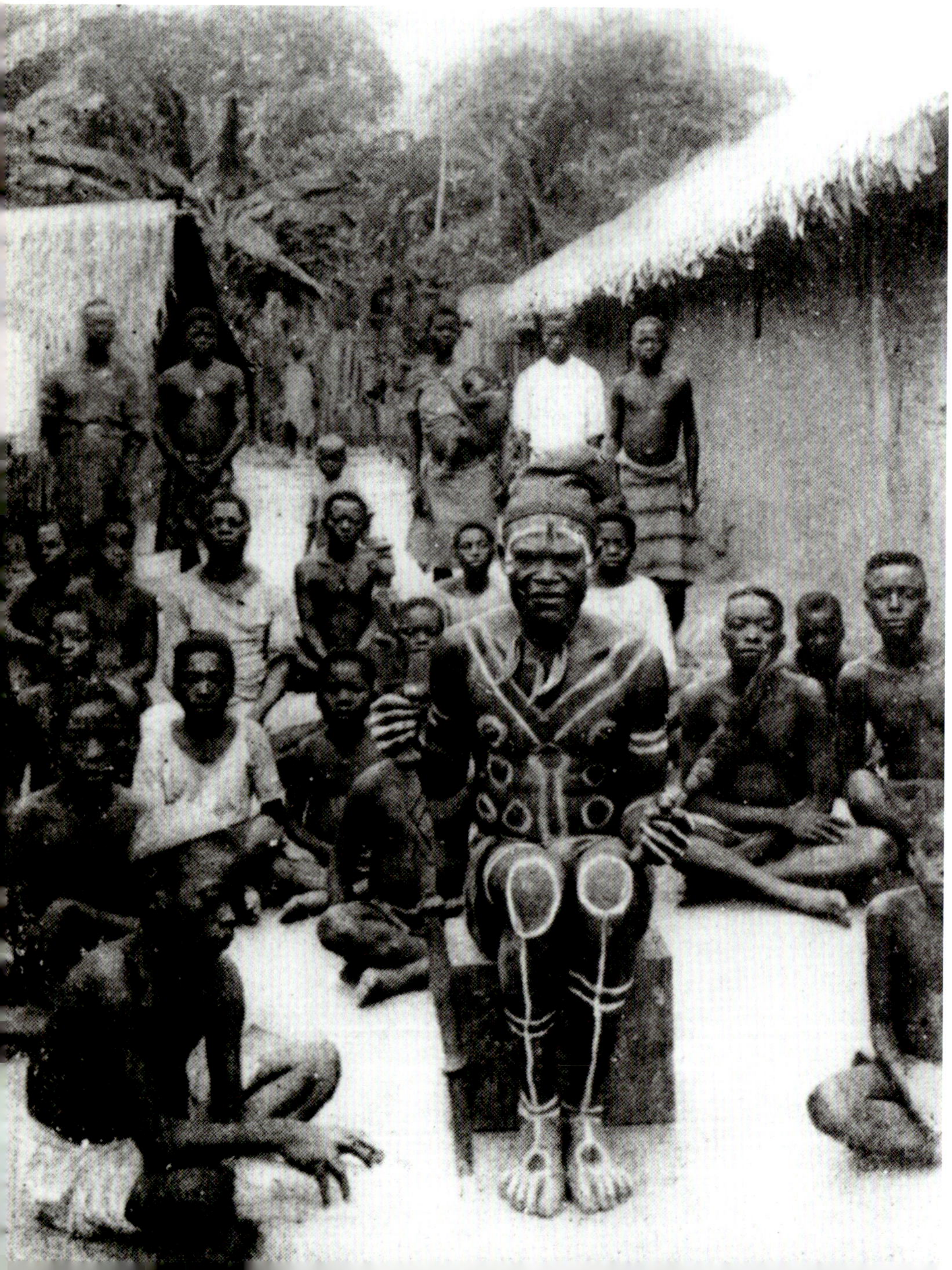

Installation of a lineage chief. Kongo, Congo (Kinshasa)
Photo: Leo Bittremieux, *c.* 1920

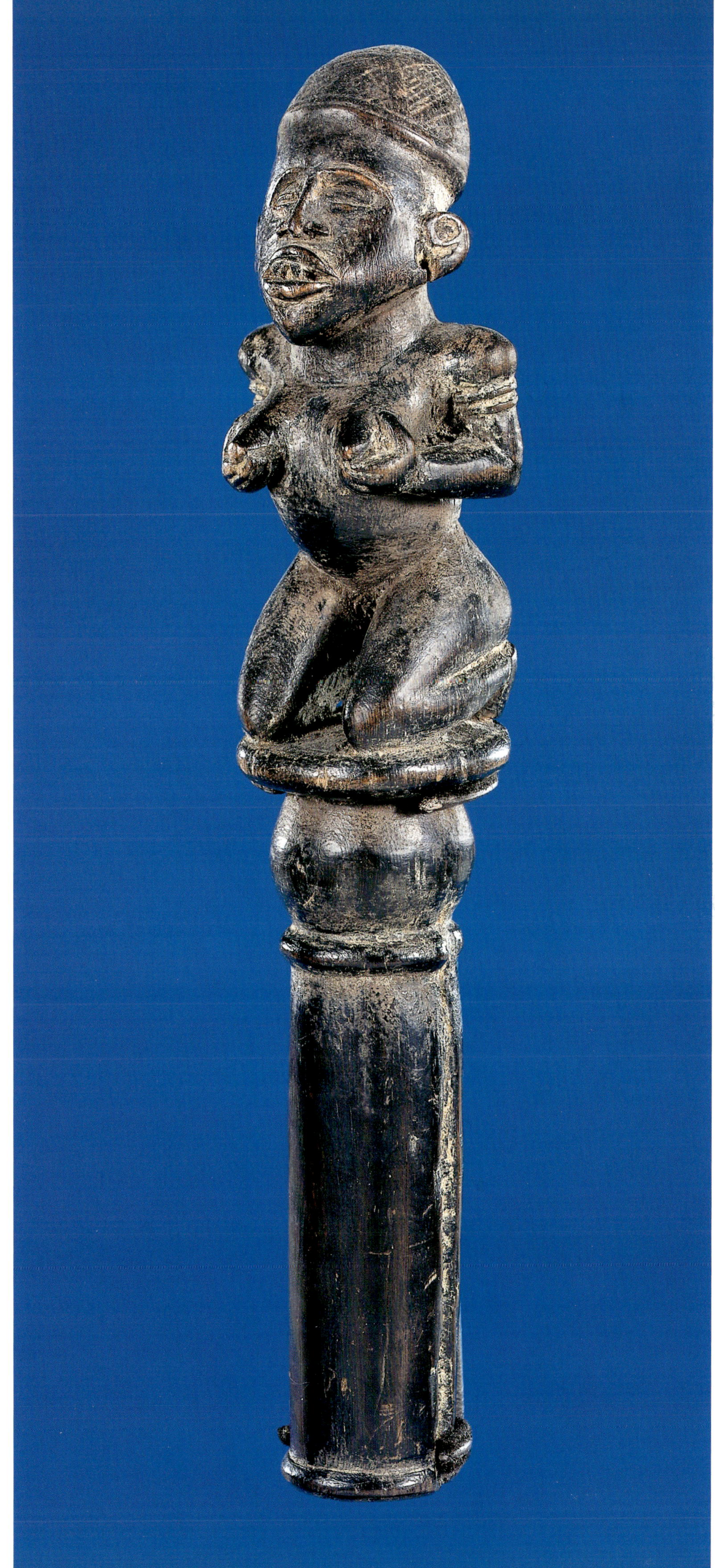

14 The Illusion of Lightness: a Baga/Nalu Headdress (*Banda*)

Dance Headdress (*Banda* or *Kumbaduba*)
Baga/Nalu, Guinea/Guinea Bissau
c. Early 20th century
Wood, polychrome, metal, L. 160 cm
Partial gift of Valerie Franklin, Los Angeles; and purchased with exchange funds from Gift of Lily and Nelson Adlin; Gift of R. Bruce Allen, from the Estate of Luther Emory Allen; Gift of Dr. and Mrs. Bernard Berk; Gift of Mrs. Sidney Burney; Gift of Mrs. Harry B. Dillehunt, Jr. in Memory of her Husband; Gift of Mrs. P.W. Dore; John Erikson Collection of Eskimo Indian Art; Gift of Mrs. Rowland H. Evans; Bequest of Lilian Sarah Greif; Gift of Irene Gulck; Gift of The Hecht Company; Gift of Mr. and Mrs. L. Manuel Hendler; Gift of Lulie P. Hooper; Gift of Mrs. Vincent Lopez; Gift of the Jamosil Foundation; Gift of Stephen and Cecilia Ludwig; Gift of the Maryland Academy of Sciences; Gift of Saidie A. May; Gift of Mr. and Mrs. Alan Meyers; Gift of Mrs. C.R. Miller; Gift of Mr. and Mrs. Vincent Price; Gift of Mr. and Mrs. Robert Rody; Gift of Mr. and Mrs. A. Harvey Schreter; Gift of Mrs. E. Ridgely Simpson; Gift of Mr. and Mrs. Leonard Whitehouse; Bequest of Florence Reese Winslow; Gift of Alan Wurtzburger
BMA 1990.2 (ex Harry Franklin, Los Angeles)

Baga and Nalu art, legends, cultural history, and ritual are permeated with the notion of struggle and cooperation between mankind and the natural features of their world. This balanced tension especially characterizes the costumed spiritual representation called Banda, one of many masks and headdresses brought into play during cultural events. The Banda mask is a composite creation, carved from a single piece of wood, incorporating the human head with its eye, nose, and its braided and crested coiffure, a crocodile jaw, antelope horns, chameleon tail, and serpent, and often a small house perched on the forehead. The whole forms a complex of elements from throughout the Baga environment. In the 1920s, with the coming of the French missionaries of Les Pères du Saint-Esprit, another architectural element entered the Baga landscape, and its forms were adopted: on the BMA headdress is a model of the two-story French ecclesiastical building with stairs and colonnades, highly abstracted, carved above the mask's forehead (Lamp 1996:136–137, 144–153).

Before the twentieth century Banda seems to have represented a high and powerful spiritual being and appeared only to privileged society elders (Appia 1943:158, 160; Bowald 1939:126, 128; *Voix* V, 7, 1930:13). It reportedly figured in ritual designed to protect the villagers against crocodile attacks, human malevolence, and various impending dangers, especially at the time of male initiation to mark the attainment of adolescence, adulthood, and elder status. It also appeared on such events as marriage, harvest celebrations, and new planting ritual, and the appearance of the new moon, all auspicious occasions. A single village might have had two or three Banda headdresses, which could appear together.

Today, Banda has disappeared from the southern cultural areas of the Baga, and it is seldom seen except in very remote Baga and Nalu villages in the North. It may appear on any special occasion, such as the visit of a dignitary, a wedding, New Year's Day, or any national public holiday. Its dance is regarded as entertainment, although there is certainly still some element of spirituality in its regard, and it is stored in its own sacred house.

The dancer, always a young man, carries the wooden headdress on top of his head. Attached to the underside is a large cape of bleached raffia falling to the dancer's knees. On top of that a shorter cloth cape is spread, tailored in several pieces, often with ruffles. Completing the ensemble are generally loose trousers, ruffles of bleached raffia at the ankles, and sometimes cloth tassels attached to the ends of the wooden horns.

The performance takes place in the evening after sundown within a circular arena formed by the crowd. When I witnessed the dance in 1987, the mask was brought out in my honor, and, as I wished to videotape the performance, a slight adjustment was made in scheduling the dance to begin while some light was still in the sky. Normally, I gather, lighting would come only, or principally, from lighted torches of grass.

Drummers played a rhythm on giant wooden slit gongs, as they did earlier in the century:

> In the evening there is a celebration.... In the village plaza lies a hollowed tree trunk which is closed on both ends. In use, different deep tones are emitted from the three, long, straight slits of different length.... Youths of the village manipulate it, working it with the ball of the left hand and with a wooden stick in the right. Right and left of it stand the drummer and the balafon player (Bowald 1939:123–125)....

Individuals from the crowd entered the circle to display their dancing ability. The guardians of Banda entered to display theirs, as a sort of riff, heightening the momentum. The participation of the audience was described in 1939 very much as it occurs today:

> [First] only one of the beautiful villagers dances. Her upper body is nude. The reflection of the flickering fires casts strange shadows on the dancing form.... Now elfish, delicate, and soft—then in a fiery whirl. Like someone possessed, she beats the naked soles of the feet upon the hard beaten earth of the village. With tightly bent elbows the lower arms spin, whirling in circles. The girl dances herself into ecstasy....
>
> Then the picture changes. A youth steps into the circle. Men dance differently. Without fervor, without fire, without haste, without overexertion. The fellow stood with his legs far apart in the circle. He makes a step to the left, one to the right, one forward, and one backward (Bowald 1939:125–126)....

Finally Banda entered the arena with a few tentative steps. The repertoire of movements, specially choreographed for Banda, again, remains today quite the same as that described in the 1930s and 40s:

> A man who has undergone a metamorphosis into a spirit, bearing the royal crocodile on his head, stands in a circle of spectators. At the sight of the monster "Banda" the women sing and clap their hands. A young girl massages his feet.... At the order of the chief, he moves into the center of the circle, where he kneels to salute those in attendance. Then he stamps his feet in place, he makes incredible leaps, and focuses upon the women (Ibrahima Sylla, 11 years

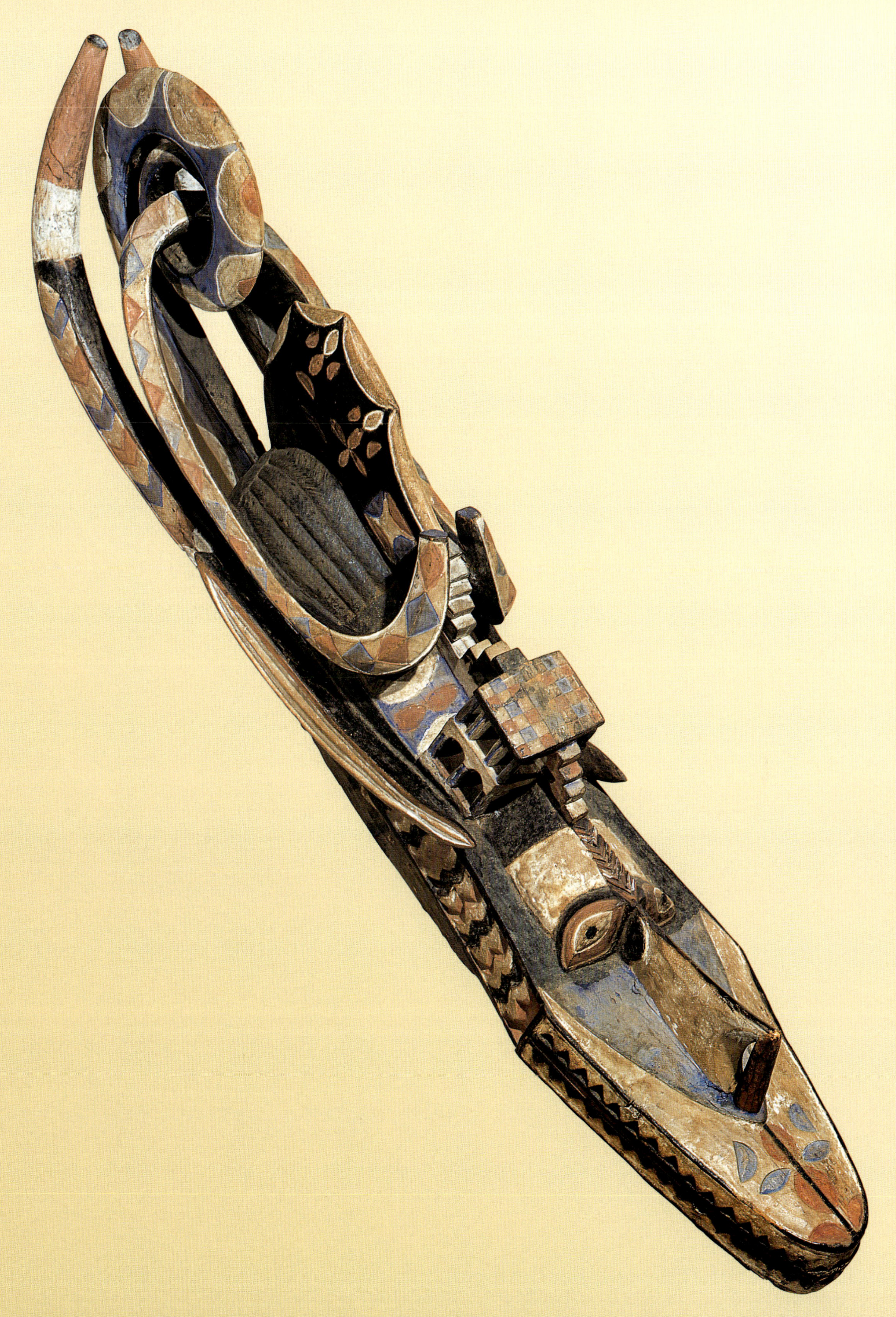

old, Susu schoolboy at Monchon, Buluñits, as reported in Appia 1943:159–160).... Screaming, the women of the village give it space. As if possessed, the "Jelibas" [musicians] hammer away at their instruments.... With the heavy mask, he executes all possible kinds of capers. Suddenly he crouches down on the ground, and in the next blink of an eye, he leaps up high like a "springing-devil" in the Jack-in-the-box, twisting his arms to twirl the mask around over his head. Now with not a trace of an earlier stilted way of walking, the dancer's leaden stiffleggedness gives way to abandon. Although everyone knows well enough who is hidden under the mask, it goes with good taste not to speak of it.

The children and women scream loudly when the spirit dancer comes close to them. If he is tired, another steps in, taking his place. Slowly, the ranks of the spectators thin, gradually the balafon and the bush drum dies out (Bowald 1939:126–128).

The dance is astonishingly vigorous—considering the formidable weight of the massive wooden headdress. One movement is an eye-dazzling, rapid shuffling of the feet while the dancer remains in place, almost hidden in a choking cloud of dust kicked up from the sandy plaza terrain. As he rests occasionally, women dance out into the circle and back, and two men, attendants of Banda, execute the same vigorous steps of Banda.

The masked dancer takes on the roles of various animals. Each time before his vigorous dance, he stands in place, and kicks out the left foot, then the right, and then scrapes each foot backward in turn, resembling a bull, in rhythmic time to the beat. Other roles imitate a serpent undulating, or a fish swimming. Like a predator bird fishing in the sea, he takes high steps, then lunges the headdress downward at an angle. Crouching down on the ground, he puts his snout to the ground, or he will shake the headdress from side to side, lower himself to the ground, shudder while making pecking motions toward the ground, then point the headdress high in the air, like the bird swallowing its fish. As a bird in flight, he circles around the space, tilting the headdress to the spectators, and flinging out the raffia with his hands, prancing with bent knees.

In the greatest spectacle of all, the dancer goes into a dizzying and weightless spin holding the headdress aloft. He twirls the headdress in a series of figure-eights, plunges to the ground, and immediately puts the headdress back on his head without missing a beat. The ecstatic crowd rushes forward to congratulate him, and the dance continues on in this vein for several hours, with various dancers taking turns under the weight of the headdress. The seemingly effortless manipulation of the mask by the most skilled of the dancers defies the appearance of this massive wooden object.

I watched the dance of Banda for more than an hour as the twilight dwindled, alternately looking through the lenses of my video camera and my single-lens reflex. The movement of the dancer wearing the headdress was so rapid, frenetic, spinning, and darting, using the whole of the sandy plaza so expansively, that, even with my art historian's eye, I could not discern the sculpted forms of the headdress. Banda form is relatively consistent, and I am thoroughly familiar with the corpus. Yet, it was not until I returned home and had the opportunity to study my slides and my video footage, that I was able to determine exactly the iconographical form of the carving. It occurred to me then, that this is as it was meant to be. This is how the carver must have seen his work as he designed and executed the form, and painted its ornamentation. It is meant to be seen kinetically, in trajectory, as a swath of lines, forms, and color.

In keeping with the overarching principle of balance, Banda dances alternately with another masked figure, Pende-Pende. This figure, costumed entirely in brightly colored cloth and raffia, represents, on the one hand, the buffoon, and on the other hand, a punisher, as opposed to the spiritually noble and benevolent character of Banda.

He goes out the day of the circumcision and chases the uncircumcised boys, called "the two-horned ones," by my consultant. He teases the housewives.... He comes and sits down to the cooked rice, which then no one dares to eat because it must be reserved for him. His role consists, among others, of amusing the initiates and the people of the village at the time of the initiation (Appia 1943:160).

In Bowald's description (1939:126), and in photographic documentation from the beginning of the twentieth century, it is clear that several Banda dancers might appear together in the same occasion, relieving each other occasionally when the other became tired. Other masks also appeared with Banda and are said to have shared a kinship of sorts, according to elders of the Baga subgroup Mandori. The "father," Banda, was the dancer, while the "son," represented by a smaller, horizontal mask, to-Bom, was the guardian and did not dance, but simply watched the father. Banda was the father, and the "spokesman" for all the other masks.

The atmosphere of the Banda dance was one of joy, excitement, and awe, with an extravagance of visual design and movement performance. Despite the heaviness of the isolated mask that we now see on museum walls, the art form as it appeared in the Baga village was one of lightness of shape, and of enormous complexity and range in all its components.

Frederick John Lamp

Banda Dance. Baga Mandori, Guinea. Photo: Frederick John Lamp, 1987

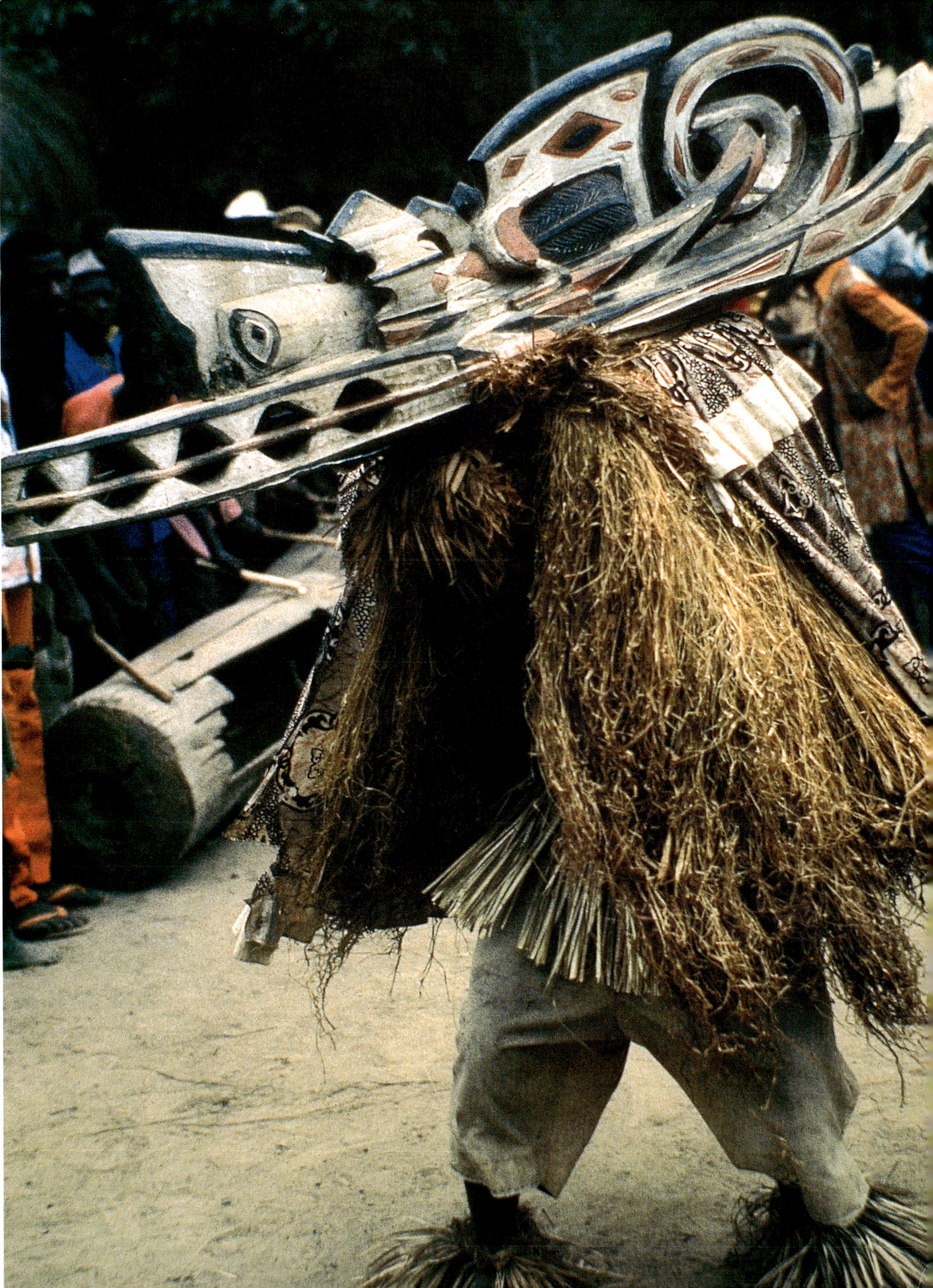

15

Steps of Aggression and Peace: a Loma/Kpelle Mask (*Kpakologi Sineï*)

Male Mask With Headdress (*Kpakologi Sineï/ Niamu/ Ngamu*)
Loma/Kpelle, Liberia/Guinea
Pòrò Association
c. Early to Mid-20th century
Wood, feathers, cloth, fur, cowrie shells, metal, hide, string, twine, H. 65 cm
Gift of A. Harvey and Phyllis K. Schreter, Baltimore
BMA 1991.390

Kpakologi, "big," is a term used to refer to male adults of advanced age, and to a pair of masks of the Loma, the Kpakologi Sineï (male) and Kpakologi Saai (female). Both these mask types have been borrowed from the neighboring Kpelle people to the south, where the male mask is called *Niamu*, or *Ngamu* (Mengrelis 1948, 1952; Bellman 1980:64).[1] Accordingly, the performance of the Loma Kpakologi is done in the Kpelle language, which is another Mande language closely related to Loma. Nevertheless, the mask has become fully incorporated into the class of Loma wooden masks referred to as *afuiti*. *Afui* is the spiritual being of the forest serving as the principal object of devotion in the male initiation society, known as the Pòrò. Kpakologi is one of the few masks, in addition to Afui and the stilt dancer, *Laniboï*, found in all Loma communities. Southern Loma generally possess fewer masks than their northern counterparts and Kpakologi is often the only masked figure performing in this area. There are also miniature forms of the Kpakologi mask, possessed by each member of the mask society. Personal miniature masks are thus much more numerous than big masks used for public performance.

The BMA Kpakologi bears the characteristic tripartite format of most Loma masks. It has a flat facial plane, a protruding forehead, a marked human-like nose and a large jaw. The big round eyes and the prominent cheekbones of the BMA mask are sometimes a feature of the Loma Kpakologi, although they are not characteristic of other Loma masks. The frayed, brownish feather headdress of the this Kpakologi bears witness to its age. If the mask were still in use in Loma ceremonies, the feathers would have been renewed. The beard made of monkey hair that has almost disappeared from the lower facial part of the mask would also have been renewed for ritual performance. Here a white adhesive material is visible to which the missing portions of the beard had been fixed. It is otherwise a well-kept example that has maintained its blank, black surface color.

The appearance of the wooden Kpakologi mask, which is worn on the forehead rather than on the face, can change dramatically in performance, depending upon whether one sees it straight on or in profile. When the masked dancer is seated and faces the audience, bending forward, the mask appears almost human. By contrast, when the masked dancer walks or rushes through the space of the village, bearing the mask horizontally, the audience perceives more clearly the bearded 'crocodile' jaw with real, metal, or wooden sculptured teeth. Then, the red inside of the mouth is also more visible. Inside the disguise, the wearer's left hand is free to move the mask's lower jaw, for instance, when it talks or rumbles, or when he takes cola nuts and money into his mouth, given by members of the audience (Harley 1941:27, Goépogui 1975:32).

The headdress of the BMA mask is made of a large bundle of feathers and a red headband decorated with three circles of seashells, which are separated by four vertical rows of seashells. In performance, a dark cloth would have enveloped the upper part of the mask wearer's body and from this a large raffia dress would cover the legs and feet. In some cases, raffia may also cover the wearer's head and shoulders. Over the cloth, both the male and female Kpakologi wear a colorful cross-shaped garment with triangular patterns, of which one cross extends over the shoulders, and the other, larger section down the chest and back. *Thoghagi* is the vernacular term for this decorative cross-shaped element made of skin, cloth, and fur, worn with a number of distinct Loma masks (seep. p. 56). Another Kpakologi element is the small two-pronged pitchfork that the wearer carries in his right hand and which is concealed by the costume. In some cases the wearer carries a short switch made of a cow's tail instead.

There are regional variations of both the male and female Kpakologi. For example, the feather headpiece is common for the male Kpakologi among northern Loma, and for the similar Landai mask of the neighboring Gbande and Kissi (Eberl-Elber 1936, Lamp 1992, Harley 1941:28), which the Loma also classify as Kpakologi. Further south in the vicinity of the Kpelle, the male Kpakologi usually wears a flat round cap similar in shape to that of the Mende Gbini and Gòboi masks (see Siegman and Perani 1980). Likewise, the raffia dress of the female Kpakologi is in some instances described as short, with the legs of the mask wearer wrapped in cloth (Bunot 1950:145). In other cases it is similar to the long dress of the male mask (see photo of Kpelle female Niamu in Bellman 1980:79). Kpakologi perform in a variety of events, such as funerals for initiation society members, blood sacrifices, commemorative ceremonies, and, more recently, national holidays and festivals. In contrast to the Kpelle Ngamu, which clearly occupies a position analogous to that of the secret Loma Afui (cf. Bellman 1980:64–67; Mengrelis 1952; Welmers 1949:230–233) the Loma male Kpakologi appears relatively frequently, usually in the daytime, and can be seen by all

Kpakologi Male Mask with Followers. Loma, Guinea. Photo: Christian K. Højbjerg, 1991

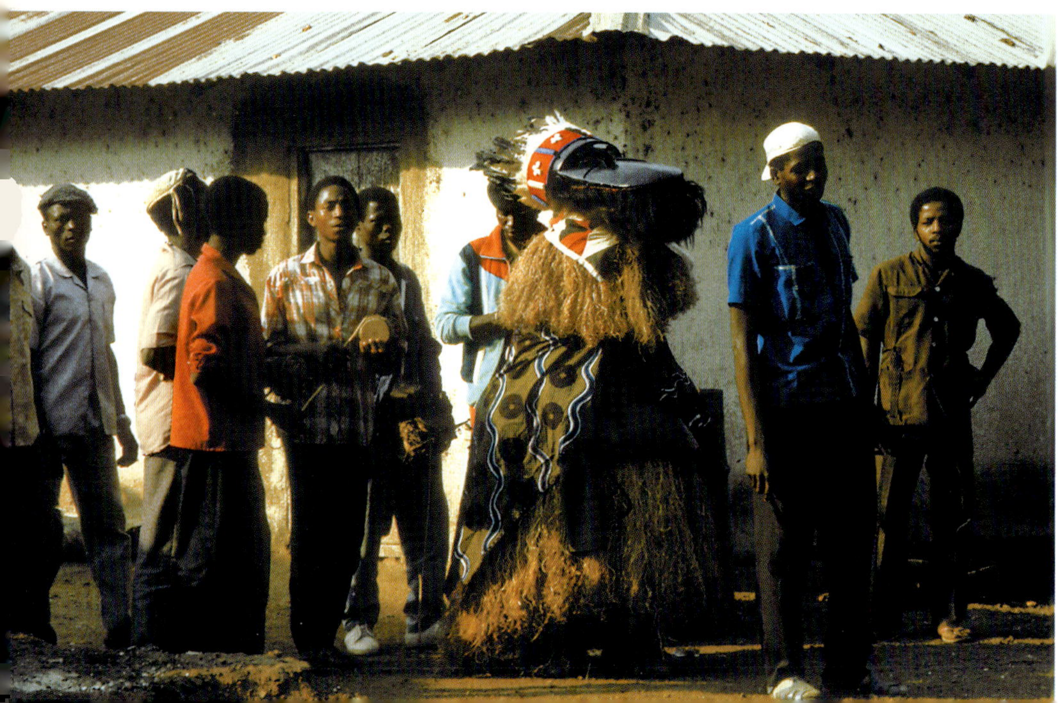

members of the community. It has been observed that the appearance of the male and female Kpakologi is feared by women and non-initiated members of the community because the masks are assumed to reveal a number of crimes, such as witchcraft, poisoning, and adultery (Gamory-Dubourdeau 1926:337), although this is not obvious in the performance. In some areas, however, the performance of the male Kpakologi is obviously staged so as to frighten a part of the audience, e.g., those that are not initiated, who keep their distance from the masked dancer.

Again, regional variations occur in the performance. The male Kpakologi of the northern Loma seems more peaceful during its public appearance, in contrast to the male Kpakologi among the southern Loma, which displays a more aggressive nature. In the south the masquerader rushes from one end of the village to the other with his attendant (*zomagi*) trying to keep up with this fearsome being of the forest. Women usually keep a safe distance from the masquerader, whereas the curious and yet frightened children cannot resist the temptation to approach the wild character. As the tension increases between mask and audience, the attendant tries to appease or beat the masquerader into submission with his whip. When he does so, the Kpakologi becomes extremely aggressive and the zomagi is then expected to protect those attending the performance. Such a scenario would be less common among the northern Loma, where the attendant functions mainly to translate the words of the immobile or slowly-moving masquerader and to ensure that the audience obeys the accepted rules of conduct for the Kpakologi performance. Some general proscriptions during the performance, which go unexplained by the guardians of the masks, are that there must be no smoke in evidence at the time, and members of the audience are not allowed to stand or sit with their legs crossed.

The female Kpakologi is formally distinguished from the male by more anthropomorphic features, as well as by a short, decorated stick on top of the mask. She does not necessarily accompany the appearance of the male Kpakologi although she may, if the village possesses both masks. By contrast to the Kpakologi Sineï, the Kpakologi Saai moves rapidly, whirling round and round, thrusting its face upward to the sky.

Christian K. Højbjerg

1 Compare also with Nyomu Kine Gbloa and Nyomou Néa among the Kono (Holas 1952) and *Landai* or *Dandai* of the Gbandi, Kissi and Loma (Eberl-Elber 1936, Plates 191–195; Germann 1933, Plate 9(1) and Plate 9(3) for the female Kpakologi; Harley 1941:27–28 for Dandai performance technique and Plate XIII for an equivalent of the Loma female Kpakologi; Lamp 1992:10). The Loma male and female Kpakologi are both illustrated in Gaisseau 1953, Plates IV and IX. Siegman notes that the Loma Kpakologi has been borrowed from the Kpelle who in turn adapted it from Kono and Mano masks (Siegman 1977:16).

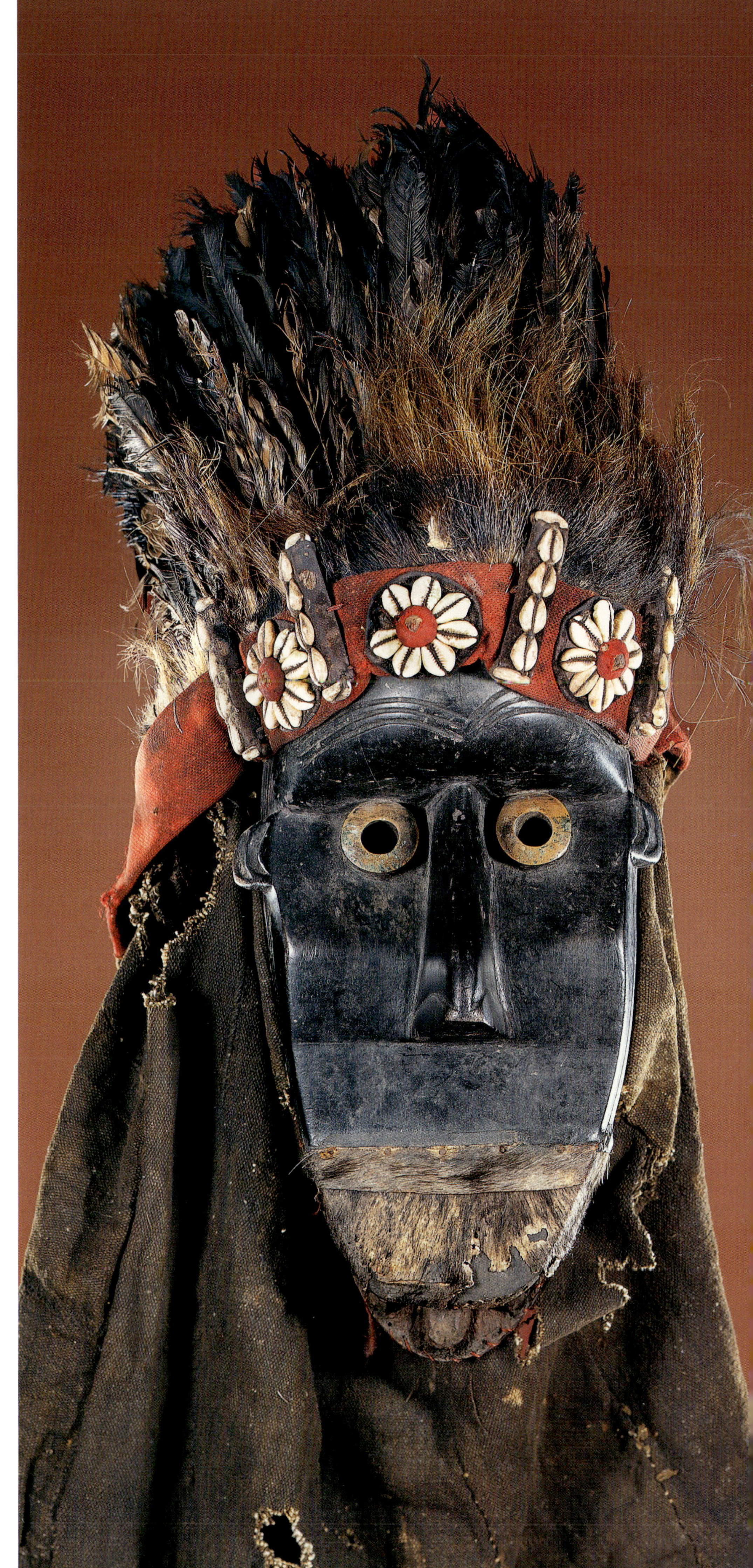

18

Protecting the Body and Spirit: a Luba Neckrest

Caryatid Neckrest
Luba, Congo (Kinshasa)
c. Early 20th century
Wood, H. 17.8 cm
Gift of Alan and Janet Wurtzburger
BMA 1954.145.91

Aesthetic considerations are of great importance to the Luba, whose concept of the beautiful is an important part of both life and art. Physical beauty is seen as a reflection of the inner self (Neyt 1988:90; Nooter-Roberts *Masterpieces* 1996:181; ghostly to any Olbrechts 1959:65–66; Roberts 1995:287; Roberts and Roberts 1996:18, 44, 85, 89, 98, 100, 107). However, beauty, whether physical or artistic, is not perceived as an intrinsic quality, but rather the result of an individual's or artist's striving for moral or artistic perfection. Hence, in order to capture the attention of the spirits, the body, mirror of the innermost being, must be made beautiful whether in the flesh or in wood. Elaborate hair styles, patterns of scarification, shining black skin, rounded forms, and half-closed lids are the standards by which beauty is measured. These characteristics of beauty and culture also communicate important information about the wearer, such as notions of self-esteem and self-worth, social standing, official title, profession, and marital and parental status.

Luba neckrests are supports that have been specially designed to protect the elaborate hairstyles worn by men and women of rank and wealth. In his inventory of objects found in a Luba household, Colle (1913:167) mentioned woven mats for sitting and sleeping, and neckrests. They are both prestigious articles created for personal use, and powerful spiritual images. Owners are so attached to their neckrests that they are often buried with them. If the body of the deceased is irretrievable, his or her neckrest may be buried in its place. In some instances, the body is buried secretly in order to protect it from being desecrated, while locks of hair, as well as the neckrest belonging to the deceased are given a public burial. The family makes offering to the spirits at the latter site. In addition, neckrests also provide protection against the antisocial spirits that, in fear of the blazing daytime sun,

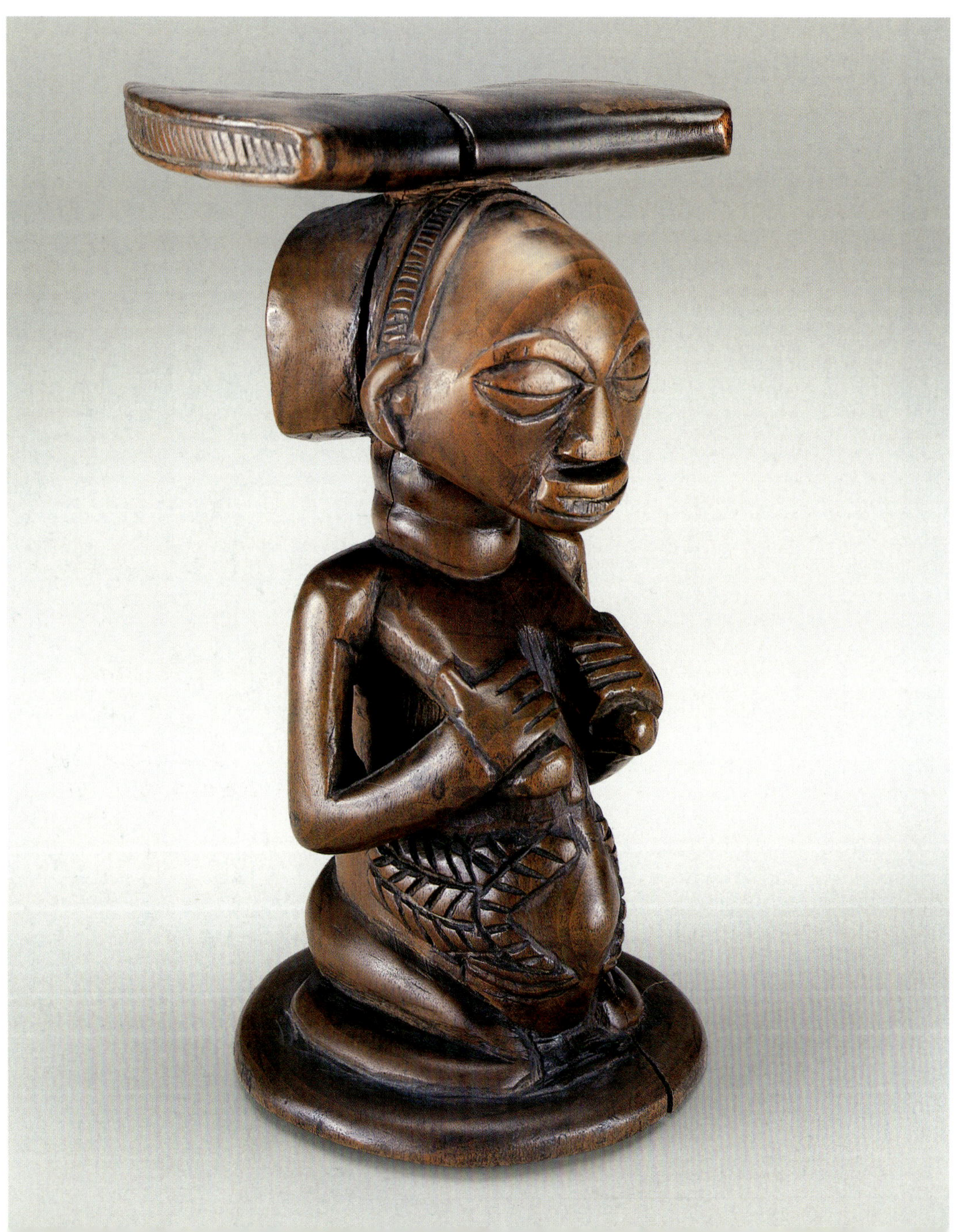

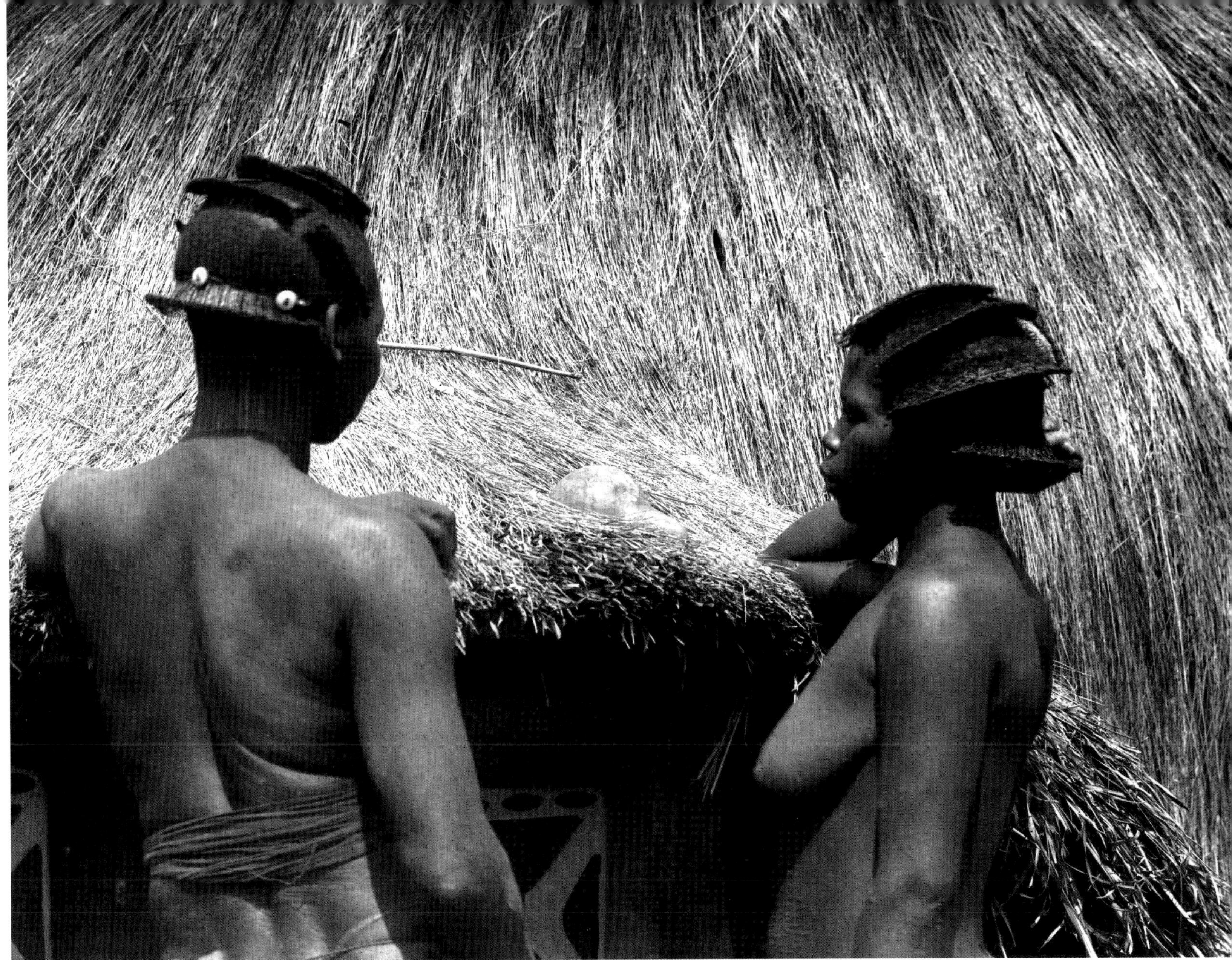

Luba women with dressed coiffure. Luba, Ngobo, Congo (Kinshasa)
Photo: Ch. Lemaire, 1899. ©Africa-Museum (Tervuren, Belgium)

roam the land at night. The nighttime usage of neckrests associates them with dreams that are believed to be communications from the spirit world, and omens of the future (Neyt 1988:90, 92; 1994:182–183; Nooter 1990:64; Nooter *Kings* 1992:324; Nooter-Roberts *Masterpieces* 1996:181; Roberts 1995:287; Roberts and Roberts 1996:98).

Although stationary in the mundane context of supporting the neck and head, spiritually-guided movement is essential in another context, where neckrests serve as instruments of divination. In Luba society, the diviner is consulted for any number of reasons, such as illness, spiritual matters, psychological problems, and legal issues (Neyt 1994:183; Nooter *Faces* 1992:16). Colle described a session in which a mother sought the help of a diviner for her sick child. The diviner's power to influence the spirits (*bwanga*) was contained in a headrest. Shaking a child's rattle with his right hand, the diviner cried out to the spirits:

> If someone is thrashing about, let him cease, if someone is cleansing the herbs, let him stop. Oh spirits of the dead who give my bwanga its power, discover for me the one responsible for the illness; tell me which one of the dead has taken over this child; reveal him, that we may pacify him with gifts (Colle 1913:382).

Following this recitation, the diviner picked up a small stick, and a straw, and blowing over the latter, he placed it in a cup, and began to move it over the surface of the neckrest while saying:

> If it is the protective spirit of the father, tell me so without delay, oh my powerful *bwang* (Colle 1913:382).

The cup continued to move over the neckrest. The diviner then addressed the guardian spirits of the child's living and dead relatives. Finally, the cup stopped, and rapped on the headrest three times, thereby signifying the identity of the culprit spirit. After paying the diviner, the mother left to make the proper offerings to the spirit who had been tormenting her child (Colle 1913:382–383).

L. M. B.

11

We Will Fight You Day or Night: a Fante Flag (*Frankaa*)

Local flags with figural images were noted by European visitors as early as 1693 along the coast of Ghana, where military institutions known as asafo ("war people") have a long history in most states of the Akan. This is especially true of the coastal Fante peoples where *asafo* developed as a defense against nearby states or more distant outsiders such as the powerful Asante to the North (Ross 1979:12–13). The original function of defense has given way, today, to social, philanthropic, and fraternal functions. Nevertheless, each local company still competes against neighboring companies for predominance, primarily through the ostentation of its arts and ceremony (Cole and Ross 1977:186).

Most asafo companies have a number of flags with prosperous groups having sixty or more. One flag is typically flown from a pole surmounting the concrete shrine (*posuban*) that is the center of most company activities. These shrines are often extravagant multi-storied forms, some in the shape of warships. The Fante often refer to the shrines as "forts," "castles," or "posts." Spaces inside may be used for meetings, company ritual, housing company spirits, and for the storage of paraphernalia, such as drums and flags. Shrine exteriors are generally adorned with multiple cement sculptures that share many of the same motifs as the flags (see Cole and Ross 1977:186–191, Ross 1980).

A new flag is commissioned by each asafo officer at his own expense from a specialist upon his installation to office. It subsequently becomes company property. A new flag may also be created for the "outdooring" or opening of a new shrine, or to replace old or tattered flags. Asafo installations are frequently timed to coincide with the principal asafo ritual of supplication to the spirits called the "path clearing" festival (*Akwambo*). Other occasions for elaborate flag displays include the royal Yam Festival, the funeral of a deceased company member, or durbars honoring visiting dignitaries.

In performance, the flag is carried by a specially trained performer called the *frankaakitanyi*, exhibiting spectacular, elaborate choreography. With education in ritual procedure and the use of spiritual power, the flag dancer is seen as having special powers normally associated with priesthood. In performance he wears a short raffia skirt from the waist to the thighs, ornamented with beads, bells, and amulets. Across his chest may be a crossed cord, and designs painted in white may decorate his forehead, chest, shoulders, and calves. This is also the ritual dress typical of traditional priests (Cole and Ross 1977:192).

Performance by the flag bearer takes place in the context of loosely-structured plays enacting past battles. Other actors perform with the flag carrier and are called "guards of the flag;" they also control the crowd of onlookers. The flag is carried

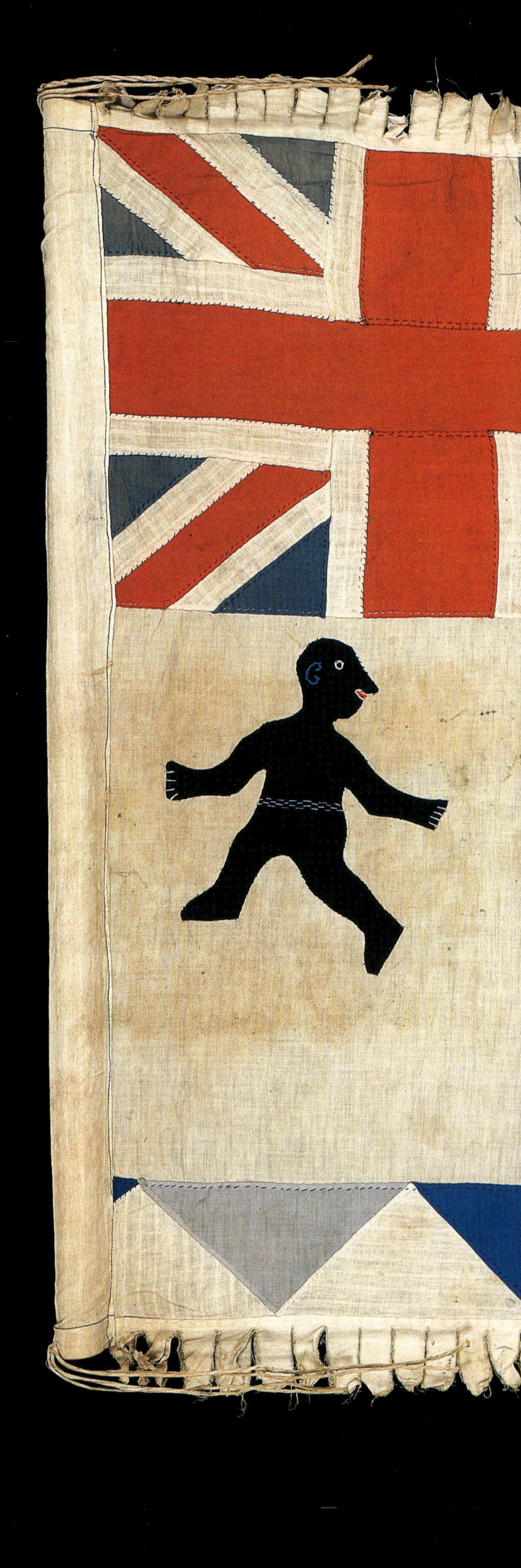

Flag (*Frankaa*)
Fante, Ghana
Asafo military company
Artist: Kobina Badowah (*c.* 1910–1999)
From Upper Kormantine (Kromantse or Kormantse)
c. 1950
Cotton and synthetic fiber, L. 135 cm
Gift of Dawn M. Liberi, Washington, D.C.
BMA 1998.375

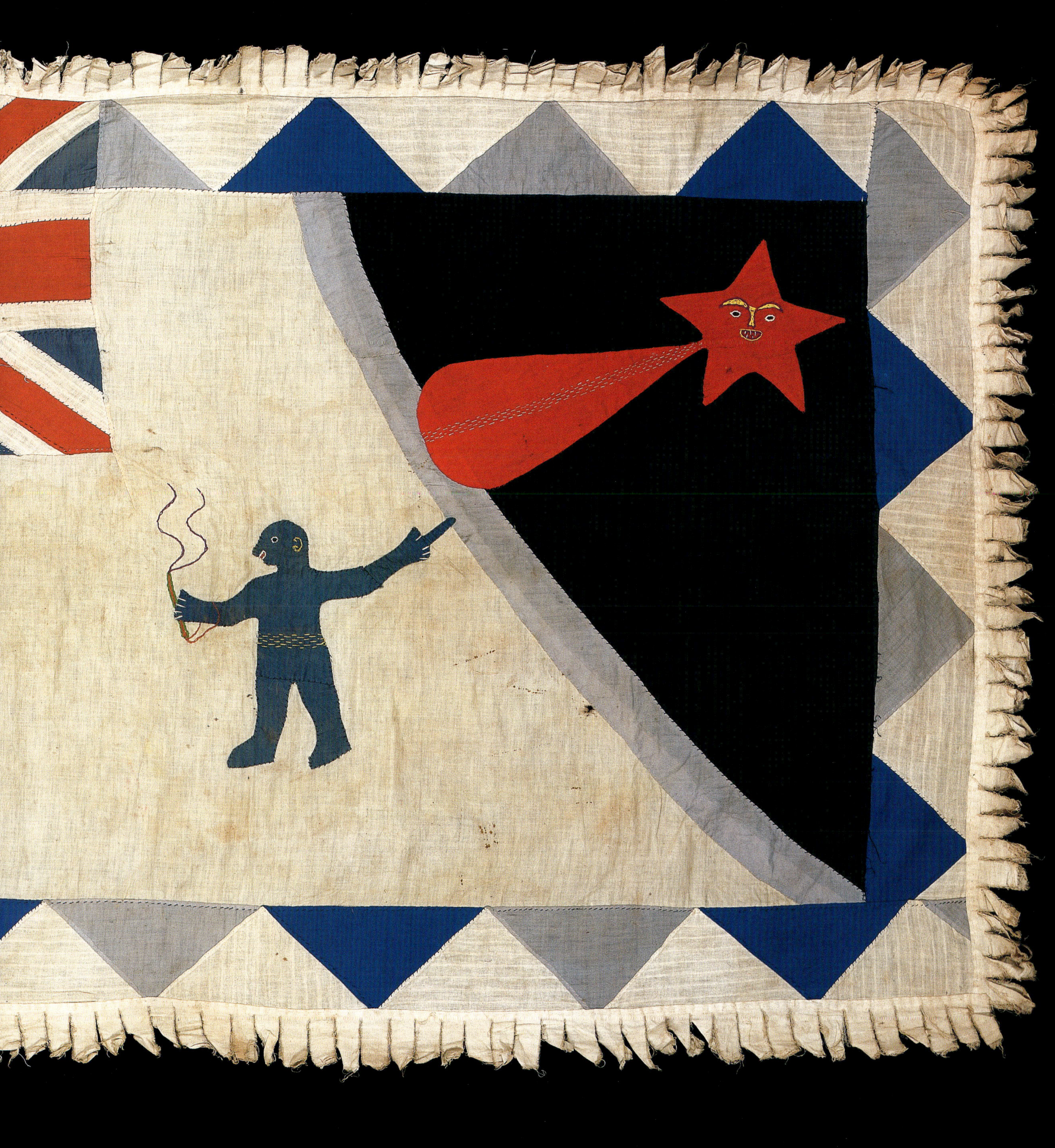

proudly into "battle," then withdrawn, wrapped around the body of the bearer, or rolled up and tossed to another soldier for protection. The performance is heightened by special gestures: the dancer may unfurl the flag, flash it to the enemy, and then lie down and sleep on it to express confidence in eventual success. He may crouch on the ground and take a mouthful of dirt, invoking the blood of buried ancestors to the fight. Or he may draw "traps," or "witch holes," on the ground to capture the enemy. Some steps are simply marvelous aesthetic embellishments—leaps, jumps, hops on one foot, twirls, and other flourishes—demonstrating the virtuosity of the dancer and heightening the entertainment value. The entire campaign is accompanied by drums, gongs, and often provocative songs. Upon the success of the battle, the flag is paraded victoriously (Ross 1979:11).

Most asafo flags are created with a combination of embroidery, appliqué, and piecework techniques as seen in the BMA example, although painted flags are also known. Flag imagery includes an enormous variety of human, animal, and plant forms as well as much of the rich material culture of the Fante. The meaning of these motifs is rooted in the extensive "oral literature" of the Akan, with proverbs being most prevalent, but including such conventionalized forms as boasts, insults, praise poems, jokes, riddles, and even lengthier folktales or historical accounts. These images and messages bolster company pride and are intended to antagonize and intimidate the enemy (see Labi 2003).

I was able to identify the origin of the BMA flag and in 2001 interviewed two sons of its maker, the late Kobina Badowah from Upper Kormantine (Kromantse) who sewed the flag around 1950. Two different ideas are embedded in the image. One is a simple boast: "We will fight you day or night" suggested by the black and white division. This exclamation is being proclaimed by the man with the whip; the other man (running way) represents the enemy from a rival company.

The second message is a proverb that interprets the large red "drop" as palm oil. The slightly varied translation of the Twi statements by three different Fante elders, including the two sons, follows:

> Where there is palm oil, you cannot spoil the place.
> Where the palm oil has fallen, do not put any rubbish there.
> Where you eat regularly, you don't spoil the place.

The senior son, Kwesi Asemtim, said in English that this meant that one should not disturb the evening meal with discord. The younger son, Kobina Tawiah, thought that the palm oil was a metaphor for blood and that the proverb argued against dishonoring the blood of the ancestors. Of course, these are not mutually exclusive possibilities.

The Union Jack in the upper corner is ubiquitous on flags created before Ghanaian independence in 1957. After independence, the new Ghanaian tricolor took its place in the canton. In either case the asafo company aligns itself with the governing authority. While many companies have retained flags with the Union Jack, just as many others have either sold off these outdated vestiges of colonialism or replaced the British ensign with the modern Ghanaian flag.

Doran H. Ross

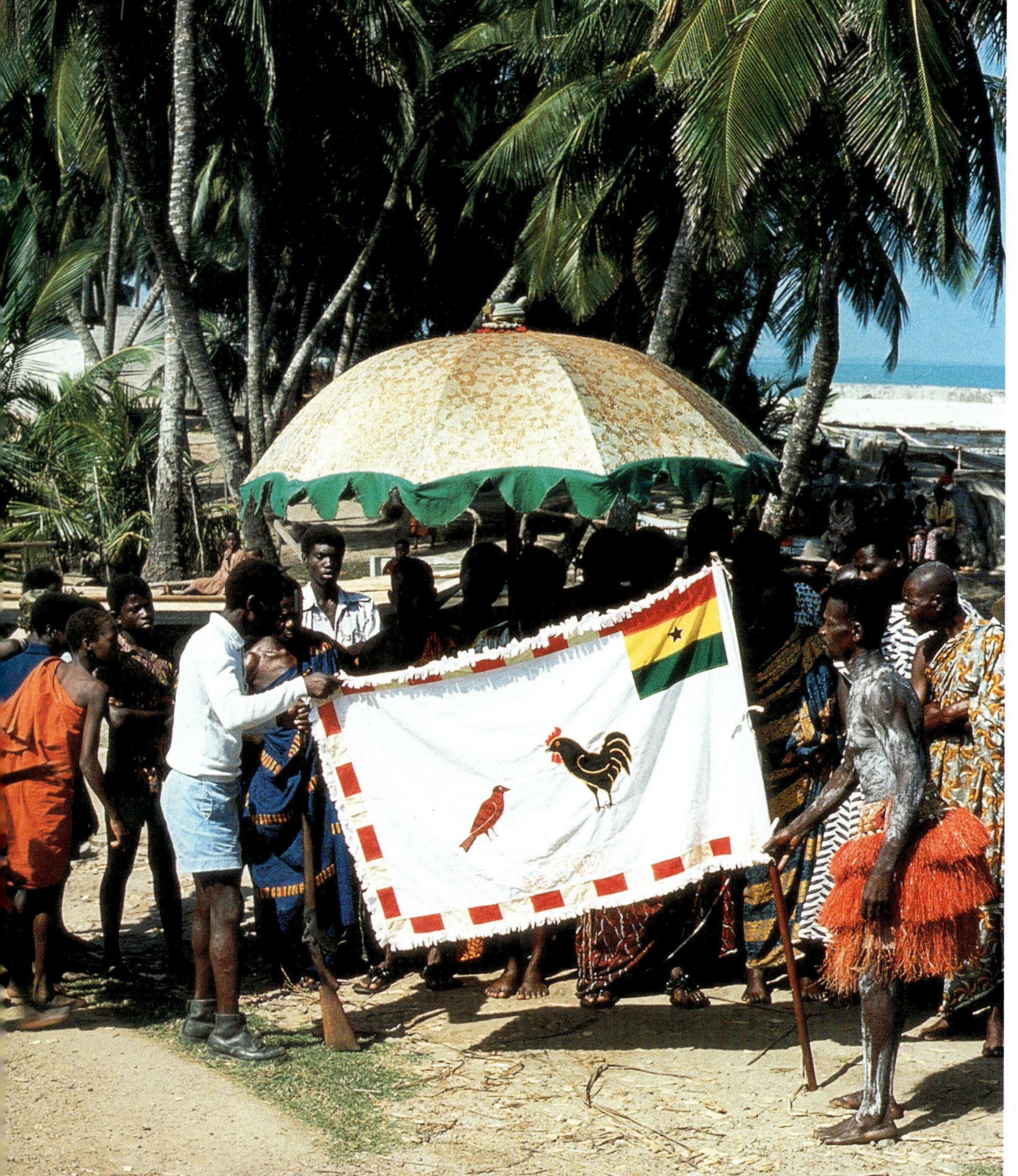

The "outdooring" of a new flag usually accompanies the installation of a new asafo officer, and entails the dancing of the flag in front of the other asafo company shrines and a presentation to the paramount chief. This ensures that the flag's colors and images do not violate the prerogatives of rival companies and are otherwise acceptable to all involved. The motif of this flag depicts the cock and the "clock-bird" (which also announces the dawn) and the flag's owners are boasting that they control the events of the day. The verbal interpretation of the motif is clearly part of the performance. From the Okyir festival, Fante, Anomabo, Ghana
Photos: Doran H. Ross, 1975

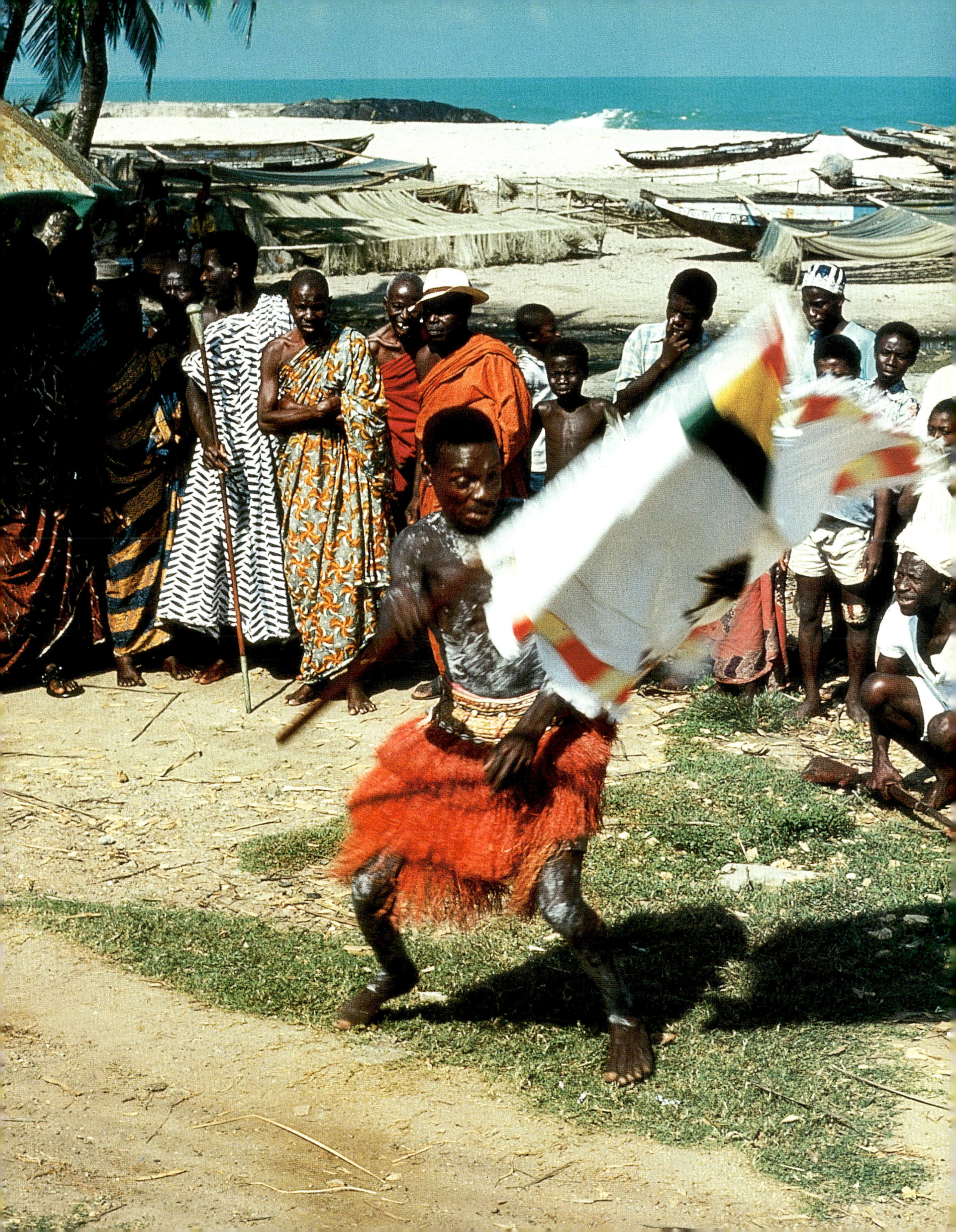

The Speed and Color of Aggression: a Mossi Mask (*Wan-Zega*)

Male "Red Mask" (*Wan-Zega*)
Mossi, Tengabisi subgroup. Burkina Faso, Boulsa region
c. Early 20th century
Wood, fiber, polychrome, H. 97.2 cm (236.2 cm with costume)
Gift of John and Patricia Garon, Bethesda, Maryland
BMA 1984.256

Mossi people would identify the BMA "Red Mask" as the head of a mask, or *wan-zugu*. Customarily, in Western collections, only the carved wooden portion of the mask is preserved; here, some costume is attached, while a considerable portion has been discarded. When people in Burkina Faso see such an object displayed in the museum as we see it here, they are reminded of a hunting trophy. They talk about the heads of animals displayed on walls of museums that they have seen in photographs. They talk about the mask as a living spirit, complete with a head, a body, a character, a spirit, a soul, a family, and even a job to perform.

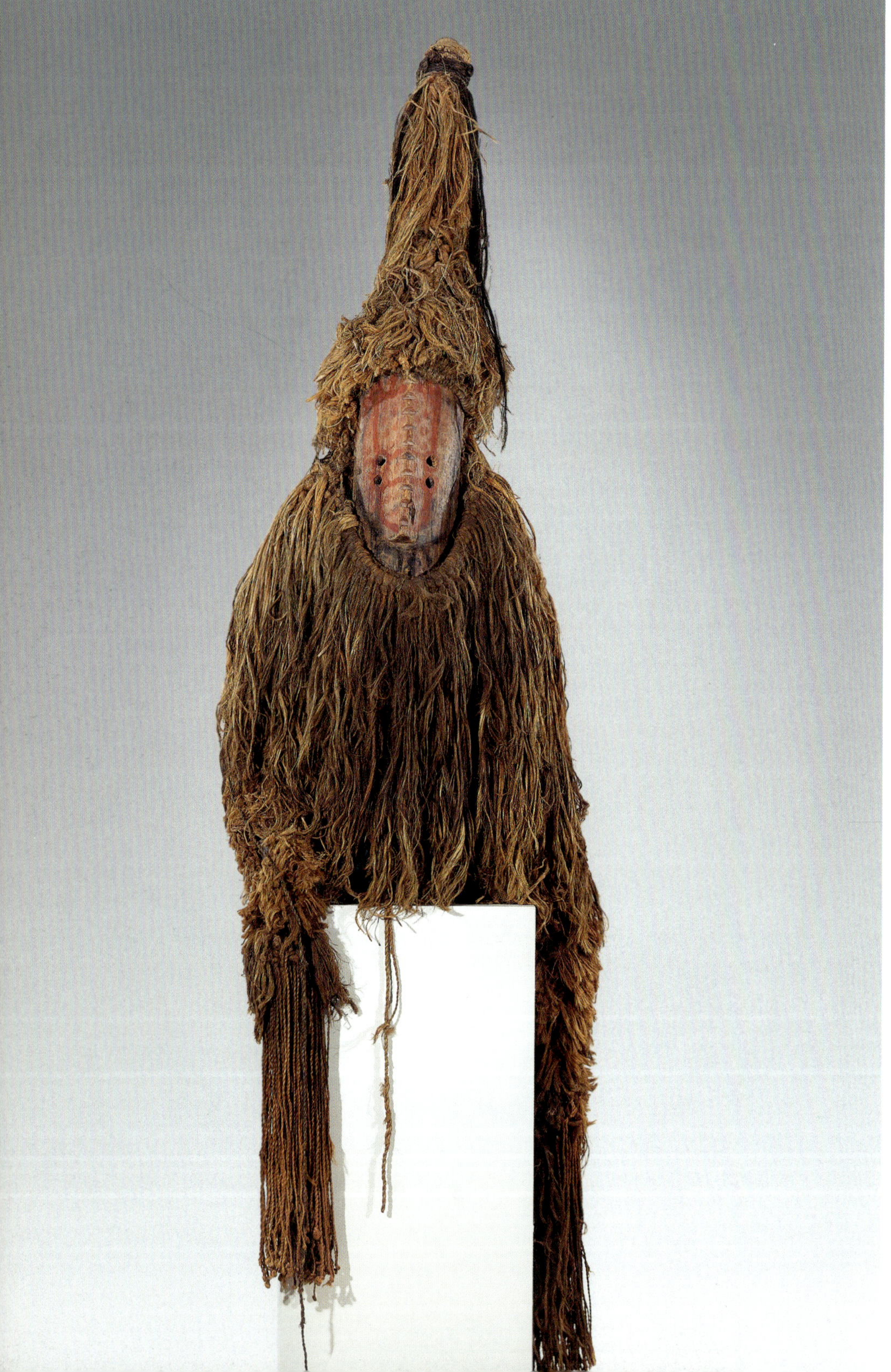

Most of the white pigment which was originally applied to the carved wooden facial portion of the BMA mask has been removed either through abrasion or has been consciously scrubbed off by an art dealer or collector. Until recently the three colors that were used both for masks and for costumes in Burkina Faso were red, white, and black. The red that colored this mask was originally obtained by grinding iron-rich stone. However in the past few decades the owners of these masks have had access to Western dyes, which can be readily purchased in the market, so it is quite common to find masks that have been dyed with pigments made by BASF in Germany.

The hemp fiber remaining on the BMA mask has obviously been used for at least one season and probably more than that, although, generally, in use, the costume is replaced each year. Hemp is commonly cultivated and is widely used as a durable material for a variety of purposes, and in Burkina Faso it is the only material that is used to make the costumes for masks.

The complete costume would consist of the carved, wooden face with a post that rises above the head. To the top of this a ball of materials is attached, which Mossi informants described, in French, as the "fetish." This magical bundle gives the mask spiritual power. Below the face of the mask, still visible on the BMA example, is a shawl or cowl made of hemp fiber, including the sleeves, which have long tassels that extend below the performer's hands. For this male mask, a pair of trousers would be added, made of the same hemp material. The full costume is made up of long strands of fiber knotted into a close-fitting fishnet body stocking, constructed to hide the body of the performer completely but at the same time to give the him great freedom of movement. Unlike other Mossi masks, the trousers make it possible for the performer to move rapidly, even to run while chasing members of the audience. In contrast, the companion female mask, whose costume is made of black fiber, wears a skirt which is bound tightly around the legs, restricting the leg movements in exactly the same way that a woman's wrapper prevents her from taking long strides. The result is that the black or female mask can neither run nor move very quickly in any direction.

There are two basic dance steps which are used by Red Masks in performance. The dance performance is accompanied by the sound of very large drums (membranophones) which are carried over the shoulder of the drummer and played with long sticks. Each of the masks performs individually.

When the mask is first called out by the drummers to perform, the steps are short and rapid with the feet moving quickly front-and-back or side-to-side while the upper body remains relatively motionless. After two or three minutes of dancing like this the rhythm of the drums changes and the mask begins to spin first in one direction and then in the opposite. As the performer rotates as fast as he can, the fibers of the costume fly outward. At the same time the large ball of magical medicine which is fastened to the top of the mask by a two-foot cord also spins outward away from the mask. When the mask reverses direction the ball on its cord regularly wraps itself up on the post to which it is attached.

This is one of three masks used by the Mossi. It is the male mask. It is accompanied by a black masker with a white face portraying a female character, and by a short masker only four feet tall, playing the role of a child spirit. All three masks are worn exclusively by men, including the black mask representing a female character. The child's mask is worn by a preadolescent boy, unless a man who is short enough can be found to play the role. These masks constitute a family of masks, inseparable, always appearing together. When the elders of the community are questioned about the relationship of the masks, their uniform response is that like humans the spirit beings of the wilderness have families of mother, father, and child. They mirror the family, kinship, and other relationships that exist among humans.

Of the three masks that appear together, only the male Red Mask has a voice. The masked performer holds a reed clamped between his teeth through which he alternately sucks and blows air, producing a very high-pitched twittering sound very much like a bird. The performer can even use this reed to communicate to the mask attendants that follow it, who call out to the performer to warn it of a stone in its path or of some other obstruction that it must avoid.

The Red Mask is aggressive. The performer carries a flexible whip made of a branch from a *neem* tree in his right hand which he uses liberally to strike out at members of the audience or anyone else who crosses its path. Throughout the performance it acts in a threatening manner, shaking its whip at almost anyone it sees. The performer often dashes towards a member of the audience it has picked out, and almost always the person flees as fast as possible to avoid being struck by the mask. On the other hand, a mask may greet each of the elders, seated at the side, touching each on the shoulder with its whip; to be struck by the mask in this case would be auspicious.

This ensemble of masks appears together in a variety of different contexts throughout the cycle of the Mossi year. The three appear at funerals, at initiations of young men, at market day performances when they entertain people who come to the village market, and finally, in the context in which I have seen them, shown here, they perform just before the beginning of the rainy season in May to close the ceremonial portion of the year.

Christopher Roy

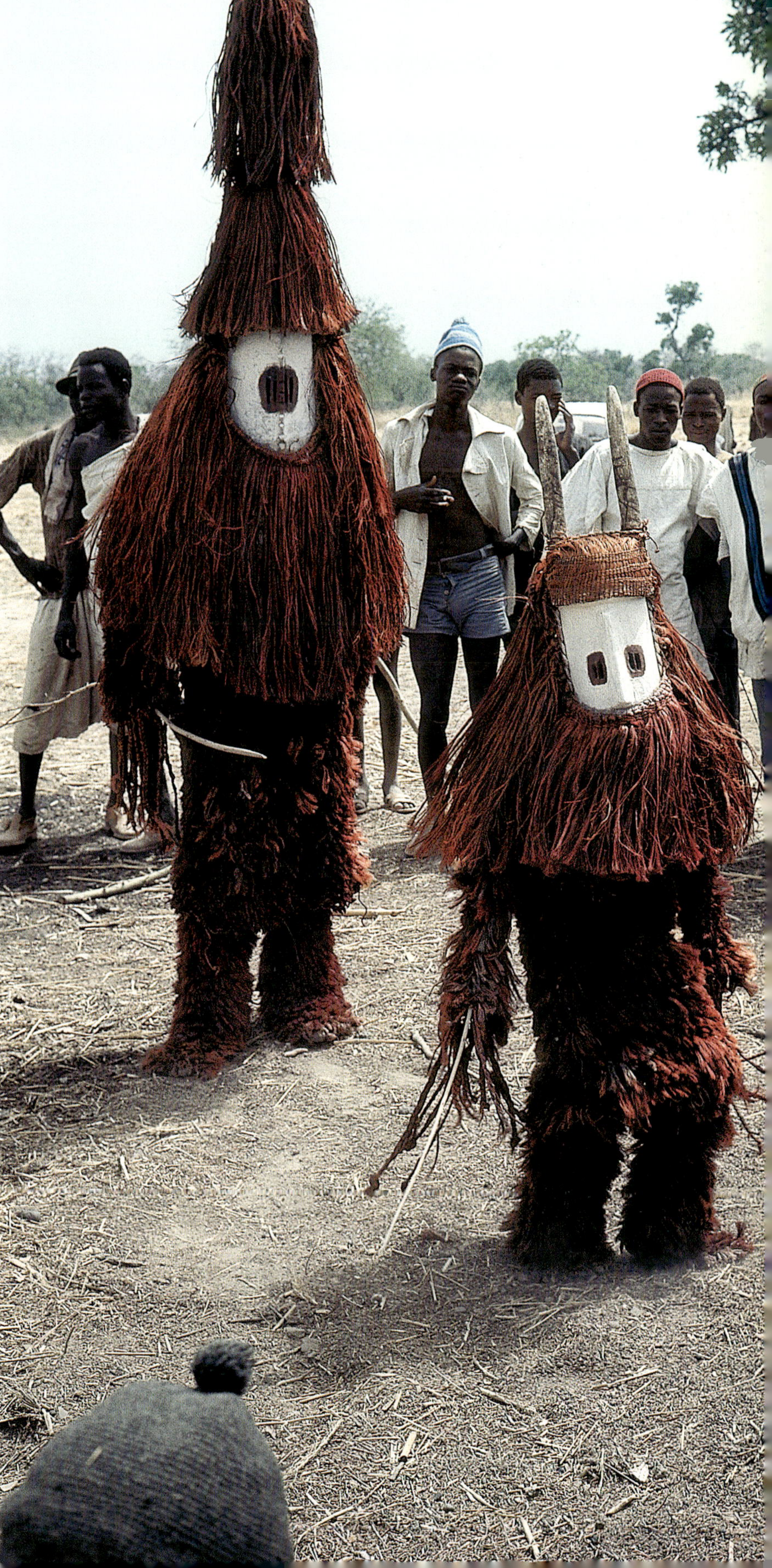

Masks at Funeral. Mossi, village of Sini, Burkina Faso
Photo: Christopher Roy, 1977

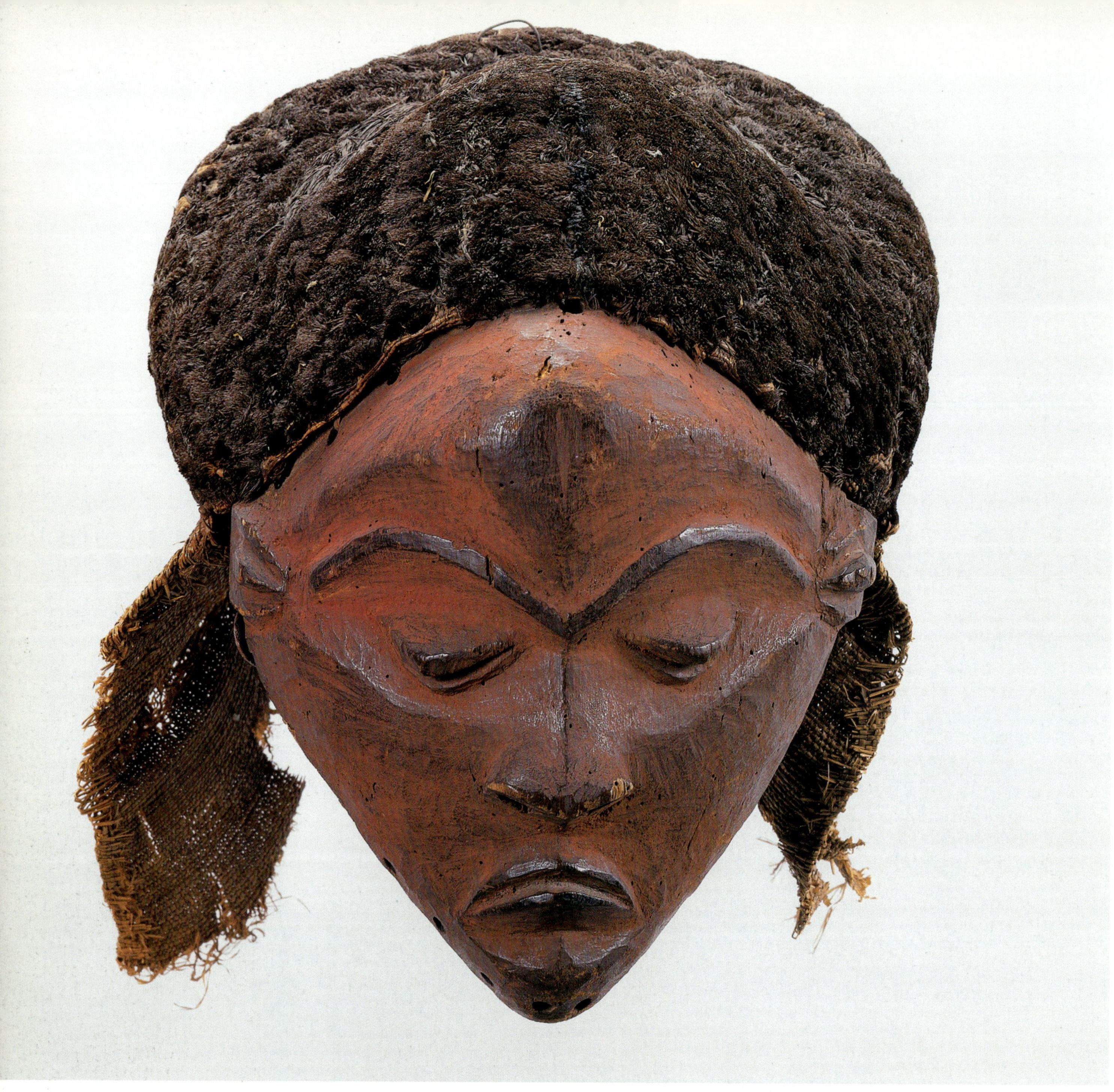

19

Dancing the Heat of Life: a Pende Mask

Mask
Central Pende, Congo (Kinshasa)
c. Early 20th century
Wood, raffia, painted with red barkwood pigment, H. 27.9 cm
Gift of Alan Wurtzburger
BMA 1954.145.73

For the Central Pende, a masquerade is literally a "dance of masks" (*ulumbu wa mbuya*) and the event a central occasion for performers seeking renown. It is the performers who invent masks by brainstorming to come up with a new dance that will draw and delight an audience. The term "mask" (*mbuya*) refers both to the "facepiece" as well as to the ensemble of dance, costume, props, and song that together create a masquerade persona. Male dancers work out the steps, costume, song, and name for new masks. They then consult a lead drummer who sets the performance to music. If their conception is radically new, dancers will consult a master sculptor able to create a headpiece that expresses the ontological essence of the new character. More often, the performer adapts a face- or headpiece from another masquerade figure.

Because many "masks" therefore share the same face, it can be impossible to assign a precise name to a headpiece, divorced from its costume and dance. The forehead mask in the collection of the BMA is a good illustration of this principle. These masks are anchored in place by a snug-fitting hat frame so that they slant off the forehead, leaving the eyes and nose of the performer below unobstructed (Strother 1998: Fig. 85). A short raffia fringe (sometimes mistaken for a "beard") is tied along the jawline and chin. From a distance, this ruff obscures the eyes and nose of the dancer from the audience, but allows him to see and breathe

Dance of Ginjinga performed by Bundula Ngoma. Pende, Kinguba, Congo (Kinshasa). Photo: Z.S. Strother, 1989

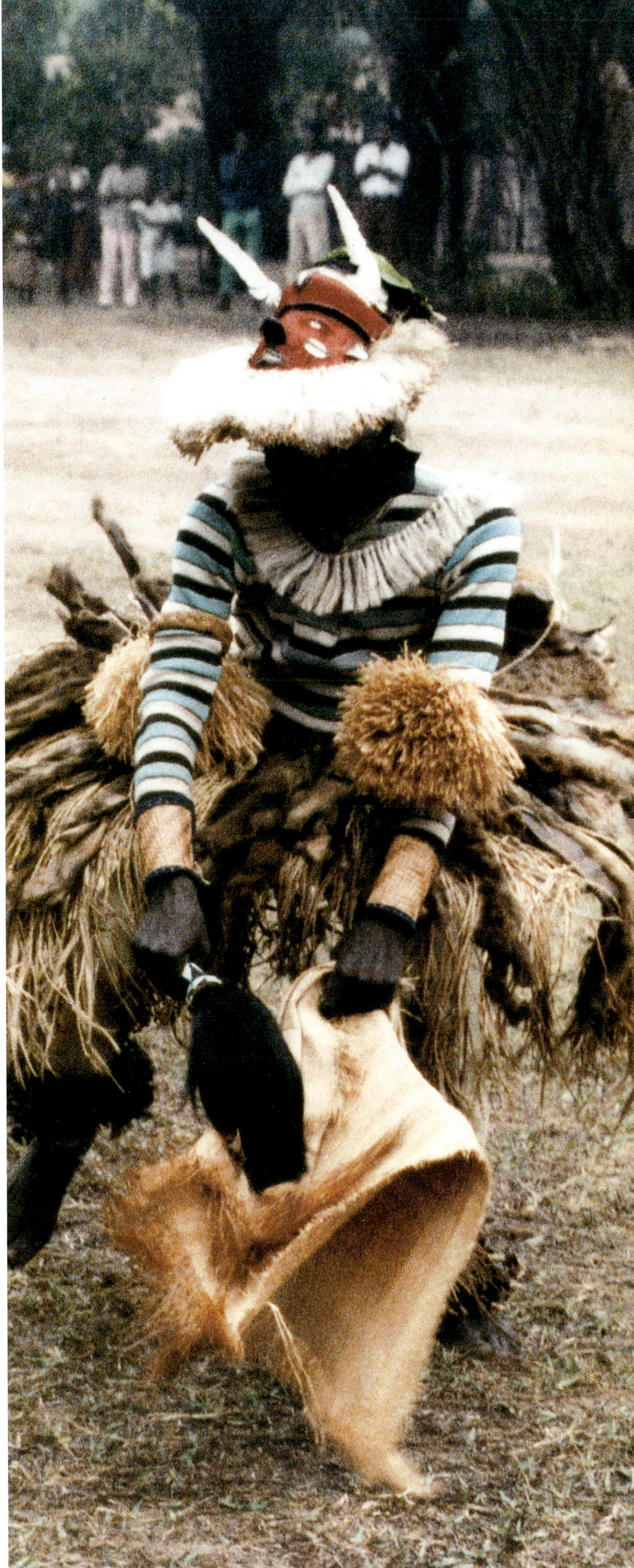

freely. The performer's face is banded below the nose with a strip of woven raffia cloth, which is sewn to the body of the costume.

Forehead masks always depict a male face (Strother 1998: 108–37) and are associated with "hot" explosions of dance. Because the performer can see and breathe normally, he may run and leap freely and maintain longer outbursts of high-aerobic activity. When the performer looks down at the ground to concentrate on his footwork, some of the audience will catch a frontal view of the facepiece. Usually, however, a work like the BMA forehead mask is conceptualized by the sculptor to be seen in profile with a clear silhouette of forehead, nose, and chin. Before each performance, the dancer refreshes the colors of the work so that they may be read across a large dance floor. The BMA mask was painted with a red barkwood paste that was also used originally as a cosmetic by both men and women to soften and tint human skin. The eyes, mouth, and hairline were usually highlighted in white and the brow singed black by a hot poker.

The BMA sculpture most likely belonged to one of four masks that were popular in the early- to mid-twentieth century among the Central Pende: Ginjinga, Pota, Galusumba, or Gabatshi [G]a Nyanga. Statistically, it is most likely to belong to Ginjinga or Pota, two of the oldest surviving Pende mask genres.[1] Pende field consultants speak with something like awe of the dance of Ginjinga. Drummers find the rhythms fast and difficult to maintain. The mask executes more *gutshiatshiela* (fast-paced, alternating footwork on the toes) than any other Central Pende mask. Part of the skill of Ginjinga's dance lay in coordinating the steps with dramatic gestures made with the performer's hoop, which is tied around the waist and covered by heavy piles of raffia braids and animal furs. Gutshiatshiela, Ginjinga advances, gutshiatshiela, he backs up. He turns to the right, gutshiatshiela, he turns to the left, gutshiatshiela. He swooshes his hoop to each side by stepping forward with one foot and then slapping down the hoop on the same side while twisting it towards the back. Then in the blink of an eye, he whirls around 180 degrees and recommences. The fast alternating steps make the foot rattles resound across the arena.

Ginjinga is considered to be a mask that showcases the athletic skills of young men in their prime. The aerobic intensity of the footwork demands great stamina and knees of iron. Several older professional dancers told me regretfully that they just did not "have the knees" for Ginjinga. Unfortunately, by 1989, young men were bored by Ginjinga and preferred more "modern" masquerades. An older dancer, Bundula Ngoma, has tried to keep the mask alive but critics rejected his performances in 1989 as "chilled." Tiring quickly, Bundula made little use of his hoop and began to flap the raffia cloth in his hand instead of slapping the ground with it. The drummer Muthamba criticized him forcefully for not turning, spinning, and swinging the hoop so that the fur and cords of his costume could fly out straight from the waist.

The dancer of Pota also requires great stamina and physical strength to support the weight of the costume. Pota is covered by many layers of raffia braids, strung from belts tied around the neck and a hoop encircling the waist. The dressers stuff the twisted raffia cords with leaves. The choice of leaves is

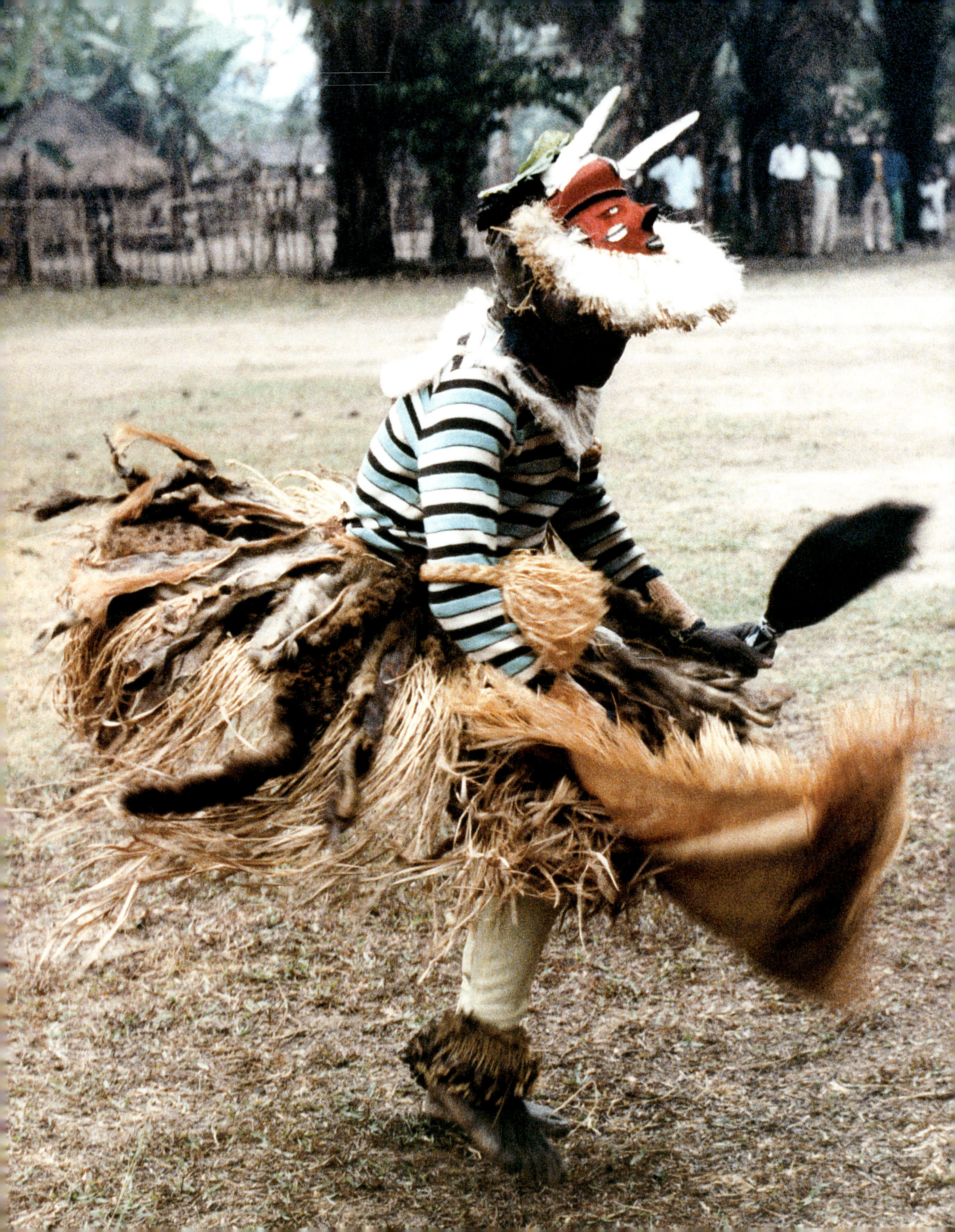

determined by what will stick best to the cords, rather than from any deep symbolism. Pota first appears in the distance as a mysterious mound of quivering leaves, the headpiece hidden under a square of raffia cloth. As he approaches, he begins to lift his feet in fast succession on his toes (gutshiatshiela). From time to time, he sweeps the leaves tied around his neck over each shoulder in succession as he "shivers" (*gudigita*) his shoulders, moving his elbows in and out. This movement from men's dance makes the leaves shake and rustle. Once Pota arrives on the dance floor, he lays down the cloth obscuring his headpiece and begins to perform a rapid-fire *gutshiatshiela* across the dance floor that sends the cords flying out. Pota punctuates the footwork with high semicircular kicks and ends each segment by throwing the rope of leaves over each shoulder in succession before changing direction.

Performers appropriated facepieces from the long-lived Pota and Ginjinga for other masks as well. The BMA mask might also represent Galusumba or Gabatshi [G]a Nyanga. Galusumba wore a costume more or less identical to Ginjinga's except that the performer carried a bow and arrow. A comedic mask, Galusumba pantomimed the stiff, jerking feints of a man attempting to aim his arrow at small birds hopping from branch to branch in the treetops.[2]

Gabatshi [G]a Nyanga is a mask connected with dancers active from *c.* 1885–1950. Its real claim to novelty lay in its costume, which was based on a fabric introduced by the Belgians (perhaps Scottish plaid). The masker wrapped the cloth around his neck and then fixed it to a hidden hoop floating above his hips. Below, he wore a second hoop, heavy with cords of twisted raffia. During the performance, the dancer twisted the upper hoop, making it tremble, flipping it up in front or back. At the climax, he would swoop the hoop over his head as he spun around, hands hidden by the fabric, raffia braids flying. He finished with powerful semicircular kicks. In its day, the dance was much admired and drew ululations of joy.

Forehead masks like the BMA work are important in facilitating the high aerobic outbursts in dance that galvanize an audience. Pende dance criticism contrasts the "heat" of life with the coolness of death. Muhenge Mutala, intiatiated *c.* 1921, explained that masquerade is capable of "making rejoice the bodies that are shivering." The cold, the aging, and the ill assume many of the same postures as they stiffen and curl up into themselves. According to Muhenge, dance warms the body and drives out the chill of incipient death. The role of masks like Ginjinga or Pota is to catch us up in excitement for their pyrotechnics so that even the weak and ill feel stronger and interested in others as well as themselves. By doing so, they strengthen the community (*gukolesa dimbo*) as much as they make it beautiful (*gubongesa dimbo*).

Z. S. Strother

1 Much of the following discussion of masked dances is drawn from Strother 1998. Readers should note that this text describes Central Pende custom, which can differ dramatically from Eastern Pende practice, even when the names of masks are identical (e.g., 1998:200–208).

2 De Sousberghe confuses the performances of Ginjinga and Galusumba perhaps because both wear almost identical costumes (1960:513, 520).

Dance of Ginjinga performed by Bundula Ngoma. Pende, Kinguba, Congo (Kinshasa)
Photo: Z. S. Strother, 1989

Khoshi Mahumbu dressed and waiting to perform with the mask Pota. He is looking down to show the forehead mask to the camera. Pende, Nyoka-Munene, Congo (Kinshasa)
Photo: Z. S. Strother, 1989

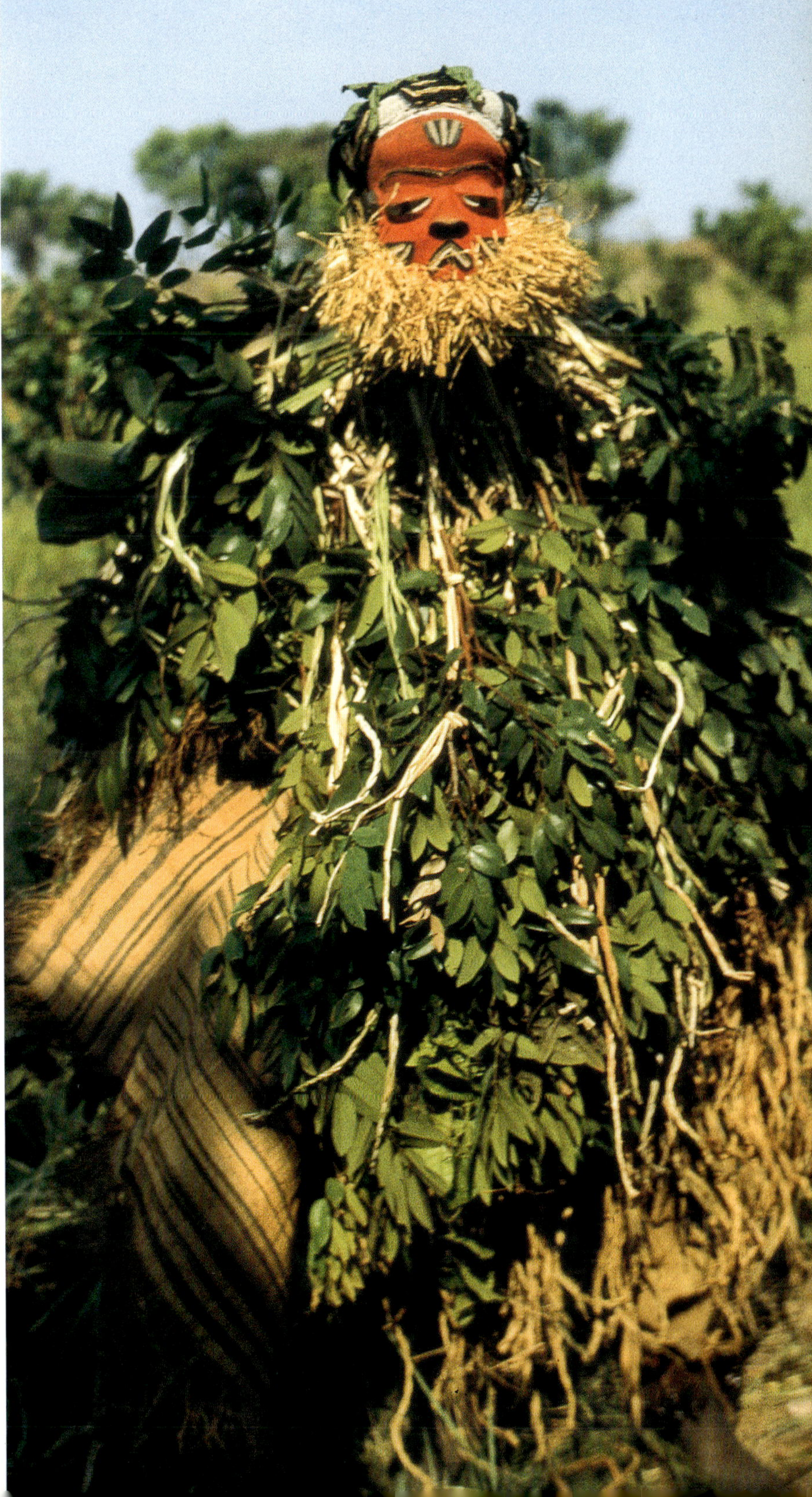

Movement in a Funerary Procession: a Kuba Mask (*Ishyeen Imaalu*)

Ishyeen Imaalu masks are found in the central and northern Kuba region among various populations including Bushoong, Ngongo, Ngeende, and Shoowa peoples. They are owned by communities that have adopted the ritual and performative practices of the initiation society known as Babende. Babende practices include masked performances for recently deceased members of the society. While the goals of the society and its funeral rituals for initiated men from the central and north are similar to those in the south, there are several key differences. An important distinction is the location of initiation rituals inside the community setting and not in a secret forest location.[1]

Ishyeen Imaalu ranks within a hierarchy of masking, and assumes a middle position between the well-known fiber and cloth mask Mukenga (Binkley 1992) and the large wooden casque or helmet mask called *Bongo*.[2] The Ishyeen Imaalu mask shares stylistic conventions with several other Kuba masks. The jutting eyes are said to resemble the eyes of a chameleon. Encircling each eye is a series of holes that form a strong decorative element and allow the masked dancer limited vision during performance. Below the eyes are a series of diagonal parallel lines. As with other masks in the region, these symbolize lines of mournful tears and suggest the primary context for the appearance of this mask—masquerades honoring recently deceased members of *Babende*.

Male Mask (*Ishyeen Imaalu*)
Kuba, Congo (Kinshasa)
c. Late 19th–early 20th century
Wood, cloth, feathers, fiber, cowrie shells, pigment, H. 40 cm
Gift of the Jamosil Foundation, Alexandria, Virginia
BMA 1989.150

An Ishyeen Imaalu mask performing at a funeral. Kuba, *Shoowa* subgroup, community of Maloong, Congo (Kinshasa). Photo: David A. Binkley and Patricia Darish, 1989

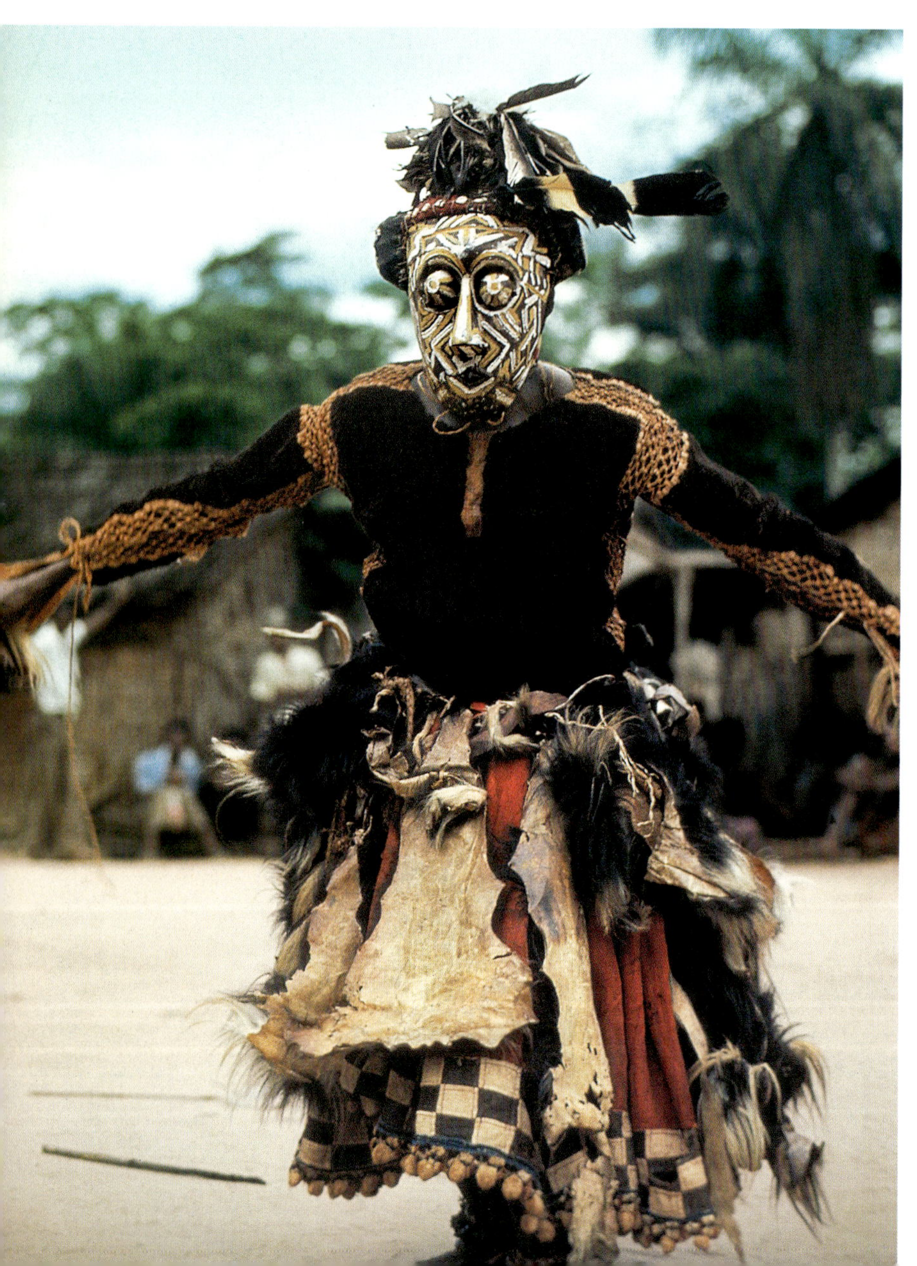

The wooden mask is attached to a framework covered with cloth that forms the top, back, and sides of the head. A distinct live characteristic is the placement of a dark brown tri-lobed hat on top of the head. Attached to the hat is a large group of feathers. Additional feathers jut out prominently from the front of the headdress. This coiffure of feathers is the same as that worn by warriors, and thus identifies the masked dancer as a warrior (*iyool*): a titled class of individuals who are charged with protecting Kuba communities from both internal and external conflict.

The mask is worn with a black raffia cloth shirt decorated with velour embroidery. String lacing attaches the front and back sections of the shirt together. The dancer also wears a men's long red raffia skirt with checkerboard borders. Over the top of the raffia skirt are secured a number of black-and-white colobus monkey skins. He wears seed rattles on each ankle and carries one or more flywhisks during performance.

The identity of masked dancers in the northern Kuba region is not as closely guarded a secret as it is in the south. During the performance of Ishyeen Imaalu described below, the dancer would at times push the mask back onto his forehead so that one could clearly see the sides of his face and then pull it down over his face.

At the Shoowa community of Maloong, I had the opportunity to see Ishyeen Imaalu perform at the funeral of an initiated man. Immediately after news of his death, several meetings with leaders of Babende, the chief of Maloong, and members of the deceased family were held to organize the schedule of funeral activities. The following day, accompanied by several drummers, Ishyeen Imaalu proceeded down the central avenue carrying a long object that resembled a tree (*kinabongu*). He was accompanied by a titled member of the initiation society (Iyool inkaan) who carried a large initiation rattle. As the Iyool inkaan moved steadily down the central avenue toward the enclosure where the body of the deceased lay in state, he would occasionally stop and shake the rattle. The masked dancer would immediately react to this sound and kick up his leg and turn quickly to the side. The dance step is identical to a very popular dance movement that is made whenever initiated men gather to dance. It appeared that the Iyool inkaan and rattle served as a fulcrum or pivot on which the mask would turn as they both proceeded down the avenue.

When Ishyeen Imaalu reached the enclosure, the kinabongu was given to several initiation society elders. Women, who were resting in the enclosure with the body of the deceased were chased away. Large mats that the women were sitting on were taken up and positioned in such a way as to obscure the "planting" of the tree in front of the pavilion. After these and other preparations were completed, children standing near by ululated or called out like roosters to signal for women to return.

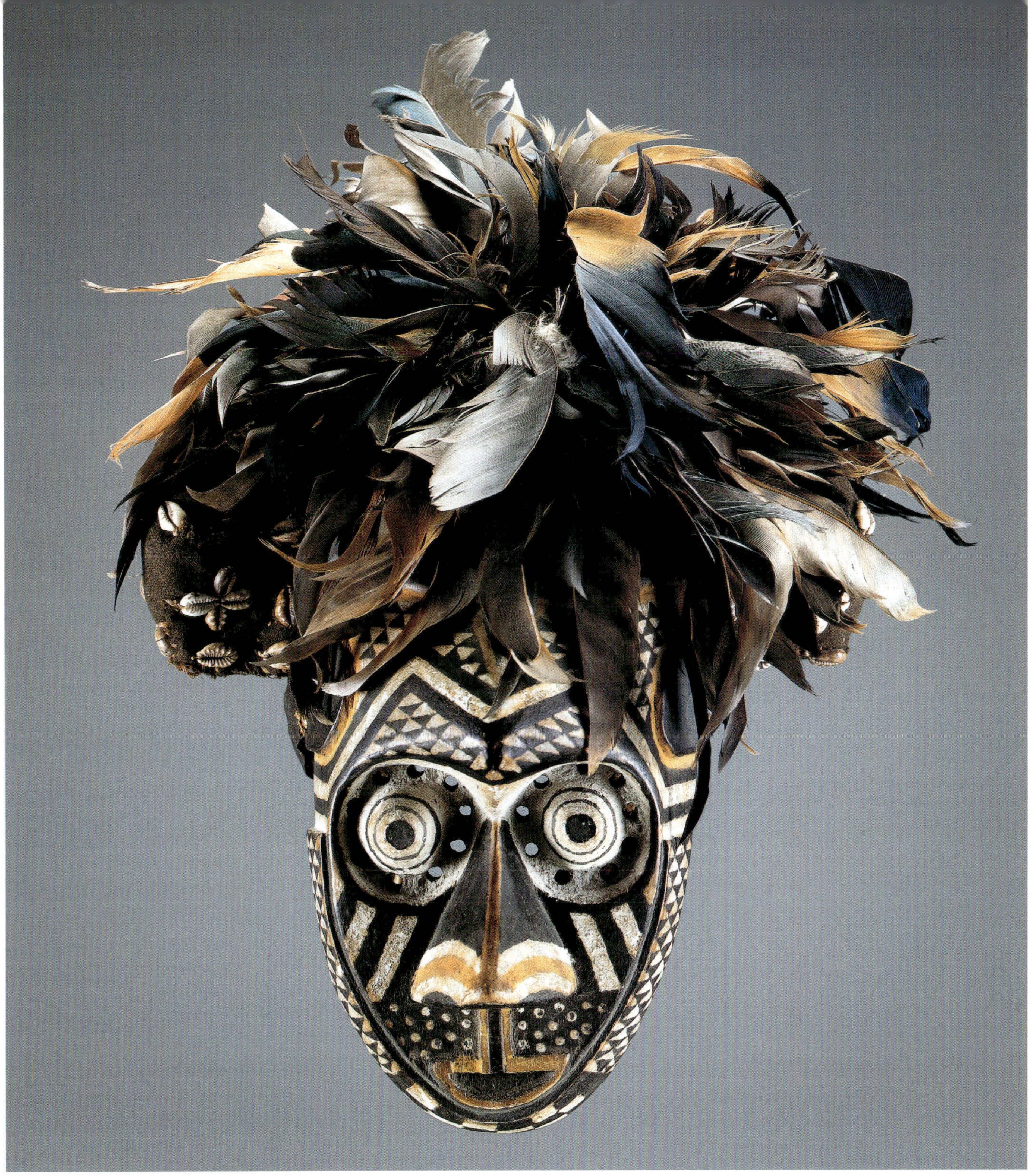

Ishyeen Imaalu then began to dance in front of the enclosure accompanied by a group of musicians. Unlike masquerade in the southern Kuba region that is confined to an area near the residence of the deceased, funerary masquerade performances in the north range over the entire central avenue. This allows for a much different style of masked performance. Among the most popular movements during masquerade is the use of the high kick and turn of the legs. At times the masked dancer would place two dance wands on the ground and then, with knees and back bent, feign to pick them up. In this regard the dancer would often glance toward the musicians which suggested that he was playing as much for the amusement of the musicians as he was for the audience of onlookers. The dancer moved towards one side of the central avenue and then toward the other. When dancing at some distance from the viewing public, he seemed to rely more on creating expressive profile gestures or "pantomime" of movements. He would then walk back toward the musicians or to the enclosure and dance vigorously, directly confronting the musicians and audience. The entire performance was a contrast of close-up, rapid foot and body movements and distant, deliberate gestures.

David A. Binkley

1 Torday and Joyce, 1910; Torday 1925; Vansina 1954, 1955, 1978; Binkley 1987, 1987b, 1990, 1996.

2 Cornet 1993 states that this mask is called *Pwoom Itok* in the Bushoong capital of Nsheng.

SOUND, MUSIC, AND SPIRIT

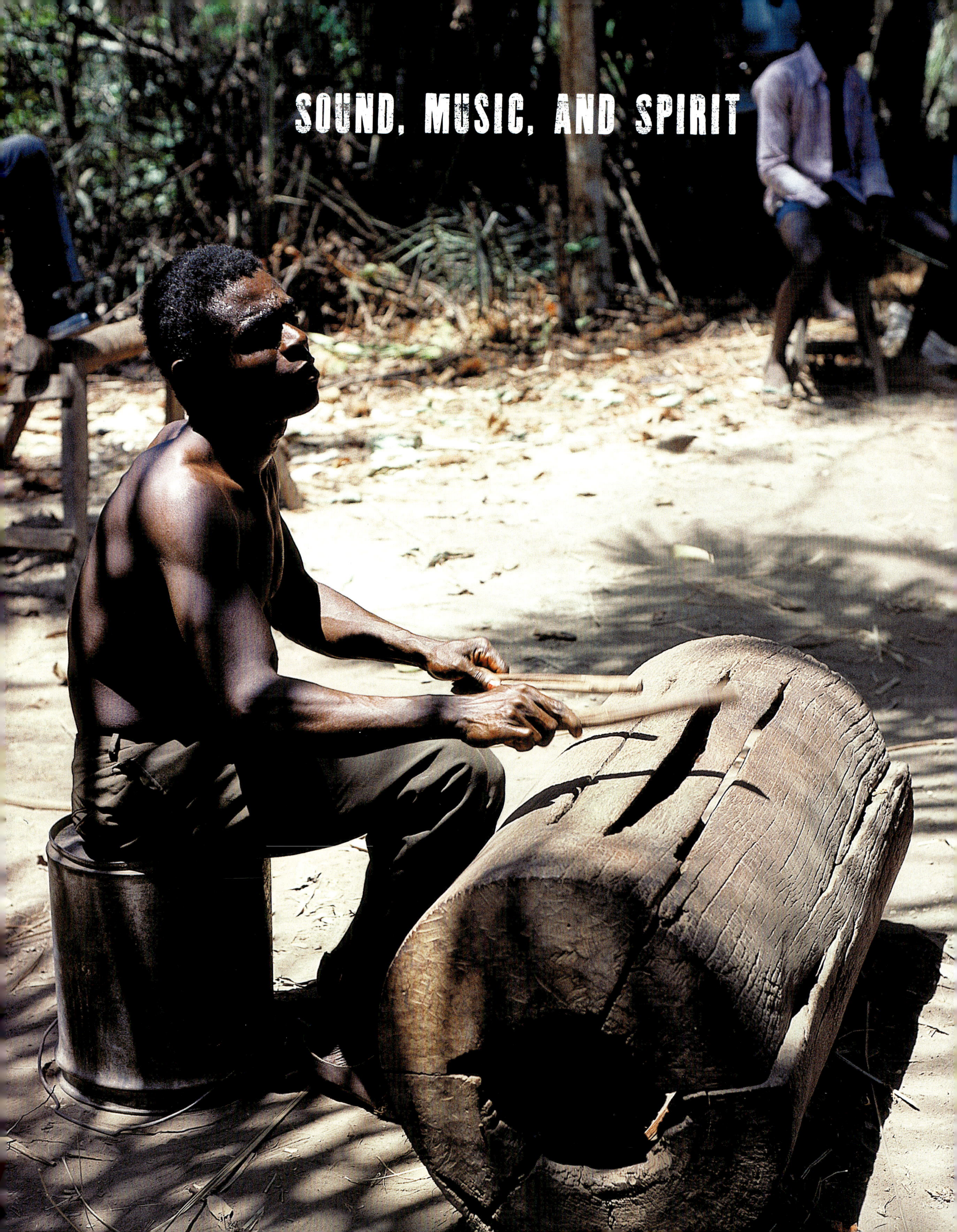

Sound is an essential component of almost all masquerades and it is frequently important to ritual involving objects placed on a shrine or used in some other way. Sources on African music used in ritual performance are comparatively few, when one considers the vast literature on material arts and culture. There is some literature on musical instruments, some on the role of music and musicians in culture, and frequent references to lyrics, but less on sound itself.

Just as the form and style of an object can locate it within a particular region of Africa, or in some cases within a particular ethnic group, so music is also diversified and style-specific.

> Questions of identity are so keenly played out in music that to neglect them impoverishes analyses. The staggering plethora of musical instruments uniquely associated with any one region and group of people should signal that these instruments and the traditions they represent are strong markers of group identity and history. For example, the nonmusical lives of Wasulu and Maninka hunters are probably not very different, but their musics are. Drums, styles of playing, and ways of dancing to them are instantly recognized, identified with, and appreciated by those who know their languages (Charry 2000:352).

Sound can be as revealing and as indicative as sculpture. It can be iconic, iconographical, symbolic, and referential, and it can be a key to cultural and personal thought and understanding about the world or about the moment. In Africa it constitutes an important site of learning. The existence of music and other man-made sounds offer a world of perception. "Because music exists, the tangible and visible cannot be the whole of the given world, something we encounter, something to which we respond" ... and its significance, going deeper than the referential, "lies not in what it points to, but in the pointing itself" (Zuckerkandl 1956:68, 71). Sound embodies sentiment, shape, energy, and intention.

In the case of the Baga D'mba performance (p. 223), specific large cylindrical drums are used exclusively for this ritual. The rhythms played on these drums were composed exclusively for the dance of D'mba. They have been handed down from generation to generation, and the original composer can no longer be identified. A set repertoire of songs exists, as well, with lyrics that are heard in no other context. As is common in African ritual, the lyrics are not what one might expect, that is, they do not seem to be about D'mba in most cases, nor do they seem to refer necessarily to the qualities that D'mba represents. Instead, they seem to introduce other themes into the event over which D'mba reigns. Lyrics refer anecdotally to events in ordinary village life, to particular people in the community, in a boasting way to the strength and endurance of particular dancers, or to personal or communal conflicts. The lyrics of one song, for example, express the sentiments of a clan leader, who is always expected to lead the group responsibly, and laud the benefit of belonging to a group:

> When it's time,
> They take my face and put it in front.
> When you have nobody—that is fearful.
> I'm afraid of that.
> Everyone help me—I have nobody.
> I am afraid this year
> because of the condition of this world.

Sound and lyrics may associate a performance with war or trouble. In some cases the music may provoke fear, in others it is offensive and repulsive, provoking a challenge. It may be used to negotiate, to encourage, or to raise the morale of a group. Some music is meant to entertain, engender pride, and to amuse. An Igbo sage has advised, however:

> Uninformed people may take these songs word-for-word, but this is a mistake. A close look at one song proves this. *Uburu Achala* means "the apple is ripe." Ignorant people think the song is about apples. The song really means "it is time to move on," and is sung when the masks and followers are ready to move from one place to another (Alexander O. Attah, in Cole and Aniakor 1984:200).

Often the most important spiritual manifestations ("art objects") are those never seen by anyone, whether savant or neophyte, because they have no physical manifestation at all but rather are manifested by a sound. This has been explored in Liberia by Edward Lifschitz (1988), who calls it "acoustic masking" because of the invisibility yet perceptibility. The Mau Kòmasu spirit (p. 236) for example, may appear as a masked character in the night, or simply as discordant sounds from musical instruments. The highest male spirit representing the Pòrò association of the Temne people in Sierra Leone is a good example. What does the spirit look like? Nobody knows. The spirit's voice is heard in several ways. An official representing him is heard in the night singing to the response of the members in chorus, or he may be heard as a low whine, interpreted by his assistant into recognizable Temne. Like other powerful spirits, the high male spirit is really a sound conducted by a sweet breeze and has no physical form. At the sound of his voice, women and the uninitiated scurry to their houses in fear. It is the sound of the spirit that allures and entraps those who foolishly refuse to yield space. The spirit resides in the forest. When he is said to want to spend time in the settlement, a miniature house suddenly appears at daybreak at the West, as if by magic. No one sees anything enter or exit the miniature house (Lamp 1982:136–141).

An experience related by Stoller (1989:113–115, 121) suggests that hearing occupies a much more critical place in sensory perception in Africa than it commonly does in the West. The ethnologist had accompanied a Songhay spiritual healer to find the spirit "double" stolen by a sorcerer from a man who, consequently, had fallen ill. After a number of preparatory rituals, they climbed a dune together where the millet husk (*duo*) had been winnowed by the women and left in a pile:

> Sorko Djibo walked into the pile of *duo* and got down on his hands and knees. He sifted through the husks, jumped up and exclaimed ... "Did you hear it?" "Hear what?" I asked dumbfounded. "Did you feel it?" "Feel what?" I wondered. "Did you see it?" "What are you talking about?" I demanded. Sorko Djibo shook his head in disbelief.... "Without sight or touch," he continued, "one can learn a great deal. But you must learn how to *hear*".... Why had I not been able to hear the bewitched man's bia ("double") as it swooshed past me on its way back to its human counterpart? Exhausted from the frustration of instructing such a dullard, Djibo lapsed into silence as we trudged down the sand dune.

When the two returned to the bewitched man, he was suddenly up and about, walking vigorously, verbose, and full of strength.

Playing the slit gong (*kèlèñ*) for a masked dance during male initiation in the sacred grove. A similar slit gong is played for the Baga D'mba (p. 223) and the Baga Banda (p. 75) masquerades. Temne, Sierra Leone. Photo: Frederick John Lamp, 1976

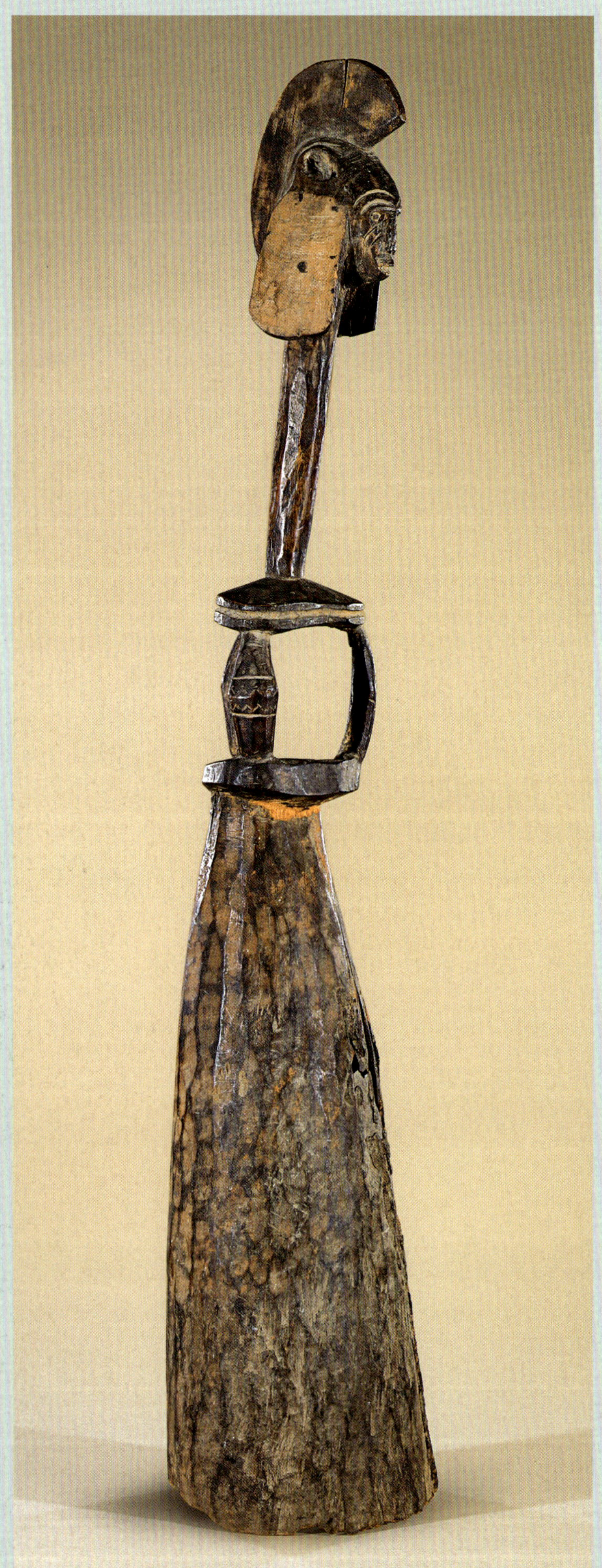

Figurative Gong, Mumuye, Nigeria
c. Late 19th–early 20th century
Wood, red pigment, H. 93.4 cm
Gift of Robert Elkin, Bethesda, Maryland
BMA 1999.596 (ex Herbert Baker, Los Angeles, 1978, who purchased it in Africa before 1969)

Sound can be used to suggest action, either in the absence of action or in collaboration with it. Drums among the Asante of Ghana, called *ntumpane* or *fontomfrom*, or talking drums, are described by Rattray (1927:286) as emitting tones or rhythms that communicate proverbs and sayings. At the town of Mampon, he catalogued seventy-seven sayings drummed on the fontomfrom drums, some as complex as:

> O Path, thou crossest the River
> O River thou crossest the Path.
> Which of you is the elder?
> We cut a Path, and it went and met the River.
> The River came forth long long ago
> It came forth from the creator of all things.

Among the Yoruba, Margaret Drewal (1992:93) shows how the drums complemented the movement of the masked dancer, and represented the same action in a different vocabulary, that of music:

> Gorilla (*Inoki*) had naturalistically carved wooden testicles and a penis painted red on the tip. He sneaked up behind unsuspecting women in the performance space, raising his penis as if he were going to rape them. Meanwhile the drums sounded an ideophonic *sabala-sabala-sa-o,* which represented aurally Gorilla's fucking gestures.

Music in African performance is indeed very visual; one can "see the music," in the words of A. M. Ipoku (Hampton 1982). In the Baga D'mba performance, the drummers form a procession, facing forward, then backward, as they move around the village plaza, leading the masked dancer. In the initiation of young men and women together into adulthood, the Baga used an immense drum usually supported by a group of figures and abstract forms, brightly colored, which could be higher than many of the men authorized play it, so that they always needed to stand on a stool in performance. This was an event in which the elder men showed their power to the youths thereby playing out generational tensions. The sound of the drum, which has never been recorded, must have struck the initiates with awe, certainly amplified by the visual magnificence of the drum. Chernoff's sexually-inspired description (1979:111) of the maneuvering between drummer and dancer, given in the previous section, underscores the unity between visible and acoustic art forms. This same kind of imagery is made extremely graphic in the dances performed by the Yaka women in Congo (Kinshasa); dancing with erotic movements of the belly and hips, the women are inspired by the vision presented by the drummers (Devisch 1990:116):

> In a tense (*ngaandzi*), erectile (*khoondzu*) posture, the male drummer holds the phallic-shaped cylindrical dance drum between his legs: some songs, particularly in the context of circumcision rituals, make the association between the drum's appealing rhythm (*dithiimba dyangoma*) and the erect penis' movement (dithiimba).

Robert Thompson (1974:262–263) recorded the advice of a Banyang chief, Defang Tarhmben: "The dancer must listen to the drum. When he is really listening he creates within himself an echo of the drum.... Once he is seeing the echo, he is dancing with pride."

Sound in African ritual may be produced by many different media and methods (Bassani & Fagg 1988, Brincard 1989, DjeDje 1999). Obviously, musical instruments are frequently used, such as drums, horns, lyres, gongs, and cymbals as in the case of the Baga D'mba (p. 223), the Loma Angbaï (p. 57), and the Mossi Wan-Zega (p. 86). Gourd rattles provide a distinctive, rhythm-identified sound (Dan Mask, p. 99). In some cases like the Cameroon masks (pp. 160, 163) a similar sound is made by anklets of bells or seed pods worn on the body. Just as with the tapping described above, Moba diviners invoke spiritual presence by clapping their hands, and with the metallic jangling of metal objects on a cord (p. 185).

Sound is efficacious spiritually, and the simple act of uttering certain sounds, names, and the lyrics of songs, sets up a dynamic that is unlike that of other artistic elements. Henry Drewal (in Ross 1994:65) describes the power of naming and praise giving vis-a-vis particular sculptural works of art among the Yoruba:

> Such names become a focus in the verbal arts of appellations (*oriki*) ... and songs (*orin*). These arts embellish the imagery associated with names, names that serve to integrate persons in a lineage, an unbroken chain of relations from departed ancestors to living relatives, ... to invoke the spiritual essence of the person, and to elevate the person by encouraging perfection and "faultless performance".... When such praises are voiced, the head becomes "inspired" or "energized" (*wú*) with the spirit of one's noble ancestry, which is calculated to encourage high achievement.

Among the Songhay of Mali and Niger, the sound of a small stringed instrument composed of a gourd, stick, and horsehair, called a *godji*, is so powerful and sacred that it can link past and present. Stoller (1989:109) was told by Adamu Jenitongo that "the godji cries for me; it cries for you; it cries for the people of Tillaberi; it cries for all the Songhay." The sound itself is like a path to be traveled; one who hears the sound is the path:

"The sound of the godji penetrates and makes us feel the presence of the ancestors, the ancients [*don borey*]. We hear the sound and know that we are on the path of the ancestors. The sound is irresistible. We cannot be unaffected by it and neither can the spirits, for when they hear it 'cry,' it penetrates them.

Just a few of our writers for this book concentrated on sound, although many writers mentioned it. In this section, Daniel Reed shows how music is used among the Dan, with masking, to manifest a spiritual being. Till Förster discusses the function of insulting lyrics by young master singers that ironically do honor to the elders. Among the Yoruba, divination is shown to be aided by sound meant to attract spiritual power. And from the Sukuma, Frank Gunderson demonstrates the use of the sweet and the acerbic in musical tribute associated with figural sculpture.

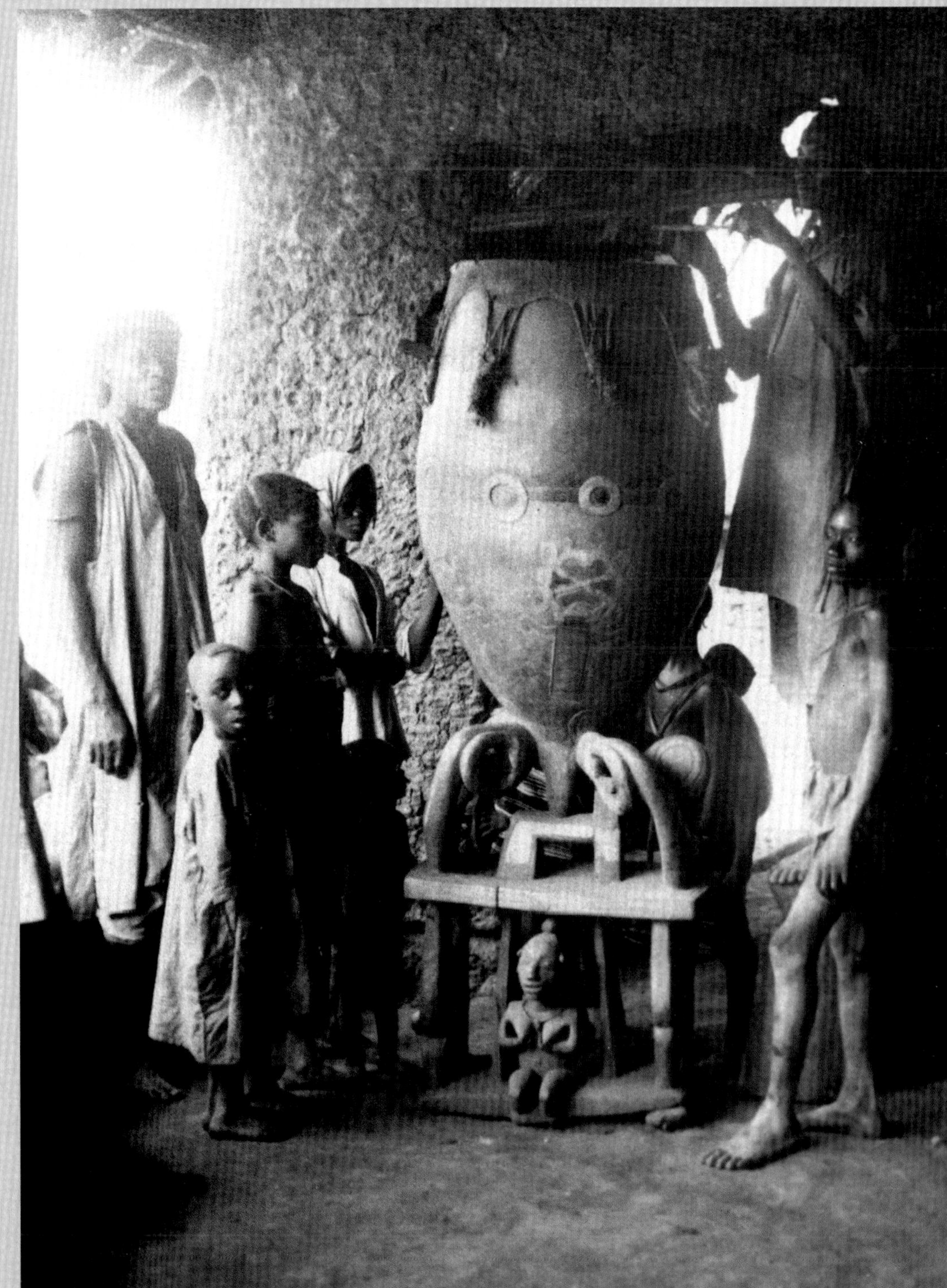

Timba drum, Baga Sitem, Katako village, Guinea
Photo: Père Soul, Pères du Saint-Esprit, *c.* 1930
Courtesy photo archive of the Pères du Saint-Esprit, Paris

21

The Transformation into Spirit through a "Constellation of Arts": a Dan Mask (*Tankë Ge*)

Mask (*Tankë Ge*/ *Tanka Gle*)
Dan, Liberia/Ivory Coast
c. Early 20th century
Wood, H. 24 cm
Bequest of Saidie A. May
BMA 1951.388
(purchased from Pierre Matisse, New York, 1947; ex Charles Ratton, Paris)

Ge (*gle* in the west and south of the Dan region), which in most scholarly literature has been translated as "mask," denotes a multi-faceted concept which has four components: the notion of a forest spirit; the particular performative form in which that spirit manifests among humans; the foundation of the traditional education that takes place in initiation; and the enactment of that education, or in other words, ideal behavior for adults in Dan society.[1] A performing Ge is thus a spirit that appears among humans as a dancing and musical embodiment of Dan social ideals and beliefs. Many types of Genu (plural) are found throughout the Dan region, each of which serve particular societal functions. Tankë Genu express Dan social ideals in the form of excellence in dance.

The Tankë Ge, as it is known among the northern Dan (called Tanka Gle in the western region), is a type of spirit whose primary function is to entertain with dance.[2] Among the northern Dan with whom I have lived and conducted research (Reed 2001, 2003), tankë translates literally as "to dance" (cf. GBA 1982).

Tankë Genu are generally called upon to dance at celebratory occasions. Historically these would include events like harvest celebrations and rites of passage such as weddings and funerals. Today, however, the list includes an array of events: tourist-oriented festivals, speeches by visiting government ministers, and various other official political public relations functions. During my most recent field research in 1997, Tankë Genu danced at many political public relations events: at a party thrown by the African Development Bank, at a ceremony honoring the opening of a new primary school in a nearby village, or to welcome the mayor back from a trip to France. In part as a result of these new opportunities in national political performance contexts, Tankë Genu perform more regularly than previously, and have grown in number compared with other types of *genu*.[3] The northern Dan region has become far more ethnically and religiously diverse over the past century, and for many of the Christians, Muslims, and members of other ethnic groups in the area, Tankë Ge performances serve as purely secular entertainment. For many Dan, however, including the performers, Tankë Ge performance remains sacred, if less so than performances of more highly sacred *genu*. Many of my consultants in the city of Man, Ivory Coast, view Tankë Ge performance as a critical enactment of their religious and ethnic identity in the increasingly pluralistic setting in which they live.

The Tankë Ge mask that hangs on the wall at the BMA is just one small (though centrally important) aspect of the visual component of the multimedia manifestation of a Tankë Ge spirit. With few exceptions,[4] among the Dan a *ge* performer must conceal his entire body, allowing no human skin to be seen. Completely concealing the body supports the belief that, in performance, all performative components—visual, sonic, movement, and other—are transformed into spirit, obliterating the human "behind the mask" of the performing Ge. Around the periphery of the forehead of the mask are holes, which are used to secure the headdress, called a *komo*, worn by the dancing performer (cf. Fischer and Himmelheber 1984:23). A tall, bonnet-shaped hat, the *komo* is made of goatskin leather, dyed in bold, striking primary colors. The komo is frequently adorned with cowrie shells and topped with a plume of goat fur that rises high above the crowd. Ringing the forehead of the mask, or attached to the komo, is a goat-skin strip covered with cowrie shells called *bla kar*, while braids of dyed cloth sometimes frame the Ge's face. The Tankë Ge's torso is generally covered by a hand-woven, traditional Dan *boubou*, in shades of blue and cream, with loose sleeves that are sewn up at their ends to conceal the hands. Through the sleeves, the performer holds flywhisks—traditional symbols of authority among the Dan. The Tankë Ge's legs are covered by hand-woven trousers that usually match the *boubou* top. Tied around the waist are colored, leather strips that drape over a (usually knee-length) raffia skirt. Iron bells are tied around the Ge's ankles, and typical footwear are comfortable, canvass sneakers well-suited for dancing.

The mask itself is effeminately beautiful, and an excellent example of what Vandenhoute called "idealized realism" (1948:8)—a phrase that gets at the heart not just of this style of carving but of the very idea of Ge and Ge performance. Thin, slit eyes, distinct, high cheekbones, a finely-carved, somewhat realistic nose and lovely protruding lips identify the Tankë Ge as a female mask (Fischer and Himmelheber 1984:9). Frequently the eyes and lips are outlined or painted in white or red; in the northern Dan region, the mask of an especially popular sub-genre of Tankë Ge, called Gedro, includes a red stripe across the eyes. The Tankë Ge mask's effeminate features are just one of several reasons that French-speaking Dan often call them "women's masks."[5] Tankë Ge masks are frequently adorned with earrings or other jewelry associated with women, and many women told me that, in contrast to the fierce and frightening visages of many other *genu*, Tankë Genu are beautiful to behold. More importantly, women involve themselves in Tankë Ge performances to a greater extent than with more highly sacred *genu*. Not only do women especially enjoy watching Tankë Genu perform, they also more frequently sing and dance along with the Ge, taking important roles in the manifestation of the spirit in performance. For all these reasons, many women cite Tankë Genu as being their favorite type of Ge.

Far from being mere accompaniment to the dancing Ge, the musical aspect of a Tankë Ge performance is every bit as much a part of the manifestation of the Ge's spirit as is its physical form. This music is called *getan*, which translates roughly as the music/dance of the Ge (Zemp 1971:69–70). *Getan* for Tankë Ge performances consists of an ensemble including three to four drums (singular, *bhaa*), a gourd rattle (*gle*) or a shaker consisting of a basket-shaped chamber filled with small pebbles or seeds (*sekpe*), and a mixed male/female vocal chorus singing songs in a call and response form. The repertoire of songs that can be sung at a Tankë Ge performance is not fixed in number, as good singers count among their talents the ability to spontaneously improvise songs to comment on a situation at hand. Many of the texts of the songs comment on some aspect of the concept of *Ge*, while others involve light-hearted themes meant to add to the joyous feeling of a Tankë Ge performance. Some Tankë Genu themselves also vocalize, punctuating the music with high-pitched

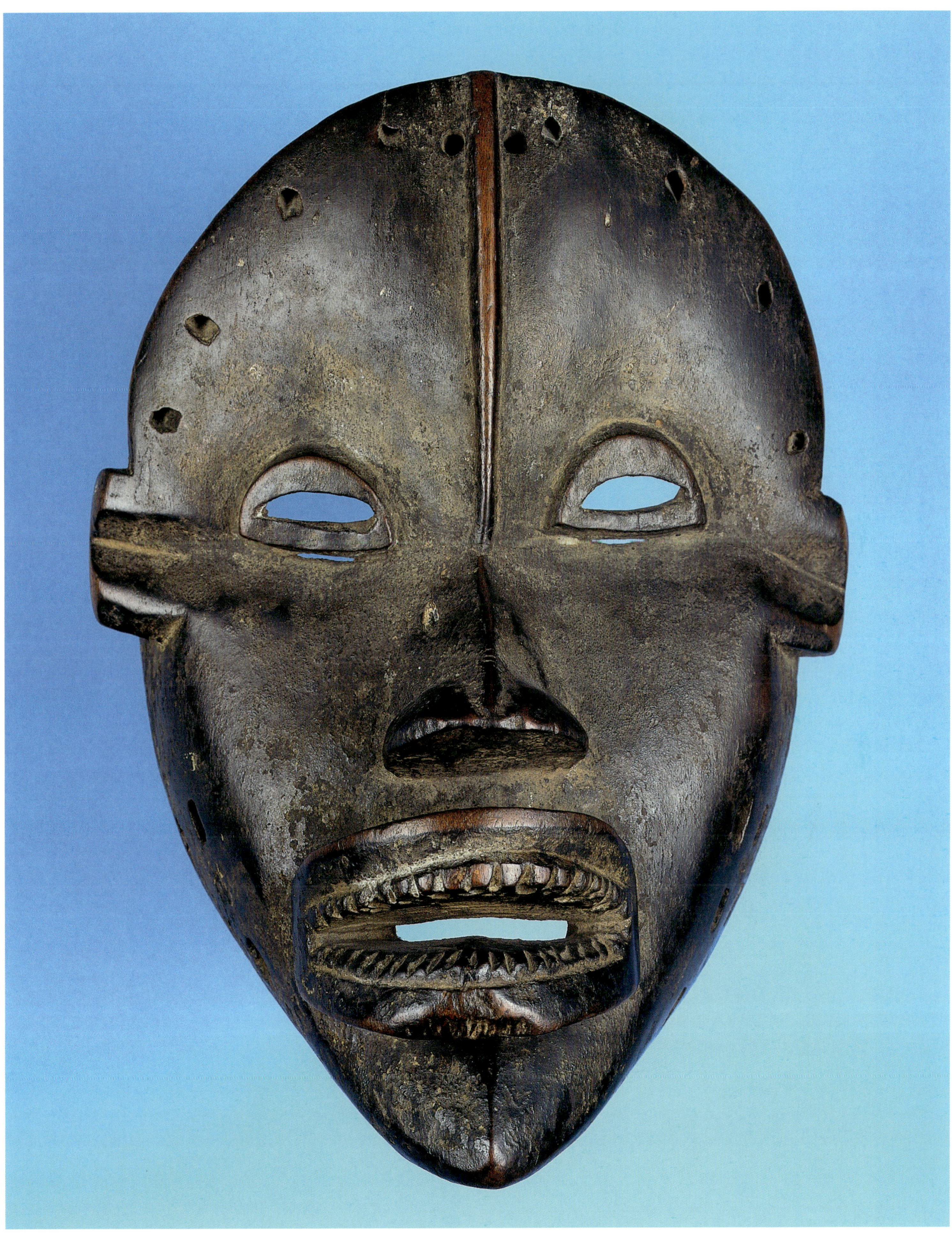

screeches or singing that recalls that of certain birds. As the vocalists sing, instrumentalists create a richly textured polyrhythm by playing repeating patterns on the drums and rattle that they artfully vary to enrich the sound and energy of the performance. Layered over these repeating parts, the master drummer (*bhaakpizoemen*) improvises and plays rehearsed solos that synchronize with the iron bells (*gbung*) on the dancing Tankë Ge's feet. The densely layered, polyrhythmic, thickly textured sound of *getan* animates the Ge, drawing the spirits to him that enable him to perform to the utmost of his ability.

The rhythmic interaction between the dancing Ge and the master drummer is the focal point of a Tankë Ge performance. Audience members not only appreciate the Ge's dancing skill but also delight in recognizing rhythmic and dance motifs that the Ge and master drummer borrow from other Dan dances, dances of other ethnic groups, and even popular songs from the radio. Incorporating such dances into his performance, the Tankë Ge demonstrates his awareness and mastery of all dances in his environs, proving himself to be the ultimate dancer around, thus manifesting behavioral ideals. Through the incorporation of popular music into what they call a "traditional" performance form, performers express identities simultaneously rooted in Dan tradition and cosmopolitan surroundings.

Though his physical features are effeminate, the Tankë Ge's comportment in performance can be aggressive and masculine. In a smooth but cocky manner, he struts around the performance space, stopping to dance, then moving on. His dance is often strong, forceful, and athletic, his torso remaining stiff as his feet speed across the ground to the rapid tempo of the music. Traditionally, a Tankë Ge performs in the center of a circle formed by the vocal chorus, the instrumentalists, and the "audience," who also contribute to the energy and sound of the performance with improvised dancing, singing, and clapping. These days, however, Tankë Genu also perform on western-style stages, which condition a greater distance between performers and audience, and encourage a more linear arrangement. The dancing Ge is always accompanied by an assistant (*gekia*), who shadows his every step, swiftly moving to adjust loose ankle bells or any other problem that might arise with the Ge's outfit, and collecting monetary gifts on the Ge's behalf.

All in all, a Tankë Ge mask can best be understood as one small part of a "constellation of arts" (Stone 1998) involving visual art, music, dance, text, and theatrical components that performers bring together to manifest a complex concept—Ge—that is at the very center of their religious and ethnic identities.

Daniel Reed

1 Genu (plural) are most fundamentally part of a pantheon of spirit intermediaries between people and God. Most of my Dan consultants agree that the spirits who manifest as Genu originate in the wilderness, in certain mountains, trees, or streams of the forest environment that surrounds human settlements in the Dan homeland region. Each Ge manifests in a particular way in performance in the world of humans, and performs for particular reasons. There are Genu for rejoicing and entertainment, Genu who direct initiation, Genu who enforce fire regulations during the dry season, and Genu who act as judges to settle conflicts, to cite just a few examples. Given that Ge is also the spiritual base of the experiential education taught during initiation, which includes a philosophy of social ideals, values, and ethics involving proper behavior for adults in Dan society, for many Dan who continue to practice what they often call "the tradition," or "the religion of our ancestors," Ge is at the root of Dan identity, of what it means to be Dan.

2 There is some slight variance in published scholarly literature as to the definition of Tanka gle, and to the classification of Genu in general. Dan sociologist GBA Daouda (1982) and I, who conducted research in the northern Dan region, found people making a distinction between Tankë Ge (dance Ge) and Trukè Ge (comedic Ge). Tankë Ge merely dance and occasionally sing, but do not play instruments (with the exception of the ankle bells on their feet); rather, they perform with an ensemble consisting of drums, a gourd rattle and a vocal chorus. Trukè Ge, on the other hand, perform either mime theatrical comedy or sing and dance to their own accompaniment, consisting of a gourd rattle, and the ankle bells on their feet. Key to the distinction is that the primary function of a Tankë Ge is to dance, while that of the Trukè Ge is to make comedy. In contradistinction, Fischer (1978) and Fischer with Himmelheber (1984), who conducted the majority of their research among western Dan in Liberia, combine under the single rubric of Tanka gle those Ge who sing, dance, and pantomime, and may be accompanied either by an ensemble or by their own gourd rattle and ankle bells. One can only speculate as to the reason(s) for this discrepancy, but regional difference and change over time are two likely factors. In any case, given regional diversity, change over time, the fact that Dan tend to classify Genu in several different ways (e.g., by form, by function, and in broad and more specific categories), and the non-dogmatic and fluid nature of the Dan religious system, creating a single system of classification is inherently problematic. Regarding the classification of Dan masks, GBA writes, "The problem is deeper than one can imagine" (1982:57).

3 Because of certain changes that have occurred during the colonial and postcolonial periods, especially the ethnic and religious diversification of the Dan region, some more highly sacred Genu no longer perform, remaining instead within the confines of sacred houses where they can be consulted in times of need.

4 The Ge lowest in the sacred hierarchy, the racing Ge or Biansè Ge (which Fischer and Himmelheber call "gunyege"), sometimes races barefoot; this is the only Dan Ge I have ever seen whose costume allowed human skin to be exposed.

5 One must not confuse this term, however—women's masks—with the Ge of the women's society called Kong, which is an entirely female affair that is never seen by men.

Tanka gle, the entertainment masquerade, singing and dancing. Dan, village of Bagamaple, Ivory Coast. Photo: Eberhard Fischer, 1975

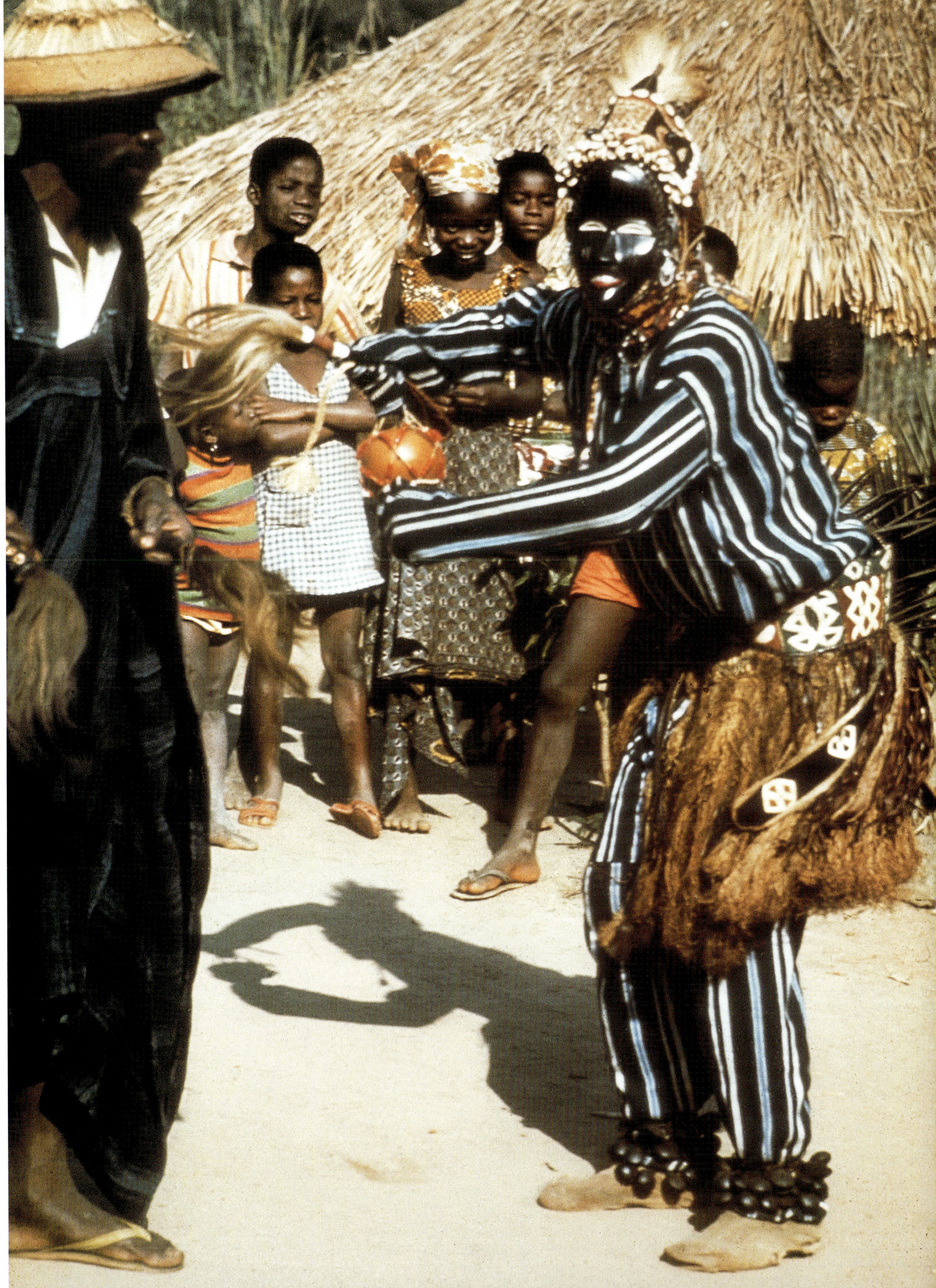

22

Songs of Insult: a Senufo Headdress (*Daagu*)

Singer's Headdress (*Daagu*)
Senufo, Ivory Coast
c. Early 20th century
Wood, reed, cotton cloth, cotton threads, cowrie shells, glass beads, feather, nails, and metal chain, H. 37 cm (helmet only)
Gift of Dr. and Mrs. Lawrence D. Pinkner, Baltimore
BMA 1998.477

Young men within each Senufo village divide themselves into age groups when they are between twelve and eighteen years old, before they are initiated into the local *Pòrò* society. In these age groups, they must take part in various rituals, the *zeu* (in the southwest), or *niyogi* (elsewhere), being the most extensive. The young men submit to a physical ordeal that culminates in a masked character whipping their naked legs with a switch. Having passed this trial, they have the right to sing songs criticizing the old men of the society and the village. The young men choose two gifted singers from the age group. Gathering in the oldest square of the village, these two singers sing together in alternation with the group.

The two singers each wear a headdress called Daagu. It consists of a wooden helmet with two horns, ears and, at the front, in most cases also a small female figure seated on a pair of downward-pointing horns. The back shows corresponding elements. The whole helmet is decorated with cowry shells and often has additional accessories. Among them are short, colored strips of fabric, remnants of which are still visible here in the BMA example, as well as long white feathers attached almost horizontally to the back part of the helmet and sometimes substituted by strips of tin or aluminum. The bottom rim of the helmet is more often than not perforated so that numerous chains can be tied to it. The longest of them are made of cowry shells and reach down to the wearer's ankles. The face is also covered with chains consisting of colored glass beads, as in this example, or plastic disks, secured by a cowry. In addition, a long cloth is attached to the back of the helmet onto which, again, cowries have been sewn. If this train is not completely covered with cowries, they are sewn on in decorative patterns as in this case. A fringe is tied to the hem of the train that often also has little brass bells attached. Very often a small, rectangular mirror is also sewn onto the train. On the train of this Daagu helmet, there is a spot left undecorated for this purpose.

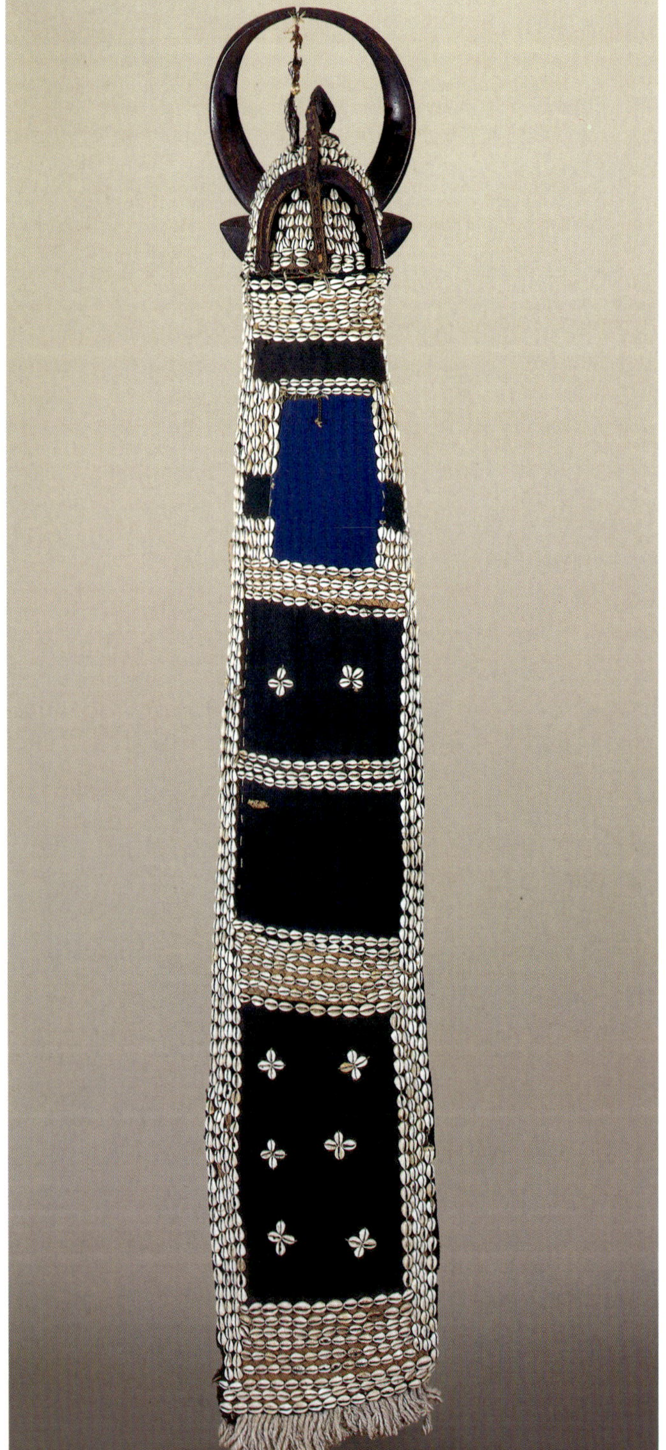

In addition to the helmet and its accessories, the singers wear a netted garment loosely thrown over the shoulders and fastened at the neck by a string. In the months prior to the ritual, the young men knot this shawl themselves out of cotton. They also put on a loincloth as is customarily worn by the initiates of the Pòrò society. This now suggests that the young men will be next to be introduced into the society.

The singers hold an iron rod in their hands, with a small female figure at the top, made in *cire perdue* technique and decorated with strips of cotton or colored cloths. This rod is called *tefalapica*, "the plowman's girl". A similar staff is used in a different context among the older boys and young men: the hoeing contests that take place on the fields ready for cultivating at the end of the rainy season. Then, it is typically carved out of wood, although the iron staff may also be used, and here the staff distinguishes those who have excelled in their work in the fields.

In connection with the zeu ritual, the singers place the rod to mark the middle of the square where they will perform. The chants start in the early evening hours and often last until the next morning. Accompanied by the remaining young men of their age group, the singers first move through the village in a long line, stopping briefly in front of the huts of the old men of the society to greet them. Afterwards, they go to the oldest farmstead of the village and perform their chants in its center. To begin, the singers proceed slowly round the square, singing of their impudence and the rare chance to be allowed to criticize the old men of the village. The singers call themselves "snakes with cleft tongues" or something similar, while the old men of the village are addressed as "droopy testicles" or "inveterate liars."

The evening is subdivided into several acts. In the second phase, the singers sit down on two stools in the middle of the square while their companions continue to dance round it. The chants are accompanied by drums and wind instruments fashioned from horns and long, tubular calabashes. The boys wear iron anklets with bells that ring with every step of the dance.

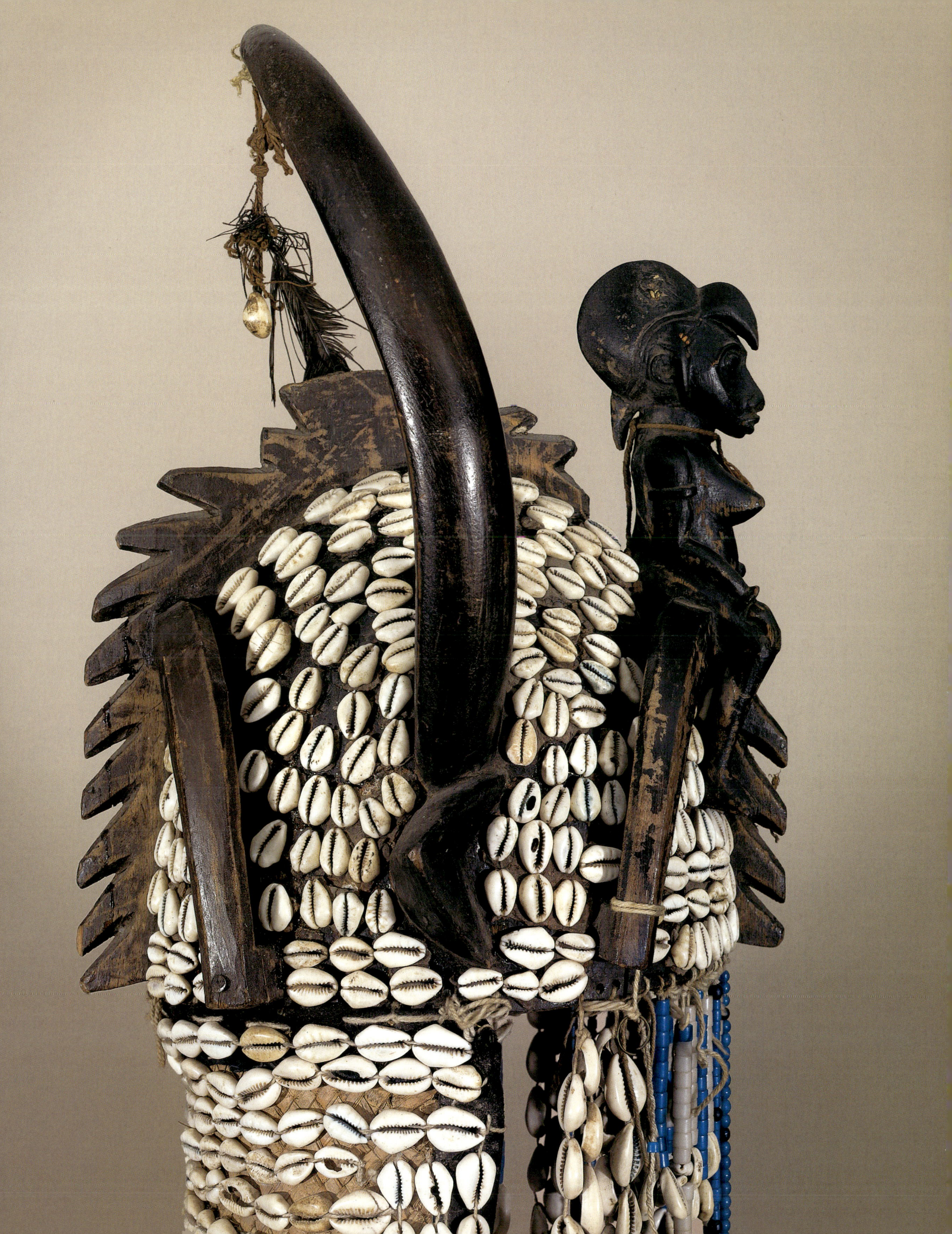

In this phase of the chants, individual old men are the preferred theme. Sometimes complete sketches are performed, with the members of the group playing the old men of the village. A typical theme is, for instance, the excessive trust the old men have in the supernatural spirits said to be living in the wilderness. A victim is imitated while the main singer describes how one or the other of the village neighbors spent all his money on these sacrifices until he had nothing left for himself: The spirits of the wilderness have a better life than the humans!

The rituals of the Pòrò society itself are bitingly picked to pieces. The appearance of the most important and most secret Pòrò mask is recreated with the masked dancers and the old men (played by the boys) of the society staggering so much that they end up falling onto the dust of the dance floor. Alcohol is held responsible for this. The singer ends with a lament: "Heaven has robbed us of the good old men, and only left behind the bad ones [here]."At the culmination of such a chant, the singers shake their garments so that the various little bells attached jingle, while other young men blow horns and fill the square with this hollow sound.

The chants of the zeu are very popular. Not only the youths, who otherwise rarely have an opportunity to criticize the old men of the village, but the older men themselves also excitedly await each performance. Everyone knows that the young men have observed everyday life in the village for months to find out the particular weakness of each individual. They have practiced the chants at a specifically arranged place in the wilderness. Once or twice a week, they would light a fire there to rehearse in the middle of the night in the glow of the flickering flames. On these occasions, young people of the same age are allowed to eavesdrop, but the old men, who are later to be criticized by the singers, are not entitled to do so. For them, the first night is meant to be a surprise. Some of the old people find the chants insulting and angrily leave the square when their turn comes. But the majority also see in the criticism a sort of tribute as well, in that only he who has fulfilled all his duties in the Pòrò society also has the right to be the subject of a song by the new age group. Criticism is also an honoring of old age, and there are old men who are quite touched when, after their many years in the society, they are addressed in this way, even if confronted with their shortcomings. Some who are not addressed in song become angry that they have not been mentioned.

The chants of the zeu are a local artistic genre, performed only in a few Senufo towns. They feed on the many allusions to individual habits and events incomprehensible to those who have not lived in the village for any length of time. One has to have shared the people's everyday life in order to understand what the singers mean and whom the young men are portraying in their sketches. In only one town, Boundiali, complete stories are told so the audience does not have to rely on intimate knowledge of everyday life.

Once the men have performed several times in their own village, they go on a tour around the neighboring settlements. The repertoire often changes in the course of this. Some allusions to specific persons are omitted in favor of generally understandable portrayals. When the young men are back from their tour, they store the costumes in order to pass them on to the next age group to be formed at the end of another six years. In the process, the most valuable accessories are removed, so that each age group has to decorate their costumes anew. Every generation tries to create particularly elaborate and attractive costumes.

Till Förster

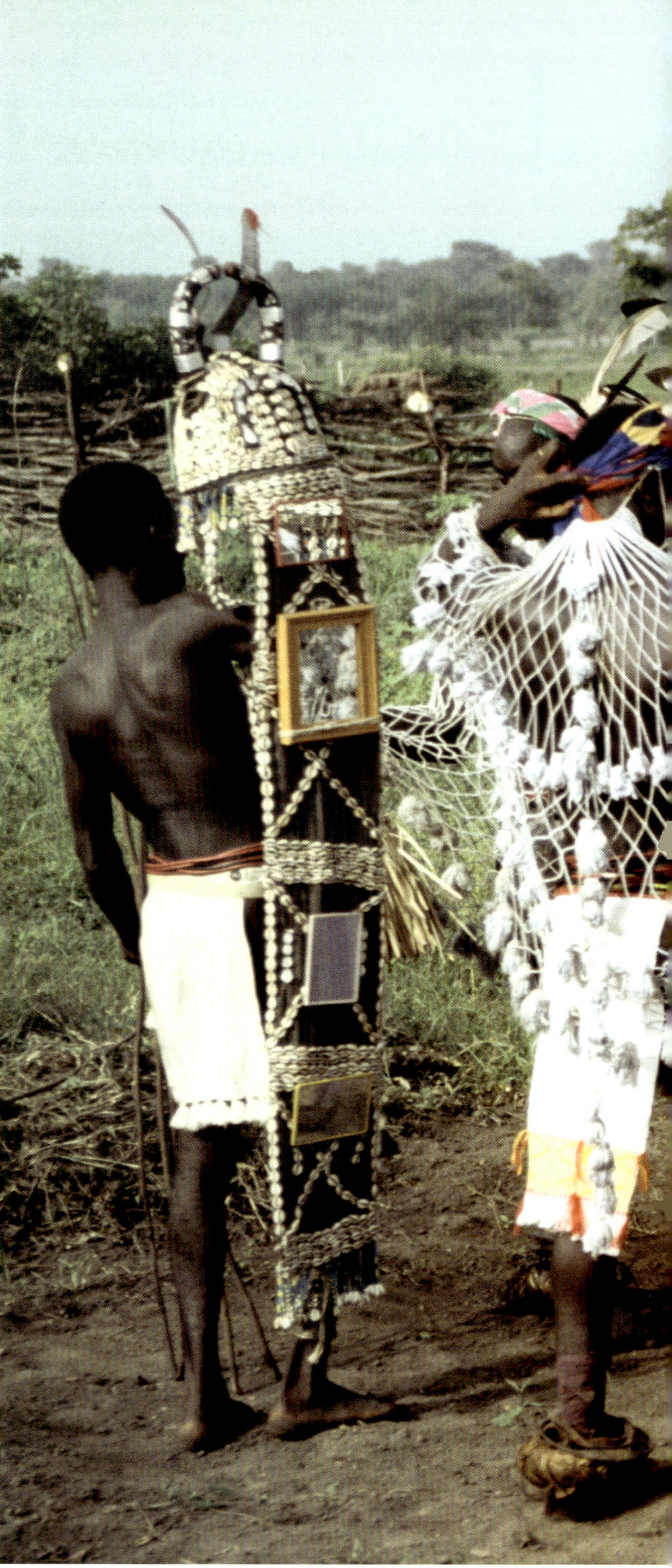

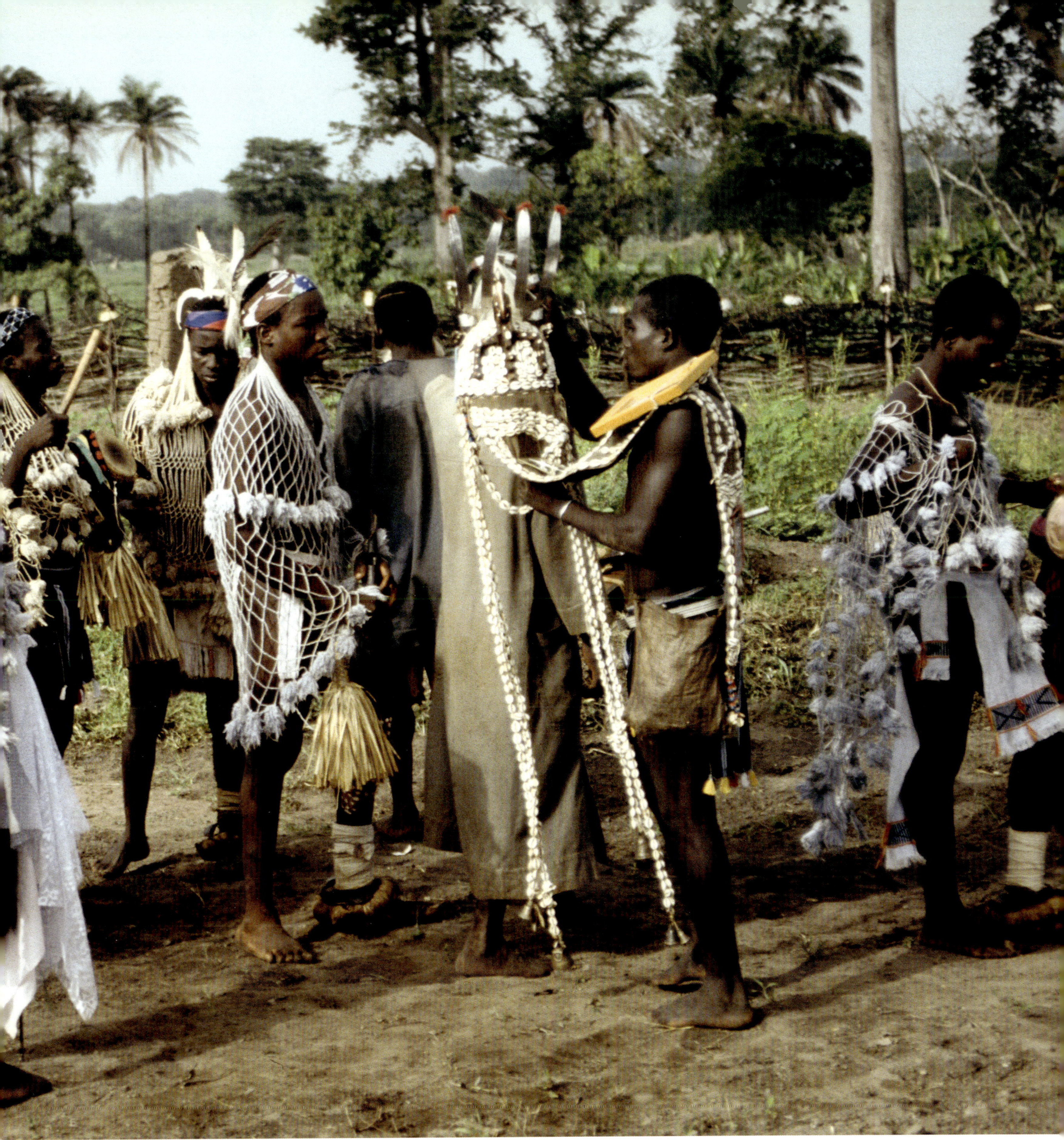

Zeu singers preparing to perform at the *kpaala*. Senufo, Nafoun, Ivory Coast
Photo: Till Förster, 1991

23

Attracting the Attention of the Spirit: a Yoruba Divination Tapper and Bowl

In Yoruba divination guided by the god, Ifa, there are several necessary elements: diviner, client, palm nuts, tray, tapper, and powder. The ivory tapper is performed by a diviner, a man who functions as a priest, known as *babalawo*, "father of secrets." The diviner trains for years to know the verses corresponding to configurations he marks on a tray (*opon*) scattered with a powder (*iyerosum*). The marks are made by his fingers and are determined by the manipulation of sixteen palm nuts (*ikin*). Many diviners have other accoutrements, such as a cow-tail switch, a bag to carry the palm nuts, and cups or elaborately carved bowls to hold them. Tappers or bells are used to tap the tray in the beginning of the divination process to attract the attention of the god, Ifa, or Orunmila, the god of wisdom and divination.

Divination occurs when an individual wishes to understand and clarify a new occurrence or problem in his or her life or before embarking on a new course of action. Diviners help determine the most appropriate sacrifices to ensure accord with the events in a person's life and with an individual's ancestors (Bascom 1969:12, 60). A newborn baby is brought to a diviner to help the parents determine the character of their child and the best way of bringing it up (M. Drewal 1992:52).

At the start of divination, the tray is placed on a mat and scattered with the powder, a dust created by termites gnawing on wood (Bascom 1969:35). The tray is placed so that the carved head of Esu, the messenger god of confusion, the crossroads, and sexuality, is opposite, facing the diviner. "Frobenius (1913:I, 252) reported that the diviner 'always turns to the East'; and an Ife informant said that long ago diviners faced East; now they can sit facing in any direction so long as Eshu is placed opposite them" (Bascom 1969:34).

Before the day's divination begins, the priest recites various verses for each object he will use during the day. Below are verses incorporating the tapper.

> Tapping the tray with the diving bell or with the handle of the cow-tail, switch, he recites, "To climb and chatter, oh to climb and chatter. If, the West African Grey Woodpecker mounts the top of a tree, it will, chatter. To climb and chatter, oh, to climb and chatter. If the Agbe bird awakes, it will chatter. To climb and chatter, oh, to climb and, chatter. If the Woodcock awakes, it will chatter. To climb and chatter, oh, to climb and chatter."...
>
> He continues, "Eshu, homage, oh" and recites several of Eshu's praise names; Osun chatters, followed by praise names of the God of Iron; Osun will chatter, followed by praise names of the Goddess of the River Osun; Sango, your homage, oh, homage" and praise names of the God of Thunder. He continues to invoke and recite the praise names of as many deities as he can, the order being unimportant after Eshu, and Ogun. He then invokes the living and the dead kings: "Kings on earth and Kings in heaven, your homage, oh" and the earth: "Ground, your homage, oh."
>
> He concludes, "Orunmila, sacrifice is offered, Orunmila, sacrifice is satisfactory; Orunmila, sacrifice come to pass": he claps his hands, and says, "Thank you, oh." The invocation addressed to Orunmila, is a prayer that the sacrifice which is offered will be acceptable to him, and that it will achieve its purpose (Bascom 1969:38–39).
>
> Palm nuts may be kept in a bowl by the diviner's side. Elaborately carved bowls, with figures of animals and human beings, sometimes in groups, are among his prized instruments of divination. Once the principal participants are seated, the diviner will "activate" the palm nuts with either prayers or a libation. If the diviner has a tapper, he will then tap the tray to assure the attention of Ifa, who determines the verses by controlling the manipulation of the palm nuts (Bascom 1969:36, 43, 104). The entire ceremony takes about a half an hour and the diviner maintains a calm, quiet atmosphere in order to concentrate on the verses which are to be recited and to better ensure the attention of the client (M. Drewal 1992:52).

Ifa Divination Bowl
Yoruba, Ketu, Republic of Benin
c. Mid-20th century
Artist: Fagbite Asamu or his son, Falola Edun
Wood, polychrome, H. 18.8 cm
Gift of Russell L. Wade, Washington, D.C.
BMA 1999.748 (purchased from Jeffrey Hamer, New York)

Bascom does not cite any use for the tapper other than in the opening moments of the divination when it is used to "open" the tray. Roache (1974:24) recalls that she has seen the priest use the tapper to make symbols in the powder on the tray. In a further use, "at the beginning of a divination session, and at other moments in the rhythmic movement of the ritual, a priest of Ifa will gently tap the point of this tapper against the edge of his divining board" (Fagg, et al., 1982:190).

The mention of the "rhythmic movement of the ritual" raises the question of whether there are prescribed movements to the process. The manipulation of the palm nuts is the only part which seems to have a specific pace associated with it. This rhythm comes more from the individual's handling than from a predetermined, measured beat. While Ifa divination is a serious undertaking, is not rigid in its procedure, and the diviner may exercise a great deal of leeway, and some levity (M. Drewal 1992:57).

The tapper and its sound are a visual and audible communication with the spirit world. "The sound punctuates prayers and invocations affirming *asé, asé* (power)—'so be it'" (C. Odugbesan, in H. Drewal 1977:15). The divination tray is provided with a hollow area carved into the underside, creating a sound chamber. When the tapper is struck against the top surface of the tray, the tray acts as a wooden gong, and the sound reverberates in order to "communicate between this world and the next" as one diviner explained to Henry Drewal (personal communication, 2003; see H. Drewal 1992:192–3). Some tappers have a clapper in the large open end by which they make the sound of the bell, rendering the audio-invocation to the spirits even richer. In response to this greeting, the spirit Orummila, reveals future events in the life of the diviner's client and prescribes ritual activities that will insure well-being, transmitted through oral narrative by the priest, drawn from a monumental body of memorized, handed-down text.

F. J. L.

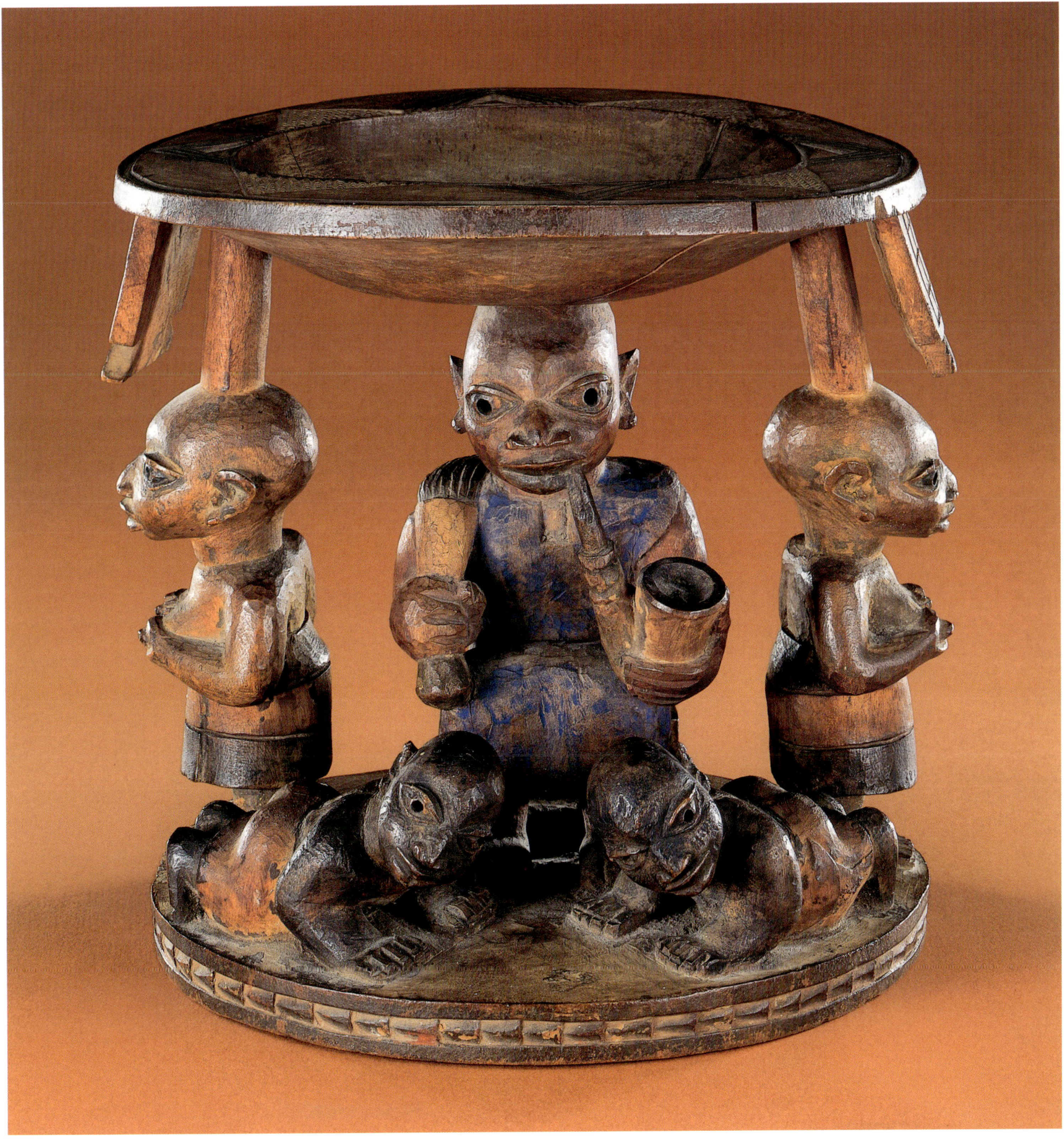

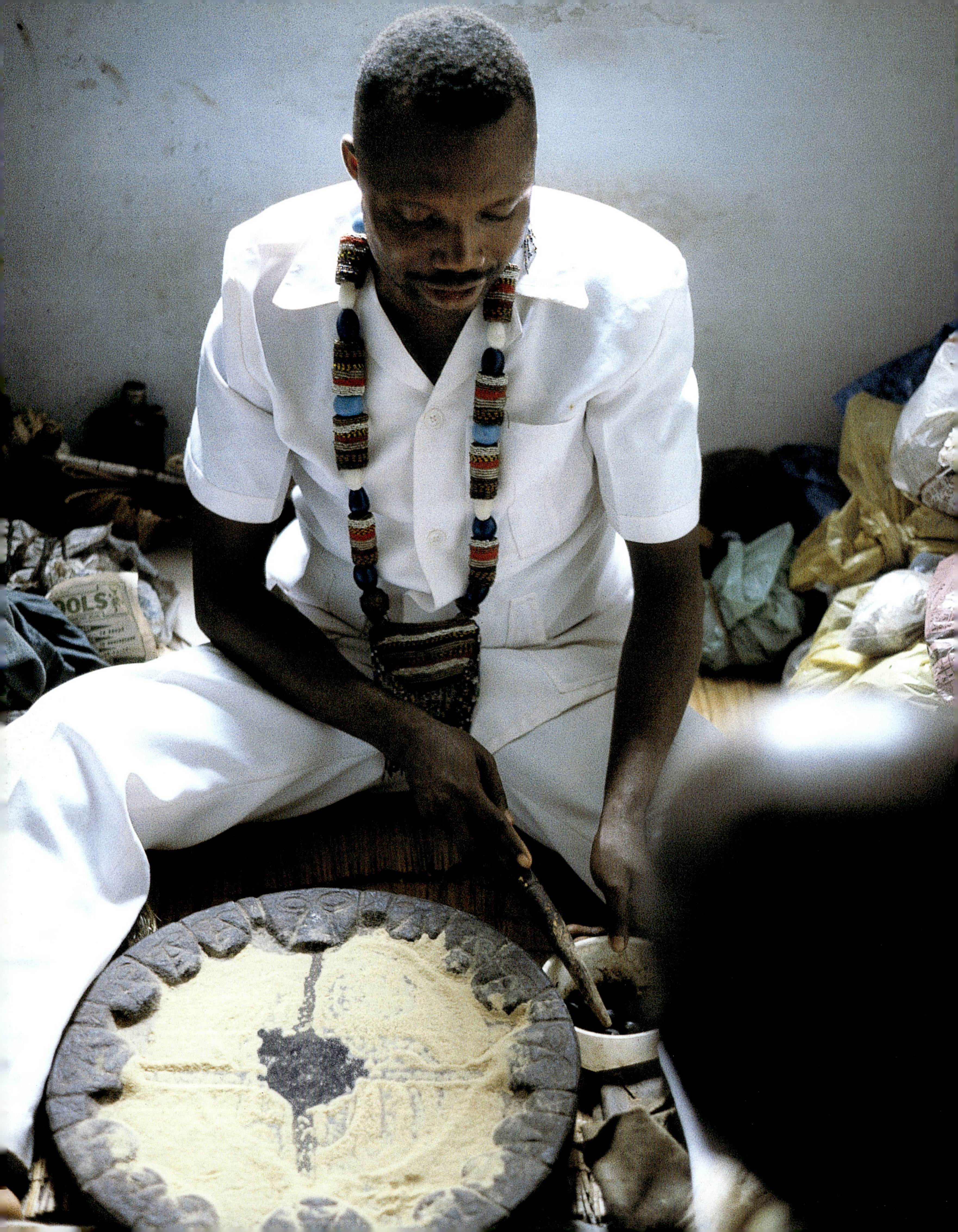

Babalawo Kolawole Ositola performing the rite of divination.
He touches sacred palm nuts (*ikin Ifa*) with the tapper while chanting a prayer to Orunmila, the deity (*orisa*) of divination. Yoruba, Nigeria
Photo: John Pemberton, 1982

Ifa Divination Tapper (*Iro Ifa*)
Yoruba, Nigeria
c. Early 20th century
Ivory, H. 30.5 cm
Gift of Alan Wurtzburger
BMA 1954.145.39

24

Tasting the Sweetness of My Songs: a Sukuma Figure (*Mabinda*)

Female Figure (*Mabinda*)
Sukuma, Tanzania
c. Early 20th century
Wood, H. 23 cm
Gift of Nancy and Robert H. Nooter, Washington, D.C.
BMA 1994.266

The Sukuma ethnic group, occupying the southern shores of Lake Victoria-Nyanza, together with their Nyamwezi relatives further south, constitute nearly six million people. Lovely carved figures such as this come to life in the context of *m'biná,* intense competitive performance events which include song duels and dance contests. Late afternoon and evening post-harvest village competitions are the primary forum of public music performance and popular entertainment. During the German colonial era in Tanganyika (1884–1914), a fierce competitive relationship between two shamanistic healing societies developed and eventually coalesced all existing Sukuma performance groups under two respective organizations, known as the Bagíika and the Bagáalu. Today, all competing farmer-musicians proudly align themselves with one side or the other of the Bagíika-Bagáalu complex, and draw their ritual, medicinal, and esoteric musical knowledge from these groups.

Sukuma dance competitions are extraordinarily complex and multivalent performance events (a comparison to a "three ring" circus would not be too far off). Though competitive dancing and narrative song duels are the main attraction, wooden puppets and figurines, known as *mabinda,* or "wonders", are a part of the arsenal of techniques, dances, songs, tricks, and the feats of acrobats (*bang'wisha*) that farmer-composers and dance leaders employ in order to draw spectators to their side of the dance arena. The BMA figure portrays a nude woman, very likely one half of a sculpted male-female pair, which in a competition would be made to pose in a variety of suggestive poses to the delight (or disgust) of the audience. Sculptures figure prominently in discussions about performance in general, and the appreciation of carved objects demonstrates the Sukuma's complex integrated tapestry of performance aesthetics. Composing a song, for instance, is compared metaphorically to carving a hoe handle, or carving a puppet, not an endeavor done in haste.

Besides the manipulation of wood figures, a list of the mabinda dance attractions that a spectator might see at any given performance could include choreographed hoe twirling, mid-air somersaults and hand walking, gender role reversal and cross dressing, feats of strength and endurance such as men pounding hoes or pestles onto the chest of another, performers being buried alive, walking on glowing embers or swallowing flames, and pretending to cook and eat bats or lizards. Mabinda attractions also include the use of "medicines," known as *bugótá,* which are used to attack dance opponents, or to draw a crowd. Bugótá are carried in antelope or wildebeast horns (*mbogoshi*). The user can bathe in its smoke, apply it on the body as if it were perfume, rub it into incisions on the body, or bury it (*kujika*) in an area on the dance arena which many people will pass.

However, all of the activities involving mabinda are really just a sideshow to the main attraction, the sung poetic discourse, with a chorus response called *wigáashe,* sung by initiates to Bagíika-Bagáalu. Wigáashe, or "sitting competitions," have for the past eighty years been the dance genre of choice at Bagíika-Bagáalu competitions, and are considered the most respected and revered of all Sukuma musical art forms. Wigáashe composers, known as *baliingi,* are full of hyperbolic self-praise concerning their authenticity and possession of the right medicine coming from the hands of the right master initiator. In sung narratives that can go on for hours, wigáashe singers expound upon personal exploits while degrading a singing opponent. Though for the most part composed, wigáashe songs have an expected element of improvisation, and composers are famous for their ability to extemporize "off the cuff." Singers insult their opponent's eating habits, drunkenness, lack of sexual vigor, or incompetence in medicinal ability, while bragging about their own compositional and singing skills, birth lineage, witchcraft knowledge, farming ability, and undefeated competitive record (real or imagined). Following is a text that illustrates further the self-praise and slander found in wigáashe songs:

> *Bulingi bo Ng'wana Majungati—, / Bo malile amaisha lulu! / Boshila akagelela lyimbo limo huna sele yi. / Huna sele kete, / Wilolela nantundagi, / Wabilemba, gugelela mng'holo yii / Olunaliponeja lwane, / Ng'wana Kiboja Ngulu, / Likarukaga ng'wigulwa lyubadanha / Hibega yii, / Nalyo, lilinamagulu, / Likasimizelaga muban'hu yii, / Lituja mugatani yii, / Kenabazungu bakabizagugema / Kubuchabucha milomo yii, / lulu bimbe yii,. / KiSukuma lulu jabayanja yii, / Bakalila kukimala nakubyulabyula yii, / Nulu ngi yugwila munomo yii, / Banonelagwa mimbo yii. / Babishindika kumigongo yii, / lulu bandole, / Bagugaiwa nimba gone, / Bakalila gukimala nakubyulabyula, / Yaniyo milimo ya Ngika, / Ng'wana Weja hii, / Wabisila shilaka mchuma, / Mamyuyi nagahahilaga, / Nung'ula najile, / Ooh, Ngwana Kanundo.*
>
> The compositional abilities of "Son of Majungati"—They are finished! / His songs have no meaning. / Empty, without meaning, / You can no longer handle your own dreams, Like the child who can't control his own urine. / Myself, if I throw out my songs, / Son of Kiboja Ngulu, / They reach so high, / Carried on shoulders. / My songs have legs, / They move about, from person to person, / You won't find them left in the trash heap. / Even the visiting Europeans make attempts, / They try and open their mouths, / So they can sing it, / Though the KiSukuma language defeats them, / They are astonished, they just bat their eyes. / Even the flies that land on my lips, / Have tasted the sweetness of my songs. (repeat) / People push themselves forward, back to back, / Just to come and look at me, / To come look at my body, / They are astonished, they just bat their eyes, / This is the work of an *Ngika,* / Son of Weja, / Made of iron, / I breathe hot air on them, / And then they just go, / Yes, the one they call "Son of Kanundo."
>
> "*Bonunu bo Mimbo ga KiSukuma,*" performed by the composer Hoja Ng'wana Butemi. / Recorded by Frank Gunderson on 9-07-1994, in Miswaki village. / Translated by Frank Gunderson and Elias Songoyi.

Sukuma wigáashe songs are testimonials laden with local and historical socio-political context, and contain the same sort of informational content as a letter to the editor to a daily local newspaper. They are also full of obscure innuendos or multivalent references whose exact meanings are known to only a few, giving them a powerful and abstract charm. Wigáashe song imagery consists of taming the wild, taming an audience, and taming that which is potentially controllable, such as clearing the bush or planting seeds, all images consistent with the culture of territorial expansion that the Sukuma have been doing for centuries. Though technically a non-labor music genre, nearly all wigáashe narratives will also have reference to farmers or farm labor, either in the form of praise, or in the form of complaint about lazy people (directed of course at the opponent). It is common to weave epithets such as *Natalalaga niganika ilima* ("I never sleep I dream of farming"), or *Tudimagi igembe chii'za* ("Let us grab the hoe properly") into the wigáashe narratives. Other common tropic images found in *wigáashe* relate to fire, such as *Jipembele makwii* ("I shall burn the big fire") or *Nasen'ha ng'wii* ("I gather firewood"), both referring to burning medicines, burning the opponent, or carrying on the tradition of the ancestors by keeping the hearth warm at night.

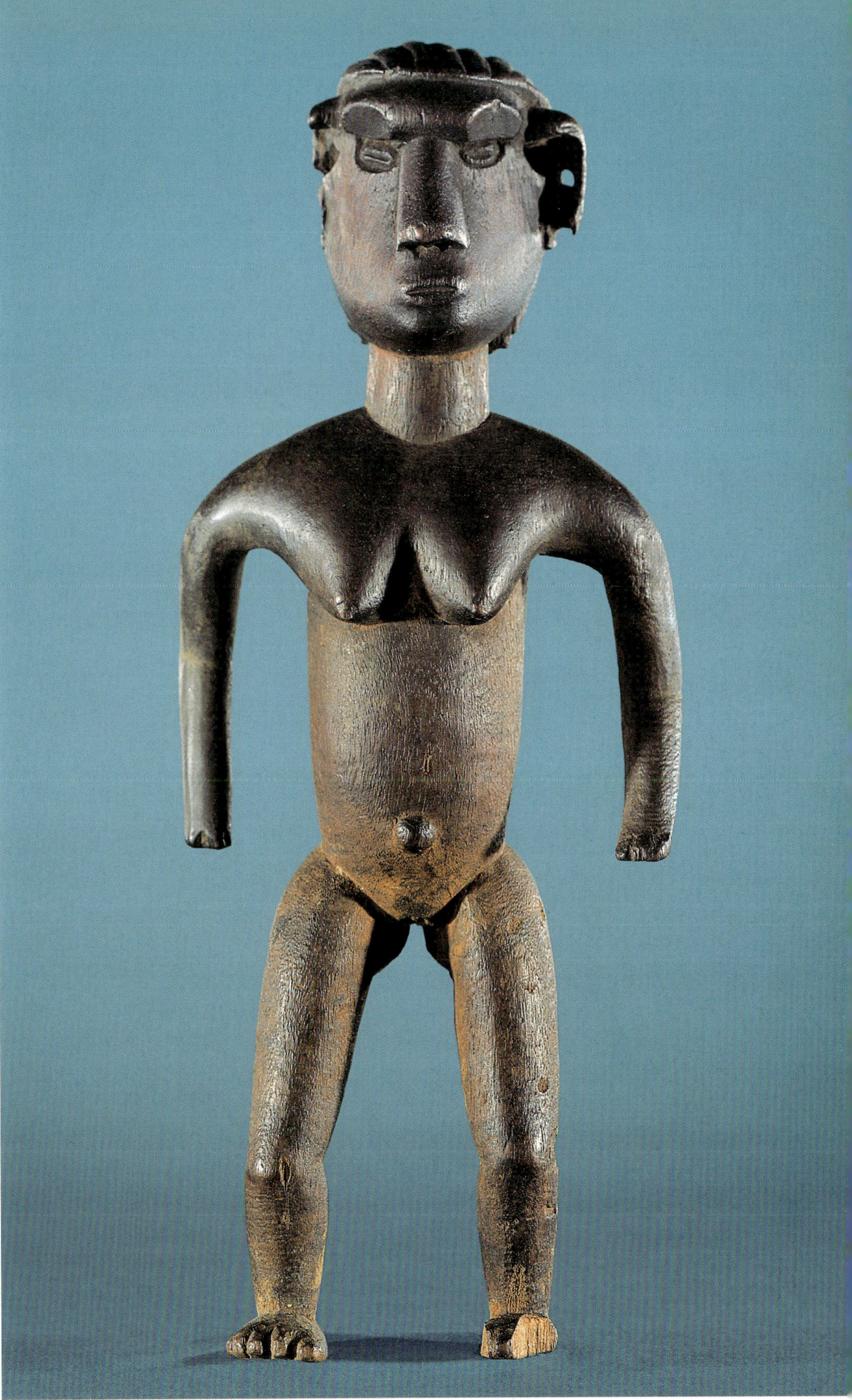

Village dance competitions between composers affiliated with the Bagíika and Bagáalu are judged in a haphazardly democratic fashion. Competing dance teams align themselves on opposing ends of a large unused open space (*lubuung'a*) or soccer field. Spectators congregate between the two competing groups, while judges *(balamuuji)* align themselves off-field near the space's halfway point. Winning dance teams are normally assessed by head count: the dance teams, musicians, and singers that attract the larger number of spectators during the allotted performance time are declared the winners. Specific procedures of adjudication vary from area to area, and performance to performance. Judges at competitions are respected members in the community, usually relatively well-off, and usually card-carrying members of the government. Judges act as neutral clock keepers and officiators, raising and lowering flags to start and stop the performances, and get council from respected elders picked from the ranks of both the Bagíika and the Bagáalu, who watch their respective sides.

The Sukuma believe that musical skill and knowledge are best transmitted in competitive environments. A farmer-composer becomes known through competition, and will only be successful if his/her performative abilities can draw listeners in competition. The cultural realm of competitive musical performance is a domain where identities are created, transmitted and negotiated, and where ground rules concerning power, status, honor, glory, and what it means to be Sukuma are most cogently expressed.

Frank Gunderson

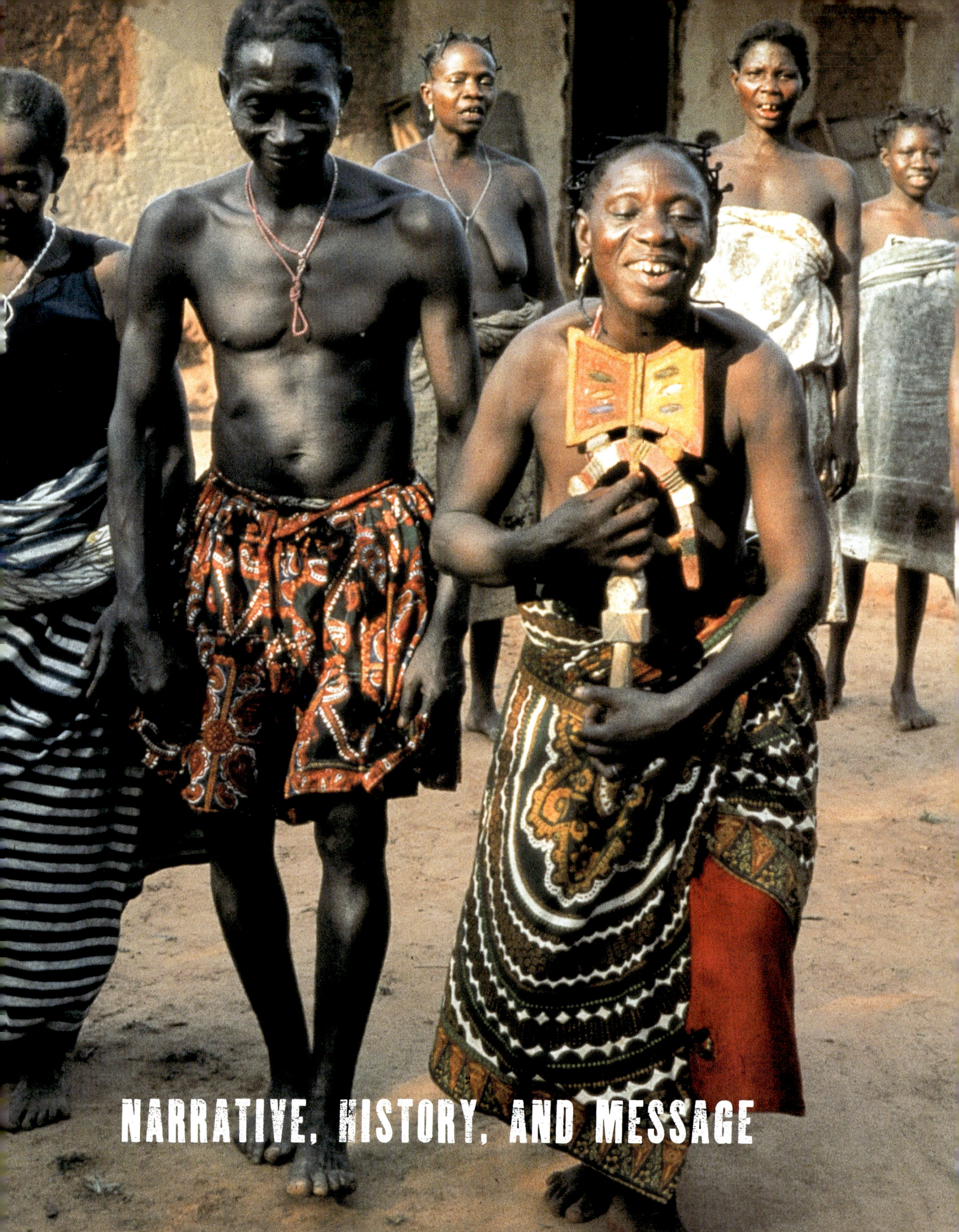

NARRATIVE, HISTORY, AND MESSAGE

A text, usually presented orally, is often an important aspect of African performance art and a prerequisite to fully understanding the work, much as a synopsis is used to follow an opera. It is generally not distributed to an audience, but simply understood. The narrative unfolds as the performance continues. This may be an account of a particular spirit or the interaction of an ancestor with earthly protagonists, for example. With an understanding of this narrative, the action takes on a comprehensible structure.

The oral, textual component of Ifa divination, examined in the last section, is central to the ritual. 256 categories (*odu*), or figures, correspond with 600 verses (*ese*) to produce 153,600 individual texts as approaches to dilemmas posed by clients of the priest. Although the texts have now been transcribed and published (Bascom 1969), for generations they were committed to memory by the priests, and recalled at each session. This is an example of very specific, codified, ritual text.

Some objects embody literal narrative in their form. Many ancient Egyptian works include inscriptions on the representative forms themselves or attached to them (p. 180, 181), introducing prayers and praise related to the image. More recent African sculpture frequently includes painted and incised symbols and script (p. 141), often esoteric. African relief carving such as shutters, architectural elements, icons, and ivory pictorial work, as well as appliquéd textiles (pp. 82, 83), is often in the form of narrative, sometimes expressing concepts, sometimes telling a story. Beadwork frequently embodies a message through its use of color and design (pp. 129, 210, 212), and, among the Ndebele (p. 48), uses script as pure design.

Other narrative text is more in the form of a backdrop to the performance, often told and retold in varying ways, containing sequence and history as the foundation for religious belief. The dance of the Ciwara (p. 169) of the Bamana of Mali is an example. Though there is no story line inherent in the movements of the two male and female dancers known as Ciwara (The Farming Beast), the Bamana savant understands the segments of religious history handed down from generation to generation that have resulted in the formation of the dance as it has been seen in this century. The form of each wooden headdress incorporates, in some regions, the head of an antelope and the body of an aardvark. The dancers who wear the headdresses are thought today to represent an "excellent farmer," that is, one who farms with an animal passion.

But the elders of the Bamana, in viewing the dance of the Ciwara, recall Bamana religious history of the supernatural being, half animal, half man, the offspring of a snake and the first being created by God, a woman known as Mousso Koroni (Old Woman). The young Ciwara learned as an infant to use his claws and a wooden stick of a particular tree which his mother had given him to cultivate the land. Not only did he become an excellent farmer, but mystically he was able to transform weeds into corn and millet. This excellent farming beast then taught his proficiency to human beings, and in this way, the Bamana learned the techniques of cultivating land and were motivated to aspire to excellence on the level of the "farming beast." Eventually, over a long period of time, human beings continued their farming but forgot about the aid the Ciwara had given them. In time, agriculture became less productive. Ciwara was disgusted by what he saw and buried himself in the ground. When the people began to see what they had done, they were sorry and they created the Ciwara headdresses to capture his attributes and to remind themselves of the gift he had given. Henceforth, the dance, following the form of the headdresses, represents the movements of the aardvark, who burrows into the soil just as a man with the hoe does, and the antelope, who demonstrates great strength and agility. The story varies from region to region among the Bamana, and there are few who know it today. Without the narrative, the dance event is little more than entertaining mime through the charging and pawing movements of the two dancers carrying male and female headdresses, surrounded by the admiring crowd from the village. The single sculpture of Ciwara as it appears in the museum gallery is a wonderful thing to see in itself, but it is stripped not only of its ornamentation and decorative attachments, its costume of fiber and cloth, its male or female pair, its drummers, its dancers, its elegant and forceful movements, but also of the narrative that gives it ethnohistorical depth and vitality, placing it within long-shared common meanings.

A Shangó possession priestess dancing with her Ose. The audience would be familiar with the sign of the double-axe representing the god of thunder and lightning, and with the extensive oral narrative of his disastrous fall as the fourth king of the ancient city of Oyo-Ile (See p. 155). Yoruba, Ohori subgroup, Nigeria
Photo: Henry John Drewal, 1975. Courtesy of the Henry John and Margaret Thompson Drewal Collection, Eliot Elisofon Photographic Archive, National Museum of African Art, Smithsonian Institution

In other cases, narrative expressly forms a dimension of the performance. Among the Temne of Sierra Leone, the guiding spirit of the initiation of young men is called Ka-Tomla, "The Guardian" (Lamp 1978). Ka-Tomla wears a costume covering his head and entire body made generally of raffia fibers. He is a completely unpredictable character, violent and angry at one moment, silly at another. When the young men enter the town during the period of their initiation, during which they are required to remain "invisible," it is Ka-Tomla who distracts the villagers through his vigorous dance. During the initiation, he guides the boys in training through role play. Taunting the boys, he asks them to come to his aid, but the boys, learning good judgment, remain wary of his tricks and taunt him in return. Ka-Tomla takes the role of a timid hunter who, once he manages to kill an animal, loudly boasts of his prowess. The boys revile him: "You were afraid to kill it all along, but when you finally killed it, then you boast." Ka-Tomla, in order to demonstrate proper masculine behavior, assumes negative roles as well as positive, the goal of which is to instill discretion in the behavior of the initiates. Throughout his performance, there is an ongoing dialogue between the spirit and the boys which helps them to negotiate their way through the various contingencies that they will encounter in life. The entire performance is immensely important to the Temne, as both art and didactic. It is the narrative component of the art form that defines the role of Ka-Tomla.

Narrative may be handed down whole, and included in performance as a completed composition. Often, however, it is a work in progress, an act of evolution:

> Improvisation on an existing stock of images and forms is the hallmark of fictional narrative of all sorts. Such tales develop during performance.... Unlike poetry and its sisters there is no moment at which a tale is composed. Innovation is only incremental from performance to performance (Vansina 1985:12).

One must assume that the narrative element in performance must always be negotiated in collaboration with other elements such as music, movement, and the smells of the moment. In the essays that follow, the imagery of a Yoruba headdress is shown by Babatunde Lawal to refer to a history of political conflict certainly well-known to the carver who produced it. A carved door of the Nupe is seen to bear a message of power in its iconography that would be understood in the area of origin. Akan goldweights and a Kuba cup are both shown to refer to aphorisms and stories in a conjunction of the verbal and visual. And beaded panels worn by the Zulu are analyzed by Carol Boram-Hays as messages of courtship.

25

The World Is Fragile.... Life Should Not Be Lived with Force: a Yoruba Headdress (*Igi Gèlèdé Oníjàkadì*)

Headdress With Wrestlers (*Igi Gèlèdé Oníjàkadì*)
Kétu Substyle, Yoruba, Republic of Benin, Gèlèdé ritual
Artist: probably Fagbite Asamu or his son, Falola Edun
c. Mid-20th Century
Wood, polychrome, H. 52.2 cm
Gift of Alan and Janet Wurtzburger
BMA 1954.32

The Gelede headdress is found mainly among the Kétu, Egbádò, Òhòrí, Ànàgó and Àwórì subgroups of the Yoruba. Although it performs in a variety of social and religious contexts (to mark important events in the life cycle or to enlist the aid of deities in times of crisis), the ultimate goal of the performance is to promote peace and happiness on earth. To this end, the headdress's performance directs much of its ritual and artistic activities toward the pacification of Ìyá Nlá, the Mother of All, the ambivalent goddess who wields the power of life and death over her offspring. For the same mother who sustains humanity through nature's abundance often destroys life through environmental hazards such as flood, drought, crop failure, infertility, forest fires, epidemics, and snake bites. According to popular belief, certain Yoruba women have direct links with Ìyá Nlá and so are capable of harnessing her powers for positive or negative purposes. These women are affectionately called *awon ìyá wa* (our mothers), receiving special homage at the beginning of most Gèlèdé performances in order to encourage them and all members of the female sex to let humanity benefit from their special endowments, most especially their procreative powers.

A typical Gèlèdé performance has two phases, a night concert and an afternoon dance session. During the night concert, a performer called Èfè (the poet or humorist), prays for the blessings of Ìyá Nlá (the Great Mother), the principal Yoruba deities (*òrìsà*), the ancestors, and all the powerful women of Yoruba society. Second, the masked dance entertains the general public with satirical performances, criticizing anti-social elements with a view to making them turn over a new leaf. In the afternoon sessions, colorfully attired performers entertain the public with intricate dances. The headdresses are usually danced in pairs, jingling their metal anklets to rhyme with the drum beats. The dancing performers do not sing, but rather convey their messages on their carved headdresses, and through the jingles of their metal anklets (Thompson 1974:203–207; H. Drewal and M. Drewal 1983: 145–151; Lawal 1996:151–152).

It should be stressed at the outset that a Gèlèdé headdress embodies specific messages which would be difficult to reconstruct in the absence of field data. Yet so much is known about Yoruba cosmology and Gèlèdé iconography that a fairly accurate interpretation of some of the popular motifs on the headdresses can be attempted by interrelating form, content, context, and oral tradition.

One of the most popular motifs is the wrestling pair such as the one depicted on the BMA headdress. Other variants of this theme show two animals (Roberts:1995:36) or, frequently, a bird and a snake locked in mortal combat. In some cases, the pair is shown standing beside or facing one another, rather than fighting. That Gèlèdé iconography places a special premium on twoness is reflected in the fact that the headdresseses are normally danced in identical pairs. The question then arises as to the significance of this phenomenon.

What immediately comes to mind is the emphasis on dualism in Yoruba cosmology. For example, nature is considered as a synthesis of the visible and invisible, the physical and metaphysical; every living individual is thought to have an unborn spirit partner (*enìkejì*) in heaven. The odd number is often associated with the negative or unpredictable and the even number with the positive or tranquil; thus the birth of twins (*ìbejì*) is expected to bring good luck to their parents, and so on (Idowu, 1962:173; Thompson 1974:204; Lawal 1996:260–262). Moreover, there is a strong belief that the cosmos is sustained by two opposing, even if interrelated forces. The deities (*òrìsà*) are usually associated with the forces of goodness or order, while the untamed spirits of the wild (*ajogun*) are associated with misfortune and disorder (Abimbola 1971:75). Hence the popular Yoruba saying: "*Tibi tire la dá ilé ayé*" (the world consists of benevolent and malevolent elements (Lawal 1996:22). Human society is thought to reflect a similar dialectic, thus making life a struggle for survival.

A closer examination of the wrestling motif on the BMA's Gèlèdé headdress reveals deeper layers of meaning. Although different colors distinguish the two figures (ocher and brown for the skin, and blue and red for the long pants), their special hairstyles (*òsù*) identify them as priests (*àwòrò*), royal messengers (*ìlàrí*), or twins (*ìbejì*) who seem to be engaged in a dramatized, rather than actual, combat. The motif reminds us of the ritualized mock battles or wrestling contests that take place during annual festivals in different parts of Yorubaland. Some of these contests commemorate an event that allegedly occurred shortly after creation when two Yoruba deities (*òrìsà*) and their followers fought one another. According to the myth, when the Supreme Being Olódùmarè decided to create the physical world (*ilé ayé*), he commissioned the creativity deity Obàtálá to do it, giving him a bag of sand and a sacred bird. But shortly after receiving this commission, Obàtálá got drunk and fell asleep by the roadside. Thereupon, a rival deity Odùduwà took the bag of sand and sacred bird, descended the sky by a chain and created the physical world at Ilé-Ifè, the sacred city of the Yoruba and widely regarded as the cradle of their culture. When Obàtálá woke up and discovered what had happened, he challenged Odùduwà and a fierce battle ensued. The Supreme Being subsequently intervened and resolved the issue, compensating Obàtálá with another commission—the privilege of molding the human image from clay (Idowu 1962:18–27). Some historians view the Obàtálá-Odùduwà conflict as reflecting a time in the distant past—between the 7th and 10th centuries CE—when an immigrant group led by Odùduwà invaded Ilé-Ifè and conquered the aboriginal population headed by Obàtálá. In the course of time, the followers of Odùduwà and Obàtálá reconciled and intermarried, agreeing to rotate the kingship among themselves (Adediran and Arifalo 1992:305–317; Adedeji 1972:321–329; Lawal 2001:498–499). As the story goes, after Odùduwà had firmly established his regime in Ile-Ife, his children and grandchildren spread to other parts of Yorubaland, founding new kingdoms, sometimes peacefully, and sometimes by force of arms (Smith 1988:14–27). This makes the wrestling motif a polysemic symbol in Yoruba art and ritual, hinting at both spiritual and temporal paradigms.

Since the BMA headdress is in the substyle of Kétu, a kingdom said to have been founded by Sopasan—a grandson of

Odùduwà somewhere between the eleventh and fourteenth centuries, it is plausible that the motif may also allude to two major conflicts in the history of the Kétu kingdom. The first has to do with the alleged subjugation of the aboriginal population of Òkè Òyán, where Sopasan first settled before the kingdom's capital was eventually established in present-day Kétu (Parrinder 1956:16–17; Smith 1988:56). The second conflict is about a succession dispute in Kétu sometimes in the fifteenth century. According to legends, when one of the ancient Kétu kings (identified in one account as Alaketu Akebiohu) died, his twin sons, Akan and Edun, competed for the throne. Realizing that his brother planned to kill him, Edun fled from Kétu, taking with him certain sacred royal symbols, without which his twin brother (Akan) could not be crowned as the king of Kétu. Edun sought refuge in the town of Ìlóbí to the southeast of Kétu. Shortly after, Akan and his group invaded Ìlóbí at night; but Edun frightened off the invaders with a device that they mistook for divine intervention. According to some informants, the device was in the form of costumed figures which later became known as Gèlèdé. In short, the two warring twins eventually reconciled and Edun returned from exile to become

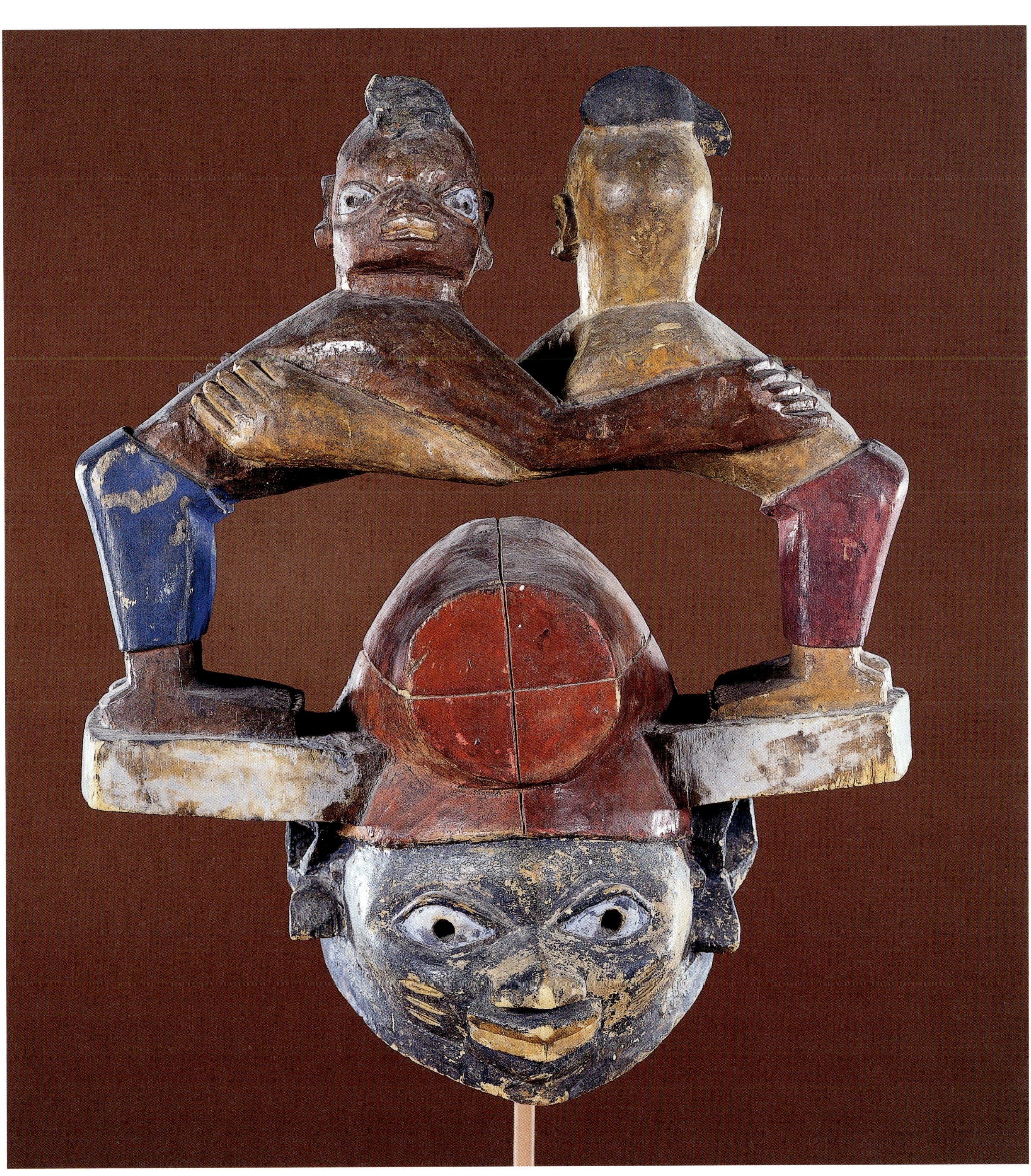

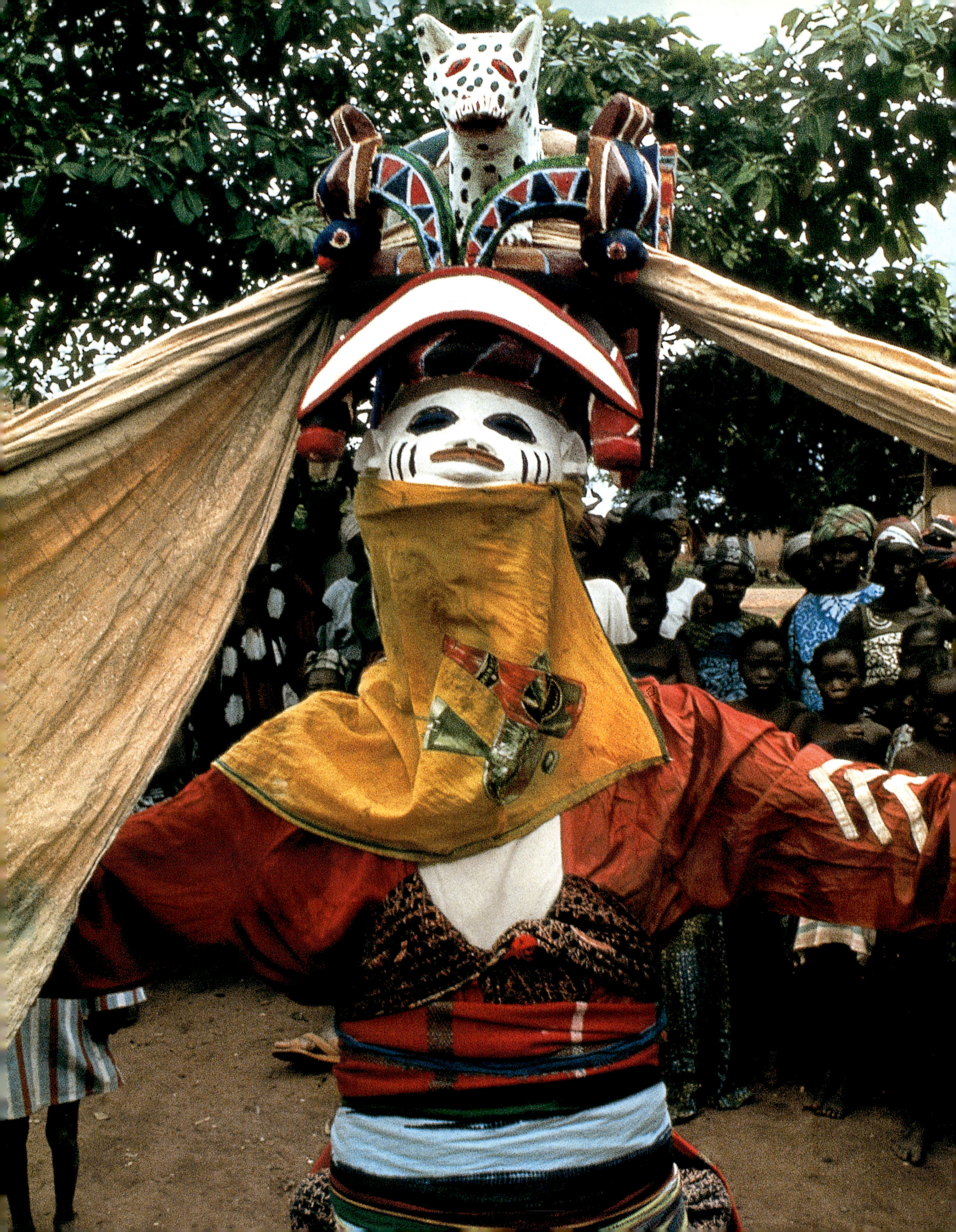

Gèlèdé dancer. Yoruba, Nigeria. Photo: Eliot Elisofon, 1971
Courtesy of the Eliot Elisofon Photographic Archive, National Museum of African Art, Smithsonian Institution

the king of Kétu (H. Drewal and M. Drewal 1983:226–231; Lawal 1996:68–70). Thereafter, the kingdom is said to have witnessed an unprecedented era of peace and prosperity until it was attacked and plundered in the eighteenth and nineteenth centuries by their neighbors, the Fon.

Some Yoruba oral traditions trace the beginnings of Gèlèdé to a ritual dance originally performed by women carrying images on their heads. According to these traditions, the men later took over the dance, wearing elaborate masks. A vestige of the original dance is evident in the "a tokun," a female guide who sometimes dances in front of a gèlèdé mask with a carved image on her head (Lawal 1996:56; fig. 3, 6). Thus, the reference to costumed figures in the nocturnal attack on Ìlóbí during the succession dispute might indicate that the Gèlèdé performance—now comprising an Efè nocturnal concert and a diurnal dance—is a synthesis of two previously separate but apparently related traditions (Lawal 1996:68–69). By the same token, could the two figures on the BMA's headdress signify this night and day aspect of Gèlèdé? Or could they represent the twin brothers who once vied for the throne of Ketu? Admittedly, twins are usually identified in Yoruba culture by their identical hairdo and dress. Could the difference in the hairstyle and the color of the body and pants of the two figures signify the disagreement between them? The human face directly below the two figures sports a headgear that is reminiscent of the wine keg surmounting a Gèlèdé headdress in the Seattle Art Museum (McClusky 2002: plate 96). However, the keg on the BMA headress is partly concealed, exposing only the rim on which a cross motif is inscribed. Denoting what the Yoruba call *oríta mérin* (a junction of four paths), this cross motif might allude to Èsù, the divine messenger of the Yoruba pantheon and the guardian of the crossroads. He is the agent provocateur who frequently makes enemies of intimate friends (including twins!), if only to create an opportunity for himself to mediate such quarrels. As the bearer of messages and sacrifices emanating from rituals, he relates opposing elements in the Yoruba cosmos, thus helping to restore order to disorder. Like the trickster phenomenon in other cultures, Èsù emblematizes what Lewis Hyde calls the "paradoxical category of sacred amorality" by which societies articulate and regulate their social life and behavior (Hyde 1998:7–10; Lawal 1974:242–243).

Thus, the confrontational pose of the pair on the BMA's Gèlèdé headdress seems to communicate much more than meets the eye. The figure on the left returns the viewer's gaze with what appears to be an uneasy calm on his face, recalling the Yoruba proverb: A hen perches on a rope; the rope feels uneasy, the hen also feels uneasy (*Adie bà l'ókùn; ara kò r'okùn; ara kò r'adìe*—Lawal 1974:248). This proverb is often quoted by Yoruba elders to plead for caution in a risky or unpredictable encounter. Why, then, should human beings (*ènìyàn*)—the wisest of Olódùmare's creations—fight one another like wild animals (*eranko*) when they can readily use their intelligence to settle disagreements in a peaceful manner? As the saying goes: Anything handled with force becomes harder; anything handled with care becomes easier (*Ohun a bá f'èsò mú kì í ni ni l'ára; ohun a bá f'agbára mú ni í le koko*—Lawal 1996:283). That this approach is critical of the Gèlèdé social agenda resonates in one of its songs (Lawal 1996:104):

Pèlé, pèlé l'alé ílé
Pèlé, pèlé, l'oorun iwo
Pèlé, pèlé, o
Ìyá Nlá, Ìya Agbo ...

Ògún 'Jàyè
Èsò l'ayé
Ìyá
Ayé kò gbè èle, o

Gently, gently descends the sun.
Gently, gently sets the night,
Gently, gently,
Great Mother, Mother of All....

Ogun 'Jaye
The world is fragile
Mother,
Life should not be lived with force

As a result, unlike other Yoruba masks (such as the Egúngún which may be employed in judicial and military actions including the execution of traitors and criminals), Gèlèdé places more emphasis on social reform through satire. And by encouraging all and sundry to relate to one another like siblings, it endeavors to create a context for both minimizing and resolving conflicts—entertaining and educating at the same time.

Performing the masked dance is expected to activate the messages embodied in the costume as well as on the carved headdress. The costume of a typical Gèlèdé consists of assorted fabrics aimed at identifying it as a male or female. Some masks may represent animals. In any event, the most sacred item on the costume are female headgears called *òjá* (baby sash) and the metal anklets (*aro*). Since Yoruba mothers normally use it to secure a child on the back, the female headgear on the Gèlèdé costume not only signifies a prayer for fertility and divine protection, but also reminds Ìyá Nlá and the powerful Yoruba women of their maternal responsibilities to humanity. The integration on the costume of headgears/baby sashes (*òjá*), contributed by individuals with different characters, is expected to metaphorically facilitate peace and social concord in the community. Although the metal anklets have aesthetic functions during the dance, their vibration is thought to ward off evil forces. As mentioned earlier, it is customary for Gèlèdé performers to dance in pairs when they synchronize their metal anklets with the music, thus evoking the virtues of collaboration and teamwork. It is this sight-and-sound harmony of costume, music, and dance that exites the audience. Some spectators may clap hands or sing along with the drummers, while others may simply allow their bodies and limbs to respond freely to the drums and the jingling of the anklets. This makes audience response part and parcel of the Gèlèdé spectacle. And as the performers move or spin to the rhythm of the drums, the wrestling figures on the headdresses suddenly cease looking like antagonists. Rather, they appear to support one another in a precarious world in which individual and corporate survival depends, for the most part, on fellowship, civility, love, and the cultivation of sociable behavior.

Babatunde Lawal

26

A Reading of a Statement of Power: Nupe Door Panels

Door Panels
Nupe, Nigeria
c. Late 19th–early 20th century
Wood, metal, Left: H. 150.5 cm; Right: H. 153 cm
Gift of Vivian L.C. Anderson, North Bethesda, Maryland
BMA 2001.417a–b
(acquired in Lagos, Nigeria, *c.* 1970)

Nupe artists, through the mid-twentieth century, carved doors with images for important families. A door (*kpako*) usually consisted of two or more panels lashed together. They were the only wooden ornamental component of traditional Nupe architecture, which was built of earth. Elaborate, carved doors were found only in the doorway to the *katamba*, the round entry hall in a Nupe compound, which consisted of many structures, especially at aristocratic and royal residences. Other doorways were screened with elaborately woven reed mats. It was primarily the *katamba* doorways of the aristocracy and the rich that were decorated with carved wooden doors to express the owner's financial means and artistic inclinations. Royal palace architecture was more severe, without plastic decoration, and the commoner's home would be completely devoid of decoration (Dmochowski 1990:3.9, 3.18).

The Nupe have been Muslim since the invasions of the Islamized Fulani in the early nineteenth century, and Nupe details are therefore conventionally abstract, and largely non-human, in keeping with Muslim preferences. On the BMA door panels there are images of Muslim slippers, weapons, two large Muslim "magic squares" (resembling Maltese crosses), two Muslim writing boards, two stools, and living creatures, among other objects. Whereas the utilitarian objects are easy to recognize, the animal figures are more stylized, and the one human figure is the most abstract of all. This reflects Muslim proscriptions against the depiction of animate creatures, especially the human.

It would be tempting to see the pattern of representations on the Nupe door as a set of hieroglyphs, similar to those found in ancient Egyptian wall texts. Yet there is no evidence that the names for things can function grammatically together as a syllabary among the Nupe. Rather, the individual images seem to function as messages in themselves. The door proclaims the agenda of the owner and the characteristics of his power, whether the motifs are chosen by him or by the carver.

In the center of both doors is a large square with a design resembling a Maltese cross. This is surely a version of the design used all across North Africa known as *khatem* ("seal") in Arabic, and across the Sahel under the Pular (Fulani) term, *hatumere.* Similar signs can be seen in Nupe house decoration. Hatumere at its most basic appears as writing designed in the form of "magic squares," in which numbers, representing letters, are used in a pattern based upon a concept of the structure of the cosmos and hierarchy of the universe. Along diagonal axes, sequential numbering may create a spiral in both directions around the center. The center square may signify Allah, or a mosque, or, in the case where it has a reflecting surface, it may represent the soul. Hatumere stands as a signifier of the power of sacred line, holy script, and sanctified space, and appears in letters, amulets, printed cloth, and a myriad of media (Prussin 1986: 74–76). On the door, it may proclaim this leader's unity with the Islamic community and especially with its more occult patterns of problem solving.

The two pairs of slippers at top right signify that he is a devout Muslim. These are shoes with only a flat sole, a leather or plastic upper front, and no heel covering, so that they can easily be removed five times a day at prayer time. Around the entrance to a mosque, one commonly sees rows of slippers and shoes belonging to worshipers inside. On this door, the slippers have been removed and placed at the entrance, as the wearer enters into the place of prayer barefooted. Another pair of shoes, shown from the soles, may refer to the same thing.

Flanking the central right hatumere, are four squares with handles, with alternating patterns of a crosshatch and an X. The two with the crosshatch designs seem to represent wooden stools, which carvers often produce, usually with a handle on either side (Stevens 1966:29–34). The two with the X designs represent wooden prayer boards used by scholars to practice writing Muslim prayers. These prayer boards suggest that the owner of this door is a learned man, who reads the Koran and can speak and write the holy script. They may also refer to the general practice of accumulating spiritual power after a writing session by drinking the ink washed off the boards. The arrangement of four squares around the central square may be designed to complete the hatumere in the standard four-by-four motif, with the fifth square in the center, symbolizing the Five Pillars of Islam and the five daily prayers (Prussin 1986:75).

Several items seem to have reference to this political leader's function in justice and displays of power. In the center of the right panel is a pistol, suggesting his prerogative to take life. On the left panel there are several weapons: two knives, a cutlass, and what is possibly a scythe. These may also have to do with his dominion over agriculture. But ornamental blades are commonly used as regalia of power from Nigeria and the Republic of Benin through Central Africa with an extraordinary repertoire of designs. The scythe, in particular, may refer to this ceremonial, processional function.

A human being, in abstract form, appears on the lower right panel. Carved, three-dimensional figures are not traditional to the Nupe, but the style of this figure closely resembles those carved by other nearby groups at this latitude in the central savanna, the Moba and LoDaaga of Togo to the West. These figures generally refer to ancestors and the ritual required to maintain their allegiance (see p. 185).

A number of animal forms appears. On the right side of the right panel is a vertical serpent, its direction unknown, as both ends are broken off. This would probably have been the hinged side of the door, as the iron latch is located on the other panel to the left. In areas to the South and East, the descending serpent has to do with spiritual power (*ashe*, among the Yoruba), as seen on the roofs of the palaces of Benin kings. The crocodile, on the left, might refer to the owner's dominion over the dark powers associated elsewhere with this water animal. Other animal forms are more obscure. On the lower left there appears to be a two-footed bird, and on the upper right a four-legged animal with a tail and long, vertical ears or horns. The meaning of these, and other unidentified forms can only be known through an understanding of the narrative shared by the Nupe.

F. J. L.

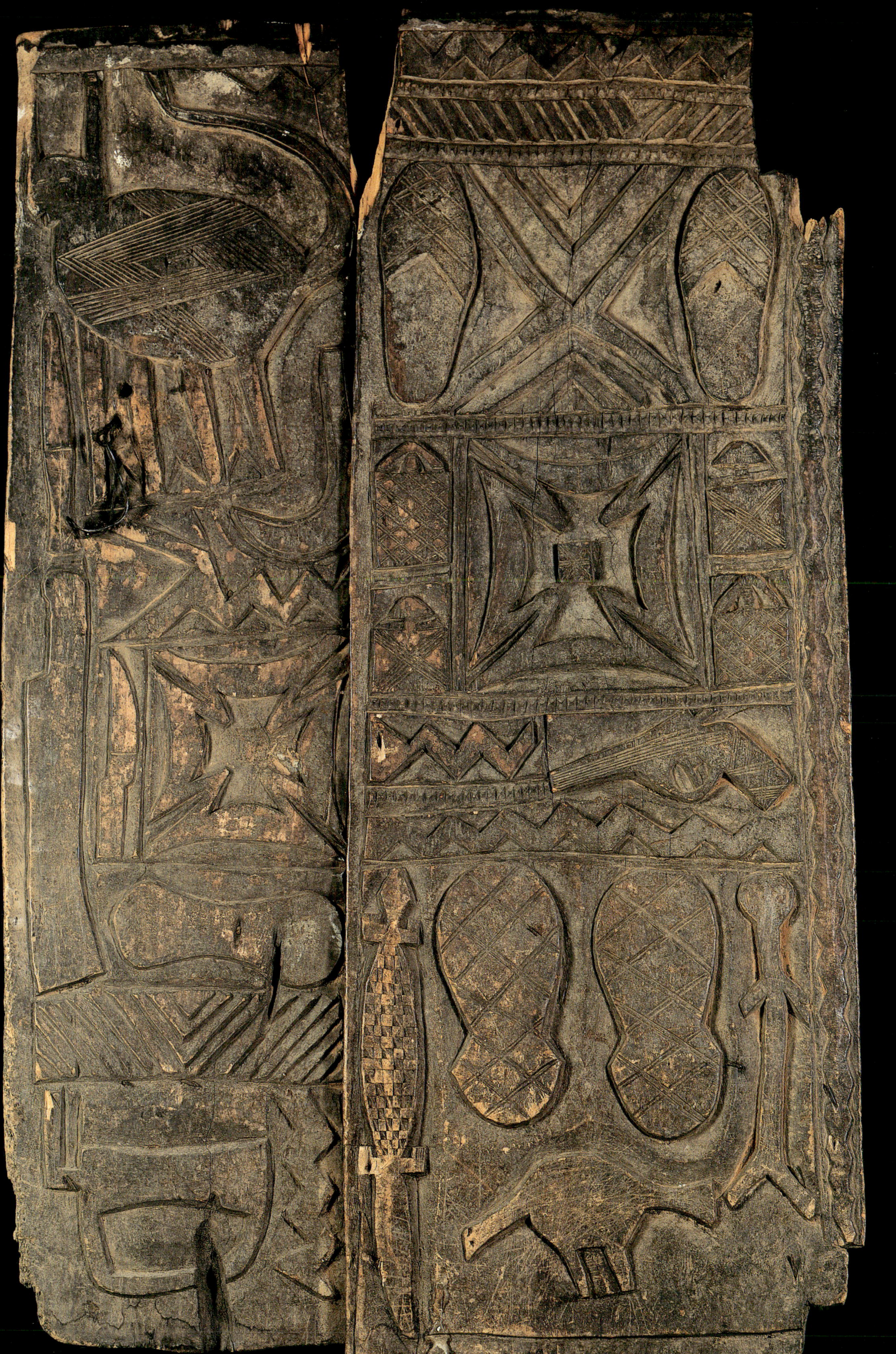

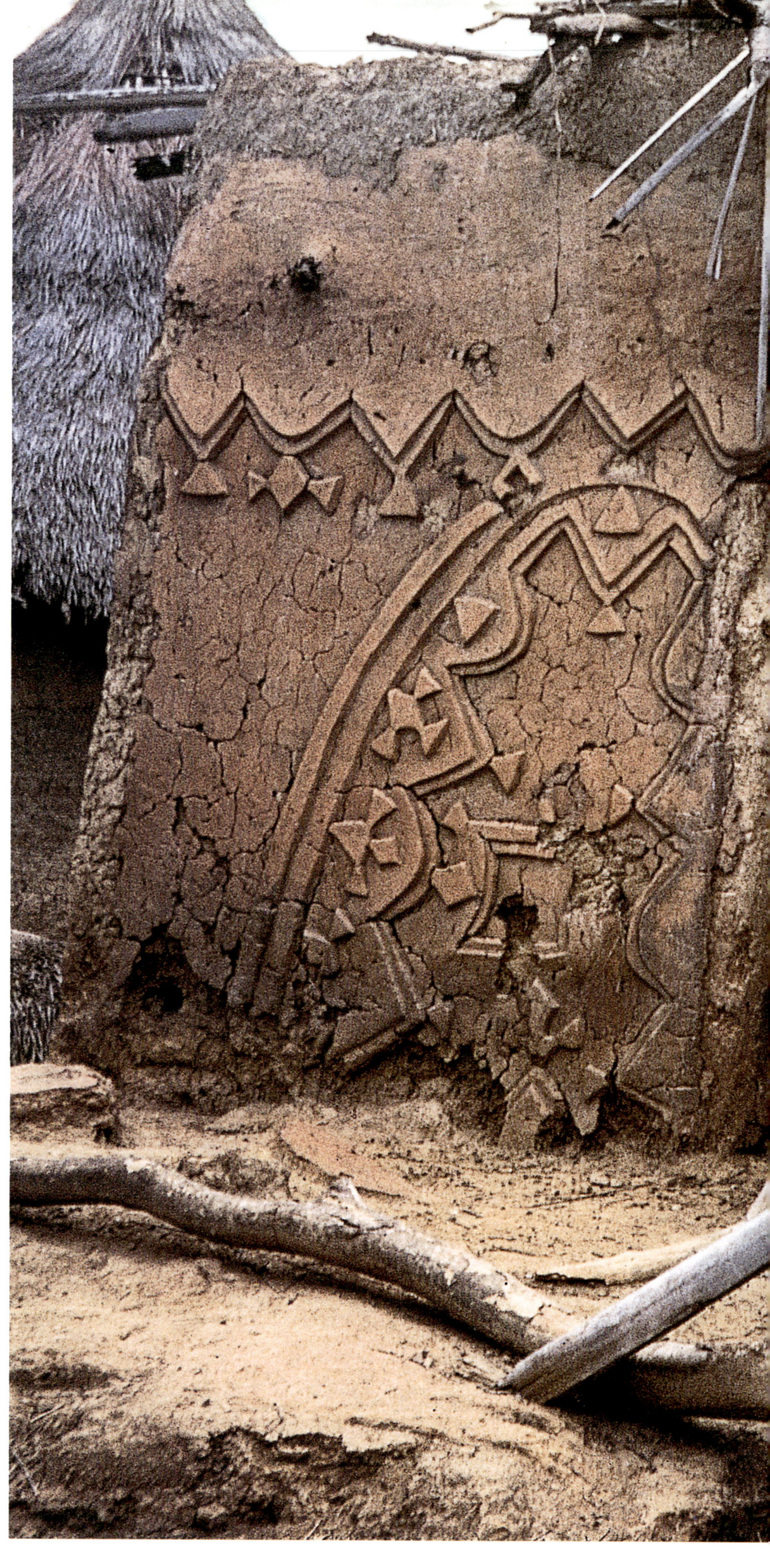

Entrance to a compound, with molded designs surrounding the doorway. Nupe, village of Tada, Nigeria
Photo: Phillips Stevens, 1965

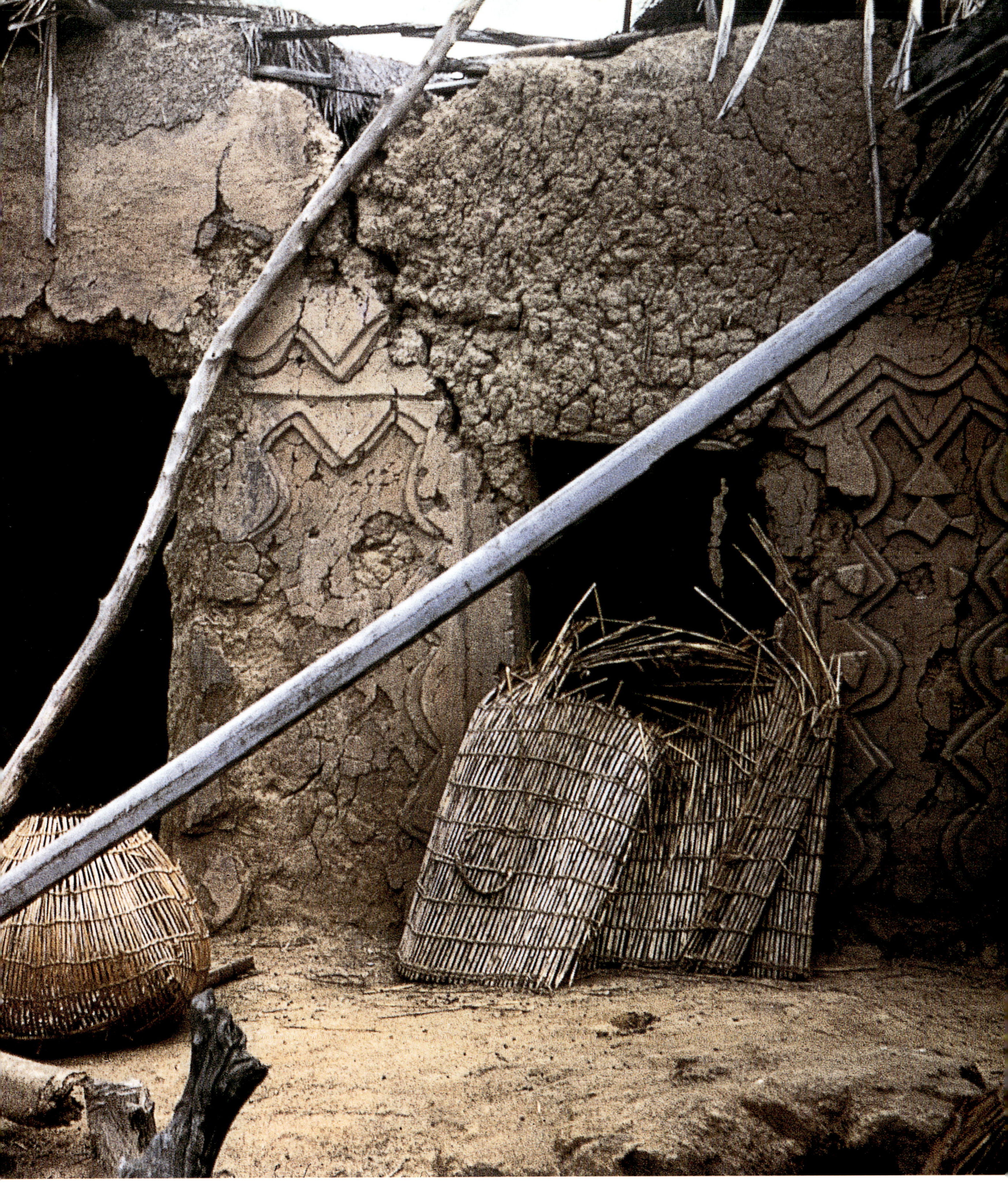

21 When It Lies behind You, Take It: Akan Goldweights (*Abrammuo*)

A chief with gold ornaments. Asante, Ghana. Photo: Eliot Elisofon, 1970 Courtesy of the Eliot Elisofon Photographic Archive, National Museum of African Art, Smithsonian Institution

Brass weights for measuring gold facilitated the accumulation of wealth and power for the Akan during the seventeenth and eighteenth centuries. At the same time that the function of the brass goldweights served to politically enhance the strength of the Akan peoples, their creation and use encouraged the reinforcement and development of cultural and social values. They were at once functional and symbolic forms of political, social, cultural, and economic power for the Akan.

Goldweights were made and used by the Asante, Baule, Fante, Akyem, Brong, Sefwi, Anyi, Nzima, and other Akan peoples primarily between the beginning of the fifteenth century and the end of the nineteenth century. A proliferation of weights and an increasing variety in their form occurred in the eighteenth and nineteenth centuries (Garrard 1980:2, 298–300; McLeod 1971:8; Cole and Ross 1977:70). When the Asante centralized their power in Kumase, they brought the best goldsmiths from subordinate Akan states to the capital (Garrard 1980:2, 298–300; McLeod 1971:8; Cole and Ross 1977:70).

The universal adoption of the gold currency amongst the Akan states resulted in a greater need for goldweights for chiefs, traders, and families. Any man who engaged in trade needed to have, or at least have access to, an assortment of goldweights (McLeod 1971:8; Garrard 1980:300). Akan men would commonly give their sons a group of goldweights when they reached adulthood (McLeod 1971:8; Garrard 1980:177; Cole and Ross 1977:76).

Conducting transactions with gold as the medium of exchange was a lengthy process (Garrard 1980:173–176). The buyer and seller of a particular commodity first agreed upon a price, the amount of gold to be exchanged. Then the buyer would weigh the appropriate quantity of gold on his own scale, using his own weights (Garrard 1980:174). The scales used to weigh gold were held over the left thumb with the palm turned upward, reducing the chance of interference from the rest of the hand (Garrard 1980:173). The seller would then use his own scales and weights to remeasure the buyer's gold. Concluding the transaction was not easy because often the buyer and seller would disagree on the measure of gold.

Thomas Edward Bowdich, a British envoy working in Kumasi early in the nineteenth century, suggested that the chief's weights were larger in mass for a given standard than weights held by other people. Bowdich may have been confused by the practice of having to pay larger fees to the chief. The chief's weights were actually supposed to be standards against which other weights could be measured (Garrard 1980:243, 174). Chiefs had their own accumulation of weights, and there was a treasurer in charge of their care. To designate that a particular collection of weights belonged to a chief, they were wrapped in a leopard skin or a piece of elephant leather from the animal's ear. The chief was not allowed to use the weights or scales, and he was not allowed to open the leather bag or chest in which the weights and scales were stored. It has been suggested that this was to protect the chief from temptation, preserving his dignity and preventing any suspicion of dishonesty. When the treasury was opened, a libation was poured, and prayers were offered to the ancestors. The treasurer would be the only person to put his hand into the treasury bag (Garrard 1980:188–192).

Goldweights were primarily used in trade, although they may have also served other purposes. Some goldweights appear to have small loops indicating they might have been worn as protective devices, charms, or amulets (Garrard 1980:201; Cole and Ross 1977:74). Sick children or other people might have worn these goldweights to bring them to good health, to bring good fortune, or to protect them from harm (Garrard 1980:201). In the Ivory Coast, a goldweight may have been included inside a brass box that contained the gold being sent as a dowry or as a payment of fines or debts (Garrard 1980:201). Goldweights were sometimes sent as messages, as a reminder of a debt or other obligation, a warning, a piece of advice, or a token of friendship (Garrard 1980:201).

The Akan language is rich with proverbs, boasts, insults, riddles, poems of praise, and folktales. Figurative weights are frequently associated with various verbal forms. The bird standing with its neck arched over its body, looking behind itself, is a common image, known as *Sankofa*. The translation of the proverb associated with Sankofa is: "When it lies behind you, take it" (Garrard 1980:205), meaning, "Use the wisdom of the past" (Garrard 1980:205). Sankofa is a common figurative weight (McLeod 1981:128).

It is not clear, however, that all figurative weights are associated with verbal phrases or that each figurative weight is associated with a single, specific proverb. Some make a clear reference to a specific phrase. Others could refer to numerous proverbs (Garrard 1980:202–210; Garrard 1979:66; Cole and Ross 1977:78; McLeod 1981:128–129). Similarly, multiple figurative weights could reflect the same idea (Appiah 1979:66). The more visually complex weights usually have only one saying, whereas more generic images, for example, animals such as the leopard, may have many references (Doran Ross, personal communication, 2002). The relationship between a goldweight and a specific proverb often reflects upon human nature and a person's position in society or the family system (Appiah 1979:66).

The ability of an Akan speaker to communicate metaphorically is evidence of the speaker's wisdom and is fundamental to earning society's respect as an elder (Appiah 1979:64). The relationship between Akan proverbs and goldweight forms may have meant that goldweights served as educational tools and mnemonic devices helping children become fluent in their proverbial language (Cole and Ross 1977:81). A very wise and proficient Akan speaker could conceal the meaning of the conversation with the use of metaphors. However, proverbs and other metaphors tend to be generational, changing over time in meaning, form, and usage. Therefore, it is difficult to know if the proverb associated with a weight by an Akan speaker at one point in time would have been the same at an earlier time. There are also variations in the use of proverbs between different Akan groups, localities, and regions (Garrard 1980:203).

Most goldweights for indigenous use were created before 1900. By the 1920s, the making of goldweights had declined, although the skill has continued until today through the work of some remarkable contemporary artists (Doran Ross, personal communication, 2002). The gold trade itself probably ended between 1895 and 1905. In 1889, the Demonetization of Gold Dust Ordinance

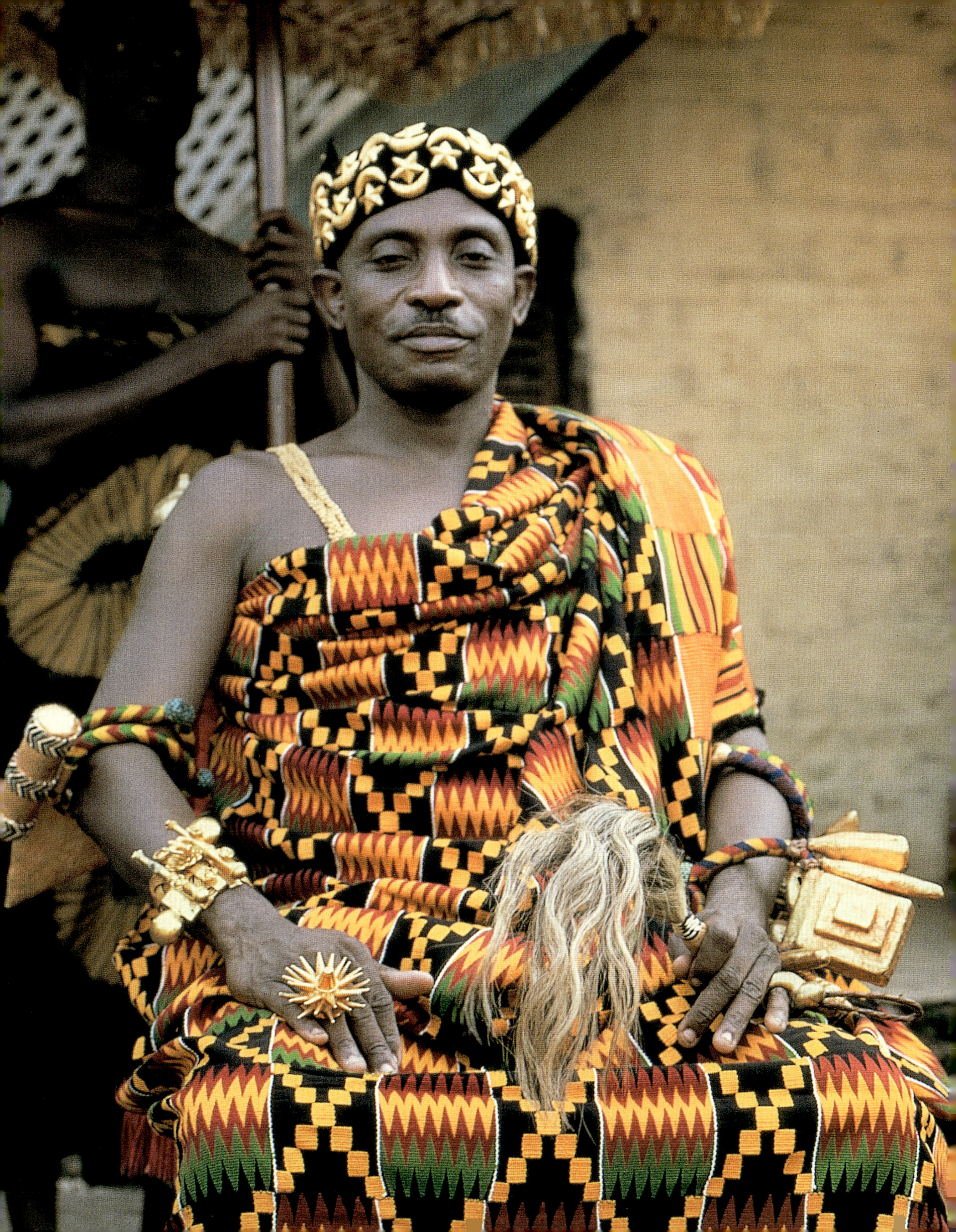

was passed in the Gold Coast, no longer allowing the use of gold dust and nuggets as currency. In 1896, the Weights and Measures Ordinance made it illegal to use Akan weights (Garrard 1980:300–304).

Throughout the early and mid-twentieth century, European and American expatriates in Ghana collected these objects, finding them easily at the markets and through personal contacts with Ghanaian owners. The Baltimore Museum of Art is the repository for 651 goldweights, as well as a broad array of brass tools and containers used in the trade. Twenty-nine of the weights were collected before 1954, purchased from American dealers, and 621 were collected in Ghanaian markets between 1968 and 1971 by the wife of the then U.S. ambassador to Ghana.

S.E.G.

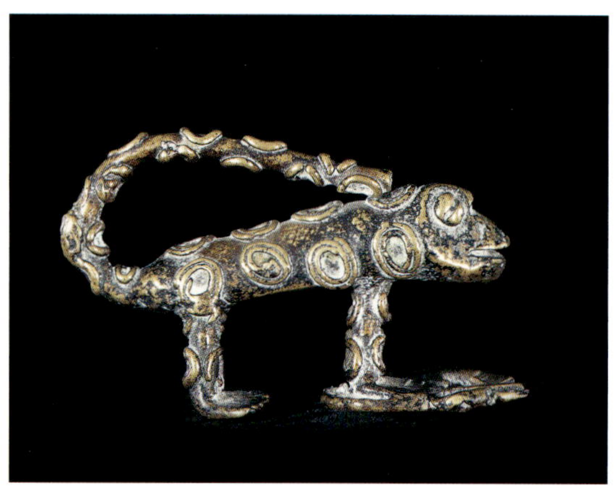

a

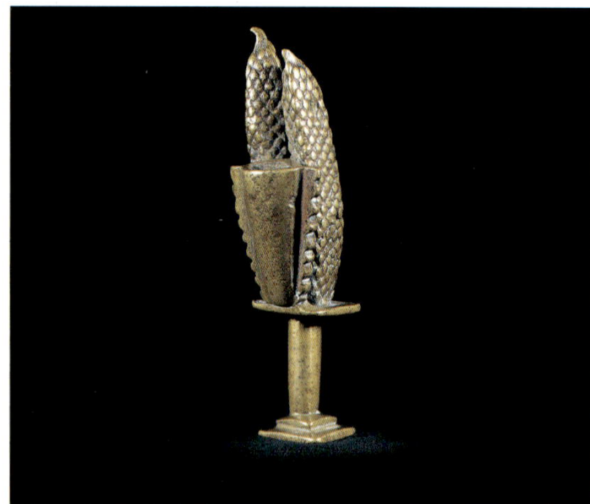

b

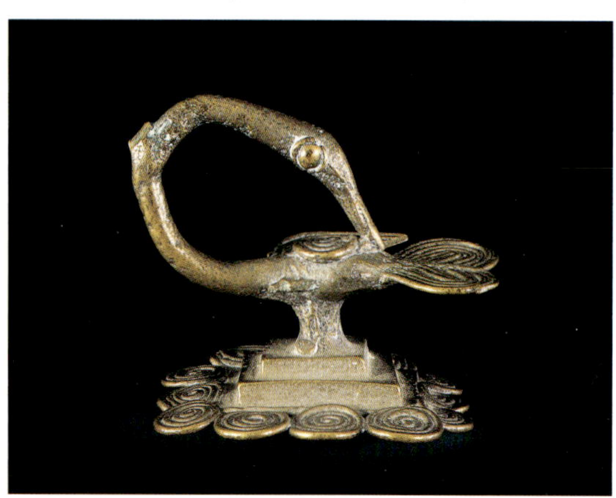

c

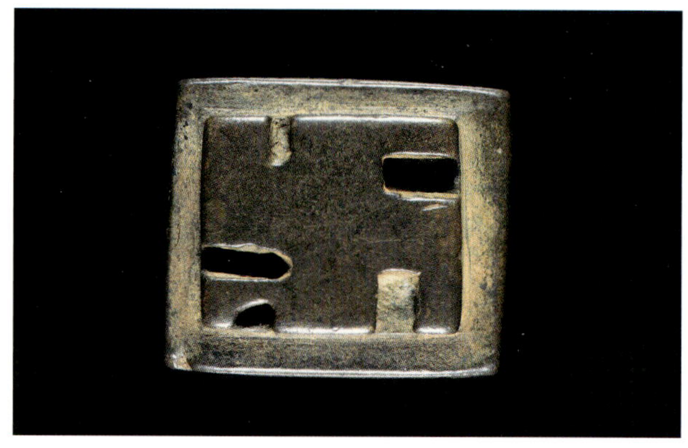

d

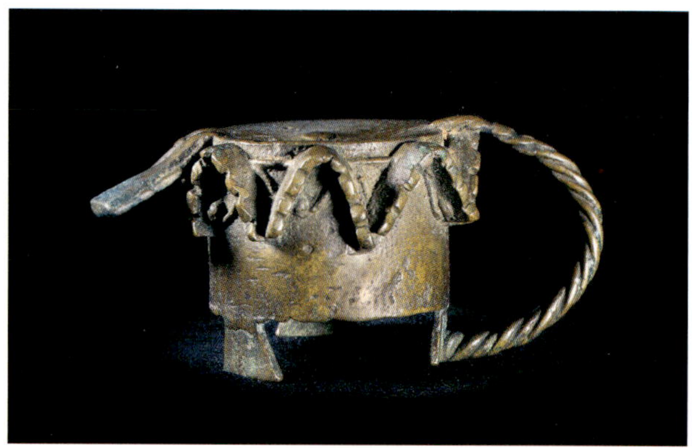

e

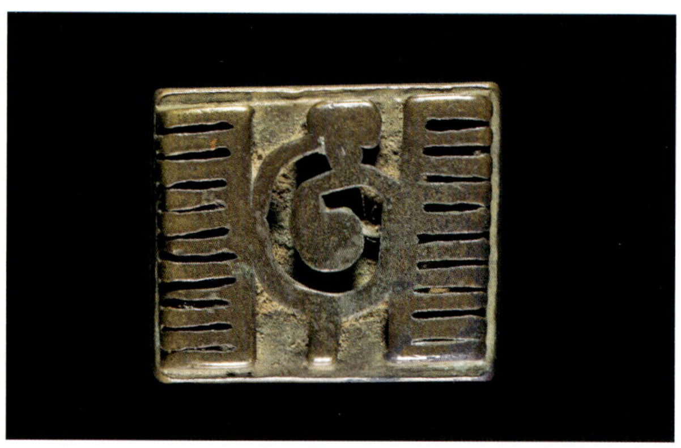

f

Gold Dust Weights (*Abrammuo*)
Akan, Ghana/Ivory Coast
c. 16th–19th century
Brass

Gift of Alan Wurtzburger
a) BMA 1954.145.31 f. (1700–1900). H. 3.2 cm
b) BMA 1954.145.31 o. (1700–1900). H. 6.9 cm
c) BMA 1954.145.31 j. (1700–1900). H. 4 cm

Gift of Helen 'Muffie' Lippincott McElhiney, Bethesda, Maryland (purchased in Ghana 1968–71)
d) BMA 1988.715. (1500–1720). H. 1 cm
e) BMA 1988.1185. (1700–1900). H. 3.5 cm
f) BMA 1988.708. (1700–1900). H. 1.2 cm
g) BMA 1988.1047. (1700–1900). H. 4.3 cm
h) BMA 1988.1131. (1700–1900). H. 3.9 cm
i) BMA 1988.1041. (1700–1900). H. 7 cm
j) BMA 1988.1087. (1700–1900). H. 1.3 cm

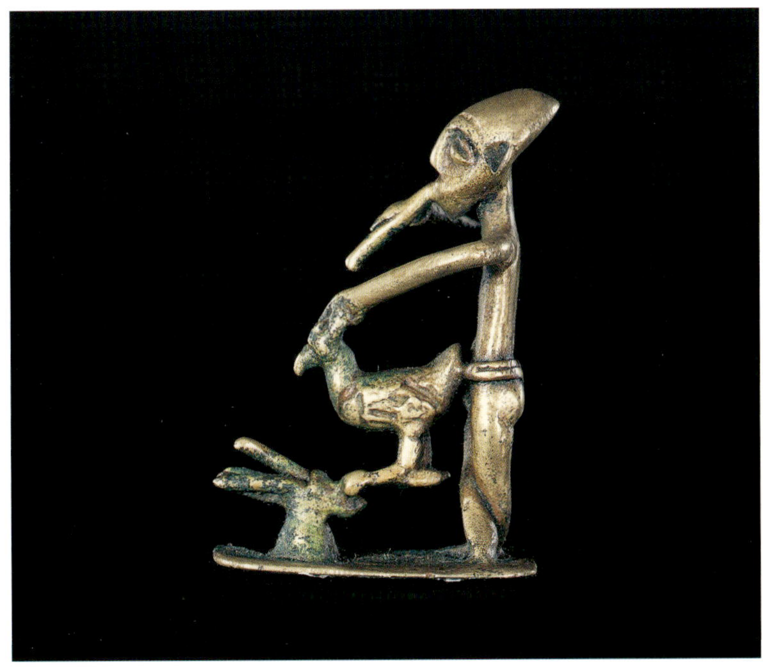
g

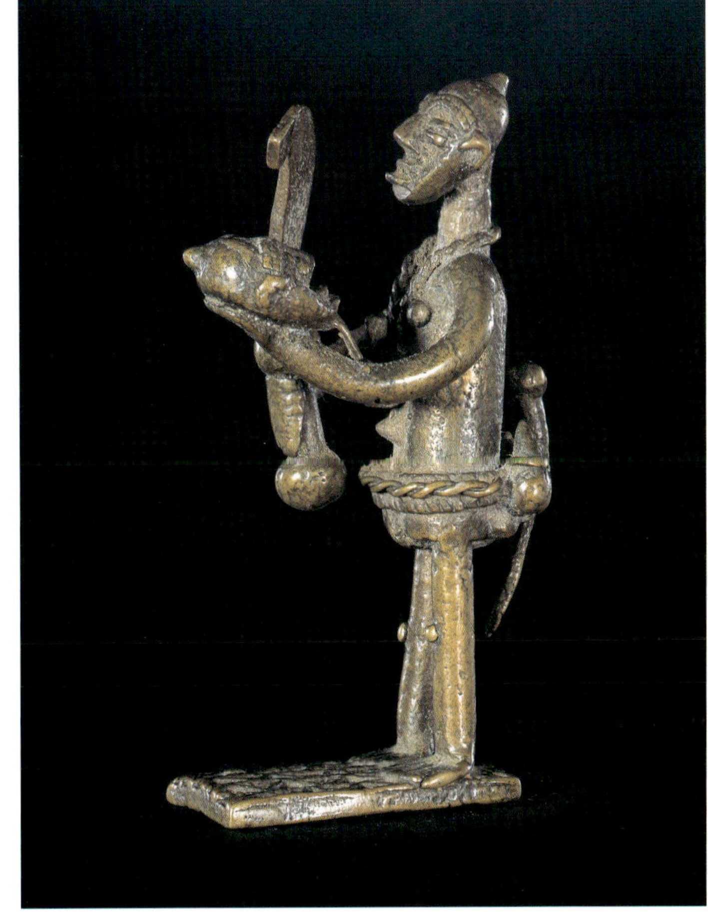
i

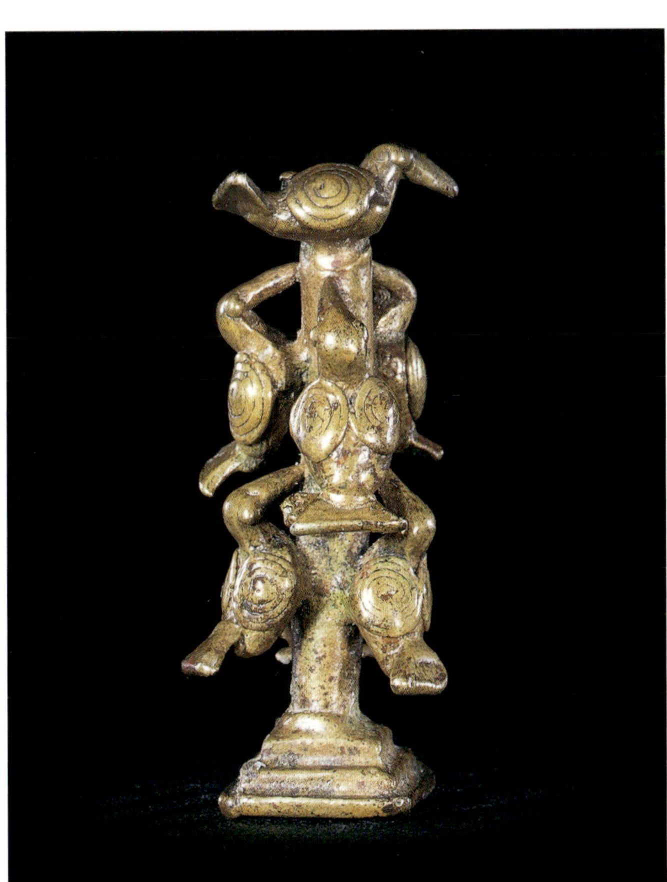
h

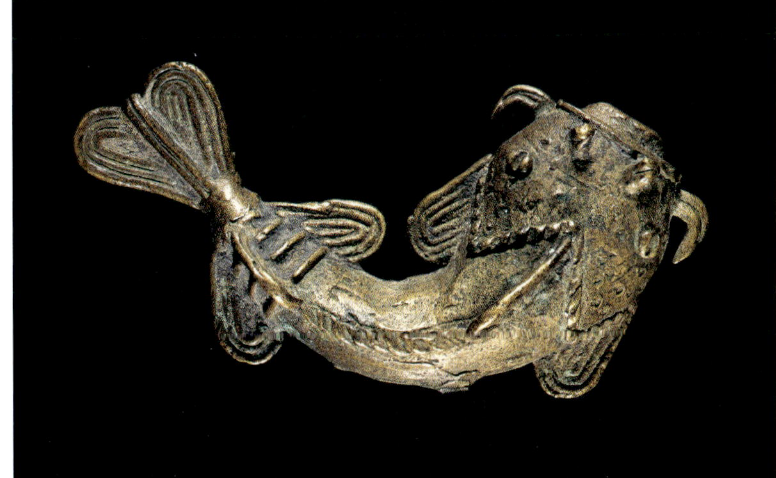
j

Man Is Like Palm Wine: a Kuba Cup

Figurative Cup
Kuba, Congo (Kinshasa)
c. 19th century
Wood, H. 18.4 cm
Gift of Alan Wurtzburger
BMA 1954.145.110

The good Kuba host or hostess provides guests with palm wine, in a time-honored ritual of hospitality. Today the cups are usually made of ordinary glass or plastic, but in the nineteenth and early twentieth centuries, they were often elaborately carved of wood, known as *mbwoong ntey*, and meant not only for drinking, but also to be appreciated as works of art in their own right. The quality of the workmanship of a cup brought recognition and honor both to the sculptor and to his patron; the cups were perceived as status symbols which spoke of the wealth, influence, and good taste of their owners. Guests drank from a communal cup which was first presented by the host to the gathered assemblage for their admiration, and then passed around (Binkley 1996:172; Cameron 1994:125; Cornet 1978:220; Koloss 1990:48; Vansina 1992:74).

Palm wine, known as *maan*, is the liquid tapped from the raffia palm tree; it has long been a popular and much appreciated drink among the Kuba. The drinking of palm wine is a social affair except for certain personages of very high rank who are prohibited from eating and drinking in public (Binkley 1996:172; Cameron 1994:125; Koloss 1990:48; Vansina 1978:183).

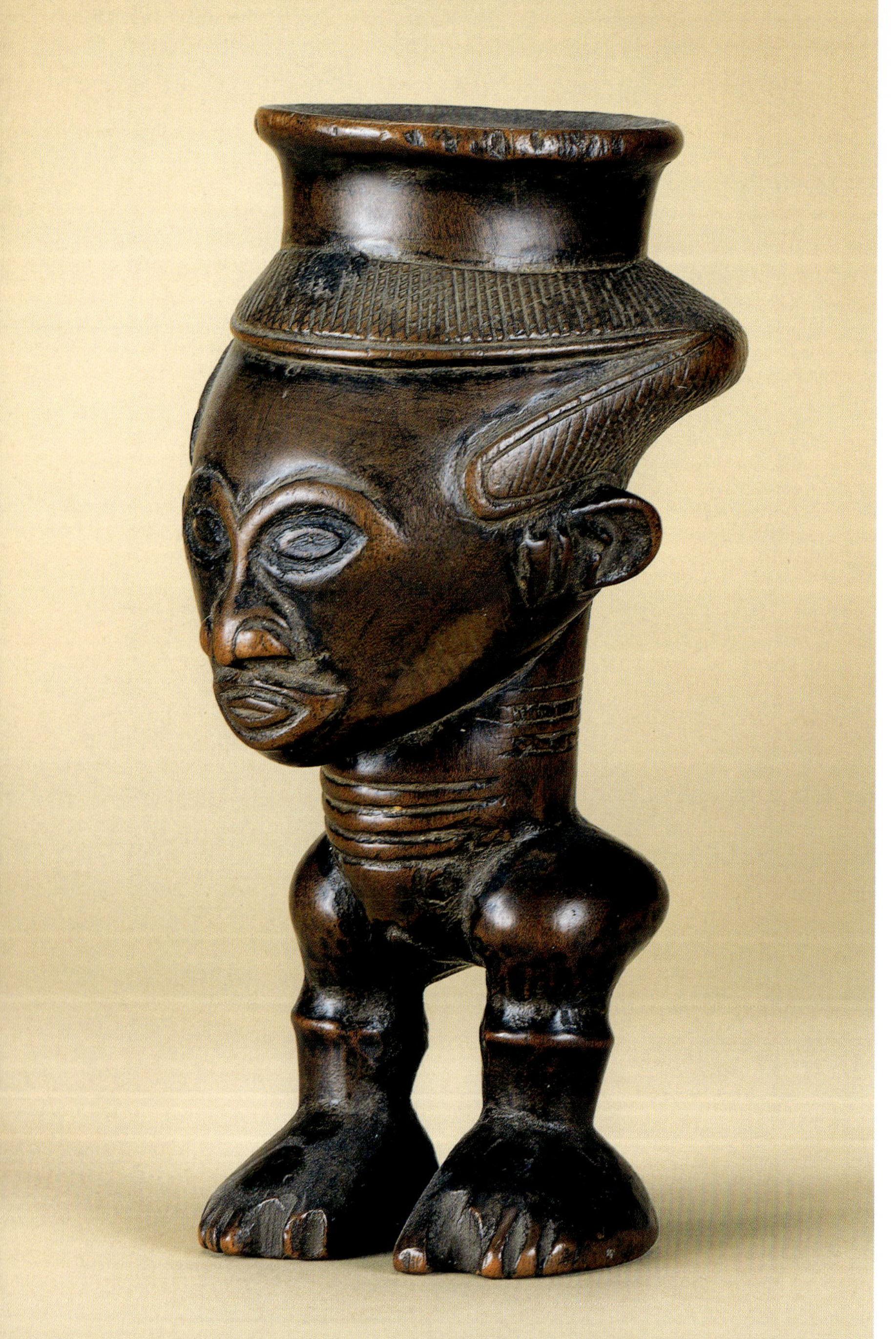

Kuba narratives contain a wealth of information about the genesis of many of their customs and practices, and they often silently and subconsciously give significance to acts which otherwise might seem mundane. In their 1910 publication, E. Torday and T. A. Joyce recorded the following narrative about the origins of the raffia palm tree:

> At the time of creation, very near to the dwelling place of the Kuba, there was a great lake which was filled with palm wine instead of water. Anytime a person was thirsty, he had but to go there and drink wine. One day, a woman whose name was Nanchamba, urinated in the lake. She was seen by a man, Boyo Bumba, who reproached her by saying: "Are you not ashamed of polluting the lake from which so many people drink? I will tell the villagers what you have done." He did this, and everyone declared that they would no longer drink wine from the lake. The next day, Boyo Bumba returned to the village and said: "See how we have been punished because of this woman; the lake is dry." And so it was. The lake had disappeared, and in its place was a gully in which four species of unknown young trees were growing. They named the trees Shamba, Mibondo, Ikari, and Diana, and paid no more attention to them, but instead continued to bemoan the loss of their lake. Years passed; the trees grew tall, creating a forest where the lake had once been. One day, a man by name of Bunyi, said to himself: "Where has the lake gone; has it not been absorbed by the trees? I am going to drill a hole, and see what the sap is like."

After several tries, always in secret, Bunyi was able to extract more and more excellent palm wine from the hole at the top of the tree. But, returning intoxicated and rowdy to the village one day, he was hauled before the king for an explanation:

> Bunyi refused to tell him the reason, except in secret. Permission was granted him to do so, and when he had told his story, the king sent a messenger to ascertain whether or not he had told the truth. When his tale had been verified, the king announced the event to the people who went and gathered the seeds of the palm trees and planted them throughout the country. Even to this day, a man may not drink palm wine by himself for fear of becoming intoxicated; he always invites friends to drink with him (Torday and Joyce 1910:235–236).

Jan Vansina tells of his participation in the 1953 Bushoong Kuba male initiation, known as *nkaan*, where palm wine played an important role in the ritual. During the initiation period the initiates were accorded certain privileges such as drinking palm wine, eating meat, and hunting. In addition, the payment of required fees for instruction was made in palm wine which the initiates tapped both mornings and evenings. The drinking of palm wine also has ties to the origins of the *nkaan*. The Kuba attribute the first *nkaan* to an incident in which Woot, their mythical ancestor, got drunk on palm wine and passed out. His sons came across him lying naked on the ground and derided him instead of offering help. His daughters, on the other hand, when they saw him in this embarrassing position, covered him up. As a result, Woot rewarded the latter by instituting the matrilineal succession, and punished the former by forcing them to undergo the first initiation (Vansina 1973:304, 306, 312, 313–314).

The drinking of palm wine is a metaphor for the Kuba, not only underlain by narrative, but giving rise to the verbal in turn. The mildness of the newly-tapped palm wine which gives way to ever-increasing potency as the day wears on is the source for a Kuba saying which compares youth and old age to the transitional phases of the wine: "Man is like palm wine: sweet youth lacks wisdom, wise old age lacks sweetness of character" (Torday 1925:143).

L. M. B.

Kuba woman holding a child. Note that the shape of the child's head resembles that of the cup. Kuba, Mushenge, Congo (Kinshasa). Photo: Hans Himmelheber, 1939

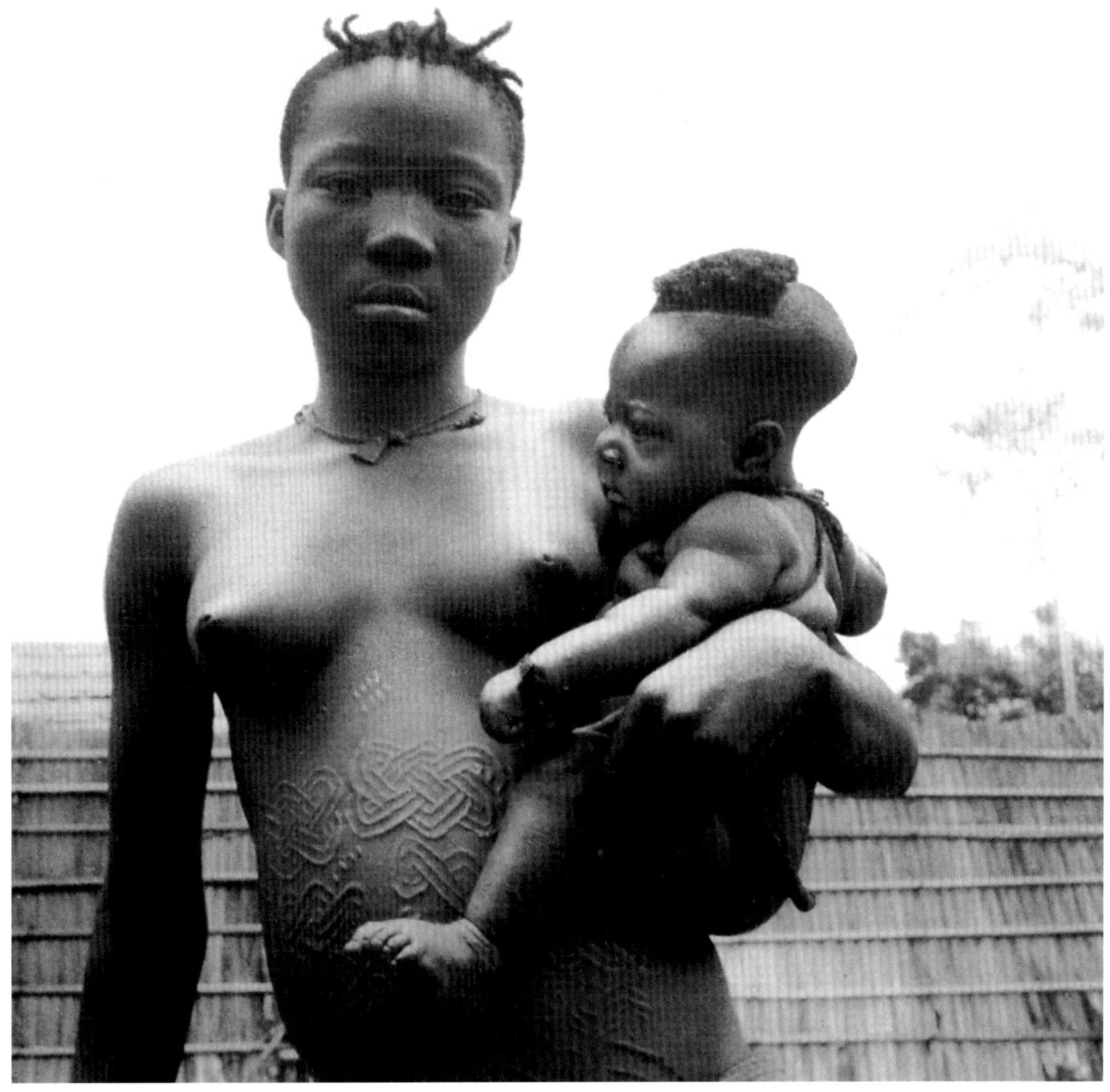

29 Personal and Social Messages: a Zulu Beaded Panel (*Ubheshwana*)

Beaded Panel (*Ubheshwana)*
Zulu, South Africa, Nongoma region
c. Mid-late 20th century
Glass beads, yarn, plastic thread, cotton thread
L. 24.5 cm
Gift of Caroline Popper, Baltimore
BMA 1990.211

Since the second half of the nineteenth century, beadwork ornaments have been an integral part of the traditionalist style of dress of Zulu men and women in South Africa, though originally restricted to the royal court and other high ranking members of society (Wood 1996:148–149). Beaded ornaments are used to adorn the body as well as communicate information about the identity of the wearer to the wider community. The dramatic color combinations and complex geometric patterns that these works feature vary according to the region and, sometimes, the generation with which the artist was connected (Boram-Hays 2000:460–461), while information about the gender and social status of an individual is conveyed by the quantity and types of beaded items donned. Worn as part of lavish displays, beadwork provides striking graphic and color complements to the other cloth, hide, fur, and/or metal elements that are part of traditional-style Zulu attire.

This rear loin covering, *ubheshwana* (pl. *obheshwana*), is a type of beaded ornament that is sometimes included in the costume of a young man or woman during courting. An ubheshwana is characterized by a large panel of woven beadwork that is attached to a plain string or beaded waistband. Though obheshwana are worn in many areas of Zululand, the distinctive red, white, black, and green color combination and interlocking rhomboid motif, said to represent a Zulu shield (Morris and Preston-Whyte 1994:51), indicate that this piece was created by an artist from the Nongoma region. Also unique to the beaded aprons of this region is the striped, bottom fringe tipped with smalls seeds, called *amalosi* seeds or Job's tears. The ragged fringe on the bottom edge of the skirt would have been restored to its original appearance before being worn. Usually only brought out on special occasions, elaborate beadwork ornaments such as obheshwana were generally kept by the owner until the pieces were beyond repair, their owners were past the appropriate age to wear the work, or the pieces fell out of fashion.

Through years of wear, small bits of dust and body dirt (*insila*) generally accumulate in some of the crevices of the beadwork. According to traditional Zulu beliefs, miscreants with special spiritual knowledge can use insila to help them commit malevolent acts against the person from whom the insila came. These small deposits of dirt, therefore, are frequently removed from a piece before it is sold, to prevent strangers from gaining access to the insila of the owner. On the BMA example, however, the deposits are still evident.

Unlike other regions of Zululand where beadwork artists changed color combinations and motifs about every twenty years, artists from the Nongoma area have been using the distinctive red, white, black, and green combination of colors and rhomboid motifs since at least the 1940s (Boram-Hays 2000:292–293). The Nongoma region is where the Zulu royal household resides, so having family ties to the Nongoma area imparts high social status on an individual. Probably because of these connections with high social prestige and strong connections to the past, the color combinations and motifs employed by the artists of this region have been less prone to change. This also has allowed beadwork ornaments in the Nongoma area to be passed down within the family, in contrast to other regions where outdated, beadwork items were usually sold or undone and the beads restrung into works of a more current style.

Obheshwana are created by young women for their own adornment or as gifts for their male suitors. When created for their own use, courting-age women wear obheshwana over their buttocks, in part, to visually enhance this region of their body. The obheshwana worn by women are part of the outfits that consisted primarily of beaded bracelets, anklelets, torso ornaments, skirts, a wide variety of necklaces, belts, head decorations, and wooden or beaded earrings. At times, metal, cloth, or beadwork decorations are also worn on the knee and/or upper arm, and, more recently, many young women have added a short, colorful cloth skirt to this combination of elements. Though all of these are not necessarily worn at once, many of them are usually included and all of the beaded items will have matching color combinations and motifs. Designed to catch the eye of potential suitors, these elaborate costumes not only enhance the body of the wearer, but also proclaim her industriousness and skill with domestic duties (Klopper 1993:30).

In contrast to women's wear, objects made from animal products and metal form the basis of Zulu men's traditional style clothing. Both courting-age and married men wear a knee length, leather, back skirt (*ibheshu*, pl. *amabheshu)* over their buttocks and a grouping of animal tails over their genitals. In addition, they can wear cow tails on their knees and upper arms, or multitudes of metal bands at the wrists, upper arms, knees, and/or ankles. Like courting-age women, young men usually don elaborate costumes to attract the attention of the opposite sex and often take an exceptional interest in their appearance.

When the young men become romantically involved with young women, they also begin to wear the beadwork ornaments that their female suitors give them, including bracelets, anklets, belts, chest decorations, many different styles of necklaces, and obheshwana. One of the most elaborate types of beadwork ornaments worn by young men, obheshwana are placed over the leather backskirt, and are usually given from women to men as expressions of love. Through established associations between different colors of beads and proverbs, young women sometimes use these beadwork gifts to communicate information about the status of the relationship between herself and her suitor (Grossert 1968:527). For instance, lavendar (*ijuba*) colored beads are associated with the saying, "I envy the dove that picks up corn grains near the door of your mother's hut", meaning "I wish I were already married to you." Other times these gifts are simply intended to be tokens of affection. Worn with pride, obheshwana and other types of beaded ornaments serve as displays of a young man's popularity with his girlfriend or girlfriends.

Traditionally, courting-age people wore their beadwork ornaments, including obheshwana, on a daily basis. While some people continue to follow this practice, many reserve such costumes for national festivals, weddings, and other special occasions. But whether in the past or present, it is at these special occasions where displays of beadwork are at their most dramatic and dynamic.

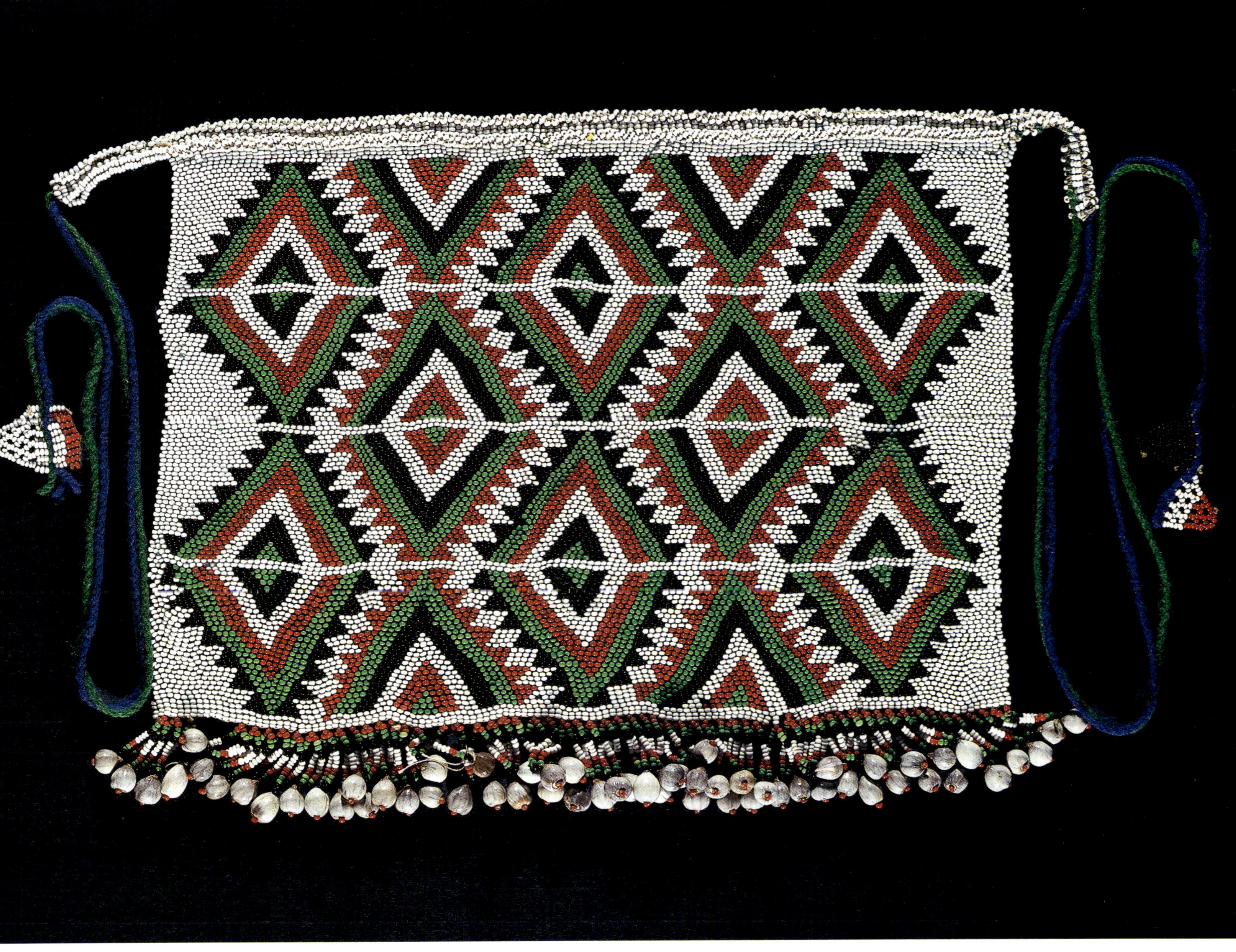

At such events, which usually take place over the period of several days, large numbers of people dressed in their finest clothes gather to celebrate with singing, dancing, and feasting.

Most of these events occur between September and December, taking advantage of the virtually guaranteed sunny and dry weather in the KwaZulu/Natal province in the spring and early summer of the Southern Hemisphere. Indeed, both of the primary Zulu national holidays, Shaka's Day and the *Umhlanga* (Reed) Ceremony, occur in September. The performances for these events are generally executed by groups of people of the same gender and age grade, and are staged in large open spaces during the daylight hours when the sun is bright in the sky. At local or family events, such as weddings, where familial ties or other types of associations bind the groups that are performing into different factions, rivalries between participating groups will often develop and infuse the performances with a highly competitive, and sometimes volatile, atmosphere. At national festivals there is a much greater emphasis on unity and the atmosphere is more regal.

Along with people of other ages, courting-age men and women, adorned in their finest attire, stage lively, choral routines and athletic dances during these special events. The dances provide a particularly vivid setting for the display of lavish pieces of beadwork such as obheshwana. Lined up in neat rows, young men dance with heavy, stomping movements that vary in tempo with the progression of the performance. The dancers are energized by the steady, brisk beats of large drums that provide rigorous, rhythmic accompaniment. With the fur and leather elements of their outfits dramatically flapping and reinforcing their actions, the performers soon raise clouds of dust in the dry open fields where the performances are staged. As the bodies of the dancers and the animal and metal elements of their costumes become unified into a synchronized, pulsating mass, the bright colors and geometric patterns of the obheshwana and other beadwork items that the young men wear stand out in contrast. Similarly, the dances performed by courting-age women are very active, athletic, and ordered. Fueled by the rhythms of drums and, frequently, the whistle of the lead dancer, the young women, aligned in rows, perform dances with quick, high, kicking steps that are visually energized by the bright colors and vivid patterns of the beadwork.

At events where the participants usually hail from the same region, the members of the same age grade and social status will wear similar outfits and beadwork featuring the same color combinations and motifs. It is a material uniformity that corresponds to the unity and mass of the choreography. Yet, the way in which these color combinations and patterns are employed can be quite diverse. So while the unified movement of the dancers and the colors and patterns of the beadwork create large, visual weights and volumes, there is also a distinctive visual intricacy within these masses. In contrast, at national festivals were people from many different regions gather, members of the same age grade may perform together as a unit and wear similar combinations of items, but the color combinations, motifs, and forms of the beadwork worn will vary widely depending upon the region from which the wearers come. During these large scale performances, people from the same region will stay together and perform within the larger national group to create distinct visual blocks embedded in the mass of people performing together. Whether is it a local or national event, observers, usually also dressed in their finest traditionalist-style clothing and beadwork, urge the performers on with choruses of clapping. With great flourish and dynamism, these dances and costumes are designed to showcase the fitness of young people in their physical prime in great visual and aural displays of mass and unity.

Obheshwana are designed to enliven the body with both color and pattern, together with other beadwork items, and metal ornaments, and animal skins and tails used in the regalia of men, and sometimes with cloth in the regalia of women. As part of daily wear, they are meant to call attention to the wearer and communicate information about his or her place within Zulu society. As part of dancing costumes, they enhance the vigorous performances of the young people who wear them with a visual energy. Bold and bright, the obheshwana of the Nongoma area are part of costumes that help signify the unity of the wearer with the larger ethnic group, region, and age grade as well distinguish him or her within the group.

Carol Boram-Hays

Detail of Zulu Beaded Panel, BMA 1990.211, showing accumulations between beads

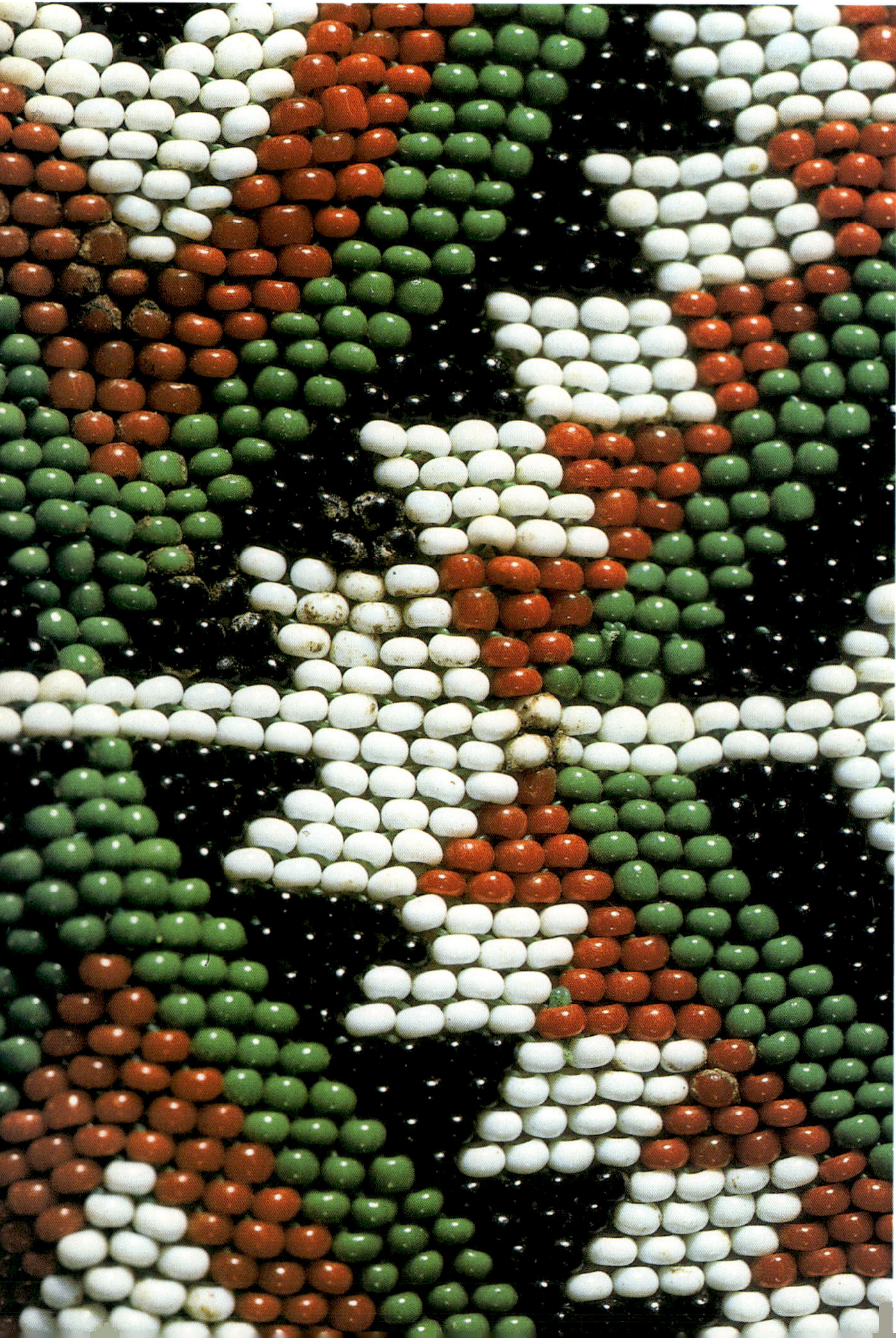

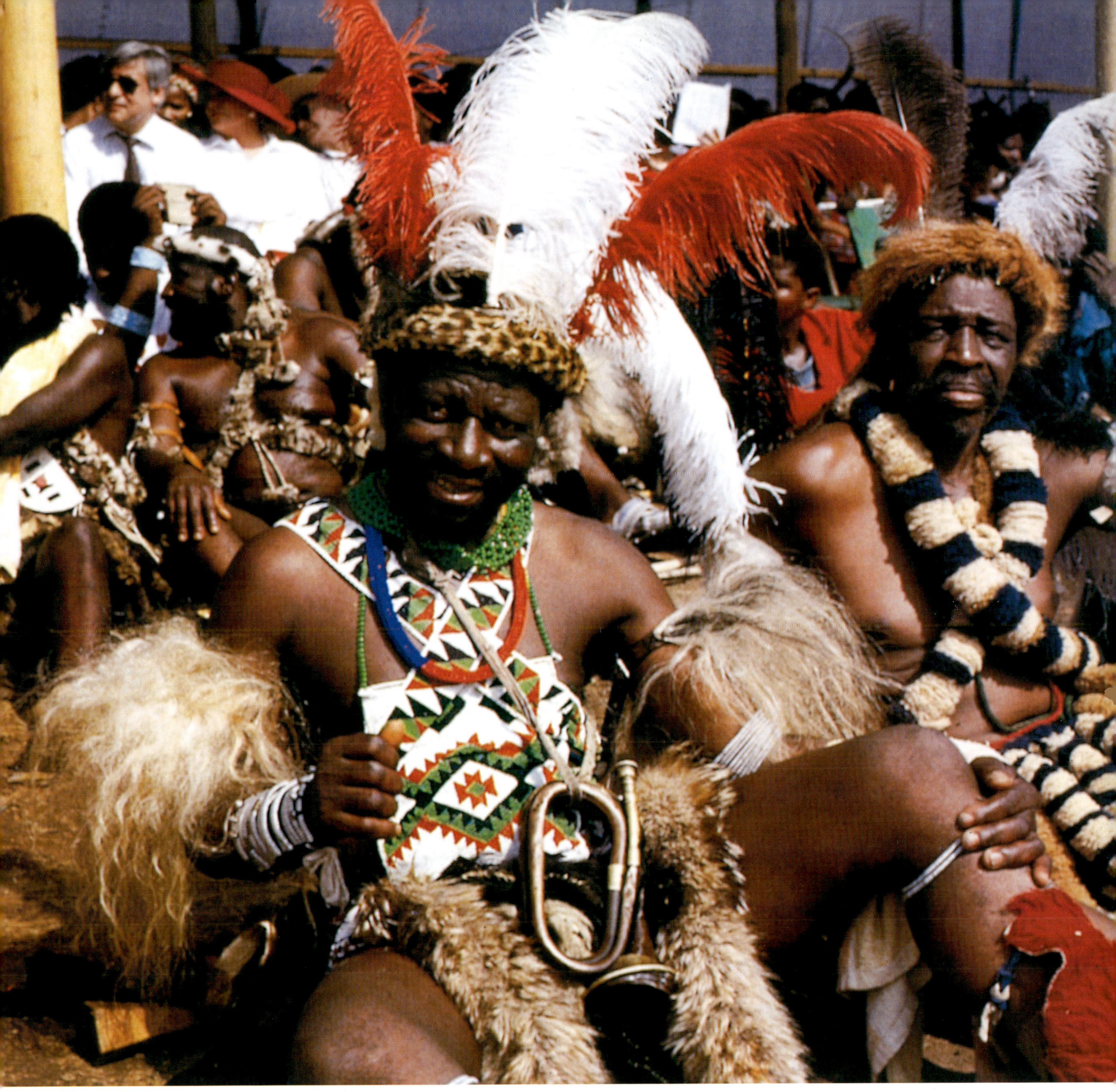

Zulu performers at the Umhlanga ceremony. South Africa
Photo: Jean Morris, 1989

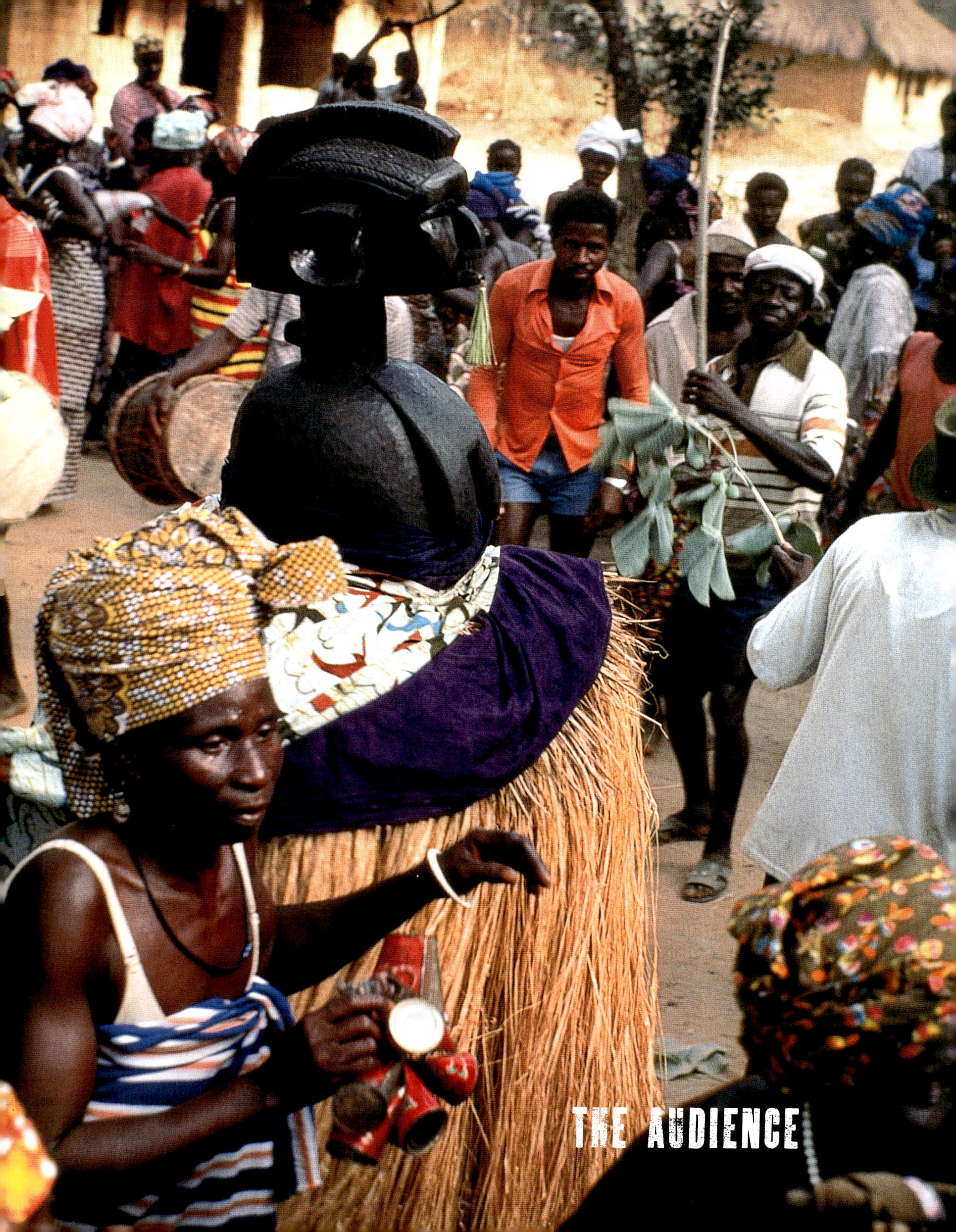

THE AUDIENCE

A performance demands a viewer as well as a performer. But in Africa the distinction between the two is not usually so clear as it is in the West. The African audience is an active participant, essentially a part of the act, an artistic element, indispensable not just to the event (as it is elsewhere) but, beyond expressing simple awe (silence) or approval (applause), is more interactive and determinative.

In the dichotomy between actors and audience in Western theater, the audience is simply the consumer. Richard Schechner (1988:61) noted that Western culture "is almost alone in demanding uniform behavior from audiences while clearly segregating audience from performers and audience from others in the area who are neither audience nor performers." Before Shakespeare, street and congregational theater were common in Europe, engaging the crowd, the product of a "spectacular society," but Shakespearean theater created a liminal space, encapsulating and "englobing the world." His stage was a macrocosm presented to the crowd, a "society of spectacle." Street theater was the "ritualized dramatization of social life" but now it became professional, institutionalized, and the "site of passage, structurally related to ritual" but distant (Hastrup 1998:33, drawing from David Chaney). A barrier is erected between actors on a proscenium stage and the audience in fixed seats, sometimes reinforced by the presence of an orchestra pit or enforced by burly guards.

The senses of seeing and hearing are privileged above all others in the Western theater. This banishing of the other senses is a way of sanitizing theater and distinguishing it from ritual—especially from the religious—which engages the congregation's participation in an emotional experience (Banes 2001:68). Bodily experiences, and, indeed, the body, are regarded with suspicion and separated from the mind to the extent that the body (the audience) and the mind, or intellect (the actor) should never meet. "Even the European stage art of dance, with its emphasis on spatial designs and spectacle, presented in a darkened proscenium theater, encourages a distanced and primarily visual attention. The stage context works against the softening of visual perception, the heightening of kinesthetic empathy, and a crossover between sensory modalities (Sklar 2001:141) ..."

Would the mask performance in Africa be an artistic event if the audience were not there to participate? The audience at a ritual event is not passive, but is involved in a call and response with the "performers" in the event. In effect, there is no "audience;" there is, rather, community participation that is integral to the art form. That is not to say that the lines are completely blurred between performer and audience. Indeed, the crowd surrounding a masked dancer is often beaten back by attendants of the masker brandishing switches or fiery torches, keeping the viewers at a distance, at least for particular segments. But the viewers are expected to fully participate in the event, through the singing of songs to which the main performer moves, often stepping individually into the dance space to dance with the masked dancer, or to take up the slack in the masker's absence during a break, thereby providing continuity and fullness to the event. Occasionally in some masked dances a member of the audience who is closely involved with the ritual will approach the masked dancer and whisper to him, giving instructions perhaps, or influencing the event in some way. The dancer, too, often aggressively interacts with the viewers. "Agency does not reside in a specific group of performers who are separate from an audience of passive spectators ... the category of audience is not distinguishable from the participant: 'the audience is part of the spectacle, is itself spectacle, and its ways of participating—audience performances—may reconstruct the nature and meaning of the spectacle itself'" (Hughes-Freeland 1998:8, quoting Charlotte Davies, same volume).

Just as the elements of music and sculpture do not necessarily share the same vocabulary and sometimes are not interintelligible, so

Dance of D'mba (see p. 223) surrounded by musicians and audience-participants. Baga Sitem, Guinea. Photo: Frederick John Lamp, 1987

the performer and audience are not necessarily on the same plane. Herbert Cole (1975) has shown in an "energy-flow" graph, how both performers and audience in the annual Odwira festival reach peaks of intensity together, at moments such as sacrifices and the "outdooring of new yam," or at the dance in the Chief's Palace. But at other moments, the audience seems to take over, while the key performers recede, such as in the visit of the elders to the Palace, or at the final sacrifices during durbar (the royal court on display). In other cases, the public is almost invisible, emotionally, as during the highly sacred purification of Black State Stools. "The brilliance of display, the boisterousness [of previous events] were suddenly held in check by total silence, lack of movement, and non-visibility.... The noise of daily living ceased, giving way to the silence of the spirit." These swellings and recedings seem to happen by some master choreography.

In the case of a shrine object, the "audience" may be one person or, rather, the supplicant at the shrine may be the principle performer, and a carved sculpture may become the audience or an instrument in the artistic ritual. The acts of the human participant define the ritual art form. Objects and actors may perform a role together. The object may act upon the participant/performer, calling upon spiritual intermediacy and self-motivation, in effect, taking the role of the performer. Perhaps games, involving objects, in which everybody plays and observes at the same time, or perhaps some Western religious ritual, such as the observance of communion, approximates African performance and the indistinguishability of the "acted upon" and the actor. Ritual practitioner and shrine may interchange:

> The altar combines not only obligatory iron and sacrifice but some of the medicines that Ogún long ago shared with Kétu followers of his forest path. An iyeye tree lends focus to the gathering of the guns, permeating them with values of nobility and collectiveness of mind. When I saw them they were festooned with three charms. But when two devotees, Elijah Adelakun and Basini Laimu, asked to be photographed, Laimu removed the charms and placed them on his body. *Abo*, a square amulet, hangs around the hunters neck: "Wear this and see things to shoot—it will work on the brain of animals, they'll get confused and become an easy mark." The bag is *apo*: "When spiritually 'tied' in the forest an animal will stop dead in its tracks and become a target." The third charm, pante, is a medicated belt: "It it is worn in the forest to make sure bullets miss your body" (Thompson 1993:182).

While audiences may be essential and participatory, they are frequently not democratic, and may be highly selective and exclusive (as Frances Harding [2002:5] has noted).[8] Attendance at certain performances of the Bamana Kòmò mask (p. 233) is restricted to blacksmiths. Drumming concerts among the Akan of Ghana, using instruments that reproduce linguistic tones, popularly known as "talking drums," are celebrated for the fact that they communicate proverbs through a pattern of pitches. But Ruth Stone (1995:262–263) adds, "Contrary to the popular view that everyone understands signaling easily, research shows that in many areas this esoteric communication is understood only by specialists and people with special training. Signaling is still used as a means to communicate with musical ensembles, particularly messages not meant for the entire audience." Some performances of the Sande or Bondo mask among the Temne or Mende (p. 175) are open only to women who have been initiated into the association. Some other Sande or Bondo masquerades are privy only to the higher official ranks, and men hide indoors in fear when the performers pass by in the night. Many men's masquerades are restricted to initiated men, and women and children run in fear when the masked performers appear (p. 79). Sometimes there is conflict between the mask and particular sections of the audience, particularly women (p. 279) Sacred groves are frequently restricted to men, although particular women officials may have some access, as in the case of the Wè (p. 43). There are many examples of masks and shrines which can never be seen or approached by ethnic outsiders (e.g., Lamp 1996:57–60).

Although in the interaction of performers and audience, there frequently does not seem to be a clear division, a quite complex structural hierarchy can in fact, be in place. In the procession of the women's coming-out of the Bondo initiation (see p. 175), all women may be considered participants, but are rather strictly assigned to prescribed roles and spatial positions, according to their rank in the initiation society. Herbert Cole (1975) has shown that in the formal seating of chiefs and their entourage during the final durbar of the Odwira festival, a strict hierarchy is imposed, resulting visually, and distinctly in plan, in a pyramid from the chief at the apex to the broad foundation of the "supporting audience." This static formation may be compared with a fluid motion by the central performers and audience participants during the main processional events.

"Audience" may consist of both the living and the dead, as most of African daily and ritual life does. The essays in this section on the Baule figure and the Bwa mask, and many others in this book, show that others are looking on, from outside our worldly sphere. The importance of these "outsiders" is signaled by Ruth Stone (1995:266):

> Ancestors and tutelary spirits must also be counted as participants in events. For though their presence may be known to a few selective insiders, they are surrogate performers who influence and most often enhance the music. Ancestors appear as spirits of deceased players who are called to attend the event. An *mbira* player sings "Gbono-kpate wee" as he invites the late player of that name to attend. And the audience knows that Gbono-kpate has arrived when the high-pitched "Oo," sung by the soloist, is heard in response.

In recent decades, the "audience" at African performances has come to include the researcher from America or Europe, visiting dignitaries (see Dan Mask, p. 99) embassy personnel, doctors, sometimes tourists, and even video operators, and crews from national television. Charles Gore (1998:79) has accounted for the emergence of video as an element in the construction of the performance event in Benin. Beginning around 1990, the video camera was viewed as intrusive, with its lighting and placement requirements, especially considering the exclusivity of some of the events, such as initiation proceedings. More recently, however, video has become almost an essential element:

> Familiarity with the technical requirements has led to participants now taking some account of the presence of the video operator.... The use of video filming shifted very rapidly from being a particular record of the event to an almost mandatory assertion of the importance of the individuals participating ... Indeed an Ohen [priest] now loses status if there is no filming of the annual festival, and members of a shrine budget for its cost in their preparations for the festival. In terms of content, the most prominent features of this filming are the amount of real-time expended and the emphasis on the numbers of participants, particularly the more eminent visitors. The more that the event is recorded in real-time (this is often a 14-day affair in the case of annual festivals), the more prestige and status are asserted.

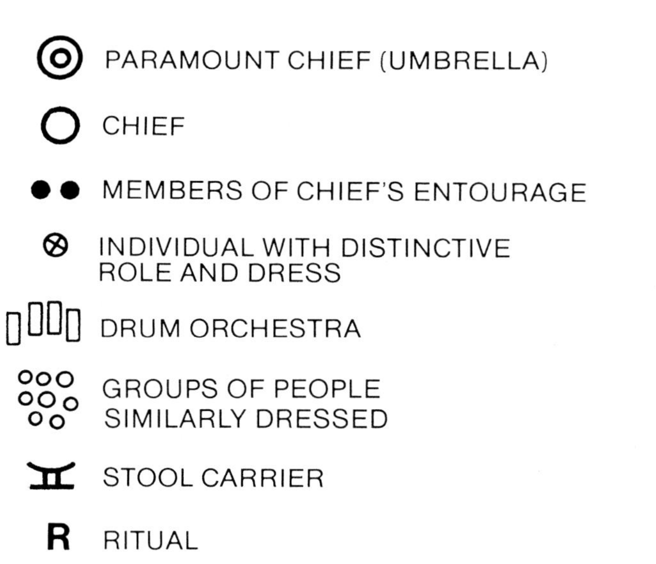

The audience is represented in a number of different ways in the essays included here. Among the Bwa, the entire community, from the very elderly to young children, contributes individual dances to the performance, as described by Emily Hanna. In the case of Baule spirit figures, the spirits themselves form an audience. For the Ejagham helmet mask, the central audience is composed of the military secret society members who sponsor the performance, and it is shown that their shifting view of the mask's symbolism has reshaped the masquerade. Yoruba spectacles, described by Henry John Drewal, deeply involve an audience steeped in understanding of forces of the cosmos. And among the Nafana, the meaning of Bedu masquerades, as analyzed by Karel Arnaut, is defined by its particular audience in place and time.

In the interaction of the group in African performances, one might look for certain factors. What are the verbal and the nonverbal aspects, and how do they interchange and engage each other? How are individual body spaces and efforts coordinated with others and incorporated? Are individual efforts unified or distinctive? Are the participants self-(body)oriented or other-(space)oriented? What are the group rhythms, and how are individual rhythms negotiated? How are individual kinespheres and action territories adapted and incorporated into the group, and how does this express a unified quality? Within the whole, are individual movements synchronic, symmetrical, or sequential? "If the observer shifts from watching an individual in a group to seeing also the forms, angles and rhythms between any two members or three or the whole group, the individuals are then seen as parts of a larger body and a whole new world of perception opens up ... so that we may now speak of a sort of social choreography" (Bartenieff 1980:129, 171).

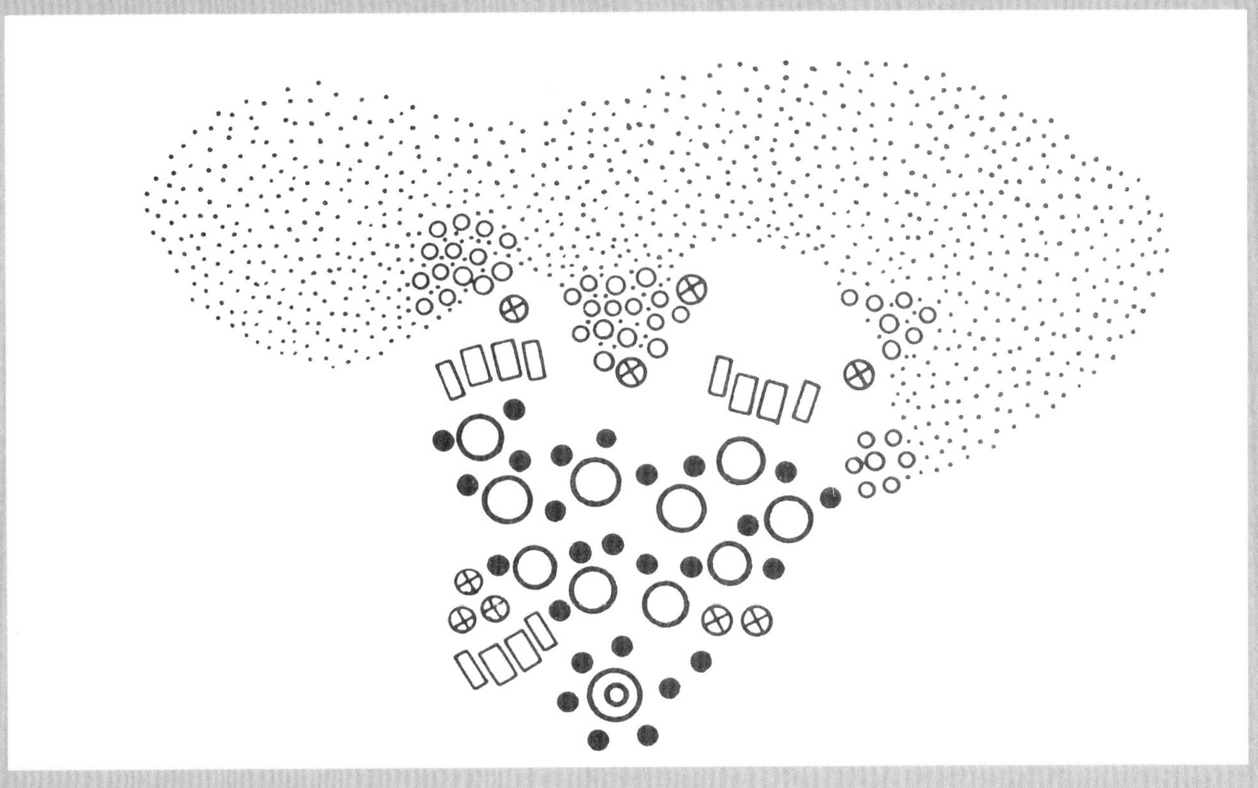

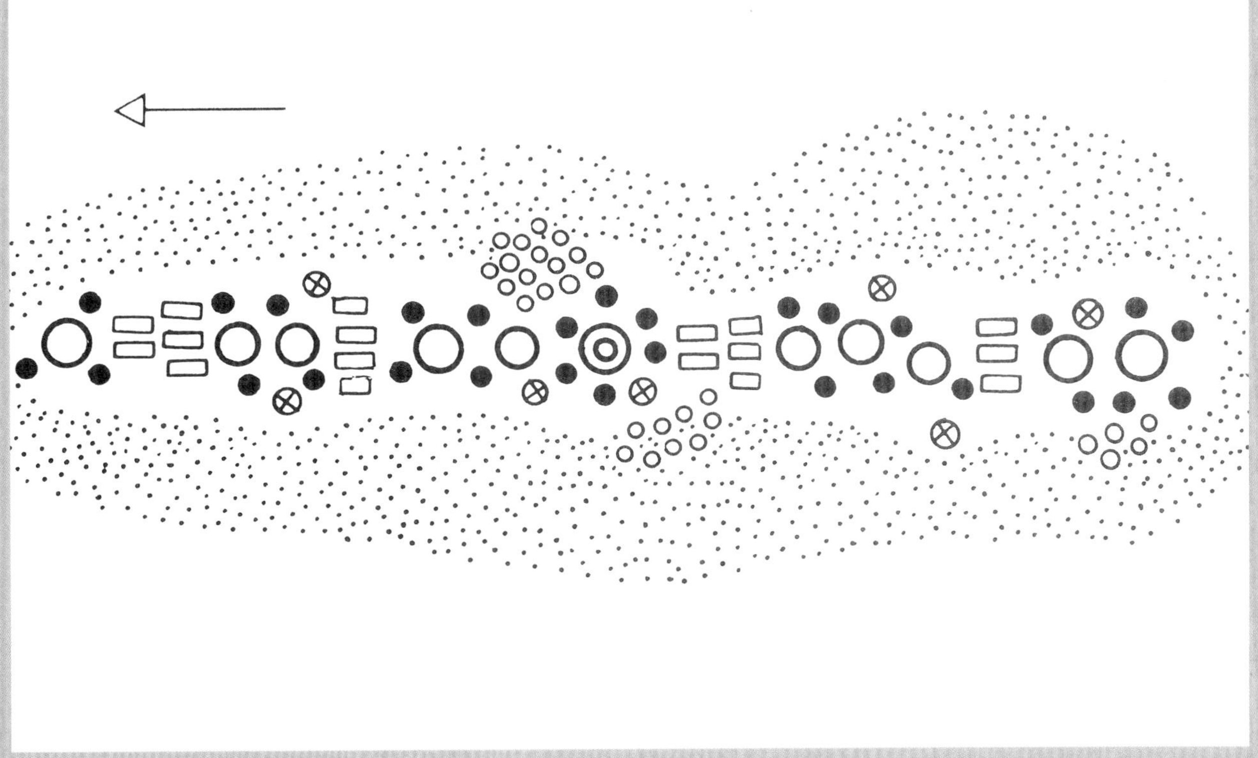

Schematic relationships of hierarchy during the Odwira festival in Akropong, Ghana.
Top: sedentary (durbar); Below: in motion (procession)
Drawing from Cole 1975

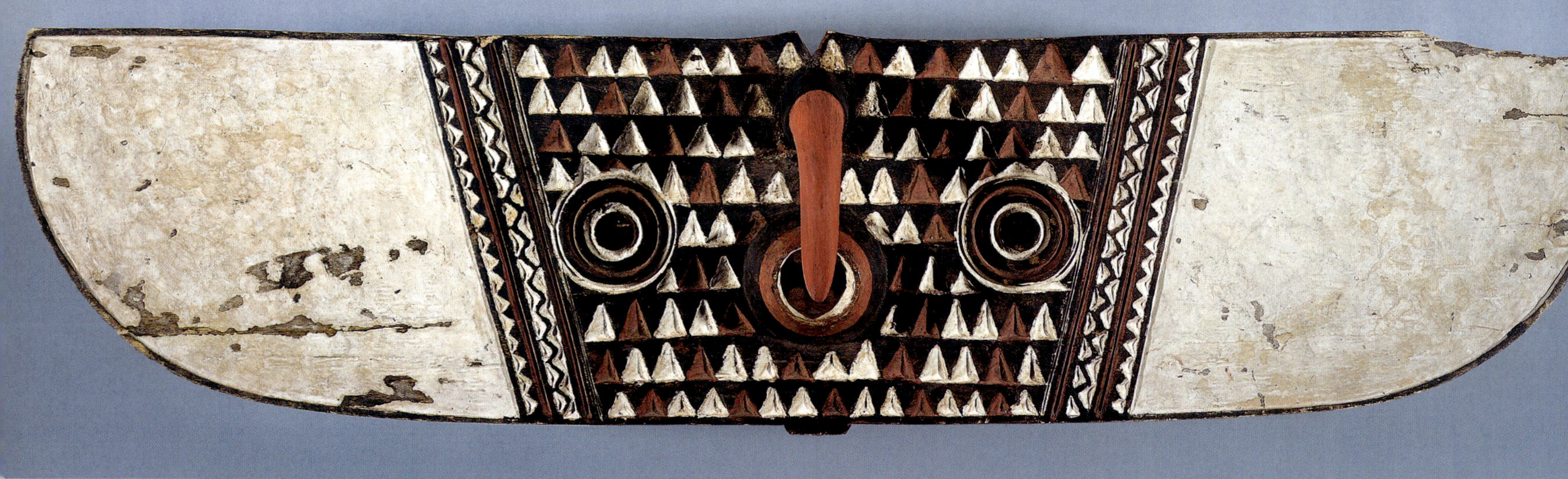

30

Dream Animals as a Link to the Spiritual World: a Bwa Mask

Mask Representing a Hawk (*Duho*)
Bwa, Burkina Faso
c. Early–mid-20th century
Wood, polychrome, resin, restoration (polyethylene, epoxy, acetone)
H. 117 cm
Gift of Gilbert and Jean Jackson, Potoma, Maryland
BMA 1995.101

Masquerade is one of the most important art forms in Bwa society, combining art, performance, ritual, and political display. The most ancient masquerade tradition in Bwa memory features masks and body costumes made entirely of leaves, vines, and grasses, which are destroyed after the performance. The BMA mask, which may represent a hawk or bat, comes from a more recent tradition of wooden masks, some with animal forms and others with long, shaped, vertical, or horizontal planks decorated with geometric patterns.

Wooden masks perform at funerals and during family initiations, both of which are held in the period following the harvest known as the dry season, between December and April. In some areas, they also perform for new year or purification ceremonies before the first seeds are planted in the ground as the rainy season begins in May. These performances are scheduled according to the season and phase of the moon, and based on divination sessions, by which ancestors are consulted for favorable dates. Word of these important events is spread to family members in distant villages during markets, which are held on a rotating basis between villages.

The masquerade performance space is located within the village, in an open area near the homes of the family or families who own the masks. During a funeral, the masks perform directly in front of the home of the deceased person as well. In some villages, the space is tight, and spectators watch the performance from the rooftops of their homes. Masks emerge into the performance space from a walled family courtyard or other private area in the mid- to late afternoon, when temperatures can be 100 degrees or more, and generally perform until nightfall. The order in which masks perform varies from village to village, but generally the vertical and horizontal plank masks, including the BMA type, emerge first, followed by animal masks such as the antelope, serpent, and buffalo.

Masks are worn with a kind of woven net jumpsuit made of hemp. Long bunches of loose hemp fibers are attached to the net, so that the dancer's body is completely concealed by the thick, shaggy, mass of fiber. The costumes, which smell of plant material and wood smoke, sometimes retain their natural straw color, but more often they are dyed reddish-orange or black. New synthetic dyes are now sometimes used, producing brilliant pinks, greens, and blues.

In the southeastern Bwa region, where this mask probably comes from, the vertical and horizontal plank masks tend to be large and quite heavy. Performances consist of spinning in place, twisting, tilting the mask from side to side, and quick, hopping footwork, somewhat like a jump rope game in the United States called "Double-Dutch." Performers wearing smaller animal masks move with much more agility, performing summersaults, large body spins, and head snaps that are not possible with the larger masks. Groups of drummers and balafone players accompany the performances, and frequently guide the dancer, who may have difficulty seeing clearly from behind the mask, with musical cues. In some villages, groups of teenage boys play carved, wooden, diamond-shaped flutes in a call-and-response chorus that sounds like the rhythmic call of cicadas.

Adult initiated men always wear the masks, but women participate closely, singing the praises of an excellent performance, and rushing up to raise the hand of a masquerader following an impressive or vigorous dance. Groups of girls and women sing praise songs, describing the strength and beauty of their family's masks, and dance in a slow-moving circle before the masks emerge. Elderly women dance in groups of two or three between individual mask performances, delighting themselves and generating an appreciative response in the audience. Despite their advanced age, they dance with great flexibility and strength, repeatedly doubling over at the waist and then arching their backs and flinging their arms out and back. On separate occasions, young boys of the family carry out their own practice masquerades with masks made of millet stalks, as they prepare for their initiations.

In spite of the increasing availability of commercial paints in a wide variety of colors, the color scheme for wooden masks remains white, red, and black. In many villages, natural pigments are still prepared to paint the wood. The white pigment, made of clay and lizard dung is a chalky wash of color through which the wood is sometimes visible. The red pigment, which has an egg binder, is a thicker colorant, and is usually slightly glossier. The round opening on vertical and horizontal plank masks, which appears to be a mouth, is always painted red. The black pigment, created by boiling plant materials with iron slag, is also thick and shiny. The masks are washed, soaked, and repainted before each performance season, and the red and black pigments, which are not water soluble, tend to build up over the years.

This mask probably represents a spirit that appeared to a Bwa villager in the form of a hawk or bat. Bwa people, who mostly live in rural farming communities, carefully observe the animals with which they share their habitat. Animals are frequently connections to the world of spirits, and the Bwa are alert for signs and contacts from the invisible world. A bird or animal appearing in a person's dream could also be interpreted by a diviner and generate the creation of a mask.

Families that use wooden masks are invited to participate in national and international arts festivals and cultural expositions, such as the Pan African Film Festival (FESPACO) held biennially in Ouagadougou. Perhaps in response to new audiences and performance opportunities, mask decoration continues to evolve and change. The flat, wooden planks are natural writing surfaces, and in some villages masks have become signboards, featuring family names or slogans of favored political parties. Images and scenes, carved in low relief, also now accompany the more traditional geometric patterns. The spirit of independence and innovation that marked the initial adoption of wooden masks continues to characterize this dynamic performance art.

Emily Hanna

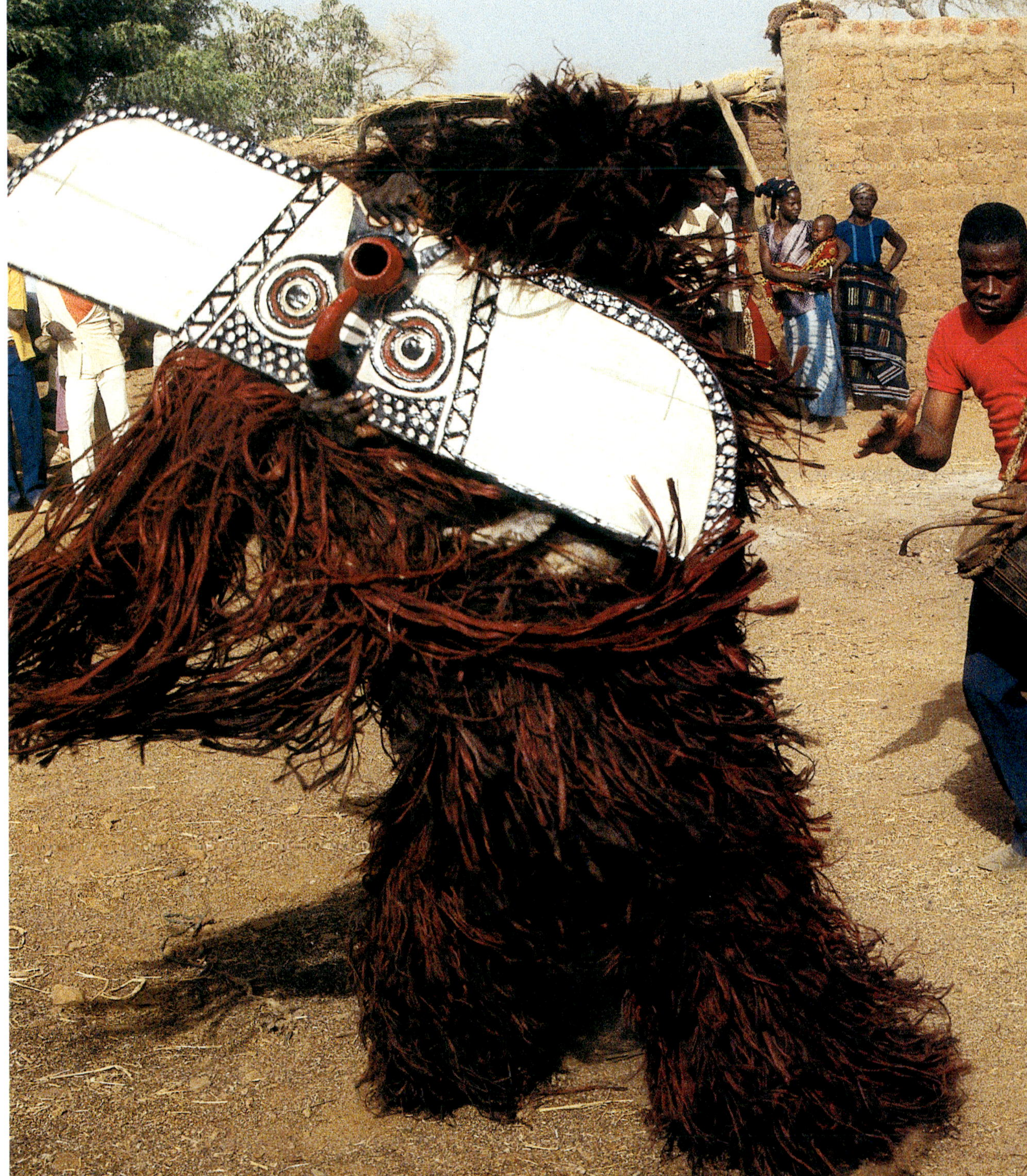

Masked Dancer at a funeral, swivelling the mask upside down. Bwa, Boni, Burkina Faso
Photo: Christopher Roy, 1985

31

The Asye Usu Can Fall On You: a Baule Figure (*Asye Usu*)

Standing Female Figure (probably *Asye Usu*)
Baule, Ivory Coast
c. Late 19th–early 20th century
Wood, beads, string, H. 37 cm
Bequest of Gertrude Rosenthal, Baltimore
BMA 1989.158

For the Baule, spiritual beings interact with human beings through the intercession of a spirit medium known as a *komien.* Komien hold their divination performances on Wednesday, the most sacred day of the week when spirits are most amenable to congress with mortal beings (Vogel 1977:56, 58; 1997:52, 62). Among those spirits from the otherworld (*blolo*) involved in human affairs are the lesser nature spirits, asye usu, often associated with carved wooden sculptures in human form (Vogel 1973:24; 1977:152, 169; 1997:92, 221, 232).

Asye usu, who may be male or female, are said to have distinctive and unpleasant physical and psychological profiles. They are generally described as ugly, disfigured, slovenly, dirty, disproportionally large or small, frightening in appearance, and uncivilized in behavior, all characteristics associated with their natural abode, the bush—the antithesis of the ordered civility, and, perforce, beauty, of the village (Vogel 1973:23; 1977:162, 169; 1997:46, 224, 239).

In some instances, an asye usu will be attracted to a particular man, woman, or child, and as a result, will seek to possess them:

> "If you are a good singer and sing in the fields, the *asye usu* can love you and fall on you [possess you]" (Vogel 1997:224, quoting Kouassi Aya).

This first violent encounter with the spirit, often occurring at a funeral, causes the possessed person to fall into a trance and flee into the bush where they will spend several days in the company of the spirits that dwell therein. This marks the beginning of a lifelong, mutually beneficial association between a spirit and the individual it has chosen to be a diviner, a komien (Vogel 1997:224–239).

Once a person has been certified as a komien, he or she must commission a beautiful and flattering wood statuette (*waka sran*) bearing the twin hallmarks of a civilized being: an elegant hair-style and scarification marks. The spirit will then move back and forth from the sculpture to the body of the komien, who, when possessed, will enter into a trance and perform divinations. The Baule believe that it is the spirit itself, hoping to create a favorable impression on future audiences at divination performances, who dictates the civilized appearance of the sculpture. While most Baule statuettes are carved in the nude, their nudity is lightly covered with an actual loincloth or, like the BMA's example, with draped beads and string, signifying that, like civilized human beings, these sculptures are not meant to be seen completely naked, a state associated with infants, the insane, and wild creatures. Were the sculpture to be ugly and unflattering, in other words, uncivilized, the asye usu would be offended, and thus inclined to cause greater trouble for the chosen individual. Since asye usu are attracted and influenced in a positive manner by that which is perceived as civilized, divination performances are performed only within the confines of a village. In fact, once an asye usu has possessed a komien, it will never return to the uncivilized bush (Vogel 1973:24; 1977:165, 169; 1980:3, 8–13, 20; 1986:85; 1997:94, 221, 224, 227, 231–232, 237).

One-on-one consultations with a komien occur in private in the diviner's shrine room. However, for the most part, consultations are part ritual and part theatre, and, as such, conducted in public in front of an audience. The Baule place great value on individuality, so not all divination performances are the same; each diviner has his or her own style. An individual performance may incorporate varied musical arrangements and dance steps, as well as more than one costume change; painting the body and face with white pigment is part of the overall costume (Vogel 1997:49, 221, 234, 237).

Vogel (1997:234, 237) gives a first-hand account of a 1972 performance given by Katake, a famous komien, in the town of Lolobo:

> Before Katake appeared, the audience and musicians had been singing and drumming for at least half an hour to "warm" the dance space. Also, Katake had entered a trance, alone in the closed shrine room where his sculptures remained. From outside we could hear him singing and the slow regular ring of his *lowre* mallet striking an iron gong. He entered the dance circle briskly accompanied by drumming and full-throated singing by his musicians. He wore a white knee-length wrapper with the usual crossed bands of specially strung *nfwe* white beads on his chest and white chalk painted on his lips and across his eyes (to see the spirits and interpret their voices). His chest, waist, and arms were thickly hung with leather-covered amulets of various shapes, and he carried his carved lowre mallet and iron gong in his hand or hanging from his waist throughout the performance. He also held plain cow-tail whisks and wore several broad rattles on his ankles, and on his head a red hat with a crest of cowrie shells and a small

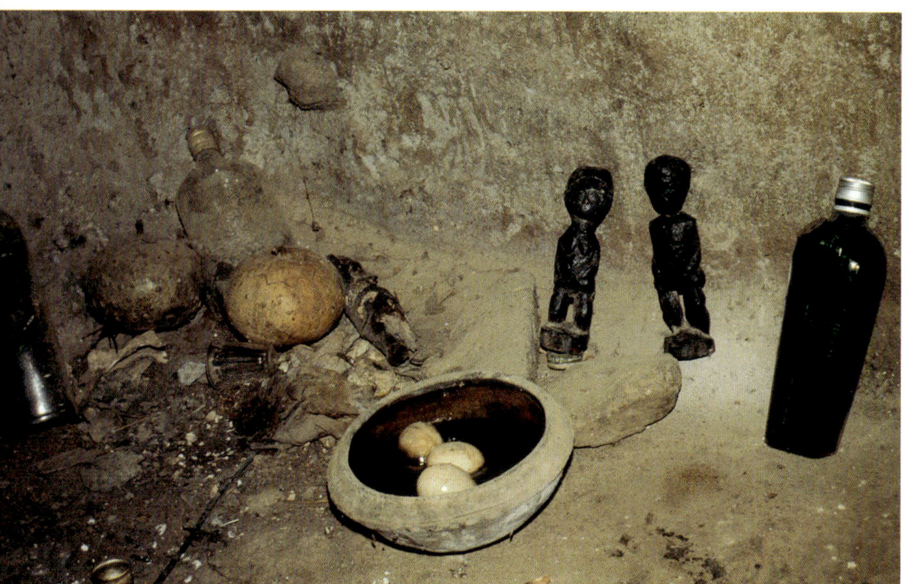

***Bo Usu* Shrine. Baule, Kouassikouassikro, Agba Katienou region, Ivory Coast**
Photo: ©Susan Vogel, 1978

bird on top.... To one side of the drummers, Katake's assistants arranged a goat skin with medicinal leaves, a piece of kaolin, a cowrie, and a coin on it; a small knife stood thrust into the ground on one side.... Katake was successively possessed by five bush spirits" (Vogel 1997:234, 237).

During this performance, the audience, recognizing the different spirits that possessed the komien, called out their names and asked them questions. The possessed komien, in turn, answered in the distinct and recognizable voices of each spirit. In addition, each spirit had its own particular dance. From time to time, members of the komien's family, as well as others in the audience entered the arena to dance, to speak with the asye usu in possesion of the komien, or to praise the diviner for his performance (Vogel 1977:167; 1997:221, 232, 237).

Generally speaking, diviners do not display their asye usu sculptures during divination performances. Instead, the asye usu, draped in cloth, remain in storage in the komien's private sleeping quarters or in small darkened shrine rooms that also serve as storage space for the komien's dance accoutrements: rattles, mallet, gong, hats, cow-tail whisks (Vogel 1977:167–168; 1997:221, 232). The decision to display the sculptures is a matter of choice for each komien. Vogel describes witnessing such a performance in the 1990's:

> "[The diviners] both had an attendant dramatically carry their sculptures into the dance place after the crowd had gathered and the musicians were drumming and singing. Their two very different sculptures were set on the ground or partly hidden by white cloth, and formed a focal point for the performance, although the audience could only see them poorly and at an angle.... At the end of the performance, as soon as the diviner abruptly left and before the audience could move, the assistant returned the sculpture to the closed room in which it was kept, the musicians still singing" (Vogel 1997:237).

Asye usu spirits demand regular offerings of earth, raw eggs, and blood from their komien. Such offerings are most often placed in pans, or the raw eggs and blood may be poured over small mounds of earth in the asye usu shrine. In most instances, offerings are not poured directly on the face and body of the sculpture for fear of marring its man-made beauty. However, on occasion, the komien might sprinkle the offerings on the figure's feet, or on dance accoutrements such as the cow-tail whisks or the komien's hat (Vogel 1977:168; 1980:3; 1997:232).

The link between an asye usu and the chosen individual lasts for a lifetime. Upon the death of a komien, his or her matrilineal relatives will clean the asye usu sculpture (or sculptures) and dance accoutrements with water and kaolin, cover them with a cotton bag, and keep them safe until that time when the spirit indicates its desire to possess another member of the same family. In rare instances, the spirit of the deceased owner will indicate that it has chosen to occupy the sculpture that once served as a home for its asye usu instead of the customary ancestral chair or stool. In that case, the chosen asye usu sculpture will be placed in the family shrine (Vogel 1973:24; 1977:164–165; 1980:2; 1997:234).

L. M. B.

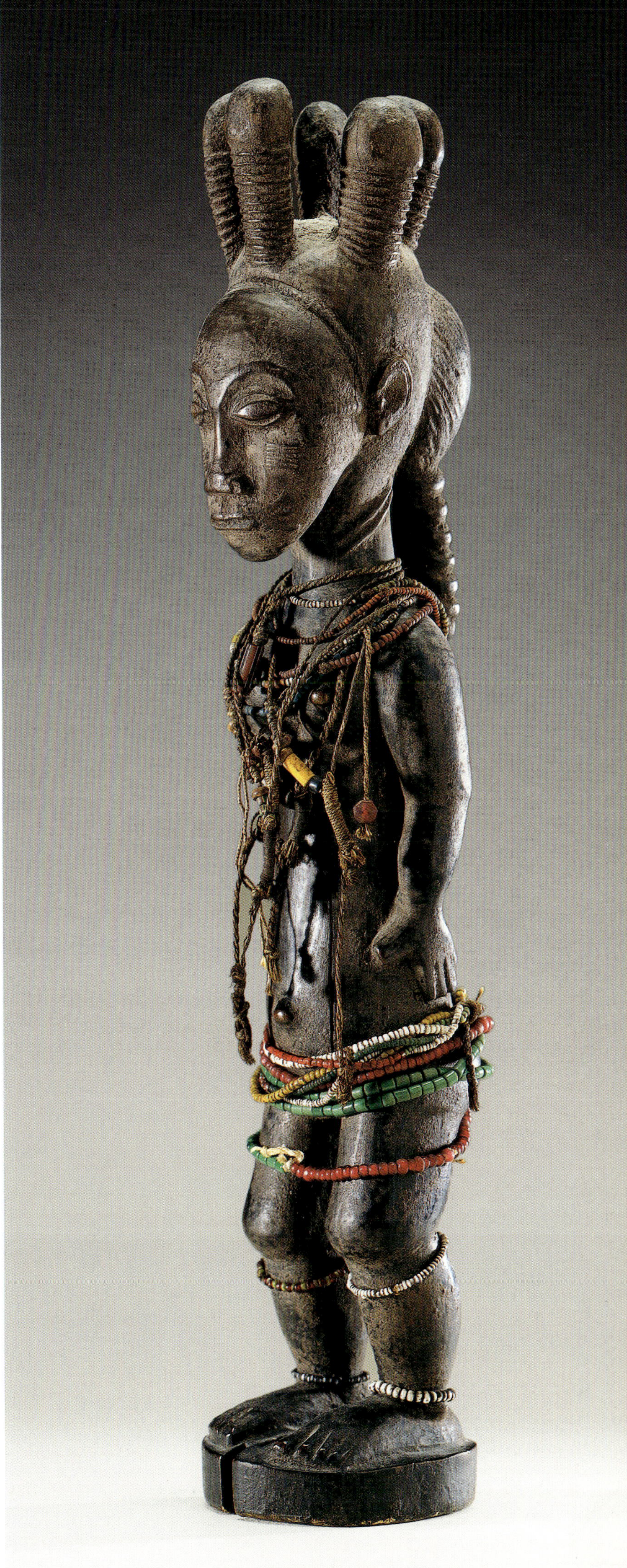

32

The Military Unit, the Festival, the Drama: an Ejagham Mask

Janus Helmet Mask
Ejagham, Akparabong subgroup, Nigeria
Ekpe Association
c. Early 20th century
Wood, antelope skin, metal, polychrome, H. 40.5 cm
Gift of Barry and Toby T. Hecht, Bethesda, Maryland
BMA 1989.369 (ex William Arnett, Atlanta)

Among the Ejagham, in the vicinity of the Cross River, social control has been, for the most part, in the hands of the secret societies, rather than political leaders. The BMA's janus mask was associated with the military secret society, the Ekpe, that exercised the political and economic power in the local community. Ekpe provided the patronage and the audience.

The BMA mask was carved in the form of a helmet big enough to rest on the shoulders. It has two faces, a dark, forward-looking side and a light-colored, rear face. The darker side has eye openings, while the lighter side has "blind" eyes made of shiny metal strips with wooden peg pupils. Traditionally, the animal skin covering stopped at the hairlines to allow the attachment of real human hair. However, the elliptical upper cranium of this mask is pierced with holes to enable the insertion of feathers and porcupine quills, which often replicated human coiffure. Today, among the Igbo for example, young men of the *ogbolo* age-grade wear conical shaped coiffures with feathers. Other archival material seems to indicate that the shaved hairline followed a regional fashion among men shared by other ethnic groups, with short-cropped hair and a characteristic indenture on the lower hairline (Mansfeld 1908:219, Fig. 147, 158; Cole and Aniakor 1984:35, Fig. 62).

There were two versions of the costume for this type of mask in use. The first was a form-fitted net costume worn with a hoop skirt. The second consisted of loosely-fitted overalls or a gown made of imported European fabrics (Jones 1984:42 ff).

Archival records of janus skin-covered masks from the beginning of the nineteenth century indicate that the BMA mask has undergone transformation due to inactivity. In actual use, shininess of the eyes, made of polished metal strips (now corroded), produced a certain realism. Senior members of the military secret society would lubricate the surface with palm oil in order to protect the skin from shrinkage. Today, cracks on the skin surface are the result of the lack of indigenous lubricants, as well as the aging process (Campbell 1982:131, 133). The painted facial decorations are intact, including Nsibidi script, a secret means of communication, in the form of two intertwined lines representing affectionate devotion between partners, located near one corner of the lips, in addition to some pseudo Nsibidi commonly seen (Campbell 1982:195 ff; Roschenthaler 1998:41 ff).

The janus mask signified a recognition of gender duality along with other opposing dichotomies deeply rooted in the creation narrative, and in the various social and political structures, as well as the secret societies. Although the sexual characteristics of the respective faces are rather ambiguous, there are some gender specific codes expressed. The contrast of the dark, forward face, and light, rear one, as a symbolic expression of sexual duality, was considered significant. The darker male face was meant to represent a fierce character. Archival records suggests that holes were bored in early masks for attaching a raffia fiber beard on the dark face. Alfred Manfeld (1908:Plates XVIII and Fig. 158) published a drawing of a janus mask with a beard, and a photograph of a soldier with an artificial beard attached to his chin. Raffia fringes or vegetable fibers were interwoven in the "hammock" that was attached just below each ear to tie the beard in place on the mask's chin (Campbell 1982:85 ff; Nicklin 1974:14).

In the context of a masquerade of the Efut people in Calabar, the significance of the two faces of the mask as a specification of two genders was interpreted as follows:

> This mask represents Tata Agbo, a man born in war, and his wife. All his brothers and sisters had been killed in combat. Only he and his wife remained. Whenever he went to battle, his wife went behind. When he shoots, she loads, till he wins. That is why when Tata Agbo died, they made that [skin-covered helmet mask] as remembrance, that the man was facing the battlefield, the wife was in back, loading. It is a double remembrance (Thompson 1974:175).

Military secret society masquerades were performed for mortuary rituals, public seasonal festivals throughout the year, and initiation ritual for the age-group organizations. Other occasions included a celebration of successful military campaigns or the accomplishment of profitable trade deals, especially if lucrative slave trafficking was involved (Campbell 1982:64).

At a designated time, the beating of the village's largest drum, *Egyuk*, marked the beginning of the "play" for the soldier's secret society. The messenger announced that the society's spiritual being, the *Okun*, had came to the village, and the masquerade was to be held in his honor. The soldiers and dancers performed in two groups. One group of performers circumambulated in an inner circle around the musicians and choir in the center, while the other group moved along the outer circle, singing and clapping their hands (Mansfeld 1908:133 ff; Talbot 1926:272).

The performance space was an open yard in front of the society's sacred pavilion called *Ekpe Ntan*. Within the space could be found a large sacrificial stone called *Buku-Nkang*, an ancestral shrine and, in some villages, a circle of monoliths. The most important masquerade character was the janus mask that performed near Ekpe Ntan. In front of the pavilion were two carved posts signifying the authority of the judges who presided there. The ambulatory movement of the performers was focused on the central objects as well as on the sacred space. With the exception of the janus dancer, participants in the event were unmasked. In the outer circle, bearded soldiers wearing helmets played aggressive roles by challenging the audience with spears, machetes, and clubs. They 'danced' their staffs and weapons moving them harmoniously to the rhythm of iron double-gongs, wedge-tuned drums, slit gongs, and percussive sticks played by men in the inner circle. The titled man, Muna, shook a rattle in each hand to guide the rhythm of the dancers. Women sitting around the periphery of the dance ring often played percussion instruments (Eyo 1996:374–375; Mansfeld 1908:212, Fig. 158; Talbot 1926:431; Thompson 1974:184).

While some dancers in the outer circle wore helmets and held spears ready to strike the observers, other performers bent their torsos and turned their heads downward. Looking downward was a gesture of subordination, and signified the respect toward the *Okun*, the spirit being honored by the masquerade. The gesture derived from the traditional belief that viewing the soldier's costumes, especially that of the janus mask by an uninitiated person, could result in capital punishment. Moreover, the function

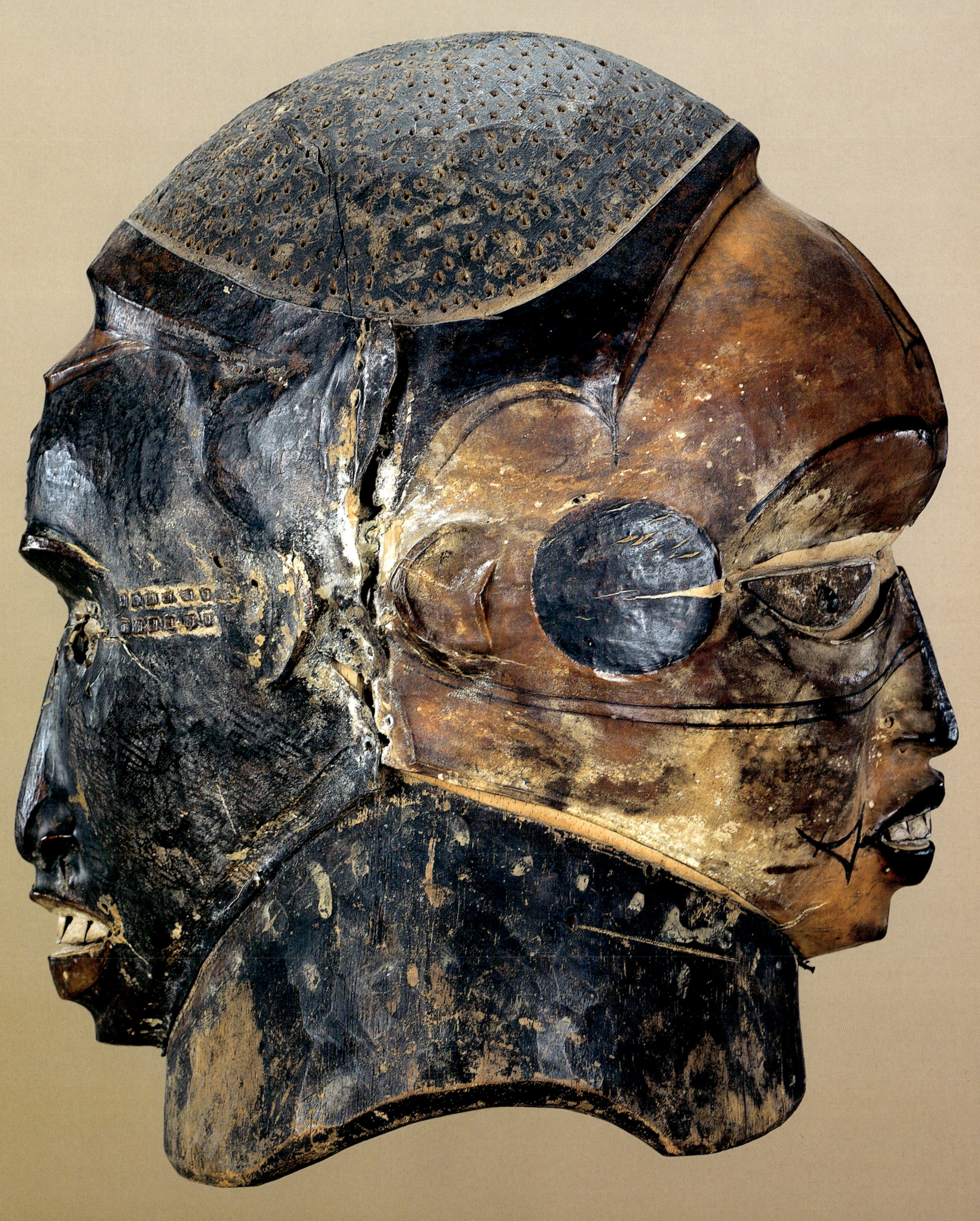

of the costume was to impress the uninitiated viewer by creating an aura of mystery and a sense of fear (Mansfeld 1908:148, Fig. 108; 157, Fig. 133; Campbell 1982:61, 72).

The Ejagham tradition has been transformed among the Efut people of Calabar into a new masquerade form, the *Ikem*, where the context of a military combat seems to have evolved into a combat of opposing genders. There, during the Ikem festival, organized for the local government, there is now a tendency for newer and more secular forms of janus masquerade. The janus character enacts some aspects of the real-life interaction between sexes, frequently taking either the male role or the female. The performance is often satirical and jocular. Although completely different in its meaning and social role, the Ikem 'play', focusing on the violent aspects of sexual behavior somehow retains the aggressive character of the soldier's secret society dance (Nicklin and Salmon 1988).

P. K.

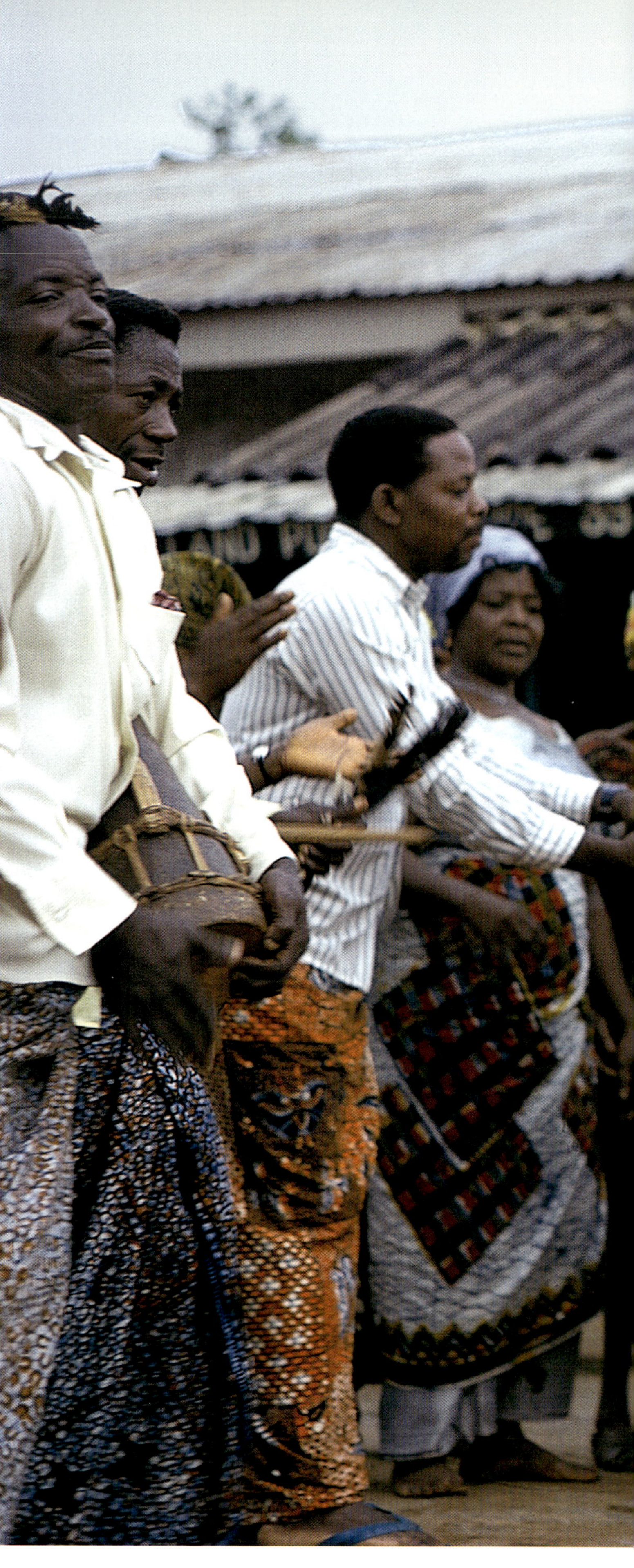

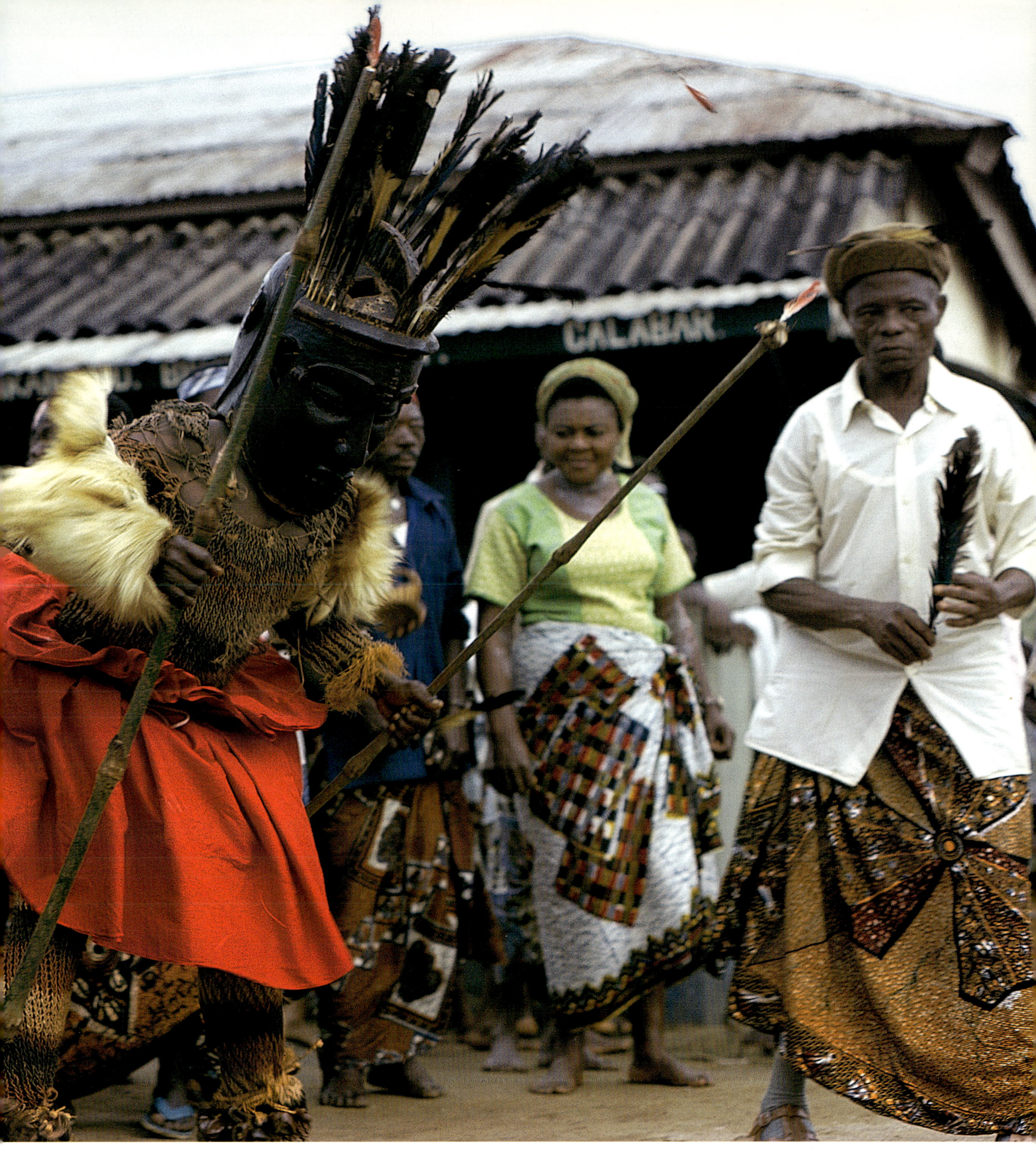

Skin-covered helmet mask. Big Qua Town, Calabar, Nigeria
Photo: Keith Nicklin, 1975

A Spectacle of Miracles: the Yoruba Forest Spirit Mask (*Aroni*)

Trickster Mask (*Aroni*)
Yoruba, Nigeria. Probably Oyo Kingdom
Egungun masquerade
c. Early 20th century
Wood, twine, polychrome, H. 28 cm
Purchased with exchange funds from Gift of Mr. and Mrs. Joseph Gerofsky; Gift of Irene Gulck; Gift of Mr. and Mrs. Alan Meyers; Gift of Dr. Joseph H. Seipp, Jr.; and Gift of Alan Wurtzburger
BMA 1983.83

The oppressive heat of the day begins to lessen as the sun angles toward the hazy horizon. In the marketplace, the excitement of the gathering crowd grows in eager anticipation of the approaching spectacle (*iran*)—a masquerade performance. Children run pushing and shoving to claim their prized places on the ground in front of their honored elders seated on folding metal chairs and improvised benches. Behind them, other men, women, and children press forward toward the performance circle, squeezing into any available space in order to see and experience the masked miracles (*idan*) that honor the spirits of departed ancestors in the Yoruba masquerade known as Egungun (M. Drewal and H. Drewal 1978; M. Drewal 1992:89–112).

Yoruba ritual performances are multi-media and multi-sensorial aesthetic experiences. They are meant to enliven and enlighten audiences as well as involve them. Thus the root of the Yoruba word for spectacle (iran) shares the same root as the word for visual representation (*aworan*). And aworan also refers to a spectator, a viewer of a performance. Thus Yoruba performances are understood as participatory—where performers and audiences interact, playing improvisationally with each other to energize the space and place of spectacles that temporarily transform reality, bringing normally invisible otherworldly forces (ancestral spirits) in the visible world to provoke wonder, reflection, and action.

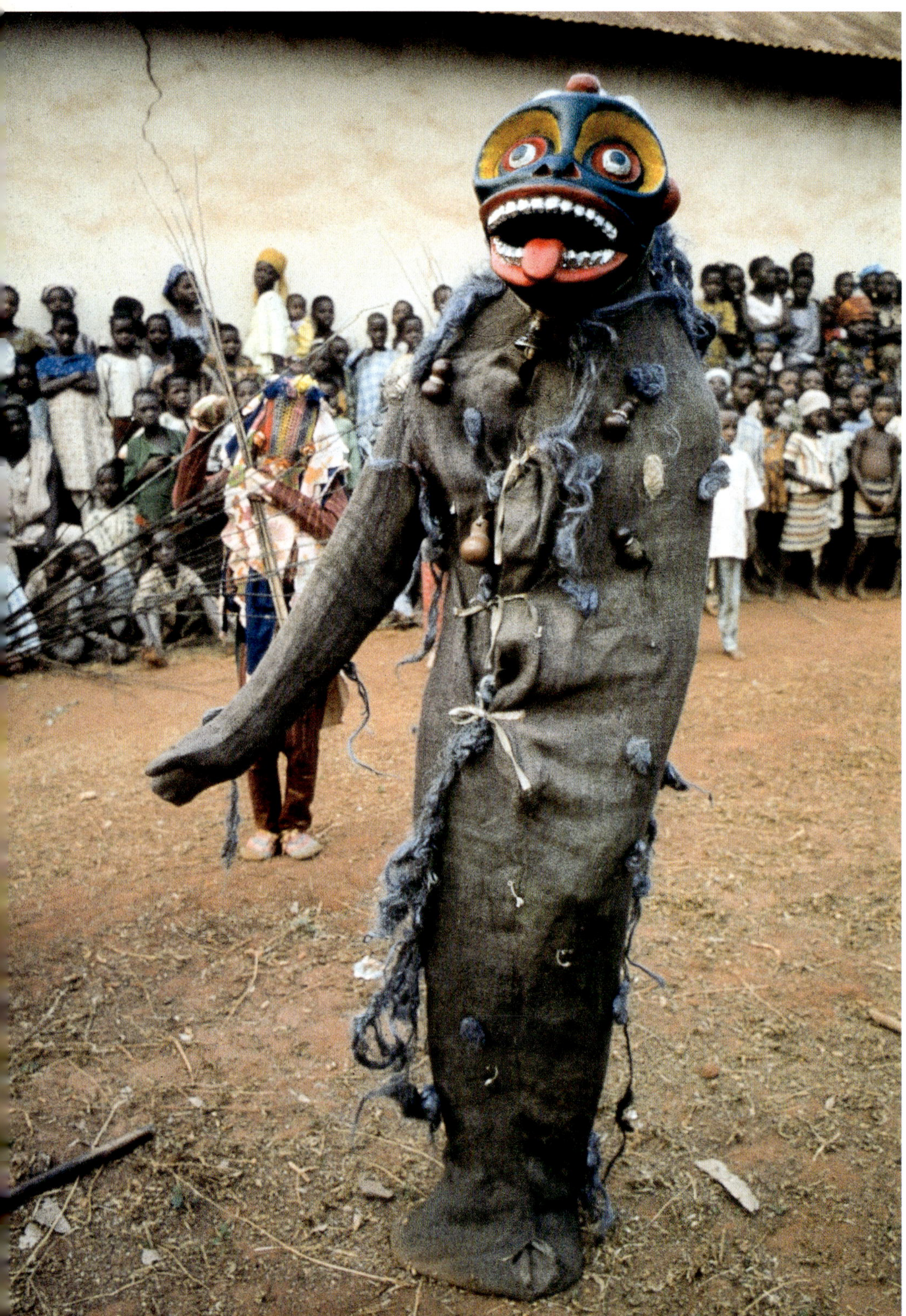

In order to comprehend the deep significance of art (*ona*) for Yoruba peoples, we must first try to understand their concepts of cosmos, creation, and place of humans and objects in this worldview. First, everything that exists—plants, animals, humans, things, places, words, songs, smells, tastes, gestures—possesses a vital force/energy or performative power known as *ase.* Through knowledge, training, and wisdom, people harness such *ase* for various purposes. Masterful artists, no matter what their medium, manipulate *ase* in their works in order to shape both the world (*aye*) and the otherworld (*orun*)—to "make things happen."

Second, life in this world is brief, transitory, and uncertain. As Yoruba say, "this world is a marketplace, the otherworld is home," and "life is a journey, the otherworld is home." Art mediates the threshold/space between marketplace and home, journey, and arrival. Art is a sacrifice, an offering to the forces in this cosmos. It embodies the unseen as well as the seen, the immaterial as well as the material.

When the Yoruba marvel at a work of art, they say it is "wonderful"—that it simultaneously creates and embodies wonder—it is a transformative and transforming experience. They understand that the "work" embodies *ase*, because the work that went into creating it—the inspirations, thoughts, toil, sweat, etc.—imbue the work with performative

Yoruba Masquerader representing Aroni, a forest spirit, Egungun Ritual. Egbada-Yoruba, Nigeria
Photo: Henry John Drewal, 1978. Courtesy of the Henry John and Margaret Thompson Drewal Collection, Eliot Elisofon Photographic Archive, National Museum of African Art, Smithsonian Institution

power. And when that object has lived a long life of use—carved, painted, touched, oiled, blessed, fed, clothed, danced, sung-to, broken, repaired, and buried—it possesses the *ase* of all it has come in contact with and becomes a powerful venerated relic.

This mask, now in the possession of The Baltimore Museum of Art, was a "miracle" (idan), part of a flexible repertoire of masquerades that are "given birth" by an "Owner-of-Miracles," the masker called Onidan. The masker and the mask belonged to the Egungun association, which functions principally for the veneration of the ancestors. Onidan, possessing the transformative, otherworldly powers of ancestral spirits, gives birth to a series of marvelous manifestations [wonder-full sights]—masquerades representing otherworldly and worldly entities: animals like snakes, crocodiles, hyenas, lions, rams, insects, monsters, and monkeys; human types such as mothers of twins, drunkards, prostitutes, brides, husbands and wives, pregnant women, foreigners like Europeans, Baribas, Hausas, and Dahomeans; and otherworldly beings such as dancing mats, devotees possessed by their gods (*orisa*), and spirits (*iwin*). The deep-set simian eyes, moveable jaw with protruding tongue, and the medicine gourd crowning the head between two horn-like forms suggest that this mask was part of an elaborate costume ensemble representing the tricksterish forest spirit known as Aroni.

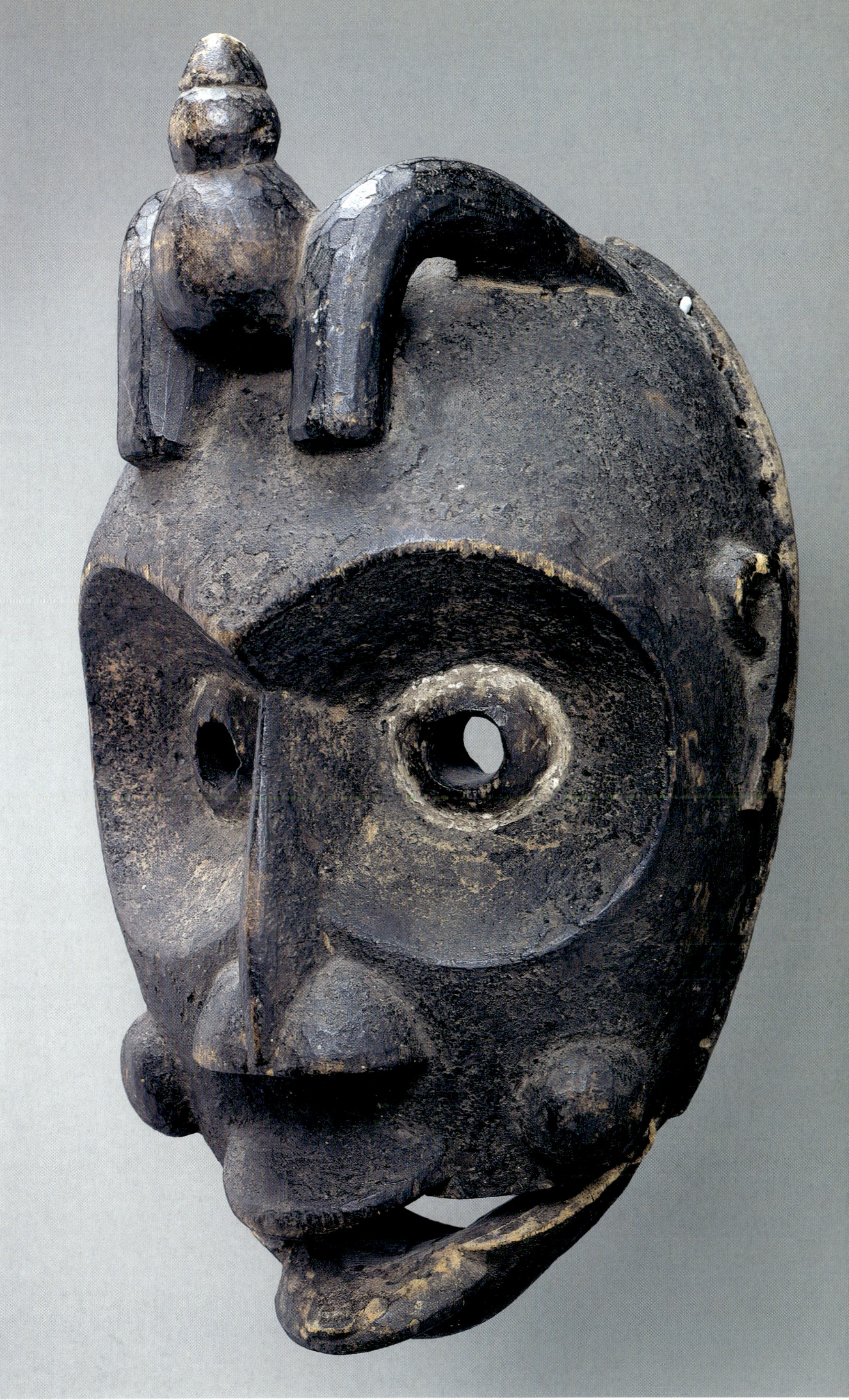

Each of these visions would appear "miraculously." Sometimes a group of Egungun set up a large encircling mat wall (that sometimes dances by itself) in the center of the performance space. At the most appropriately dramatic moment, the mat wall will collapse to reveal a miracle like a fish or crocodile with snapping, gaping jaws into which people will cautiously throw coins to show their appreciation. At other times the "miracles" will appear out of nowhere. Monkey masquerader jump down out of trees or from rooftops. Hyenas and lions suddenly appear and race through the crowd, chasing and terrorizing small children who scatter in all directions. Foreigner-masqueraders mime their cultural stereotypes—a European couple holds hands, kisses, and exchanges love notes on scraps of paper. A Dahomean warrior smokes a pipe as wields an axe, menacing spectators as he moves through the space.

Being a forest spirit, Aroni ensembles often include natural materials to evoke its habitat beyond the cultural centers of Yoruba cities and towns. Some I have witnessed have masks attached to rough burlap costumes (painted green) bedecked in roots, leaves, vines, and medicine gourds. Aroni lore describes it as a spirit with one arm and one leg, so the costuming creates this image —the masquerader hops around on its "one leg," sometimes holding onto a long wooden staff with its "single arm." Masked attendants escort it about the performance area as drummers play rhythms associated with songs for Aroni and audience members give alms and sometimes come forward to seek blessings. A fickle forest spirit, Aroni can help or hinder hunters and others who enter its realm. Using its magical medicines, Aroni brings game to hunters, teaches them herbal cures, or makes them lose their way and perish. Though it does not speak during the performance, its articulated jaw and protruding tongue suggest magical incantations, words of power.

Henry John Drewal

The Many Publics of the Bedu Masquerade: Nafana Male and Female Masks

Male and Female Masks (*Bedu*)
Nafana, Ivory Coast, Tambi village
Artist: Koffi Djereba (d. 1994)
1968
Wood (from the buttress roots of the silk-cotton tree: Bombacaceae Ceiba pentandra), fiber (from the bark of the baobab tree: Bombacaceae Adansonia digitata), pigment, Male: H. 140 cm; Female: H. 180 cm
Purchased with exchange funds from Gift from the Collection of Albert D. and Esther Lazarus Goldman, Baltimore; Gift of Howard B. Marshall, New York; Gift of Mr. and Mrs. John J. McCavitt, Plantation, Florida; Gift of A. Harvey and Phyllis K. Schreter, Baltimore; and Gift of Daniel Solomon, M. D., Los Angeles
BMA 2003.66.1–.2 (exported by Drid Williams from the Ivory Coast in 1970; performed in a ceremony in Tambi in 1969; commission from the artist by Drid Williams in 1968)

Participating in the Bedu masquerade is an annual activity for many inhabitants of east-central Ivory Coast, in and around the ancient trading town of Bondoukou, along the border with Ghana. Since the fourteenth century, multiple waves of migrations, intensive long-distance trade and military occupation by various groups, have turned the city and the region of Bondoukou into an ethnic mosaic including village quarters of Mande, Hausa, Fulani, Gur, and Twi (Akan). These factions share annual communal festivals which mobilize villagers across ethnic, family, religious, and gender divisions, and often include the Bedu masquerade.

Drid Williams and René Bravmann—the first anthropologists to have provided descriptions of Bedu—immediately noticed the inclusive, communal character of the masquerade as one of its most outstanding features. Precisely "its public nature, its lack of esoteric ritual, and its concerns for the health and prosperity of all," Bravmann (1974: 117–118) argues, encourages the many Muslims of the region to participate in the masquerade alongside their pagan and Catholic neighbors. After all, Williams (1968:20) explains: "the Bedu rites are a communal purification phenomenon. No one remains uninvolved." As well as bringing the community together, the many activities surrounding the Bedu masquerade mark neat divisions between gender, age, and sometimes ethnic-religious groups.

Depending on the ritual calendar which is negotiated among the different ethnic and religious groups or quarters, villages set up Bedu performances during their new year festivals which can last one to several weeks, but always take place sometime during the dry season (November to March). Bedu is a night masquerade that features one or more maskers—these are male initiates who carry a tall plank mask from the chest up and are dressed in a bark costume that covers their entire body. The large circle of people demarcating Bedu's moving space, consists of a small group of drum-playing musicians, and a large active audience of children, adults and elders, men and women, locals and invitees from other villages, who move counter clockwise while clapping their hands and singing songs. However, this joint convivial activity is only the tip of the iceberg and the culminating point of a series of festive and technical activities which mobilize different groups of specialists and ritual constituencies.

Every year, the mask is symbolically brought back from the bush to the village by adult male initiates. In some villages this event coincides with a nightly trip of children who go out into the bush to collect the brown/red and white pigment (clay and kaolin, respectively) with which the

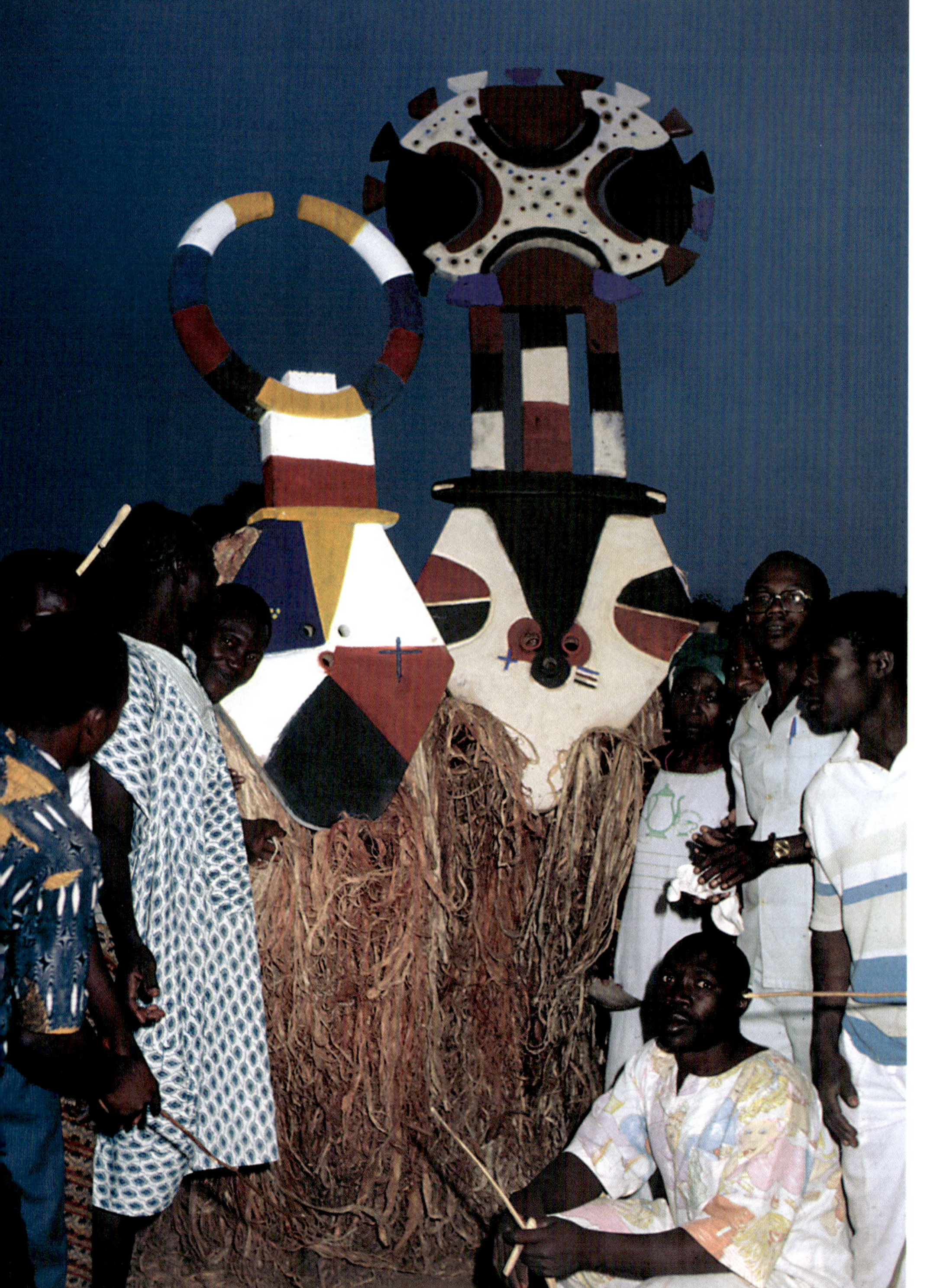

Bedu Masquerade. Nafana, Tambi, Bondoukou region, Ivory Coast. Photo: Raymond Silverman, 1987

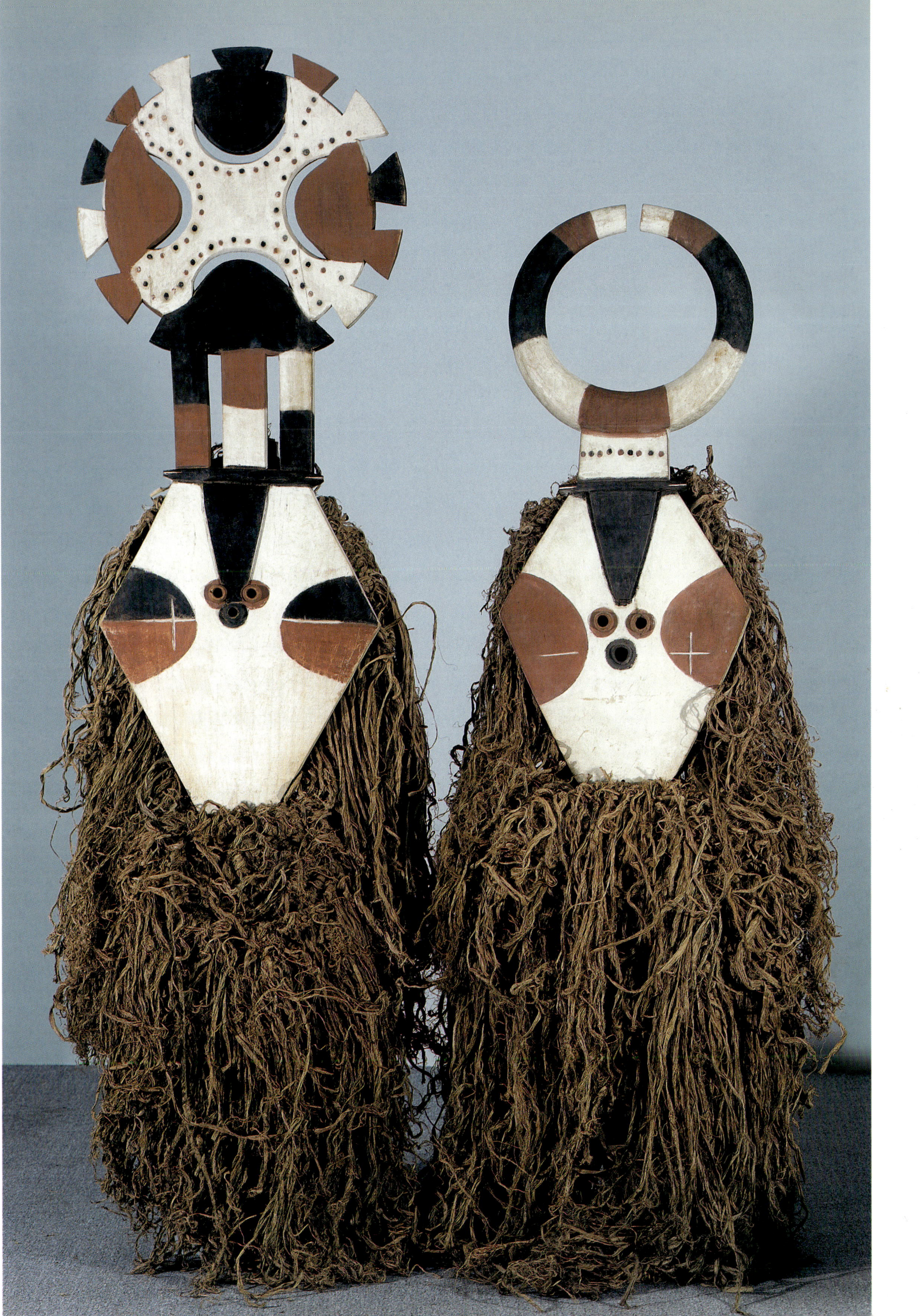

Bedu mask is repainted a couple of days later by a group of female specialists. This painting ceremony is called the "washing" and it runs almost parallel with the "feeding," that is the activity of making the Bedu mask costume. One morning a large group of male adults go out into the bush and beat several layers of bark off a baobab tree. The strips of bark are knotted to three ropes of different sizes which form the "shirt" (short), the "skirt" (long), and the "overcoat" (thick) of the three-piece Bedu costume.

This idiom of washing, feeding, and dressing clearly expresses the idea of domestication and cultivation. As it happens, the original Bedu is portrayed as a wild animal whose transfer to the village involves a process of "subjection," i.e., making a more manageable and refined effigy of the original "beast." This process of domestication is also represented in the subsequent Bedu-related performances. While during the preliminary phase the somewhat aggressive and unruly "male" Bedu masks (with horns) play an important part, during the later stages the more serene and civilized "female" Bedu masks (with the disk-like superstructure) are at the center of attention.

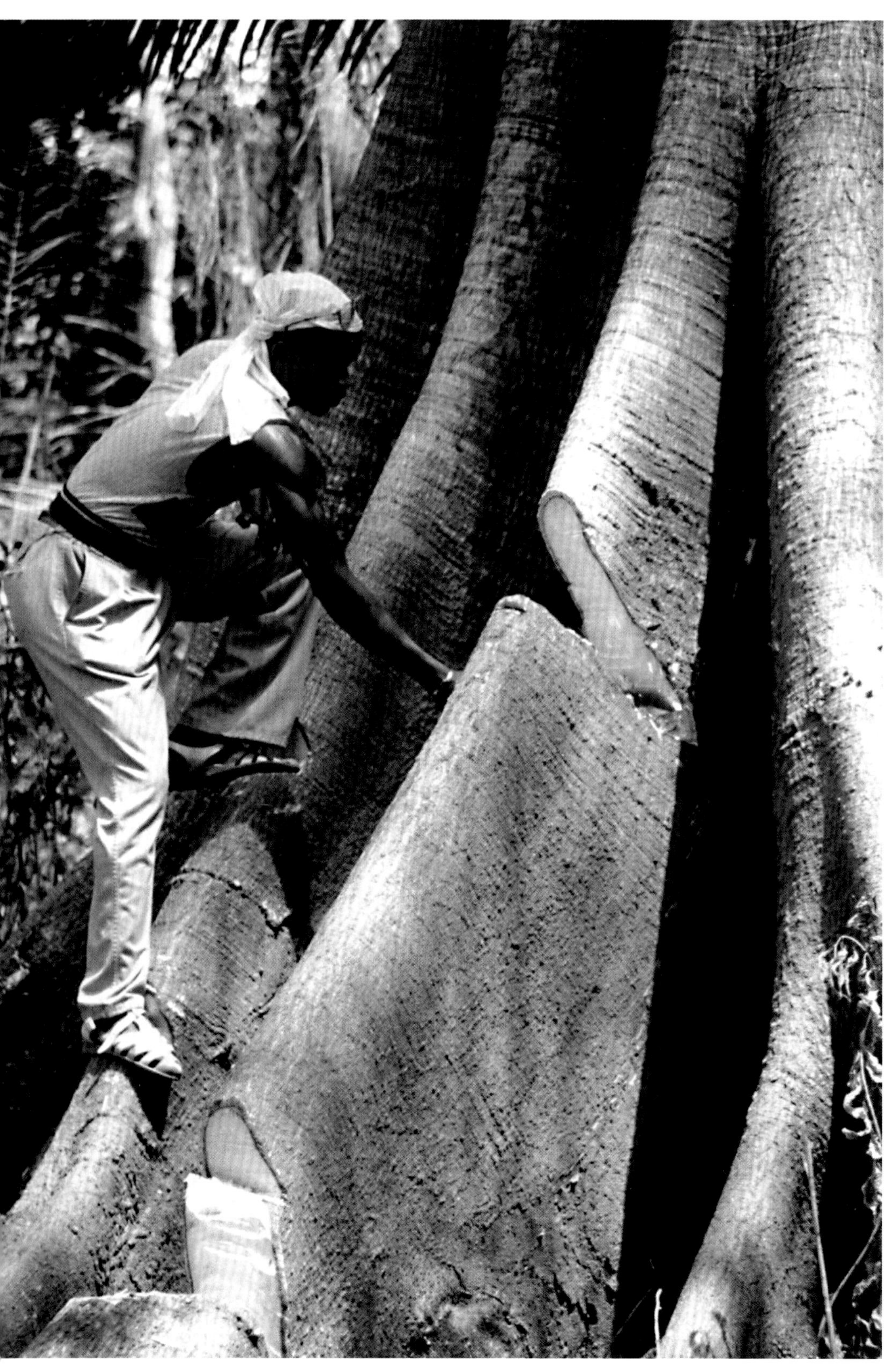

The preparatory work of the different gender groups overlaps with the ritual period called *Zòrògò*. A typical Zorogo dance shows a circle consisting of male and female sections which insult each other in call-and-response songs. At times, the circle breaks up into two gendered groups who shout at each other while naming the genitalia of the other sex. The Zorogo period paves the way for, but can occasionally spill over into, the period of Bedu dances. In that case the "male" Bedu can be seen joining into the Zorogo dances and occasionally (playfully) intervening—using his whip—when matters seem to get out of hand.

However, any formal appearance of Bedu masks is preceded by the only ceremony conducted during daylight: the presentation of the freshly "washed/painted" and properly "fed/dressed" masks to the village. The Bedu masks form a procession together with an ambulant group of male musicians and female singers who traverse the different village quarters. The Bedu masks go around blessing (the word that is often used is "cleansing") the houses of the people who died during the previous year, as well as many elders and babies of the village. From then onwards nightly masquerades are organized regularly for the next days or weeks, staging mainly the "female" Bedu masks. During these performances all gender, age, and other divisions are publicly set aside and the active audience sings solemn songs in honour of Bedu who is temporarily made to represent the highest moral authority in the village.

While during the weeks of preparatory work (painting and dressing) and liminal ritual activity (Zorogo), gender divisions become heavily thematized; later on, near the end of the new year festival, the Bedu performances stress the political and ethnic dimensions (and divisions) of communal life. First, one can observe a certain incompatibility between Bedu and the village chief. Bedu often "belongs" to a kin group different from the one of the village leader. This family, for instance, appoints among its members a Bedu chief, a kind of impresario who organizes the performance calendar, coaches the teams of female painters, male costume-makers, and musicians, and instructs the maskers. The "Bedu family" also has a special relationship to the ancestral land—the fields and bush beyond the confines of the village which is

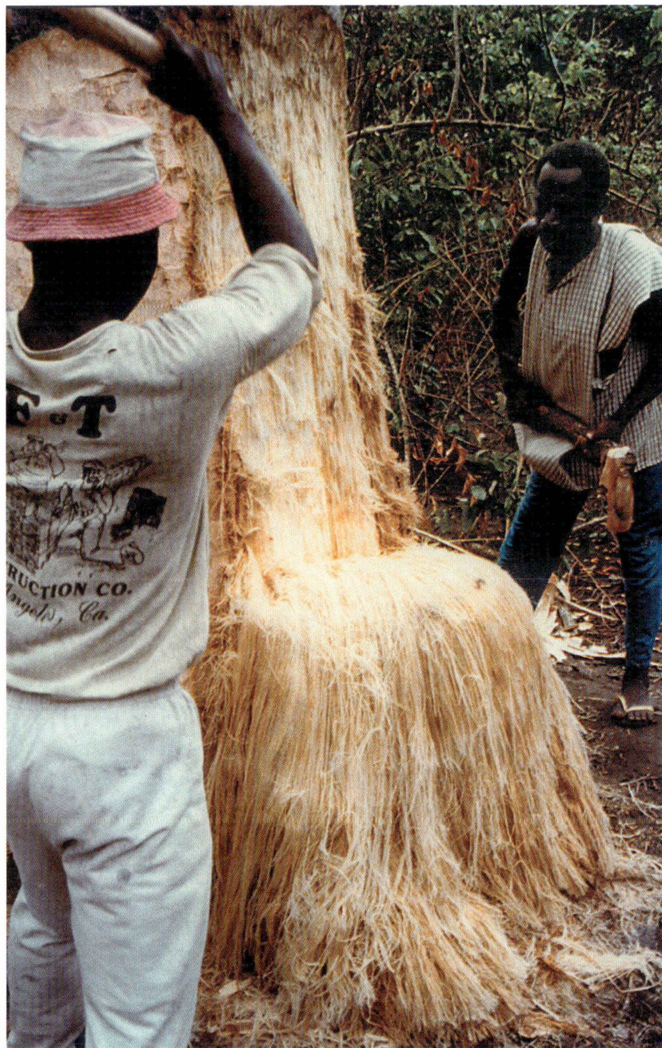

A man cutting the buttress roots of the silk-cotton tree. Nafana, Ivory Coast
Photo: Karel Arnaut

Two men beating layers of bark off a baobab tree. Nafana, Ivory Coast
Photo: Karel Arnaut

ruled over, during normal times, by the village chief. The annual and temporary transfer of the bush creature Bedu to the village is the occasion to remember the earliest origins of the village which involved the domestication of the bush and the cultivation of the land. The new year festival therefore recalls the ancestors in general and the founders of the village as well as the "owners" of the land in particular. In other words, Bedu triggers recollections about the foundation of the political power of the village chief and his kin group, and the authority of the kin groups or ethnic groups who provided the land on which the village was built. Such recollections tend to relativize (or interrogate) the power of the village chief who may sometimes even bar the Bedu mask from entering his village quarter during the annual presentation.

Also, in the city of Bondoukou, Bedu evokes delicate power balances between the owners of the city (the mainly Muslim Jula) and the owners of the land/earth (the mainly Catholic or "traditionalist" Gbin and Nafana families). Over the last decades, this opposition between Jula and non-Jula has come to dominate the Bedu masquerade to the extent that the gender theme has almost completely disappeared. Moreover, in Bondoukou city, Bedu performances have been taken over by the younger generations who have turned the annual Bedu masquerade into a spectacular game of sports that is attended by hundreds of urban youngsters. In the weeks preceding the annual remembrance of the foundation of Bondoukou by the Gbin and the Nafana, a young Nafana wearing the Bedu mask and accompanied by a dozen of his friends ventures into the city and is challenged by a multitude of Muslim Jula adolescents who playfully offend the masker. The game consists in Bedu identifying a particularly provocative "Jula" teenager, pursuing him in a spectacular race along the main roads and through the narrow pathways in between the compounds, in order to strike him with his whip. If Bedu is successful in thrashing the Muslim youngster, the latter in his turn is insulted, not only by the Nafana youngsters but also by his Jula mates. The insult they shout at him is "alaji"—in fact a Muslim honorific title (El Hadj), which for the occasion signifies weakness and defeat.

If in the urban context of Bondoukou, the ethno-religious opposition has come to dominate the Bedu performances, in rural areas one can detect a certain "Zoroification" of Bedu. In many villages the Zorogo reciprocal insulting of men and women may overshadow the entire sequence of Bedu performances to the extent that typical Zorogo songs are chanted in front of the solemn 'female' Bedu mask. Generally speaking, Bedu performances rather stress (gender or ethno-religious) oppositions while the solemn, conciliatory Bedu dances pulling together the 'whole community' have lost importance.

"Zoroification" may allow the villagers to push the sensitive and increasingly contested issues of land ownership and political authority into the background. In Bondoukou city, the kind of ethno-religious opposition at the foreground of the Bedu masquerade is dramatically played out on the national political scene of the Ivory Coast. Over the last decade the political landscape has been marked by an acerbating antagonism between autochthonous Ivorians and a vaguely defined group of allochthonus characterized as Muslims and often designated by the term 'Jula'. In September 2002 this antagonism led the country into a civil war which has been dividing the country into two with Bondoukou situated along the front line. Due to the curfew, no Bedu performances were staged at Bondoukou city last year. Having lost already some of its conciliatory powers, Bedu could not surmount its ritual constituency staging a real fight instead of a mock one.

Karel Arnaut

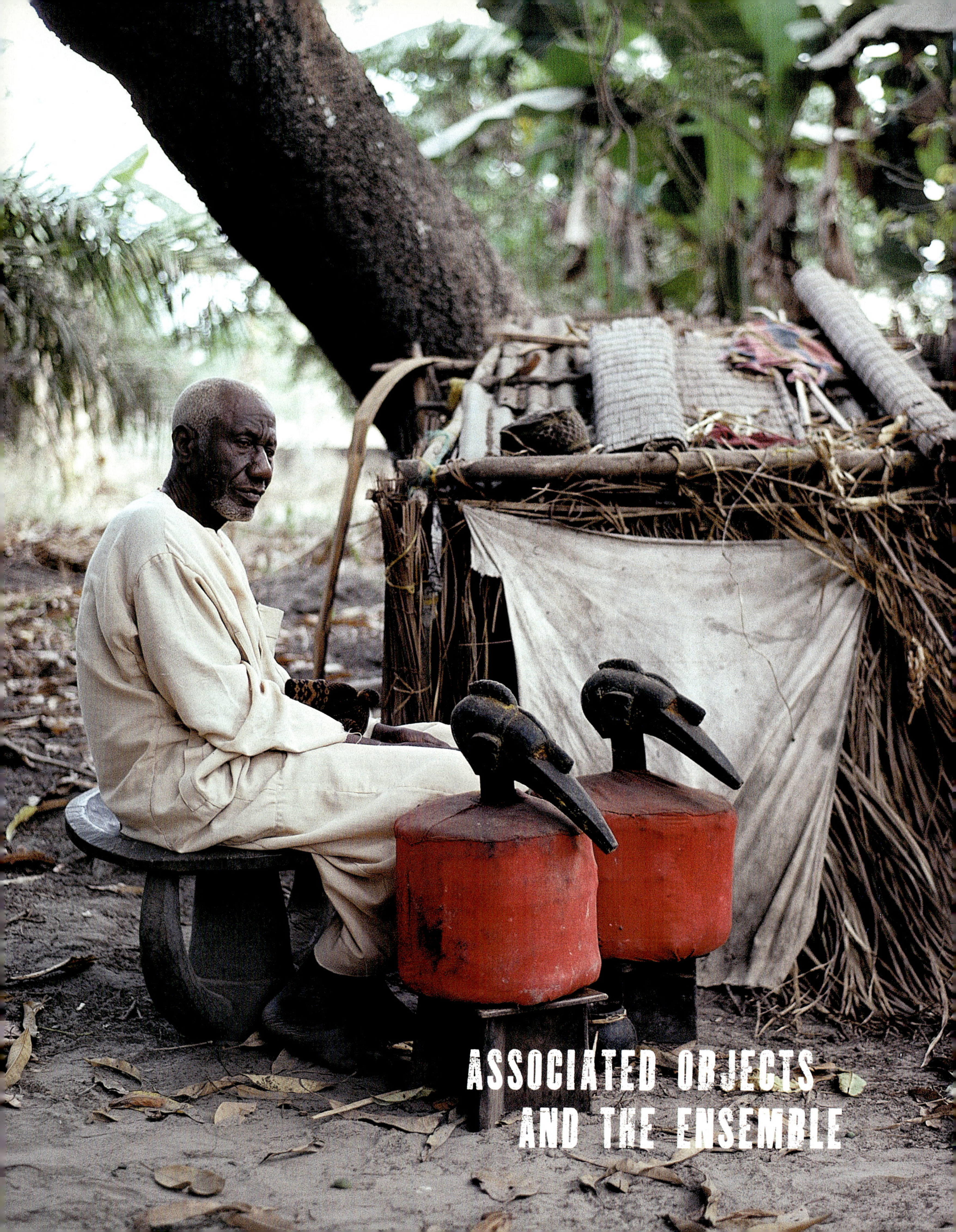

ASSOCIATED OBJECTS AND THE ENSEMBLE

The essays here examining multiple elements of performance have one concern in common: the ensemble. Henry John Drewal, Herbert M. Cole, and Suzan Elizabeth Gagliardi discuss shrine ensembles among the Yoruba, Asante, and Lobi that merge with singing, drumming, and dancing as a "chorus of visual praise offerings." Cameroon masks are regarded by Tamara Northern as forming a standard cast of characters representing a lineage. For the Baga, I analyze the interaction and contrast of two headdresses that invoke the powers of transition versus tradition. The pairing of male and female masks raises different kinds of issues—political, cosmological, spiritual, social, and kinesthetic—among the Kuba, the Bamana, and are examined, respectively, by David Binkley and Stephen Wooten. And in my discussion of the Mende Sande mask, I contrast matched and opposing aesthetic presentations.

In the modernist concept of the art museum gallery, with its gray or white walls, sparse installation, and silence, only a vacuum surrounds the art object, except for the "magic" between the single object and the viewer. Postmodern concepts of the museum tend to posit the gallery environment as context, bearing messages about ourselves and our use of art, including that from Africa. This may have little to do with the intentions of the artists.

In the African artistic context, however, there is an intended, active "sociability" that informs that artistic entity. The object is in dialogue with other objects, whether on a shrine or in a performance.

Masks and headdresses are often danced in pairs, sometimes identically (p. 115), sometimes diametrically opposed (p. 223), or in some relationship to each other. Some are danced in groups (pp. 160, 163), in a single event, in sequence, or on different occasions, but referring to each other through narrative or some ethnohistorical construct.

An obvious pairing is in the case of the Yoruba twin figures (Ibeji) (p. 261). A figure is carved at the death of a twin among the Yoruba in order to commemorate its spirit and placate the dead twin so that the latter does not try to entice the living twin to join him or her in the other world. In all cases, the twin figures function in the context of the pair. When there is a living twin, the wooden twin figure functions in ritual with the living twin, is cared for by the mother and treated just as the living twin—it is given food, anointed with oil, clothed, given jewelry, and carried in the arms of the mother. Should the second twin die, a second figure, identical to the first except for a gender differentiation, as the case may be, is made to accompany the first figure and treated in ritual in just the same way.

Often a family has a collection of these figures, up to ten or twenty, all kept in a basket as a community of twins. The physical art form comprises the basket and any such multiple miniature figures huddled together and forming a whole. Recent collections include plastic dolls as well as wooden figures. Such collections are often presented in public performance. In this instance, the collection constitutes the art form, not the individual object—this does not preclude the mother from regarding each of these twin figures individually. Frances Harding noted how:

> specific carvings remind the mother of an individual child who died.... She will recognize differences in the quality of carvings but this may not reconcile with her most cherished memory or with the carving's function as a mnemonic of a child quite apart from its role as an item of religious belief.... [In a museum] each carving can only be seen as a three-dimensional form whose qualities can only lie on the surface, the proportion, etc. [In the Yoruba context] collectively, they seem matured and softened by their relationship to each other within the confines of the basket (in personal communication, 2003).

A pair of a-Tshol headdresses serving as shrine figures in the possession of an elder. The a-Tshol is also complementary to the a-Bil-ña-Tshol (p. 164–65). Baga Sitem, Guinea. Photo: Frederick John Lamp, 1992

Among the Yoruba, identical images appear in the dance of the Gèlèdé headdress (p. 115). Typically, two nearly identical headdresses are given identical gender attributions, and worn by two male dancers who are costumed identically (although exceptions have been documented). The dualism of the Gèlèdé performance is referential. The doubling of power as we have seen in the expression of twin figures is a quintessentially Yoruba expression, important here in the context of the affirmation of the extraordinary powers of older women. Doubling is a convention that mothers understand and that the community attributes to motherhood. However, Gèlèdé headdresses are generally collected singly, and to my knowledge, no museum exhibit in the West contains a pair.

There are many cases in African art—probably many more than scholars have realized—in which a beautiful mask is opposed by a counterpart that represents its antithesis (of beauty, uprightness, and admirable comportment). The two masks, negative and positive, do not necessarily dance at the same time, but they are assigned ritual entrances, each of which is as important as the other. Most often it is the beautiful mask that has been collected by Europeans and Americans and is best known, but the ugly or antisocial mask is often just as or more important to the Africans, bearing more spiritual power. The ugly mask often is a cruder version of the beautiful mask and therefore not as attractive to collectors.

The two female masks, Sowo and Gonde, among the Mende, are a perfect example of this disparity. For the Mende, one can hardly speak of the Sowo without reference to Gonde. Sowo (p. 175) is beautiful; the mask is finely carved. The dance is elegant and refined. Sowo represents the ideal in female behavior. Her opposite is Gonde, who is antisocial, anti-aesthetic, of ill-repute, coarse, grotesque, slovenly, in other words, everything that the Mende woman aspires not to be. Sowo's mask is finely carved with exquisite coiffure, polished to a deep, dark sheen, and completed with a full costume of finely stripped wood or raffia fiber, dyed a deep black. Gonde, on the other hand, is masked with a broken or crudely carved wooden helmet, and her costume is a disheveled collection of rags, fiber, and scraps of this and that. Without the less desirable Gonde, Sowo has no situational meaning. Sowo and Gonde define each other.

Often a stationary work of art is assembled in which every object has ritual and aesthetic importance. Here, the single wooden figure, although it may delight the viewer in its own right, may not suffice as an effective ritual form, but only as an element in an ensemble of varying forms which "works" as a whole. On a shrine, a wooden sculpture may be placed with other similar sculptures to form a community such as in representations of the ancestors of a village, and they may be associated, either singly, in pairs, or in groups, with other dissimilar objects such as bells, glasses, bowls, baskets, pottery, stones, even Coca Cola bottles, imported cloth, carcasses of reptiles, or parts from an automobile. Like the configuration of elements described above that are often attached to masks, objects placed in proximity to a shrine figure are generally prescribed by a ritual practitioner, a diviner, or a healer in order to effect well-being or a more specific change. Herbert Cole (personal communication, 2003) sees the Akan Tano shrine as "the meeting place or mediating place of people and the supernatural."

Robert Thompson detailed the importance of shrine ensembles, or "altars," in Black religion on both sides of the Atlantic, in his groundbreaking exhibition and catalogue, *Face of the Gods* (1993). One important shrine to *Shangó*, the Yoruba royal god of lightning and thunder, well demonstrates the power of the accumulation of varying physical elements. Shangó, himself, is not represented in sculpture, except through the gathering of attributes. Thompson (p. 236) first quotes the German anthropologist, Leo Frobenius, in 1910:

> A lofty, long and very deep recess made a gap in the row of fantastically carved and brightly painted columns. These were sculpted with horsemen, men climbing trees, monkeys, women, gods, and all sorts of mythological carved work. The dark chamber behind revealed a gorgeous red ceiling, pedestals with stone axes on them, wooden figures, cowrie-shell hangings and empty bottles.

Charles Gore (1998:71) described similar shrines among the nearby Edo of Benin erected in the course of initiation to the particular deity, in which the sculptured object of art may not occupy first place, but rather defines the relationship of deity to shrine. The efficacy of the shrine depends upon the inclusion of key objects "which define and articulate the relations of the initiate with that deity," and include a pot, water from the river, leaves associated with the deity, and other objects.

> "Other artefacts, such as statues, are embellishments which are introduced at shrines after initiation to enhance its prestige. They remain an elaboration or a reiteration of the basic and fundamental relationship between the initiate and the deity, although indicating the mutual benefits of the relationship as the material success brought by the deity provides the means to embellish the shrine."

Thompson goes on to describe in more detail the objects in the interior of the Yoruba shrine to Shangó:

> [Thunder wallets], seven of them, appear on the wall of the altar. They function both as receptacles for ritual paraphernalia and as virtual hangings.... Each wallet bears four panels in which appears the figure of a human with tailed headdress [striking] an asymmetrical pose right hand up, left hand down, recalling thundergod choreography....
>
> On the altar are placed four terracotta broad-mouthed vessels [*ikoko*], which serve as stands for calabashes in which ritual paraphernalia are stored. The most elaborate, at right, [is] emblazoned with a representation of a fish-legged deity flanked by devotees brandishing thunder-axes.... To the right of the figurated ikoko appears the carved wooden image of a seated dog, [an] animal specially associated with Shangó. To the right ... a thunder-ax....
>
> In the middle of the altar the eye picks out, stored in an open container, the reclining image of a twin and the jutting point of the horn of the Harnessed Antelope [*iwo igala*] for Orisha Oge, a deity closely associated with the thundergod.

He continues (p. 234), "It is ritually impertinent to read objects on Shangó's altar—thunder-ax, twin statuette—as furniture. These are colleagues.... "

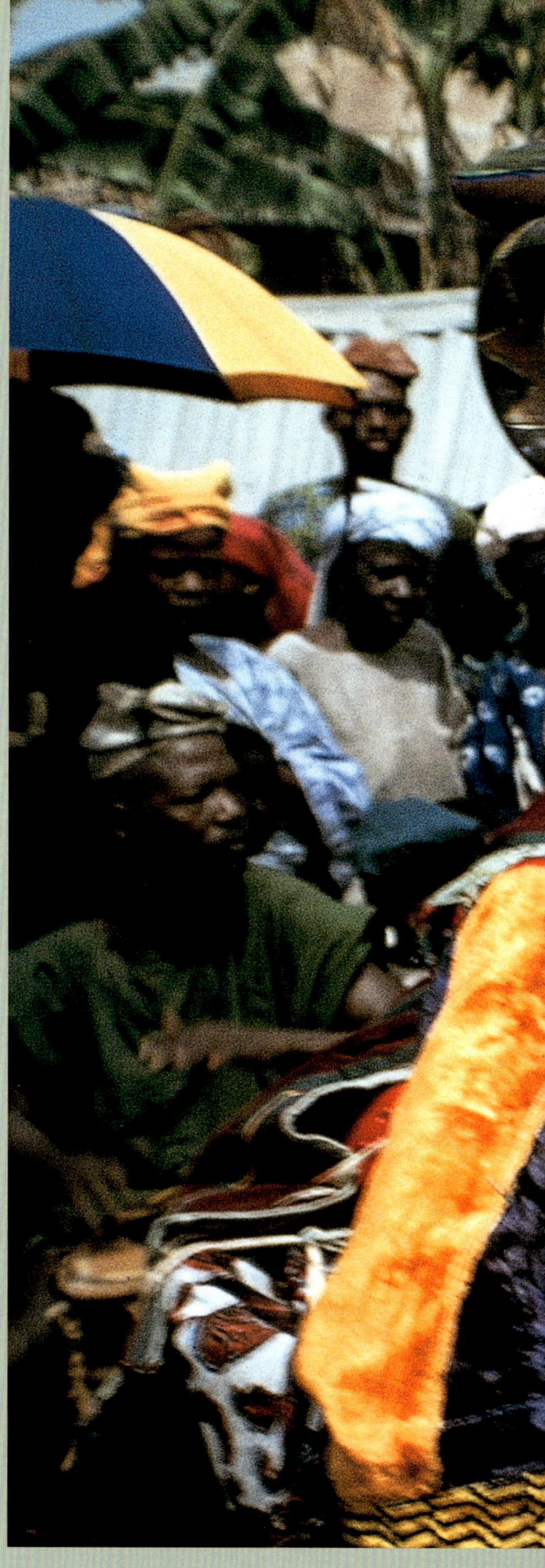

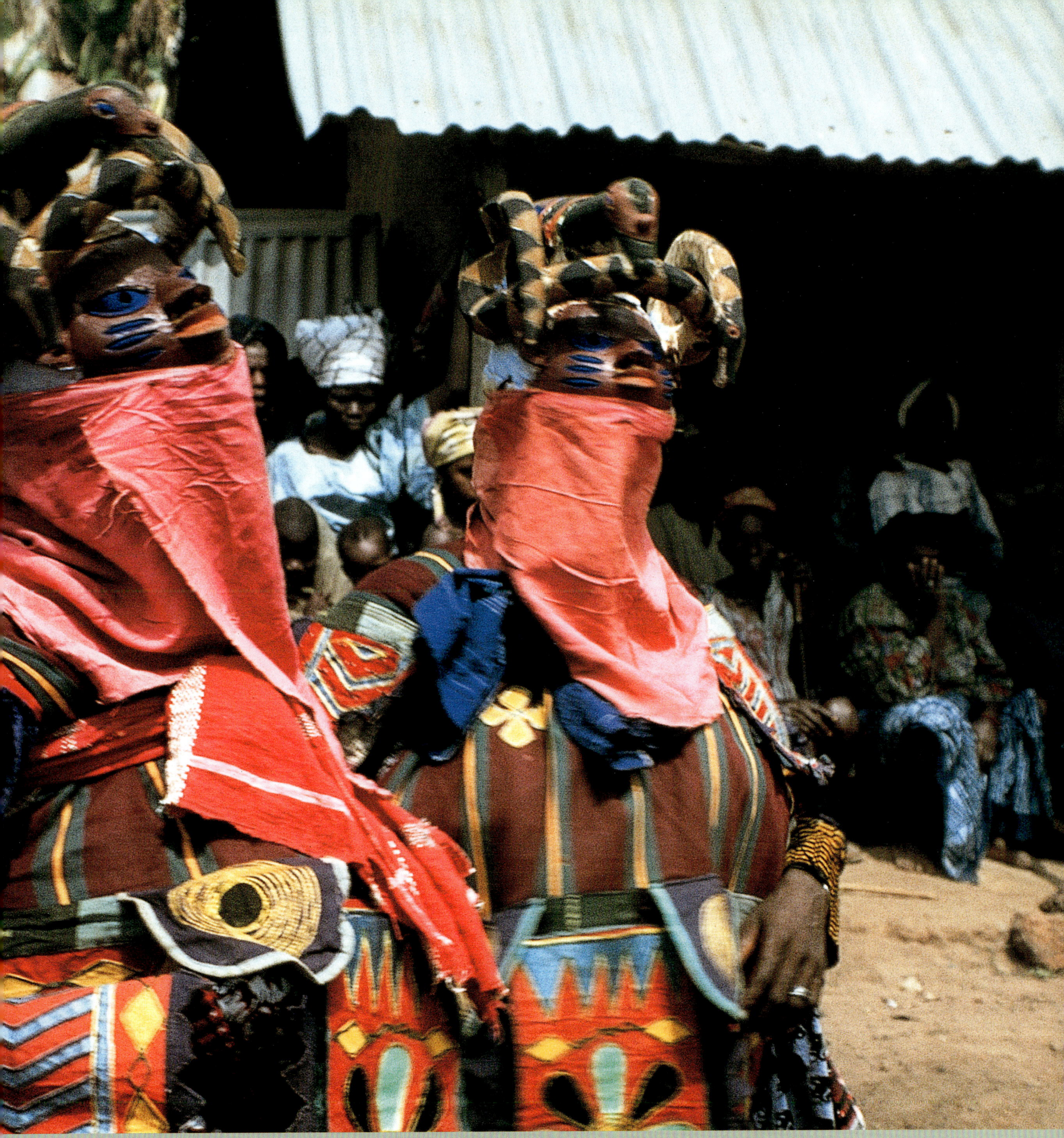

A pair of identical Gèlèdé dancers. Yoruba, Nigeria. Photo: Eliot Elisofon, 1971
Courtesy of the Eliot Elisofon Photographic Archive, National Museum of African Art, Smithsonian Institution

A Chorus of Visual Praise Offerings: a Yoruba Staff (*Ose Shangó*)

Staff for a Devotee of the God Shangó (Ose Shangó)
Yoruba, Nigeria
c. Late 19th century
Wood, H. 48 cm
Gift of Bernice Barth, Los Angeles
BMA 1991.123

Staffs for the thundergod, Shangó, (Ose Shangó) exist in two contexts—in the gestures of dances and rituals, and as shrine decorations. As dance implements, they are usually held in the left hand by devotees (as shown in the sculpture itself) during ceremonies, processions, and trance dances. They are the insignia of religious initiation and affliation. To the sharp, staccato rhythms of Shangó's sacred drum, the *bata*, devotees whirl, stamp their feet, give high kicks, and wing their shoulder blades/scapulas to mark and accentuate the rapid musical beats that evoke the active energy and potency of the god. The movement of the wands in the dance may vary. Sometimes they are raised high in the air and brought down swiftly in forceful, sweeping gestures toward the earth, evoking the flash of lightening, the crack of thunder, and the raining down of thundercelts—neolithic stone axe blades like the ones shown in the sculpture. These are signs of Shangó's presence and retributive power. At other moments, they may be cradled in the arms like a precious child, or embraced and pressed to the chest. All are gestures of respect and devotion for a deity who can be both kind and gentle, harsh and volatile. Note the shiny smoothness of the well-worn staff handle that attests to its countless ceremonial outings in the loving hands of its former owner. A carved loop at the bottom of the handle would have been used to hold a leather strap so the staff could be dangled from the wrist, freeing the devotee's hands for other actions.

The other setting for such staffs is on the altars for Shangó where they join many other ritual objects to beautify sacred space, attract the deity, and focus the worship of Shangó followers. One Shangó shrine among the Egbado-Yoruba is filled with ritual objects. On the darkened and raised earthen platform there are several fired clay vessels holding thundercelts (*edun ara*). Being associated with hot lightning and the wrath of the deity, they are often immersed in cooling water. Covering one of these in the foreground is a forged metal dance staff with its double-bladed form at the top. White chicken feathers and other remnants of offerings mark the front edge of the platform and floor. Leaning in front of the main whitened vessel are three carved wooden Shangó staffs. All have been painted in either natural dyes or commercial enamel paint, and one has been decorated with cloth. Covering the large white vessel are several gourd bowls containing three sacred gourd rattles (*sere*) used to invoke Shangó, as well as other smaller, non-figurative dance staffs. At other times they may be placed against a back wall of the altar or hung suspended from the rafters or a wall using the leather strap. The multiplication of arts—carved pedestals, bowls, and staffs, decorated bowls, leather bags, metal staffs, etc.—create a

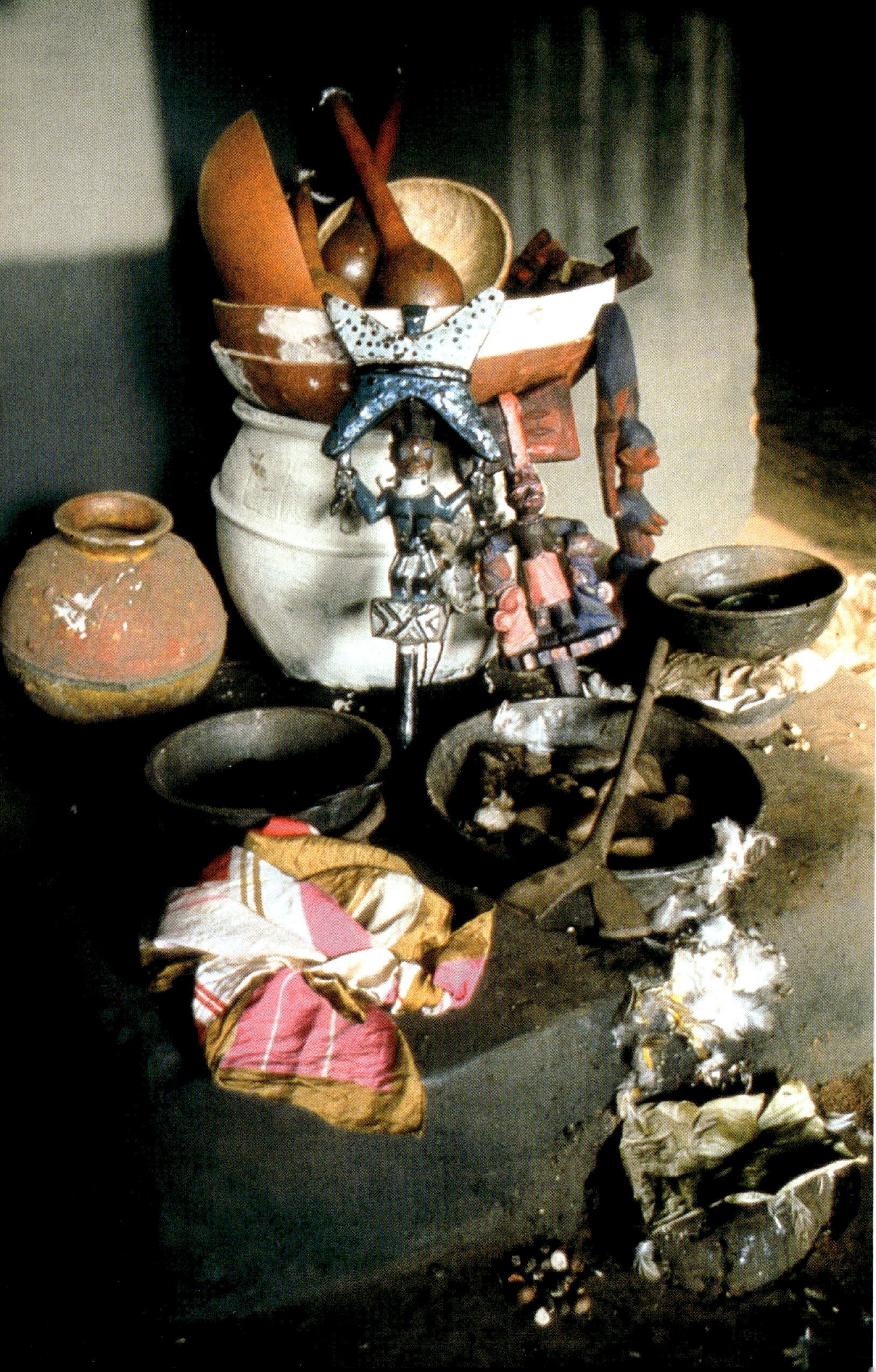

Shangó shrine. Egbado-Yoruba, Nigeria. Photo: Henry John Drewal, 1978. Courtesy of the Henry John and Margaret Thompson Drewal Collection, Eliot Elisofon Photographic Archive, National Museum of African Art, Smithsonian Institution

kind of chorus of visual praise offerings to Shangó that accompany the singing, drumming, and dancing that would fill such a shrine room on ritual occasions.

Remnants of the original polychromed surface can be seen in the sculpture's incised designs. Red and white are Shangó's symbolic colors. While these often appear in his art, artists and patrons are free to choose other hues to beautify works. Often staffs are decorated not only with colors, but with actual jewelry (necklaces, bracelets, earrings) and sometimes clothing. The figure in the sculpture, a representation of a Shangó devotee, is often a portrait of the staff's owner—the decorations reinforce this connection. Staff decorations are generally renewed for ceremonial occasions and annual festivals. These can be done by its owner, an artist, or any family members and friends. Staffs are often passed down within families or devotion societies, although sometimes divination determines that a person's ritual items should be buried with the body to accompany them in the afterlife. At other times, divination indicates that the objects should be destroyed, to honor and mark the owner's departure for the otherworld (*orun*). The lives of such objects thus resemble those of their owners or inheritors.

Henry John Drewal

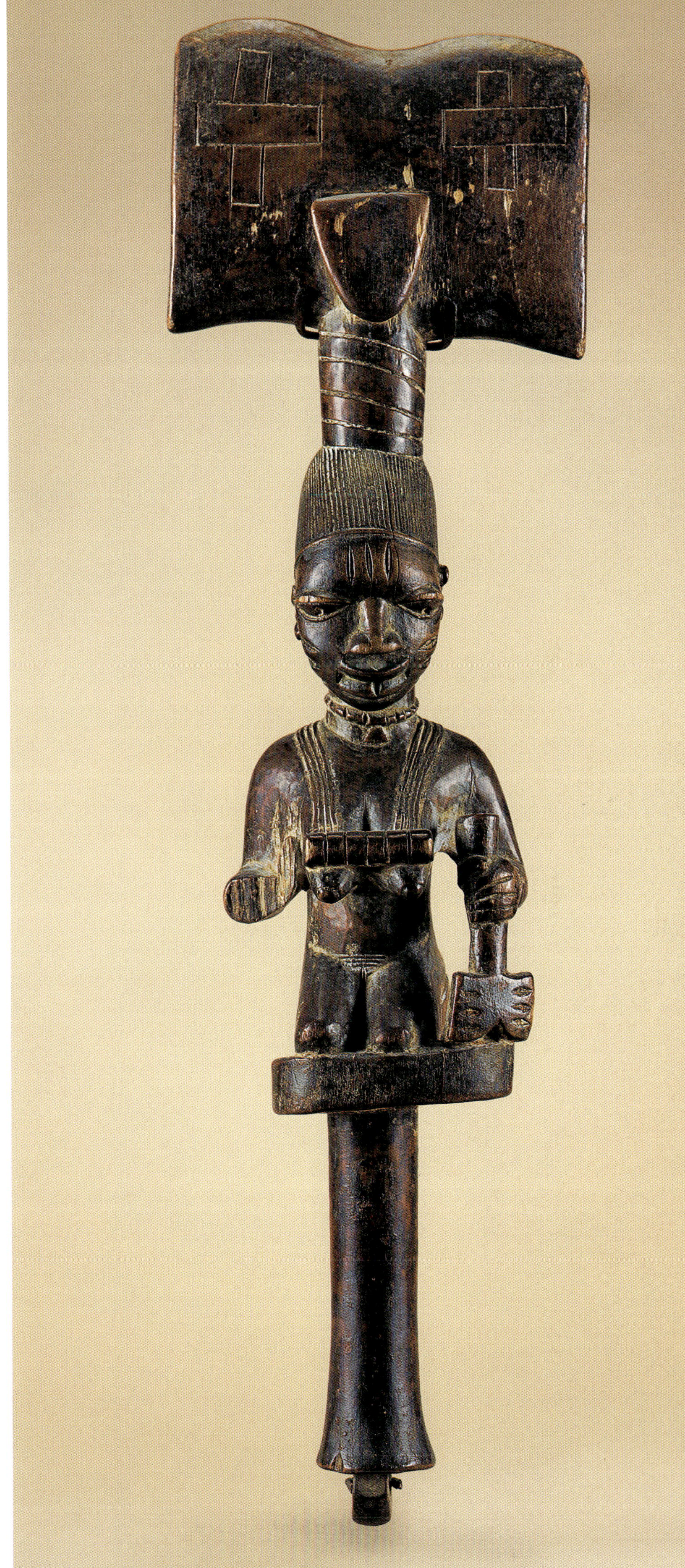

The Aura of Power and Mystery: an Asante Figure (*Akua'ba*)

The precise history of any African art object is often difficult or impossible to reconstruct. This is especially true of common objects such as this small blackened figure in the BMA collection, an object type that exists in the thousands—perhaps hundreds of thousands. This simplified human figure, called Akua'ba (plural, Akua'mma), comes from the Akan peoples of Ghana, most probably from the Asante, based on its style. In the case of what may be called "climax" or unique forms of great historical importance, such as the Asante Golden Stool, there is such a cultural centrality that their histories are reasonably well known. The very numerous, small, disc-headed Akua'mma, mostly anonymous as to owner and artist when they come to us, are virtually undocumented individually. Occasional examples can be attributed to specific artists, but attempts to discern the history of any given Akua'ba by "reading" its surface—scarification marks, wear or use patterns, color or attached beads, for example—reveal very little.

Female Figure (*Akua'ba*)
Asante, Ghana
c. Mid-20th century
Wood, beads, H. 28 cm
Gift of Robert and Nancy Nooter, Washington, D.C.
BMA 1985.287

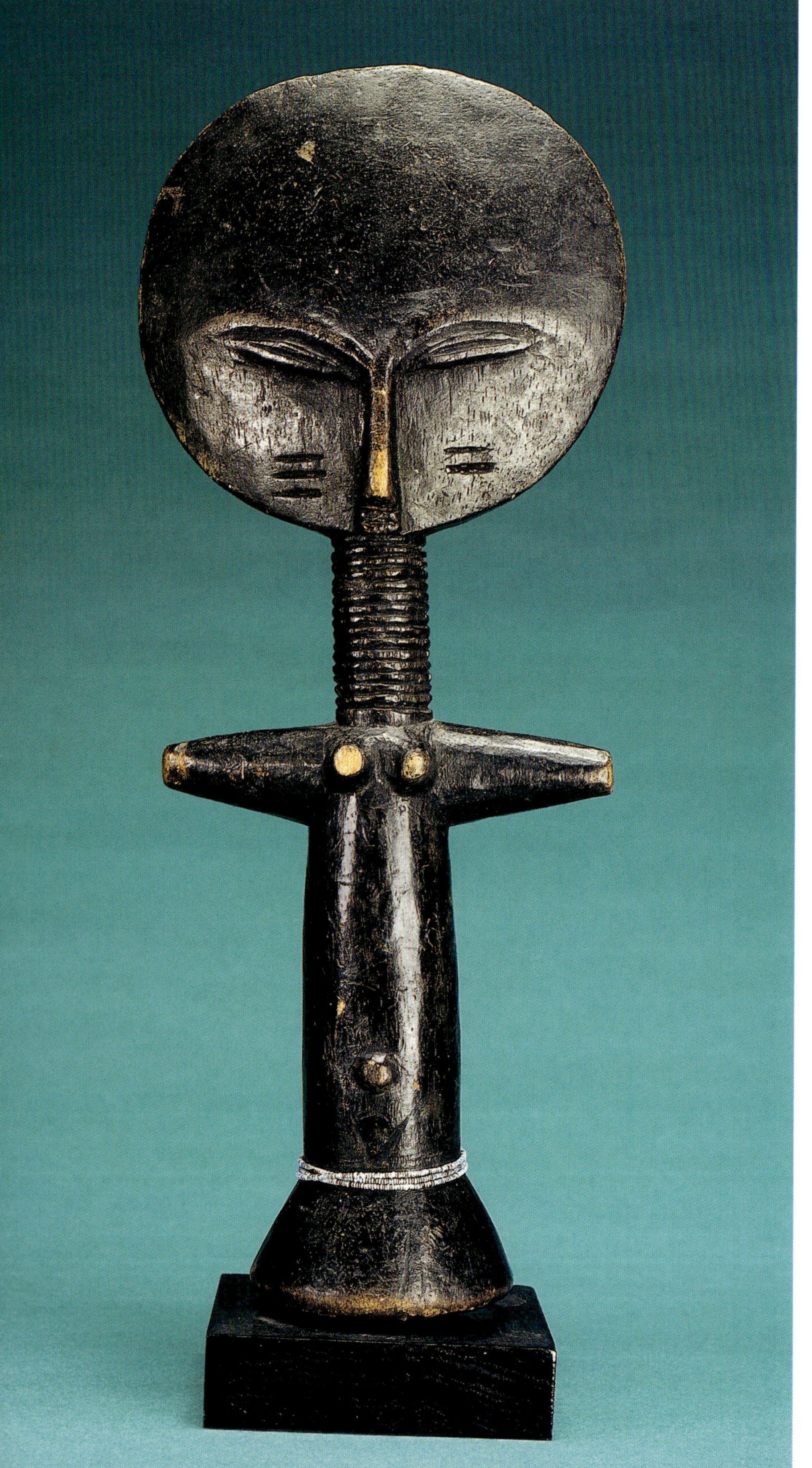

The common legend about the origin of these figures may be briefly recounted. Many years ago, a married Asante woman named Akua (meaning "Born on Wednesday") wanted to have a baby, but was barren. She consulted a priest, who told her to commission a carving of a small child and treat the image as if it were her own baby. She did so. She, fed, bathed and clothed the carving, and carried it on her back, as living infants are carried. People in the village saw her with a wooden head poking out of her wrapper, and teased: "Look at Akua's child" (Akua'ba in Twi, the Akan/Asante language). But Akua soon conceived and later gave birth to a beautiful girl baby. Generations of Akan women have followed her legendary example.

The function of these figures in contributing to a woman's conception, benign pregnancy and the safe birth of a preferably female child (because the Akan are a matrilineal people) has been recorded frequently. Three particular contexts of use are documented. First, these small images are cared for as in the legend and "worn" or carried on their backs by pregnant women and those hoping to conceive.

Second, in some few instances, the figures may be entrusted to children, as recorded by Malcolm McLeod (1981:166):

> Young (premenarche) girls were given these carvings to play with; it was believed that by looking upon a well-formed doll a woman was influenced or assisted to bear a good-looking child. A link of some sort was conceived between the form and quality of the doll and the child eventually born.

Third, we know that Akua'mma are placed in shrines, normally to the river god, Tano. Tano is well known across central and southern Ghana for his ability to help with both conception and a successful birth. The reason most Akua'mma are situated in shrines is that they have been returned to the shrines as thank offerings to the god and its custodian, after aiding the new mother in conceiving and in delivering safely.

Diviners send barren or hopeful women to local Tano shrines, which exist in the hundreds throughout the large Akan region, and they generally suggest that the woman procure an Akua'ba to take along. Sometimes the husband or another amateur carves the image, but more commonly, it is professionally carved. At the shrine the priest or priestess conducts a ceremony with the figure, consecrating it by invoking the power of Tano to help the woman in her plight. At one shrine I documented, the priest first placed the woman's Akua'ba figure on the shrine, invoking Tano.

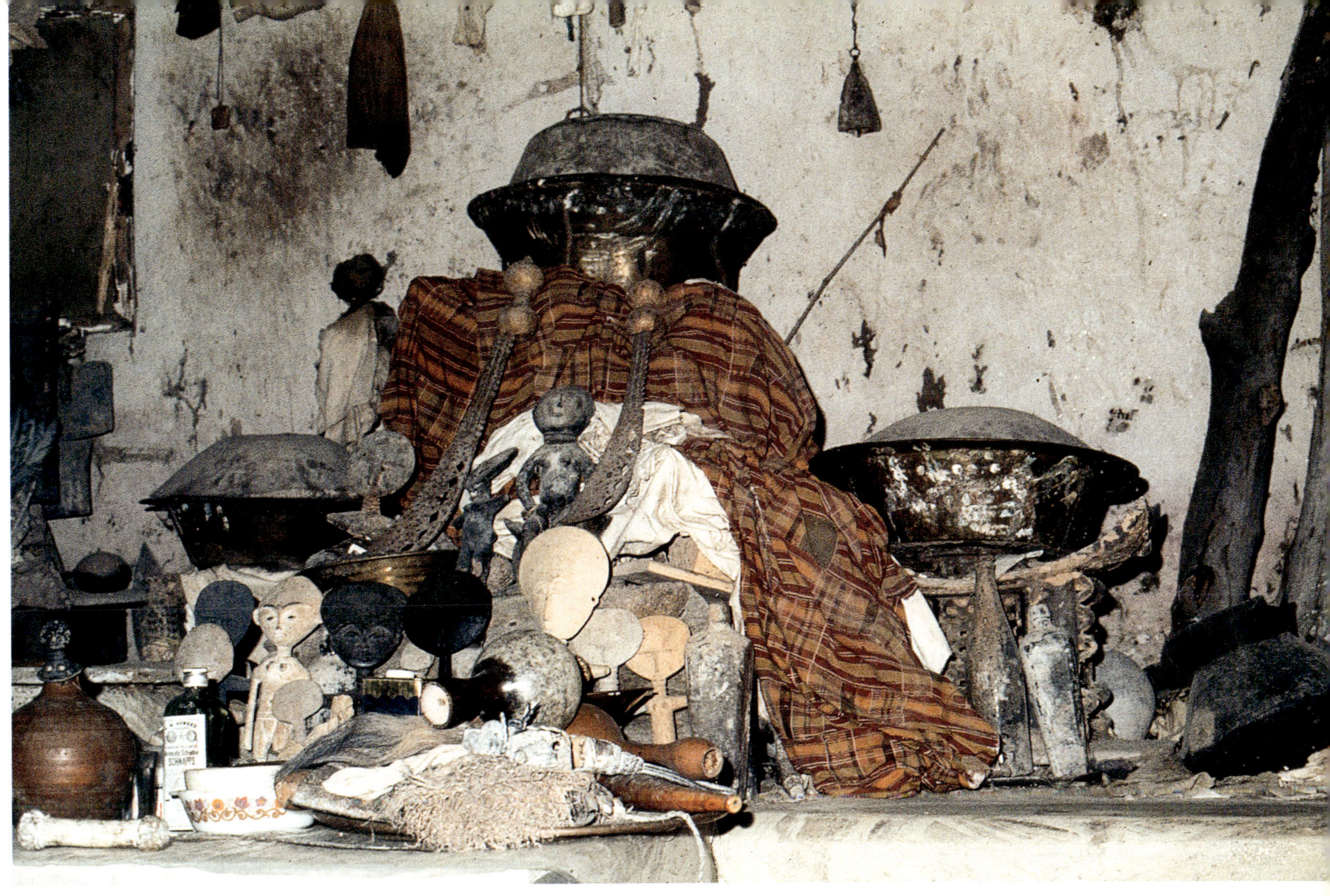

Tano shrine in an Asante community with many Akua'ma in varied styles which have been returned to Tano in thanks for his intercession in conception and/or childbirth. This shrine contains many separate altars to Tano, referred to as "Tano's children," each contained in its own brass pan. Asante, near Kumasi, Ghana. Photo: Herbert M. Cole, 1972

The priest then helped her tie it to her back with a cloth baby wrapper, along with a seated female terra-cotta figure permanently kept at the shrine. He prayed, asking Tano's help for her. The Akua'ba was taken away by the woman, while the terra-cotta was returned to its place on the shrine, where it could be similarly employed in future consecrations. Sometimes a woman may be given medicine to drink or apply to her body, and an image may also be rubbed with an empowering substance or sacrificial blood. The hopeful woman also makes an offering at the shrine, in some cases a baby chick or egg, in others, money. Before the woman left the shrine I photographed, she was instructed by the priest to return her Akua'ba to Tano after the child had lived for a few years. Hence the accumulation of Akua'mma in most Tano shrines, although it is clear that not all these small figures find their way back.

Surely the rituals empowering Akua'mma must be highly variable, as are both the shrines and figures themselves. Akua'mma exist in several regional styles (Asante, Fante, and Brong being the most common), and in any one shrine, which presumably draws mostly on its immediate region, there will be several variant Akua'mma. Differences in size, style, color, and relative naturalism remind us of the variability of human agency and process. The accumulated numbers of images attest to the power of that shrine and its priest, as well as Tano.

The small figures become part of an ensemble, an accumulation of forms and effects that characterize most shrines on the continent, and that contribute to the aura of power and mystery that is, in many instances, consciously invoked by shrine custodians. Included here are brass basins (containing a mixture of substances forming the sacred essence of the gods and their relatives seen to be present), cloth, swords, sacrificial offerings and their residues (bottles of spirits or schnapps, eggs, canned milk, blood), stools (present but hidden by cloth), sometimes books, pictures, candles, medicines, powder and/or other items, and of course the Akua'mma. The most important and focal elements of these shrines are normally the brass pans and their sacred ingredients. The number and nature of the Akua'mma appear to be arbitrary.

As every Akua'ba is different from others, so is every shrine the unique product of its custodians' and constituents' preferences and needs, and thus its history. Some shrines have several figures other than the common Akua'mma, such as mother and child images, or fully naturalistic standing female figures, or those depicting a priest with an egg in one hand and a symbolic sword in the other. Each of these is referred to as an Akua'ba although that word appears to have been invented for the disc-headed figures such as the one in the BMA collection. The reasons for such broadened naming, alas, have been lost in the mists of history.

Herbert M. Cole

Sculptural Biographies: a Lobi Figure

Female Figure
Lobi and other group identifications
Northwestern Ghana, northeastern Ivory Coast, and southern Burkina Faso
c. Early 20th century
Wood, H 59.7 cm
Gift of Robert and Mary Cumming, Baltimore
BMA 1983.66 (purchased from Issaka Zango, New York; ex J.J. Klejman Gallery, New York)

The Lobi peoples carve wooden sculptures that assist them in their daily lives. These may be placed in shrines that are located in, on, or around compounds, or may be used in divinatory consultations. As component parts of shrines or as divinatory tools, figurative sculptures serve as intermediaries between the world of human beings and the world of the *thila*, or nature spirits. The figures often experience a life cycle comprising their initial conception, their creation in the material world, their use in shrines or in divination, and finally, their decay.

In Lobi cosmological thought, the thila are capable of directly intervening in the daily lives of human beings, whereas the high creator god is removed from such mundane concerns. Unlike the creator god, the thila can make themselves manifest in the material world through natural and constructed objects, including certain figurative sculptures. Through the work of those men, and sometimes women, called upon by the thila to divine, mediation is brought about between humans and thila. Diviners interpret various signs provided by the thila in the natural world and communicate the concerns and demands of the thila to their human clients. Individual thila request relationships with individual human beings, often by introducing themselves through physical objects or animals found in the bush. When these objects or animals cross individuals' paths more than once or when people face inexplicable illness or trouble with their work or family lives, they frequently consult a diviner. Such consultations are held in private with divinatory tools sometimes including cowrie shells and figurative sculptures, and they often reveal that the thila are demanding greater attention in a person's life. To serve the thila, people erect, maintain, and modify shrines, perform sacrifices, and stage festivals.

The conception of many wooden figurative sculptures begins when the thila are perceived to call upon people to augment their

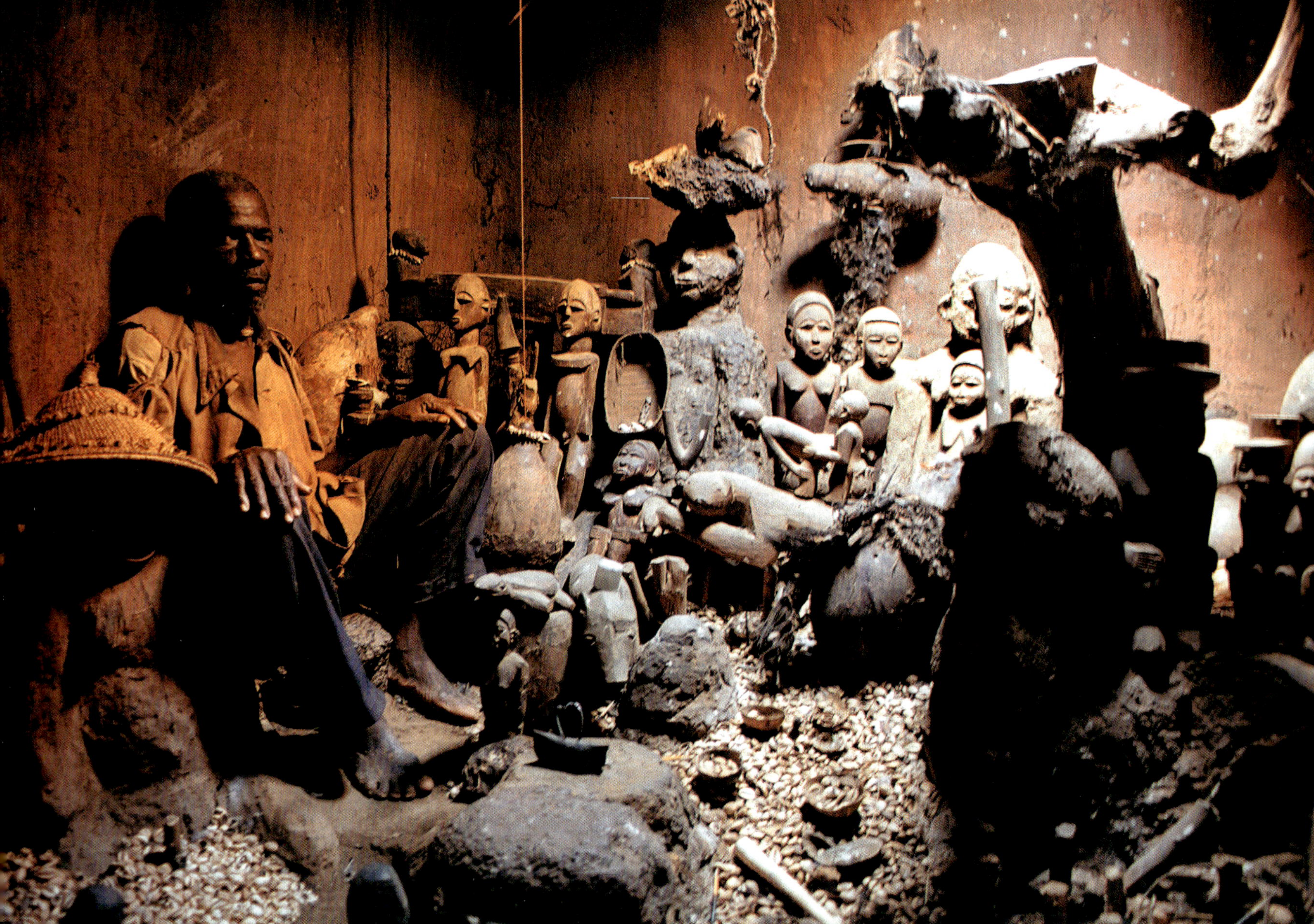

Sib Tâdjalté, a priest, sitting next to the family altar. Lobi, Department of Kampti, Burkina Faso
Photo: Huib Blom, 1999

individual shrines. Shrines can be elaborated upon in many ways, depending upon the specific demands of the spirits. However, the thila frequently call for new sculptures to be carved and placed on their shrines, and in so doing, dictate the specific form the figure is to take. The thila usually do not specify the type of wood or size of the figure, although in some instances they may.

While many figures resemble persons, they assume a variety of characteristics and postures and are not intended to refer to specific individuals, for portraits of the living or dead would be dangerous to those represented. Anthropomorphic Lobi figures may stand with their arms at their sides or with their arms extended above their heads. Alternatively, they may have features that are unusual amongst human beings, including Janus heads or unusual numbers of limbs. Piet Meyer (1981) believes the variety of pose and form in Lobi figures provides personal arsenals tailored to individual concerns and problems, to fight against antisocial forces, address the sorrows of death, and assist in the accomplishment of personal endeavors such as marriage or fertility. However the size of the figure does not necessarily affect or reflect its effectiveness.

The figures are usually placed upright on the appropriate shrines once they have been carved to the specifications of the thila. If satisfied with the offering, the spirits are seen to work to redress the problems plaguing the individual who commissioned the figure. A figure that has served its usefulness often becomes damaged by termites or other environmental conditions.

While anthropomorphic figures found amongst the Lobi in their houses and around their villages commonly experience this process of conception, life and decay, other anthropomorphic figures possess different biographies. These may be in the hands of people removed from the original ritual context, such as non-Lobi, or Lobi who profess other religious faiths or who no longer need to supplicate the specific thila for whom a figure was carved. Other Lobi within the ritual context may simply find that the figures have served their usefulness for one reason or another. Such individuals may remove the figures from their shrines while still active. These figures are often sold to neighboring traders and foreign collectors, through whose hands they migrate into museums and independent collections.

Susan Elizabeth Gagliardi

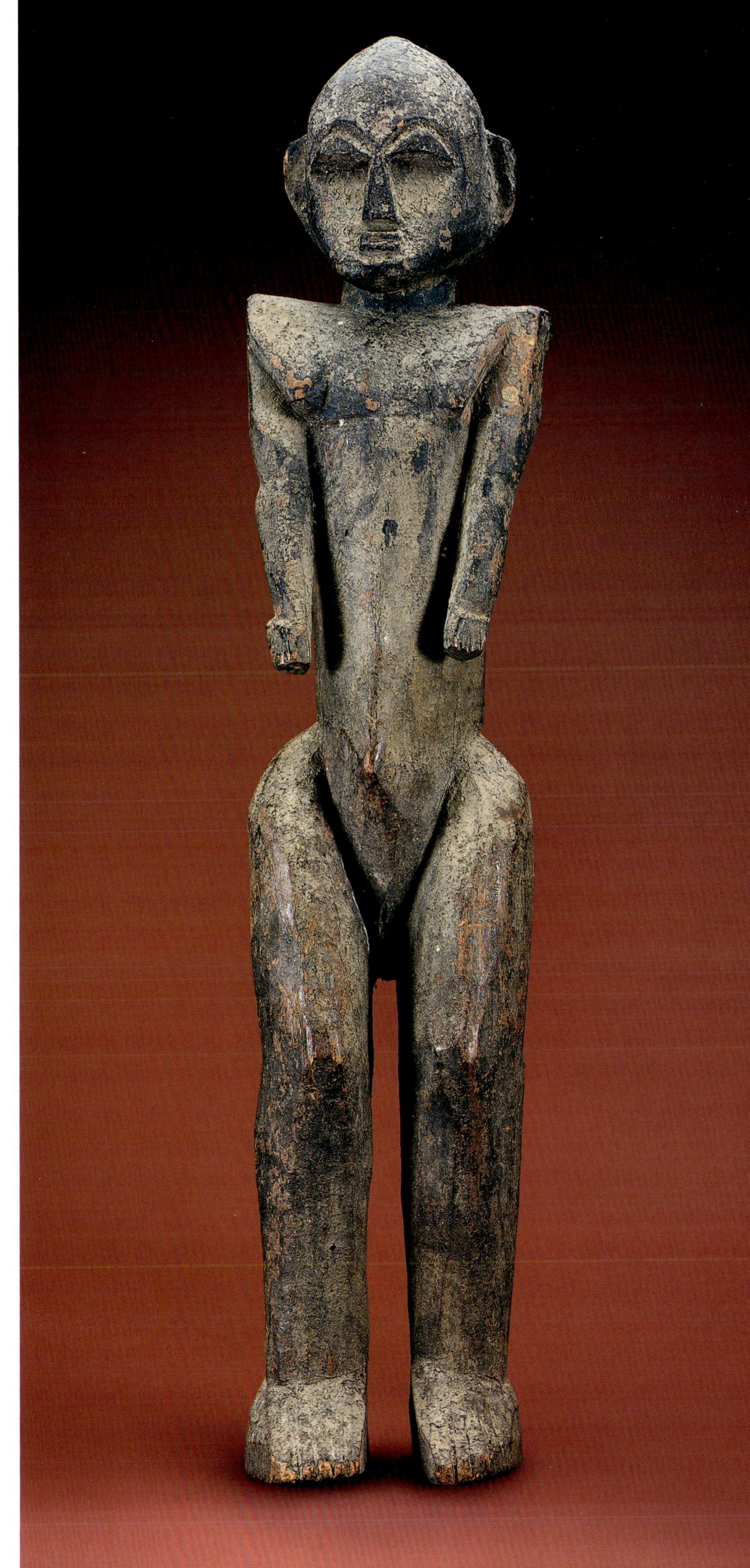

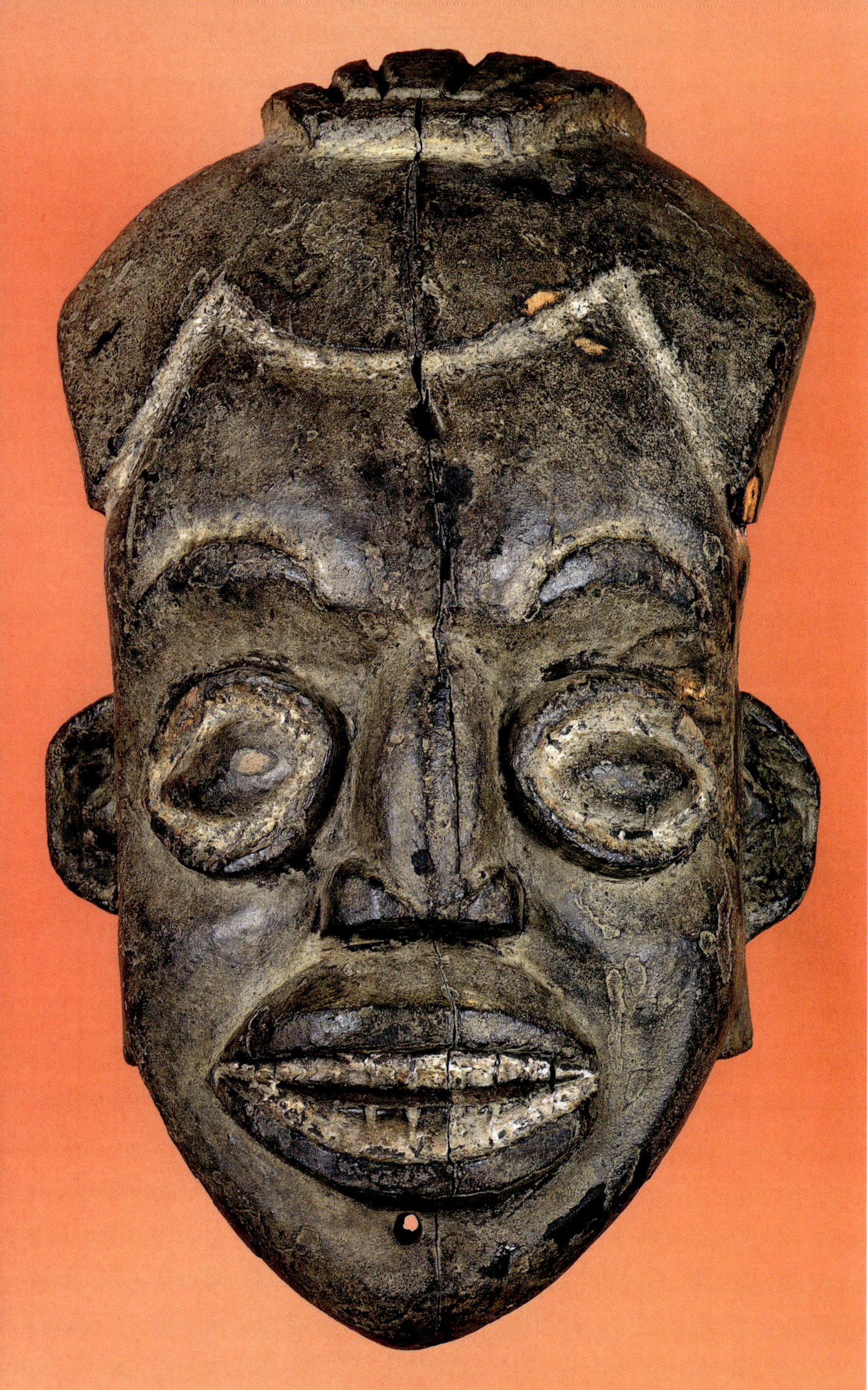

Female Headdress (*Ngoin*)
Kom, Cameroon
c. Early 20th century
Wood, H. 38.1 cm
Gift of A. Harvey and Phyllis K. Schreter, Baltimore
BMA 1984.271

38

The Spectacle of Lineage and Hierarchy: Two Cameroon Headdresses

Headdresses of the Cameroon Grassfields resemble masks, but they are worn at a slight angle atop the head of the dancer whose face is covered by a mask of see-through fabric. The performer holds the headdress in place by a string leading through the small hole in the chin. A large costume of cloth completes the performer's concealment.

Both of these headdress types are a part of an ensemble that is characteristically found throughout the kingdoms of the Cameroon Grassfields. Such ensembles perform under the auspices of the palace and its affiliated regulatory society, or Kwifoyn, which is dominated by ranked male representatives of the kingdom's important lineages. Accordingly, one can classify Cameroon Grassfields masks and headdresses into two broad categories, those belonging to the palace and Kwifoyn, and those belonging to individual lineages, a more private form of ownership that is nevertheless licensed by and to some degree under the control of Kwifoyn. The number of lineage headdresses in any given kingdom is by far the greater; it has also increased dramatically since the 1960s coinciding with national independence as well as global tourism.

The majority of Cameroon headdresses in American collections are lineage headdresses, as are the two examples here, the human-face headdress from Kom, and the zoomorphic headdress from one of the smaller kingdoms to the North of Kom where this hybrid bovine style is more common than in other areas. A lineage headdress ensemble has a standard cast of characters in human, animal, and hybrid forms; the principal animal representations include leopard, elephant, buffalo/bovine configurations, and birds. All of them demonstrate by their specific symbolic references the hierarchical powers of male authority in the kingdom (Northern, 1984).

Lineage headdresss and their garments are kept concealed in separate cloth bags in their respective compound storage huts. They are accessible only to the qualified male lineage members who dance them and who practice randomly with their musicians throughout the year without the headdresses, but wearing the ubiquitous pair of ankle rattles made of several dense layers of dried seedpods. These rehearsals take place in an inner courtyard of the home compound in an ambiance of laughter, jokes, and palm wine merriment—happy social gatherings that also serve the practical purpose of inspecting the dance vestments to see if repairs are needed. These would be undertaken by one of the men handy with a needle. Masquerade vestments are sewn by a tailor in the community; as generously-styled cloth tunics, they do not require the same special skills that were necessary for the old, traditional garments, some of which were densely covered with human hair or feathers. These would have been made in secret by a specialist in the regulatory society compound.

The public performance of headdress groups centers on commemorative death celebrations, "cry-dies," of royals and commoner power brokers of the kingdom who are wealthy lineage heads with large compounds (with many male and female dependents of all ages) and who are themselves the principal quasi-private owners of headdress groups. Cry-dies take place in the dry season, preferably shortly after the harvest (November through January) when food is plentiful. They are expensive events requiring the hosting lineage to provide food and drink for the participation of extended family members as well as palace and Kwifoyn representatives.

By their commemorative nature death celebrations take place months or even years after a death occurrs; their timing is decided by Kwifoyn in consultation with the deceased's family. Only a Fon's death requires his public commemoration as soon as his successor is installed, thus conflating this ultimate royal cry-die with the public installation ceremony of the new king, and reaffirming the unbroken continuity of the office of kingship. This event may extend over three weeks, the longest of celebrations, with all headdresses of the kingdom worn in performances sequentially on the open public square in front of the palace—the kingdom's official public ceremonial space—where large festive crowds gather to look on.

However, by far the most common and regular appearances of lineage headdress groups are at the cry-dies of lineage elders throughout the kingdom. They are celebrated from two to five days depending on the social rank of the deceased; as with all else in these kingdoms, there is also a hierarchy of celebrations: the higher the status of the ancestor, the longer and larger his cry-die. A representation of Kwifoyn headdresses will usually open the cry-die on the first day with solemn and awe-inspiring performances freighted with the authority of officialdom. They will be followed on subsequent days by groups of lineage headdresses, performing one after the other, from about ten to as many as thirty per day. Since the respective headdress groups do not perform simultaneously or mix together, this assures exposure of and attention to one ensemble at a time for about twenty minutes. In contrast to the Kwifoyn headdress appearances, lineage headdresses generate an aura of mundane entertainment and the excitement of a festivity.

These performances take place in an inner courtyard of the host family's compound; this large open rectangle is tightly surrounded by one-story houses whose corrugated tin roofs extend to provide veranda-like shady spaces. Cry-dies are well publicized daytime events beginning in late morning to early afternoon and ending before sundown (at 6:00 p.m.). Both costumed characters and audience are exposed to a high, bright sun, spending the day in the heat, sweat, red dust, food, and sour palm wine odors of a celebration's hustle and bustle. As public events, cry-dies are open to anybody who can make the often long walk from a distant compound, and since the people are accustomed to long hikes, many spectators join the host family members simply for the spectacle of masquerade. Strategically positioned at the main entrance to the compound one may find a diviner or "native doctor" with his paraphernalia from which he sells "small medicine" to men and women (fertility incentives top the list).

Spectators arrive in good time to crowd into the shade along the buildings and to see the orchestra comprised of a xylophone of banana tree logs and one to two tall cylindrical drums set up toward one side of the rectangular arena, leaving the middle free for the masked dancers. Once the musicians begin to warm up, the audience respectfully lines the rectangle of the dance space, children are kept from darting about, and very few spectators ever attempt to cross the dance arena, and, if so, only men. The crowd is contained but relaxed, not awestricken and silent as at a Kwifoyn masked performance where, in a manner of speaking, one could hear a penny drop. As the afternoon wears on, a more casual attitude gradually takes over and, in the dance breaks, when no performers with headdresses are present, family members may walk over to mingle with the musicians or even circle the instruments with their own improvised dance steps.

Meanwhile many of the participating headdress ensembles enter from the rear at the far side of the compound directly into a building reserved as a staging area for the dancing characters. Here the dancers receive food and drink consisting of *fufu,* a firmly textured maize porridge, roasted chicken or—if it is a wealthy compound—goat, and a spicy dipping sauce. Meat, which is not eaten on a daily basis, is a mandatory item for this occasion. The lead dancer is served first and only when he signals his assent may the others join. This is also the time and place to reenergize and strengthen the headdresses by reemphasizing their facial features (hairline, eyes, teeth) with white kaolin powder and to apply the required potent "medicinal" substances that heighten the agency of the headdresses.

At the headdress ensemble's entry into the courtyard, its lead character, Nkang, signals the musicians to begin playing as a hush settles over the crowd. The costumed characters follow Nkang in single file, looping around the perimeter of the arena to the slow rhythmic progression of the music almost brushing the solid wall

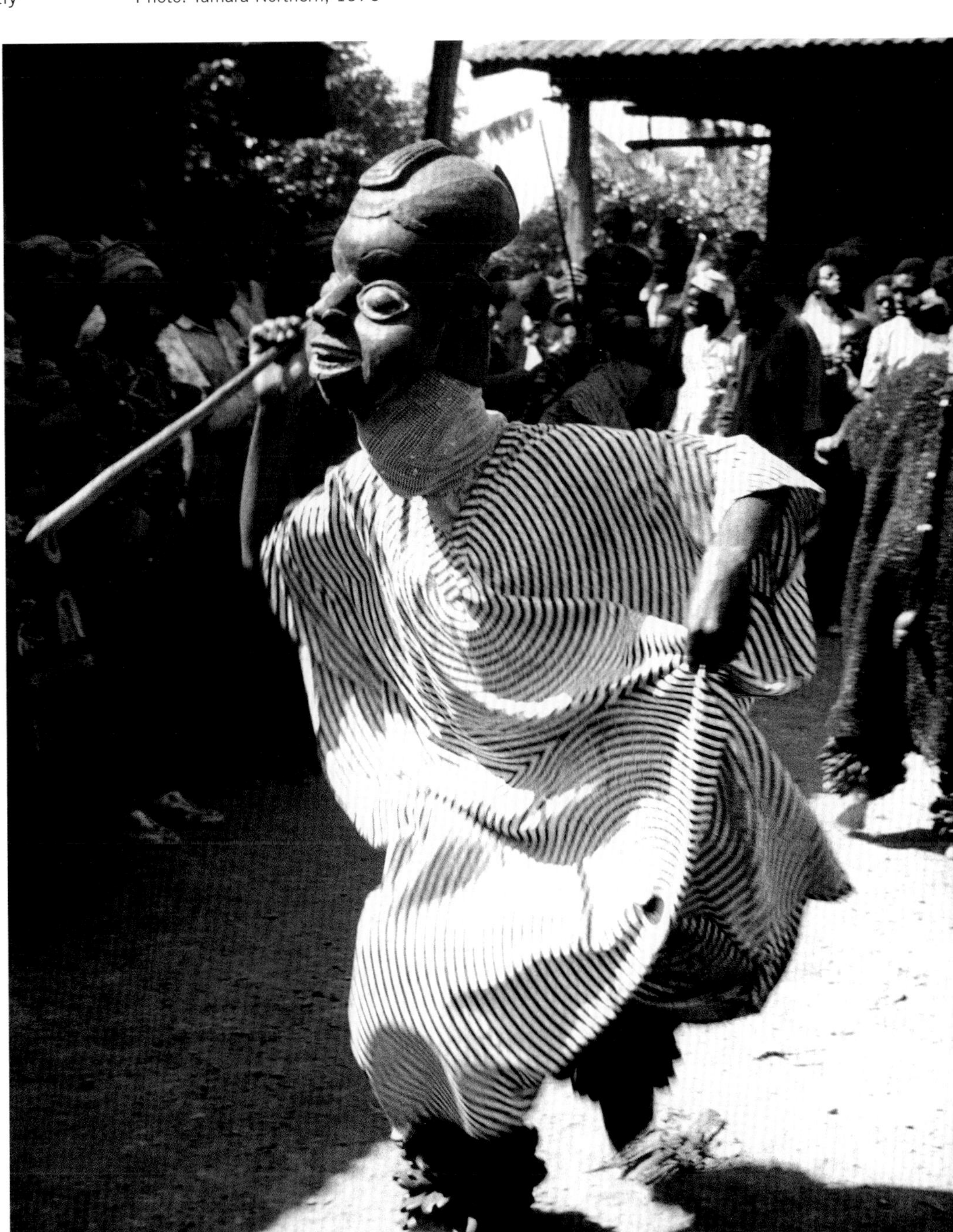

Ngoin daintily gesturing during a solo. Her mask group performing on the third and last day of this death celebration belongs to Fai Manko. Ngashie Quarter, Kingdom of Oku, Cameroon
Photo: Tamara Northern, 1976

of spectators. As the music gains momentum, with successive crescendos, individual characters break out of the line into the central space to dance and gesture in their very own style, filling the arena with moving, circling, pairing, stomping dancers who at that time improvise a choreography in relationship to each other.

This human-face headdress (p. 160) is a female image, Ngoin, the obligatory companion to Nkang, and by etiquette—at times disregarded—the second character to enter. In large headdress groups there will be more than one Ngoin, the second and third ones taking a position toward the end of the line-up. Ngoin has a brown or near black patination with kaolin accents—traces of which are still visible in the BMA example—giving heightened definition to teeth, eyes, brows, and hairline. She has as her defining female feature a central elliptical hairdress analogous to that of royal wives. For a performance this hairpiece is rubbed with palm oil and red camwood powder, a ritually sanctioned practice, just as it is also applied to the royal wives, themselves, in ritual proceedings. Ngoin's vestment has traditionally been a tunic of royal, blue-and-white, resist-dye cotton cloth which, however, during the past three or four decades, has been replaced by less expensive, typically colourful, and boldly patterned cotton fabric.

As a female persona Ngoin's style of dancing is demure, coy, and measured; she daintily waves a decorative flywhisk, now often substituted for by a less expensive, simple, long, wooden staff. Ngoin is the only female character in the ensemble and her dance style—with vivacious movements—is choreographed in clear distinction to that of the male characters who all, to varying degrees, represent power and aggression. However, there is some flexibility for all dancers to exercise their agency. Thus Ngoin will work up to occasional fast solo swirls which catch the audience's attention and generate appreciative murmurs of acknowledgement.

The onlookers are not entirely passive; as the dancers stream in and out of the arena they engage with them in modest ways, albeit always mindful of the proper distance to be maintained. For example, a spectator may reward a character's virtuoso performance with a small gift of money, a cigarette, or the like. Such "dashes" must be placed on the ground as the costumed character passes by; etiquette does not allow an unqualified spectator to touch the characters. Others may shout and gesture in unison with the sound of the rhythmic stomping of ankle rattles. The end of the performance is signaled by Nkang who places his foot on the xylophone; the music fades, and the characters regroup to head toward the entrance/exit to unwind in their house of seclusion. In a few minutes the spectacle will be repeated by the next headdress group.

The hybrid male headdress shown here (p. 163) has as its most prominent characteristic a wide jaw with a set of once whitened, glaring teeth. This feature identifies the headdress as being related to the prototype of buffalo representations. The buffalo is one of the royal referent animals which signify power, might, and aggression. With typically formidable jaws and sweeping horns, four or five of these headdresses are a part of every lineage headdress group. In the BMA example, the horns of the headdress have been configured into clusters of burls as they would adorn both sides of a textile cap headdress worn for prestige by royalty. Here two major symbols of power, human and animal, have been integrated to form a new hybrid headdress form that ironically enlarges the family of headdresses with aggressively displayed, open jaws with bared teeth.

For performances, this headdress was also renewed with kaolin on its eyes, ears, and double row of teeth. Buffalo headdresses and their hybrid derivatives, such as this example, wear a garment of no particular distinction; it is a large, industrial cotton tunic in black or a patterned design that covers the dancer from neck to ankle. Before the

Buffalo Headdress
Cameroon, perhaps Bafumbum Kingdom
c. Early 20th century
Wood, H 45.7 cm
Friends of Art Fund
BMA 1973.69 (purchased from Jakaria Sillah)

Two Buffalo Masks in solo counterpoise performance during a death celebration. Ngashie Quarter, Kingdom of Oku, Cameroon. Photo: Tamara Northern, 1976

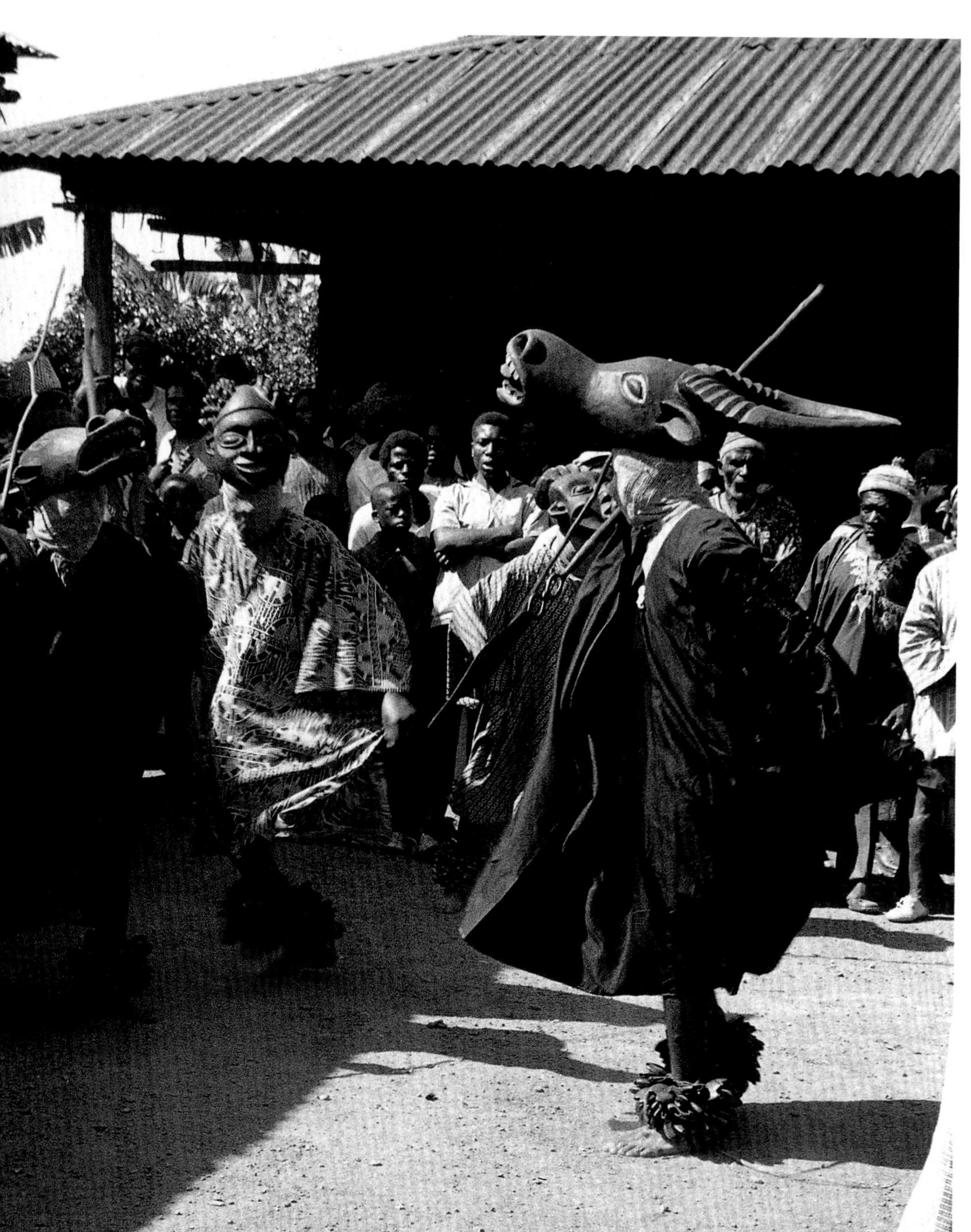

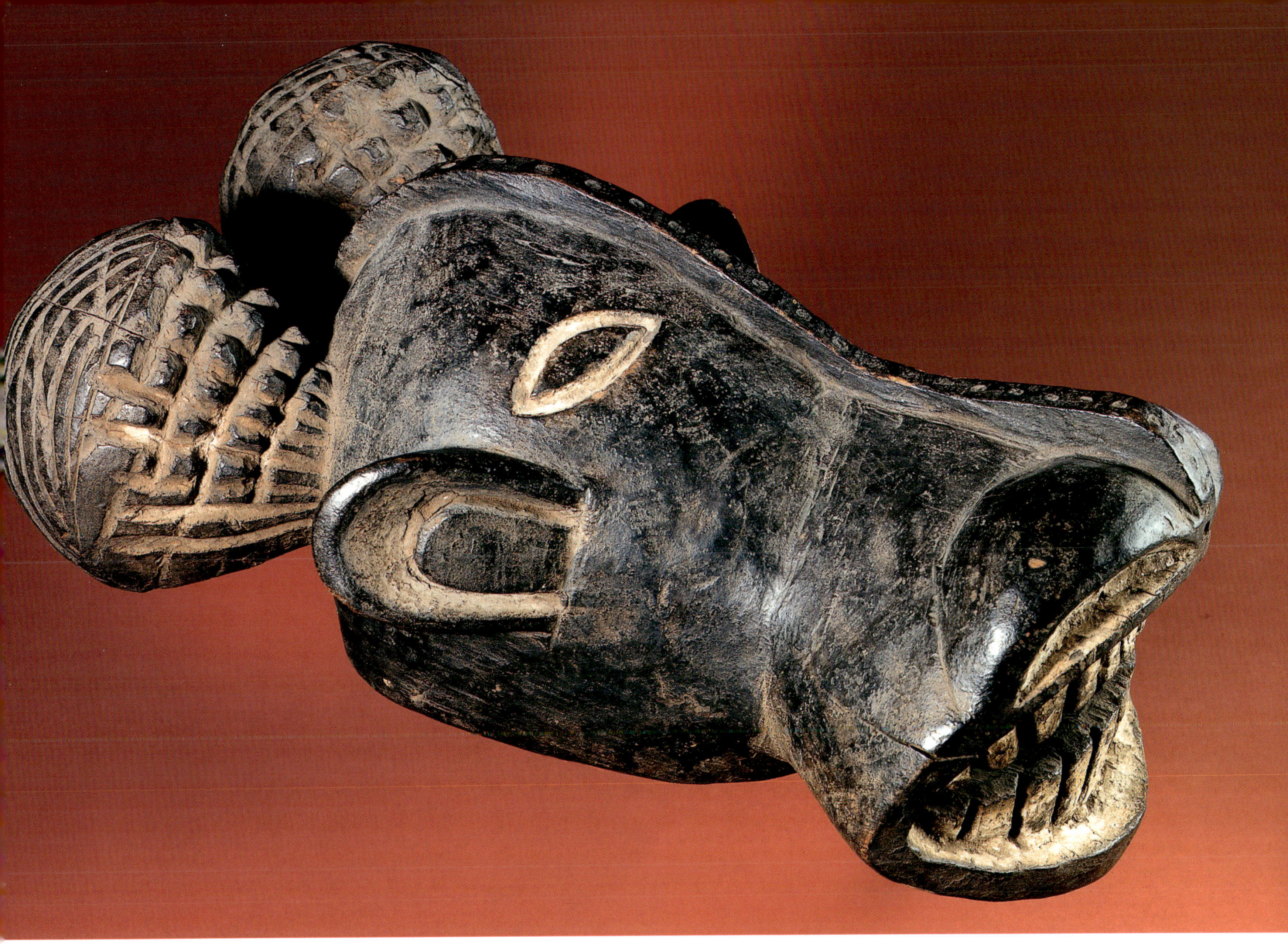

modern tendency to homogenize dance vestments, this may well have been different. Particularly strong buffalo headdresses of the regulatory society, for example, have been known to wear a feather-covered garment. It is, however, less likely that this could have applied to the hybrid headdress type, which had a limited distribution, and was small in number, indicating a headdress of lower rank relative to the others.

These characters are positioned toward the end of the dance line-up where as many as five follow each other. They hold long, wooden staffs or simple sticks in one or both hands and gesture with them aggressively when breaking out of the line to dance their solos. At that time their movements are fast and erratic, not in imitation of the natural animal, but rather to give a performance of unbridled strength which is made more impressive when some of them confront each other, or they move together in unison and counterpoise. These dancers are often characterized by unbridled exuberance, as is the crowd, giving them the loudest acclaim. But on Nkang's closing signal, they reign in and retreat with their group until another cry-die invites their participation.

The headdresses' disappearance from the public eye, however, does not mean "out of sight, out of mind." On the contrary, the icon of the wooden headdress in the form of a face has for centuries been imprinted upon people's minds. Thus when issues of right and wrong arise in the broad spectrum of life it is the wooden face that comes to mind as the visual symbol of their culture's norms of justice and retribution. While the dance garment is necessary for the performance aspect it is but an adjunct to the wooden face headdress that encompasses core cultural values. Headdress forms have for long periods of time, perhaps centuries, remained constant, but the corresponding "costumes" come and go. The changing fashion in dance garments seems to have come full circle: from mere coverings of the dancer's body, to elaborate and differentiated vestments, and back to current ordinary fabric coverings. The headdress of wood may be but a fragment in the context of performance, but in the larger cultural context it is the part that matters most for its profound and lasting expressive value.

It should be noted that the above portrayal is that of a long tradition which has successively changed under colonial domination, nationhood, gaining literacy rates combined with our Western-style education, and all the influences of an interdependent modern world. While some features of the headdress and masquerade complex have been retained, much of the performance etiquette no longer applies. The entertainment value of a masquerade—formerly but a part of its purpose—now dominates, and, in an unprecedented break with tradition, women may now mingle with the masked characters in a performance.

Tamara Northern

39

Air and Water, the Vertical and Horizontal, Tradition Versus Transition: a Baga Headdress (*A-Bil-ña-Tshol*)

Model Canoe Headdress (*A-Bil-ña-Tshol*)
Baga, Guinea
c. Early 20th century
Wood, polychrome, pitch, L. 199 cm
Purchased as the gift of Charles W. Newhall III, Owings Mills, Maryland
BMA 2001.287 (purchased through Sotheby's New York; ex an American collector; ex Jacques Boussard, Paris; ex Jacqueline and Maurice Nicaud, Paris, collected in Guinea *c.* 1954)

A-Bil-ña-Tshol, "The Medicine Canoe," is a long, flat panel, carved along both sides with abstract and geometric designs painted in brilliant colors. At the front, a circular, coiled form protrudes, as a prow ornament. At the rear is a pointed projection, resembling that of some canoes, where the rower would sit. Along the top edge are six protrusions resembling model houses. And between them, on the top edge, are holes stuffed with pitch.

My first exposure to the existence of the a-Bil-ña-Tshol dance came in 1987 in the course of a demonstration of the dance of *a-Tshol* ("The Medicine"), an important bird headdress, where the two performed together, occupying the same space and time. The fact that only two examples exist in Western collections, apparently, may mean that its use was not widespread, or that it was either not recognized as collectible or, once collected, was lost in misattribution. Testimony from Baga elders suggests a long continuity. A former dancer tells how it was danced and maintained:

> A-Bil-ña-Tshol did not have a *kà-lò-kà-pòn* [a sacred house] as did a-Tshol [the long-beaked bird headdress]. The person who bore it in dance would guard it in his bedroom. A-Bil-ña-Tshol was for the initiation, *kà-Bɛrɛ-Tshol* [for the boys and girls].... The day of the dance, I decorated it with cloths and handkerchiefs and I wore it to go dance. It was kept in equilibrium on the head by a thin cord attached at the front and held in the teeth of the bearer.... The boys and girls could, on invitation, go to dance in a neighboring village. It was on this occasion, above all, that a-Bil-ña-Tshol was danced (elder savant, Tolkotsh, Sitemu, 1992).

The a-Bil-ña-Tshol was borne on its bottom, long edge, atop the head in ritual, without any special costume. On the top of the head, resting on a coiled headtie, would be placed a hemispherical socle with a groove, resembling the head of a metalscrew, into which the center of the long edge of the panel would be fitted. Short sticks would be thrust through small openings along the top edge of the board, and cloth streamers would be attached. The long panel would then be balanced as the bearer danced within the perimeter of a circle, with its painted sides facing the audience. The image would be one of a decorated, floating, two-dimensional canoe.

Beating an iron gong, the dancer in 1987 moved agilely, with slightly flexed knees, floating his body back and forth across the space, taking quick, small, measured steps, and maintaining the same height. Intermittently, he was joined by another dancer bearing the headdress, a-Tshol, representing the head of a bird with a long beak (Lamp 1996:87–103). The two dancers never confronted each other, usually moving in opposite directions. Occasionally a-Bil-ña-Tshol would follow a-Tshol.

Aside from several other photo and video documentations I made of the dance of a-Tshol, alone, the only other photographic record of the dance was made by Michel Renaudeau (HOA-QUI, Paris). Here, the dance of the bird headdress is accompanied by the hoisting of a real canoe above the heads of a number of men. This confirms the association of canoes, either real or abstract, with the dance of a-Tshol, although Baga consultants who were questioned on this association were ambiguous and divided on whether there is, in fact, a ritual relationship between the two. Nevertheless, the record presents a curious dyad, on which, perhaps, the full artistic context may shed some light.

Songs associated with a-Bil-ña-Tshol had to do with contemporary matters, often with a nautical edge. The following two songs describe a change for the better, bringing work, imports, and new markets since the military takeover in 1984 from the previous totalitarian Marxist regime:

> *wali mbe* [Susu] / *sà nànk nò mò* / *nañ kali Allah* [Susu]
> ... / *tɛn da ri fɛ* / *wololo nà nànk-o....*

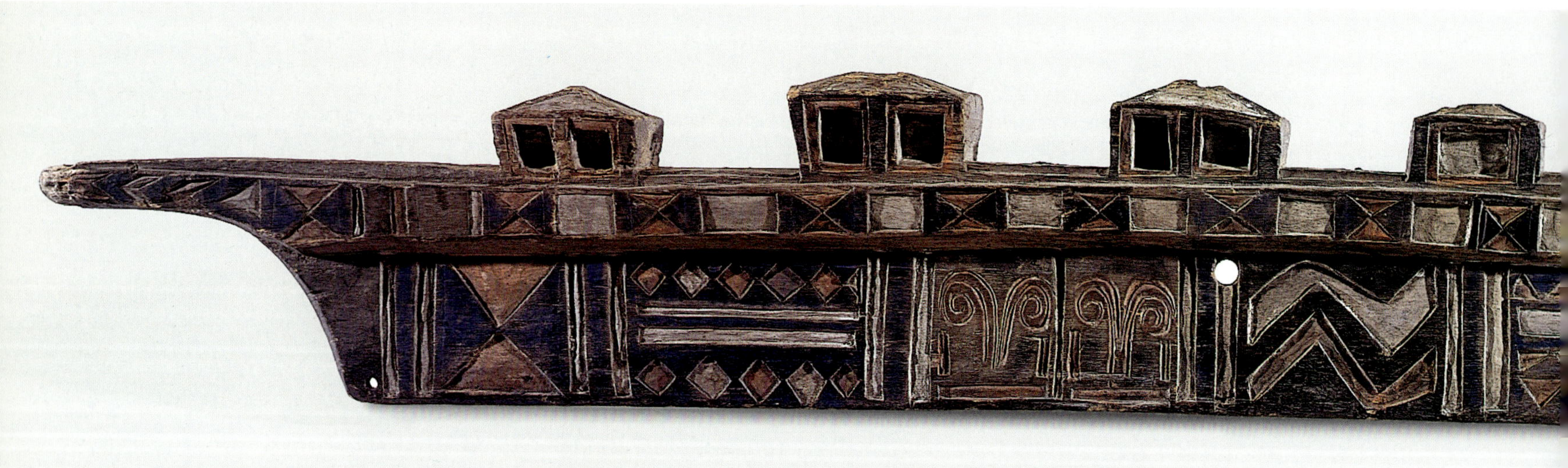

kòntòfili [Susu] / *nkɛ kà-na yi nò mò* / *nke ki-lip-o* / *a-bil neñ der* / *neñ kɛrɛ tshà-loto* / *ya kuri ya militer....*

The work / we are seeing now— / I swear to God ... / It was not so before. / Oh, dear me, look.... / The trouble / we had before— / All that is ended. / A boat has come / bringing clothes / During the military regime....

A-tshol, the complementary pair, is represented by a long-beaked bird head on a long, slim neck thrust into a separately-carved base often in the form of a round stool. In Baga ritual, the bird is frequently a spiritual messenger, coming down from on high. The stool is of the type that would only belong to an elder, a member of the council of elders that traditionally, before the imposition of chiefs by the French colonial administration, ruled absolutely in every Baga community. The personal names given to a-Tshol reveal that it is somehow identified with God, the supreme creator, and although this identity seems to be somewhat ambiguous, some consultants clearly see a-Tshol as God. If so, it is God seen in the likeness of an elder, who, in turn, is seen in the likeness of a bird. As such, it is the defender of Baga traditions handed down from the ancestors (Lamp 1996 *Art*:87–103).

Going on the assumption that complementary masquerades generally embody oppositions, what can we make of a-Bil-ña-Tshol, knowing what we do of a-Tshol? If a-Tshol represents the vertical, traditional descent of power from the highest spiritual source, the realm of God and the ancestors, what would the complement be in the context of the blessings of welfare? The form of a-Bil-ña-Tshol is the boat or canoe, found ubiquitously in the coastal islands were most Baga live. The canoe is used principally in trade, to take agricultural products to market, and to return with merchandise from other villages and other ethnic groups. A-Bil-ña-Tshol, then, as the second song above alludes, would relate to the benefits brought, not down from the ancestors, but across, horizontally, from the outside world, not by tradition, but by transition.

But another allusion compounds the metaphor, according to Mohammed Bangoura (1991:34):

Apart from the intimate relations between man and woman, it is believed in Baga society that it is the spirits (*a-kàrfin*) who distribute children, who they send by way of the sea. Each year the women would get together to organize dances at the edge of the great wells of the village where the spirits would offer them children. Children born in the same month were considered to have been sent in the same canoe.

This calls to mind the notions of conception and birth held by the relatives of the Baga, the Temne, further south. Here, the serpent is the bearer of fertility (Lamp 1985:38–39). Women wishing to become pregnant would wear a serpent's skeleton around their waists, among other associated ritual acts. Among most of the peoples to the south, in Sierra Leone, these rituals are thoroughly imbued with the notion that the serpent is the harbinger of pregnancy, and, in fact, the serpent among the Baga is represented by a headdress, *a-Mantsho-ña-Tshol*, that has to do with beginnings and with the fertility of young men and women going through initiation into adulthood (Lamp 1996 *Art*:76–85). In this context, therefore, and extremely poignant comparison is found in an illustration of a wall painting found among the Bidjogo, just to the north of the Baga (Quintino 1964: Fig. 4). It pictures a serpent with a coiled circle at its end (compare the a-Bil-ña-Tshol), and bearing human figures on its back, as if acting as a canoe. The image of fertility is further reinforced on this example of the a-Bil-ña-Tshol by the row of model houses on top. Model Baga houses are found carved on a number of Baga masks and headdresses, and seem always to refer to the excitement and the erotic sense that surrounds a young man's marriage to a young woman, at which point he is authorized, for the first time, to build his own house, and to carry his young bride there (Lamp 1996 *Art*:111).

The image of the canoe, in this sense, may relate to the creative role of the spiritual world in human fecundity, just as the image of a-Tshol, in profile resembling a hoe, relates to the creation of the God, Kanu, in the realm of agricultural fertility. The world of the spirits, a-kàrfin, has little to do with the world of the Supreme God; the realm of the former occupies the same relative space as that of mankind, while the realm of the latter is remote, not of this world. The sea-going spirit, a-Bil-ña-Tshol, and the airborne spirit, a-Tshol, dance in the same space at the same time, but in their crisscrossing paths they never meet.

Frederick John Lamp

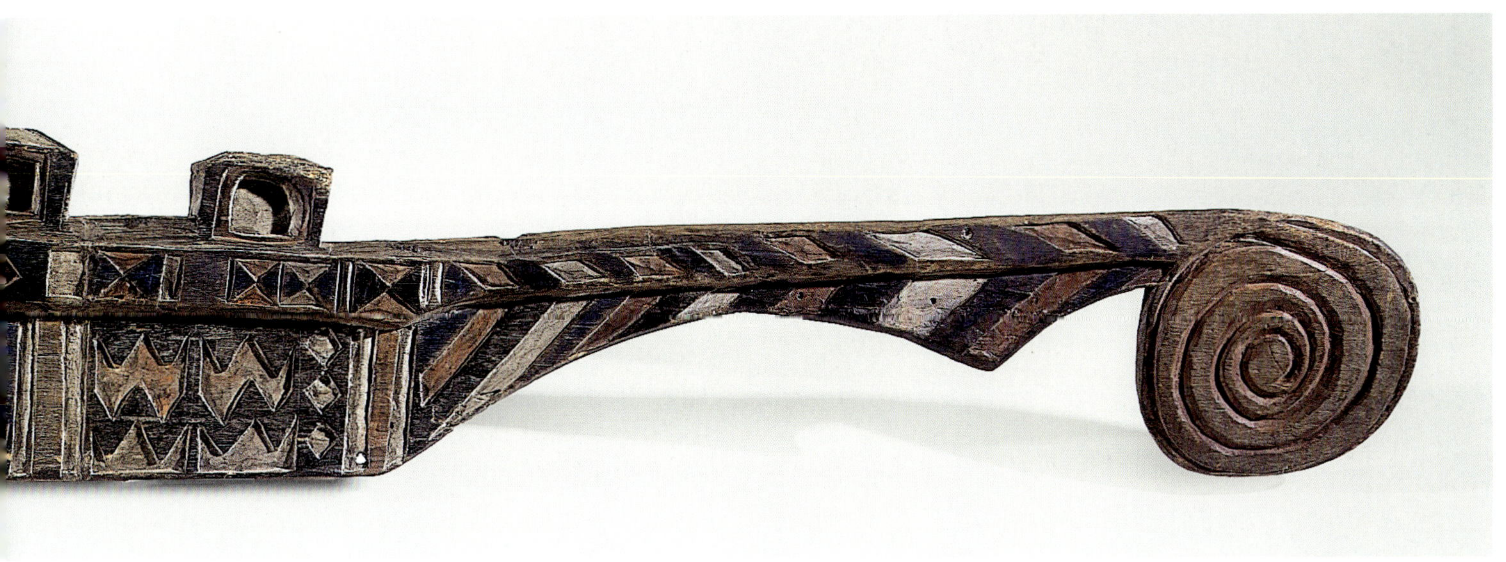

Dance of a-Bil-ña-Tshol and a-Tshol. Baga Sitem, Guinea
Photo: Frederick John Lamp, 1987

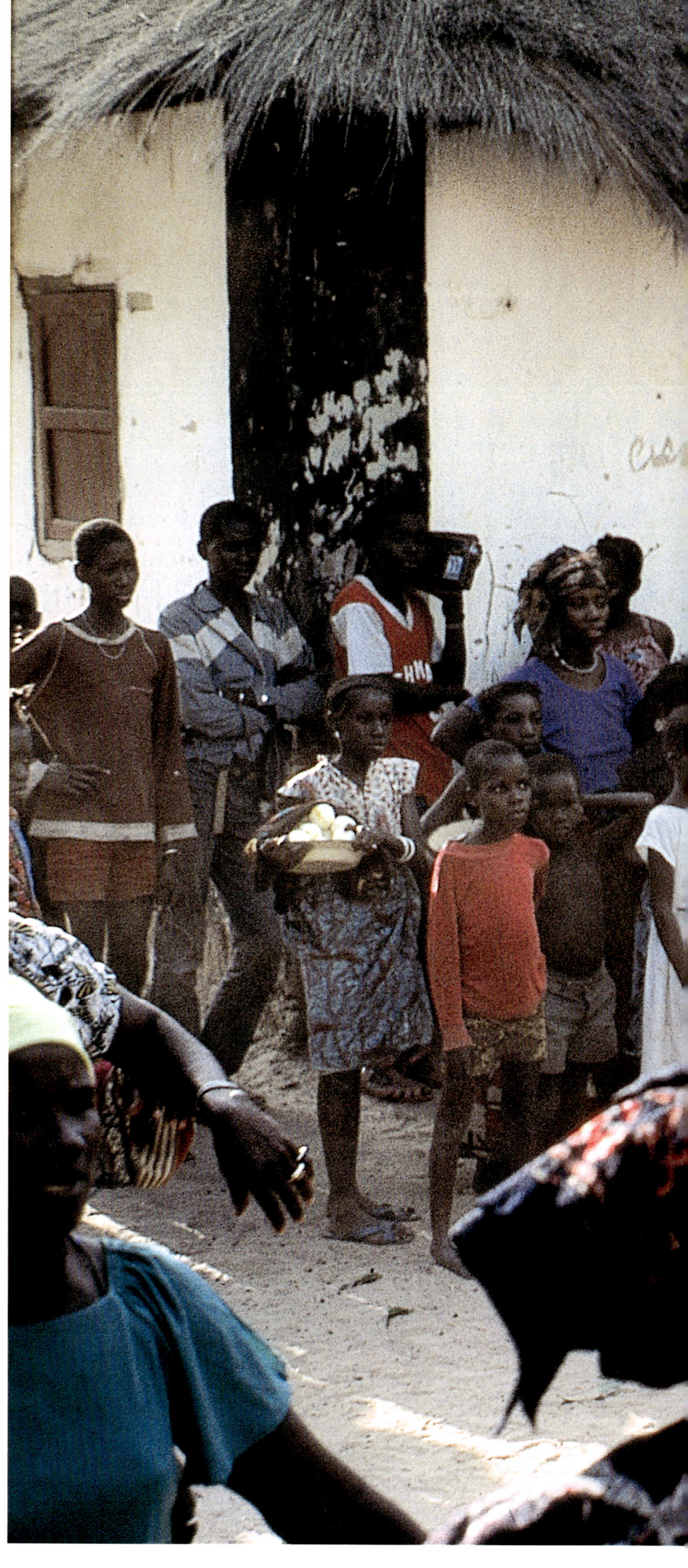

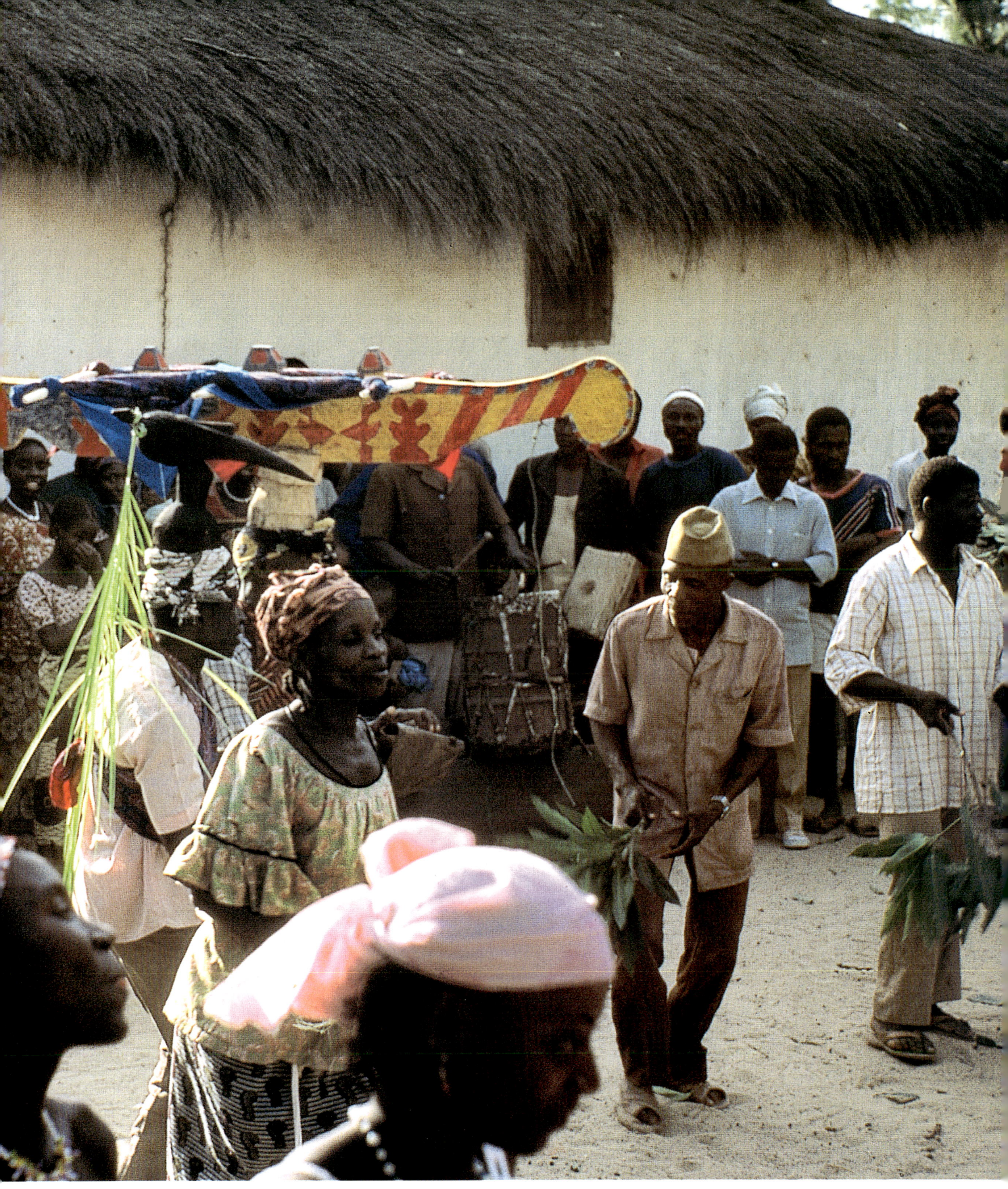

40

Where Is My Mate? The Importance of Complementarity: a Bamana Headdress (*Ciwara*)

Female Antelope/Anteater Headdress (*Ciwara*)
Bamana, Mali
c. Early 20th century
Wood, metal, thread, L. 61 cm
Gift of Alan Wurtzburger
BMA 1954.145.1

What a beautiful object—so elegant, so refined. However, it is so isolated, so alone. After more than a decade of ethnographic research among Bamana farmers in rural Mali, I have come to see and understand objects like this as constituent elements of a complex whole. Doseke Jara, a Bamana elder I respect a great deal, would refer to such a single object as *waraninje*: a little white (empty) *wara*, a Ciwara headdress without meaning or power. He contrasts such Ciwaraw (plural of Ciwara) with Ciwaraw *yereyere*—objects that are enmeshed in a complex and powerful artistic and cultural environment.

In the Bamana world, objects such as this always come in pairs—one male and one female—symbolizing the union of mythical half-animal, half-human beings that taught their ancestors to farm, and the productive union of men and women throughout time. As Doseke told me, "Anything that reproduces must come in male and female form. So, for Ciwara you can never have one without the other." When Bamana people think of these headdresses, they think about them in pairs, just as they think about many aspects of their cultural world.

Blacksmith-sculptors (*numuw*) produce the wooden Ciwara headdresses, and a wide range of important items for individual farmers and for farming communities. The relationship between blacksmith-sculptors and farmers is ancient and complementary. According to Bamana oral tradition, smiths played an instrumental role in the development of the farming way of life. The original smith is said to have fashioned the first farming tools and created the first Ciwara headdresses to honor the beings that brought agriculture to the Bamana. Since that time, blacksmith-sculptors and farmers have forged a symbiotic relationship. The smiths have worked iron and wood to create tools central to the very existence of agriculturalists. In the farmers' hands these implements mediate the human interface with the environment. The smiths' contributions occur on another plane as well. As sculptors, their creation of headdresses enables a symbolic cultivation process, wherein farmers nurture the essence or spirit of agriculture and in turn harvest its blessings and support.

A few years ago, a blacksmith-sculptor named Zoumana let me watch him as he carved a pair of Ciwara figures for me. Once the carving was finished, he blackened and oiled the finished surface. "They should really shine," he said. Then he indicated that it was time for the village women to dress the Ciwaraw, and I learned that gender complementarity extends into the artistic realm as well. The women bought red thread, silver hoop earrings, and plastic bead necklaces in the nearby market. They dressed the Ciwaraw, tying thread into the nose piercings and various ear piercings, setting the earrings into several ear holes, draping the forms with necklaces. The BMA Ciwara shows signs of a similar dressing process.

Ciwaraw made for performance would need a costume and accoutrements. A small basket (*seki*) would be attached to each figure so it could be worn on the head. Each one would need a fiber veil to be attached to the basket to mask the performer's face. There would be mudcloth suits that each performer would wear. The performers would need sticks to hold in each hand to insure four-point, antelope-like contact while moving about the dance space. There would be drums and songs that accompany each outing of the headdresses. Perhaps most significantly the performers would need power objects (*basiw*) to accompany the Ciwara headdresses. These are saturated with *nyama*, the vital force.

Finally, when Ciwaraw perform they "come out" in an environment rich with nuance and complexity—aural, visual, social and religious. In a sense, they come out into a context where the dressing process is completed. The details of one particular performance are illustrative.

It is late afternoon in April. The long hot dry season is coming to an end and members of a traditional farming community on the Mande Plateau in central Mali are looking forward to the return of the rains and to the start of a new farming season. As part of their transition into a new cycle, the community holds a day-long celebration. Residents have been eating and visiting all day and the time is coming for a series of public mask performances. A small group of young men standing under the village's main shade tree create a welcoming rhythmic layer by beating their drums. A melody emerges in the voices of young women who are singing praise for their Ciwaraw. By forming an encompassing circle, the young and old, male and female residents of the community frame a performance space for the Ciwaraw.

Feeling the rhythm, hearing the songs, the Ciwaraw are drawn forth into the performance circle. They make their way into the midst of the assembly. Upon entering the circle, each does a turnabout before making a pass through the open space. A girl shadows each performer; she fans her Ciwara, disseminating its energy, or nyama, into the air. As they pass the drummers and the singers, the Ciwara offer their greetings, "Whoo, Whoo, Whoo!" As they pass the elders, the Ciwaraw honor them with cries as well.

As they gaze upon their Ciwaraw, the elders reflect on the acts they have undertaken hours before to honor and empower the masked characters. In the morning, the elders offered chicken blood, the juice of kola nuts, and millet gruel to the power objects, or basiw, associated with Ciwaraw, in recognition of the power Ciwaraw have over agricultural and social reproduction in the community. As he cut the throats of the chickens, an elder offered words of thanks for the benefits the community received in the months preceding and asked for support in the days to come. He asked for safety in the field, plentiful harvests, and numerous healthy births. If the Ciwara forces are supportive they will protect the farmers from lethal snake bites, and errant blows from sharp hoes, they will stimulate strong rains, bountiful crops, and the arrival of robust babies.

Meanwhile, children frolic to and fro, young men gather together to chat and smoke, young women connect with friends, old men and women gather with their age mates as they mark another annual cycle. Through its excitement the crowd conveys a sense of welcome to the Ciwaraw; their claps, their smiles, and their joyful cries create a nurturing environment. Despite their excitement, all those assembled know that they cannot come between the male and female Ciwaraw when they are performing—the pair is inseparable. Anyone who breaks up the pair will suffer from tremendous back pain or worse, death.

The Ciwaraw make their way back to their point of entry and crouch, listening to the beat of the drums and the lines of the songs. When the rhythm section switches to a faster pace, the female Ciwara rises and enters the performance arena, moving briskly along the outer perimeter in a hop-skip fashion. The performer circles the space several times; the audience becomes excited and their applause encourages him. After several spirited passes, he retreats to the sidelines and the male makes its rounds. Both Ciwaraw, having completed their initial circuits, settle down for a brief respite. Members of the audience chat among themselves; the drummers tune their instruments; the singers catch their breath.

A few minutes later the beat returns and another song begins. The male enters the performance space and makes his way toward the center. Rays of light from the setting sun trickle though the giant shade tree and fall on the crouching Ciwara. He thrusts a hand into the air to reveal something to the audience. What is he holding? A razor blade. He shows the blade to those assembled, pausing a bit longer to be sure the elders see the blade. In the meanwhile the female has joined him in the center. Now, having ensured that the object has been recognized, the male Ciwara places the blade into his mouth. He returns his open hand to his stick and segues into a spirited dance, chewing dramatically on the blade within his mouth. He makes his way toward the drummers and spurts blood in their direction. He moves over to the male elders and repeats this act. Those gathered register approval with shouts of praise and amazement. The Ciwara quickly circles the space and takes up a position alongside the female.

The female dances into the opening and crouches in the center. The performer gestures to the sidelines and a young man emerges with several burning sticks, freshly drawn from a nearby hearth. The Ciwara shows the glowing sticks to the crowd before chewing at them in a ravenous fashion. The embers consumed, the Ciwara completes a rapid circuit through the space before rejoining her mate on the sidelines. Reunited, the couple makes its exit.

The audience punctuates their departure with applause. The dust raised by the movements of the energetic dancers begins to settle and children dash into the arena to exhibit their dance moves. Other masked performers with hyena masks, the *Namanikunw*, dance as tricksters, agents of mischief and levity. As twilight nears, a new group of musicians assemble under the shade tree, and three performers, the *Cebilenkew*, appear, costumed from head to toe in traditional mudcloth, each holding a set of small sticks. Their acrobatic performance is well received.

Throughout the afternoon, the connection between the various performers and the audience is intimate and complementary. There is clearly a synergy between those with masks and those without. Over the course of several hours the community has drawn together to mark a turning point in their lives, a shift from a long dry season to a short but critically important wet season: a time of interdependence and hard work. As potent symbols of unity and productivity, the Ciwaraw have helped solidify the community and have given its members energy for the new farming season. In Doseke Jara's terms, these are Ciwaraw *yereyere*: true Ciwaraw. They are a gendered pair and they are enmeshed in a complex web of artistic expression and cultural meaning.

Stephen R. Wooten

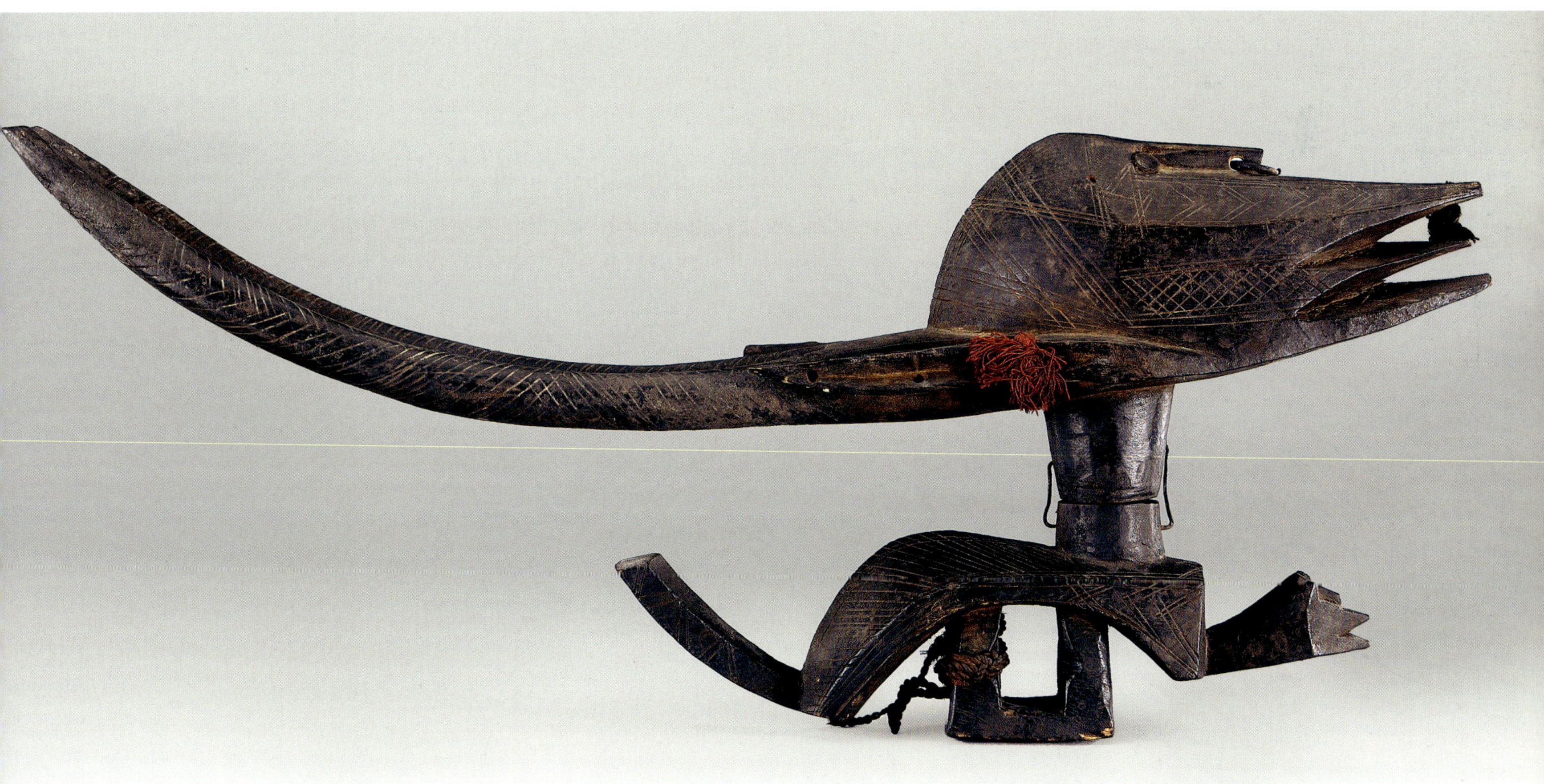

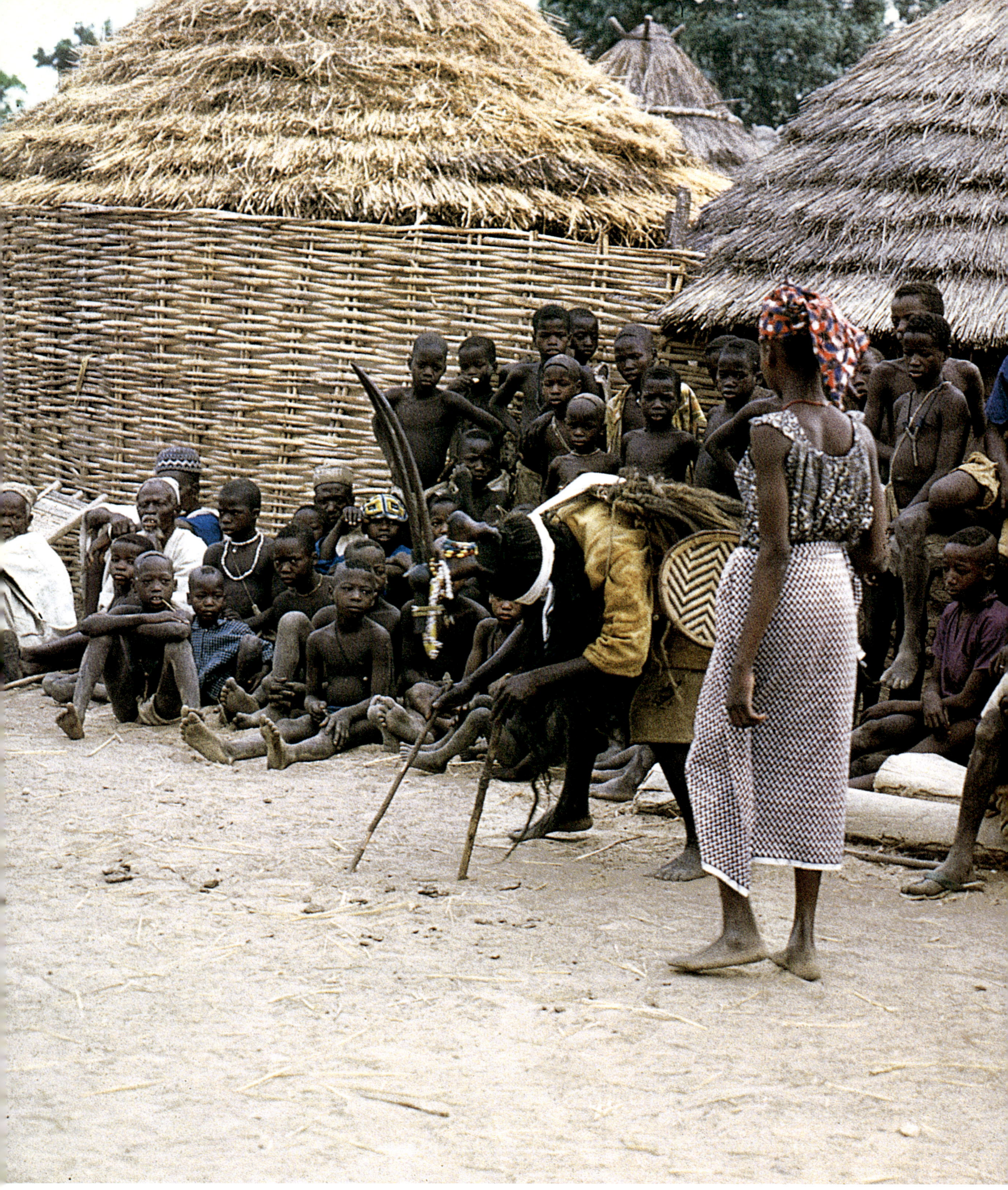

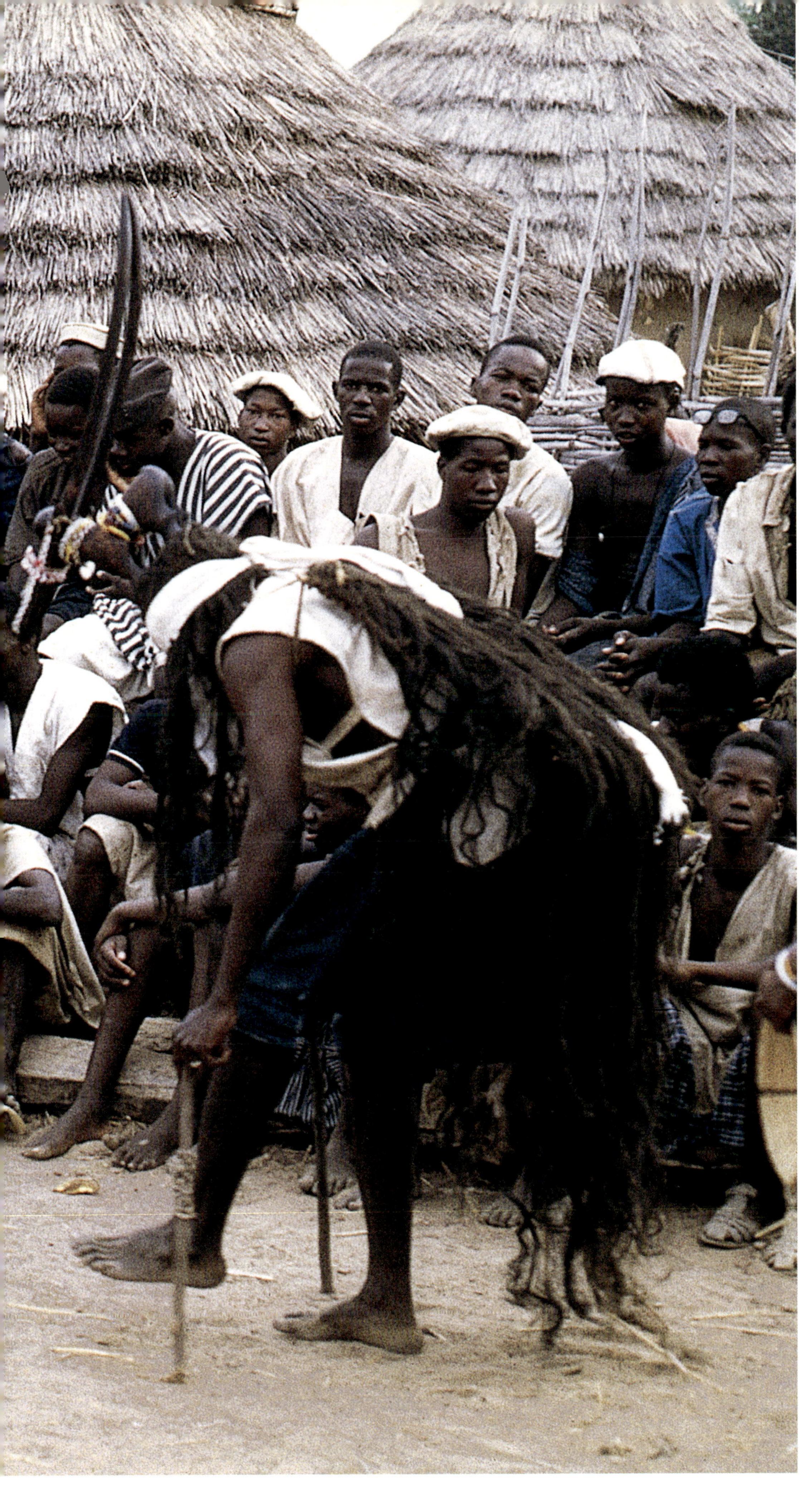

Male and Female Figures Beginning the Ciwara Dance. Bamana, Mali
Photo: Pascal James Imperato, 1970

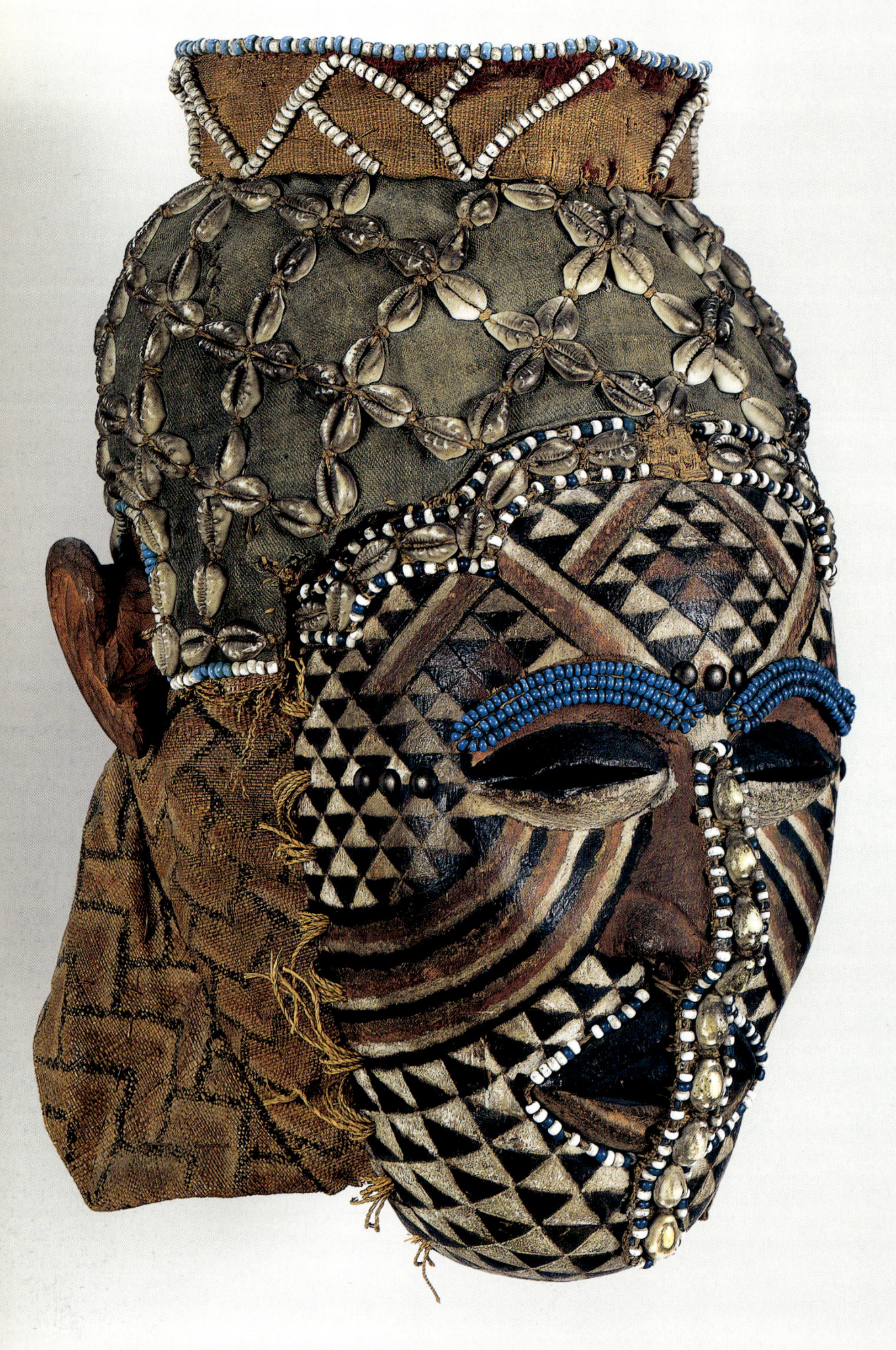

Female Mask (*Ngady Mwaash*)
Kuba, Congo (Kinshasa)
c. Late 19th–early 20th century
Wood, metal, fiber, beads, cowrie shells, paint, cotton, raffia, H. 34.3 cm
Gift of Alan Wurtzburger
BMA 1954.145.77

41

Ideology of Male and Female Movement: a Kuba Mask (*Ngady Mwaash*)

Although many publications designate the Kuba female mask, Ngady Mwaash, as a royal mask appearing primarily at the royal capital of Nsheng, in fact, performances of Ngady Mwaash have only been documented in the Southern Kuba region. In the South, certain Bushoong communities live side by side with a larger number of Northern Kete communities, some of whose histories predate the arrival of the Bushoong in the region. Here, Bushoong men trace the origin of their initiation rituals (*Nkaan*) and a number of mask types associated with Nkaan ritual practice to the Northern Kete (Vansina 1945, 1978; Binkley 1987b).

In Bushoong communities, the name Ngady Mwaash translates as "female mask." Like a number of other central and southern Kuba mask types, the prototype for the Ngady Mwaash type mask is a Northern Kete mask called *Mukasha ka Muadi*, which also literally means "female mask." Both the Kuba and the Kete masks exhibit similar morphological details; however, the Ngady Mwaash mask type usually displays more pronounced and elaborate polychrome geometric patterning, shells, and beaded decoration on the face and head of the mask, and more elaborate costume details than its Kete counterpart. Like other masking traditions localized in the central and southern Kuba region, the surface decoration of the mask is a riot of contrasting geometric patterns, including triangles and parallel lines. The complexity of this decoration is heightened by the addition of colored beads outlining the brow ridge and mouth. A beaded and cowrie shell decorated strip of cloth is attached to the bridge of the nose and across the mouth and chin of the mask, as with other mask types. Parallel lines, painted diagonally across the cheeks of the mask, symbolize tears that are shed at the death of a member of the initiation society. This stylistic convention, found on other Kuba masks as well, underscores the primary context for masquerade performance in the region: funerals of recently deceased members of the men's initiation society (nkaan) (see p. 92).[3] Masquerade performance is a prerequisite at funerals in which societal members and relatives and friends of the deceased celebrate the departed's life while mourning his death.

The physical characteristics and techniques employed in the construction of Ngady Mwaash are similar to other face masks in the region. The carved and painted wooden face is attached to a framework covered with cloth that forms the top, back, and sides of the head. Two wooden ears and cowrie shell and beaded decoration cover the surface of the cloth head. A distinct characteristic of Ngady mwaash is the placement of a triangular shaped hat centered on the head of the mask. The form of this hat is identical to those worn by Bushoong female diviners. Its appearance on the mask suggests an association with the world of nature spirits (*ngesh*)—the powerful beings to whom diviners attribute their supernatural powers.

The costume for Ngady Mwaash consists of a hide or cloth shirt and leggings painted with a black-and-white triangular patterning. Small wooden dowels are often attached to the front of the shirt to represent breasts. The masked dancer, always a man, wears a long woman's embroidered skirt wrapped around the waist, and over the top of this skirt a short decorated overskirt is held in place by a belt. Beaded bandoliers decorated with cowrie shells are often worn criss-crossed over the chest. The masked dancer wears cowrie laden armbands and legbands and usually carries a flywhisk as an additional symbol of elevated status.

During masked performances, Ngady Mwaash never appears alone but always in the company of a male masked figure such as *Mwaash aMbooy* or *Bwoom* in the context of funeral masquerade. In this region, funeral masquerades take place in an area near the residence of the deceased. Performances occur in the afternoon on the day the deceased is to be buried. The dancing area is often densely lined with onlookers who have come to bid a final farewell to the deceased and to witness the masquerade.

Among the Kuba, male and female masked figures never dance together but take turns appearing for short periods within the performance area. The following description was documented at a funeral masquerade in which Bwoom and Ngady mwaash performed in the Southern Bushoong community of Boganciala in 1982. The masquerade began with the performance of Bwoom. Because of the confined dancing area and the proximity of the spectators to the masquerade figures, the performance of powerful male masked figures like Bwoom are characterized by an aggressive but restrained style. Bwoom forcibly stamps his feet, lunges forward and then abruptly stops and just as abruptly moves off in another direction. These movements are accompanied by threatening, jabbing gestures made with a short sword. To witness the masked figure's performance is to sense the tension between highly controlled but unpredictable power and authority. The observer is uneasy—will the mask suddenly lose control and strike someone? After a short performance, lasting no more than five minutes, the masked dancer retires to a chair that has been placed at the edge of the circle. Then, Ngady Mwaash, who has been standing on the sidelines, enters the arena.[1] The performance of the female mask is in marked contrast to the aggressive style of the male mask. Her performance style is sensuous in performance as the body, legs, arms, and hands of the dancer move in fluid gestures. Hand and arm gestures are accentuated with the use of the flywhisk held in one hand. The long skirt and overskirt worn by the Ngady Mwaash masked dancers prohibit the flamboyant torso and leg movement characteristic of male masquerade performances. Masquerade dance movements approximate closely the individual styles of men and women at funeral dances in the area. The movements and gestures of male masked figures may be characterized as heavy, dellberate, and decidedly earthbound while the movements of female masked dancers are graceful and more vertical in orientation, appearing at times to defy gravity. These clearly opposing performance styles, like the gender of masks, overtly express the ideology of initiated men who control masquerade performance.[2] Funeral masquerades aggressively reinforce opposition toward the uninitiated, especially women (Binkley 1990).

David A. Binkley

1 In the temporal world, chairs are reserved for men. Therefore, the Ngady Mwaash masked dancer does not sit in a chair. Rather the figure stands at the sidelines or sits on a mat that has been placed near the dancing area for this purpose.

2 Surprisingly few masks in the region are designated as feminine in gender. These include Ngady Mwaash and one other mask, the raffia or wooden versions of the initiation mask *Kamakengu* (Binkley 1987b, 1990, 1996).

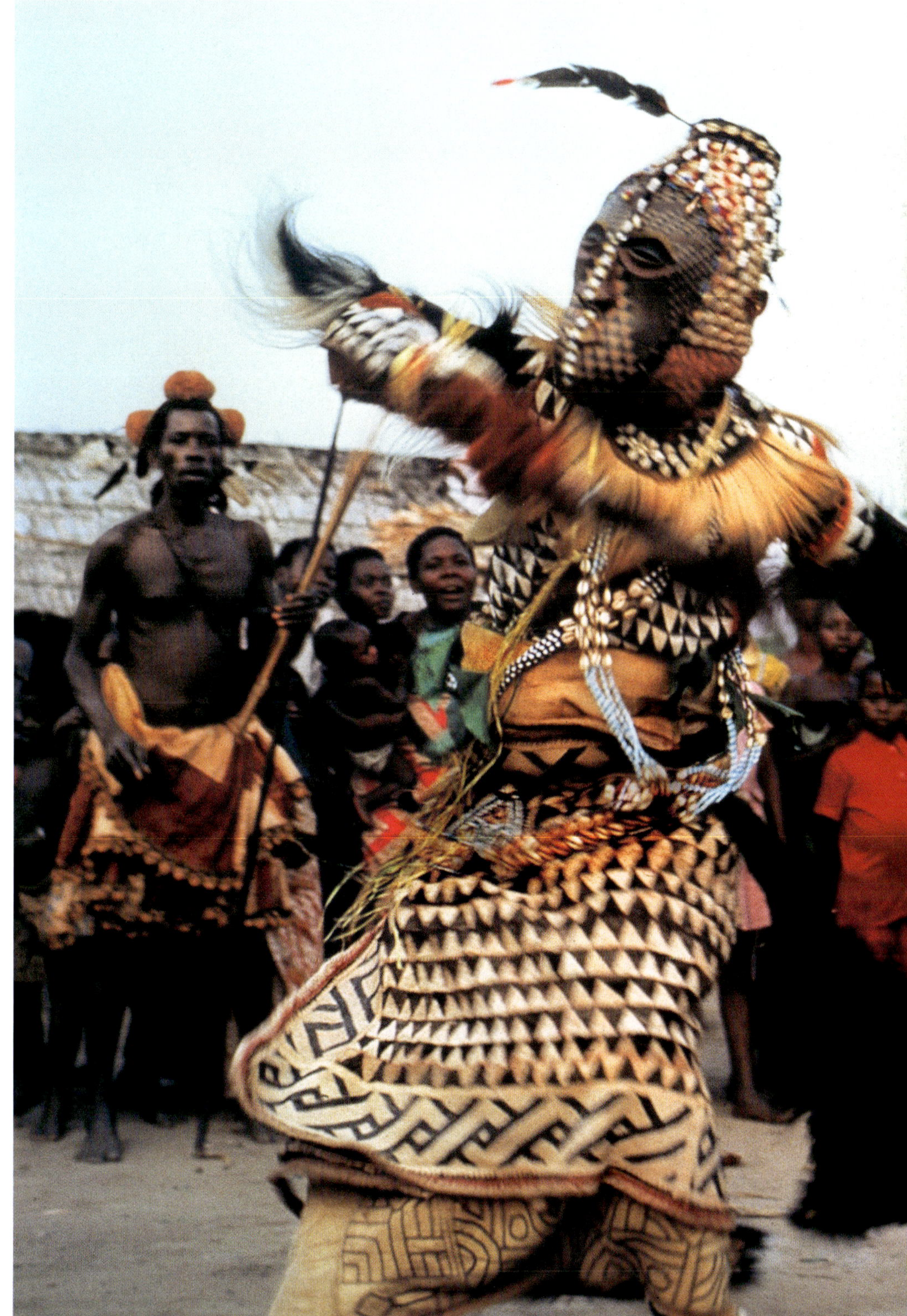

Ngady Mwaash performs at a funeral for an initiated man.
Southern Kuba, Community of Boganciala, Congo (Kinshasa)
Photo: Patricia Darish and David A. Binkley, 1982

42

Transcendent Womanhood and the Scavenger: a Mende Mask (*Ndoli Jowei*)

Female Ancestral Mask (*Ndoli Jowei / Sowo / Nòwo*)
Mende, Sande/Bondo Association, Sierra Leone
c. Early–mid-20th century
Wood, black pigment, H. 40.1 cm
Purchased as the gift of Helen and Howard Benedict, Tiburon, California, in Memory of Alan and Janet Wurtzburger
BMA 1984.50 (purchased from Alpha Sadu Thiam, Monrovia, Liberia)

With the widespread disintegration of Sierra Leone into chaos in the past decade, little is known outside about the current state of the institutions that had flourished and enriched human life. In the hope that the masquerade and women's society described here will be continued in some fashion, I have used the present tense.

The masquerade at hand is shared loosely, and variably, throughout the southern and western half of Sierra Leone by the Mende, Bom, Kim, southern Bullom, and southwestern Temne, as well as in northwestern Liberia among the Vai and Gola, and in some variation among the Bassa. All of these groups use the mask in the context of a women's organization, known as Sande throughout most of the southern distribution, but known as Bondo among the Bullom, Temne, and also other northern Sierra Leone groups that do not use the mask. The spirit of the women was documented throughout Sierra Leone as Nòwo in early twentieth-century literature (Lamp 1985: 28–30, 98), but is now known among the Mende as Ndoli Jowei (Phillips 1995:94, 189).

The masked character appears in dance wearing a black, wooden helmet mask, a gown of black raffia attached to the mask and falling below the knees, and black or dark cloth covering the arms, hands, legs, and feet. A white strip of cloth is usually attached to the pinnacle of the mask, left to fall down the back. Bells would be attached behind the waist, jingling as she moves. A number of amulets in the form of stuffed sheep horns or leather Muslim packets would be attached to protect the masker from spiritual harm. In her left hand, she would carry a broom switch. The costume today often includes a variety of materials disdained only a couple of decades ago, such as tennis shoes. Ruth Phillips (1995:53) found that when she tried to get Sande leaders to show her the masks without producing an entire masquerade, the leaders were immovable, responding "Could you go out without your head?"

Among the Mende the Ndoli Jowei dances at several key events during the initiations of young girls into female adulthood, as observed by Phillips (1995:81–86), Ndoli Jowei accompanies the Sande women parading into and around the town from the initiation grove at the beginning of initiation. About two weeks later, she dances publicly throughout the night to herald the coming of the new initiates brought to town for the first time. The next day, the girls enter the town in single file, wearing white face paint and accompanied by Ndoli Jowei. After a couple of months in initiation, the girls are finally released in a four-day ceremony, during which a number of Ndoli Jowei dancers, sometimes five or six, make their appearance. On the final morning, Ndoli Jowei leads the initiates, polished with oil, to the river, the sacred home of the Sande spirits, for a ritual washing. Ndoli Jowei, however, does not enter the presence of more powerful Sande spiritual beings. Then the girls are dressed in their finest clothes and jewelry and led back to the town under a canopy held by the women of Sande, led by Ndoli Jowei. The girls are installed in the central meeting pavilion, where they remain seated for several days, feasting and receiving the accolades of their townspeople and relatives.

In dance, an attendant Sande officer carries a straw mat used to screen the dancer if she needs privacy for costume adjustments, and she calls out the dancer's professional masking name to introduce her to the crowd (Phillips 1995:101–111). A cluster of Sande members around her dance, sing, and provide a rhythm by shaking their gourd rattles, called *segbura*. These rattles are filled with seeds, and are held in a net sewn with other seeds on the outside. Men joined them beating conical drums called *sangbei* and large wooden slit gongs. The dancer usually dances close to the drummers and faces them.

The Ndoli Jowei dances each dance separately, in turn. The steps of the dance are rapid and abrupt, with intricate footwork and individual variation. The dancer dips and swirls in wide circles, and the thick black raffia flares out dramatically. Often her movements, especially in her first appearance, are sudden and unpredictable, as characterized in some personal names given to individual masked dancers: *Gbuawei*, "Sudden Appearance," or *Kpema*, "Hide-and-Seek" (Phillips 1995:101). Just as often, the dancers stand or sit quietly, observing the proceedings (Lamp 1982: Fig. 151). In the final ceremonies, the masked dancer waits with dignity to receive money as tribute from the families of initiates for her role in the initiation. A Sande official always accompanies the dancer, who announces her coming, picks up stray raffia that falls from her costume, fans her continually, and covers her from the public eye with a mat if she wishes to remove the mask for fresh air and rest. Kenneth Little (1951:252) described the dance steps:

> The style of the dance includes a darting and skipping movement taken almost at the run, like the preliminary strides of an expert skater on the rink. There are side to side inclinations of the head and shoulders—both turned in opposite directions and complicated pirouettes on the balls of the feet. While waiting to dance, the spirit feigns restlessness, scatters the crowd about her, and has to be 'pacified' by her attendant.

The crowd surrounding the dance space of Ndoli Jowei is always in good humor, full of energy and merriment. The masked dancer sometimes mingles with the crowd when not dancing, caressing Sande women (see Phillips 1995: Fig. 8.3) or flirting with the men (Lamp 1982: Fig. 177). Although Ndoli Jowei is silent, even while dancing vigorously, some personal names given to individual dancers express the general character of the event: *Sòlɛ*, "Noisy," or *Mòjɛ*, "Laughter" Phillips (1995:101).

As the picture of beautiful and righteous ancestral womanhood, Ndoli Jowei is understood to be the positive side of dual nature. Her counterpart is called Gonde, whom Sylvia Boone (1986:39) has described as "disreputable ..., the 'anti-aesthetic' mask—coarse, unkempt, gross; the top is broken or grotesque, the costume a pile of junk and scraps." The mask may be an old, deteriorated, discarded mask, often splattered with paint, or it may be a mask carved originally to represent Gonde, with grotesque or crude features. The costume is a disheveled accumulation of fiber and rags, often festooned with discarded objects such as bones, tin cans, and shells. Ndoli Jowei (Sowo, Nòwo), on the other hand,

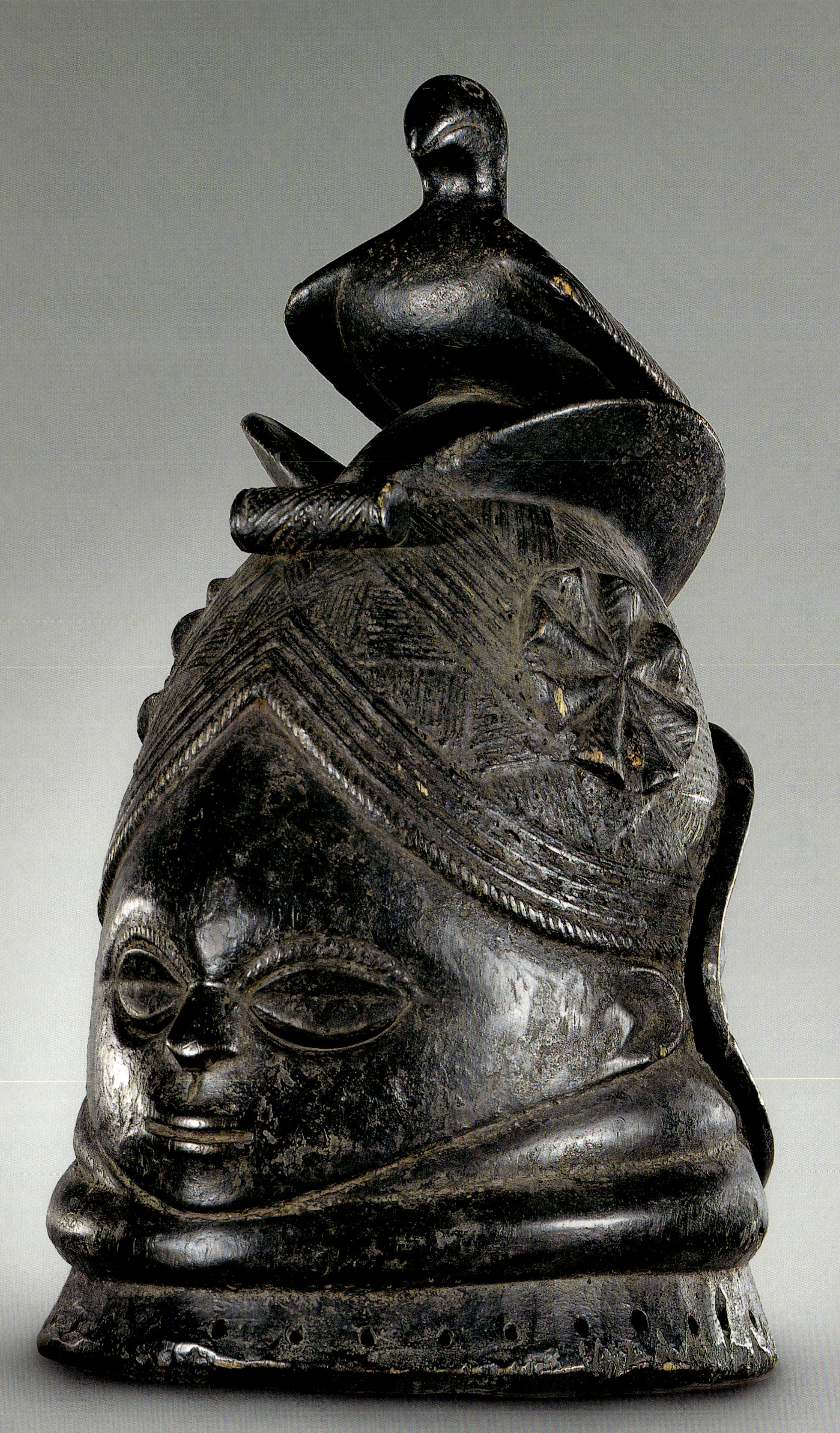

Boone has described as "the classic image of transcendent womanhood—beautiful, elegant, serious, sumptuous, and with an aura of grandeur."

While Ndoli Jowei wears a full body covering, the Gonde dancer often exposes her arms and legs and sometimes even the face. "One song sung about *gonde* goes, '*gonde* is shameless, she's not ashamed to show her face'" (Phillips 1995:90). Gonde's behavior is reprehensible. Not only does she push her mask up over her head, but she sometimes confronts spectators to demand money. Another song mocks *gonde's* poverty: "*Gonde* has not yet eaten ... she's roaming the darkness for food" (Phillips 1995:90). Although Gonde may be disgusting herself, she is a reminder of what not to become: "the blotched figure strides about shaking a bundle of switches at wrongdoers of either sex and all ages, reminding all who watch the public ceremony of Sande's power to catch and punishing transgressors even if they

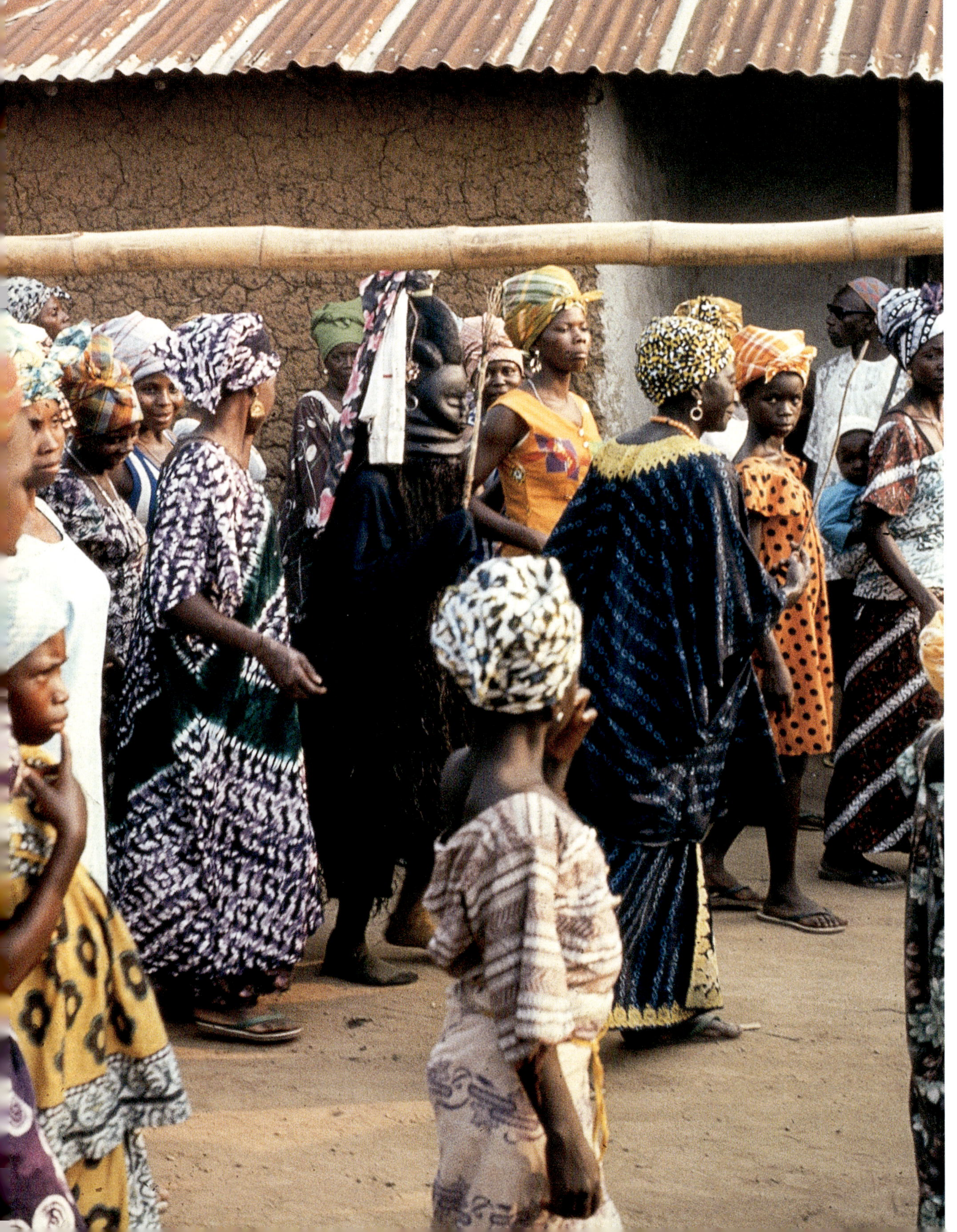

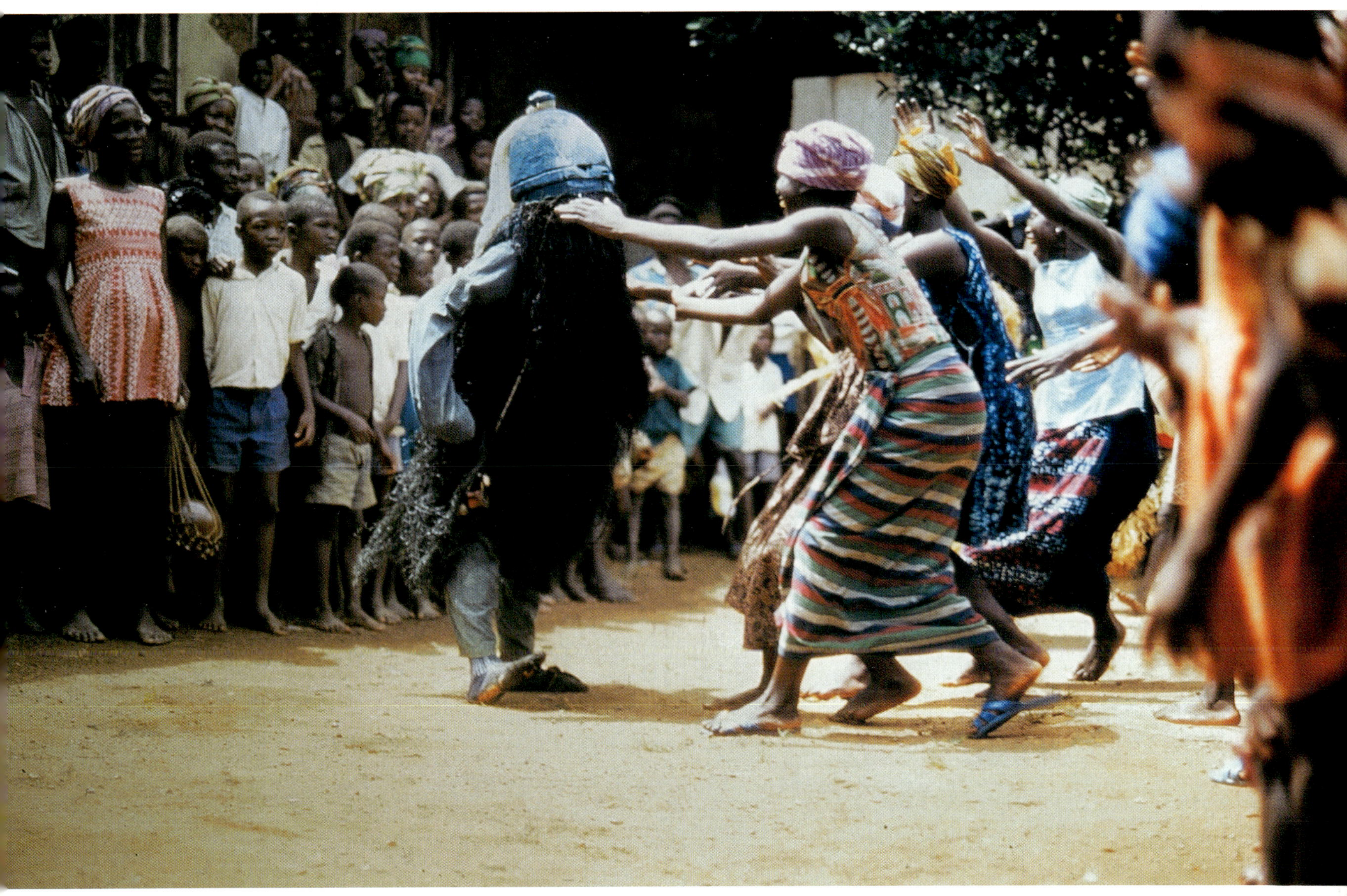

Women attempting to chase the anti-aesthetic dancer, Gonde, from the performance space. Mende, Ngiyehun Village, Luawa Chiefdom, Sierra Leone. Photo: Ruth Phillips, 1972

sin in secret" (MacCormack 1979:35). Sometime Gonde tries to interfere with the performance, and she is chased away by the women in charge, but most often, she dances separately, at another time.

As indicated above, Nòwo/Ndoli Jowei is not the most powerful spirit in Sande/Bondo. There are several spirit beings specifically associated with Sande and Bondo, and most are purely conceptual. It seems to be in keeping with the nature of the spiritual being that it is the non-masked, unseen spirits who are most powerful and critical to the ritual.

Frederick John Lamp

Final procession of the coming out of initiates of Bondo with Nòwo in lead. Temne, Gbiri, Sierra Leone. Photo: Frederick John Lamp, 1976

STAGING: SPACE, ARCHITECTURE, AND ENCLOSURE

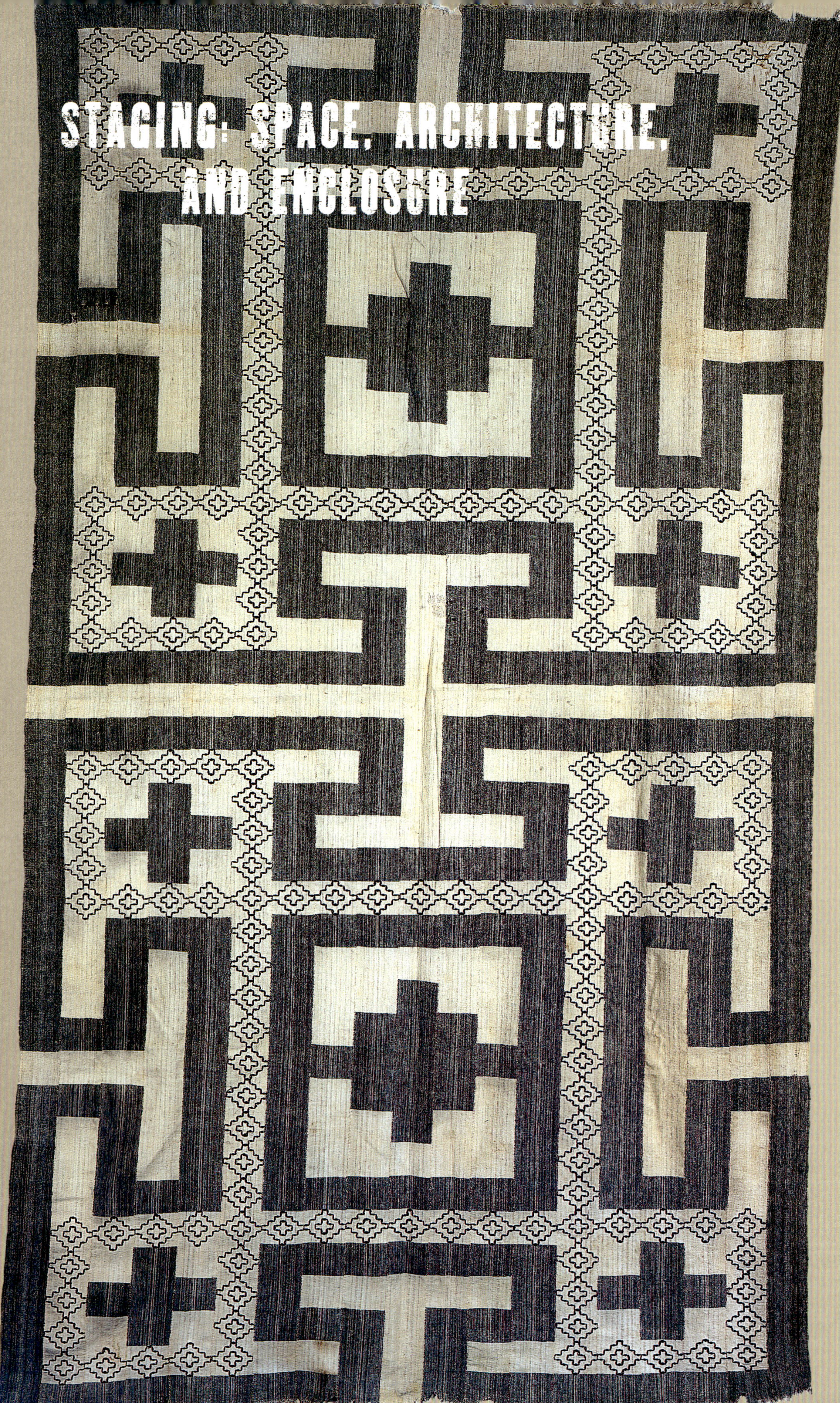

The setting, or staging, of the symbols of the Yoruba god, *Shangó*, discussed in the previous section, leads directly to a consideration of the stage set, if we are to think of African art as a performance art. Here we consider the space in which the action takes place, in which the stationary objects reside, and on which they depend. In the essays that follow, cardinal direction is seen to be critical in the ancient Egyptian use of jars to store the viscera of the deceased, discussed by Thomas Kittredge. For the Moba, discussed by Christine Mullen Kreamer, the positioning of wooden figures in the context of divination and other ritual is critical for contact with God and the spirits, in male and female contexts. Ibibio/Annang masks define inner and outer social spaces—the underworld and our own, ancestral circles, and the home—as described by Jill Salmons. Figures of the Pende discussed here, used to decorate the pinnacle of a chief's ritual house, mark a center from which radiates the welfare of the village. In coastal Sierra Leone, carved stone figures dating back 500 years or more may relate to contemporary shrines of stones placed in an east-west configuration, with anthills, which I discuss as a reference to the cycle of life and death, and of the rising and setting sun. Apart from this configuration, the stones are of absolutely no value.

The ancient stone figures are said by the current inhabitants of the region, the Mende, to have been carved by the original landowners. The Mende simply find these objects and use them in a number of different ways, most often placing the figures upright in a remote area of the farm. Here, the figures were expected to guard the rice crop and to make it productive through their special spiritual powers. In this setting, the figures were seldom seen by the general population, but they were used by the farmer in very private ritual in order to keep their power effective. Visually then, they are minuscule, or invisible, in relation to a vast space, yet in another context, their visual impact changes. This use of the stones has never been specifically documented, and we do not know how critical an exact placement is within the farm.

Among Kissi people of Guinea, similar stone figures were collected and set in shrines together with other objects such as simple stone cylinders, pebbles, miniature wooden pestles, stone celts, metal tools, and polished stone axes (see below). These collections tended to be placed on a large, raised earthen altar, under the shelter of a small pavilion or a veranda roof. Here, the objects were clustered tightly, not meant to be seen fully in the round. It is the mass, not the individual carving, that has the greatest visual effect as well as the greatest spiritual power.

Among the Kuba of Congo (Kinshasa), the use of the mask *Ngady Mwaash* (p. 172) is an excellent lesson in the study of both associated objects and staging. Ngaady Mwaash is best comprehended in relationship to other masked characters who go by the names of Mwaash aMbooy and Bwoom. These characters are said to represent a number of different qualities and personalities varying according to the informant and the region (David Binkley, personal communication, 2003). By most published accounts from the Kuba capital, which differ from those of the southern Kuba, Mwaash aMbooy is a royal male figure related to or identified with the first mythical king of the Kuba, Woot. Ngady Mwaash, is variously the wife of Mwaash aMbooy or his sister—in any case, a highly placed royal female. *Bwoom* is described as a commoner, a Pygmy, an original land owner (that is, someone who has been overthrown), a slave of the king, a nature spirit, and the last of nine sons of the mythical Woot—thus, a son without power. These three masks appeared in performance worn by male dancers, but according to Jan Vansina (1973) they also appeared in the context of initiation attached to a raffia screen held up by a framework of wooden poles, featuring three triangular peaks. On the peak to the left was hung the mask of Mwaash aMbooy along with a lesser mask representing Woot's child. On the peak to the right was the mask of Bwoom. Other masks appeared, such as Yool on the center peak as the incarnation of Woot as enforcer as well as another mask with a Janus head referring to the dual realms of the village and surrounding bush. In the center, literally and figuratively, was the image of Ngady Mwaash, referring also to the garden found between village and bush. Suffice it to say that it presents a set of spatial relationships, both static and kinetic, between the elements on the raffia screen. How would the image be conceived by young male initiates who are symbolically cut off in exiting through Mwaash aMbooy's legs and finally emerging through the legs of Ngady Mwaash?

Blanket
Gola/Vai/Mende, Liberia/Sierra Leone
c. Early 20th century
Cotton, L. 252 cm
Purchase with exchange funds from eight donors
BMA 1998.480 (collected in Liberia between 1923–1929 by the parents of purchase source [Bruce Bussell]: Pauline Bussell and Conrad Turner Bussell, Supervisor of Customs and Financial Advisor to President King of Liberia)

In field research in Africa on the spatial context of a work of art, and its theatricality, we might address some of the following questions. On the subject of orientation: how would the art form relate spatially to other objects within the prescribed space? Would it be enclosed and not accessible visually, or would the space around it be open and inviting? Do others freely enter the space or is it restricted; and if they do, under what circumstances and by what routes? Which forms of space are more important than others? How do the viewers use the space? Would the viewer be invited to interact closely with the mask, as in the case with the Mende Ndoli Jowei (p. 175) where its beauty is to be examined, or would the viewer be discouraged from coming close, as in the case of the Makonde/Yao mask (p. 214), risking the annoyance of the spirits? Is the use of space arbitrary or is it prescribed?

What of markers? What natural and fabricated objects mark the space, the entrances, and the exits? What are the shapes of the architecture that surround the object, and how does it relate to them? How does the performance use the corners, the borders, and points of entry? How does it use east, west, north, and south? How would the performance change if the space were changed? What are the possible parameters of spatial configuration with the same art form?

What are the sequences in the use of specific spaces? What are the vectors of movement within the space? Do the movements require vistas, courtyards, plazas, or small corners? Turner (1986:73–76) urges us to concentrate on how space is processualized and temporalized in the course of the performance.

Ancestral altar with stone figures. Kissi, Guinea. Photo: Denise Paulme, *c.* 1950

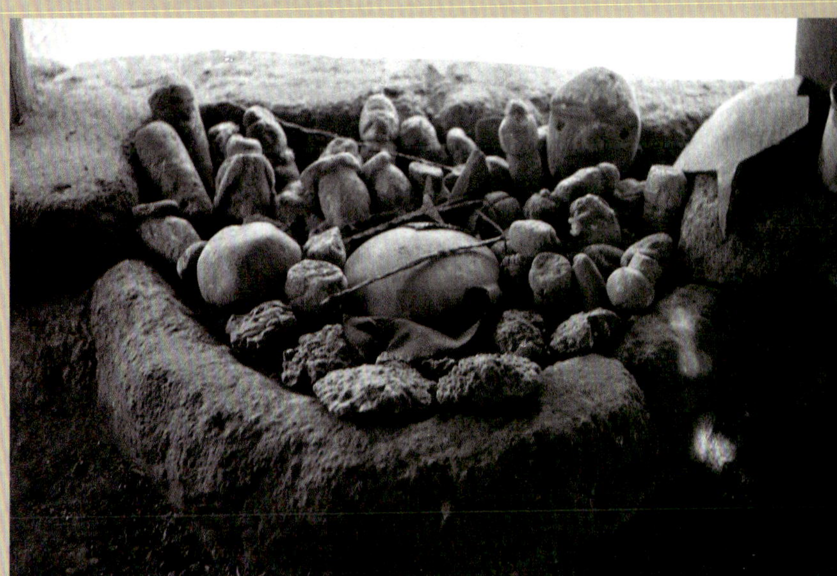

43

Orienting the Body: Egyptian Viscera Jars

Set of Viscera Jars for Psamtik
Egypt, Area of Qusae (Middle Egypt)
Early Dynasty XXVI, 664–*c.* 600 BC
Alabaster, carbon black pigment, unidentified substance
H. a) 27 cm; c) 24 cm; b) 24.2 cm; d) 25.4 cm (in order as illustrated)
Gift of Robert Garrett
BMA 1956.132a–d

During the Predynastic Period, the ancient Egyptians chose to bury their dead directly in the desert sand. This resulted, unexpectedly, in the complete desiccation of the corpse, preserving it to an exceptional degree. However, over time, ancient Egyptian mortuary practice became more elaborate, the dead being instead interred in coffins and tombs, thus eliminating this contact with the hot sand. As early as Dynasty 1, mummification developed as an alternate means of arresting the disintegration of the corpse. This allowed the deceased's body to reunite with his spirit, and become a replica of Osiris, the Egyptian god of the underworld (*Lexikon* I:610–1).

Mummification was a complicated procedure, lasting seventy days, for which the ancient Egyptians have left us no detailed descriptions. However, Egyptologists have been able to reconstruct this process by drawing on information gleaned from the scientific examination of mummies, and from the experimental embalming of animal and human remains. The first major step was the removal of all the deceased's viscera, save for the heart and kidneys. A "Reader" priest supervised the process, reciting appropriate formulas in the presence of the "Official of the Secret of the Embalming Workshop." Attending the process were the "Embalmer of Anubis" (black god with the head of a young jackal—black was the color of rebirth), the "Chancellors of the God," who handled valuable objects used in the operations, and the other officiants called *Ut* or *Wet* (Desroches-Noblecourt 1963:222). The corpse was then subjected to a lengthy drying process with natron (a mixture of carbonate, bicarbonate, chloride, and sulfate of sodium), treated with various unguents and resins,

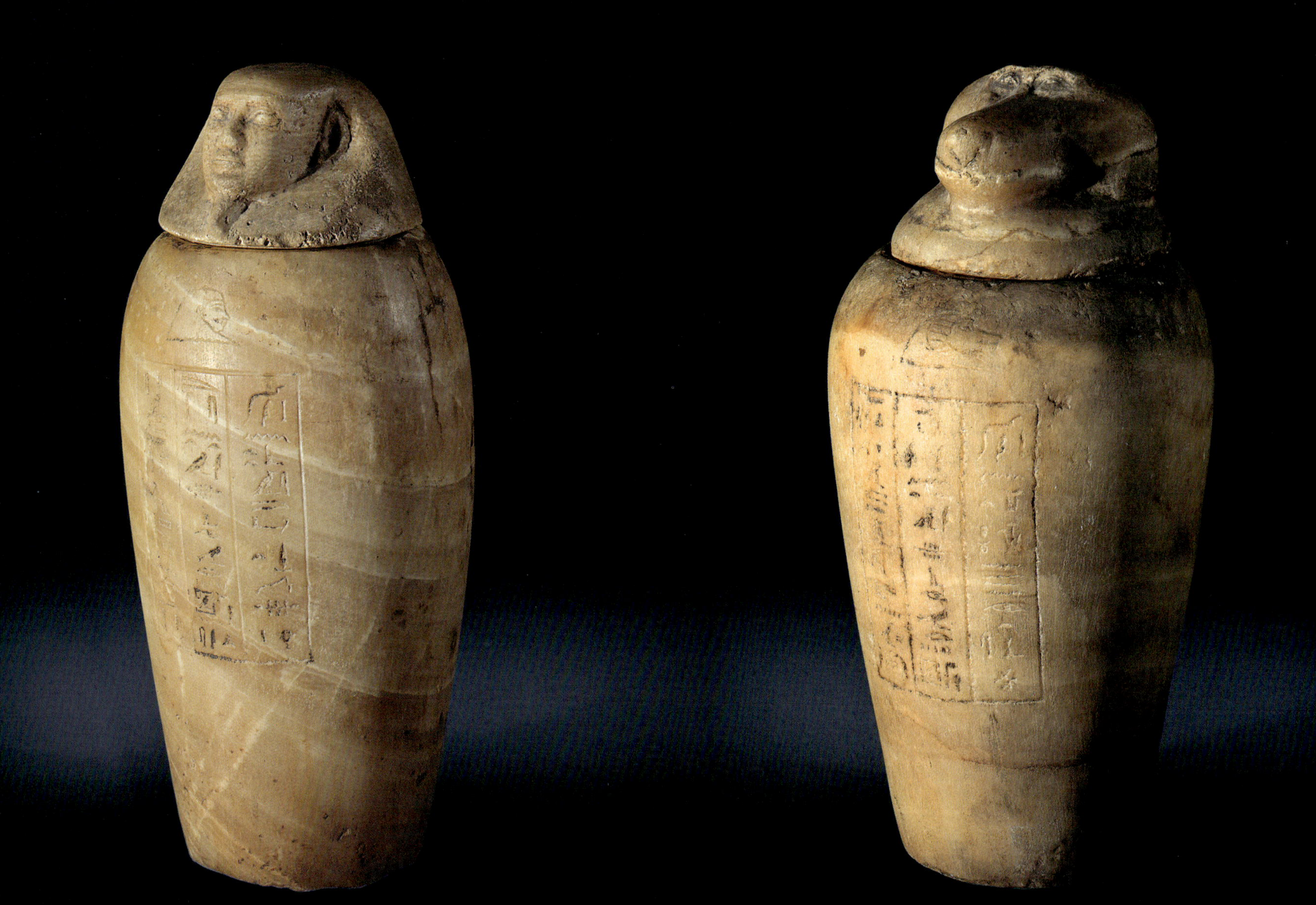

wrapped in hundreds of yards of linen, and supplied with a number of protective amulets. Throughout this entire process, mortuary priests performed rituals and recited religious formulas (*Lexikon* I:611–3).

After the major organs (liver, stomach, lungs, and intestines) had been removed, they were placed in four viscera jars, which were made of alabaster (whose clear white color symbolized purity) (Aufrere 1991:696), wood, limestone, faience, or pottery (Doxey 1997:248). These viscera jars were often kept together in a rectangular chest of stone or wood, which would have been included in the funeral procession. In the *Papyrus of Ani*, from the 19th Dynasty, a funeral procession is depicted with the viscera chest on a sledge drawn by four men behind the hearse and its mourners. The chest is decorated with painted designs and festooned with lotus blossoms and on the top is the figure of a jackal. Finally, after the procession, the chest would have been interred with the deceased in the tomb. In the event that there was no viscera chest to accompany the burial at the tomb, the viscera jars would be placed at the end of the coffin (*Lexikon* III:317).

In this set of four viscera jars, at the top of each jar body there is a profile depiction of the lid that is supposed to go with that particular jar. These images served as assembly instructions for the workers who finished the tombs and placed the burial goods in it, but who were not educated in the actual rituals and unable to read hieroglyphs (Betsy Bryan, personal communication).

These depictions and the jar lids themselves represent the heads of the four sons of the god Horus, who were minor deities, as they did not have their own cults (Dodson 1996:562). From the 12th Dynasty onwards, they were charged with the protection of the aforementioned four major organs (Brovarski 1978: Introduction; Germer 1997:53). In the late 18th Dynasty the viscera jar lids actually took the form of the four sons' heads, a practice that remained constant down into the Late Period (Doxey 1997:248). Each of the four sons was responsible for one particular organ, had his own protector goddess, and corresponded to one cardinal direction:

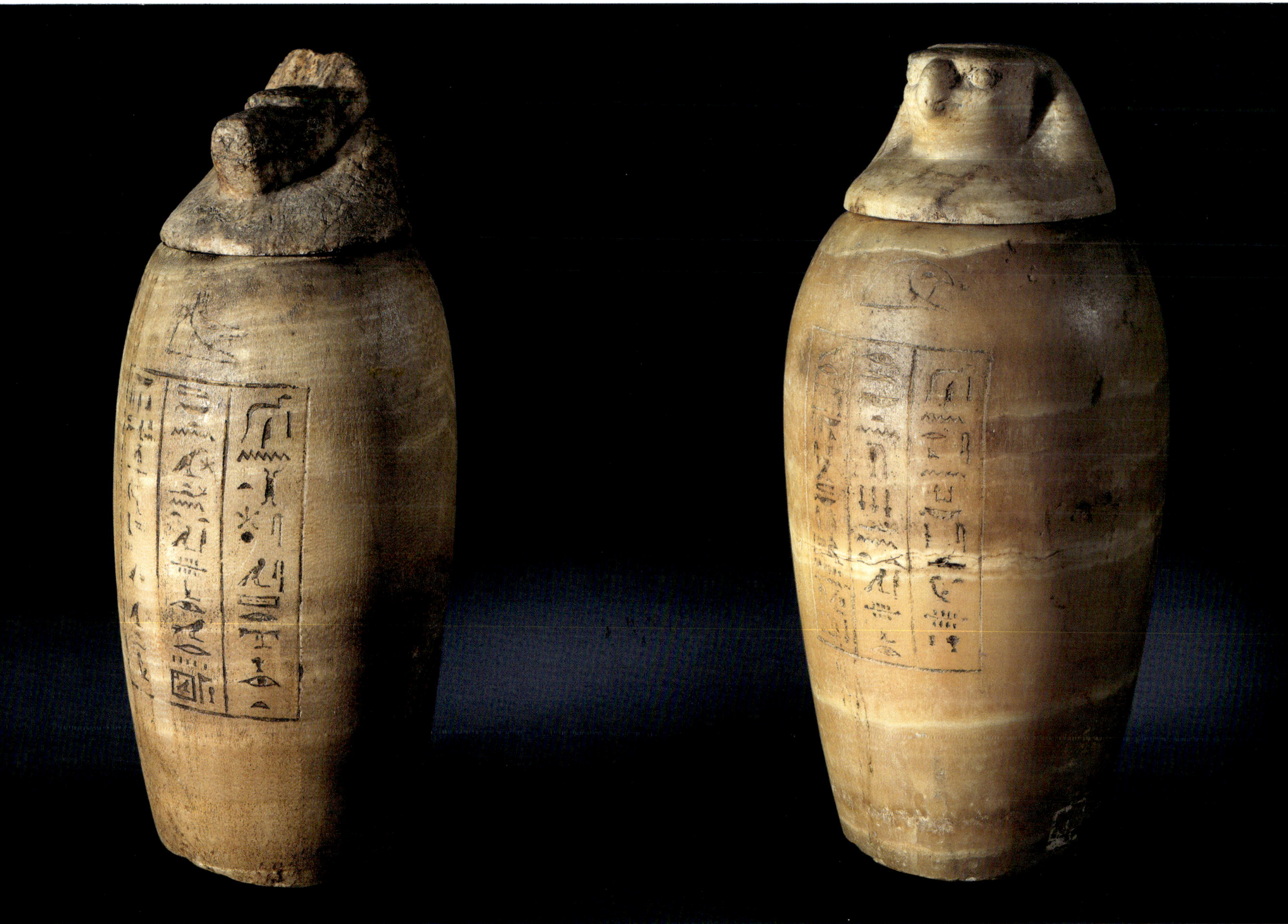

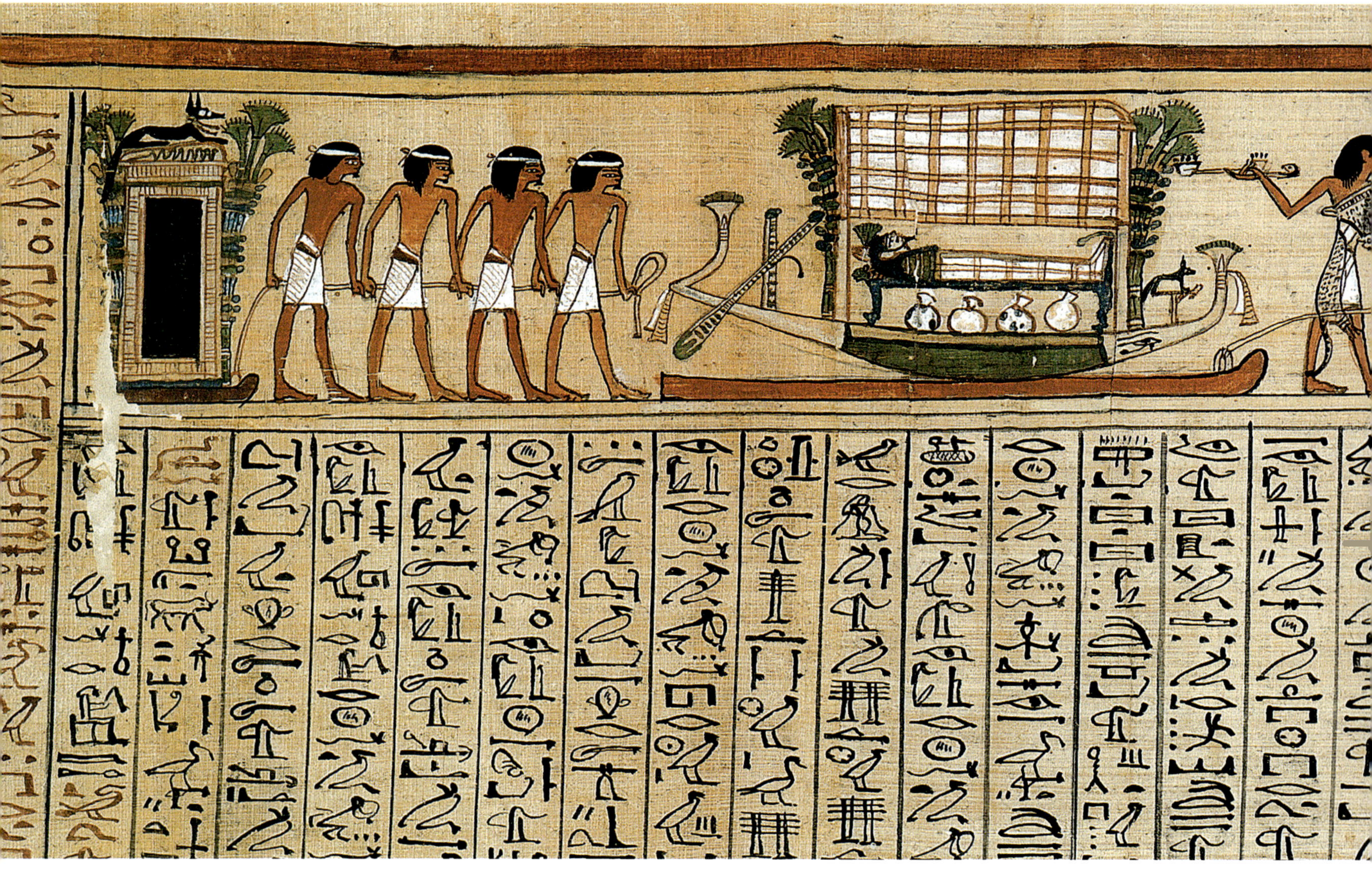

Human-headed Imseti, protected by Isis, for the liver: South

Baboon-headed Hapi, protected by Nephthys, for the lungs: North

Jackal-headed Dewamutef, protected by Neith, for the stomach: East

Falcon-headed Kebehsenuef, protected by Selket, for the intestines: West

Given the Egyptian attention to the importance of sequence in processions, it is curious that, in the depictions of viscera jars in paintings and other scenes (where the viscera jar lids are distinguished by the heads of the four sons of Horus), the order in which the jars are placed is not consistent. But the most frequently found sequence is that given above. In a study by Lamp in 2003 in eleven depictions of viscera jars documented (where the heads are differentiated), this is the only sequence that is clearly found more than once (five out of eleven), and it is the most frequent order (thirty-four out of forty-eight) in the depiction of full figures representing the four sons of Horus. This seems to imply the order in which the four jars should have been placed on the funeral sledge, which may or may not have been consistent. In some cases, the viscera jars are in pairs facing the center, in which case the sequence is ambiguous, but this may refer to their placement in the four corners of the burial chest.

On each jar body, below the profile depiction of each jar lid, there are three columns of inscription, filled in with carbon black, which are to be read from right to left. These inscriptions reveal that the four viscera jars were made as one set for an individual named Psamtik. They also describe the actions of each of the four protector goddesses, as well as listing the deceased's titles, and the name of his mother.

Imseti (human-headed) (p. 180, left):
"[right] *Words spoken by Isis: May (I) seize the opponent, and may (I) protect* [center] *Imseti, that which is in (me). The protection of Osiris (referring to the deceased Psamtik), the great one of the five, and priest of Hathor, mistress of Qusae,* [left] *Psamtik, the one born of Khered/ Neni-shebu, is Imseti.*"

Hapi (baboon-headed) (p. 180, right):
"[right] *Words spoken by Nephthys: May (I) conceal the secret, and may (I) protect* [center] *Hapi, that which is in (me). The protection of Osiris, the great one of the five, and priest of Hathor,* [left] *mistress of Qusae, Psamtik, the one born of Khered/ Neni-shebu, is Hapi.*"

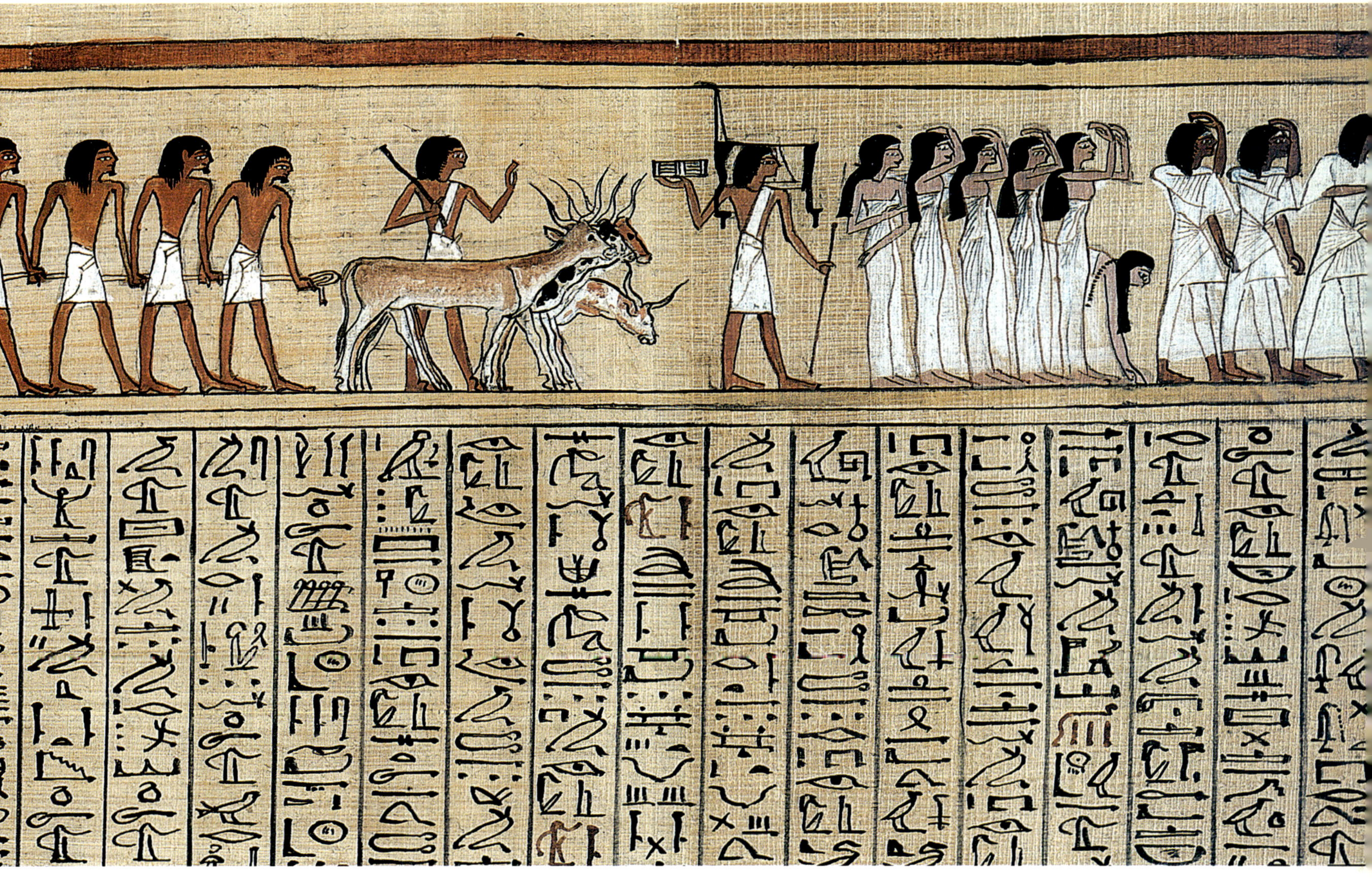

Funeral Procession with Chest of Viscera Jars. From *Book of the Dead of Ani.* Egypt, Dynasty XIX. Photo: ©The British Museum

Dewamutef (jackal-headed) (p. 181, left):
"[right] *Words spoken by Neith: May (I) spend the morning, and may (I) spend the evening, making* [center] *protection for Dewamutef, that which is in (me). The protection of Osiris, the great one of the five, and priest of Hathor,* [left] *mistress of Qusae, Psamtik, the one born of Khered/Neni-shebu, is Dewamutef.*"

Kebehsenuef (falcon-headed) (p. 181, right):
"[right] *Words spoken by Selket for your ka: May I keep watch,* [center] *protecting Kebehsenuef, that which is in (me). The protection of Osiris,* [left] *the great one of the five, and priest of Hathor, mistress of Qusae, Psamtik, the one born of Khered/Neni-shebu, is Kebehsenuef.*"

The name Psamtik, by virtue of its popularity among several kings of Dynasty 26, indicates a probable date within that dynasty, and it is not mentioned prior to this period. Curiously, the name of Psamtik's mother, Khered/Neni-shebu, appears nowhere else. The inscriptions are of a type which date to Dynasty 26 or later (Sethe 1934:229, Note 12). In addition, alabaster was a popular choice for viscera jars of Dynasty 26 and later. Finally, a Dynasty 26 through Dynasty 30 date is indicated by the form of the wig on the BMA model (p. 180, left), as it covers the throat, as well as through the presence of a divine beard (Reisner 1899:70).

However, if one were to look only at the style of the human-head jar lid of Imseti, one would be inclined to assign this set to the earlier 25th Dynasty, the rule of the Nubian (Kushite) kings. Several of the head's features are observed in sculpture of the 25th Dynasty, the so-called "Kushite style:" the round head, the short nose, the full lips set close beneath the nose, and the very full cheeks (Robins 1997:217–8). However, this style did continue into the beginning of the 26th Dynasty, ironically, as the rulers of this dynasty were not Nubian, but from the northern city of Sais in the Western Delta. They would not have had Nubian features, yet they maintained the Nubian style for a time even in their own portraits.

Thomas Kittredge

44

Seeing Between Worlds: a Moba Figure

Human Figure
Moba, Togo/Ghana
c. Mid-20th century
Wood, H. 52 cm
Gift of Robert and Mary Cumming, Baltimore
BMA 1993.595

Among the Moba of northern Togo and Ghana, minimally carved human figures (*tchitcheri*, pl.; *tchitcherik*, s.)[1] of an attenuated, abstract style are most often created on the advice of a *djabat*, or diviner (Kreamer 1987). With the exception of certain large and imposing sculptures (*tchitcheri sakab*, pl.; *tchicherik sakwa*, s.) usually planted in the ground and associated with village founders and lineage shrines, or with offerings dedicated to the hunt, most Moba figure sculptures function as part of offerings at shrines dedicated to individual and family concerns.

The first performative context involving tchitcheri is that of divination. Many diviners use figures, called *bountàrrà tchitcheri*, to enhance their abilities to "see the truth clearly ... to see into two worlds ... [like] a fish [that] can see you coming toward the water and can flee, but can see clearly in the water, too" (Interview with Kondoeil Bangànar, Nano, 31 January 1990). Diviners rely on the power of bountàrrà tchitcheri, as one diviner noted, to "wander around the village at night ... to see the problems" that clients bring to them the next day during consultations. Some may be small, portable iron or wooden figures—a single figure or two figures bound together—that are stored in a diviner's goatskin bag as part of his mobile tool kit. During a divination session, these may be kept within the diviner's sack, hidden from view, or may be brought out and placed to one side as visual reinforcement of the diviner's powers. For diviners who work only at home—particularly female diviners—larger wooden figures may be employed.

Seated within the cool, dark environment of the compound vestibule or in a shaded area of the inner courtyard, a diviner will position himself or herself opposite the client. God and the ancestors are alerted by the diviner to the proceedings in the typical way that the Moba announce their presence when calling on neighbors: by clapping the hands together, asking to be recognized, and then stating in a straightforward manner the purpose of their visit. To outsiders, the approach might seem informal and lacking in the solemnity one might associate with ritual activity. But from a Moba point of view, these auditory cues conform to norms of politeness that govern social interactions with the living as well as the spirits. Background activity—family members chatting and going about their tasks, children playing or watching the divination session—continue within proximity of the consultation and rarely distract from the proceedings.

The divination session then begins. For a male diviner, this is usually done through numerous manipulations of the *gbañi*, the primary divination tool that is an assemblage of eight leather strands to which are affixed earth-packed animal horns, seed pods, corn cobs, pieces of worked iron and recycled metal, and a range of found objects such as Bic pen tops and plastic hair curlers. The diviner takes the eight strands, wound into a bundle, and taps them several times on the floor, an action that produces a metallic jangling sound as the pieces of iron and recycled automobile and bicycle parts hit the hard-packed earthen floor. This action separates the strands a bit and allows for an interpretation of the relationships that are formed by adjacent strands. Female diviners are prohibited from using the gbañi, relying instead on cowrie shells, kola nuts, and other items that are cast onto the earthen floor and manipulated in their work. A physical and psychic connection between diviner and client is established through joined hands and the use of a metal or wooden staff that is held by both parties and tapped on various combinations of divinatory materials. In a low tone, questions are asked and responses given, and where the staff periodically rests is relevant to the interpretation and advice the diviner offers. Further, the conversational tone of the diviner's statements does not diminish the intent to seek spiritual guidance in the work to be accomplished.

Throughout the proceedings, there is often little reference by the diviner or the client to the divinatory figures, the bountàrrà tchitcheri, that give diviners their insights, though their power and presence is tacitly understood whether or not the figures are seen and used during the consultation. However, the divinatory setting is a critical one, for it is during a consultation that a diviner might inform a client that he or she should commission the carving of a figure, a tchitcherik. The function of the shrine figure is determined at that time—whether it is to represent a specific ancestor and in what ceremonial contexts the figure is to be used.

The second performative context for Moba figure carvings is in offerings made at shrines.[2] One or more carved wooden figures, associated with the different shrines common to most Moba rural households, are placed in proximity to the earthen shrine area and share in the offerings. The figures function as "collaborators" to enhance the efficacy of the offerings (Interview with shrine priest Lebentik, Malàbat: 26 January 1990) designed to protect against misfortune and ensure good health and prosperity.

The mid-sized height of the BMA figure places it within a genre of figures usually associated with household concerns. Their form is largely indistinguishable one from the next. Without the collection data that would identify its gender (as the BMA example does not have distinguishing sexual characteristics) and its precise, original contexts, it is impossible to determine its intended use. There are at least three possibilities, all of them in fairly common use in Moba country.

The first, *kpiem tchitcheri,* are carved for the dead and rest in proximity to ancestral shrines. Female figures are generally located within the interior space of the family compound while male figures are kept in the compound vestibule, a space that is viewed as male and exterior.

Bawount tchitcheri are created for the ceremony of *bat*, a ritual that identifies one's potential to be a diviner (*djabat*). During divination, an individual learns that he or she is "followed by *bat*" (Interview with Kondoeil, Nano, 28 February 1990) and, thus, must undertake a *bat* ceremony in order to avoid misfortune and achieve individual and family peace, good health, and prosperity. A wooden figure, created specifically for the ceremony and only by a carver who has similarly performed his own *bat*, is placed in the earthen offering area identified as *bawount*. For a man, this sacrificial area is located outside the client's compound and often to the side of the vestibule entrance. For a woman, her earthen bawount shrine is usually constructed in her sleeping room. Presided over by a senior diviner, the ceremony involves animal offerings, assisted by the client who serves and consumes millet

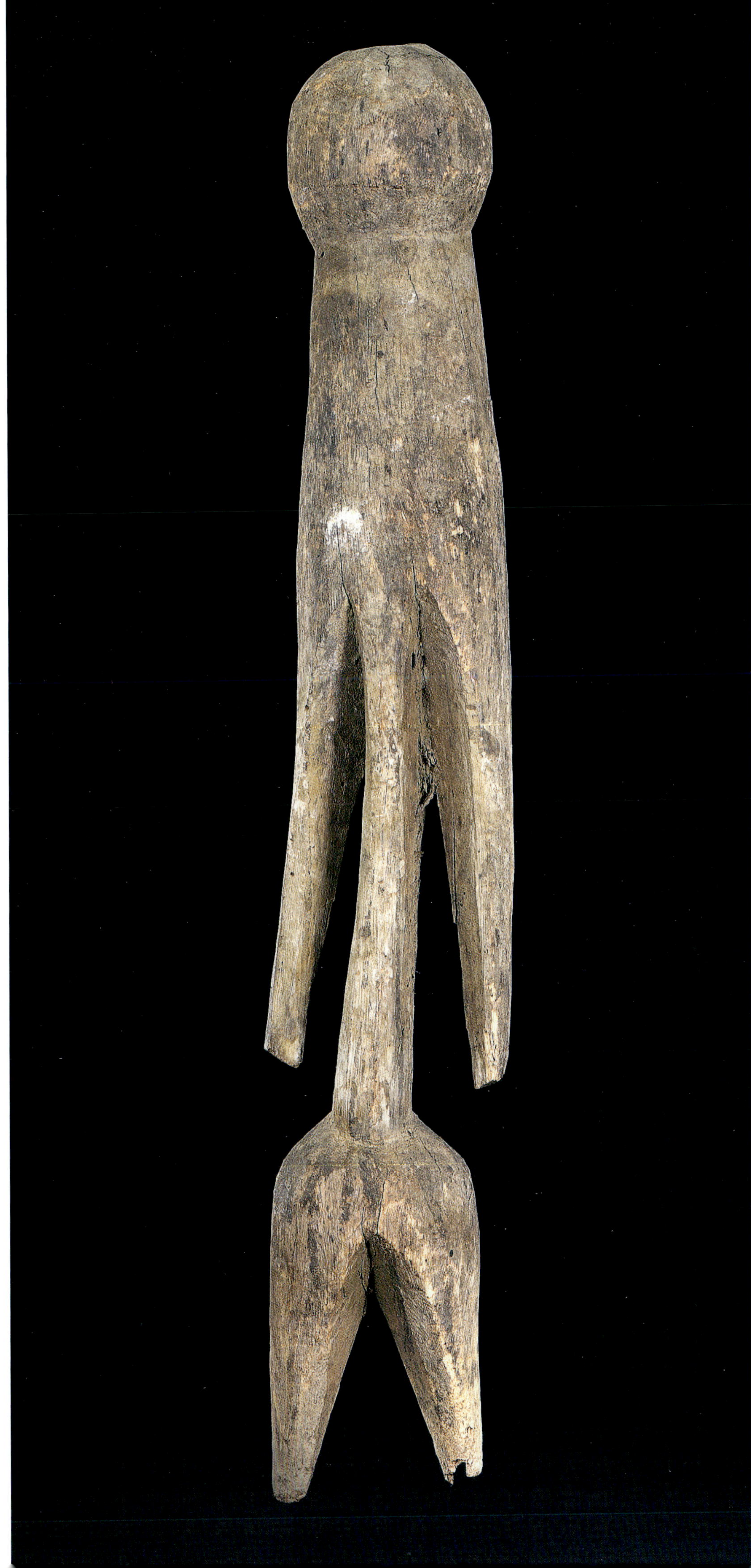

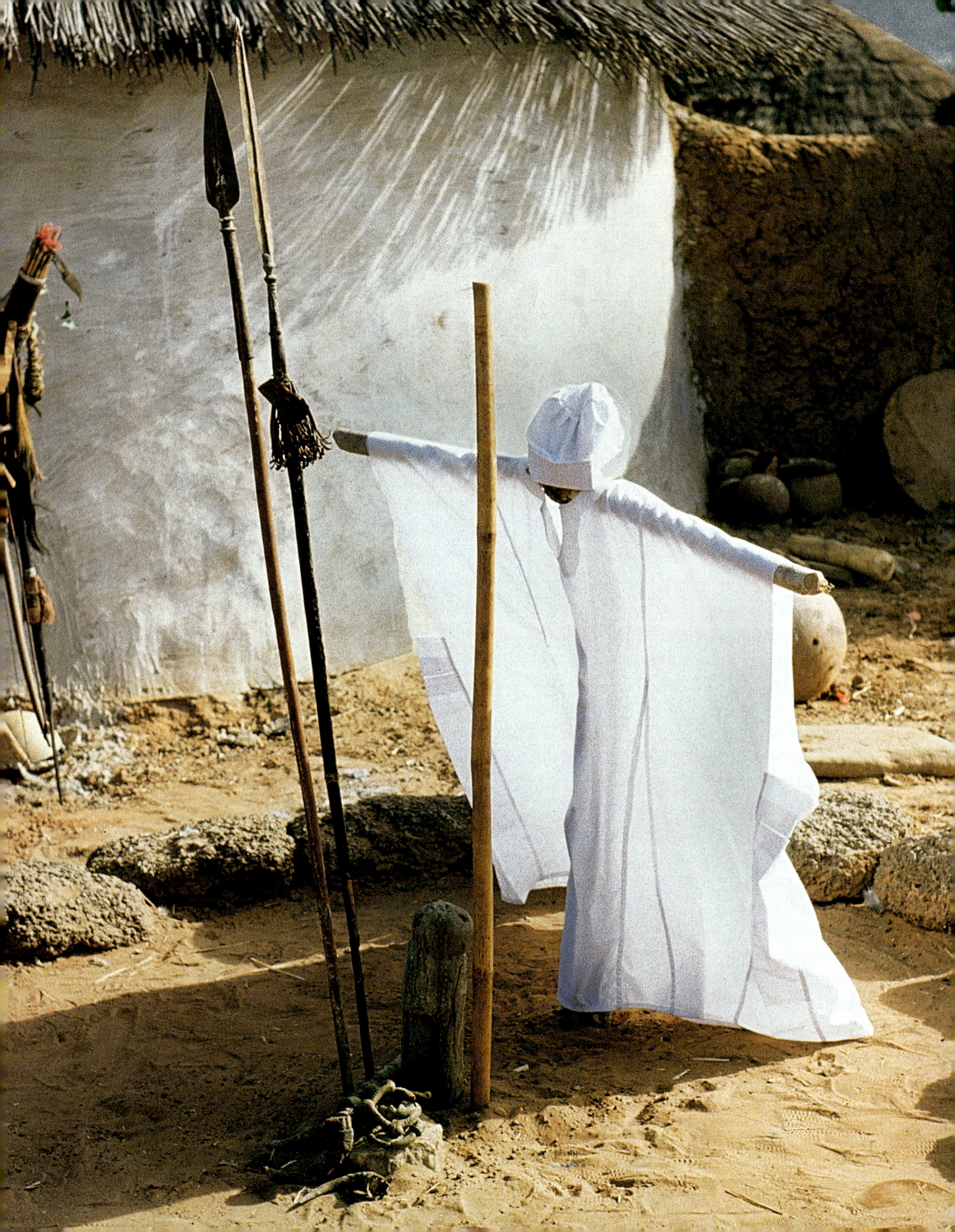

Shrine with a carved wooden figure "collaborating" in the offering. Moba, village of Nasiet, Togo. Photo: Christine Mullen Kreamer, 1980

beer that has been prepared for the ceremony, and who "dances *bat*" throughout the night. Bawount tchitcheri are brought outside periodically for ceremonies.

A third category of figures, *saara tchitcheri*, may represent specific family ancestors but are kept outside in the sacrificial area and, thus, are generally considered male. They are used in offerings designed to bring peace and health to the family. The positive, generous qualities associated with *saara*[3] are indicated by an emphasis on sweet foods and white animal offerings (usually fowl, sometimes a goat or ram) that are shared with children who attend the ceremony.

In February 1990, in the village of Nasiet, I observed a particularly impressive *saara* ceremony held late in the afternoon on the occasion of the public announcement of the death of the Nasiet chief (which had occurred months earlier). To prepare for the ceremony, the sacrificial circle for the offerings, located outside the compound vestibule, was swept clean by a young woman of the household. In its center was a saara tchitcherik, planted in the ground (see opposite). Objects belonging to the deceased chief were placed on the shrine: five brass bracelets, two shrine horns, two spears planted in the ground blades up, a staff, and a hunting stick. Two crossed sticks supported the chief's white hat and smock. Once these items were assembled, a woman from the family mixed water, millet flour, milk, honey, and millet cakes together in a large calabash to form a sort of porridge. At this point, men from the family performed the animal sacrifices, slitting the throat of each animal and dripping some of its blood on the wooden shrine figure and the shrine horns. Feathers and hair from the sacrificial animals were also applied to the figure and horns. As with most Moba ritual activity, there is much animated discussion and advice about the process, what to put out and where, as elders—mostly men, but occasionally older women, too—bring their collective experience to bear in instructing some of the younger participants about the proper steps to follow to ensure a successful offering.

A transcription of some of the ritual invocations gives a sense of the straightforward, conversational style typical of Moba offerings:

> ... Your sweet meal!
> There is millet ... milk ... cakes ... millet flour.
> It is all inside. Take and give to the former chiefs.
> ... Embrace it with the left hand and the right hand.
> That the cool re-enters,
> That the heat does not re-enter [the house].
> One does not live in a house [full] of heat [anger, problems]
> (Nasiet, 9 February 1990).

Some of the *saara* porridge was ladled onto the shrine, including the wooden figure, and kola nuts were brought out and shared among the adults present, with three white kola nuts left on the shrine as an offering. Then the fun began for the children as the senior wife of the deceased chief ladled out small portions of porridge to them, most of whom were from the deceased's immediate and extended family. A calabash was circulated among the adults to collect small donations of money. When most of the children had consumed their porridge, the rest was poured into a large metal basin and a jostling 'free-for-all' among the children took place. A similarly good-natured melée took place when the calabash full of donations was upended and the children scrambled for the money. Adults and children alike enjoyed this sharing of the wealth that seems part and parcel of the goodwill that *saara* ceremonies engender.

Wood figure carvings function as integral components of Moba shrine configurations. As objects variously connected with personal guardians, family ancestors, village founders, and "the eye of the fish" or the ability to see into two worlds, Moba wooden figures play a critical role in forging strong connections for the living with God and the ancestral spirits. Though a precise determination of type and function is impossible in the absence of collection data once the figure carving is removed from its cultural setting, one can say with certainty that Moba figure carvings embody notions of power and the ability to make things happen, particularly in the contexts of divination and shrine offerings.

Christine Mullen Kreamer

1 Other sources note different—but clearly related—spellings for these figures: *cicilg* or *cicilig*, s.; pl. *cicili*. (Zwernemann 1998); *cicilk*, s.; *cicili*, pl. (de Surgy 1983, 1986); *kikirriga*, s.; *kikirri*, pl. (Frobenius 1913:430).

2 While the general formula—ritual invocations, libations, and, at times, sacrificial offerings—are followed and conducted by a man of the household, the type and intention of the offerings varies depending on the shrine that is the focal point of the offerings.

3 This term may be derived from the Arabic, *sadaqa* (in English characters), as it is found elsewhere in West Africa, for example among the Temne of Sierra Leone (Frederick Lamp, personal communication, 2003).

Spaces of Inclusion and Exclusion: an Ibibio/Annang Mask

Mask
Ibibio/Annang, Akwa Ibom State, Nigeria
Ekpo Association
c. Early 20th century
Wood, black pigment, H. 31.2 cm
Gift of Alan Wurtzburger
BMA 1954.145.52

Ekpo, a person's eternal soul, either transmigrates to the underworld at death to await reincarnation (*obio ekpo*) or becomes an evil ghost, as John Messenger (1973:119–120) was told among the Annang in the early 1950s. Ghosts, *ekpo onyon* (soul above), are those souls of the dead that cannot enter the underworld but are doomed to travel about the earth for all time, homeless and alone. This destiny depends on the person's earthly activities and judgment by the community and the spirit world. For example, if a person was found guilty of a serious crime against the community, he would have been killed and his body thrown into the "bad bush" where ghosts were believed to reside. Or if a person developed a terrible disfigurement, such as leprosy, smallpox, or gangosa, this would be considered to be divine retribution, in which case, at death, likewise, the body would be thrown into the bad bush. Ghosts are therefore named according to the evil acts they committed before death. If a person poisoned another, his wandering soul is called *ifot* (poison) *ekpo*, whilst *mfumfum ekpo* is the ghost of one who has committed suicide or murder. A thief becomes an *ino ekpo* ghost whilst an *ntuntan ekpo* represents one who was poor, homeless, and without close relatives in his lifetime (another indication of supernatural punishment for some grave misdemeanor).

The Ekpo society is a crucial instrument in the hands of the village chiefs. "It serves as an enforcement arm of the village government ... (and) ... provides an outlet for youths and men to channel their energies into activities which are beneficial to the community" (Akpan 1994:49). The enforcement of rules and regulations affecting every aspect of day-to-day life is given powerful spiritual sanctity through the appearance of the ancestors. Every village has an Ekpo lodge, *ejo ekpo*. Everything concerning the society laws, ceremonies, and masks is kept there. Every community also had a section of the sacred forest, where the *ekpo* spirits were said to roam.

The principal event in which the ekpo appear usually lasts three weeks, and is held at the end of the harvest season. Each area performs the rituals of the season in different ways. Among the central Annang, following the preparation of the sacred grove, the masqueraders accompany the villagers singing and parading throughout the village. This is followed by a period when members continually meet to drink and sing at night in the forest grove. Each village also has a number of open areas, *anwa*, focal points in the compounds of the main families. During the main season Ekpo masqueraders visit these by day to pay their respects and perform. In the past, all women, children, and non-initiates have been excluded from these rituals.

Ekpo/Ekpe Masked Dancer with Pathological Mask. Anang Ibibio, in Uzuakoli village of the Isu/Item Igbo, Nigeria. Photo: G. I. Jones. Courtesy of Cambridge University Museum of Archaeology and Anthropology

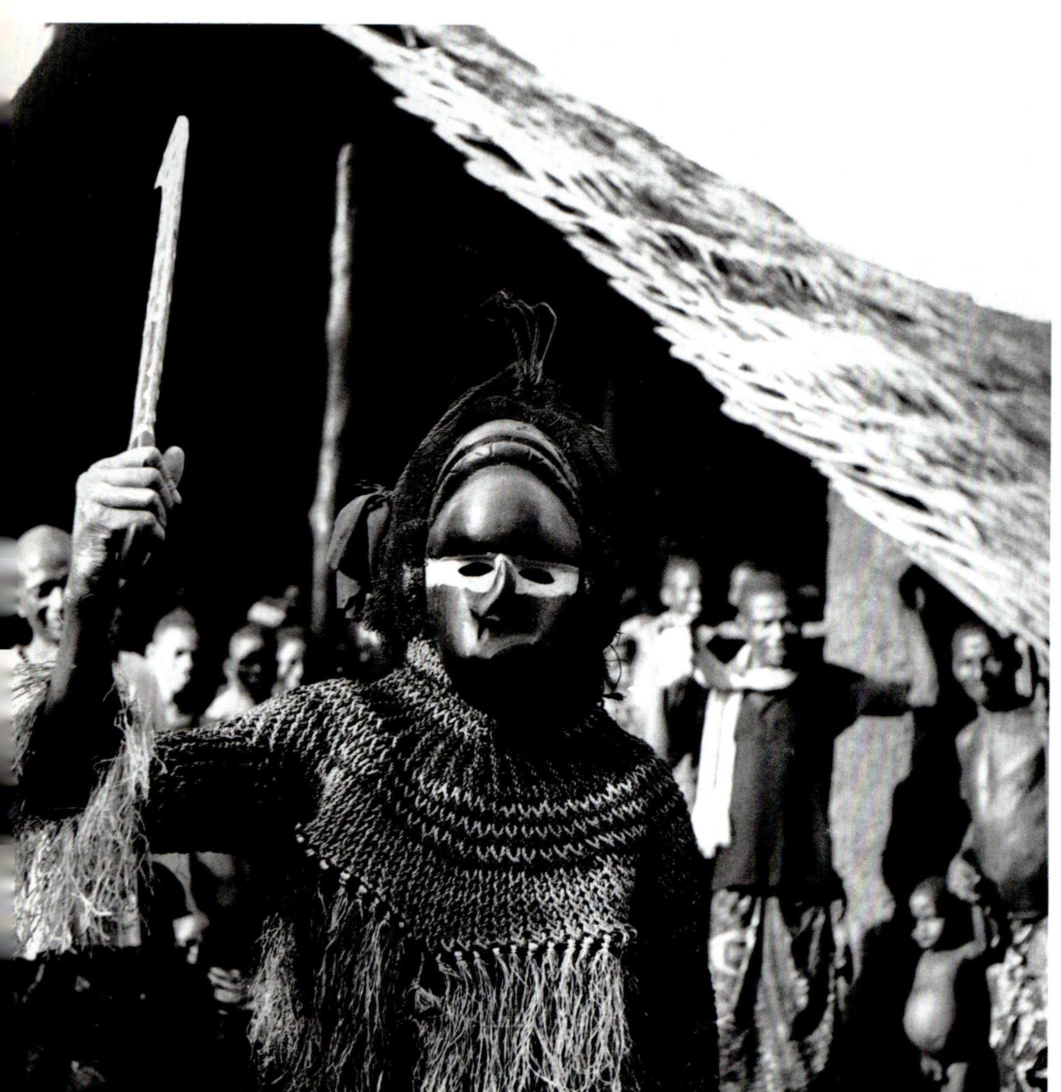

On the first and last days of the harvest season a public performance takes place at the most important market place, when all women and non-initiates are allowed to watch. First, the drums are set up on one side of the open area. Then all the old members of the society, dressed in their best clothes and carrying palm fronds and ceremonial knives, but not dressed in masquerade costume, dance in front of the drums and walk round the market square. In some Annang villages masqueraders representing *mfon ekpo* (beautiful souls) will appear at the market place on this occasion. Messenger (1973:122) was told that good and bad ghosts never intermingle because souls and ghosts from *obio ekpo* roam the earth at different times and do not meet each other.

Once the *idiok ekpo* (evil souls) have arrived, the family ritual leader draws a circle in the sand, and each time a new masquerader comes near the spot he is lured into the circle before performing—this is to invoke the spirits in the underworld to witness and guide the performances. The leader sings:

Akpan akanawan,
atime ikwa ibom ku ntuai nte eyen atuai eka.
Eyen ama atuari eka, udut, itieke aba

The first son of an old woman who uses an
ancient knife,

don't pull at me like a child pulls at its mother.
When a child does this the mother has no
strength again.

In other words the masqueraders should not get out of control.

The idiok ekpo (evil ghosts) masqueraders queue up to perform, one after the other, in front of the musical instruments, before joining their fellow members. Eventually the entire group appears, buzzing around the arena like angry wasps, lunging unpredictably into the crowds, and occasionally fighting each other, jumping, running, swirling with vivacious energy. It is recognised that once a *mbop* (mask) is put on, the soul of the ancestor possesses the soul of the wearer, so the masquerader can now commit any type of havoc and nobody will question his action. Any wild Ekpo masquerader who becomes violently possessed can be tamed by the touching of the mask with an egg or fowl, with some traditional invocations and prayers.

The final performance of the Ekpo season is called *ekpo ndok*, "ancestors knock on wood." During the final week, masqueraders venture out daily, so women have to keep food and water ready for this period and remain indoors on pain of death. Ekpo would mute their bells and silently steal up on non-initiates, on occasions even breaking into their houses and attacking them. On the final day they go to the market and upset stalls, spill oil and garri on the ground, and they stand on the paths leading to the market and demand gifts. After the completion of Ekpo rituals, women and children sweep out their houses, consume any uneaten food, and attach leaves, *afai,* to their doors to indicate that the ekpo have left their houses. They will then lock their doors. At a given signal in the middle of the night, women and children beat on the doors, shouting *ekpo ka, ekpo ka* ("Ancestors go away"). Once this has been done the following day life returns to normal in the full knowledge that the ancestors have been duly recognised and have now returned, satisfied, to the underworld.

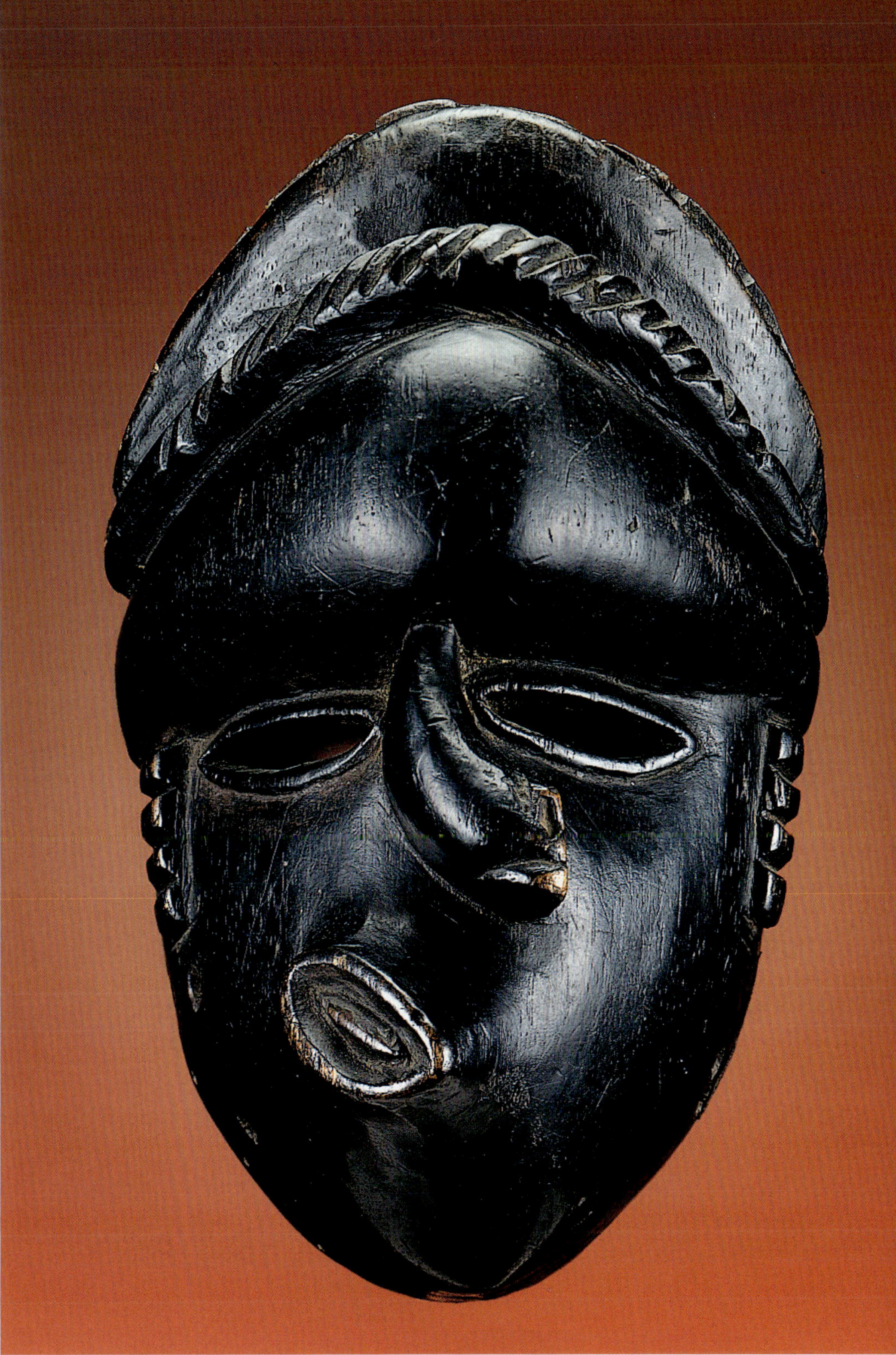

The styles of Ekpo masquerade costumes and performances vary greatly from village to village. However, throughout the region the overall colour for the idiok ekpo (evil souls) masks and costumes is black, to represent the fact that ghosts come out at nighttime, as opposed to the light-coloured costumes worn by the beautiful spirits, mfon ekpo, who move around during the day.

"The masks must be frightening in order to invoke the threat of force and authority necessary for the masked characters to maintain order" (Akpan 94.53). In Ukana Akpan, ekpo has a red face with a real skull on top, whilst others have white painted teeth and eyes. In the Ibesikpo area, the really dangerous mask is called *umiana ekpo*—bloodthirsty—and the face and costume are both red. Red is often used to accentuate mouths and tongues, and to depict sores. Certain masks depict animal or bird forms, including the cow, goat, and owl, and represent *ukpong ikot*, the aspect of human nature, considered a soul, that is emotional and instinctive, as opposed to *ukpong*, human nature that is cultured and restrained. Others still are an amalgam of human and animal characteristics. Some masks consist of a central face surrounded by numerous smaller faces or surmounted by carvings of skulls or human heads. Some human face masks depict hideous diseases such as yaws, gangosa (a severe vitamin deficiency which destroys the membranes of the nose), leprosy, or smallpox, reminders of the diseases sent as punishment to particularly evil transgressors before their transition to ghosthood. Other masks, such as the one in this collection, are carved to represent ugliness, either through distorted, deformed or exaggerated features.

Jill Salmons

46

You Are the Center, You Are the Village: a Pende Rooftop Figure (*Kishikishi*)

The Kishikishi rooftop sculptures of the Eastern Kasai Pende are the single most important decorative element found on a *kibulu*, the ritual house of the great chiefs who, according to Pende testimony, are the source of fertility and life, and the principal mediators between the ancestors and the people (Biebuyck 1985:222–223; de Sousberghe 1955:77; Strother 1993:158).

The kibulu is a two-room square structure with a narrow entrance way; a center pole (*muhandji*) supports a domed or pyramid-shaped thatched roof. The larger room is the living quarters of the *mwatha mwadi*, the chief's first wife who supervises all tasks assigned to women, among which is the cultivation of crops. In this room the chief's bed is kept along with the special mat on which he sits when passing judgment, a few selected official insignia, and the tribute collected from lesser chiefs. In addition to the chief and the mwatha mwadi, only their children, and a few privileged ministers may enter this area. A small closed doorway leads from the mwatha mwadi's living space into the second room, the kifumu or treasury room, in which the chief's coffin; special protective medicines; the three chief's insignia masks (Kipoko, Pumbu, and Panya Ngombe), and other ritual objects are stored. Access to the kifumu is restricted to the *pungo*, the chief's first minister; not even the chief may enter this room. A palisade (*tsungu*) creates a courtyard in the front of the kibulu. This enclosed area provides a private place in which the chief may meet with his ministers and important visitors. A kibulu also has a hidden secret door which is used when the chief's body is removed after his death (Biebuyck 1985:222, 234–235, 245; de Sousberghe 1953:10–11; 1955:75; Strother 1993:158–165).

After a chief has been formally instituted, he spends the night on the ground where his kibulu is to be erected. Once construction begins, it must be completed in one day. All of the chief's subjects are expected to contribute either their labor or building materials. The first step is the installation of the center post (muhandji) that supports the roof. This important initial work is done before daybreak by the chief and his ministers. When the hole for the post has been dug, the first minister places protective medicine in it, together with seeds and grains cultivated by the Pende, as well as other ritual foods and objects (Biebuyck 1985:246; de Sousberghe 1955:78, 80–81; Strother 1993:158).

During the construction of his kibulu in 1988, Chief Nzambi addressed the ritual center pole, and through it the ancestors, with the following prayer:

> You are the center pole of the house, you are the village with its people, fields, and forest. We have given you all the seeds for cultivation so that you may grip the earth as the seeds [roots] grip the earth over there. All seeds grow, may you grow [as] the seeds grow, so that the women may give birth, so that the children may give birth, so that there may be a lot of palm wine, so that the hunters may kill [their prey] with their guns (Strother 1993:161).

The construction of a kibulu is accompanied by the playing of the musical instruments that had been stored in the former chief's ritual house, and, in the late afternoon and evening as the work nears completion, by the performance of masquerades. It is at

Rooftop Figure (*Kishikishi*)
Pende (Eastern), Congo (Kinshasa)
c. Mid–late 20th century
Artist: Kaseya Tambwe Makumbi of Kandolo-Mututwa
Wood, red, black, and white pigment, H. 115.5 cm
Gift of Robert Elkin, Bethesda, Maryland
BMA 1998.371 (purchased from Sitta Sillah on September 21, 1979)

this time that the Panya Ngombe mask, one of the three chief's ritual masks stored in the kifumu, makes its only appearance. When the kibulu is finished, the upright structures of the house are blessed with the blood of sacrificed animals, and late that night the treasury from the former chief's kibulu is taken to the newly built treasury room. After this ritual, the old kibulu is abandoned, and left to deteriorate (de Sousberghe 1955:78, 80–81; Strother 1993:158, 161).

All Eastern Pende ritual houses, whether they belong to a great chief (one who owns his land) or to one of lesser rank, are decorated with carved and painted lintels and doorposts framing the entrance, carved masks on the palisade, and, most prominent of all, a rooftop sculpture which rests on the ritual center pole. Kibulu decoration is governed by a strict hierarchy, and only a great chief is entitled to carve a Panya Ngombe mask on the lintel, and decorate the roof with a sculpture depicting a human female figure (as opposed to depictions of animals and birds). The carvings indicate the chief's supremacy and power; the doorway sculptures act as the chief's personal spiritual guardians, while the rooftop sculpture offers protection to the entire village (Biebuyck 1985: 245–247; Cornet 1978:134; de Sousberghe 1955:77, 79–80; 1958:122–125; Strother 1993:170–171, 176).

Earlier figural rooftop sculptures found on the kibulu of great chiefs depicted a standing female figure, thought to represent the chief's wife, holding a ritual axe in her left hand and a ceremonial cup in her right hand, or a female figure surrounded by several smaller figures (Biebuyck 1985:246–247; de Sousberghe 1955:77–78, 1958:63–64, 123, 126; Strother 1993:172). The Museum's sculpture is an example of a relatively new figural rooftop sculpture, known as Kishikishi, that became popular among the Eastern Kasai Pende toward the middle of the twentieth century. Like the earlier figures, the female figure holds a ceremonial cup in her right hand (the BMA's figure is missing part of its right arm), but emphasizes her maternity with a child on her left hip. The creation of this rooftop mother and child figure is credited to Kaseya Tambwe from the village of Kandolo-Mututwa (de Sousberghe 1955:78–79;1958:125–126; Strother 1993:172;1998:134–135).

L. M. B.

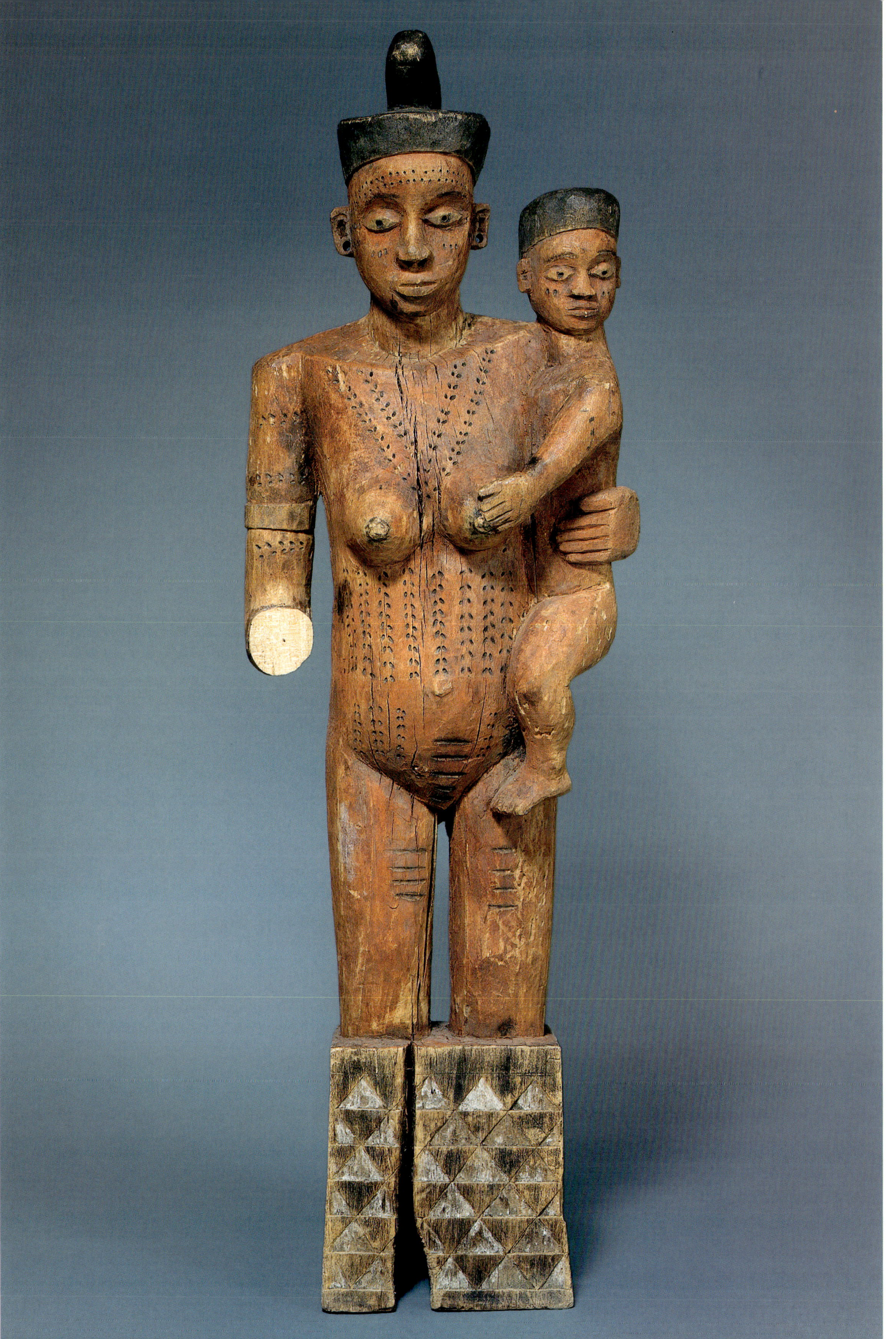

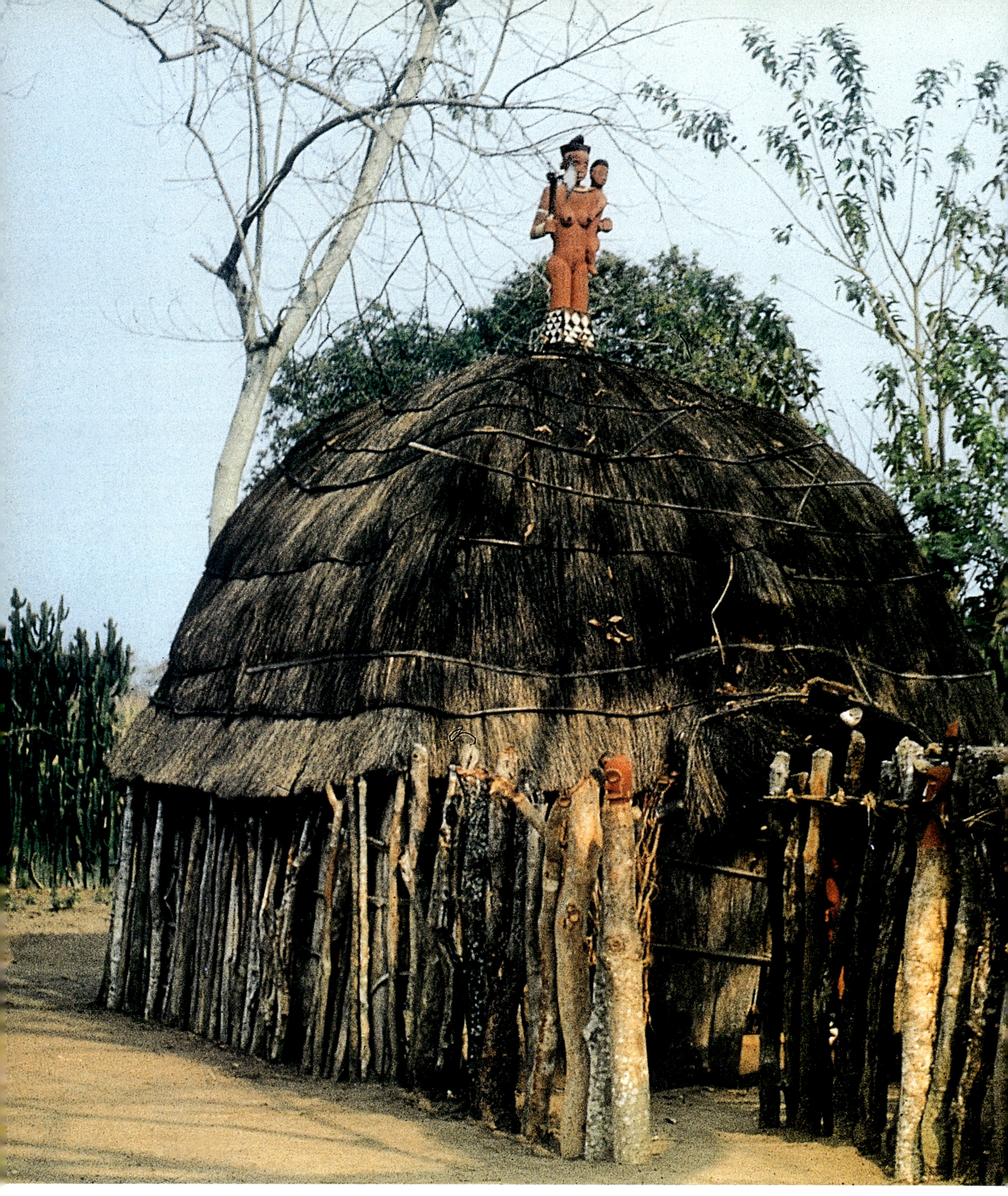

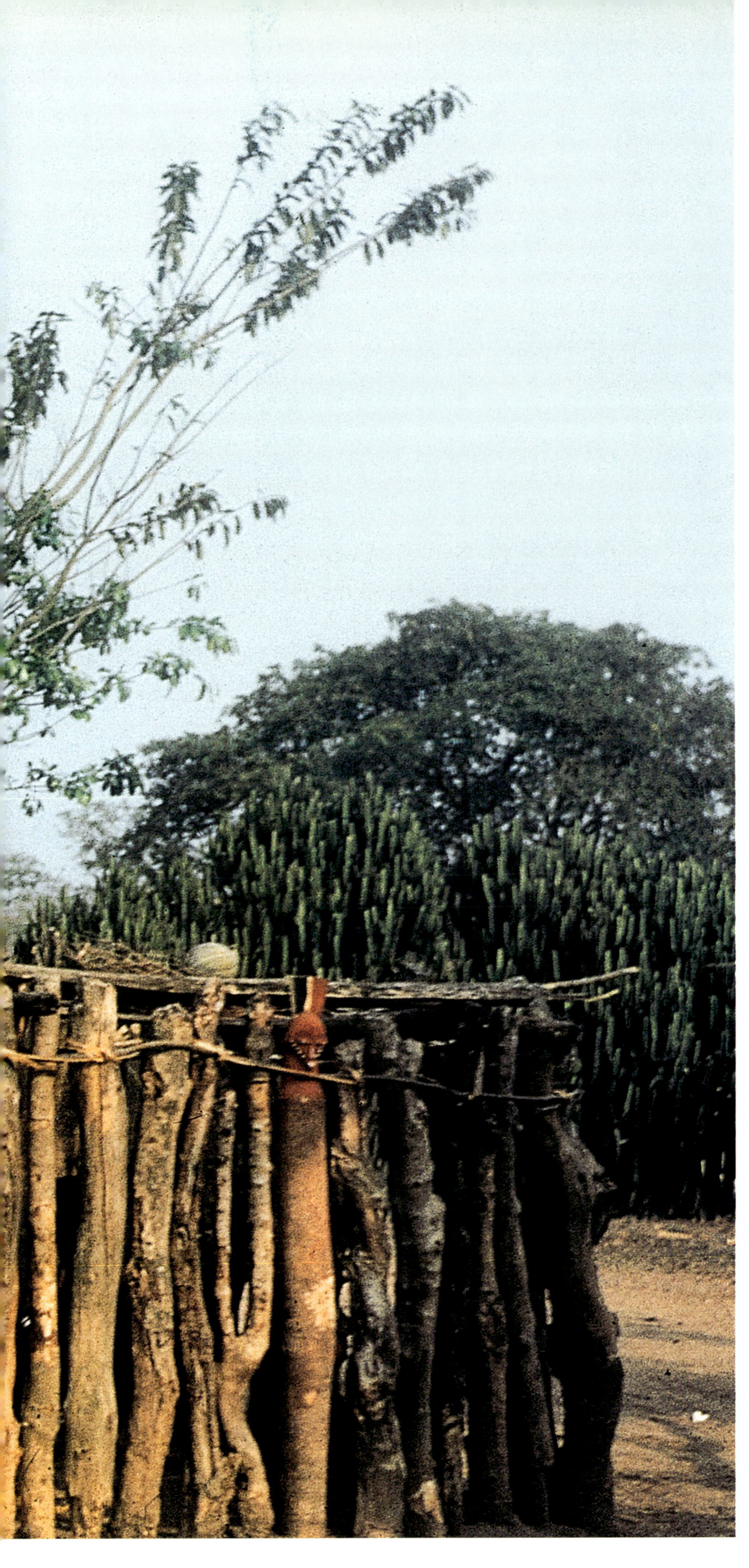

The Kibulu of Pende Chief Kombo-Kiboto. Pende, Congo (Kinshasa)
Photo: Léon de Sousberghe, 1955. Courtesy of the Eliot Elisofon Photographic Archive, National Museum of African Art, Smithsonian Institution

47

It Is the East That Has Power: Sapi Stone and Wood Figures

Male Figure Mounted on an Elephant
Sapi, Sierra Leone
Before 1550
Steatite, H. 10.3 cm
Gift of Alan Wurtzburger
BMA 1954.145.15

Along the coast of Sierra Leone an immense number of small, carved stone figures have been found by local farmers and miners, mainly among the Mende and southern Bullom people. Most have been found singly, beneath the soil or in river beds. One early European visitor was told that the figures were found often in clusters of up to fifty buried in tumuli (Rütimeyer 1901:197). The Mende, whose ancestors migrated into the area from the Northeast, today believe that the figures in stone represent the previous landowners, and that the figures were already extant when they originally arrived (Parsons 1964:XIII). Those who preceded them were a people known as the Sapi in the sixteenth century, whose descendants in this area today are the Bullom, Gola, and Temne.

Within the corpus of stone figures from the coastal area of Sierra Leone there are a fair number of representations of an animal that seems to be the elephant. At least ten of these are mounted by a male human figure. The BMA figure is a rider mounted upon an elephant, as indicated by the creases of skin and the small trunk. There is no record of elephants ever having been used to carry riders in West Africa, but this is most certainly a metaphorical rather than a literal juxtaposition, supported by data from the present-day Temne, just to the north. Hieratic or socially supporting relationships are often indicated through the use of vertical superstructure in sculpture. The elephant is a royal metaphor suggesting the king's strength based upon the support of a broad constituency. The elephant's tail and tusk are emblems of chieftaincy, and slaying an elephant was a prerequisite for the founding of a settlement, perhaps as a metaphor for the displacement of prior power. The transformation from human to elephant represents the movement from life to death. In an oral narrative the elephant is rewarded by God with its great size because it had carried the chief (of the animals) on its back. The chief's hammock, in which he is carried in procession, has been associated with the elephant. And the killing of an elephant has always required tribute to the chief. It seems reasonable to assume, from its broad base today, that the association between chief and elephant is one of long standing.

Many figures are holding a bowl in two hands. Many also depict smaller single or multiple figures in front of the main character. Female figures are found, but much less frequently than the male. The BMA standing female figure is possibly unique in that the bowl seems to be resting upon the head of a truncated, smaller human figure. The carrying of a vessel on the head of a subordinate, of course, is commonly seen today, as it must have been many hundreds of years ago. Damage to the face of the main female figure was likely incurred by a hoe digging into the soil where it would have been found.

These stone figures from Sierra Leone were probably all made before the mid-sixteenth century, but were not clearly documented in ritual use by contemporary European writers (although some vague references exist). We cannot say with any certainty who the figures represent, who made them, how they were used, or when such carving began and ended. But an interesting account by André Thevet in 1575 on the destruction of stone figures by the "barbarians" was interpreted by Paul Hair (1969:1032), as a possible reference to the type of figure considered here, which may appear to some observers as "gargoylesque" or frog-like:

> In this part of the South there is a rock where was found, in my time, the likeness of a great toad or frog, in the [medium] of stone, which was split and broken by the barbarians of the country, as big as the head of a man, so well carved that everyone judged it to be truly lifelike: and around it are a good number of small pointed shells [my translation].

I have previously given evidence from historical and linguistic sources that the Temne were in the vicinity at sometime in the past (Lamp 1983 & 1991), although it is impossible to say whether they had a hand in the carving or use of these figures. But current ritual use of stones and carved stone figures in ancestral shrines among the Temne and the Kissi (close linguistic relatives of the Bullom on the Sierra Leone/Guinea border), suggests a possible identity and ritual use of the ancient

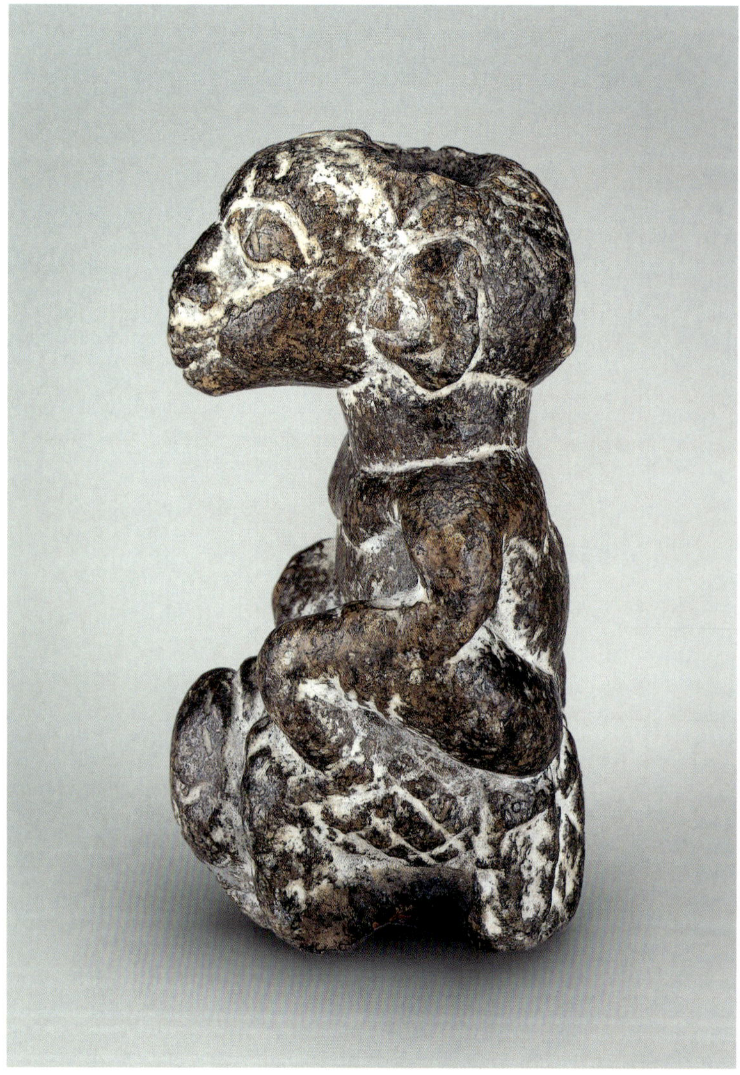

Female Figure
Sapi, Sierra Leone
Before 1550
Steatite, H. 22 cm
Gift of Phyllis K. and A. Harvey Schreter, Baltimore
BMA 1999.486

Male Figure
Sierra Leone, Sefadu District, Yafe Sewafe village
Testing by accelerator mass spectrometry: calibrated age of 1258–1379 A.D. (at a 68% confidence interval) or 1190–1394 A.D. (at 95%)
Wood, H. 19.4 cm
Gift of Elliott and Marcia Harris, Pikesville, Maryland
BMA 1991.85 (purchased from Jeremiah Cole, Freetown, 1985; ex Father Victor Mosele, Makeni, Sierra Leone; excavated by previous owner in mining operation near the village of Yafe Sewafe, vicinity of Sefadu, Eastern Province, Sierra Leone)

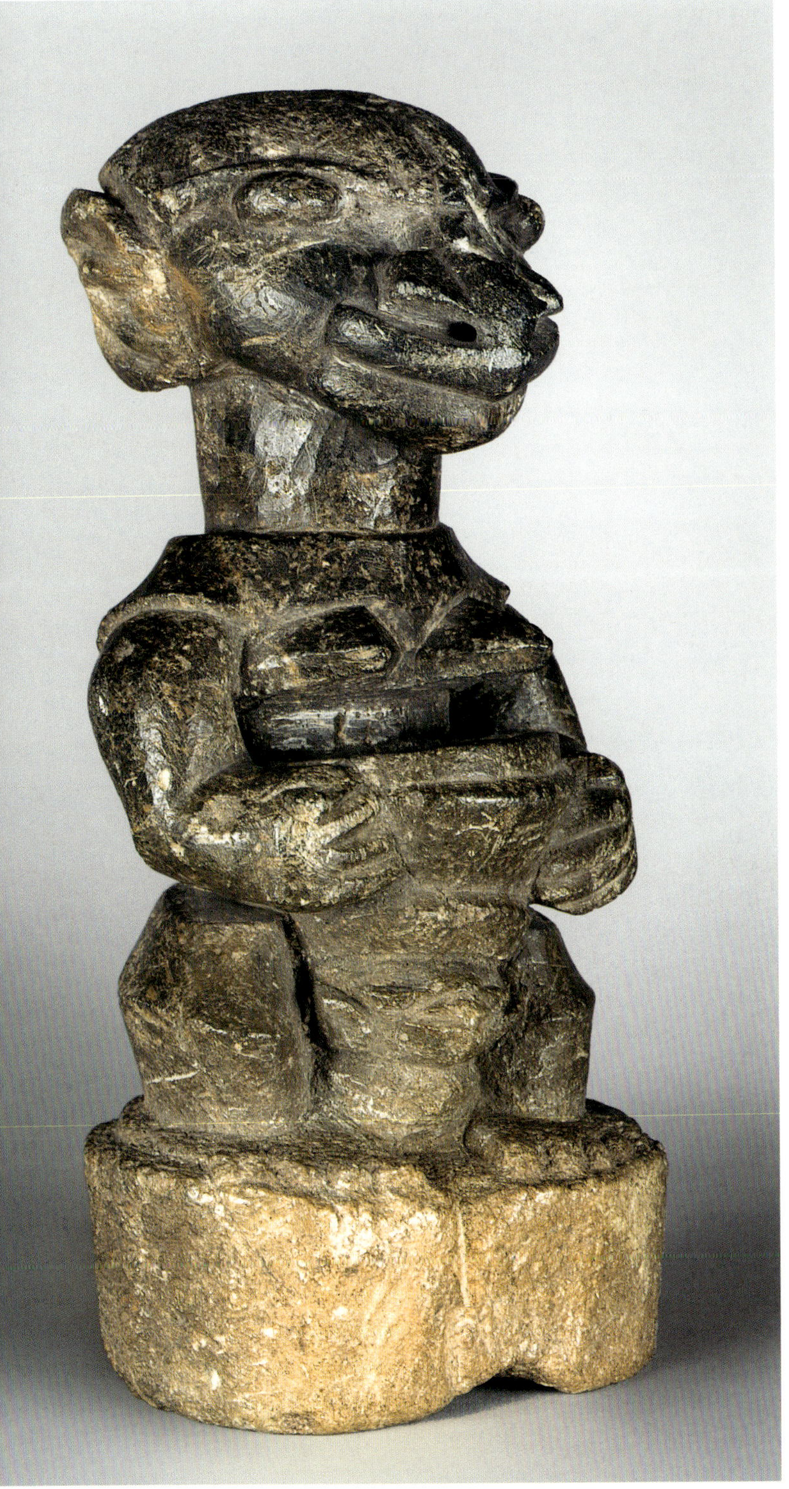

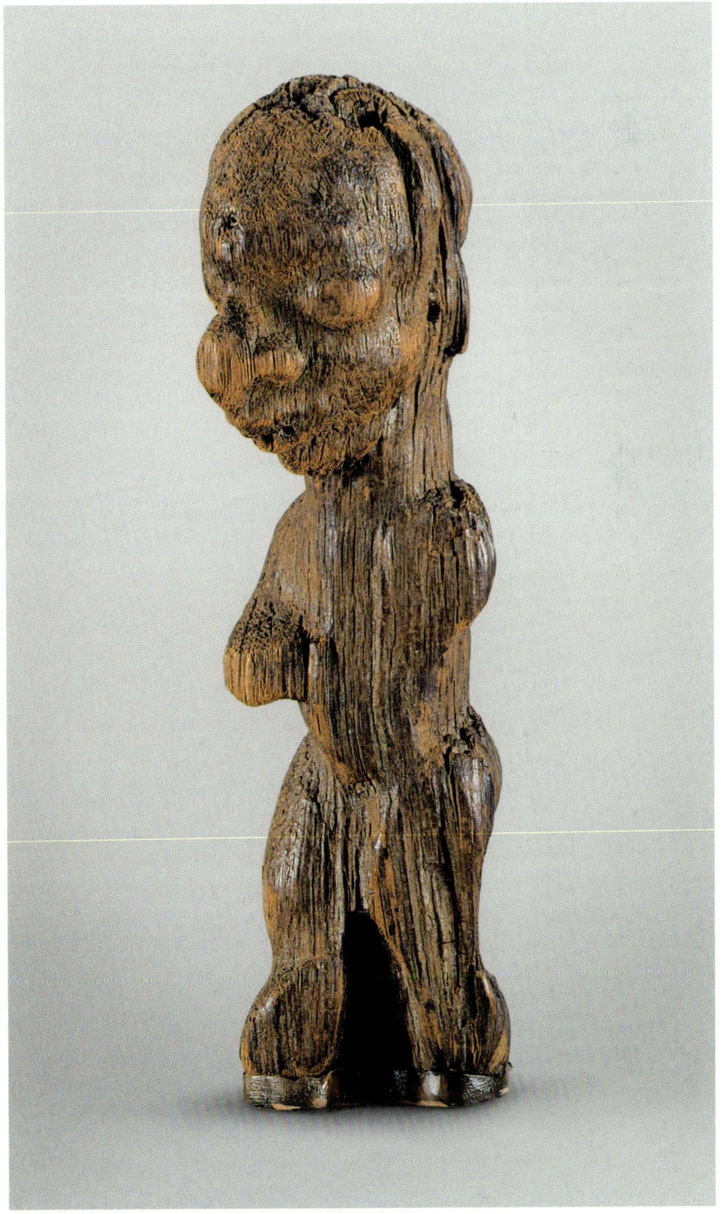

stone figures. These contemporary stones represent important deceased persons, such as chiefs and kings. Historical sources from the sixteenth and seventeenth centuries suggest a speculative continuity. Valentim Fernandes (1951:75) in 1506, referring probably to the Temne, said that they "love to make idols of wood and stone," as "a memorial of all those who have died," specifying wood figures for commoners and slaves, suggesting the deduction that the figures commemorating "honorable men" may have been carved of stone. In 1619 the French general Beaulieu (Hair 1974:43–44), visiting the Temne, wrote of "little figurines grotesquely shaped ... and also little mounds of black soil shaped like sugar loaves (which I have heard are the nests of ants)." And in 1664, André de Faro (1945:89) described a similar shrine, but containing only uncarved stones, among the Temne, exactly as they are today.

House of Stones (*boro ma-sar*). Temne, Port Loko, Sierra Leone
Photo: Frederick John Lamp, 1979

Chief carried in his hammock, a symbolic "elephant," heralded by an olifant blower. Mende, Sierra Leone. Photo: Frederick John Lamp, 1979

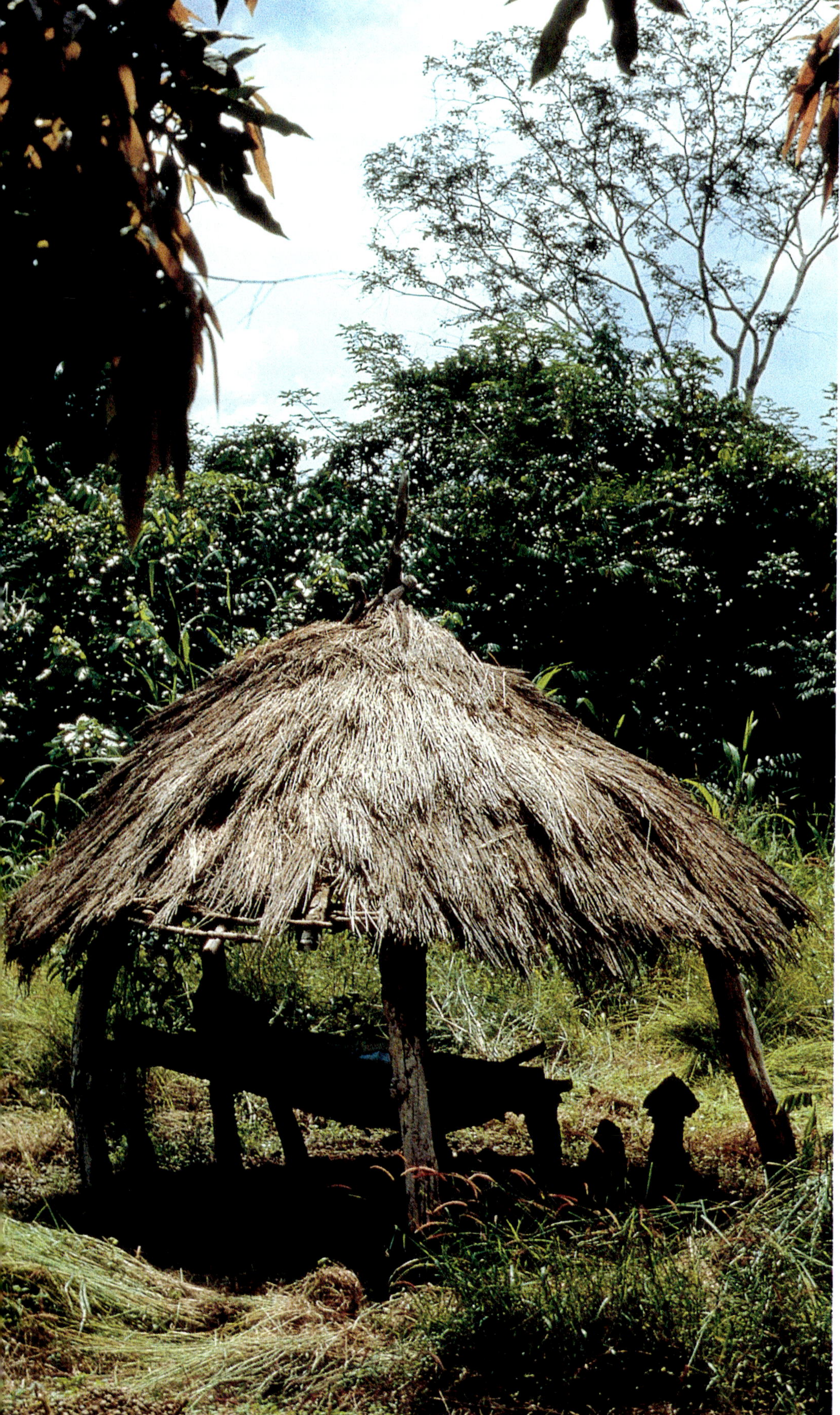

Along the road leading east from many Temne towns may be found a miniature pavilion. Within it is a platform covered with a mat, on top of which small stones are placed. Beside the platform on the ground are small, mushroom-shaped anthills. The shrine is called the *boro ma-sar*, the "house of stones."

Several days after the burial of a politically important person, such as a chief, a stone is selected from his or her gravesite by a relative and is placed in the *boro ma-sar* as a remembrance. It may be any stone but usually is about the size of a person's fist (as described by de Faro) or larger for a paramount chief. The official caretaker knows the identity of each stone. Over generations the identity of particular stones may be lost, and these eventually may be buried in a pit together in a ritual cleaning of the site.

Each year after harvest (February-March) a ceremony is conducted in which the people contribute a sacrifice of rice flour and a fowl or goat. The stones are washed, replaced on a new mat, and covered with new, clean cloths. Palm wine is poured on the ground, the animals are slaughtered, the meat is shared among the participants, and the rice flour and bones are scattered among the stones, very much like sacrifices described by Fernandes (1506), Beaulieu (1619), and de Faro (1664) (Lamp 1983 & 1991). As each stone is taken up in turn, beginning first with those of the most recently deceased, a prayer to each of the past chiefs invokes their intercession for the prosperity and health of the village. The ceremony takes place at sunrise.

The placement in the East is critical. East, the place of sunrise, is the direction from which the ancestors came, in Temne oral narrative. West is where the dead are buried, and ritually it is the West that is associated with death and destruction. The boro ma-sar is a place of ancestral regeneration.

Within the shrine, cardinal orientation is critical. The stones are located on the eastern side, laid

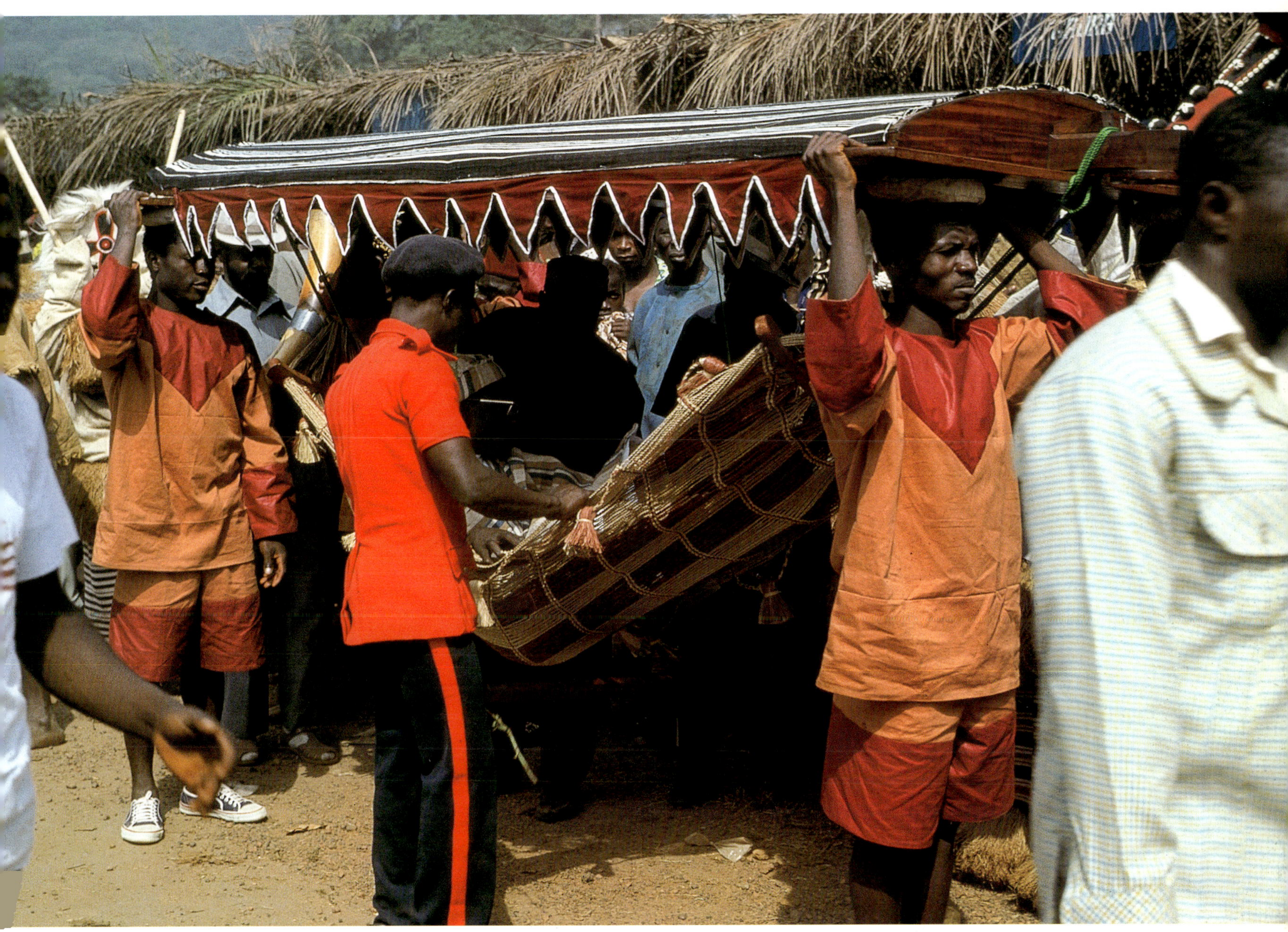

upon a folded mat and covered with a white cloth, as a person sleeping. While the stones refer to the regeneration of the powers of the dead and the bringing down of ancestral truth and guidance, the anthills refer to the aged, death, the entering of the earth by the deceased, and the medium through which the dead are approached. Like the corpse, the anthill is an empty shell from which life has departed. The anthill is placed in the West, opposite the stones.

Whether the ancient stones were used in this way, we will never know. But it is fairly clear from their iconography that they, too, were carved to commemorate important men and women, and perhaps were placed clustered in community shrines.

Frederick John Lamp

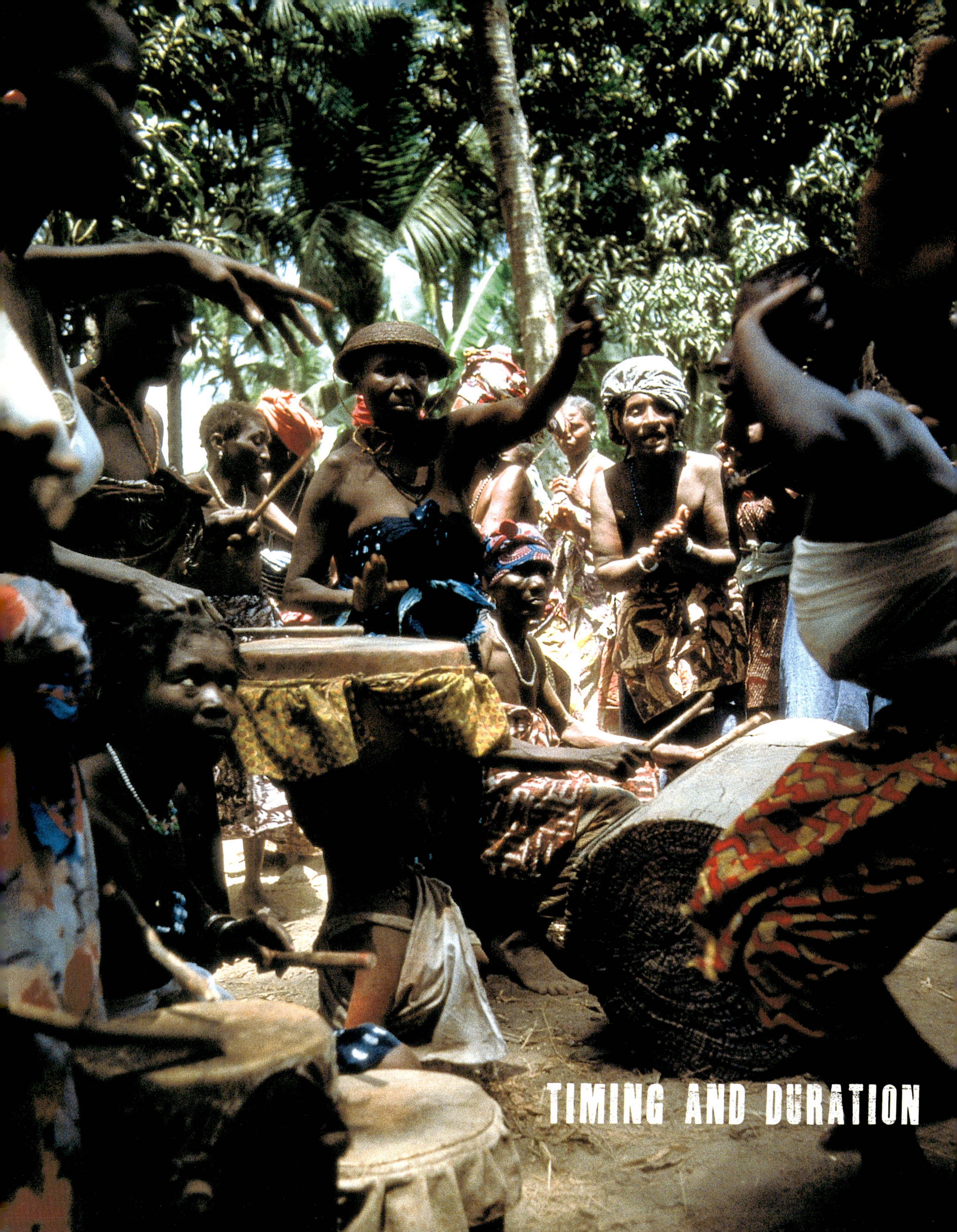

TIMING AND DURATION

Anyone who has ever acted in the theater understands the critical importance of timing to performance. In Africa, metric beats in the progression of events are often specific to artforms. Certain events must happen only at particular times of the year, month, or day (only at full moon or dusk, for example). Some shrine ritual might be composed of ongoing events that occur over a period of years. Some objects are meant to be seen in a split second and then never seen again. Others are posted publicly and permanently to be contemplated and continually reviewed.

Annual cycles, initiations, marriage, seasonal patterns, night and day, and the divisions of the day are the structure upon which performances are hung. Many African societies operate on an indigenous calendar geared to agricultural cycles and the moon or sun, and the use of the Islamic calendar and the Gregorian calendar is often interchangeable, offering national and religious holidays, New Year's Day, and commercial days. Months of the Temne of Sierra Leone are often named for their activities: "Let's marry" (*tanàntia*: November-December), "Play games" (*wolwol*: January-February), "New cultivation of the farms" (*bàfu*: March-April), or "Let's reap" (*taròkànè*: October-November). The playing of games, and such serious plays as masked dance, is most intense during wolwol, for example. The relative days of the week are expressed in terms of kinship: for example, "two days after tomorrow," *ò-wont ka ro-sòkòñ*, is literally "the brother of the far dawning." Times of the day reflects not only the position of the sun but also human activity, for example, *ràfoi*, the evening after dinner, is the "[time] of ease." The Temne think of cosmic time as a person in motion, turning from East to West (Lamp 1982).

Throughout this book, essays on individual performance contexts emphasize that notions of time, timing, and tempo are critical, as in discussions of the history and definition of the *Sogo bò* theater (p. 273) related by Arnoldi (1995:107). Timing is tied to the beginning and the end of the dry season, late afternoon, and the full moon, when "people temporarily suspended their commonly held feelings, beliefs, and attitudes toward the night as a locus of danger ... secrecy, antisocial behavior, and treachery."

The Baga D'mba headdress (p. 223) is danced only during the daytime, unlike most Baga masks which appear after dark. The stones (see pp. 194, 195) in the Temne shrine described in a previous section are handled in ancestral ritual only at the break of dawn, a time synonymous with the birth of mankind and, symbolically, the birth of individual infants. The principal dance of the Nòwo of the Temne (see the Mende, p. 175) and their neighbors is at dawn, perhaps referring to the fluttering of butterflies at this time of day.

Duration can vary widely. Male and female masks of the southern Bullom in Sierra Leone, called Rong, appear to the people only once a year, and very briefly, in a flash; those who are not vigilant miss seeing the masks. Certain masks of the Baga of Guinea representing the highest male spirit appeared only once in every fifteen years. Initiated men were invited to approach this formidable spiritual presence, but the rest of the community had to be content to glimpse the monumental image from afar, and only at brief intervals (Lamp 1996 *Art*:57–63). Yoruba Gelede maskers (p. 115), on the other hand, prolong their performances with a variety of masks for many hours through the day and night. This extended repetition may be fatiguing to the outsider accustomed to more varied movement within shorter time frames. I observed the dance of Buluñits women in Guinea celebrating an initiation of the Keke female association (p. 198). The dance went on continuously for several days, during which women became possessed through the constant vibrations of the music and rhythm beat out on caryatid drums. It seemed that any concept of time that I had brought with me now meant nothing.

Dance and drumming of the women's Keke initiation Buluñits, Guinea. Photo: Frederick John Lamp, 1987

The pace of an object in motion is critical. The Baga D'mba wafts slowly and elegantly around the plaza, sometimes pausing for five or ten minutes. In contrast, movement of the Yoruba Gelede dancers is swift and vigorous, replete with eye-dazzling step patterns and a dashing from one end of the arena to another.

Research on African masking, and even on the use of stationary shrines, might involve some of the following questions. Is this a fast or slow object? Would it appear during the daytime or at night, in the morning, in the afternoon, at dusk or at dawn? What measure of steps would it employ? Would the timing be consistent or would it be erratic and unpredictable? How often might it appear or how often might one have access to it? Would it be accessible on a continuing basis or would it appear for only an instant? Is this an object meant to be examined, or to be only fleetingly glimpsed. How is the timing of the performance situated within a system of time reckoning. How does it reveal a balance that the "society tries to maintain between 'mobility and fixity,' between 'the social and the individual' and between instances of particularity and concepts of 'the eternal,' even when such oppositions may superficially seem contradictory" (Williams 2000:182). To what extent is the timing determined by a text, a choreography, a tradition, or, alternatively, by serendipity, human intention, agency, assertion, and creative performance.

Essays in this section deal with various aspects of timing and duration. Till Förster discusses time considerations of Senufo funerary ritual in the use of the Pònyugu mask. In the case of Kuba textiles, significance is shown to be heightened according to particular ritual scheduling. Maasai ornaments are seen is critical to identifying human time segments. Laurel Birch de Aguilar shows how, in fleeting appearances, the masks of the Yao and Mekonde mark moments of passage. And, special stools of the Lobi are analyzed by Susan Elizabeth Gagliardi in terms of gendered sequences of three and four.

Detail of Lobi Figurative Stool (p. 216), with seated male and female figures corresponding to complementary sequences of three and four, respectively.

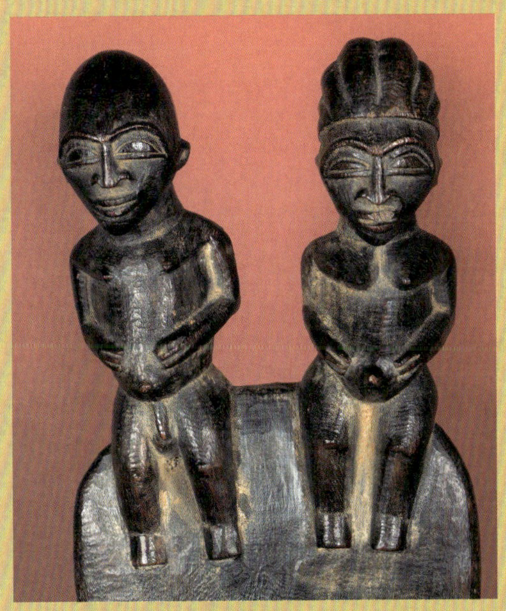

48

Alienating the Living from the Dead: a Senufo Mask (*Pònyugu*)

Mask (*Pònyugu*)
Senufo, Ivory Coast
c. Late 19th century
Wood, L. 99.7 cm
Purchased as the gift of Janet Wurtzburger
BMA 1966.17 (ex Helena Rubenstein; collected by F. H. Lem)

The Pòrò societies of the Senufo are organized in local initiation centers found in small clearings of the sacred groves at the edge of the village. Each initiation center has, among others, one main mask that, like the society itself, is simply referred to by the village public as *Pòri*, "The Pòrò." It appears at the time of burial ceremonies.

Outside the ritual context, the wooden headdress of the mask is called Pònyugu, "Head of Pòrò." This expression is used especially among the carvers who make the wooden headdress. Creating the Pòrò masks is among a carver's most important tasks. Since the masks are relatively large, the wood used has to be lightweight. Consequently, the masks are not very durable and frequently have to be replaced as early as after one initiation cycle of six years. Generally they are replaced after approximately twelve years, and in Senufo territory, there are very few masks more than thirty years old.

The iconography of the masks largely depends on the requirements of the patrons, that is the initiation center, wanting to replace an old mask. More often than not, they want the new mask to be similar to the previous one, so it is recognizable for the members of the society and maintains the local identity of the particular Pòrò society. That is why for the patrons, above all for the elders of the village societies, clearly differentiated iconographies can be distinguished. However, one of the constant characteristics is the composite form of the mask representing different animal species. It belongs to the zoomorphic helmet masks that are widespread in West Africa. The long horns are assumed to be those of the antelope or, if they are flat, of the buffalo, the long jaws are those of the crocodile or warthog, the ears belong to the hyena, while on the head the chameleon is depicted. All these animals play a role in the etiological tales of the Senufo where they have helped to create the beginning of the world. According to a few of the carvers, the eye area and the nose are thought to be human. Small mirrors may be set into the eyes. Depending on the region and the local initiation center, one or another element of the chimera may also be missing or replaced by something different.

In some initiation centers, the wooden body of the mask is dyed a deep black, while in others it is decorated in color, mainly in red and white. The blackening or the painting are regularly renewed by the initiates of the society.

Many ordinary members of the society and even some of the masked dancers themselves know it simply as a "wild creature." This is due not only to the extensive rules of secrecy surrounding the appearance of the mask, but also its costume, under which the wooden headdress is sometimes difficult to discern. The costume is not made by the carvers but, as a rule, by one or several members of the society themselves. It consists of a long, one-piece garment made of cotton painted in geometric patterns. In former times, nothing but vegetable dyes were used; nowadays, more and more industrially produced dyes are used as well. Around the neck of the wearer, several bundles of dyed raffia fibers are often tied, as well as furs and skins of various wild animals. The masks of the blacksmiths have a particularly large number of such furs. In addition, the wooden mask is crowned by one or several bundles of feathers, porcupine quills, and similar materials. An elder of the society initially makes a sacrifice or offers other ritual substances in order to impart power to the mask as well as to its wearer. Some of these ritual substances are packed into goat horns tied to the mask. In the BMA mask, they appear partly as a carved relief on the wooden body. For use in a funeral, if the mask belongs to the same initiation center as the deceased, bundles of the fresh leaves of a species of Dracaena (probably Dracaena arborea) are put on top of it, prior to the funeral.

The masked dancer carries a small iron bell. During the ritual, it is incessantly shaken and warns all the uninitiated of the approaching mask. In addition, he carries a cylindrical drum with a skin head at each end, about the length of a forearm. It is the most important accessory of the mask since, with the help of this drum, the masquerade ritual serves to separate the body from "the shadow," or "life force," of the deceased during burial ceremonies.

At the beginning of the ritual, the mask leaves the Pòrò society grove at the edge of the village together with a long line of the initiated members. While the initiated proceed only very slowly, the mask runs beside them and into the courtyards of the village. In most cases, it is accompanied by a young initiate who sometimes also takes the bell and shakes it to warn all the women and children of the presence of the mask. Pònyugu may be seen by only the members of the society and the closest relatives of the deceased.

On the first day of the festivities, the performance route leads to the shelter of the society in the village where the frail old men sit down if they are no longer able to continue to walk in the long line of the Pòrò members. Here the masquerader stops to beat an increasingly fast roll on the small cylindrical drum. As a rule, several masks from different initiation centers convene here. Later, they proceed to the farmstead of the deceased, where the corpse has been placed in its hut, wrapped in a cloth, and guarded by some of the close relatives who ward off the flies. In front of the door, masqueraders stand still and beat their drums.

One or two days later, the masqueraders again appear in the courtyard of the deceased where the corpse has already been carried outside and sewn into cloths. They place their drums directly on the torso of the cadaver and again beat their roll. The drum has to be placed on the corpse lengthwise and must be beaten on the side pointing towards the feet. This is said to ensure that the "shadow" does not leave the body of the deceased through the head and that it finds the right way to the village of the dead.

Some Pòrò masqueraders even climb up on the corpse where they move to the rhythms of other drums beaten by the young initiates of the society. Their macabre performance is less a dance step than a violent tossing to and fro of the body, interrupted by spasmodic backwards and forwards movements. It is spontaneously interpreted by many as an imitation of the sexual act—performed by a wild creature nobody knows how to categorize clearly. This incongruity is meant to jar the sensibilities of the relatives of the deceased, serving to detach the shapeless bundle containing the cadaver from their memories of a relative. It is a process of

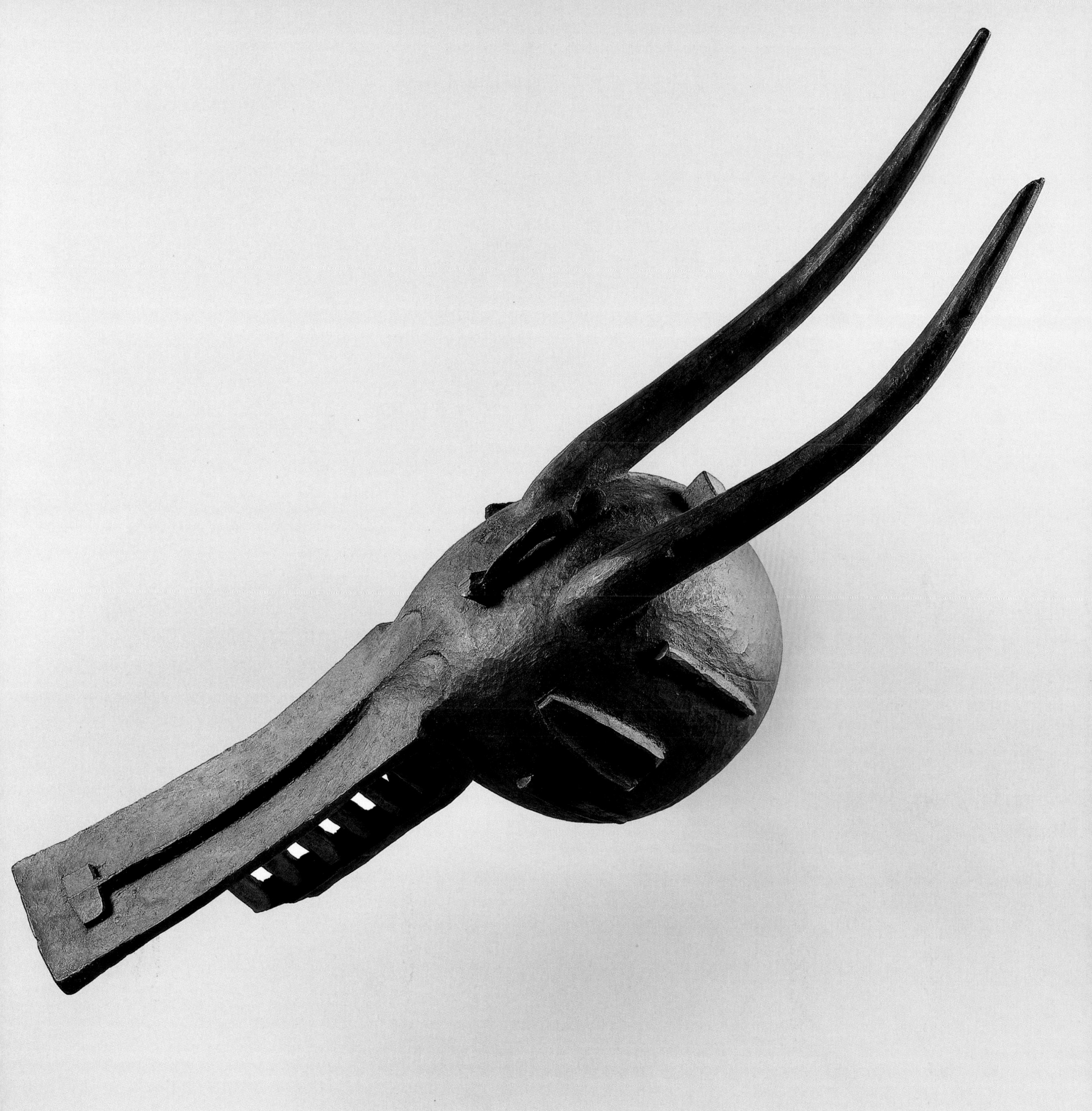

alienation, allowing them to part from the deceased through an act of disjunction.

Due to their central position in the burial ceremonies, the zoomorphic helmet masks are widespread throughout Senufoland. Only the villages and regions totally converted to Islam do not have such masks. In larger towns, the timing of the mask's appearance has changed. The strict rules of secrecy have loosened there, and frequently the masks appear at receptions where they demonstrate loyalty to national politicians. They bow deeply in front of the office bearers and receive donations of money, varying according to the generosity of the politician. These appearances are open to the public.

Till Förster

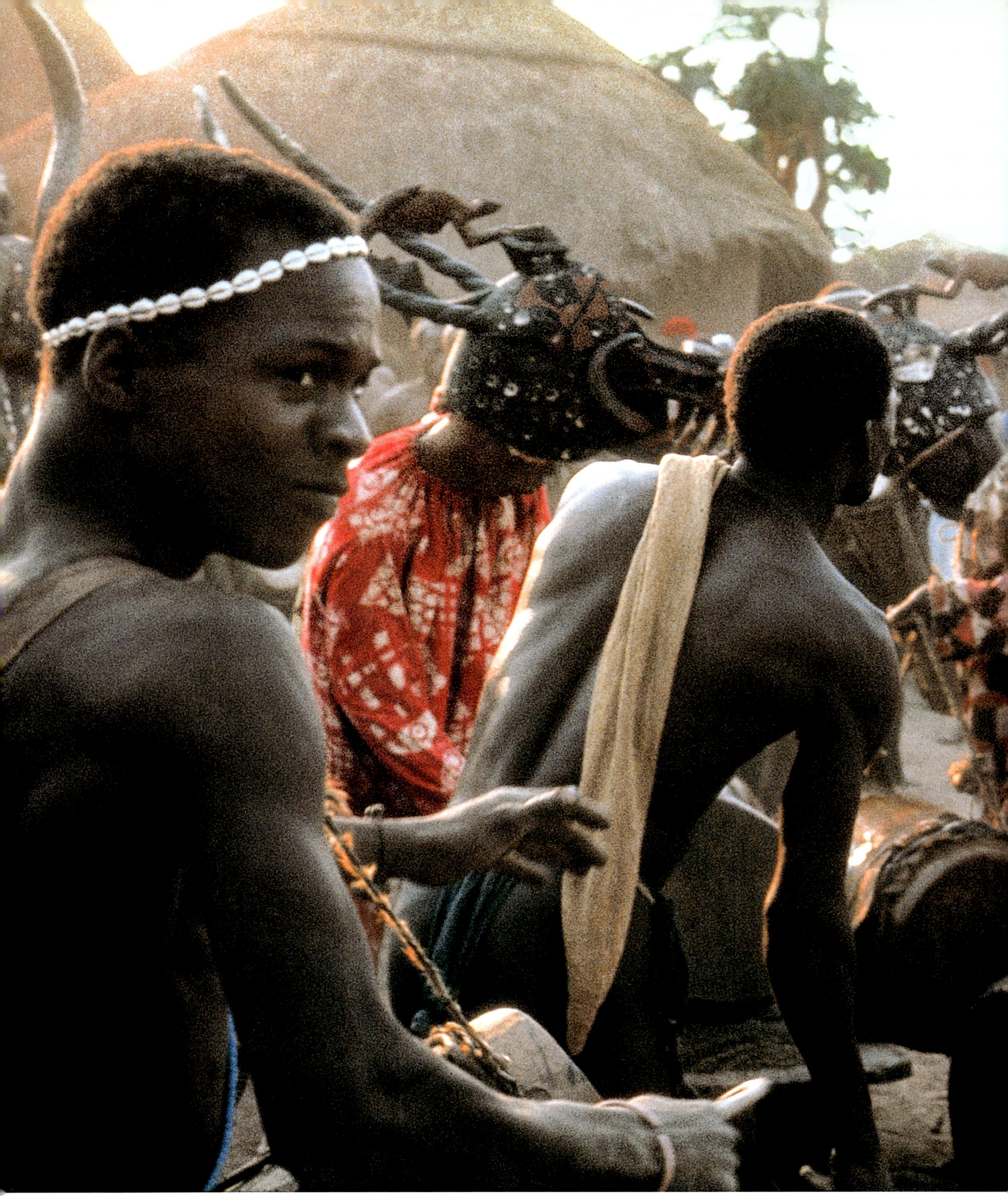

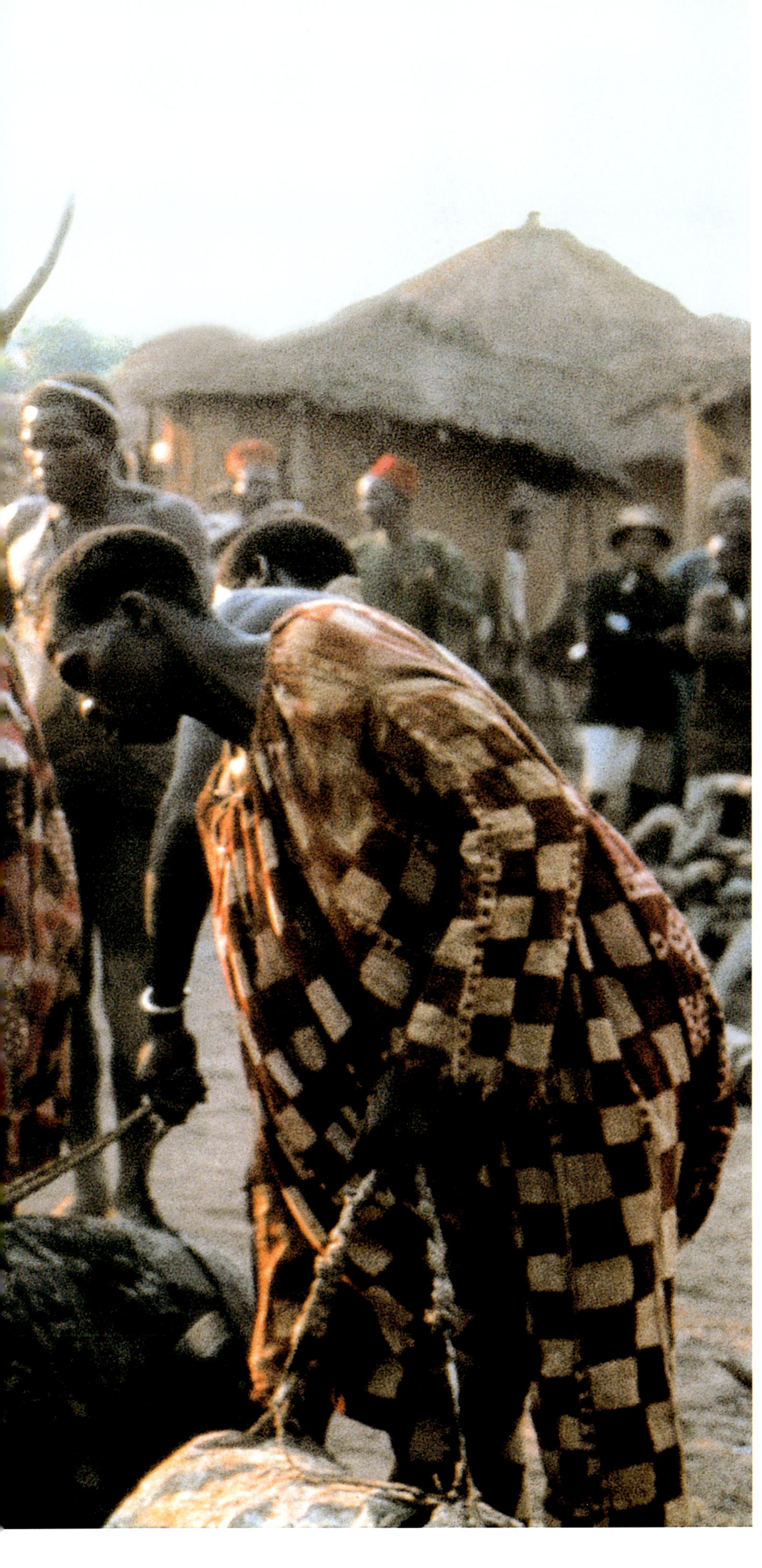

Two Pònyugu performers, each representing a distinct sacred grove association of Pòro, at a funeral. Senufo, Fodonon subgroup, Kufuru dialect, Ivory Coast. Photo: Anita Glaze, 1970

49 This Opportunity to Dance: Kuba Textiles

Raffia Pile Cloth
Kuba, Congo (Kinshasa)
c. Early–mid-20th century
Raffia, L. 54 cm
Gift of Phillip Lee Davis, Key West, Florida
BMA 2002.694

The Kuba are renowned for their woven raffia cloth which they dye and decorate with embroidery and appliqué, and, in particular, for their velvety pile work. Both textiles represent ancient art forms documented from the early seventeenth century. The Bushoong subgroup of the Kuba, centered at the capital, were so closely identified with their raffia textiles that another name for them was *bambal*, "people of the cloth" (Vansina 1978:191).

Among the Kuba, the weaving and decorating of cloth is strictly divided by gender. Young boys prepare the raffia fibers; men do the weaving on hand looms. Women do the needlework, embroidery, appliqué, and pile work using an iron needle. Both men and women soak and pound the woven cloth to make it supple. Dyeing is the work of women. Both men and women fashion garments from the prepared and embellished cloth (Adams 1978:24, 34–36; 1981: 232; Cornet 1982:184–185; Mack 1980:165).

Needlework is done from memory. Decorative patterns tend to be linear and geometric; creativity is encouraged. Patterns are never repeated endlessly, rather they change abruptly, thereby creating a sense of the unexpected. This design discontinuation is a deliberate aesthetic choice (Adams 1978:24; 1981:232; Mack 1980:164–165, 167, 169). Robert Farris Thompson (1974:10–13) has described the rhythmic thinking that may underlie designs such as we see in the Kuba pile cloth. He draws upon Hegel's interpretation of the German verb, *aufheben*, as "suspension and preservation," in which we find "an affirmative and indeed richer and more concrete determination." Although there is equal stress to each beat (or motif, in the case of textile), as in "swing," in jazz, it is made complex by an off-beat phrasing of "canceled beats or rhythmic elision."

Timing, in another sense, is important to the woven raffia skirt with its appliqué design, contrasting dark embroidery, and ruffled border (made by binding the cloth over a curled rattan stick). It is a ceremonial garment created and worn exclusively by the women of the royal household when participating in a royal celebration such as an *itul/ncec*. Such skirts are highly valued, and may not be bought. Women either inherit them, make their own, or receive one as a form of compensation (Adams 1978: 30–31; Cornet 1982:276; Schaedler 1987:393).

An itul (organized by a highranking man) or a ncec (organized by a royal woman) is one of the most prestigious and popular of Kuba festivals. Its high cost means that it is performed only rarely. In 1953 Jan Vansina witnessed a royal *ncec* organized by Kyéén, one of the king's daughters. The ncec was announced two weeks in advance by the king, and lasted seventeen days. During the first weeks the dances were held outdoors in a great square on Saturdays and Sundays. During the final week they were held every day, twice per day, mornings and evenings (Cornet 1980:28–29; 1982:272–273; Vansina 1964:122–125).

Kyéén, her only sister, the king's sisters, and other women in the royal line of succession, as well as most of the young men of the capital participated in the dances. The women wore ceremonial skirts, red in the morning and naturally-colored (white) in the evening. The dancers formed two concentric circles, men on the inside and women on the outside. The two groups moved in opposite directions, changing course every five minutes or so. Drums accompanied the dancers, who also sang songs, many of which praised the generosity of the king and of the organizer of the *ncec*, such as: "Today is the song of the Kweemy clan who has given us this opportunity to dance," and "Today we are very happy in our village" (Vansina 1964:123).

Most itul/ncec celebrations end with a dance-masquerade that represents the conflict between the king's sons and those who, in a matrilineal succession, are the king's heirs. The royal sons are represented by a fierce beast who is said to be ravaging the countryside, and the heirs by the royal wives and/or other women in the line of succession who hunt and slay the animal, thereby symbolizing the ultimate triumph of the matrilineal heirs over the royal sons (Vansina 1964:122–125).

This final event is generally performed over a two-day period: part one, a lament and catalogue of the ravages inflicted by the beast, on the evening of the first day, and part two, the capture and slaying of the beast, on the afternoon of the second day. In 1953 the latter performance took place on the last day after the morning dance. The populace gathered on one side of the square, and just before the beginning of the masquerade, the king and his entourage, dressed in their ceremonial regalia, entered and took their places. The dancers were the royal princesses and other women in the line of succession, who, on this occasion, wore embroidered ceremonial naturally-colored raffia skirts. Kyéén, her face painted with lines, and dressed in an elaborate costume with an eagle-feathered headdress performed the role of the beast—in this masquerade, an eagle. While the women were dancing in the center of the square, Kyéén zig-zagged from the sidelines and attempted to strike one of the king's sisters who tried to avoid her. After an hour of this, the beast emerged from the sidelines accompanied by four of the women in the line of succession each carrying a rifle. The beast tried once again to strike the dancing women, and after several such attempts, one of the armed women killed it. Another woman then took a piece of cloth (part of the beast's garment meant to represent its entrails) and presented it to the king, whereupon the dance masquerade came to an abrupt end (Vansina 1964:122–125).

L. M. B.

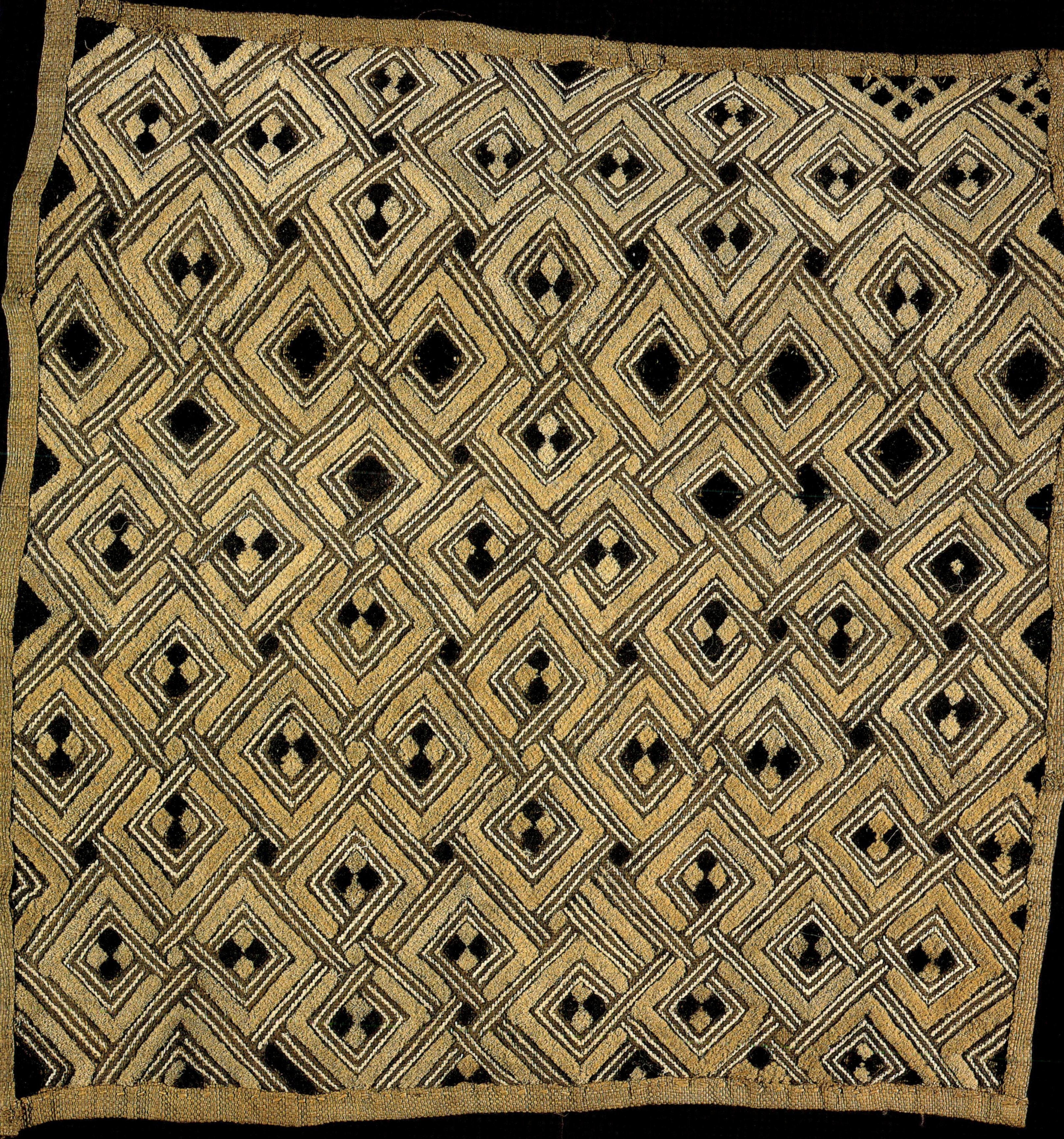

Woman's Skirt
Kuba, Congo (Kinshasa)
c. Early–mid-20th century
Raffia, rattan, H. 194 cm
Gift of Mr. and Mrs. Frank J. Gilliam
BMA 1968.25.10

Wives of Nyim (king) Mbop Mabiinc maMbekey recite his genealogy. Kuba, Mushenge, Congo (Kinshasa). Photo: Eliot Elisofon, 1955. Courtesy of the Eliot Elisofon Photographic Archive. National Museum of African Art, Smithsonian Institution

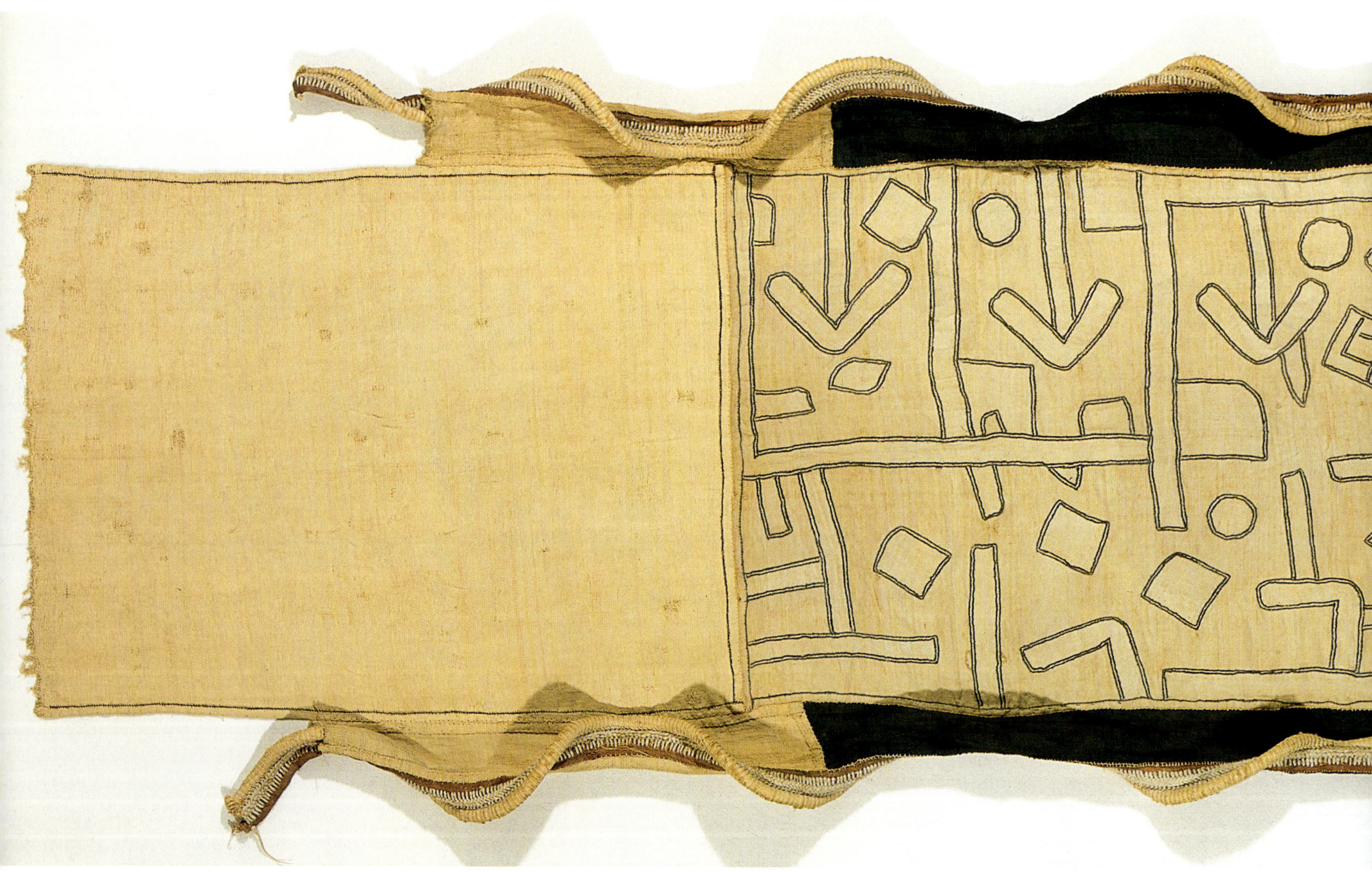

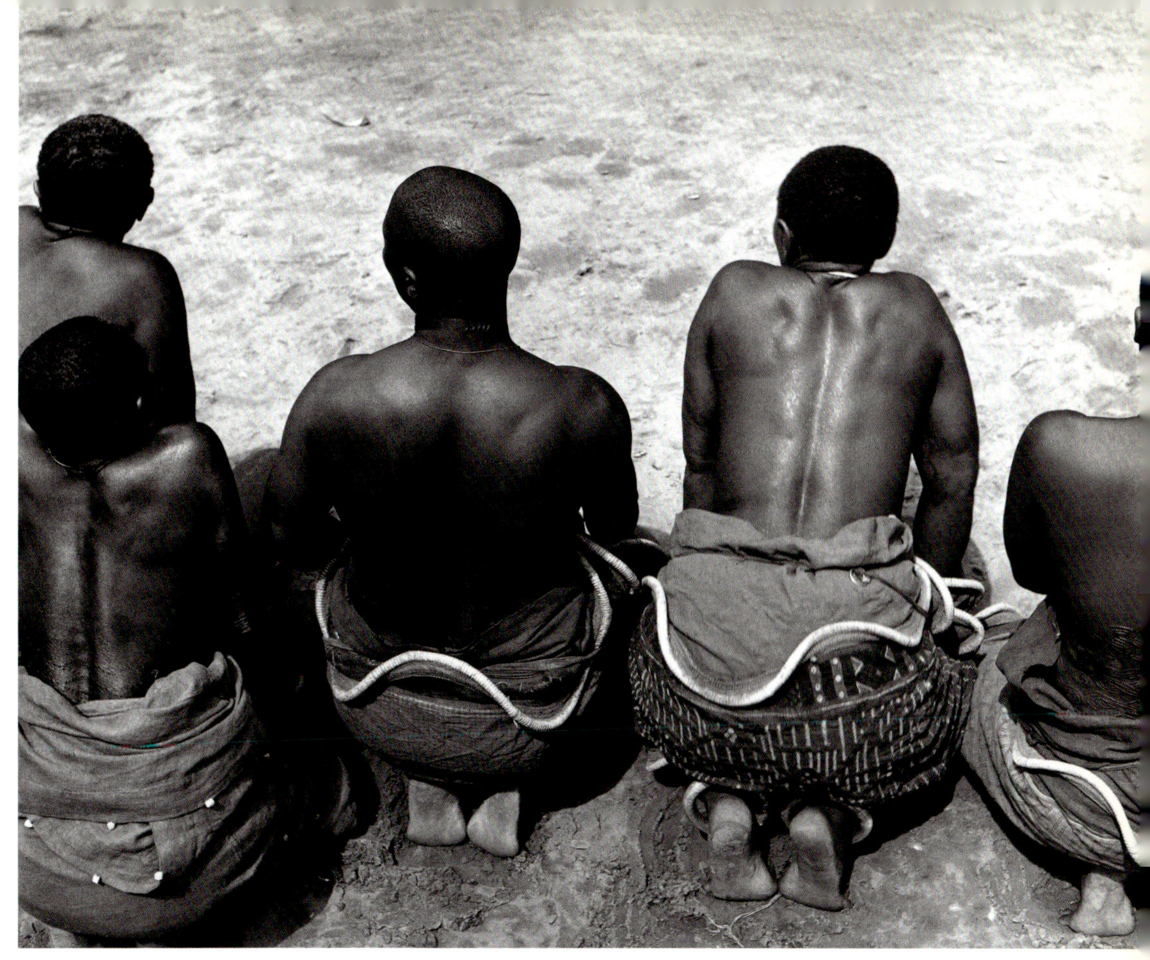

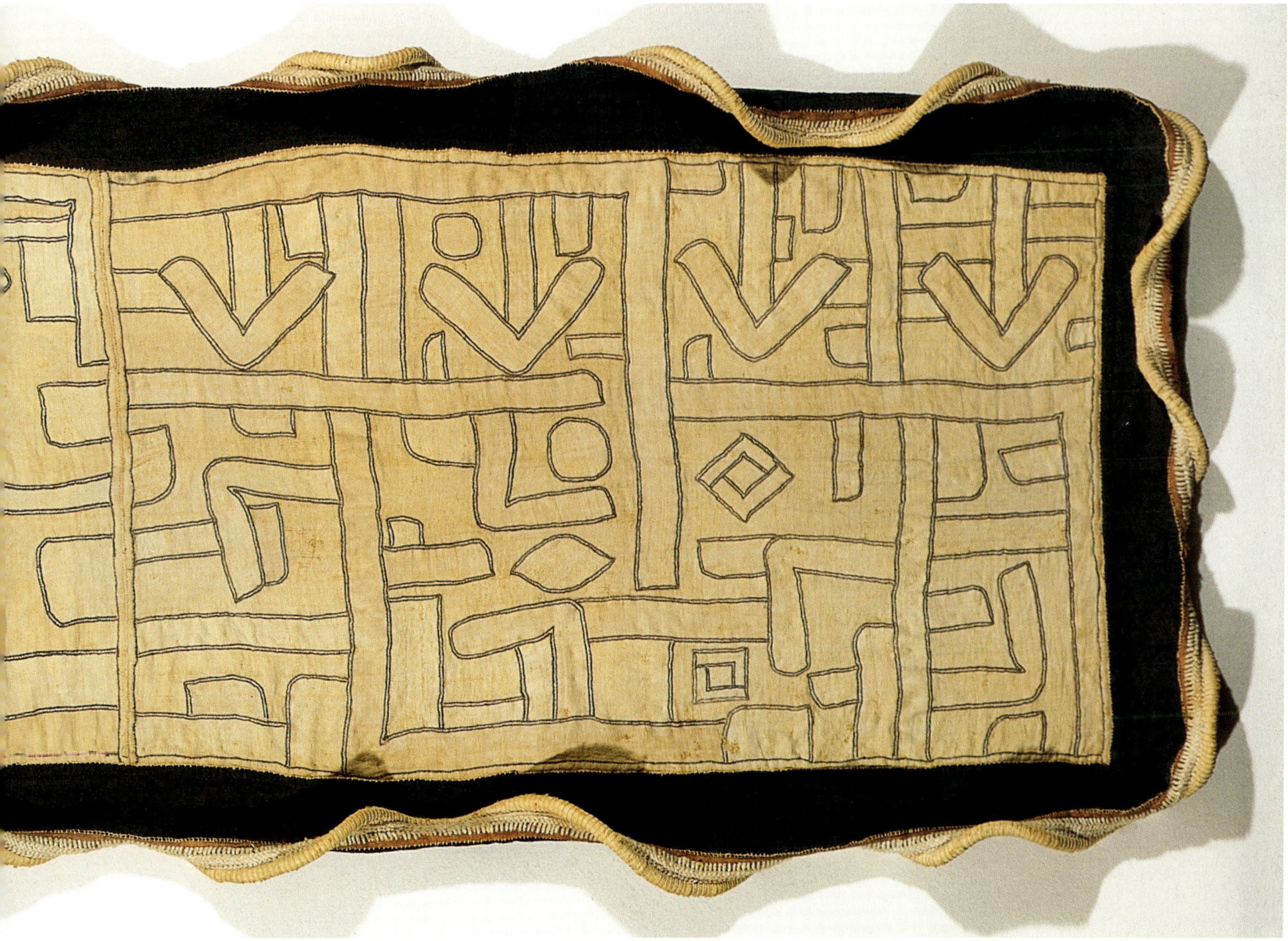

50

The Fleeting Flamboyance of the Warrior: Maasai Ornamentation

Man's Belt (*enkeene pus*)
Maasai, Tanzania
c. Mid-20th century
Glass beads, hide, L. 108.5 cm
Gift of Nancy and Robert H. Nooter, Washington, D.C.
BMA 1994.293

Warriors wearing the lion's mane headdress (*Olawaru*) and belt (*Enkeene Pus*). Maasai, Kenya/Tanzania. Photo: ©Angela Fisher

Like other pastoral peoples, the cattle-herding Maasai have no monumental art or architecture. Their semi-nomadic lifestyle dictates that their art must be portable, and, as a result of this limitation, artistic expression has found its most important outlet in the creation of jewelry and other body ornamentation, such as torso/leg painting and hairstyling (Fisher 1984:13–14, 19; Klumpp 1987:63–66, 182, 186; Saitoti 1980:18, 20, 128, 129, 136).

Maasai artistic principles are based on a philosophy that credits the attainment of balance and harmony in life to the interaction of opposites such as men (strong) and women (weak), or the alternation of opposites such as the cycle of night (dark) and day (light). The one god, *Enkai* (sky), is endowed with two opposing natures: one, the source of all that is beneficial, and the other, the source of all iniquity. In order to achieve visual balance and harmony in their ornamental beadwork, the Maasai artist expresses the principle of duality through the use of color schemes that they see as contrasting and/or complementary, such as black and white (contrasting: dark-strong/light-weak), and blue and orange (complementary: dark-strong/light-weak). Other color schemes play with light and dark variations of different hues. Color areas are separated by the use of either black or white beaded lines or shapes (Klumpp 1987:51, 80–86, 93, 105, 184–185, 188; Klumpp and Kratz 1993:205–207; Saitoti 1980:26).

Since this use of dark and light is applied on a relative scale, it can be the cause of confusion for the non-Maasai. For instance, orange is read as dark-strong next to green or yellow, but light-weak next to red or blue. Blue, whether saturated, a tone, a shade, or a tint, is always perceived as dark-strong, and is, in fact, interchangeable with black, the ultimate dark-strong. Although it is permissible to use two dark-strong colors next to one another (blue/red), it is never acceptable to juxtapose two light-weak colors (yellow/green). This flexible approach to the use of color allows the artist to fully explore both the visual excitement, as well as the underlying symbolism attached to color, such as blue, a reference to the sky/*Enkai*, and green, the color of the grass that feeds the herds, and is watered by rain, a gift from *Enkai* (Fisher 1984:27; Klumpp 1987:49–51, 93, 105, 184–185, 188; Saitoti 1980:30).

A Maasai man goes through three stages during his lifetime: child, warrior, and elder (each stage being subdivided). A young child lives at home until approximately the age of twelve when he undergoes circumcision (*Emurata*), at which time he becomes a junior warrior, protector of people and cattle, and leaves home to wander among the herds in the company of other warriors. Finally, after several years, he makes the transition from warrior to junior elder during the *Eunoto* ritual (Amin et al 1987:100; Fisher 1984:8, 14–15, 27, 29; Klumpp 1987:56, 57–59, 134, 171–172, 184, 272–273; Saitoti 1980:28, 29, 52, 57–59, 82–83, 97, 181, 196, 199; Sankan 1970:25–35).

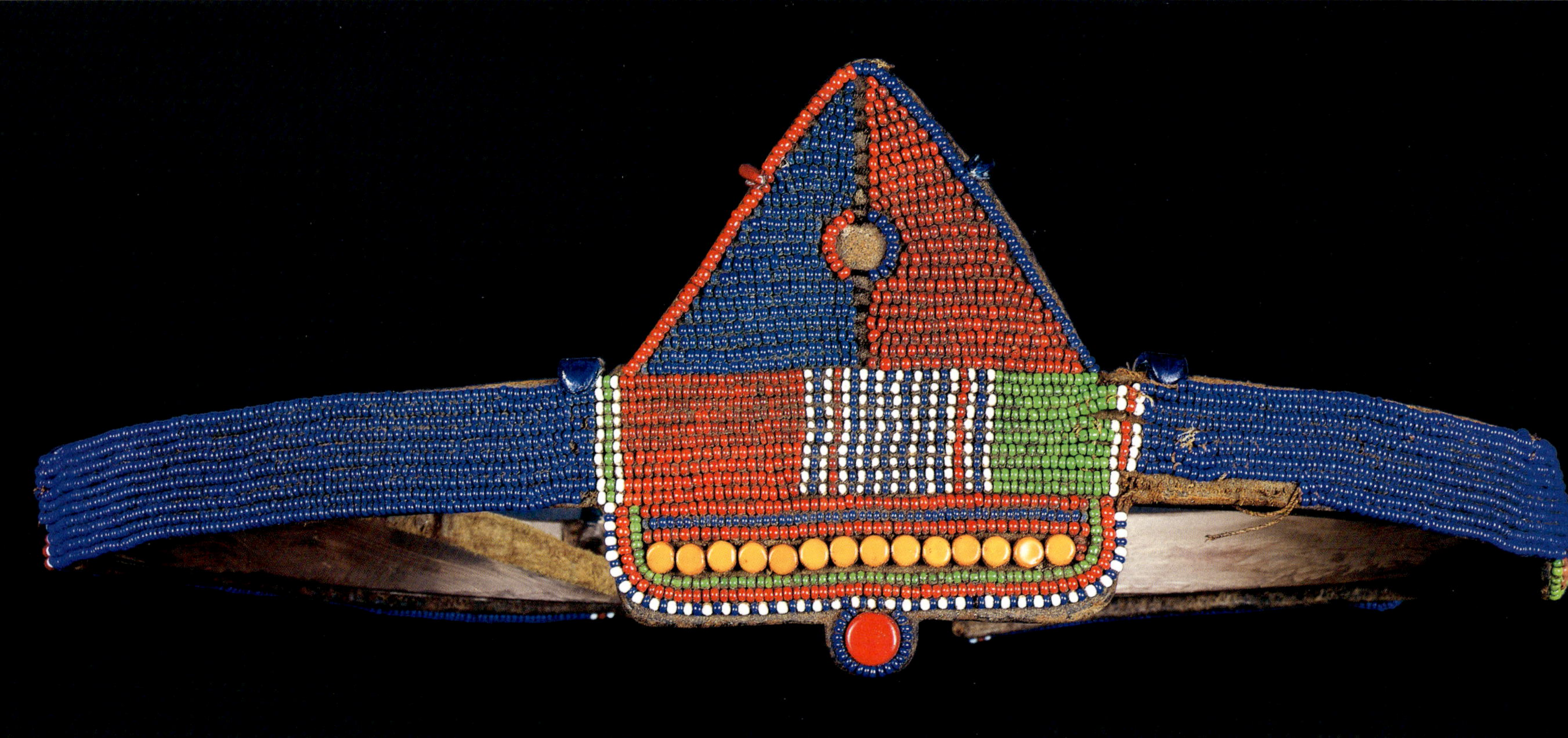

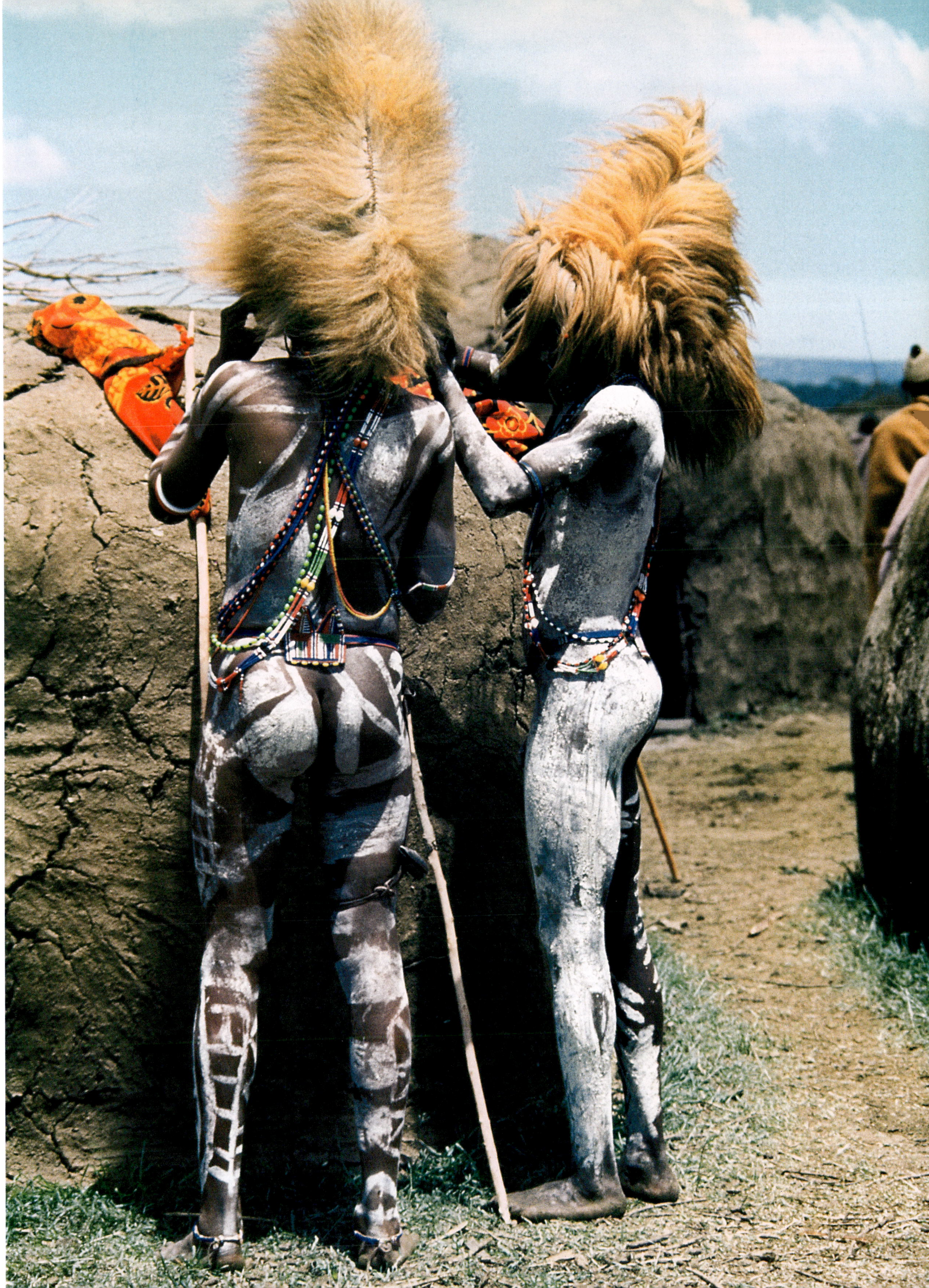

The Eunoto festival is one of the major Maasai ceremonial events. It may last as long as ten days, and is at once a rite-of-passage, theatrical event, and joyous community celebration. Since the Eunoto occurs only every seven to fourteen years, hundreds of warriors participate each time (Amin et al 1987: 100–103; Fisher 1984:8, 14–15, 27, 29; Klumpp 1987:58, 273; Saitoti 1980:156, 167). In an account of a 1968 Eunoto originally recorded in Maa, the language of the Maasai, by Benjamin ole Maora and Konana ole Mulei, a witness describes the pungent smells that filled the air:

> "A Maasai kaleidoscope of changing and combining odours of dry grass, camphor bush, cattle dung, sour milk, and wood smoke" (Amin et al 1987:102).

Appearances are very important to the Maasai, thus a young warrior, who "is the embodiment of beauty for the Maasai" (Klumpp 1987:171), and whose "body, occupation and behavior are considered the finest" (Klumpp 1987:171) takes exceptional pride in his hairstyle, dress, beaded jewelry, and torso/leg painting:

> Warriors are expected to spend a great deal of time and attention tending to their appearance, primping, and swaggering. They spend hours in small groups doing each other's hair and organizing their ornament assemblages while flirting with girls who are to be cajoled into making or giving them ornaments (Klumpp 1987:172).

This preoccupation with appearances is expected to cease once a young man has made the transition from warrior to elder. In addition to exchanging his arms for the wooden staff of a herder, and having his head shaved during the Eunoto ritual, the young warrior also removes his flamboyant ornaments never to wear them again. As an elder, he will be far more circumspect in his dress, hairstyle, and ornamentation (Amin et al 1987:100; Fisher 1984:29; Klumpp 1987:172, 273).

Although the fashioning of beaded ornaments is forbidden to men, the warriors not only select and pay for the beads, but also have a say in the choice of colors and patterns. The ornaments are designed and made for the warriors as gifts by their admiring mothers, sisters, and girlfriends. (Fisher 1984:19; Klumpp 1987: 64–65, 171–172, 175, 187; Saitoti 1980:83, 136).

The belt (p. 208) is part of a warrior's trappings, known as the "blue belt" (*enkeene pus*) (Klumpp 1987:101, 171, Fig. 97, p. 240), and worn with the triangular design (pointing up) resting in the small of the back (Fisher 1984:19; Saitoti 1980:137). The beads are *isaen* (small beads—a term used to refer to beads in general, and the smallest beads in particular) and *entepe* (larger flat beads) (Klumpp 1987:192, 275, 277); the backing is animal hide. The colors are both contrasting and complementary. The narrow belt portion makes use of a blue and red color pairing

Armband (*olkatarr enkaina*)
Maasai, Tanzania
c. Mid-20th century
Glass beads, hide, W. 10.2 cm
Gift of Nancy and Robert H. Nooter, Washington, D.C.
BMA 1994.282

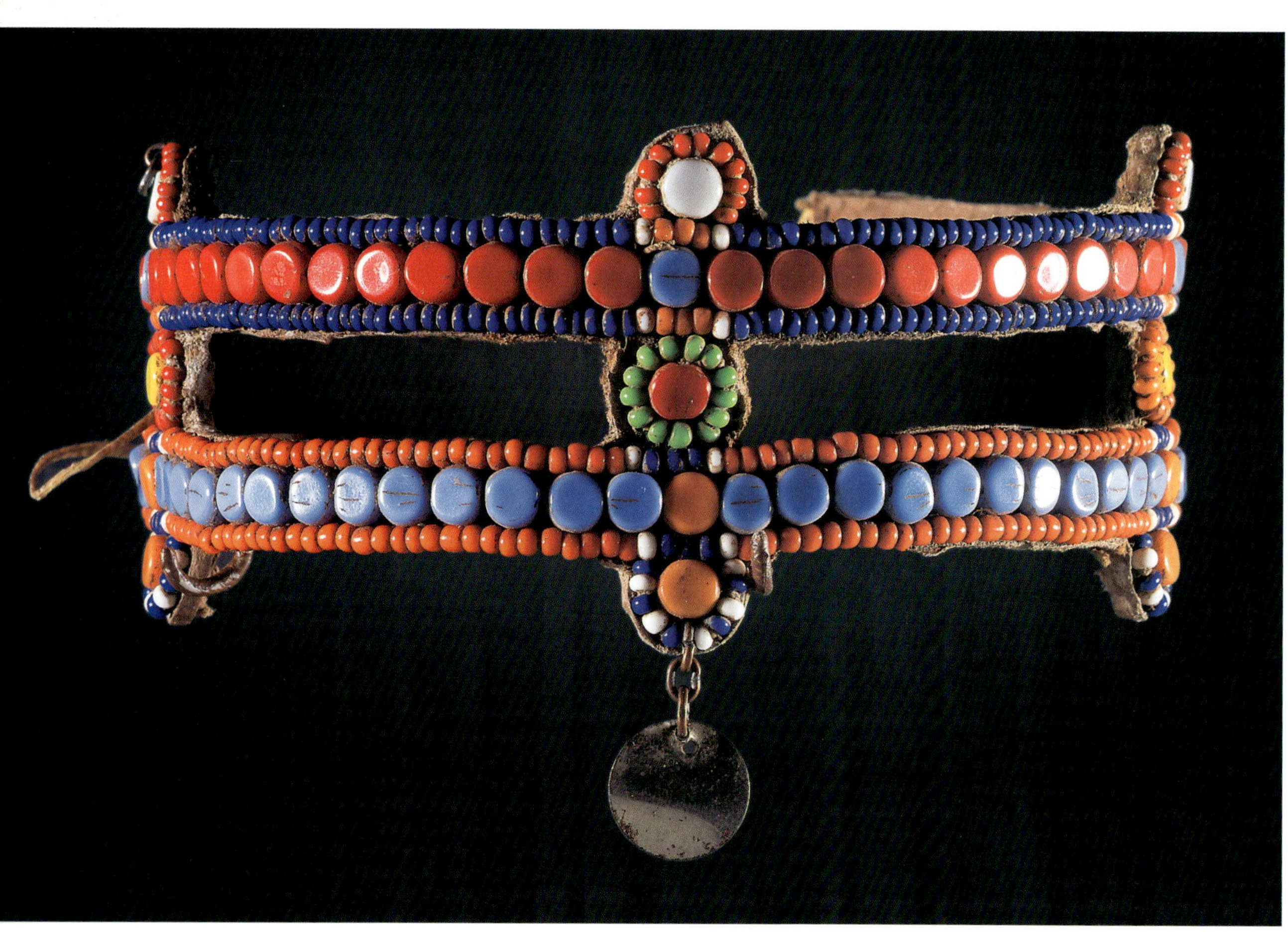

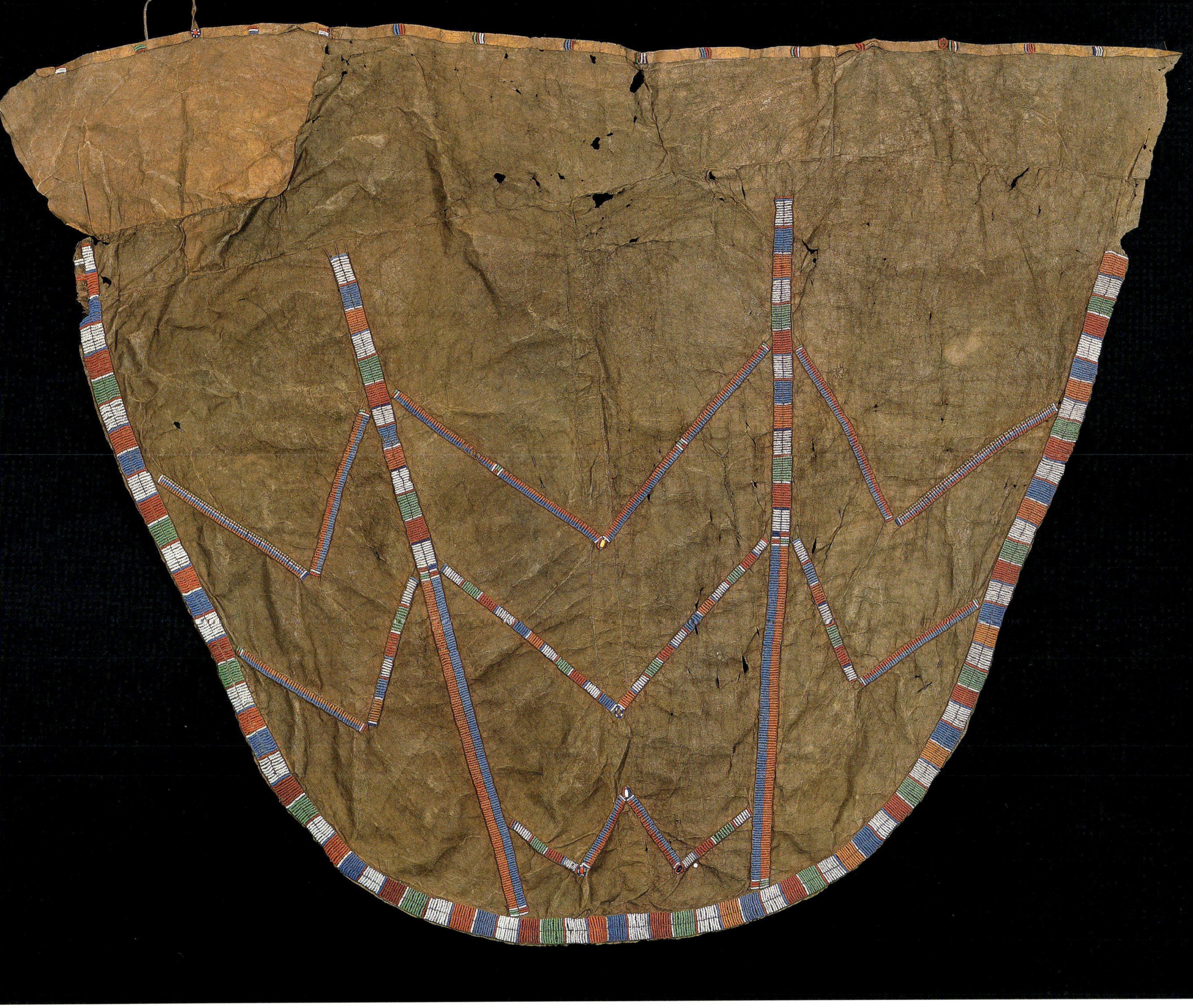

(contrasting: dark-strong/dark-strong) in which the color blue is predominant. The pairs in the triangle are the same blue and red plus green and red (complementary: light-weak/dark-strong) and green and orange, a juxtaposition that is read as contrasting: light-weak/dark-strong (Klumpp 1987:83).

Armbands that circle the upper arm are worn by both young warriors and their girlfriends. The style of the BMA's two armbands suggests that they are of the type known as *olkatarr enkaina* (Klumpp 1987:100, Fig. 88 p. 236). The BMA example (p. 212), has three projecting strips, and bears a color scheme of predominantly contrasting blue and red (dark-strong/dark-strong) and complementary red and green (dark-strong/light-weak) with touches of white. The backing material is animal hide. The BMA example of a double armband (p. 210), is crossed by three vertical strips. The beads are both *isaen* and *entepe*. The color scheme is complementary blue and orange (dark-strong/light-weak) with small decorative touches of blue, green, yellow, and white; a flat metal disc hangs in the center (Klumpp 1987:185; Klumpp and Kratz 1993:205).

The BMA's cape (above) is an article of women's clothing. Known as *enkishopo*, it is part of the clothing ensemble that

Woman's Cape (enkishopo)
Maasai, Tanzania
c. Mid-20th century
glass beads, hide, H. 63.5 cm
Gift of Nancy and Robert H. Nooter, Washington, D.C.
BMA 1994.269

Armband (*Olkatarr Enkaina*)
Maasai, Tanzania
c. Mid-20th century
Glass beads, hide, W. 14.5 cm
Gift of Nancy and Robert H. Nooter, Washington, D.C.
BMA 1994.281

includes a skirt and one or more drapes for the upper torso. It has a distinctive beaded edge and chevron pattern on the back created from small beads (isaen) (Klumpp 1987:102, 192, 243, 275). The cape's border is made up of alternating complementary color pairs: blue and orange (complementary: dark-strong/light-weak), and green and red (complementary: light-weak/dark-strong). This color set (blue/orange/white/red/green) is considered by the Maasai to be the most desirable (Klumpp 1987:83). The same color scheme, in a different design, decorates the back of the cape.

L. M. B.

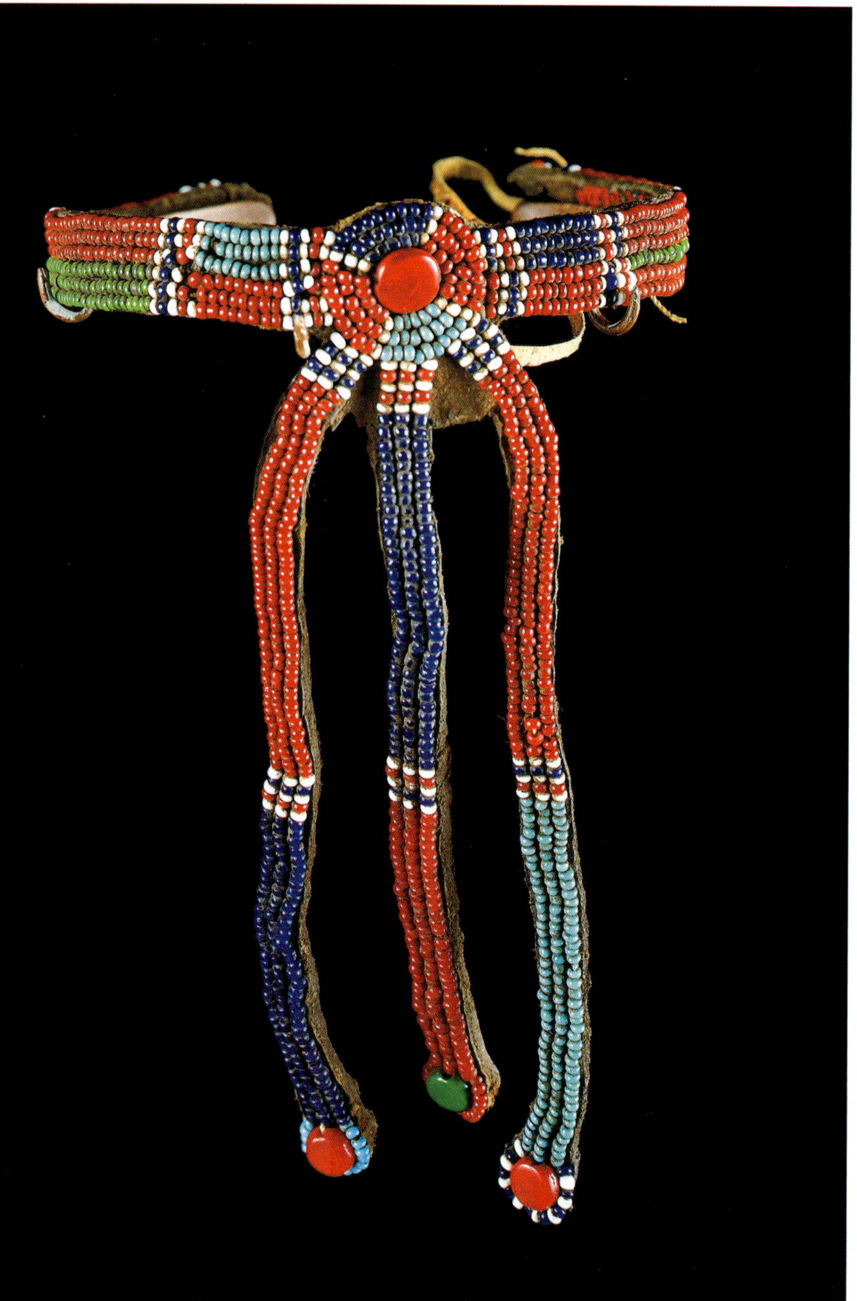

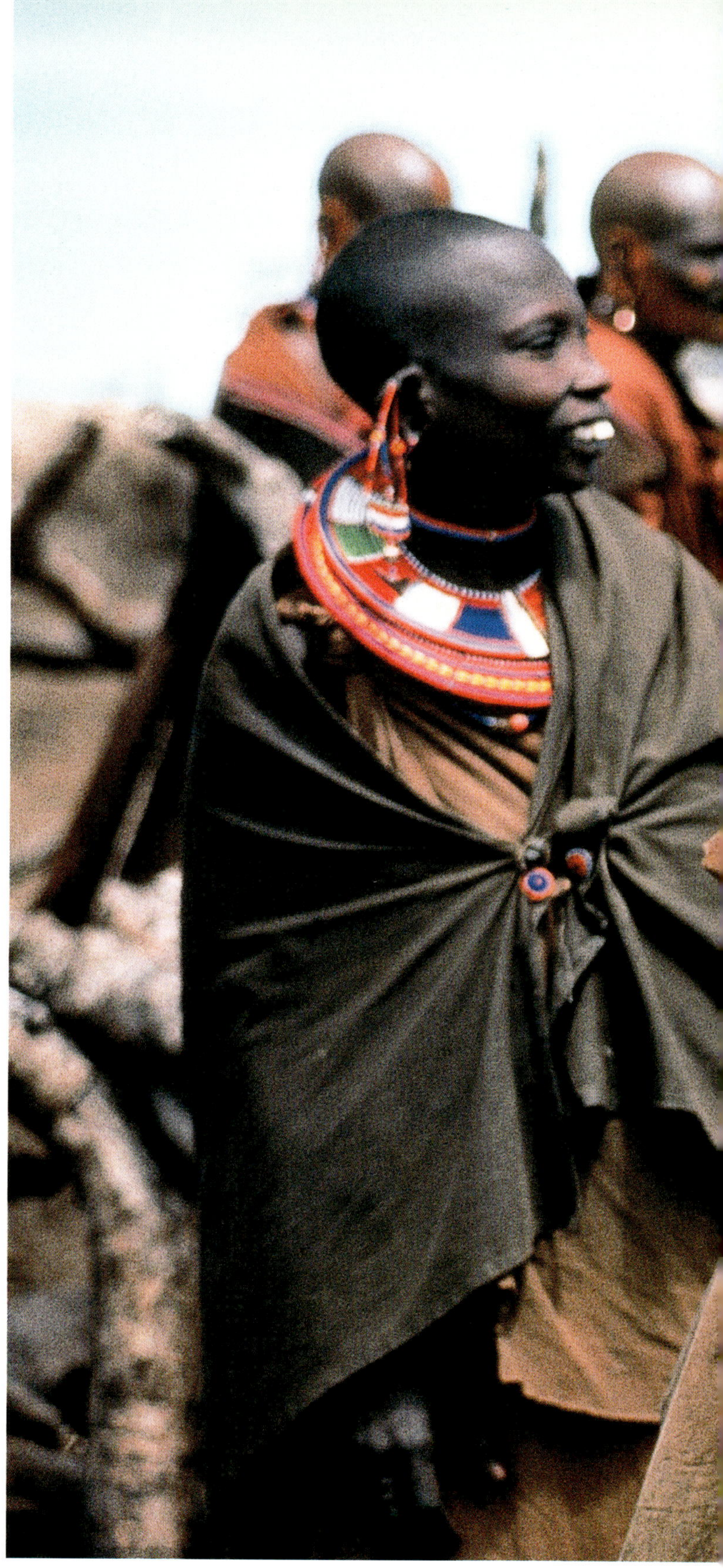

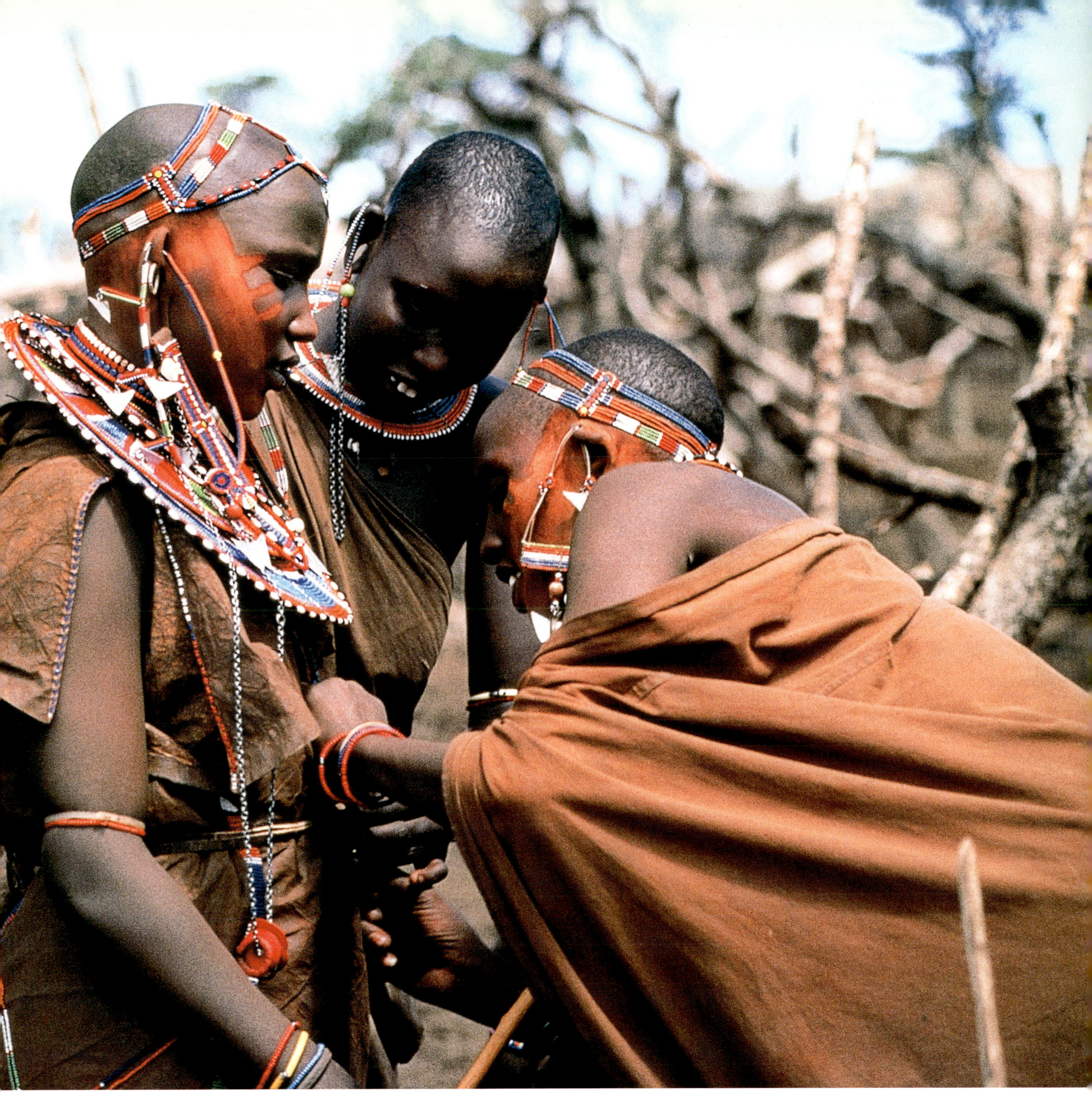

A young bride is prepared by her friends and family, all in their finest garments.
Maasai, Kenya/Tanzania. Photo: ©Carol Beckwith

Marking Passage in Momentary Appearances: a Yao Mask

The mask in southeastern Africa is an object seen only fleetingly, glimpsed in moments of performance. It is in this context, a brief moment full of movement, sound, and color, that this mask appears. The mask then disappears, hidden from sight until the next masquerade occasion. These occasions are carefully constructed events organized within the hierarchy of the village chief, chief's wife, ritual leaders, and elders, and are events that signify change in society, particularly death and life.

The Yao, Makonde, and Chewa, on the borders of Tanzania, Malawi, and northern Mozambique, share customs marking change such as funerals, selection of a new village chief, and the initiation of the young into adult society. Each event marks a death, an actual death, or a ritual death as in the initiation when a young person leaves the days of youth behind, and is initiated into new life as an adult. Masks such as this one appear in each of these events. The mask itself is alive and evocative, emotive, and capable of transforming society only in the context of these constructed social events. In these moments of performance the mask is the identity of a spirit, a person who has died and returned in this time of change. The spirit is the entire image; mask, dancer, costume, rattles, headdress. The mask is never publicly displayed on its own.

Female Mask
Yao, Tanzania
c. Mid-20th century
Wood, hair, metal, kaolin, H. 20 cm
Gift of Nancy and Robert H. Nooter, Washington, D.C.
BMA 1994.265

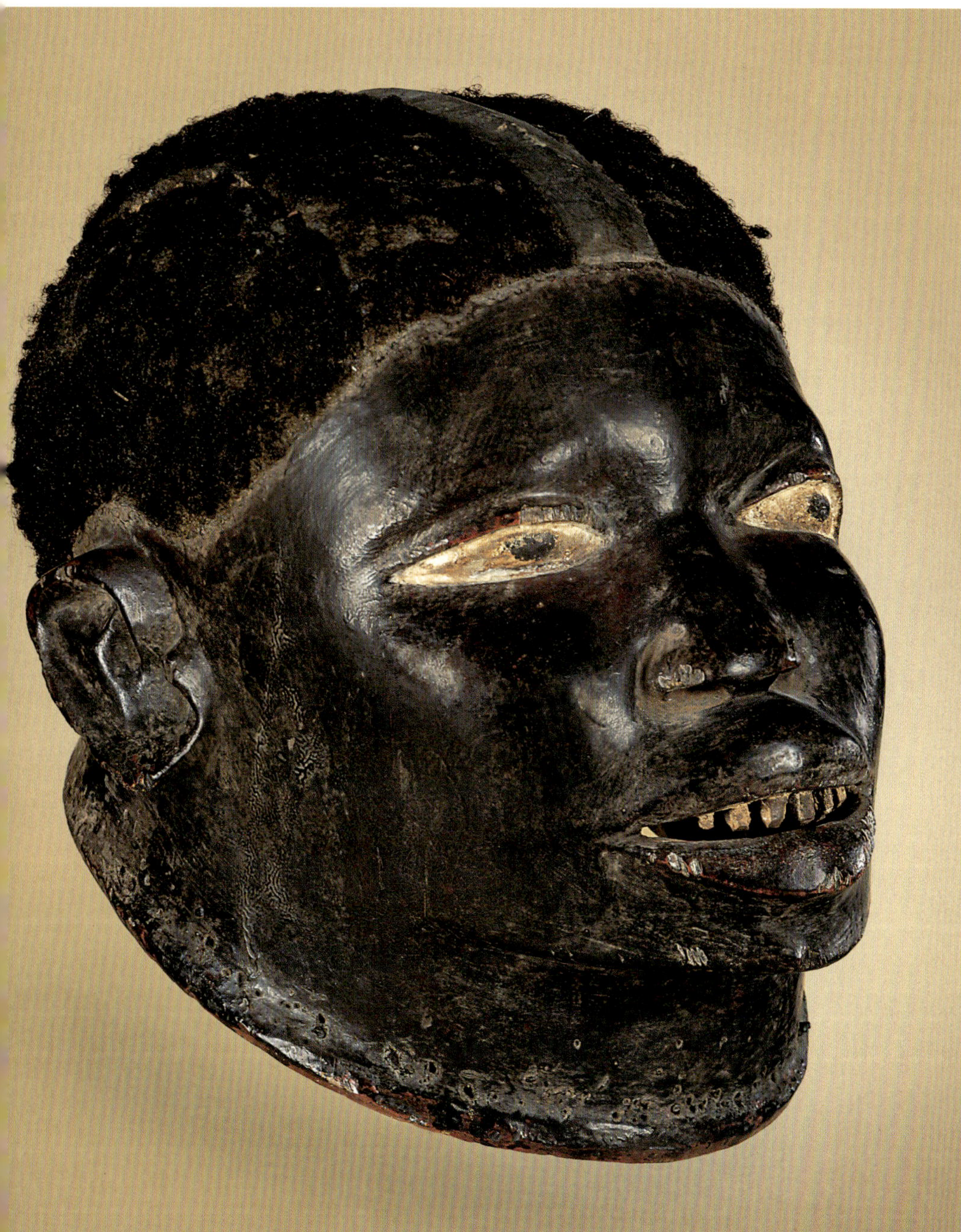

In the context of a museum exhibit, the Chewa would say the mask hangs as a dead mask, devoid of all power, empty of spirit. In fact, even in the performance, the distance between the mask and the observers is strictly controlled. In some cases, the audience is reminded not to look too closely at the masks in song, and those who stare are labeled fools because they risk annoying the spirits, and who may inflict mischievous punishment. In any case, observance is difficult as in performance the mask is rarely still. The dances are strenuous, and the mask is mostly in movement. Further, the mask is submerged in a rage of feathers and raffia, hides or wigs, and cloths comprising various headdresses and coverings that allow only the face and sometimes part of the head to be seen. Some of the masks are literally hidden until the moment the dancer throws back his head of feathers to reveal the face. Dancers kick up clouds of red dust further obscuring the mask in a veil of fine earth.

Within this moment of performance the mask conveys a host of ideas, emotions, and associations. Each mask performance is a reenactment of the reunion of the living and the dead, and the presence of the spirits. Each individual mask has its own particular significance, recognized by the audience in various ways.

The individual mask is remembered from performance to performance. Some will know the dancer and others will only know the character the mask portrays through the dance, movements, song, rhythm of the drums, and costume. Some masks are considered humorous, and others tragic or dangerous, and still others convey irony and satire for those who understand the joke.

Wooden face masks such as this one are spirits of the dead returned to the village. The actual character of this mask cannot be known without documentation about the performance. We can only know that this mask is female. Its performance would convey a particular significance of being a woman in this society. As men perform the masks, this female mask is worn by a male dancer. Women call out the songs of the spirits, and the 'voice' of the mask is that of the senior women in the performance.

One assistant said to me revealingly, "all things come in pairs." Although this mask could be danced alone, rather than in a group, it would have had a male pair, most likely a senior male mask, perhaps the mask of a chief. The use of black pigments and carving in the traditional style of the mask indicates it is a mask of a respected person, one with ritual power or leadership in the society.

As a representation of a deceased, respected woman in society, the mask would convey the character of a woman with some power to influence events, and was therefore dangerous. The movements of such a female mask in Chewa dance would involve a fast, competent whirling motion, sudden stops with one arm perfectly horizontal near the chin of the mask, and a slight moving of the head in a tilt to one side, and a nodding motion, giving the face a living dimension. The dancer's movement in conjunction with the expressionless face conjures the aura of fear in a face that does not change, shift, relax from its unsmiling presence. The total masked dancer appears as a moving, living being and an nonliving spirit enigma at the same time. From whirling in circles, face downward with rising dust and loud drums, to a sudden stillness, quiet, and exposed face slightly nodding, the changed image from life to unreal death is heightened and imparted ever more forcefully.

Female masks with such ritual power have associations beyond the pairing with a male mask. Senior women who are advisers, ritual leaders, wives of chiefs, and, indeed, in some cases, chiefs themselves, play critical, powerful roles in society, including the continuation of the masked events. Female masks are associated with matrilineal customs, special relationships with spirits and prophets, and allegiance to the ancestresses to whom all people all related. Female masks represent the mothers of all.

As the mask and performance convey this powerful image of women, the society echoes this image in the initiation of girls into womanhood stressing the important role women have in ritual power, fertility, and matriliny. In the fleeting moments of performance, the audience witnesses the presence of the female spirit returning to the village, whispering messages to the people in song, dance, rhythm, color, costume, and the mask.

Laurel Birch de Aguilar

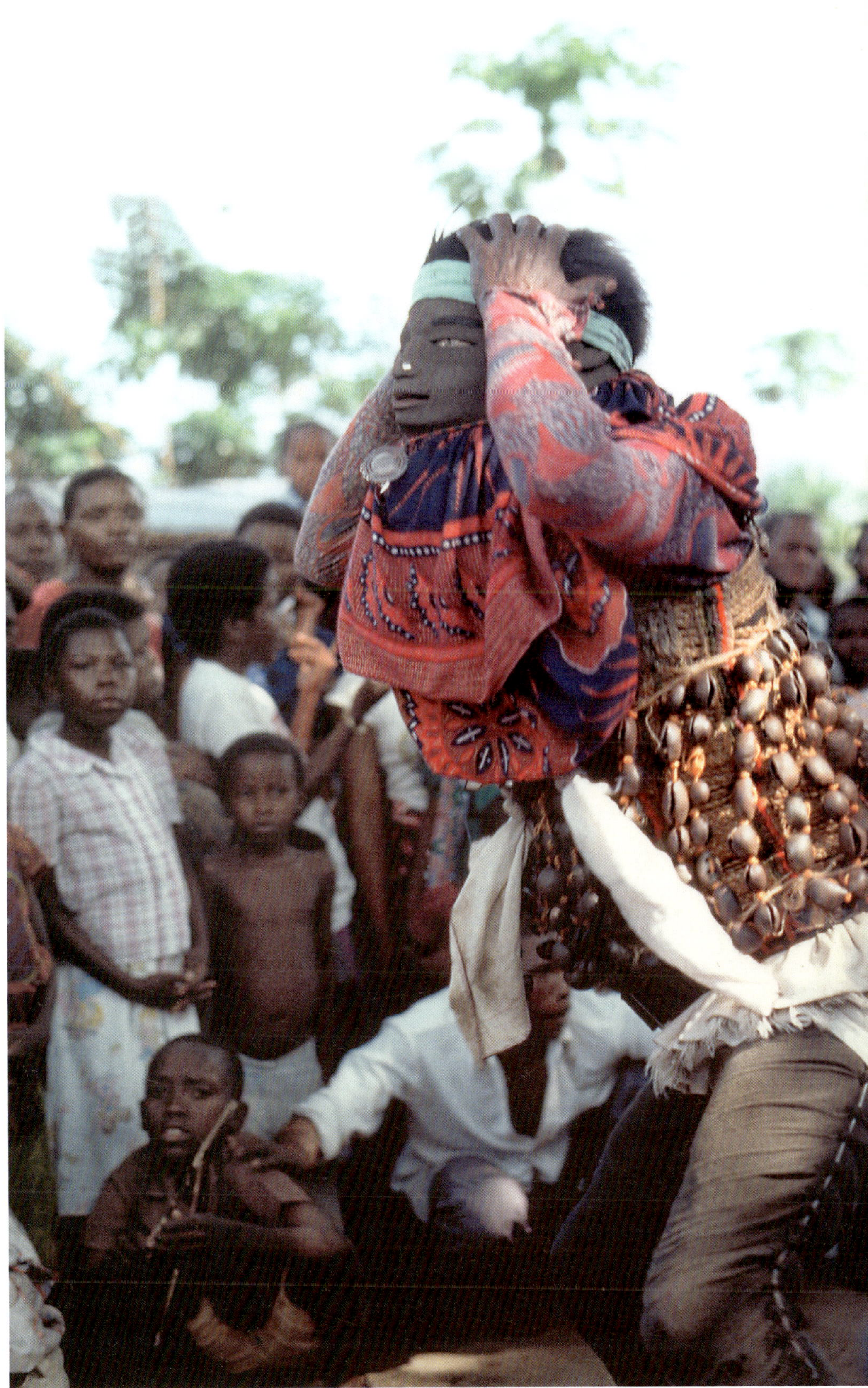

Dancer wearing a Lipiko mask. Makonde, Dar es Salaam, Tanzania. Photo: ©abm—archives barbier-mueller, 1990

52 Gendered Seats—Gendered Space and Time: a Lobi Stool

Figurative Stool
Lobi and other group identifications
Northwestern Ghana, northeastern Ivory Coast, and southern Burkina Faso
c. Mid-20th century
Wood, H. 19.4 cm
Gift of Phyllis K. and A. Harvey Schreter, Baltimore
BMA 1996.125

The stools carved and used by Lobi men and women reflect gendered divisions that are evident in the spaces and timing of Lobi performance.[1] Stools for men are distinctive in form with three legs, and are sometimes adorned with anthropomorphic or zoomorphic forms. The seats are supported by two legs of equal length at one end and a third longer leg that extends at a diagonal from the other end of the seat. Stools used by women are supported by either three or four legs of equal length. While there can be some variance in the sizes and shapes of both men's and women's stools, there is no ambiguity between the form and function of those for each gender. The former are destined for use and display in numerous public settings while the latter generally remain in the domestic sphere. Rarely does a man lend his stool to another. In order to protect the child inside the womb, pregnant women are apparently prohibited from sitting on men's stools (Antongini and Spini 1981:112–3).

The stool in the BMA collection is a man's stool. The pair of male and female figures joining the seat seem to be solely decorative (see p. 199). However, the Lobi also carve wooden figures that stand collectively in shrines, serving as intermediaries between the visible and invisible worlds (see p. 159). Figures placed in shrines are sometimes carved in pairs and are understood as twins, not as married couples (Meyer 1981:54).

Men often carry their personal stools to markets and funerals, the most frequent public gatherings they attend. When the seat of the stool is turned vertically, or diagonally, as the men carry it over their shoulders, these figures appear as if they are sitting on the stool. In seating, the owner places the stool so that the long leg extends to their right or left side.

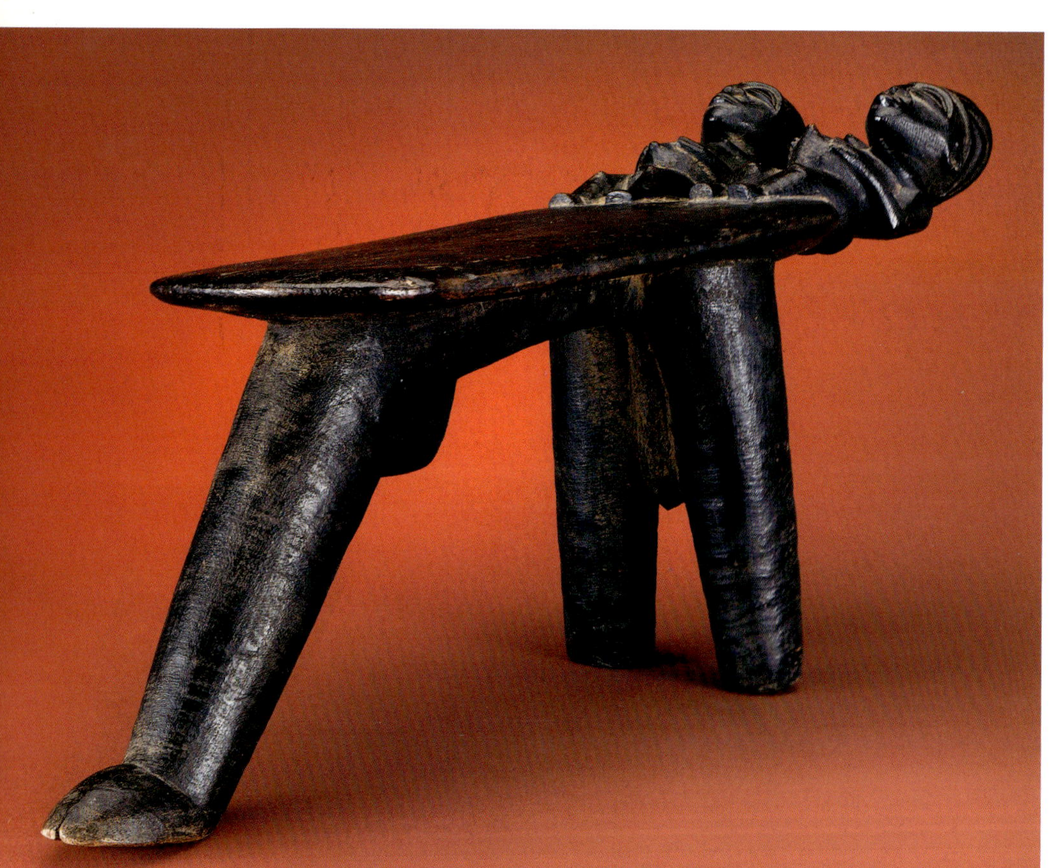

Men and women sit in separate spaces at markets and funerals. At both markets and funerals, older men congregate near the women selling *pito*, beer brewed locally from millet. They drink and talk together, sitting on their stools or on the ground. At markets, women sit together on logs, overturned metal pans, or on the ground, while they cook food and talk to their friends. At funerals, women sit on the ground with their legs stretched out straight before them. Unless a woman is selling *pito* to the men at a funeral, she generally locates herself with other women and children near the corpse, the xylophone players, and the dancing. While men also dance at funerals, and both genders mingle about marketplaces, the space where men and women congregate at both markets and funerals is demarcated for each.

Markets and funerals around the Black Volta River are sites of economic exchange as well as social interaction, and they provide fertile ground for conflict. Men's stools may sometimes be used as weapons on these occasions. People plan weddings at markets and funerals, and new unions may be contested. Sometimes a man or his brothers and friends surreptitiously make arrangements for his marriage to a woman. They agree on a time when one of the man's friends or brothers can come to the house where the woman is staying and bring her to one of their houses. When she arrives at the new house, she remains there for a few days. If a man perceives that another man is trying to take his wife from him or is angry that she has recently left him, he may confront the offending man or group of men. In an ensuing brawl, the three-legged stool may be employed as a club; a man grabs the long leg and hits the other man with the two shorter legs (Grace Longpal, personal communication, 2001).

Three-legged stools may also play a role in the Lobi initiation process when children enter adulthood. This process involves an arduous journey that brings them to the banks of the Black Volta River. Fathers often give their sons three-legged stools to protect them from unknown forces as they embark on their initiation route, journeying across space and into adulthood and masculinity (Palé Kouinthé, in Bognolo 1993:389).

The distinction between male and female evidenced in the forms of Lobi stools and the spatial division of the marketplace and of the funeral is also manifested in temporal aspects of funerary performance and display. When a woman dies, pots belonging to other women in the community are sometimes displayed on a table near the corpse, in a demonstration of commonality with the deceased. When a man dies, however, men from the community display their weapons. Before the body is buried, members of the deceased's clan (and deceased's husband's clan, if the deceased was a married female) encircle the body with clan materials clutched in their hands (Grace Longpal, personal communication, 2001; Emmanuel Sorgbum, personal communication, 2001). Following the burial, objects that the deceased used when he or she was living are commonly placed over the grave. For men, these often include the three-legged stools, representing his gender.

Three and four—the number of legs generally associated with men's and women's stools respectively—are pervasive in Lobi ritual. But there is wide variation in the understanding of and explanations for these associations between three and four, and male and female.

Three men from the Northern Region, Ghana who each identified themselves as Birifor, one of the Lobi peoples, each provided a different example of, or reason for, this numerology. Moses Sorbum Dakpelo (personal communication, 2001) said that when a baby is born, it traditionally is brought before the gods of the father and is initiated to those gods. A mixture of water, herbs, and three roots is used to wash the baby. A baby boy is washed three times, and a baby girl four times. This initiation is then the beginning of doing things three times for males and four times for females. When a woman is married, she is initiated to the gods of her husband in a similar way. When she dies, she is encircled four times, first by the husband's family, and then by her natal family. Similarly, a man's corpse is encircled three times by his natal family.

Pastor Daniel Tampour (personal communication, 2001) described *padøør*, the period after a woman has just given birth, during which she is considered to be unclean and people are prohibited from eating food she has cooked or using firewood that is in her house. If the woman gives birth to a boy, this period is three months long. If she gives birth to a girl, this period is four months long.

Banaar (personal communication, 2001), the keeper of a local Birifor shrine, provided yet another explanation, stating that a woman is afforded more chances than a man. A woman's responsibilities include going to the farm and collecting firewood as well as preparing food at home. As a woman has more responsibilities than a man, she is given greater cosmological consideration. It is also a sign of respect towards a woman to grant her the larger number. He further stated that a man and a woman could not function without each other, as the thumb and four fingers could not function without each other. The thumb is *daba*, or man, and the four fingers are *pøø*, or the wives.

The BMA stool exemplifies Lobi conceptions of gender as they are made manifest in Lobi objects, spaces, timing, and repetition of ritual performance.

Susan Elizabeth Gagliardi

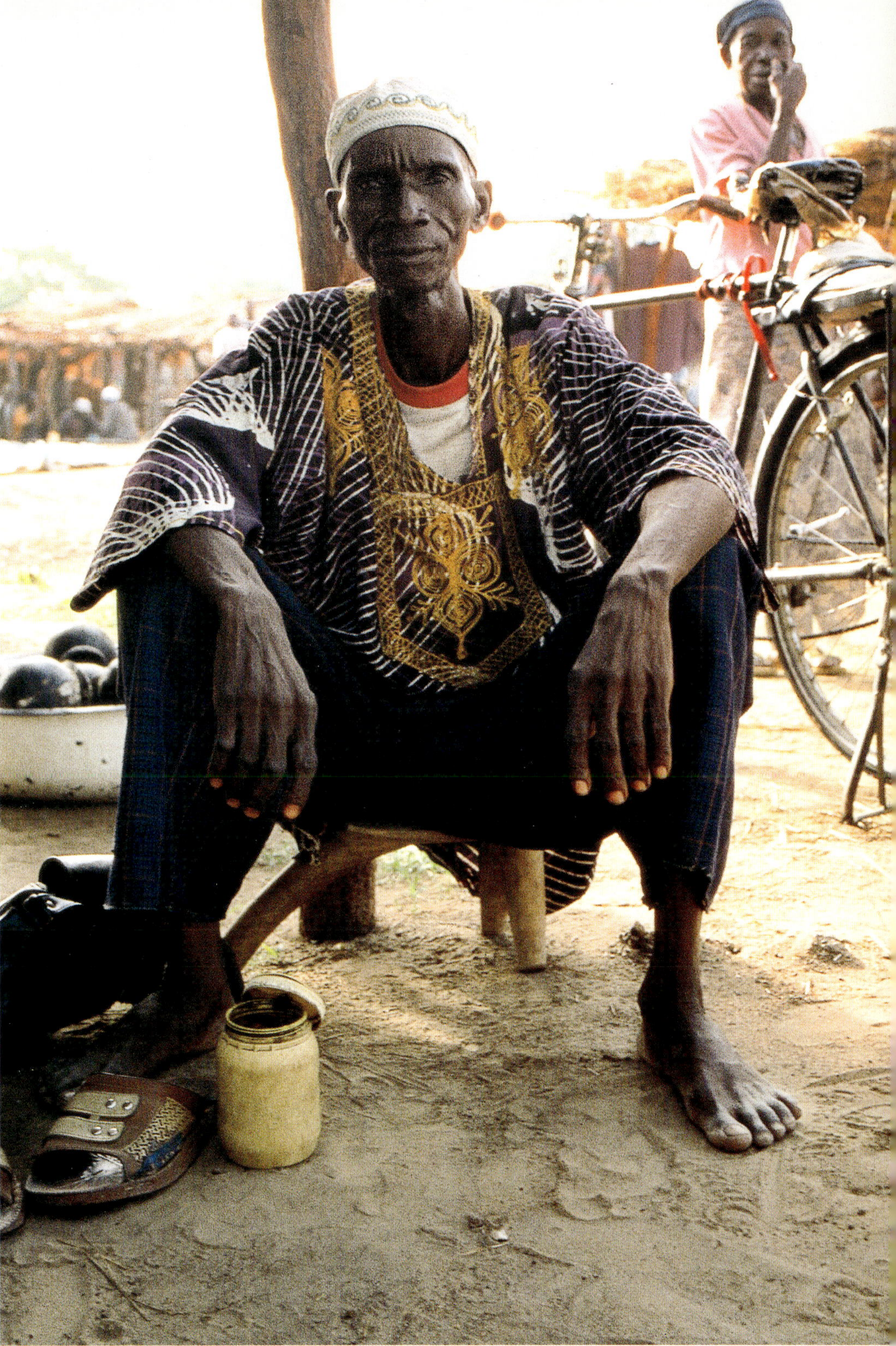

Timotey (from Danvaar) sitting on a stool at the Gbonbonduri Market. Gbonbonduri, Northern Region, Ghana. Photo: Susan Elizabeth Gagliardi, 2001

1 'Lobi' is a term commonly used in literature and by governments to refer to some of the people who live in the geographic region around the Black Volta River (Goody 1967). It often refers to peoples known by other terms, including Mewø, Birifor, and Dagara. The term can have pejorative connotations and often, during the ten months of fieldwork I conducted in Ghana between September 2000 and July 2001, I found that the term was avoided when people identified themselves. The languages spoken by these peoples are sometimes, but not always, mutually intelligible. 'Lobi' seems to be more of a directional term, used to indicate one's neighbors, than a self-referent (Goody 1967).

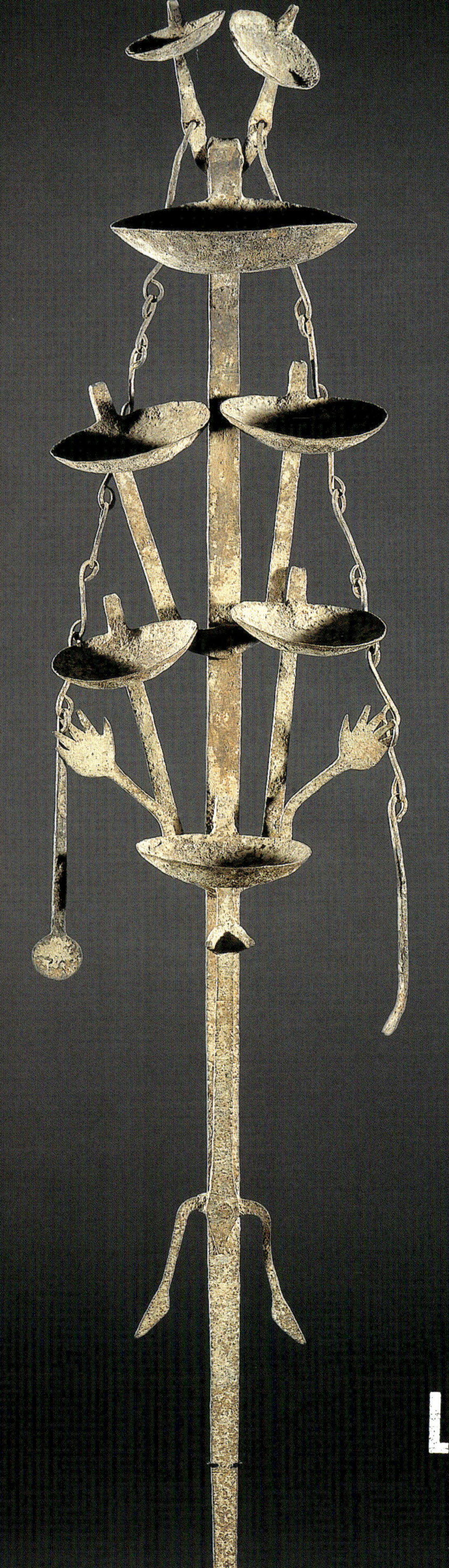

LIGHTING AND VISUAL ACCESS

Just as in Western theater, lighting in African performance is essential to its success or failure. Lighting can help to define the subject and meaning. Certain objects are meant to appear brilliantly in the bright sun of the dry season. Others must be shrouded in the dimness of dusk or dawn. Still others may be seen only vaguely in the flickering light of a torch at night, and others not seen at all but only heard. In a museum, all the objects may be displayed with similar lighting, or rather equally subdued, often in order to conform to conservation requirements, or under spotlights, à la Cartier. How different the objects would appear in indigenous contexts! An African person who had only witnessed a particular mask performed in the dim light of dusk might not recognize it displayed in the gallery illuminated by a bright spotlight.

Philip Dark (1973:27) remarked on the transformation that museums and photographers bring to African art, particularly in the case of Benin (Edo) brass memorial objects (e.g. p. 245), "set apart, emanating a tranquility, a beauty, remote and strange and witnessed to the remarkable skill of a great artist, a work of art indeed. But the Edo never saw these objects nor regarded them in the matter we do."

> Let it be remembered how conditioned we have become to many objects by the many illustrations we see of them. There is little doubt that clever lighting can bring out in photographs of Benin objects, as of others, qualities which are not there when they are seen face to face in a museum and which are certainly absent in the gloom of a shrine. As an exercise in creativity on the part of the photographer this enhancement of objects to yield new aesthetic facets is commendable, but it should be remembered that this is the field of illusion, a field real and worthy of study *per se*, but one which distorts the factors of natural vision and the cultural context proper to its function.

Among the Baga, most dances are performed after sundown, often in the darkness of night. Accompanying the masked dancer is a circle of young men carrying lighted torches made of bundles of grass. One of the principal headdresses danced at the time of a wedding is a female bust called "Signal," among other names. The surface of the bust, representing the skin of the young woman, is usually painted a brilliant red, using commercial paint. Seen in the daylight, the headdress is bright and colorful (p. 220) just as is much of its surroundings: the people in their clothing of different colors, the grass, the trees, and flowers. But it is in the dance in the darkness of night that the flashiness of Signal can be appreciated (p. 221). At one moment,

Oil Lamp with Anthropomorphic Arms and Legs
Bamana, Mali
c. Late 19th century
Iron, H. 89 cm
Gift of Nancy and Robert H. Nooter, Washington, D.C.
BMA 1985.283

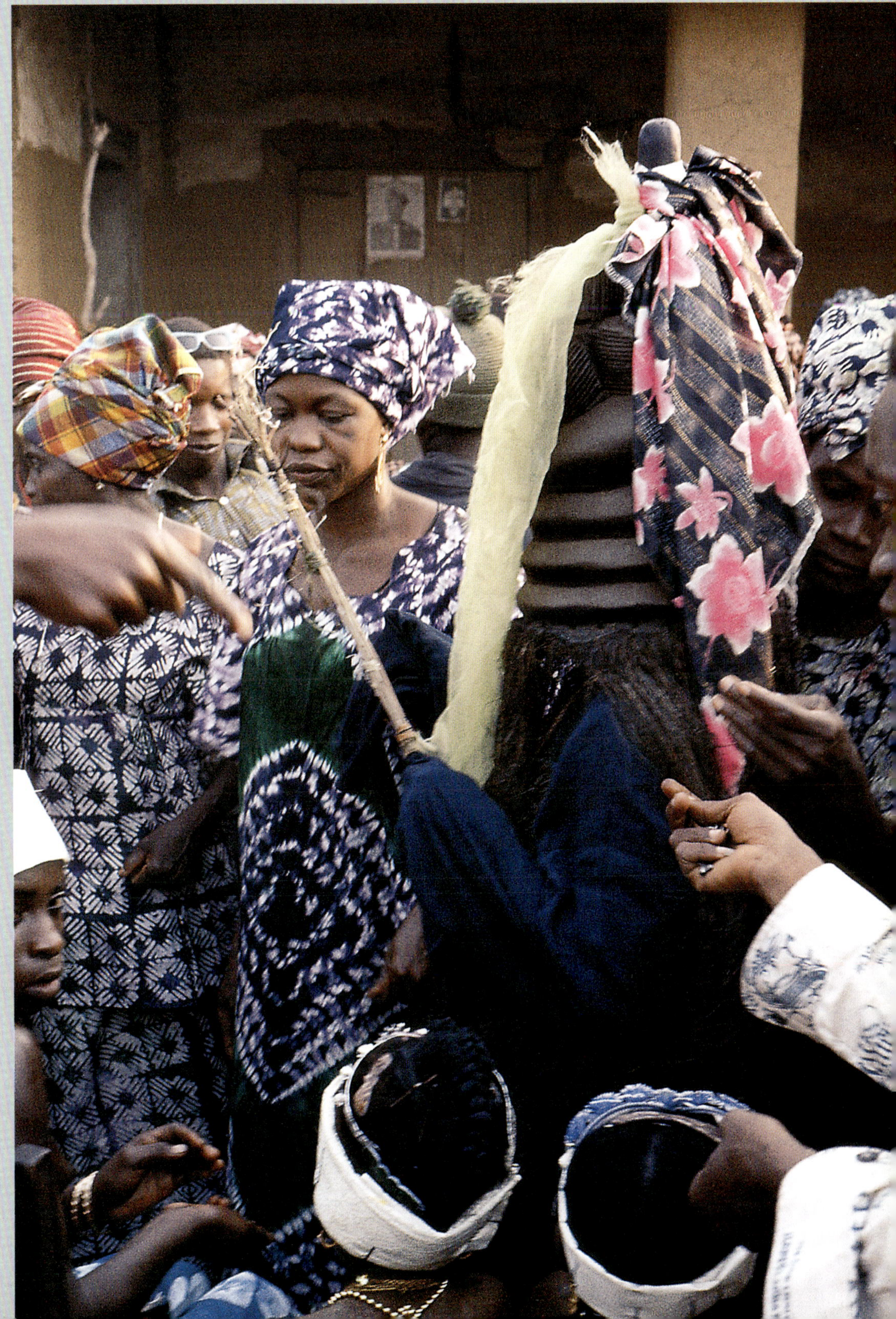

By sunrise, the dance of the Nöwo (Ndoli Jowei) masquerader has finished, and she takes her place silently in the procession of women at the coming-out of young female initiates. Temne, Sierra Leone. Photo: Frederick John Lamp, 1976

the headdress is seen dimly, at a distance, or even up close. At another, she passes quickly into the brilliance of a cluster of torches, and her red image dazzles, if only for a glimmering instant. To the Baga observer, the image of Signal then appears variously in changing views from dim and enticing to brilliant and aggressive, contrasting startlingly with the blackness surrounding her.

Susan Vogel (1997) has analyzed the use of art objects by the Baule in terms of their visibility, determined by darkness and light, as well as other means of obscurity and revelation. The world of the Baule, close to the equator, is one of equals segments of darkness and light, and until the introduction of electricity in the 1980s, evenings were spent in the dark, full of life, socializing, and moving about the village. She sees the non-visibility of art objects having more to do with ambiguity than with fear (p. 127):

> In Baule thinking, darkness is a neutral reality, not a lack of light but an alternative state. Obscurity is both accepted as a normal inconvenience and experienced as positive, useful, and pleasurable.... Night and darkness provide a way of knowing and experiencing in which understanding is actually deepened by ambiguity and fed by imagination and memory.

To summarize the above, there are variety of lighting issues that the researcher observing a work of African art might consider. Should the object and the performance be bathed in brilliance, or should it be seen dimly? Should the illumination be constant or should it be modulated? Are there varying circumstances in which the object is used and seen with varying lighting? Is the lighting important to the meaning of the object? Does a change in lighting change the meaning? How does the lighting define the form? Should the object be seen only partially? Should the object be seen at all?

The following essays examine the issues of lighting and visual access in various ways. On the D'mba mask of the Baga, I contrast the worn condition of the BMA example with the performance context of a high, black polish to the wood, studded with brilliant copper tacks, taking place in the hot, dry season in full sunlight, the mask flashing like the sun's rays as the dancer twirls through the crowd. Accessibility through lighting and positioning are important in the use of heddle pulleys that I discuss from the Baule, Dogon, and Senufo. Inaccessibility and hidden storage, on the other hand, are pertinent to iron currency used by the Kwele. Darkness is the essence of the Kòmò mask of the Manding peoples, which only the members of the male Kòmò association are permitted to "see," and even then, in the night, they would perceive little more than the sparks of fire that are made to fly out from the snout of the beast. From a related Manding people and a similar ritual context, the Mau mask, likewise, significantly inhabits the night, as described by Marie-Noël Verger-Fèvre.

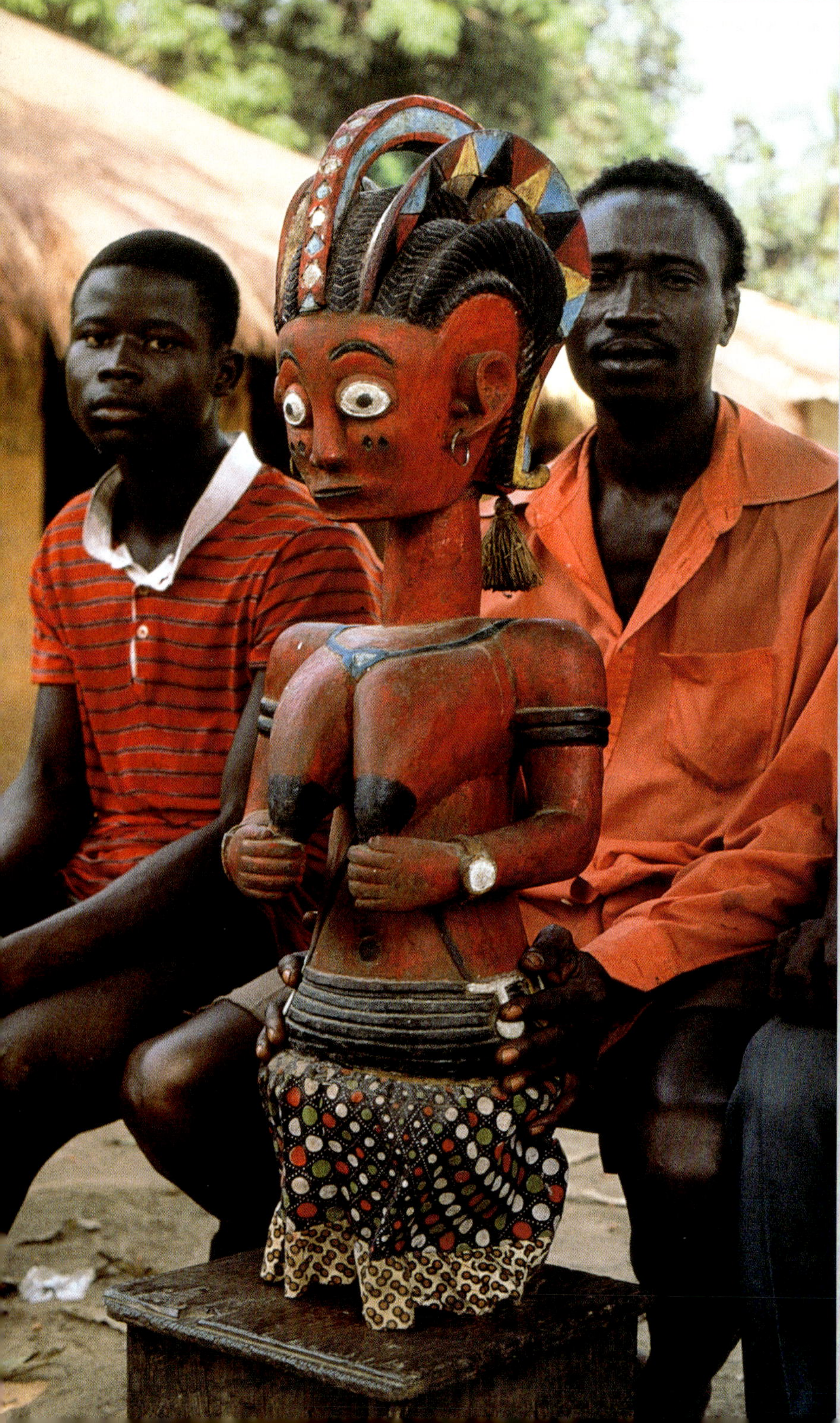

Signal Headdress in Daylight. Baga Sitem, Guinea
Photo: Frederick John Lamp, 1987

Dance of Signal at Night. Baga Sitem, Guinea
Photo: Frederick John Lamp, 1992

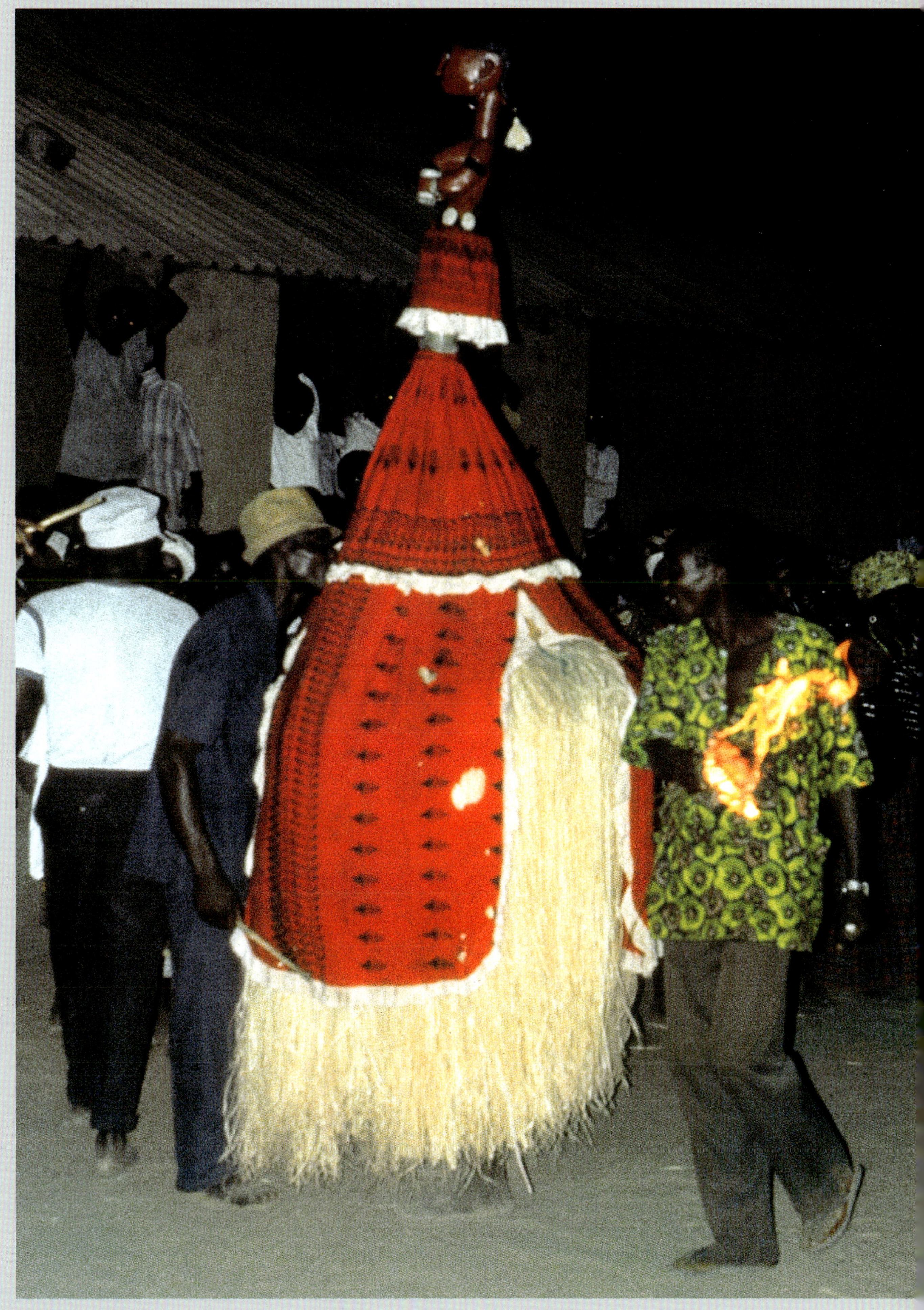

53

Sun, Fire, and Variations on Womanhood: a Baga/Buluñits Mask (*D'mba*)

Dance Mask with Superstructure (*D'mba*)
Baga/Buluñits perhaps Monchon village, Guinea
c. Late 19th–mid-20th century
Wood, metal, H. 125 cm
Gift of Alan Wurtzburger, Baltimore
BMA 1957.97 (purchased from J. J. Klejman, New York)

D'mba represents the best in humankind, characterized by the dressed bust of a mature woman with flat pendant breasts. The ideal of femininity is expressed in her unquestionable comportment, her vigorous, yet elegant movement, her refinement of coiffure, cosmetics, adornment, and dress, and the evidence, in her breasts, of her selfless devotion to the nurturing of children. In performance (danced by a young man), she would appear primarily at weddings, funerals, planting rituals, harvest festivals, and ceremonies of hospitality. She would be surrounded by members of her clan group, a circle of men immediately around her, and a wider circle of women beyond them, all within a dance space surrounded by the rest of the villagers. Her appearances ended generally in the 1950s because of a combination of Islamic, French colonial, and nationalistic pressures, but in the 1980s she experienced a limited revival in particular villages (Lamp 1996:154–181, 223–259).

In performance, the male dancer rests the underside of the mask superstructure on his own head, with a headpad to soften the weight. The superstructure towers above, with a costume of dark indigo cloth draped over the wooden shoulders but exposing the breasts, and a bulky palm-fiber skirt is suspended from the dancer's waist, attached to the wooden legs. In some cases in the past, D'mba's ears were adorned with a U-shaped wooden ornament, painted in bright colors, with triangular designs. The dancer inside, who is all but invisible to the crowd (except for his feet and calves), holds the mask by the front legs, and looks through the small holes pierced between the breasts.

D'mba dances only in the daytime, under the brilliant sun of the dry season, from early morning to late afternoon. Perhaps the reason lies in an iconic association of D'mba with light.

In a ritual covering several days and nights, as most major rituals did in the past, if the songs and dances of D'mba were continued during the night, the men would carry lighted grass torches in the place of D'mba and would reproduce her movements. Bohumil Holas (1947:61) reported that, after the disappearance of the mask in particular villages at mid-century, people continued to perform the dances, with the carrying of a lighted torch in D'mbas place.

The association of torches with D'mba was so strong that her dance was prohibited during the time of most intense heat, in July–August, just before the rice harvest. It was at this time that the elders were in consultation with the ancestral spirits over the timing of the coming harvest. The prohibitions seem to form a class having to do with the dangers of fires igniting in the extreme heat when the rice fields were beginning to mature (Bangura 1972:68–61):

> No carrying of fire in the fields or along the paths.
> No gathering of dead twigs or dry grass.
> No pounding or splitting wood in the night.
> No dance of D'mba (although other masks and headdresses were permitted).

The identity of D'mba with the illumination of fire has to do with the brilliance of D'mba, polished to a black sheen for each performance, and studded with bright brass tacks—"black beauty glittering in the sunshine," as one Baga consultant put it (Niane 1982:63). "To be brilliant, to shine," is expressed by the word *yamba* in the Susu language (Lacan 1942:396), and could be the origin of Yamban, the name for D'mba among the neighboring Pukur, who also use the mask.

Her performance in the bright sunlight is enhanced through the surface treatment of the mask. Accenting the black surface there are usually rows of flashy brass tacks delineating the lines of decoration on the face, neck, and breasts. For each new performance of D'mba, the mask would be blackened anew and polished with oil to a high sheen. Those masks in collections now bearing an eroded and bare wood surface, such as the BMA D'mba, must have been already withdrawn from service in the dance for some time, or perhaps were exposed to the elements in storage, before they were collected by runners and dealers.

The dance of D'mba cannot be fully understood without the dance of her antithesis, *D'mba-da-Tshol*. As D'mba is the epitome of beauty, comportment, and devotion, so D'mba-da-Tshol is the image of all that can go wrong with human nature. She is represented by a small, grotesque, female bust headdress often with a bulbous forehead, single eye, single ear, crooked nose, twisted mouth, jutting jaw, and single breast. Her costume is a disheveled mess of straw, grass, raffia, old banana leaves, and dirty rags. Her dance is chaotic, with dissonant music, and wildly aggressive movement. D'mba-da-Tshol is the D'mba of the elder men, bearing more volatile power than D'mba in her role as an agent of transformation, as signified in the meaning of her name, the "D'mba of Medicine." She dances at the funerals of male elders, and occasionally at weddings. Dancing alternately with D'mba, never at the same time, she provides an amusing, yet frightening counterbalance to the elegant and reassuring dance of D'mba.

The dance of D'mba begins with the appearance of a line of drummers dancing while beating their drums, in single file, followed by the D'mba dancer from behind a house, moving gradually to the central plaza. D'mba executes both sedate and vigorous steps, sometimes twirling, now pacing delicately, occasionally lying down completely on the ground, helped by assistants, and then standing up again. The crowd cheers wildly after D'mba floats around the perimeter of the circle, suddenly whirls around, and stops abruptly. According to consultants, some movements in the past were absolutely spectacular, such as dancing on top of the roofs of houses or on a couple of narrow tree trunks spanning a river, or lifting the massive mask high, twirling it above the head. The dancer had to be extremely muscular and agile as well, to perform such movements under the wooden mask that could weigh close to 100 pounds (the BMA example, in its eroded state, weighs 83 pounds).

Musical instruments include two different kinds of drums and a slit gong, and occasionally antelope horn trumpets. The drummers accompanying D'mba normally number four or five today, but a dozen, thirty, or forty was not uncommon in the past (*Voix*, VII, 9, 1932:14; XI, 11, 1936:3). *sɛñgbe*, is a large, cylindrical drum with a head at each end, connected by hide cords. It has a low musical pitch, and is slung from the shoulder to hang at the thighs by a cord, and beaten with a single, straight baton. In contrast, one

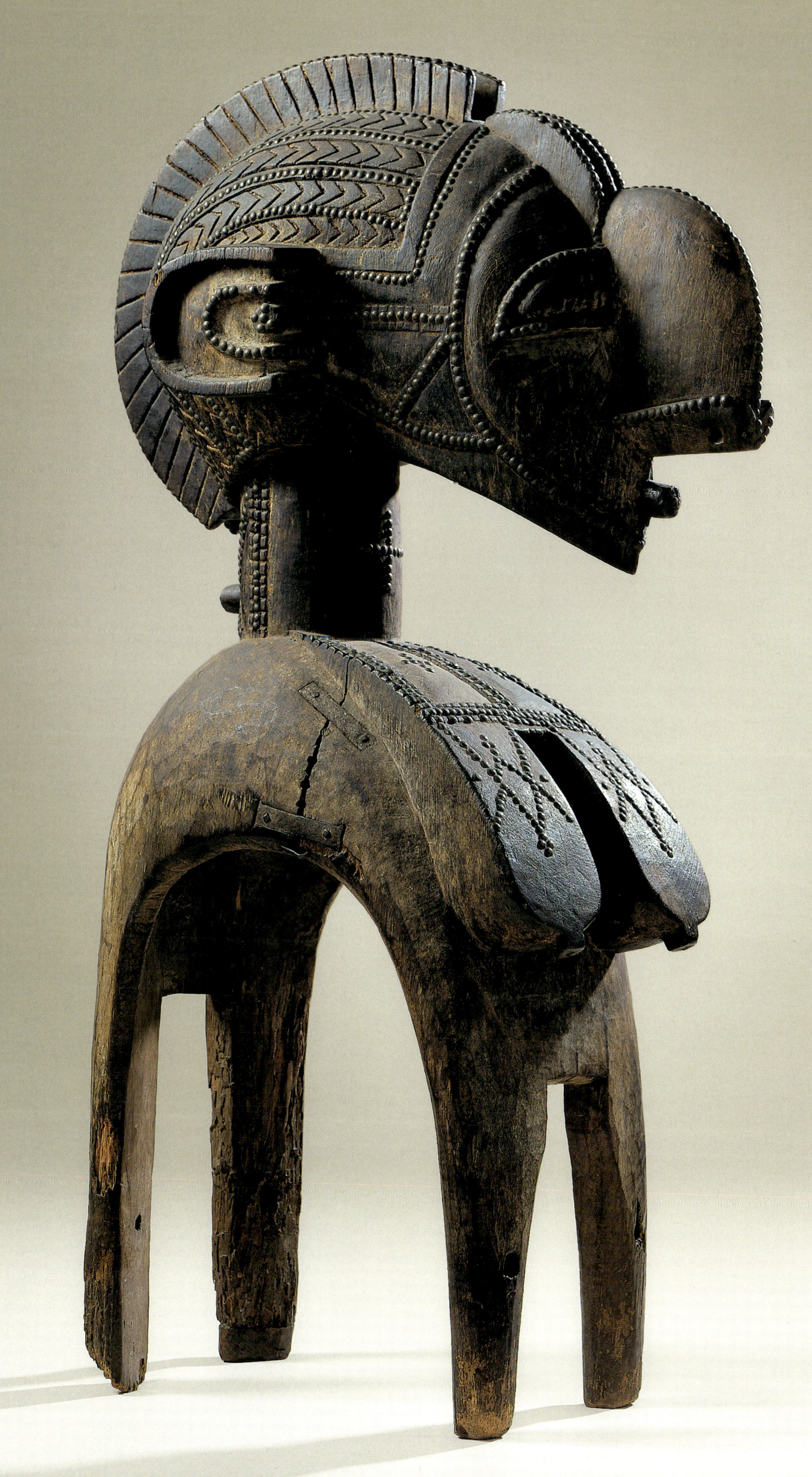

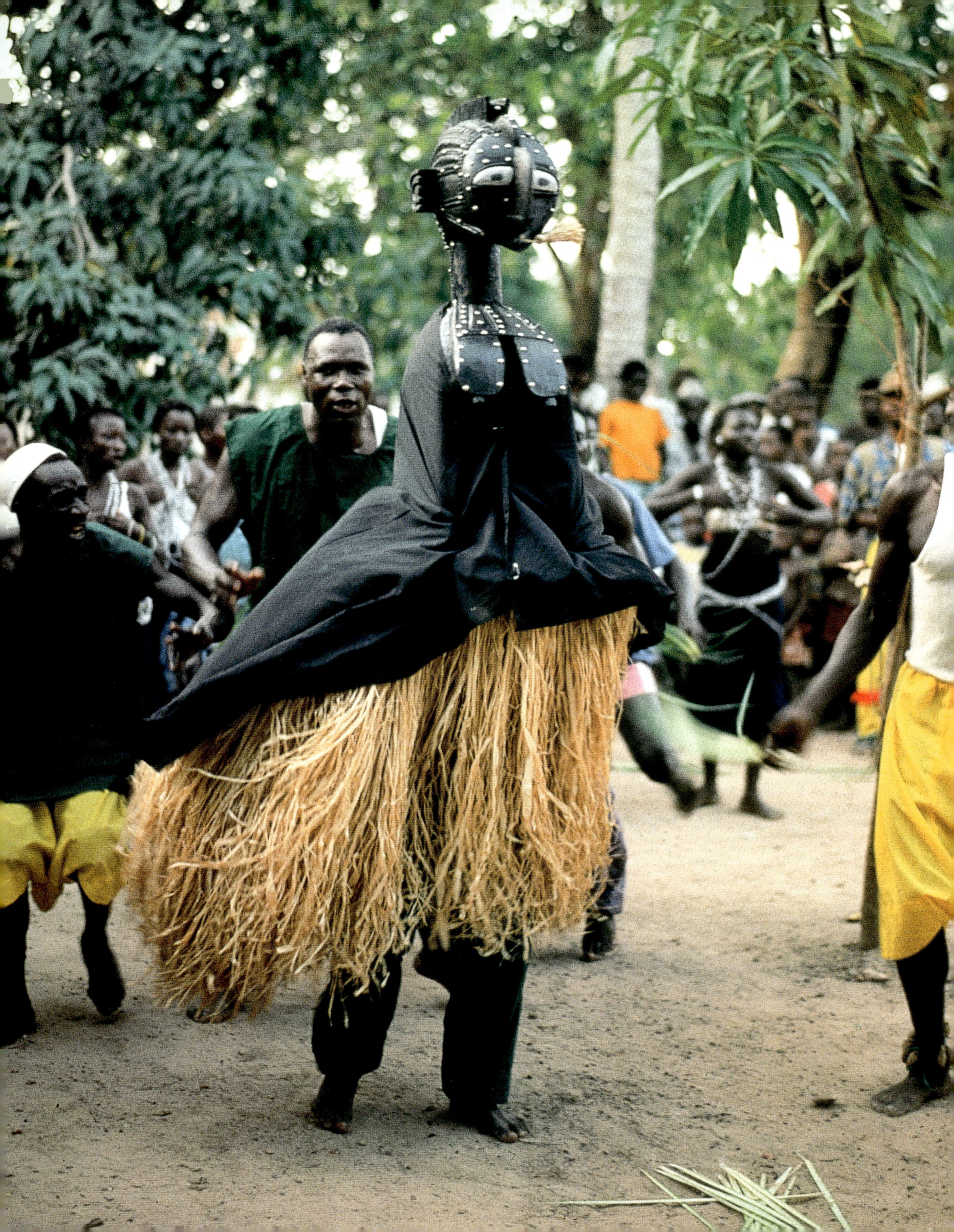

Dance of D'mba. Baga Sitem, Guinea. Photo: Frederick John Lamp, 1990

Dance of D'mba-da-Tshol. Baga Sitem, Guinea. Photo: Frederick John Lamp, 1987

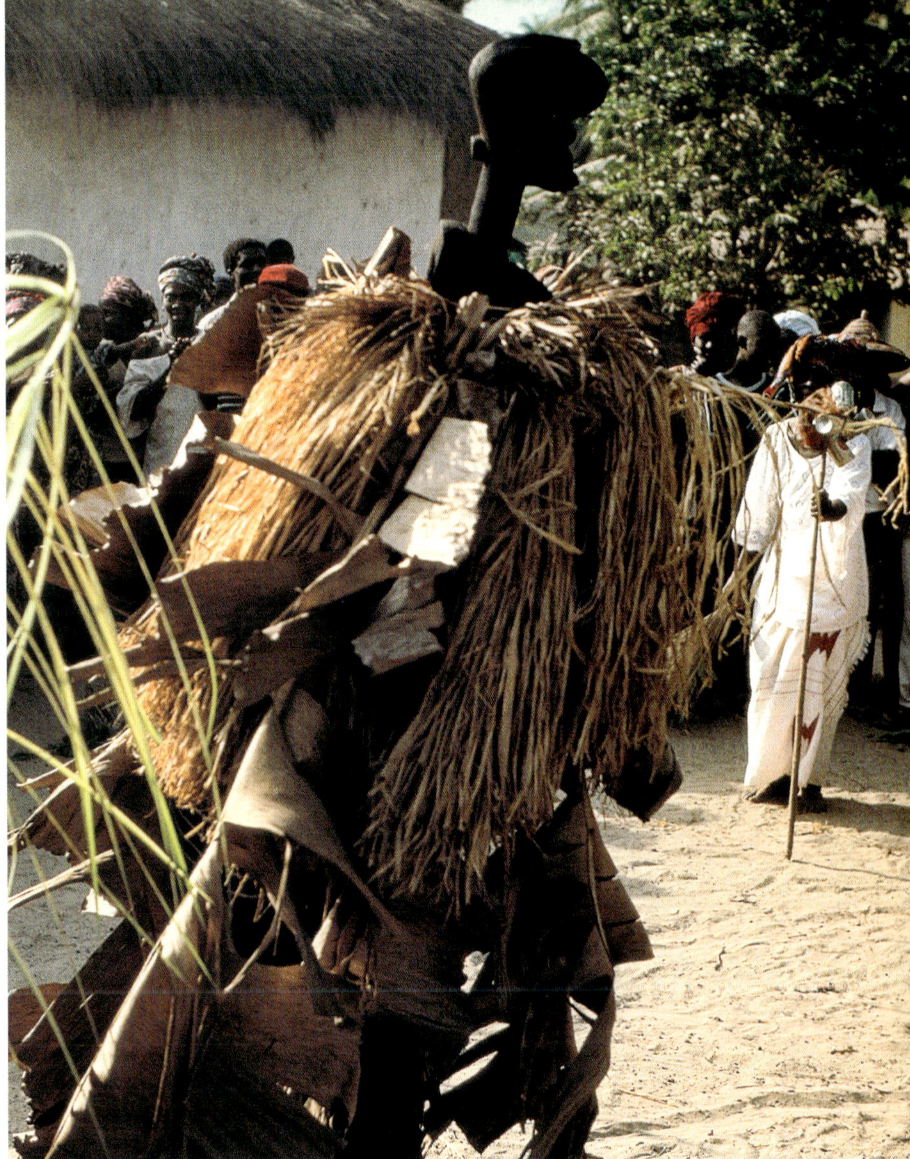

or two drummers follow the others, using a small, single-headed or double-headed drum, *te-señgbe*, with a much higher musical pitch, beaten with a straight or curved stick. Behind the drummers' waists a cluster of metal bells is hung, and metal castanets (*sanda*) are hung at the ankles. The drummers perform a dance in synchronization, first facing inward toward the circle for one or two measures, then turning to face outward for the same number of measures, and periodically reversing their progression of movement clockwise from counterclockwise. Foot patterns follow a counterpoint to the rhythm, e.g. on every second note.

A study of the drumming in five different Baga Sitemu villages has been made by Daniel Treviño (personal communication, 1998), a drummer who trained in Guinea, using my audio- and videotapes made in 1987. He has categorized the rhythm in Western musical notation as a 12/8 time signature:

> A measure (bar) consists of 12 notes, organized in four groups of 3. The main pulse, or downbeat, occurs on the first note of each 3 notes ... [as in] "Hickory dickory dock...." The first two words of this rhyme have three syllables each ... [each] equivalent to one note, making each word three notes long. Stringing together four words "hickory dickory hickory dickory," results in 4 groups of 3, or 12 syllables (notes) total ..., the downbeat or pulse of this 4-word sentence is represented by the hic- and dic- syllables (notes). The second and third syllables (notes) of each word can be referred to as "upbeats." Thus in this example, a downbeat is followed by two upbeats....
>
> The small drum or slit gong provided the reference tempo ... 120 ±5 beats/min., without any variation in pattern [except in one village].... The small drum usually provided only upbeats, resulting in a rhythmic pattern which left the downbeats to be played (or not played, according to the variation) by the cylindrical drums.... No two villages played the same pattern on the cylindrical drums. In fact, the recordings from three of the villages ... also revealed two or three variations within each village.

Today, the dance normally takes place in the large central village plaza within a circle formed by all the villagers. In the past, the space of the principal dance was the plaza in the center of a circle of houses belonging to the specific clan owning the D'mba. Routes of procession also spread throughout the village so that each clan could display its dancing to each other clan. Normally a village had two to five clans, each owning a D'mba, and each reserving a special sacred grove with a particular point of entrance into the village at the site of the clan quarters. D'mba would pause at particular points in traversing the village to pay homage to certain elders. On occasion, a clan might travel on foot with its D'mba to a neighboring village to demonstrate their virtuosity.

In dance, the crowd of men and women take an active part in giving homage to D'mba. Onlooking men (and sometimes women) frequently slap D'mba's breasts in an affirmation of her fecund durability and in homage to her nurturing power. This was said also to endow the actor with fecundity (Boris Kegel-Konietzko, personal communication, 1983). Women sing the songs, which men join only in the chorus. Women carry fans, long staffs hung with rattles, branches with leaves, or fly whisks. Women throw rice at D'mba. One particular woman, in the past, was charged with the task of following D'mba and collecting all the stray pieces of raffia that might fall from her costume, and she would also monitor the energy level of the D'mba dancer (Bangura 1972:53). Sick children could be thrown over top of D'mba from one relative to another in order to bring about a cure (Niane 1982:63).

Songs lyrics often carry social admonitions, in a metaphorical frame that to the outsider may seem ambiguous. Some of these admonitions can be summarized as follows: Don't be obstinate when taking part in a court case, respect your in-laws, don't be duplicitous in politics, don't be vain and boastful (see Sound, Music, and Spirit, p. 94) don't gossip, don't listen to rumors, show respect for the dead, and perform your ancestral ritual. Others relate to personal and family problems: The demise of a family due to feuds, death due to witchcraft, the need for the clan to back its leading elder, the lack of hospitality. Some have to do with D'mba: An appeal for a new house to shelter D'mba, with the coming of the rains, or an appeal to the elders for permission to dance.

Frederick John Lamp

54

We Cannot Live Without Such Beautiful Things: Weaving Heddle Pulleys

The loom used for West African narrow-strip weaving generally consists of a frame of three or four posts sunk into the ground to form a triangular or rectangular enclosure, connected by horizontal supports. The weaver sits inside the frame. In front of the weaver just below his waist is a cross bar known as the breast beam or belly stick. It is on this stick that the beginning of the warp threads (lengthwise threads) are attached. The warp extends out in front of the weaver often several meters beyond the front of the loom, where they are tied to a wooden frame and anchored by a stone in order to keep the threads taut.

Weaving Heddle Pulleys Ornamented with (shown from left to right) a Mask, a Bird, a Human Face, and Double Human Figures
137–138) Senufo, Ivory Coast/Burkina Faso/Mali
140) Baule, Ivory Coast;
141) Dogon, Mali
c. Late 19th–early 20th century
Wood, H. 16 cm; 7.2 cm; 8.9 cm; 16.6 cm
Gift of Howard and Jane Cohen, Baltimore
BMA 1995.137, .138, .140, .141

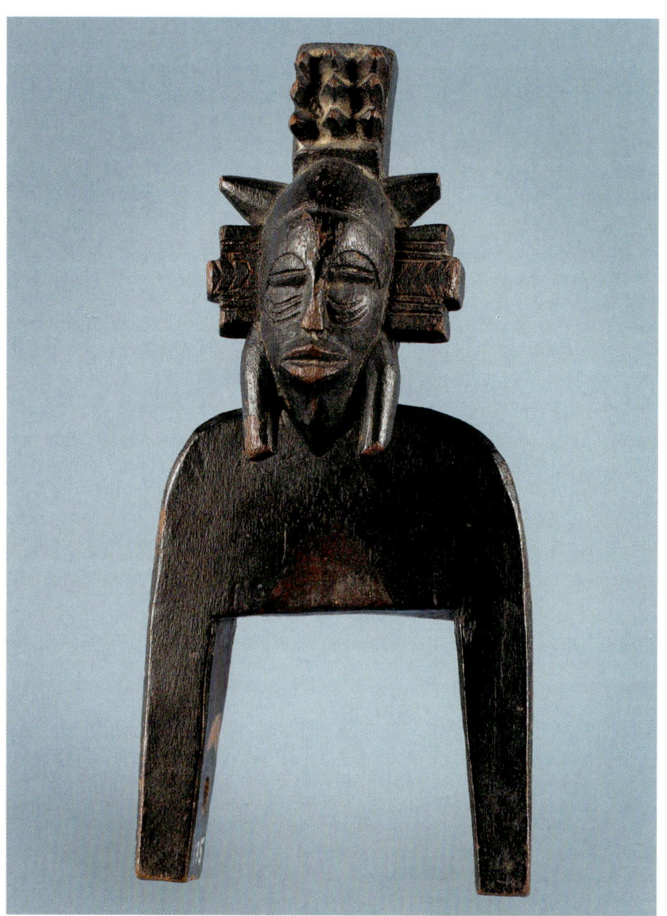

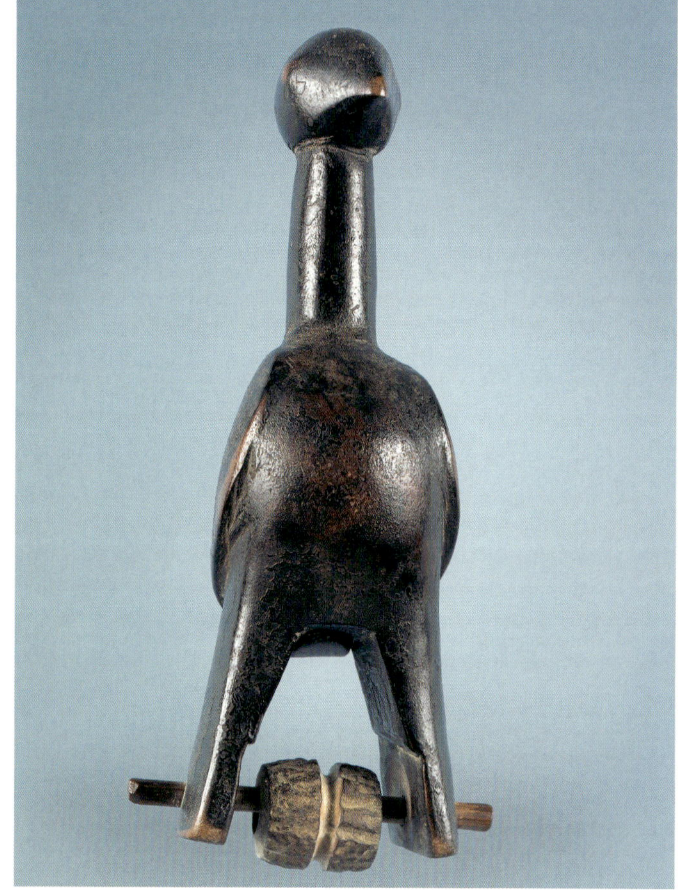

From the bar crossing over the top of the loom, the pulley hangs down just above the weaver's face. A cord passes over the pulley's spool: its two ends are attached to harnesses. Each harness consists of two horizontal bars about seven inches long joined by a series of vertical threads known as the heddles. Each of the heddles is looped in the middle, and through those loops the warp threads pass, divided alternately between the two harnesses. The harnesses are attached to foot pedals below. By depressing one of the foot peddles, a harness lowers one set of warp threads and raises the other, leaving a space between the two sets of warp threads and permitting a wooden sword or shuttle to pass through, carrying the weft or crosswise threads. As the strip is woven, it is wound around the breast beam. The many varieties of looms have been described by Alistair and Venice Lamb (1975). Pulleys with representational carving largely went out of use by the last quarter of the twentieth century.

African art tends to be utilitarian and, conversely, utilitarian objects have often been given the attention worthy of art. Combs, utensils, headrests, weights for measuring gold dust, weapons, and even the heddle pulleys or bobbins used on hand looms for the weaving of textiles were often carved in the shape of living beings, ancestral beings, and spirit masks or decorated with symbolic or abstract designs. Most weavers today insist that the decorated pulley did not represent a spiritual power (Boyer 1993, Förster 1998, Vogel 1997), even when it depicts a sacred mask, but was displayed simply for pleasure, both formally and even kinesthetically. "Each sweep of the shuttle turned the pulley head charmingly from side to side, as if it was shaking its head at the weaver" (Vogel 1997:272). Han Himmelheber (1960) once asked a carver of the Guro people of the Ivory Coast why they insisted on creating such intricately carved wooden pulleys for their looms when a simple cord would do. The carver replied: "We cannot live without such beautiful things."

Vogel (1997:272) makes an important distinction between sacred objects depicted on pulleys and the sacred objects themselves, in terms of access. Human figures, masks, and emblems of the ceremonial societies often are exclusive, not meant to be seen by the general public—at least on any regular basis—and sometimes are essentially inaccessible to the normal person, often kept and used in relative darkness. The pulley, on the other hand, is on display, in the bright daylight sun, as the weaver generally works outdoors. People often gather around to admire his work, and to spend time chatting. If a decorated pulley is used, it can be seen closely and contemplated, as one would view a piece of sculpture in a garden. The Baule use terms like *nyin* (gaze), in phrases such as "to look fixedly, to take a good long look," "to give a real stare, to get a proper look," when they talk about looking at pulleys and other ornamented utilitarian objects, but never in reference to ritual art. Perhaps because of this, such miniature utilitarian objects are often more finely carved than are the ritual objects they mimic. They are meant to be highly visible, open, observed under bright light.

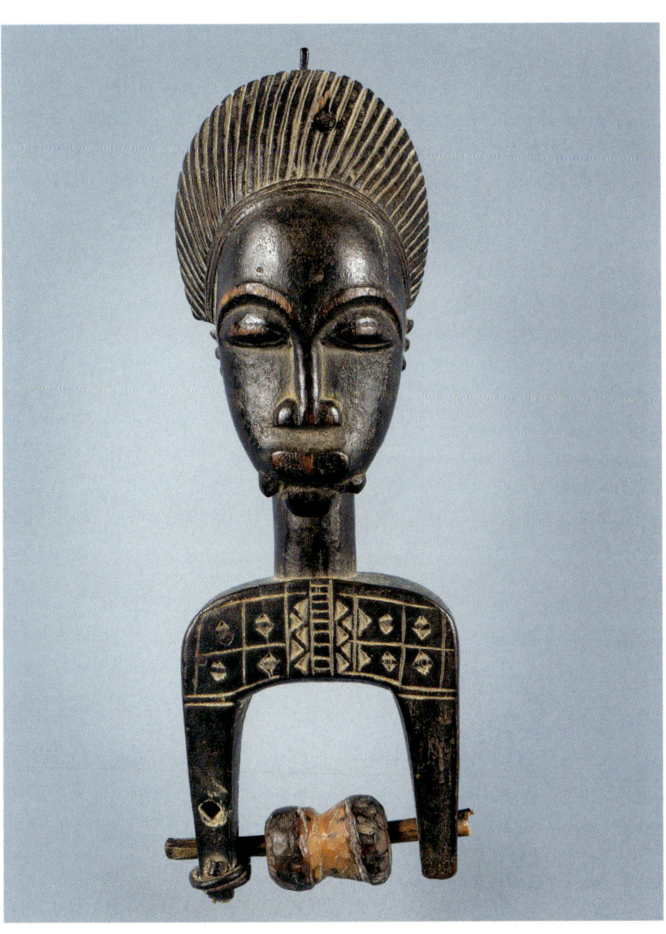

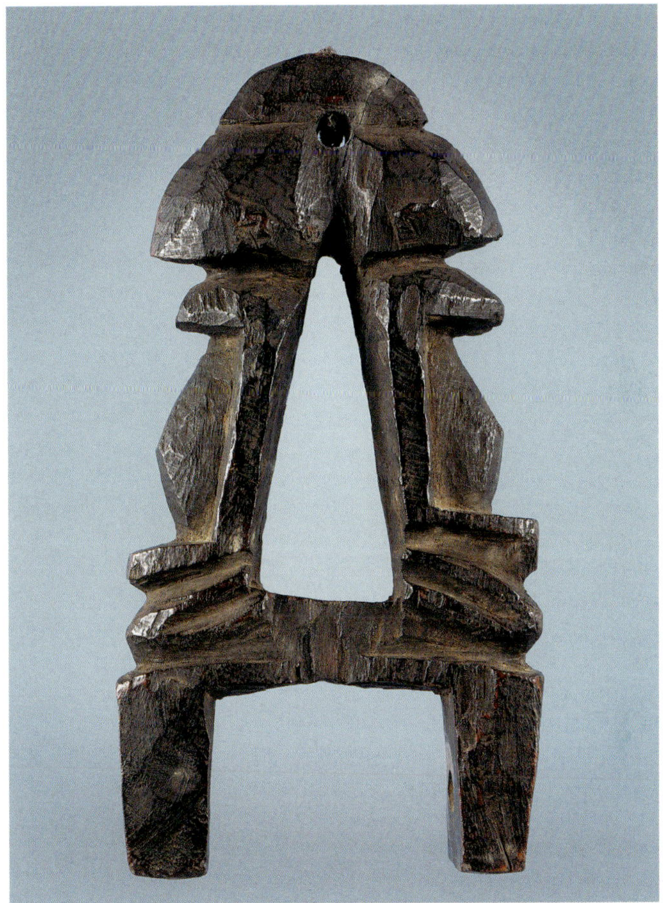

At the same time, pulley forms evolve from communal sets of knowledge and reverence that the weaver would share. Spiritual conceptions of gods, ancestors, or forces within given religious groups are not necessarily bound to one particular mode, such as a dance mask, or a carried charm, but may be interpreted in different forms by believers with different interests and occupations. The sacred *nommos* or primordial ancestors, of the Dogon, for example, are carved on their doors and house posts, on dance headdresses, ritual figures, and loom pulleys. They also may be recalled in folk stories recounted by aged minstrels, or invoked in the choreography of traditional dance. The ancestor representation found in clan masks of the Senufo *Pòrò* society, and the *Porpianong*, primordial animal and symbol of gestation for the neophyte males during their period of rebirth as adults, certainly bear important, personal, emotive meaning to the Senufo weaver that they would not bear for outsiders. It seems reasonable to assume that some "inspiration" was given to the weaver as he worked, observing, all the while, his representational pulley bearing such strongly spiritual associations. The spiritual resources developed by weavers are discussed with no one. The weaver is reluctant to reveal the symbolic meaning of the pulley, and frequently, a most treasured pulley will not even be used on the weaver's loom, but will be kept in a secret place while he uses an ordinary, unornamented pulley on the loom itself, according to Bobbo Ahiagble, an Ewe weaver from Ghana (in personal communication, 1975). Ahiagble explained how pulleys can have meaning:

> The figures on the pulleys relate to the personal experiences of the weaver and his family. If, for example, a weaver moves his family and household paraphenalia from one compound to another using a mule to transport them, he may have a pulley carved depicting that image.

This pulley serves as a reminder of the event and is kept in the family to be used as a mnemonic device in passing the information from one generation to the next.

If a weaver achieves prominence through his work, he affects his community favorably, and a portrait pulley may be carved in his honor after he dies. Although the portrait does not necessarily bear a likeness to its model, certain typical features might reveal his identity. Bobbo Ahiagble said, "If I bring honor to my name, a member of my family may have a pulley carved after my death. The pulley may be called 'Bobbo' or 'Father of Weavers' or any such name."

As he weaves, a weaver might sing a song related to the pulley he sees in front of him, for example, a song that Ahiagble recalled that refers to a pulley carved in the form of a horse and rider, referring to symbols of beauty, skill, and status:

Man's Wrapper
Ewe, Togo
c. Mid-20th century
Cotton, L. 300 cm
Gift of Russell L. Wade, Washington, D.C.
BMA 1999.751

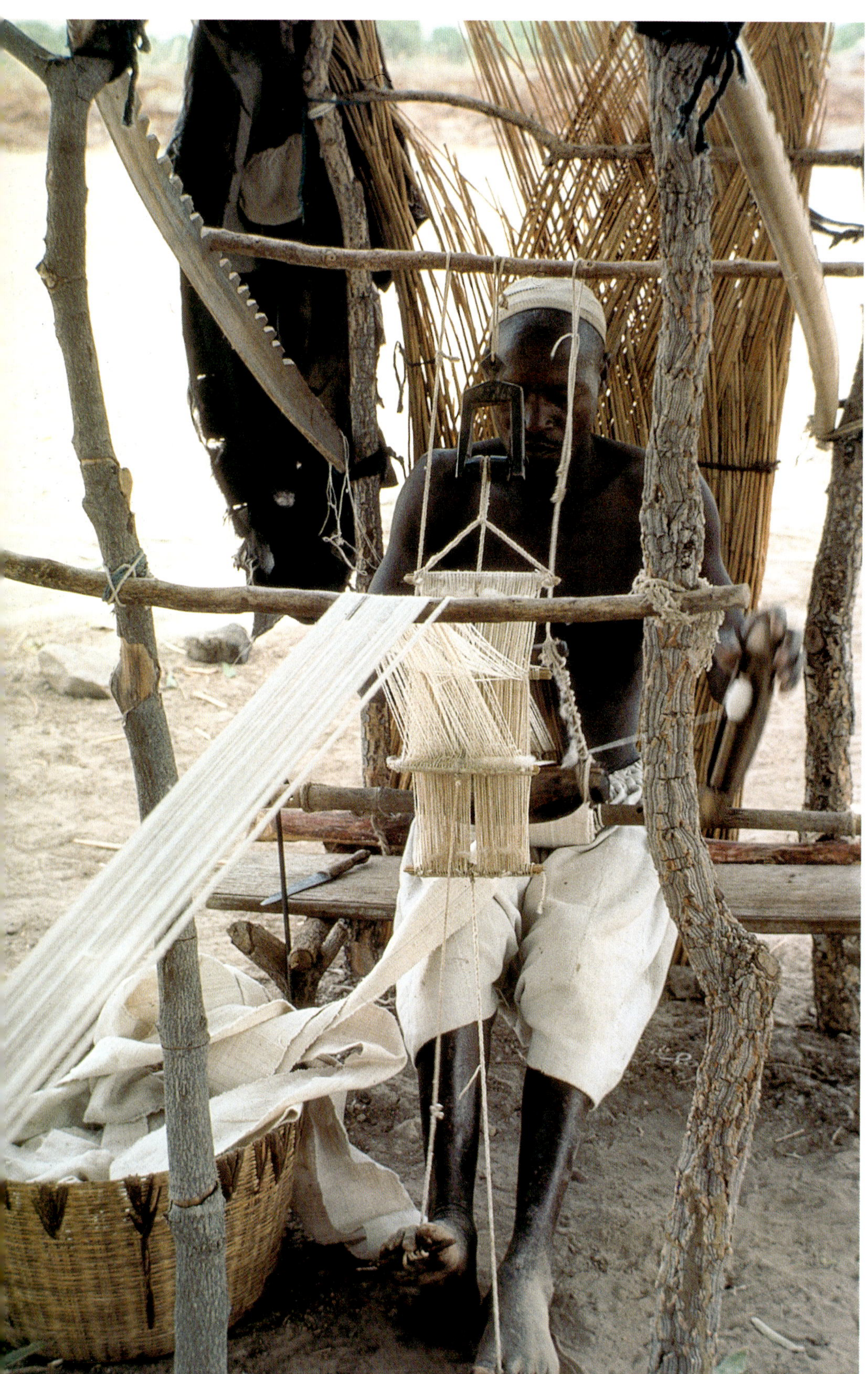

Bamana Weaver. Gao village (Koulikoro area), Mali
Photo: Frederick John Lamp, 1976

> Look at my eyebrows.
> They actually completely cover my eyes.
> I can sing like a bird.
> Look at me—I am wearing shoes and riding
> a horse.
> Who feels he can challenge me?

Birds are common figures on pulleys from the Ivory Coast. The Ewe term for "pulley" is simply "bird" (*xevi*) in reference to the similarity between the nest of the bird and the weaving loom apparatus. The concept relates to Yoruba practice where a pulley of purely functional design may be suspended from a tree branch to the loom, so that tree spirits may descend upon the weaver as he works (Ahiagble, personal communication, 1978). Birds, like pulleys, throughout West Africa, are thought to convey spiritual messages to humankind.

One of these pulleys is carved with a miniature *Kodòli-yèhè* mask like those used among the Fono Senufo of the Ivory Coast. The face mask represents a beautiful woman, and belongs to the blacksmith's class, employed by the junior grade of *Pòrò* in their initiation process. At a funeral for a Pòrò member, the mask is performed to provide entertainment in a climactic buildup of events just before burial, in the all-night watch after burial, and during second burial festivals. This is not an exclusive mask, and may be seen in performance by anyone (Förster 1988:29–32; Glaze 1981:125–131, 210–11).

The Dogon pulley, from Mali, with back-to-back figures recalls the original ancestors of the Dogon and their common legacy in bringing gifts to humankind from God. Each of the eight *nommo* was dual-sexed, with either the male or the female element dominant. In their procreative union, the eight nommo sometimes appear as only four individuals, but they also appear as couples joined back to back.

"The loom is a holy place," said Bobbo Ahiagble (personal communication, 1975). It is a shelter for the weaver which women and children are forbidden to enter. If an Ewe child should accidentally fall into the loom's shelter, a sacrifice of a ram must be made to cleanse the shrine through ritual. When

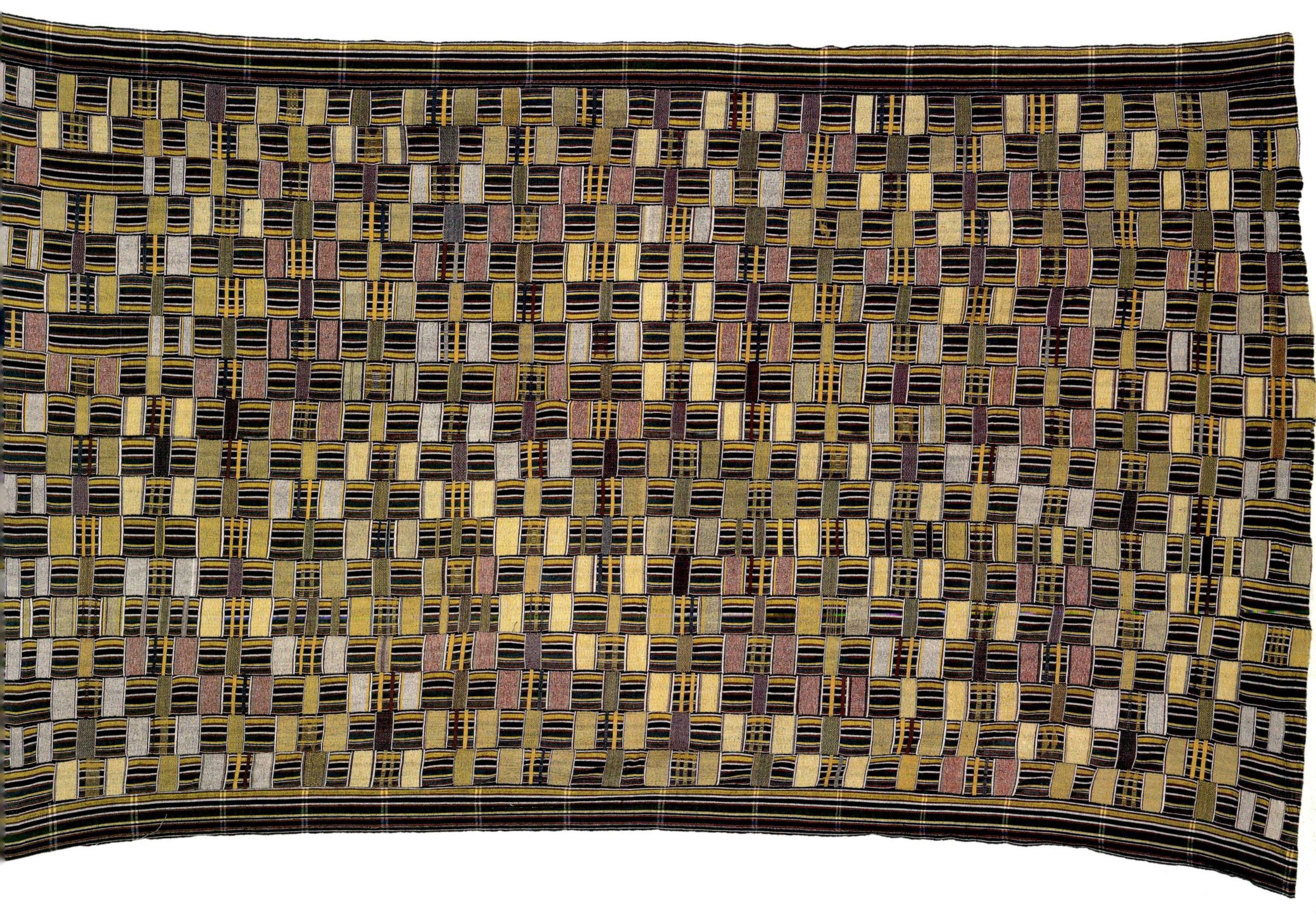

the child reaches adulthood and is finally permitted to sit in the large loom and weave, he is emotionally moved by the honor. Rattray (1927:234) recounted elaborate rituals of purification and sacrifice before an Asante weaver could sit within the loom. An old Asante loom must not be broken, burned, or have any of its parts used as a weapon to strike another. If accidently broken, a fowl must be sacrificed.

The Dogon sage, Ogotemmeli (in Griaule 1972), had a particular view of Dogon spiritual origins, which may or may not have been shared by his compatriots, or by weavers themselves, but he saw weaving, the loom, and the pulley, in a cosmic light. In his view, the seventh being, or nommo, brought the gifts of the spoken word and the woven cloth. As he spoke the word, he spat out eighty threads of cotton which were distributed between his upper teeth and eight more threads from between his lower teeth, constituting the alternating threads of the warp. A stud in his nose served as a moveable pulley and a stud in his lower lip served as the shuttle to which were attached the threads of the weft. By opening and closing his jaws, he alternately separated the warp threads, and with the top tips of his forked tongue the nommo pushed the shuttle back and forth. As he emitted the spoken word it was woven into the thread and formed in the cloth.

This linguistic relationship between text and textile is found in African and European languages. According to Ogotemmeli, *soy*, meaning "cloth" and "word" is also the number "seven," which represents the unity of spiritual forces and man's daily existence. "The word is in the sound of the pulley and the shuttle. The name of the pulley means 'creaking of the word.'" As the weaver works, the bright sight and sound of the pulley, hanging just above his work in the clear sky, remind him of the nommo's dual gift. It is a rather wonderful image, which may have been simply the intellectual vision of one African philosopher.

Frederick John Lamp

The Hidden Power of Status: a Kwele Currency Piece (*Zong*)

Currency Piece (*Zong*)
Kwele (western), Congo (Brazzaville)
c. 18th–19th century
Iron, camwood, H. 51.3 cm
Purchased in Honor of Burton "Buddy" Rosen with funds contributed by his Friends.
BMA 1999.174 (purchased from Mona Gavigan, Gallery Affrica, Washington D.C., in 1999)

There may be a certain irony in the fact that African iron currency pieces such as this were a favorite of the modern artist, Henri Matisse, who copied their forms in two dimensions. In the early twentieth-century, French traders adapted the form of the Kwele currency piece, *zong*, in the production of flat forms cut from German-made sheet iron, resembling an anchor, a well-known emblem of colonial power, which they, in turn, distributed for use by the Kwele in trading, and which went by the term *mondjos*. The traders preferred the use of their own currency, by which they could control exchange rates, to the standard coinage that was introduced and promoted by the French colonial government. None of these European-made pieces appear to be extant today, as the Kwele, in a further twist, appropriated them by forging somewhat irregular ridges down the middle, in recollection of the earlier zong, and twisting and forging the points of the anchor blade to form "ears," creating a newer, hand-crafted, less regular form of Kwele currency called *mandjong*. Their adaptation offers a clue to the formal intention of the *zong* (Dupre 1995).

Kwele consultants told Dupre (1995:87–88) that the form of the twentieth-century mandjong is a zoomorphic abstraction, with a head, long extended ears, a chest and body, ending below in a tail. Alternatively it was interpreted as a knife blade with other blades and razors attached at its tip. The same interpretation might apply to its prototype, the nineteenth-century zong. Some scholars, following the zoomorphic or humanoid interpretation, see a similarity between the "head" with bilateral projections and a style of Kwele mask that conventionally has long, arching, horn-like projections on either side.

Two hundred Zande and Mobenge currency blades displayed in a marriage settlement. Congo (Kinshasa). Photo: H. Goldstein, 1952. ©Africa-Museum (Tervuren, Belgium)

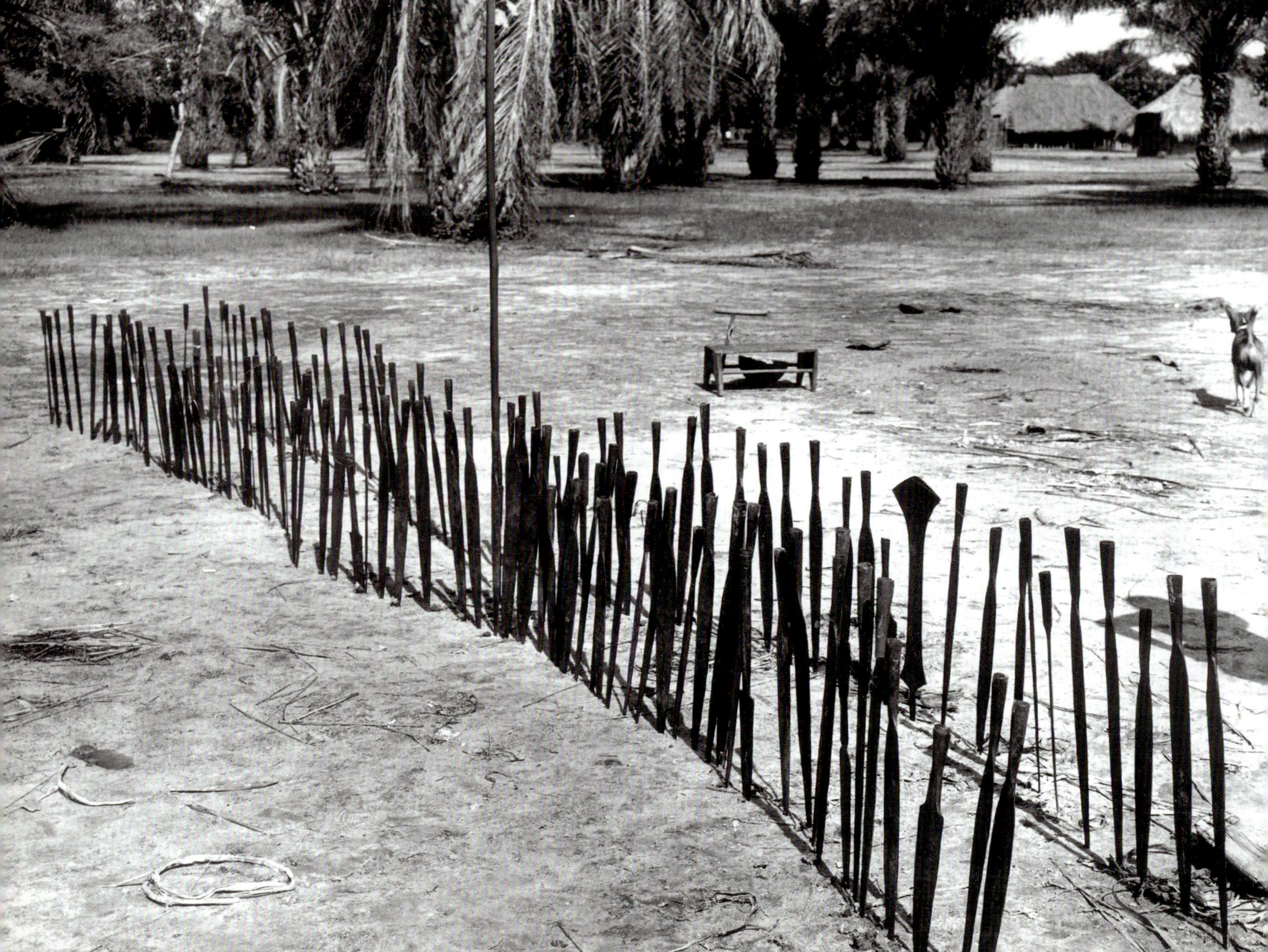

These iron currency pieces were used by wealthy families and chiefs through the mid-twentieth century in exchange, only among a small group of western Kwele, usually as an offering from the family of the groom to the family of a bride to secure their approval of the marriage. The giving of these gifts, which might also include prepared food, hunting dogs, poultry, mats, basketry, hunting nets, raffia- and bark-cloth clothing, elephant tusks, and a great number of other iron objects such as tools, weapons, bells, and jewelry, began before the marriage was formalized, and continued throughout the life of a married couple. Male relatives of the bride were the ones who determined what gifts should be given, based upon their own needs. The *mezong* (plural of *zong*) were usually presented in packets of ten, wrapped in fibers, and called *mbwanza emwas*, "the principal payment" (Dupre 1995:84–85).

Dupre (1995:85) has shown that the *zong* also actively signals status. Sometimes just a few mezong are given by the fiancé to the bride's family on his first visit, indicating his preference of exchange, or as the Kwele term it, *esumedo*, a word otherwise used to designate "a mark made on a forest that is to be cleared." At some time after the marriage, the new wife pays a visit back to her own family of birth. For the journey, she is dressed in a civet-cat skin, and decorated with black pigment, and she bears a *zong* in each hand to proclaim her new status as a bride to everyone along the route.

Among some groups in Central Africa it has been documented that, at the formalizing of the marriage contract, the collection of currency pieces would be displayed for the guests to see (Blackmun & Hautelet 1990:38, plate 15), but this does not seem to have been the case among the Kwele. The goods given in exchange for marriage held value in storage, as savings. Metal objects such as this were often conserved in mud from the edge of a river that would tend to erode the surface of the iron, or they were carefully packaged and hidden away above the cooking fire, a most private, familial area, obscured from public view. It was the fact of their retention in darkness and visual inaccessibility that rendered them political instruments, actively maintaining contracts of marriage and social alignment (Dupre 1995:86).

F. J. L.

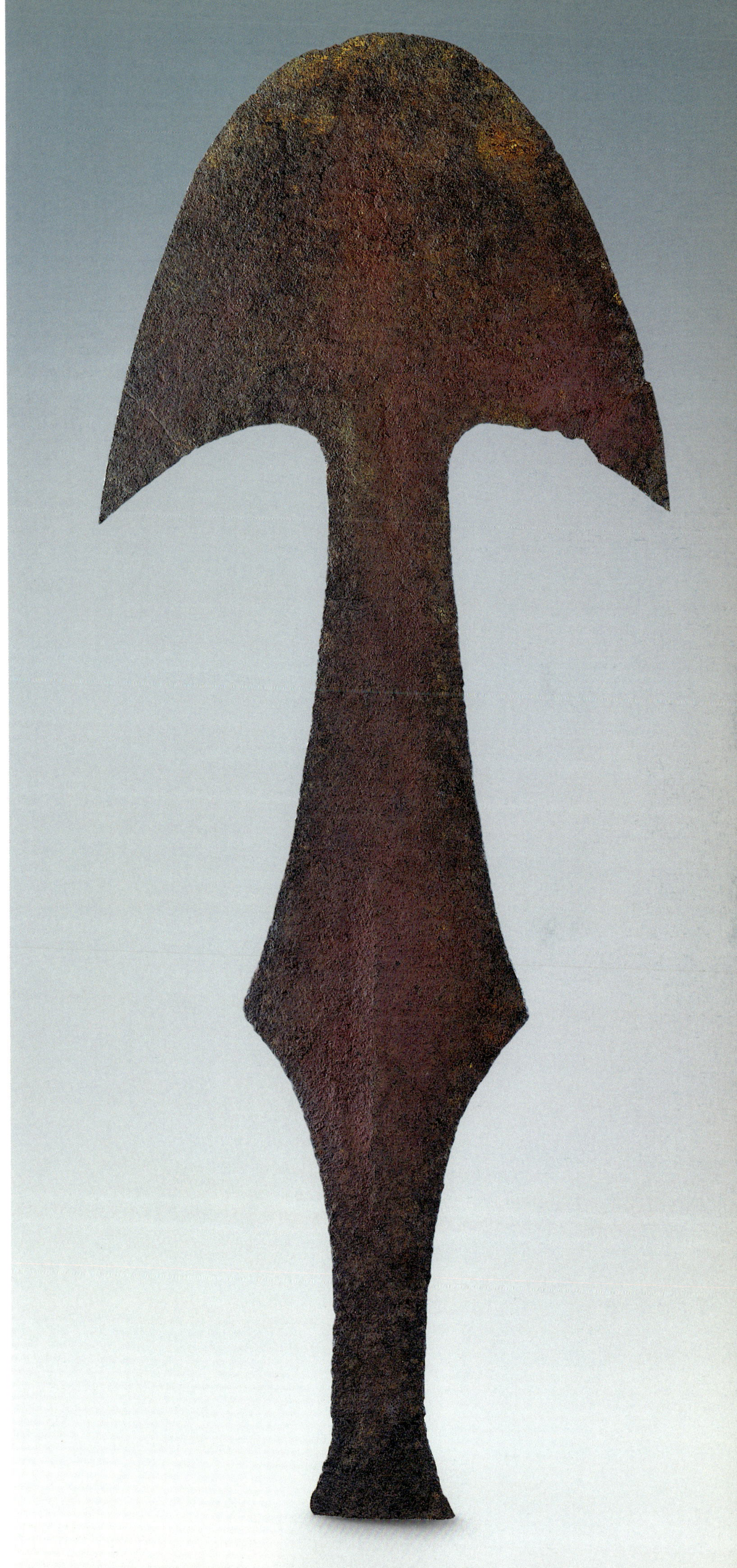

56

You Haven't Seen the Wild Beast: a Manding Headdress (*Kòmò Kun*)

Headdress: Head of Kòmò (*Kòmò Kun*)
Manding/Minianka, Mali/Guinea
Kòmò Association
c. Early 20th century
Wood, various animal horns, bird's skull, fiber, grasses, porcupine quills, encrustation, mirror, antelope horns (restoration), H. 36.9 cm
Gift of Robert and Mary Cumming, Baltimore
BMA 1983.79 (ex Harold Malt, Coconut Grove, Florida; ex Daniel Levandowski)

Blacksmiths, who make the beastly, "exquisitely horrific" Kòmò Kun, are a special class dispersed throughout the territory of the Manding and other neighboring groups (McNaughton 2001:175, 182). Because of their work with fire and iron, they are credited with the ability to harness and channel dangerous power for communal good. Only the blacksmiths may hold leadership titles in Kòmò and make the headdresses (McNaughton 1988:130), while those of the musicians class, the *jeliw*, are excluded (David Conrad, personal communication, 2001).

The headdress incorporates several forms, most prominently the head of a beast (*wara*), often cited as the hyena (McNaughton 1979:32), who figures in the narrative of Kòmò, for example, in the opening initiation ceremonies when the members chant: "The [boys entering initiation] are going to die, one after the other; the old hyena has called no one; welcome to all; let them be spoiled! Let them be shaped! Old hyena! Because you have called no one"—which is to say that the initiates have come to face the ordeals of Kòmò on their own volition and not at a command from the great hyena spirit who oversees Kòmò (Dieterlen & Cissé 1972:255). The hyena spirit or "the old hyena," alludes to the qualities of reason and intellectual capacity, and thus raison d'être. Testimonies given to Brett-Smith (1997) go further to suggest that the open jaws of a wild and frightening animal are only a metaphor for the headdress's real and esoteric identity as the forbidden and rapacious vagina which the boys will soon encounter after initiation.

The headdress is associated with the night in several ways. The hyena is a scavenger in the night. Dieterlen & Cissé (1972: 253–55) have described the annual Kòmò ceremonies, in which one of the songs performed has to do with "the divine, ancient hyena," here given the name, "jaturu":

> Black jaturu!
> Turn yourself around [dance].
> Son-in-law of the holder of the black gold! [i.e. profound knowledge]
> Turn yourself around [dance].

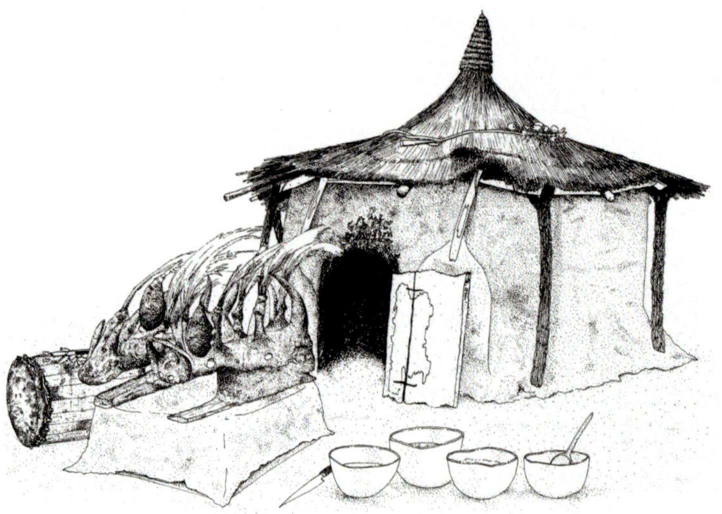

Here, the hyena of the night is revealed to be the word, or manifestation, of Faaro, the great serpent spirit of creation, who possesses the profound knowledge necessary to Kòmò. "Turnaround" (*i yelema*) suggests his capacity to transform himself into Faaro (David Conrad, pers. comm., 2001), and accompanying the sound, the initiates dance a zigzag movement suggesting that of the serpent.

Most data indicate that the Kòmò Kun was danced primarily during the night. Each headdress may have a personal name, and, although there are many names, one such name was recorded as "The Darkness of the Town Gwarankò" (Gwarankò-Dibi) (McNaughton 1979:30, 40). Dieterlen & Cissé (1972:277) recorded a ceremony in the darkness of night, in the obscurity of new moon, without the faintest firelight. But generally it was danced by the light of a great bonfire called "the fire of Kòmò" (p. 236–237). In the three extant field photographs, however, the Kòmò Kun dancers appear in daylight, and this confirms data in both McNaughton (1988) and the earlier work by Dieterlen and Cissé (1972). Two of these photographs may have been staged for the photographer (Hahner-Herzog, et al., 1997; Goldwater 1960). In Zahan (1974), the single Kòmò dancer is clearly with the initiation group in the wooded grove.

Acquisition of materials to apply to the headdress is personalized by the blacksmith creator, in the manner of a "recipe," so that no two blacksmiths' work would be the same or would function the same way. He searches for the right horns and quills, symbols of animal aggression, and emblems of the blacksmith's wisdom. He may dig a new well in order to obtain fresh unblemished water to produce medicines to attach. Herbs would be sought for particular effects, mixed by the smith, and reduced to desired forms. A chicken may be sacrificed to ensure success. The feathers of a vulture may be clustered at the top of the headdress. The resulting accumulation of materials is regarded as a *dalilu*, a prescribed combination of spiritually powerful items designed to effect a result (Dieterlen & Cissé 1972:48; McNaughton 1988:133).

The heavily encrusted surface of the headdress is produced by applying a mixture of black clay, leaves, powdered minerals, powdered bone, masticated millet, sacrificial blood, and possibly other undocumented materials. Periodic blood sacrifices enrich the encrustation. Germaine Dieterlen & her Bamana collaborator, Y. Cissé (1972:51), believed that these ingredients symbolized the order of the universe and were seen to reflect the humid matrix of creation and to effect human reproduction. A very old

Two masks displayed in front of a Kòmò shrine. Kòmò Association, Minianka, Mali. Sketch: Philippe Jespers

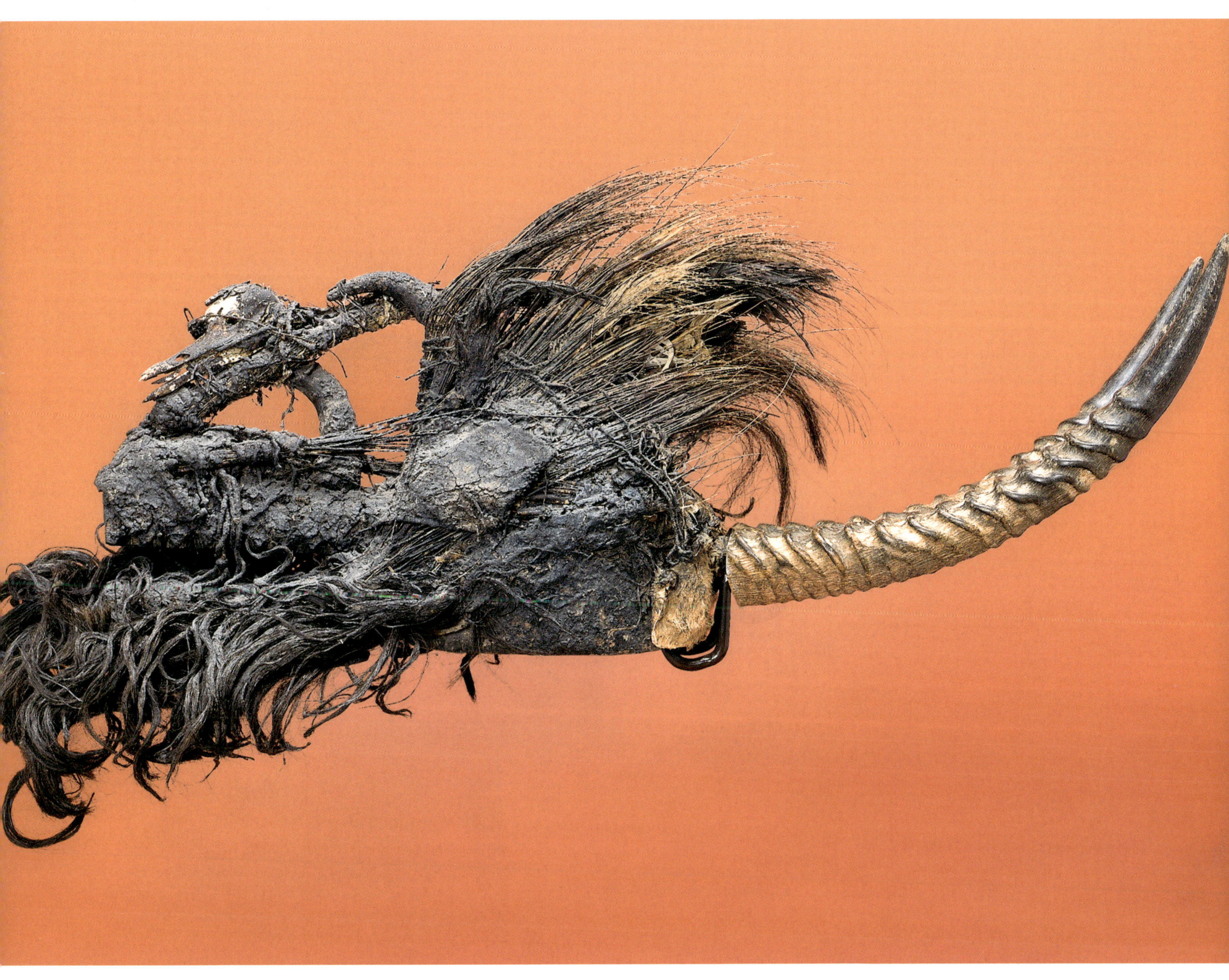

Kòmò headdress would have accumulated a spectacular array of added materials and thus would have acquired extraordinary power (*nyama*). The Manding compare old headdresses with new during Kòmò performances, with song lyrics such as: "... you've seen many Kòmò—You haven't seen the wild beast." (McNaughton 1988:135, 138).

The Kòmò headdress is concealed in extreme secrecy by Kòmò members, who are forbidden even to speak the name before uninitiated persons. The headdresses function not only as a dance headdresses but as shrine pieces, placed upon an altar upon which blood sacrifices are made. This has been described in detail by Philippe Jespers (1995:41–44) for the Minianka. On the path to the sacred forest to the west of the village lies a circular clearing whose entrance faces east to catch the first rays of the rising sun; this is the site of a small sacred house. Inside, on a platform, a number of headdresses are placed, "upon which one 'prays' and 'sacrifices' so that they always appear entirely covered with dense, coagulated coats of blood, giving them their deep black colour." The "things of Kòmò," are said to be alive and to "talk among themselves," which utterances are manifested in the appearance of cracks, coagulated blood, the slipping of parts, and other subtle signs of change in movement. Here, on the altar, the headdresses are referred to as "pieces of the body," and one addresses them as "you who go to the foundation."

Brett-Smith (1997:89) in her argument for a sexual reading of the headdress form, relates a report by Dieterlen that the initiate is forced to lick the headdress and the metal hooks that the masked dancer carries. The initiate swears that he will place Kòmò ahead of everything else in his life, even his father and mother. If the metaphor is correct, this would be a highly prohibited act, as cunnilingus, and even looking at the vagina, is forbidden to a man.

Thus in his transgression, the initiate is placed at the mercy and fully within the domain of Kòmò.

The costume of the Kòmò Kun, called the "sheath of Kòmò," consists of a loose cotton gown, gathered and sewn in accordion pleats. This cloth was customarily laid over a barrel-shaped wooden framework consisting of seven hoops. To the outside of the cloth gown, apparently sometimes pierced through and fixed to the wooden framework, are attached the large feathers of the vulture, or, in some areas, especially around Segou, the guinea fowl, chicken, or hornbill. The cloth gown, itself, in the case of some of the most sacred Kòmò headdresses, was said to have been sewn together with twenty-two bands of strip-woven cloth (Dieterlen & Cissé 1972:51–52; McNaughton 1979:31; McNaughton 1988:135–136). In addition, costumes are often covered with amulets, to heighten the spiritual power. So important are these attachments, that one of the names the Bamana give to the costume is "the largest amulet" (*sèbèn-den-kunbaba*) (McNaughton 1979:31).

When the headdresses were taken out of the shrine to dance, they are said by the Minianka to "rise," and one addresses them at this point as "you and the conversation." This refers to their relationship now to the sky and the source of prophetic speech (Jespers 1995:44, 51, 53). Before putting on the headdress, the dancer would hold it in his hand, saying, "I cannot carry the force of the world," referring to the composite elements of the headdress and to the complex of sacred signs symbolized by its feathered costume. Taking on the headdress and costume, the dancer is said to be "penetrated" by sacred knowledge. He trembles, enters into a trance, and ceases to be of this world. This trance possession lasts several hours, after which the dancer gives, in a muted, unintelligible voice, the "news of the universe" (Dieterlen & Cissé 1972:53–54).

As described by Jespers (1995:49–50), the costumed performers arrive at the entrance to the village, advancing with small steps, turning occasionally, descending into the village with "great majesty." Each dancer demonstrates his power through the theatrical acumen of his dance. Some may dance on stilts. Some claim the ability to spit fire, which would dramatically light up the night. Others spout water, or stamp on the ground forcing a fountain of water to spring from the spot (McNaughton 1988:142–143). The movement can be acrobatic and swift. The dancer may hoist the headdress up high at the end of a long stick thrust up through the costume (Henry 1910:148; McNaughton 1979:41; Monteil 1924:271). The tie formed by the headdress and its costume connecting earth and sky dictates that the dancer should never leave the ground, but should keep both feet on the ground, pressing down with knees slightly bent, but facing the sky with the headdress. When a pair of masked dancers approaches an initiate, they turn to each other and crouch down in perfect synchronization, spreading their huge costumes (Jespers 1995:50, 52).

The music of Kòmò included "dramatic and sometimes ominous or eerie drumming," using a variety of drums including the large *jembe* (McNaughton 2001:175). Charry (2000:8) calls it "threatening and private." A whistle, forged in iron or copper, would be held by the masked dancer and sounded throughout the dance. The whistle represented the whistling of the wind, "the voice of the cries of the wind," and its sounds ranged from the quietly melodic ("the voice of the murmur of the universe," i.e., birth) to the shrill ("the voice of the mourners, the cries of the universe," i.e., death) (Dieterlen & Cissé 1972:53, 272). The sound has been described also by Henry (1910:147) as a noise that freezes one with terror. Accompanying the dance, musicians would strike up a cacophony of sounds on cymbals, iron gongs, whistles, and trumpets, symbolizing, according to Dieterlen & Cissé (1972:237), "the children of the voice of God."

In 1949–50, inquiries undertaken by Germaine Dieterlen and Youssouf Cissé (1972:52–54, 215–217, 236–237, 252–255, 272–274, 277–282, 290–293) resulted in an elaborate account of the initiation, including the acts of the costumed dancer. Songs sung and orations given by the dancer have to do with invocations to Kòmò spirits ("good spirits of the birth givers of Komo"—p. 272), protection for children ("I will not let them [the sorcerers] 'eat' anyone's child today"—p. 277), and prayers for the dead ("Faaro is before you; Faaro is behind you ... This is your salute"—p. 290). McNaughton (1988:141) recorded a song in which the Kòmò masked dancer appears to offer comfort to the unfortunate and to warn the smug and privileged ("Fortunate slave [whose luck will change] do shut up [be patient], All mornings don't bleach the same way").

Accompanying the costumed performer is always the bard, or interpreter, and spiritual representative, who was known as the "Mouth of the Beast." The Kòmò performer speaks in a dramatic and unclear voice, and uses a kazoo-like voice disguiser. The sound has been described also by McNaughton (1979:33) as an extremely loud bellowing. For a new performance, he may compose new songs containing responses to questions previously put to him by those seeking his counsel. Following the song he may stop and speak to address the crowd. Whether singing or speaking, his voice is distorted: at times he would tremble, going into a trance while uttering unintelligible words. His words would then be rendered again in common language by his bard (Dieterlen & Cissé 1972:236–237; McNaughton 2001:175–176; 1979:39). Colleyn & Clippel (1998:144–147) transcribe an extensive song delivered by the costumed performer and translated by his assistant.

During Kòmò performances, all uninitiated persons must hide indoors. The exclusivity of the Kòmò dance and prohibition against spying in the night by non-initiated persons is expressed in a chant delivered by the masked dancer and repeated by the initiates, who have had a glimpse of the headdress in action just before dawn (Dieterlen & Cissé 1972:274):

> Behold Komo!
> One who is not permitted to see Komo,
> If he looks anyway
> And goes to recount this back at home!
> [Even] one who is at the end of his life would not recount this at home
> The Earth is lightened (Dawn breaks), and I have seen the Komo.

During one particular step of Kòmò initiation, the nineteenth, as reported by Dieterlen & Cissé (1972:236–37), the Kòmò Kun is said to appear in a series of acts. This step was entitled "children of the folded wings" (referring to the wings of the vulture). The Kòmò Kun headdress and costume was hoisted on its pole for the ceremony, and at one point the praise singer took up the chant of Kòmò, referring to the sacred vulture, curiously, by a man's given name, Zan (or Nzan), and emphasizing how powerful his descent (Dieterlen & Cissé 1972:237):

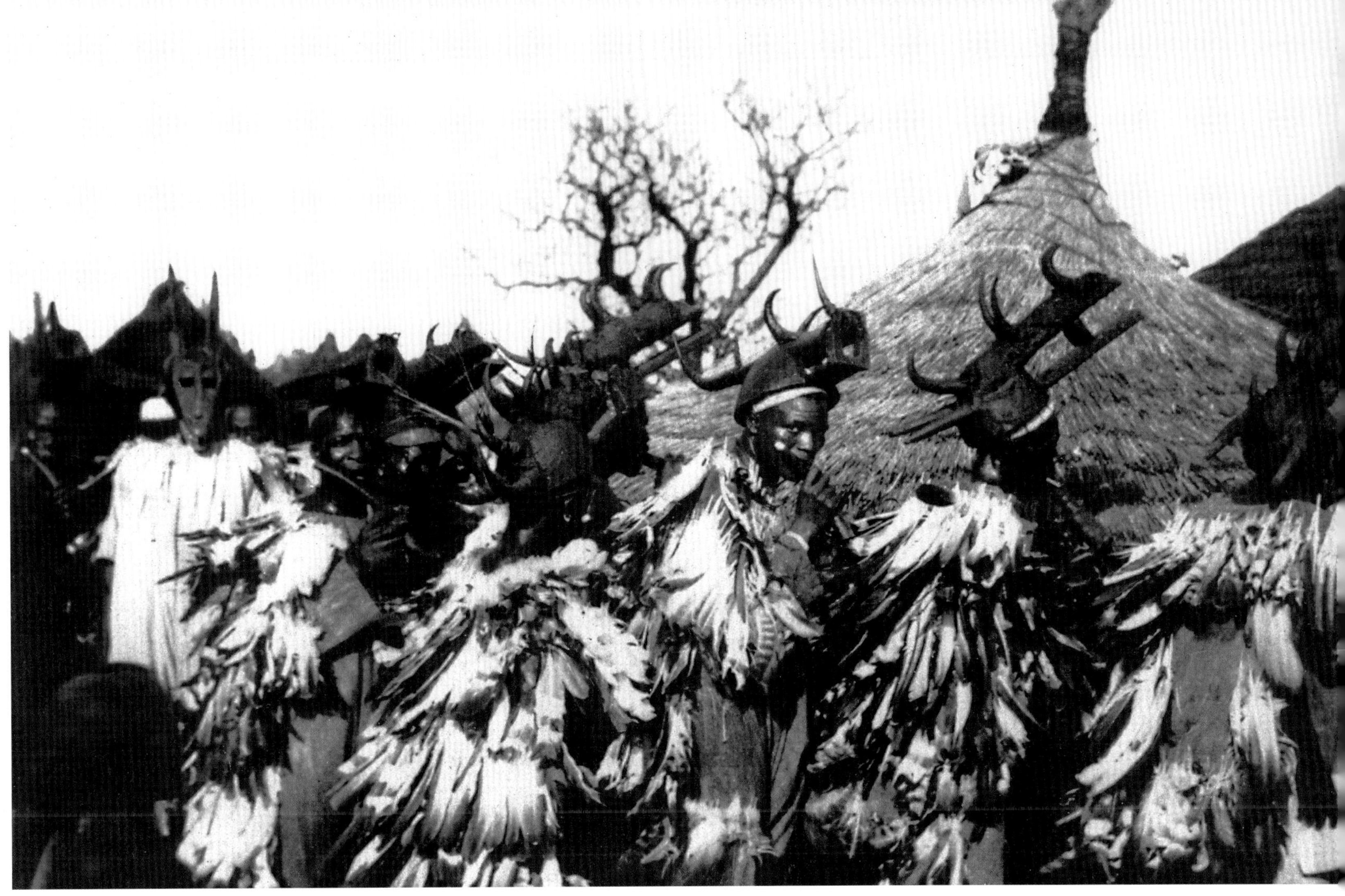

A Group of Kòmò Dancers. Kòmò Association, Guinea. Photo: ©abm—archives barbier-mueller

Zan of the powerful wings.
Zan of the powerful hooves.
The great bird with four wings!
The bird who scratches [the earth] from the sky
Would dig a well in the rock if he descended.

The costume of vulture feathers recalls a sacred narrative in which the vulture was credited with bringing Kòmò knowledge from the spiritual world to earth (Dieterlen & Cissé 1972:236). The vulture, a daytime creature, is the guardian of "white knowledge," the clear, open, knowledge of spiritual origin. As an eater of carrion, the vulture is regarded as inoffensive. As the most imposing bird, physically, the vulture is the patron of royalty, of war, of hunting, and especially of the traditional priesthood and of death. It is seen as oblivious to the vicissitudes of life on earth (Dieterlen & Cissé 1972:27). As the bearer of spiritual knowledge, the vulture is consulted by diviners, and its feathers on the Kòmò costume allude to the Kòmò performer's power to divine (McNaughton 1988:137).

In the annual Kòmò ceremonies of sacrifice to the spirits, the spokesman of the event proclaims his fidelity to "'the old hyena who, it is said, is at the origin of everything among the Bamana: the 'old beast' is in the night; the night is obscurity; what is this obscurity, if not the secret, the mystery of original void and the history of the final void.'" The chief of Kòmò responds: "'What you have said is reasonable. The hyena is a 'great thing' in the affairs of Komo. . . .'" As the vulture feasts on carrion in the daytime, it leaves the remainder to the hyena, at night, who leaves nothing, "'not even a trace'" (Dieterlen & Cissé 1972:265).

The hyena, in sacred narrative, is a fisher, splashing about in the sacred sea of the great overseer of the universe and the earth, the "master of water," Faaro. As a "fisher," *kòmò*, it gives its appellation to the ritual association itself, in the view of Dieterlen & Cissé (1972:26). The hyena is said by the Manding to devour sorcerers (who are often previously blacksmiths), and the blacksmith (presumably an honorable one) is thought able to become a hyena. The hyena is said to possess enormous knowledge about the bush and its secrets (McNaughton 1988:137). A timid animal that feeds normally on carrion, the hyena is credited with an extraordinary sense of smell and of foresight. As a nocturnal creature, living in holes in the earth, the hyena has become, for the Manding, a symbol of secrets of "black knowledge," of the knowledge of fertility, maternity, religion, dances, and songs (Dieterlen & Cissé 1972:26)—in essence, the business of Kòmò.

F. J. L.

51

The Invisible Scourer of the Deep: a Mau Mask (*Kòmasu*)

Male Mask Representing a Hyena (*Kòmasu*)
Mau/Worodugu, Region of Touba, Ivory Coast/Guinea
Kòma Association
c. Late 19th–early 20th century
Wood, goat and sheep horns, cloth, string, encrustation, nails, H. 107.5 cm
Gift of Nancy and Robert H. Nooter, Washington, D.C.
BMA 1985.281 (obtained in Monrovia, Liberia, in 1966)

The Kòma association is found among the Mau and Worodugu peoples of the Manding language group, who are closely related to the Malinke and Bamana. It is an initiation society whose essential purpose is to fight against sorcery. Membership is obligatory for all males in the Mau villages. Initiated men of Kòma are divided into three age grades: the carriers of the hoe (*lawati*), the elder men's grade; the carriers of the fibers (*futi*), for the mature men; and the carriers of the bells (*weendiiou tii*), for the young circumcised men (Diabate 1985:11).

When danger threatens the community, or when a Kòma dignitary dies, one or another mask would be invoked by the higher level Kòma members to preside over rituals of protection and honor. On these occasions, when the masks appear, only the men may be present, while the women and children remain inside their houses.

The principal male mask is called Kòmasu, "the Kòma Hyena," among the Mau, Kòmasuni among the Worodugu, and Kòmasuruku (searcher or scourer of the pond, i.e. of deep, dark or obscure things) at the village of Krikouma. It plays an extremely important, central role in the village, under the supervision of a higher, and more refined mask, the female Kòmaba. Malevolent spirits are attracted to the extraordinary power of Kòmaba, and Kòmasu can be said to be her "warrior," driving out and annihilating these forces. The malevolent spirits are sorcerers appearing in the guise of animals or other material forms in order to accomplish their crimes with impunity. Kòmasu is the only mask that possesses the clairvoyance necessary to detect their trickery.

The BMA mask has a border of small conical protruberances ornamenting the surface of the upper mandible of the beak, which may suggest the stylized teeth of a hyena, although they are usually on the insides (Sanogo 1985:184). The hyena is significant because it is known for its ability to see at night as well as by day, and because it is ferocious and dedicated to the hunt; it is said to enter the village often during the night to seize domesticated animals such as cattle, chasing its prey through the village. In the spiritual conception of the Mau, the hyena's talent for double vision enables it to see into obscurity and to detect those who have contrived to conceal themselves within particular animals, or other forms, within the village.

The beak of the mask, however, does not formally resemble the snout of the hyena, but rather the beak of the calao, a grain-eating bird very common in these agricultural regions. The calao, in oral narrative, is considered a primordial animal which brought the oil palm nut, one of the sources of wealth of this region. On certain Kòmaba masks, in fact, a palm nut is represented between the two extremities of the mandibles (Musée de l'Homme, Paris, accession number 62-74-1; Verger-Fèvre 1980: vol 2: A–1). The addition of the calao adds another dimension to the mask, integrating into the performance a body of known oral narrative of origins.

After a new mask is carved by the blacksmith, it does not become clearly efficacious until the installation ceremony presided over by the Kòmati, the head of Kòma, in the presence of all the initiated men. Here it is put in contact with the ancient masks that have been retired and conserved in the Kòmabwo, the sacred house, in order to be impregnated by their power. All the masks present are splattered with the blood of a sacrificial victim, a black dog. Three red roosters are offered to the mask in sacrifice. Goat or sheep horns are attached to the mask, filled with protective substances designed to render the mask invulnerable to the spells of sorcerers. A "medicine bag" nailed to its forehead further augments its powers.

The Kòmasu costume is elaborate. Long raffia fibers attached around the perimeter of the mask, evoke long tresses. His cotton tunic is dyed ochre, sewn closed at the end of the sleeves, and covered with a great number of amulets, just as the tunic of hunters. He wears a long and thick fiber skirt. Fiber anklets also give an allusion to the category of initiated men to whom this mask belongs, the futi, the carriers of the fibers. An example of the mask published by Holas (1969: Fig. 54) shows that it may be surmounted by feathers, probably those of the vulture. The BMA mask, as well as some others, has a number of holes around its rim used to attach its costume; but because of the great weight of the mask, the dancer generally does not tie the mask to his head, but simply holds the mask by the beak. This beak serves in dance, as a grip for the dancer's hand so that he may hold it against his face or raise it up if he needs to slide the mask over his head.

According to Mamadou Diabate (personal correspondence 1989) the Kòmasu masquerader generally appeared during the night, but it could also appear in the daytime. "The villagers are alerted to the arrival of the masks of Kòma by a number of cries. The cries of the Kòmasuni imitate the cries of the hyena,"

Mother of the Masks (*Kòmaba*). Mau, Ivory Coast. *c.* Early 20th century. Wood, hide, metal, H. 39 cm. Courtesy of the Musée de l'Homme, Paris. M.H. 62-74-1

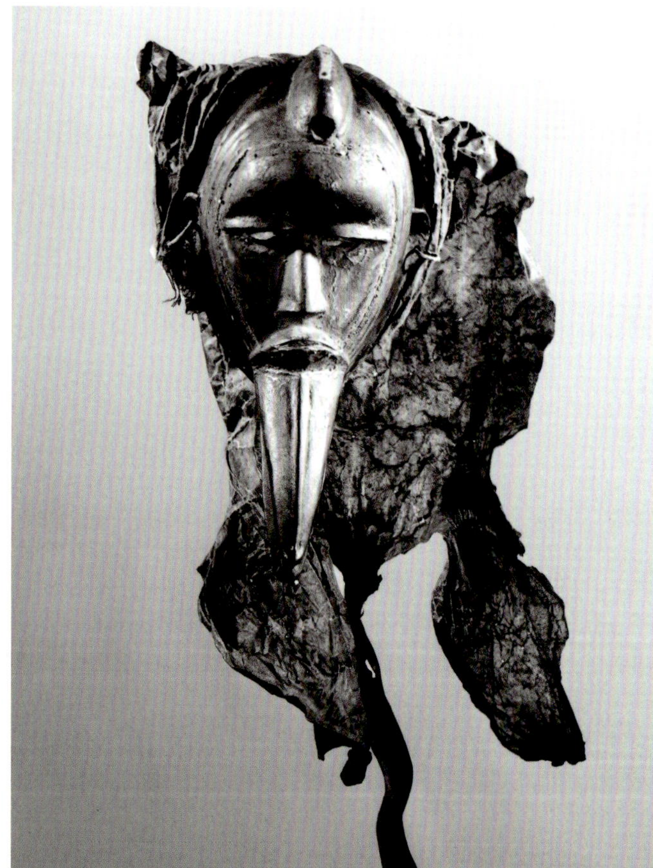

demonstrated by one consultant at Krikouma, in the Souin Canton, as "houp, houp, rrrou...." The masquerader speeds around the outside of the village to slaughter all the carriers of evil forces who roam the bush at night. He circulates around the perimeter so rapidly, repeating his cry, that he seems to be in several places at once, suggesting ubiquity. The utmost importance of the voice of Kòmasu is critical: at times the spirit is represented not by the mask but simply by the discordant sounds made by musical instruments.

Kòmasu, and all the other masks, as well as the head of Kòma, the Kòmati or Kòmatiki, are subordinate to the female mask, known most commonly as Kòmaba, "The Eldest of Kòma," that is, the most powerful. More generically she is known as the "Mother of the Masks," Maboba. In the Mau region of Touba, the mask occasionally goes by the name of Manbola, "Great Mother," or Musokoni, "The Little Old Woman" (Diabate 1985:20).

The latter name derives from that of a deity of the closely-related Bamana people, Musokoroni, because of the influence of the Bamana Kòmò association upon the Manding Kòma to the south. For the Mau, Musokoni is a sort of civilizing, feminine hero, who helped their ancestor find the wooden mask, and who entrusted the weapons of the hunt to him, as well as the ritual means of protection to shield him against attacks by the vengeful spirits of the fallen game. The Kòma stories of origin are as numerous as the villages themselves and their Kòma chapters. They generally tell of the voice that was heard by the ancestral hunter, commanding him, "The mask may be found in this tree—dig it out and carry it to the village," and announcing the prohibitions of the mask, "never to be seen by a fecund woman, nor by the uncircumcised."

The mask of the female Kòmaba, like the male, is surmounted by a coiffure of vulture feathers. The male dancer of the female mask is dressed with a costume also similar to that of Kòmasu. A cotton cloth covers the nape of the neck and the shoulders; the tunic, dyed with indigo, and stitched at the end of the sleeves, is covered with amulets. An overgarment of a fiber skirt, from the belt to the feet, confers upon the whole an impression of great majesty. This is accentuated by the comportment, slow, hesitant, and graceful, of the character, supporting himself on two high canes, as if he were a very old woman. He is armed with a lance and a sword, miniaturized and spiritually powerful.

Kòmaba, herself, attempts to draw out the sorcerers of the village by imitating the call of the owl. The owl is said to be used by the sorcerers as a spirit proxy. It is this solicitation of the sorcerers that necessitates the coming out of the male masquerader, Kòmasu, to vanquish them as described earlier.

Kòmaba's appearances are announced by other cryers. Their salute alludes to a lack of training of the young men in the professions of their fathers, and the task of Kòma to initiate them into adulthood:

> Hey! Hey! Hey! Hey! Death, oh death! Death! Oh death! Kill my enemy! If the son of the hunter eats bones, it is because the hunt has been bad. If the son of the fisherman drowns in the river, it is because the fishing has been bad. If the son of the cultivator lacks yam tubers, it is because the harvest has been bad, the land sad. The mother of the masks will soon come out to light up the world (Sanogo 1985:124).

Marie-Noël Verger-Fèvre

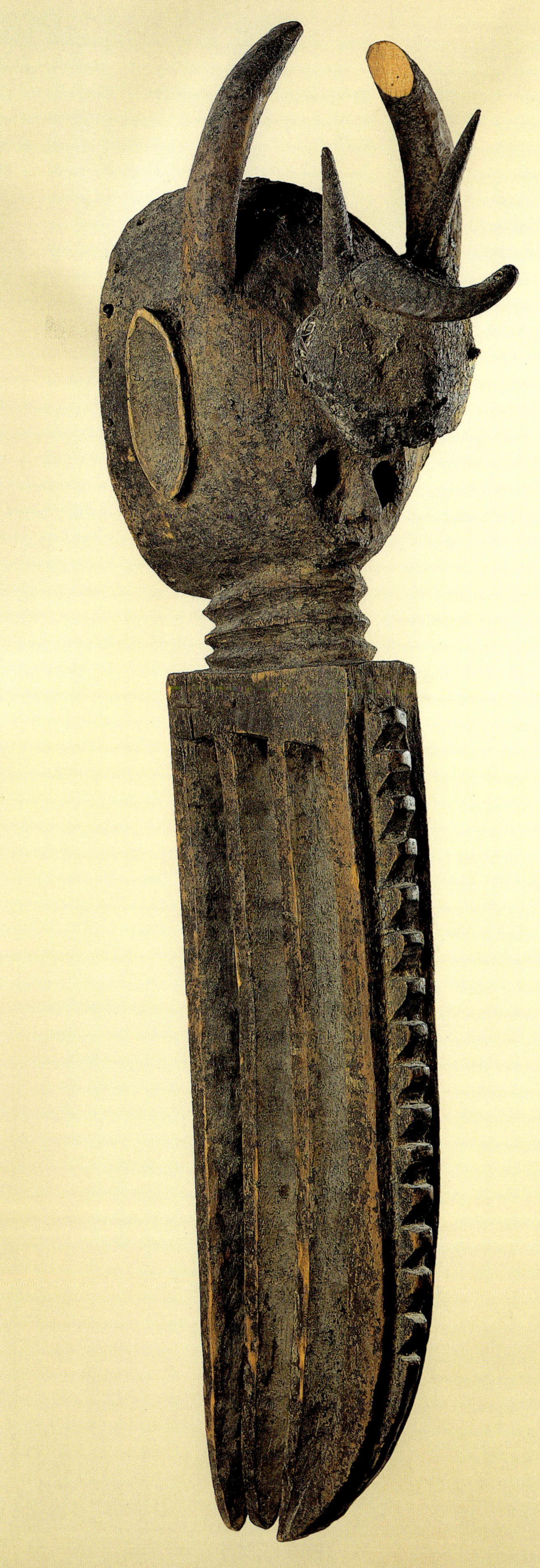

THE OLFACTORY

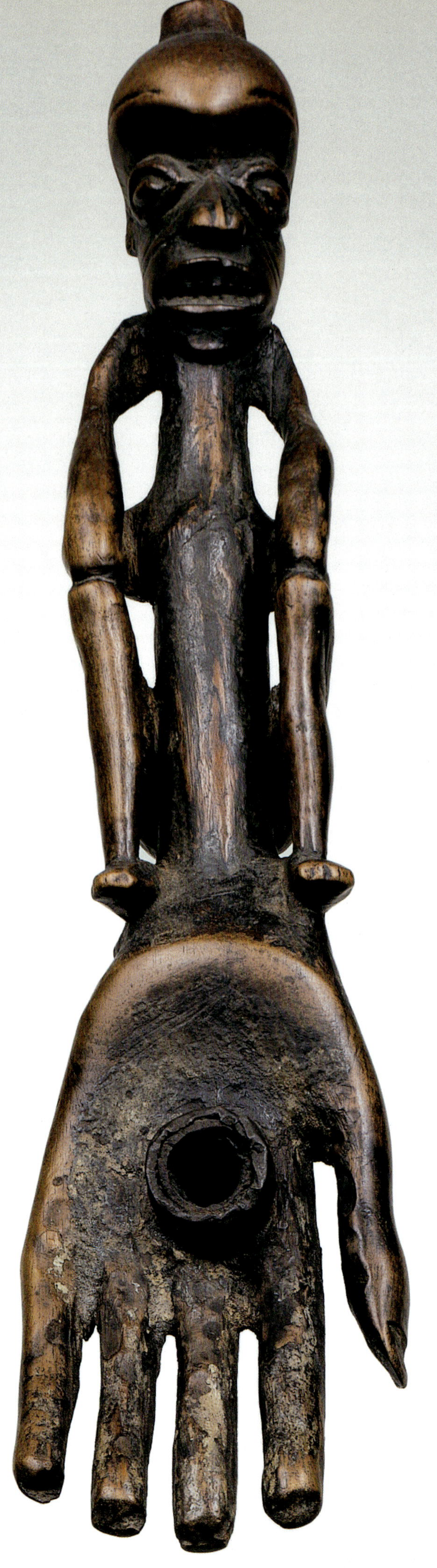

In the process of compiling this book, it became apparent that there are certain African concerns that emerge in the literature, and in some of the invited essays included here, that are rarely concerns in Western performance, where the Western model of theater is inadequate. These involve human senses other than those of sight and hearing usually privileged in the West. In several essays introduced below and in the next section, there surfaced just a few fascinating references to smell, taste, and touch. In this section, some analysis of the significance of smell, and the nose, is brought forward from Z. S. Strother's research among the Pende. The effects of prescribed odors and organic substances among the Kongo is noted by Wyatt MacGaffey. The use of blood sacrifice in Benin shrines to the ancestors is examined in view of the contrast between the olfactory repugnance and the artistic refinement of the individual objects. Raymond Silverman discusses the aromatic preparation of both vessels and bodies among the Borana.

Although contemporary theater in the West generally disdains the introduction of smells into performance, except as humor in "scratch-and-sniff," it is more respected in Western religious services, especially Roman Catholic, and historically the olfactory held an honored place in theater, as well. Sally Banes (2001) describes olfactory devices in the nineteenth century used to create meaning in performance, and maintains that "there is a total, integrated sensory image (or flow of images) created in the theater, of which the olfactory effect may be one component." Rather than redundantly paralleling what is already apparent visually and orally in the performance, the olfactory is a mnemonic in its own right, either supporting the messages provided by other contributing media, or, in some cases, subverting them (Turner 1986:23–24). In some contemporary Western theater, scents have been used, such as the odor of crushed herbs or a smelly stream in Teresa May's 1993 performance, *Dragon Island*, to evoke distant memories, and in other cases, in theater and and religious performance, burning incense refers to the sacred, or frames the entire event as sacred. Some smells may serve as icons, resembling and standing for material things such as feces, certain foods, or liquids. Other smells may relate naturally to something else, as an index, such as stagnant water and a malevolent spiritual character. Others may be truly symbolic, such as incense to evoke the spiritual, with no natural relationship.

At the Monell Chemical Senses Center in Philadelphia, the significance of odor is thought to be culture-specific, with enormous potential for insight as well as efficacy in marketing, military strategy, and many other contexts. Pam Dalton, a scientist there, says that "Smell is under-respected. It's like the Rodney Dangerfield of the senses." Another scientist at the Center, George Preti, has written that the odor of men's armpit secretions may be so powerful as to stimulate women's fertility cycles (*The Baltimore Sun*, Jan. 30, 2002: 1E, 8E).

The power of the olfactory is certainly known to African ritual specialists. In divination, particularly, "All senses must be heightened and be receptive.... It is significant, for example, that one of the least investigated senses, the olfactory, is the most closely linked by the brain to memory, a critical dimension that must be revised in the divinatory enterprise (Philip Peek, in Pemberton 2000:27).

In African ritual, the evocation of smelled memories is often essential to the creation of spiritual identity and power. For the Temne of Sierra Leone, the sense of smell is of paramount importance in ritual, arguably more so than sight, especially in communication between the spirit world and our own. When a sacrifice of food is made to the spirit of the dead, the spirit is said to be unable to see the food or actually eat it, but "The deceased, they assert, enjoys only the smell or warm steam of the dish" (Schlenker 1851:130). Human beings can smell the breezes, including a particularly unpleasant breeze (*a-kès*), of the spiritual world (*ro-sòki*). Among the Kuranko of Sierra Leone, anthropologist Michael Jackson (1977:200) found that rank in male initiation was characterized by scent, suggesting a heightened sensory perception:

> At Sukurela I observed four young initiated boys taunting a group of youngsters with the refrain, *'Oh bilakore, i ma ta, i sume n n'toro la'* ('Oh *bilakore*, go away from me, your smell disturbs me'). Upon asking them what they meant by these words they explained that uninitiated boys smell quite different from initiates and they asked me, rather surprised by my ignorance, whether I could not smell the difference.

Useful odors are frequently employed by spiritual mediums in order to effect positive relations between the world of living and the world of the spirits. Spiritual beings, themselves, have special preferences for particular kinds of aromas. Among the Tabwa of Congo (Kinshasa), wild, aromatic basil is either used or explicitly avoided in ritual of spirit possession (Allen Roberts, personal communication, 2003). Aromatic plants and extracts, as well as imported incense is used in northeastern Tanzania to purify ritual spaces and persons in healing rituals in order to attract a particular spiritual presence or to induce spirit possession in either the healer or the patient. These materials can be burned so that the smoke envelopes the sacred space and the people in it and is inhaled for internal saturation, or rubbed on the body in strategic places (Barbara Thompson, personal communication, 2003). Among the Mijkenda and other groups of the Tanzanian coast, "a diviner often takes sniffs of tobacco snuff to divine or to go into possession ..., the spirit was always called by burning the proper incense for the spirit type, along with the proper musical rhythms and songs, and foods and other gifts ... both to attract the spirit and to be possessed by it (Linda Giles, personal communication, 2003). Frank Gunderson, in his essay earlier on the Sukuma figure, detailed how the performance of "wonders" involved a performer's bathing in the smoke of particular "medicines" in order to entice his audience and attack his competitors.

David Morris (2002) has shown a fascinating correlation between scent, and desire, repulsion, and the flow of water, in which the quality of odors is intentional and efficacious in ritual among the Khoisan of South Africa:

> *Buchu*, which is a mix of aromatic herbs used in rites (particular female puberty rites), served to 'cool', or counter, potentially harmful potency, including body odours. [In oral narrative] It was on account of a young woman's scent that "the Rain" went to her, ... desiring to take her away ... [but] she calmed him to sleep—with buchu—while she "stole softly away." The Rain returned to his spring while she burned buchu, concealing her scent of *//khou*.... Weather, which threatened angry storms and lightning, or drought, could similarly be controlled by means of "smoke": rain-making was carried out by burning hair, finger nails, fat, or antelope horns ..., "smoke medicine" was made by dropping a hot coal into a buchu mixture inside a tortoise shell container....

Figurative Pipe
Lulua, Congo (Kinshasa)
c. Early 20th century
Wood, metal, H. 34.3 cm
Gift of Alan Wurtzburger
BMA 1954.145.84

The olfactory element in personal adornment is well-known, for both women and men in Africa, in body oils, coiffure dressing, garments, and adornment (see p. 129). Ancient Egyptian royal and noble women wore cones of incense on top of their heads as adornment, both physical and olfactory, which were also ephemeral, as they melted into the top of the head and through the coiffure. North African and East African jewelry today is sometimes designed to include fragrances to heighten women's allure (Christine Kreamer, Herbert Cole, personal communication, 2003).

Just as there are desirable, efficacious scents, there are also scents that must be avoided because of their negative effects. The desired and the undesired, however, are not necessarily aligned with the pleasant and the unpleasant. For example, the aromatic herbs of buchu, the sweet smell of rain, as well as "smelly medicines" and "blood-soaked tunics" (described below) are all efficacious and desirable to achieve positive ends. Among spiritual mediums in Zimbabwe, on the other hand, some normally desirable things are prohibited probably because of their associations. The mediums must avoid onions and pepper, commonly used in preparing foods, because they are strong-smelling and because they are "hot," contradicting the essential qualities of the mediums who are associated with cooling rain and water. They must also avoid scented soaps, which prohibition may arise out of a disdain for spiritually incompatible European essences (Lan 1985).

The negative, the evil, and the antisocial, as well as positive spiritual entities, may be detected through scent. Paul Stoller (1989:5) writes, "In Songhay, one can taste kinship, smell witches, and hear the ancestors." The importance of smell among many Bantu cultures mandates the position of the "'Sniffer,' a specialist, who can 'sniff out' the likes of bad medicine, antisocial individuals and other such unwanted and malevolent entities" (Barbara Thompson, personal communication, 2003). Among the Pende, divination involves breathing deeply from a horn packed tightly with herbs and medicines whose odor refers the diviner to criminals, sorcerers, the dead, or ritual violations that can be distinguished as precisely as fingerprints. While singing or posing questions, such as "What is causing this illness?" or "Is a person responsible?" the diviner would take long draughts from the antelope's horn. Pende mask wearers reenact this sniffing divination, sniffing at an empty horn inserted into the ground or using a rattle to substitute for the horn, where scent, sound, and physical properties share identity:

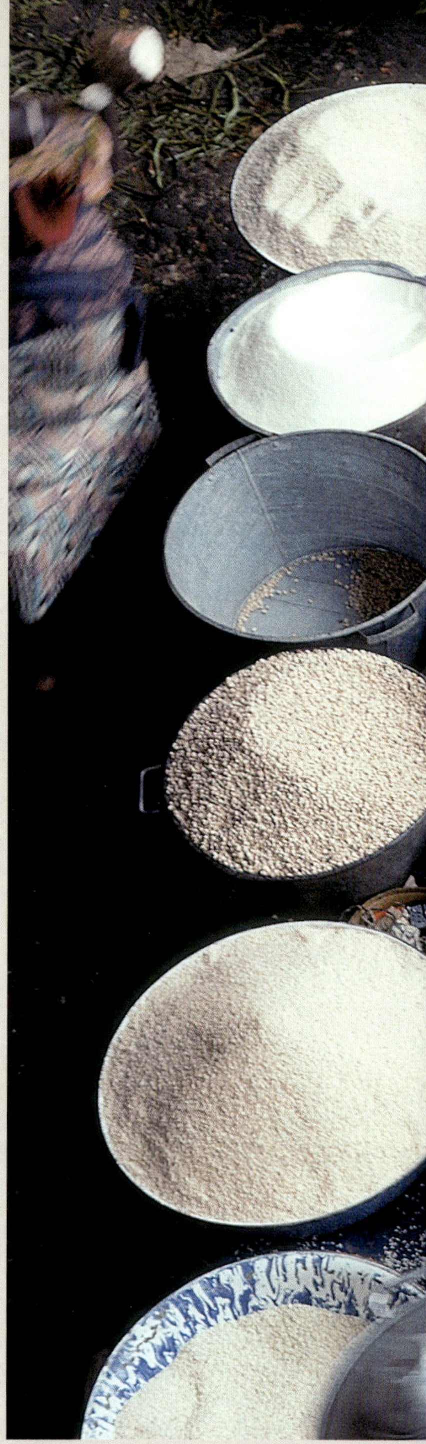

> He would sniff, and in response the tempo of the rattles grew faster, *che-che-che, che-che-che*, as the drama heightened. Exegetes explained that the fast tempo and high pitch of the rattle(s) mimic the whine adopted by the diviner on the verge of making a discovery.... To achieve the proper tone for the rattle professional dancers ... prefer to fill it with a mix of [tiny seeds] with little pieces of metal (Strother, in Pemberton 2000:103).

Material art objects, consisting of mask, headdress, and costume of grasses, leaves, fibers, and many other objects, often have a distinctive smell, and one wonders whether the odor, as well as the appearance, the consistency, or the color, and other factors, is critical in the choice of materials. Ritual throughout Africa often takes place in the heat of the daytime sun during the dry season, when the pleasant and unpleasant scent of human beings can be particularly salient whether of body ointments and powders, perspiration, or other secretions. Yoruba staffs upon which members of the Awoopa society swear oaths are coated with a thick, black sacrificial residue, "which exudes a powerful odor. Smell as well as sight contribute to one's experience of their aura. Their texture, opacity, and scent together evoke the idea of an awesome, hidden knowledge and power whose presence is made all the more culpable by the open display of secrecy" (Henry Drewal, in Ross 1994:68). The environment itself, of sun, dust, vegetation, and village setting can be full of particular odors, changing by the seasons and by human interaction. The preparation of accompanying ritual feasts often permeates the space of the performance. The stench of animal sacrifice is sometimes present. In Igbo Okoroshi masked performance, medicines are burned to protect the performers (Herbert Cole, personal communication, 2003). The odor from burning substances, whether in sacrifice, heating the drumheads to tighten them, or the lighting of grass torches at night, is frequently a noticeable aspect.

Henry Drewal (personal communication, 2003) shows how the sense of smell, along with an appeal to other senses, was significant in the iconography of a particular masquerade:

> At Abeokuta in 1978, a warrior ancestral masker's powerful aura, its performative power or *ase*, resided not only in its striking colors

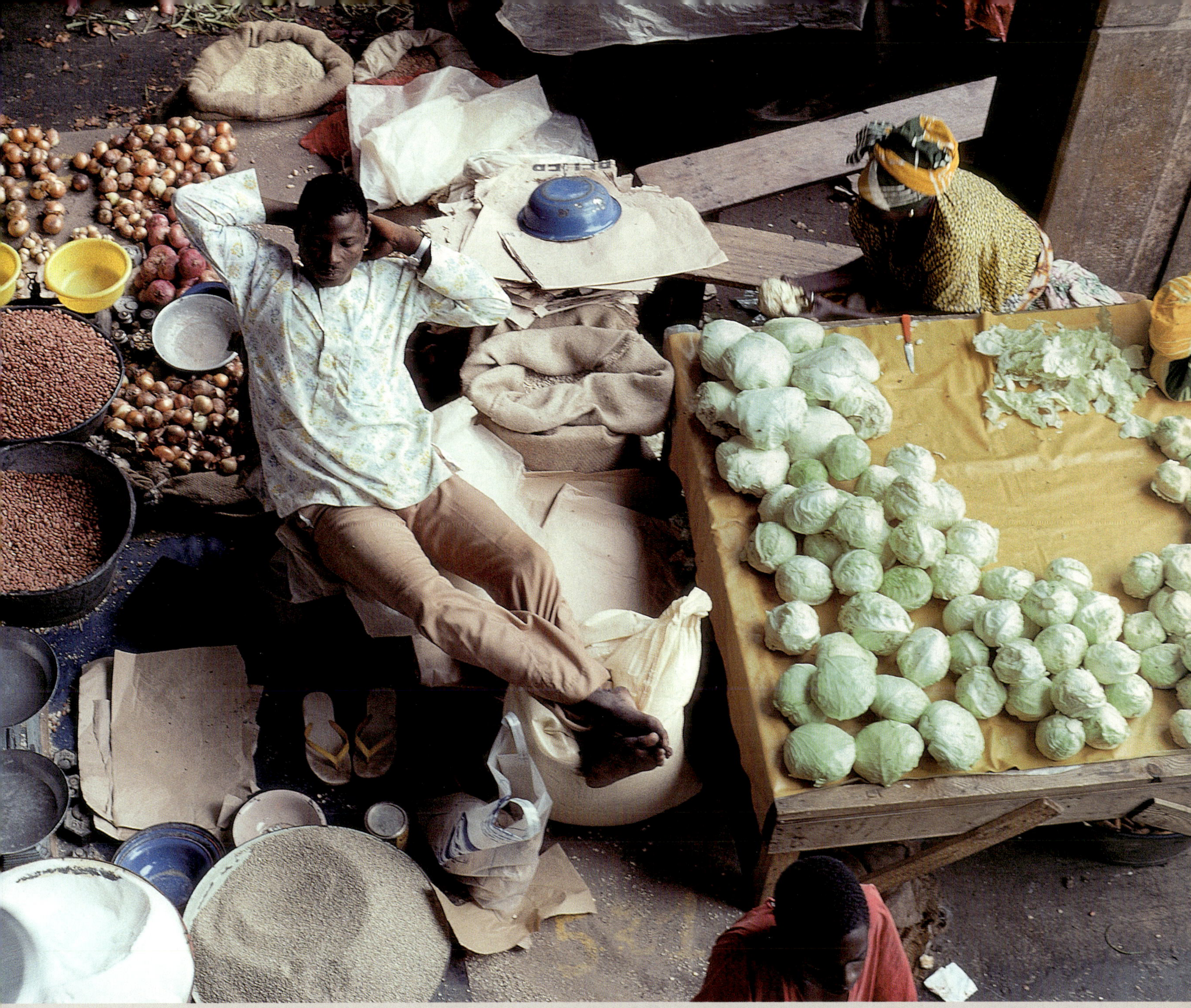

A vendor and his produce in the Trechville Market, a particularly aromatic and pungent place, from which ritual practitioners often purchase their olfactory effects. Abidjan, Ivory Coast. Photo: Frederick John Lamp, 1976

and assemblage of power packets attached to its costume, but other elements as well: the powerful chorus of words of praise that energized it; the kinetic energy of its dance amplified by accompanying dancers and the rushing, boisterous crowd; the pulsing beat of the drum ensemble; and especially the pervasive, overpowering stench that emanated from its blood-soaked tunic!

There are many questions raised by the discussion here that could be considered in the interpretation of African performance. Are messages communicated in smells? Is there intentionality, i.e., is odor introduced in order to achieve a goal? Or is it incidental, appearing by serendipity, but used as a medium as a part of the improvisation process? How do scents and their perception distinguish levels of rank within the context of ritual secrecy? Is there a scent memory, can smells be recalled and classified? Is there iconography of smells, i.e. do smells stand for something, do they have meaning? Does odor have power?

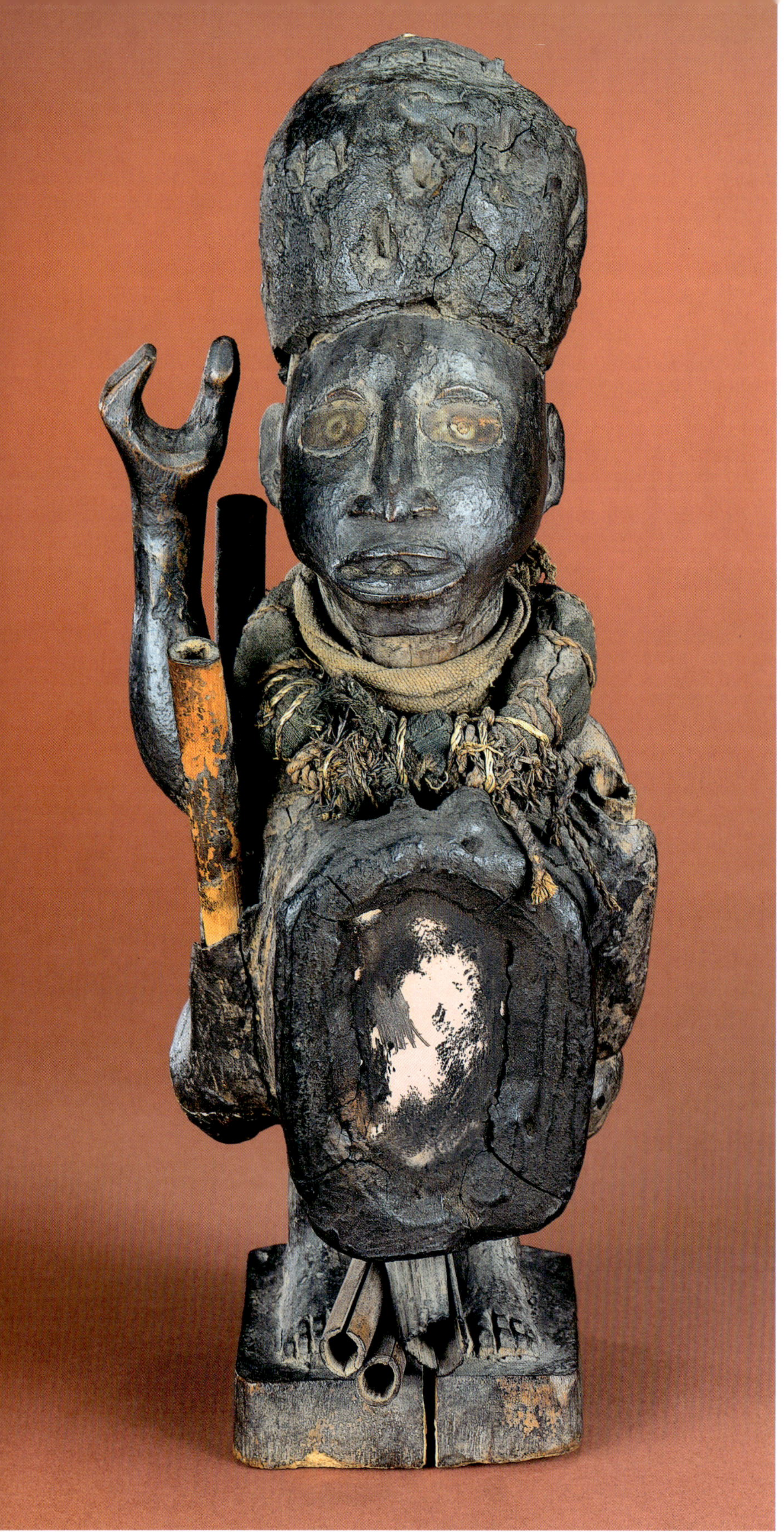

Male Figure (*Nduda*)
Kongo. Mayombe District, Congo (Kinshasa)
c. Early 20th century
Wood, glass, stalks of elephant grass, resin, cloth, unidentified materials
H. 27.5 cm
Gift of Alan Wurtzburger
BMA 1954.145.67

58 Substances and Smells in the Pursuit of Evil: a Kongo Figure (*Nduda*)

Nduda was an obscure *nkisi* widely used in the northern part of Mayombe, the western province of what is now the Democratic Republic of Congo. An nkisi (pl. *minkisi*) is a personalized force from the invisible land of the dead that has chosen, or been induced, to submit itself to human control effected through ritual performances. The performances, together with the rules to be observed by people who have dealings with the nkisi, are just as much part of the whole as the focal object that we may now find in a museum.

The missionary ethnographer Bittremieux (1936:164) described Nduda as "little devils that protect people and their habitations; usually in the form of a little man with a gun that shoots sorcerers." Sometimes they were called Mpanzu, named after the corrosive ulcers they are said to cause, but some kinds of Mpanzu are quite unrelated; it would be a mistake to think of these categories as tightly characterized and bounded. Nduda was also used to protect warriors from harm in battle. It might seem that these two functions are distinct, but in Kongo to this day diviners describe their struggle with the hidden forces of sorcery as "war." A characteristic of Nduda is its "guns," made from stalks of elephant grass loaded with gunpowder. They are called *mata ma mpimpa*, "night guns," because sorcerers operate in darkness, or *nduuda*, from a root meaning "bang."

This figure originally had four such weapons, symmetrically displayed. It has also lost the spear or dagger once held aloft in its right hand, in the manner of much larger and even more aggressive minkisi called Nkondi. A more serious loss, typical of minkisi in collections, is that of the bag or bags of medicines that originally accompanied the figure. Several such bags belonging to Nduda are found in the Kongo collection of the Ethnographic Museum, Stockholm, where, conversely, the carved figure tends to be missing. That particular collection is made up in large part of items that the missionary collectors considered less interesting to look at than carved figures and therefore relegated to the museum. The medicine bags, several in the form of a small knotted bag suitable for carrying into battle, are also armed with "guns."

The figure itself has medicines contained in the pack on the head, in the collar bundle, and under the mirror on the belly. It has more weapons stowed between its legs. The mirror, sealed with resin, is the "eyes" of the nkisi, with which it detects the approach of sorcerers; the patina of blood and other materials on the mirror does not effectively obscure Nduda's "night vision" for seeing sorcerers. We do not know in detail what the requisite medicines were, either for this Nduda or for Nduda in general, but a couple of indigenous texts roughly contemporary with the piece (early twentieth century), and from the same area, give some idea of the composition or empowerment of the nkisi (MacGaffey 1991).

"Medicines," in general, earn their place in an nkisi by verbal or other associations with the specific attributes the device was supposed to acquire. These are described in indigenous texts in KiKongo given in full elsewhere (MacGaffey 1991 and 2000), along with detailed accounts of the cultural and historical contexts of Kongo minkisi. According to a text by Timothy Babutidi, Nduda contained the head of a harmless green snake, a reference to the dead in the cemetery where it was created:

> If someone wants to compose the nkisi he goes with the nganga [the expert for this nkisi] to the cemetery, where they make an enclosure of palm branches and begin to prepare medicines which they put in the figure; they then fire two shots and return to the village, leaving the nkisi on the grave. They leave it there to make people think that the ghosts themselves complete the medicine packet. The next morning they fire another shot to announce themselves, and retrieve the nkisi (MacGaffey 1991:109).

Even from these fragments we can see that both the ritual and the medicines "say" that violent powers derived from the dead are being mobilized to deal with the danger of sorcery.

Another text, by Joseph Lwamba, describes a different compositional procedure, but one equally marked by signs of violence:

> They explode gunpowder on a stone. They take a knife [presumably the knife now missing from the figure], brandish it in the air and then bang it on the ground. And they pour the blood of a goat over the nkisi."

Then they sang a [deliberately obscure] song which mentions "twigs."

Twigs are mentioned again in a song included in another text which specifies that the nganga "shakes" his whistle while leading the troops into battle. The complete interpretation of these lyrics is unclear, but seems to be:

> The grasshopper carried his brother, they carry each other!
> The sorcerer, a bundle of twigs I have held, when you go, I will remain.
>
> *Koko neti mpangi andi banatene.*
> *Koyi kwanga dya binsafi nsimbani ngeye bukwenda mono nasaala.*

Lwamba continued, "For treatment [of sickness caused by a sorcerer, or by breaking a rule of the nkisi] they go to a stream. The two assistants stand in the water, cut a chicken, pour blood over the nkisi, and strike the nganga with twigs [which may partially explain the reference to twigs in the songs]. Then they go back to the village, slaughter the chicken and eat it." The nganga here (who could be male or female) was called Lubwilu or Lusobo, both names implying combativeness. The nganga was closely identified with the nkisi; beating the nganga was equivalent to provoking the nkisi to attack the sorcerer, as it had already been encouraged to do by the blood of the goat and, more recently, the chicken. The nkisi was activated by an invocation: "Whoever has me in his grip, a sorcerer, male or female, do you Mpanzu hunt him down, however he may come." The afflicted person might be anointed with blood of a goat, as the nkisi had been when it was composed.

Some documentation exists on nganga performances. There are photographs which showed that some *banganga* (pl. of nganga) clearly put on a show with elaborate accoutrements, but not all did. Some still do, but in modernized form incorporating what are evidently ancient elements. It is unlikely that there were conventional gestures or movements, apart from spectacular trembling. There was a vocabulary of smells, but little detail has been given. Divination for sorcery is *fyela*, "to sniff out." Basil was used to induce ecstasy. Taste figures in the use of bitter roots and leaves, some of which are munkwiza, mindudi-ndudi, and mambuzu, but the rationales are elusive.

"Nduda is kept in the roof of the house, or high up on the outside, to watch for any sorcerer coming to do harm to the owner, his wife or his children" (Joseph Lwamba). The nkisi was not simply stowed away and forgotten; it controlled the behavior of its owner and others, who were obliged to observe certain prohibitions: the patient treated by this nkisi might not eat pork or plantains; the nganga might not eat certain kinds of vegetables either. These rules were "enacted medicines," so to speak, referring by association to undesirable effects one hoped to avoid; both pork and plantains suggested the "eating" of human flesh by sorcerers. If a misfortune befell him, the owner would know that he had broken a rule, that his nkisi had been profaned and would have to be reconstituted. It was also profaned if anyone who had not composed the nkisi touched it.

Wyatt MacGaffey

A female Nganga interrogates her nkisi (in the white box between her feet) in front of a male figure covered with white clay, feathers, and other things. Photo: Guy Mols, *c.* 1900, from Lehuard 1989

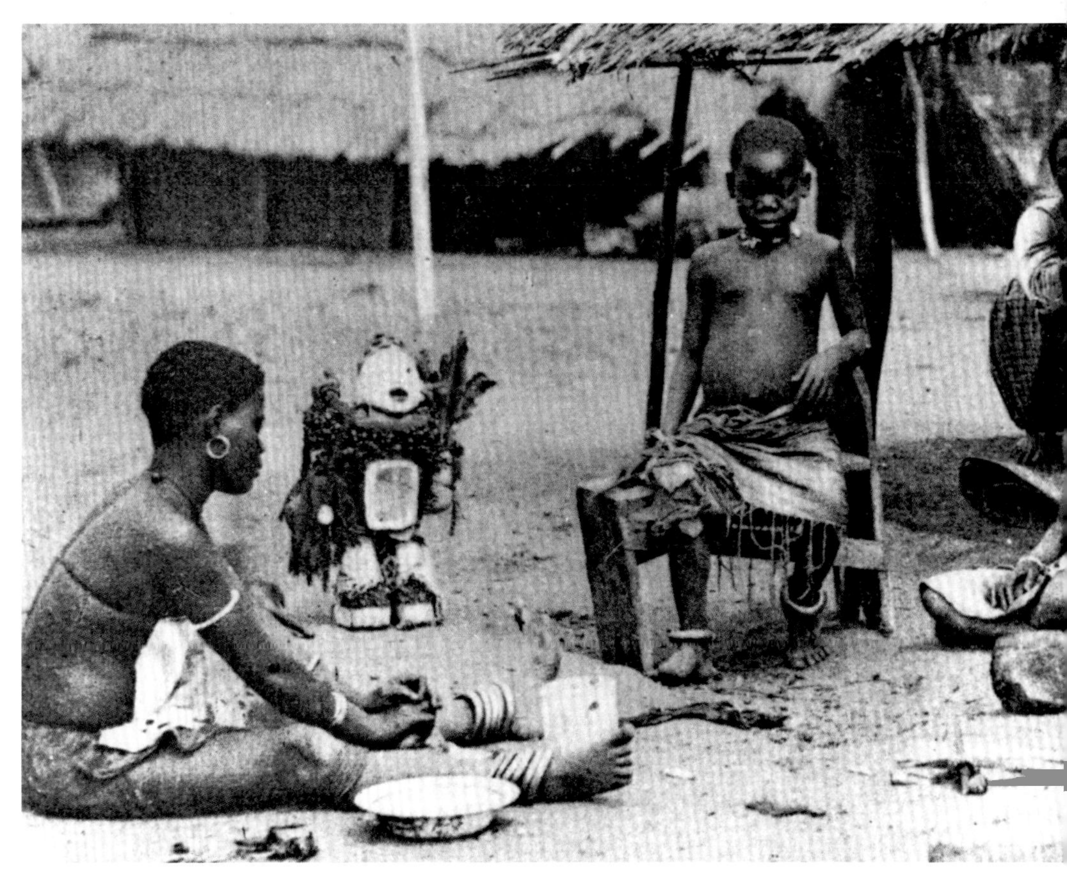

59 Blood Sacrifice and the Official Memory: a Benin Head

Head Representing a King
Edo, Kingdom of Benin, Nigeria
c. 1816–1888
Copper alloy, H. 51.5 cm
Gift of Alan Wurtzburger
BMA 1954.145.44

The Kingdom of Benin, with its rich history of royalty, nobility, and artists' guilds, going back more than ten centuries, has good reason to honor its dead. Benin City, the capital, and the site of the palace of the Oba (King), is saturated with ritual sites, including shrines to the ancestors, of every type. Individual people set up personal shrines to the inhabitants of the spiritual world in order to enter into a relationship with them. Many households include ancestral shrines to maintain the power of their forebears. Community shrines are the center of activities led by a priest (*ohen*) who develops a regular clientele, with days of worship, devotees, and institutionalized song, dance, and music. And the Oba, who, by force of his office, is considered to be in direct contact with the spiritual world, maintains some of the most important shrines that articulate his role and traditions and those of his predecessors (C. Gore 1998:68–69).

Heads such as this were not portraits but they memorialized the deceased Oba as an impersonalized divinity (Dark and 1973: 18). On an ancestral shrine at the king's palace, this head would have shared space with numerous other objects including similar heads, iron and brass state swords, and an elaborate multi-figural group in copper alloy depicting the deceased king and his courtiers. On top of the metal heads would be placed huge, soaring, carved ivory tusks, probably meant to channel spiritual energies up through the point at the top, controlling powerful forces in the air. Several copper brass bells, placed on the shrine, were available to be rung to announce the commencement of a service (Girshick 1995:78, 85). A collection of dozens of wooden ancestral rattle staffs furthered the aspect of sound, insuring that the dead would hear the words of the living in supplication (Dark 1981:139). The entire ensemble presented a formidable image of power. In the nineteenth century, houses throughout the city were said also to contain altars in a special alcove, with "carved elephants' tusks, clay figures, heads of bronze and wood, figures of birds, water-pots, four-sided bells ... and other objects" (Read & Dalton 1899:8; Girshick, 1995:88, and Dark, 1973:36, however, restrict copper-alloy heads to royalty). When the British invaded Benin in 1897 and sacked the royal palace, they found seventeen royal altars in the palace alone. Today there is one altar for the reigning king, four for his immediate predecessors, and one for all earlier kings (Cole 2001:319–321).

The ancestral kings represented on the royal shrine needed to be fed. Blood sacrifices were periodically offered to invoke the benevolence of the kings and promote the prosperity of the kingdom. There is an abundance of documentation that prior to the coming of the British in 1897, human sacrifice was an important source of blood as well as flesh for ritual feasts, documented by Paula Girshick (1999:70–78; 1995:100). She quotes (1999:129) from Alonzo de Sandoval, writing in 1627: "At certain times of the year, in honor of his dead [ancestors], the king gives festivals which last for three days; at these they sacrifice sixteen thousand souls, men and women." Some of the individual art objects on shrines were said to be so thoroughly covered under layers of blood

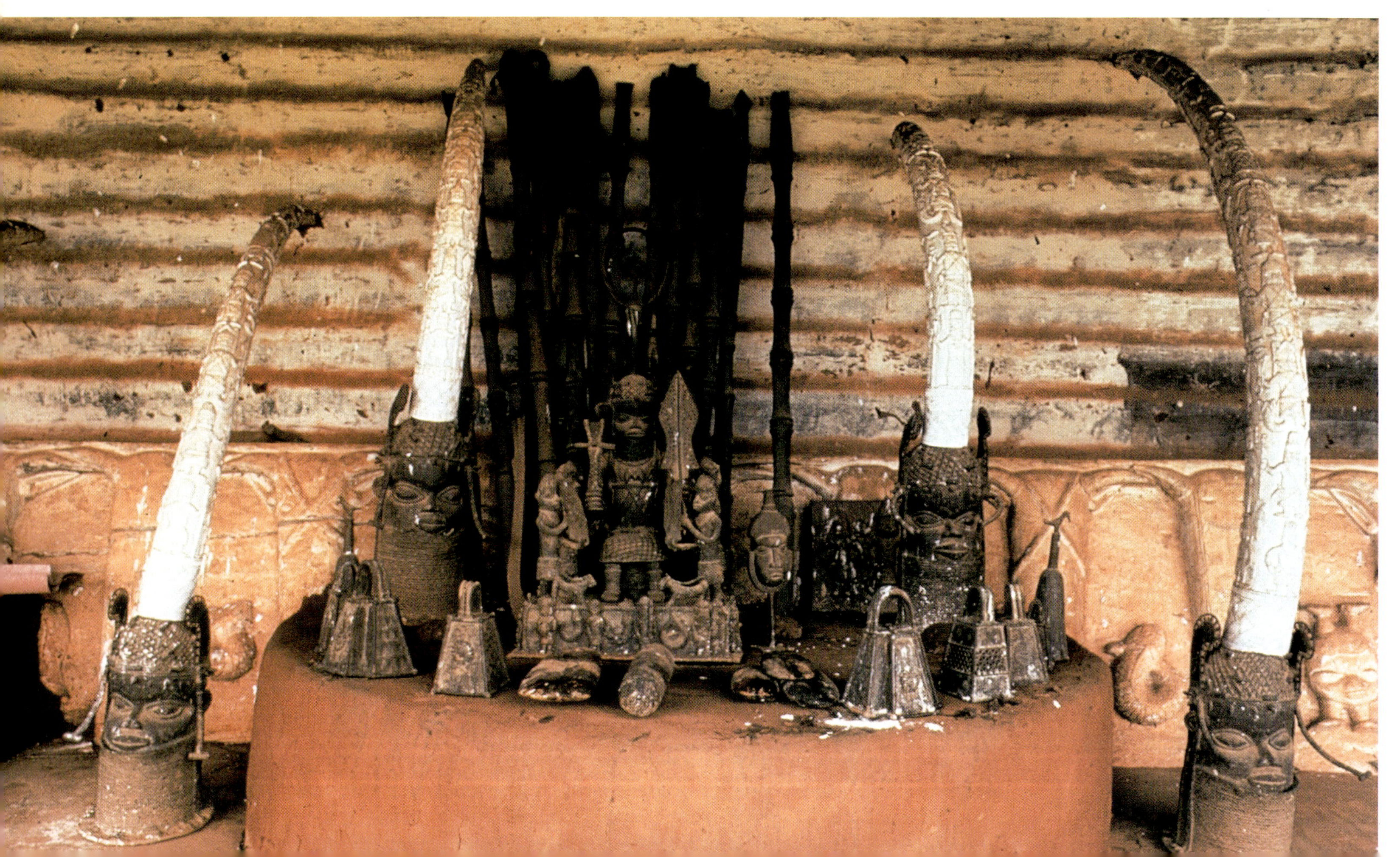

Altar Dedicated to Oba Ovonramwen *c.* 1914, Benin City, Nigeria. Photo: Eliot Elisofon, 1970. Courtesy of the Eliot Elisofon Photographic Archives, National Museum of African Art, Smithsonian Institution

(of both human and animal sacrifices) that their forms were barely discernible, leading Admiral Rawson, in 1897, to the position that, in order to bring an end to human sacrifice, the art objects and their owners, the Edo people, had to be separated (Fagg 1981:21). Many hundreds of human sacrifices were carried out by the last of the independent kings, Oba Ovoranmwen, during the six weeks just before the British invasion, in a desperate attempt to propitiate the gods, ancestors, and powerful spirits, in order to save the kingdom from destruction. The stench of the rotting blood everywhere turned the stomachs of the British invaders, and bolstered their arguments for plunder and domination. When we compare the setting of darkly-patinaed, finely-crafted, copper-alloy Benin sculptures presented pristinely in glass cases in art museum displays, in the manner of a Bernini bronze, we get no hint of the thickly sensory, saturated, formidable, and threatening character of these shrines. Even a photograph of the shrine, especially one from the twentieth century, cannot communicate this.

Read and Dalton (1899:6–7) published testimony given collectively from seven chiefs of Benin on particular annual sacrifices, including the anniversary of the death of Oba Adolo conducted by his son, Oba Ovoranmwen, before his exile by the British:

> For this, the great sacrifice of the year, 12 men were taken, 12 cows, 12 goats, 12 sheep, and 12 fowls. The offerings were brought into the big compound, and put in line in front of and facing the altar. Then *Overami* [Ovonramwen], dressed in very fine clothes, came in, and calling *Adolo* his father very loudly by name, said like this: 'Oh, *Adolo* our father, look out for all *Ado* [Edo people]! Don't let any sickness come to us. Look after me and my people, our slaves, cows, goats, and fowls, and everything in the farms.' Then the men who were in front were led to the well at the back of the compound, with gags tied in their mouths, and held each by four strong men. The executioners cut off their heads, which, with the bodies, were thrown into the pit. The animals were killed near the altar, and the blood from them was sprinkled on the big ivories and brass work.

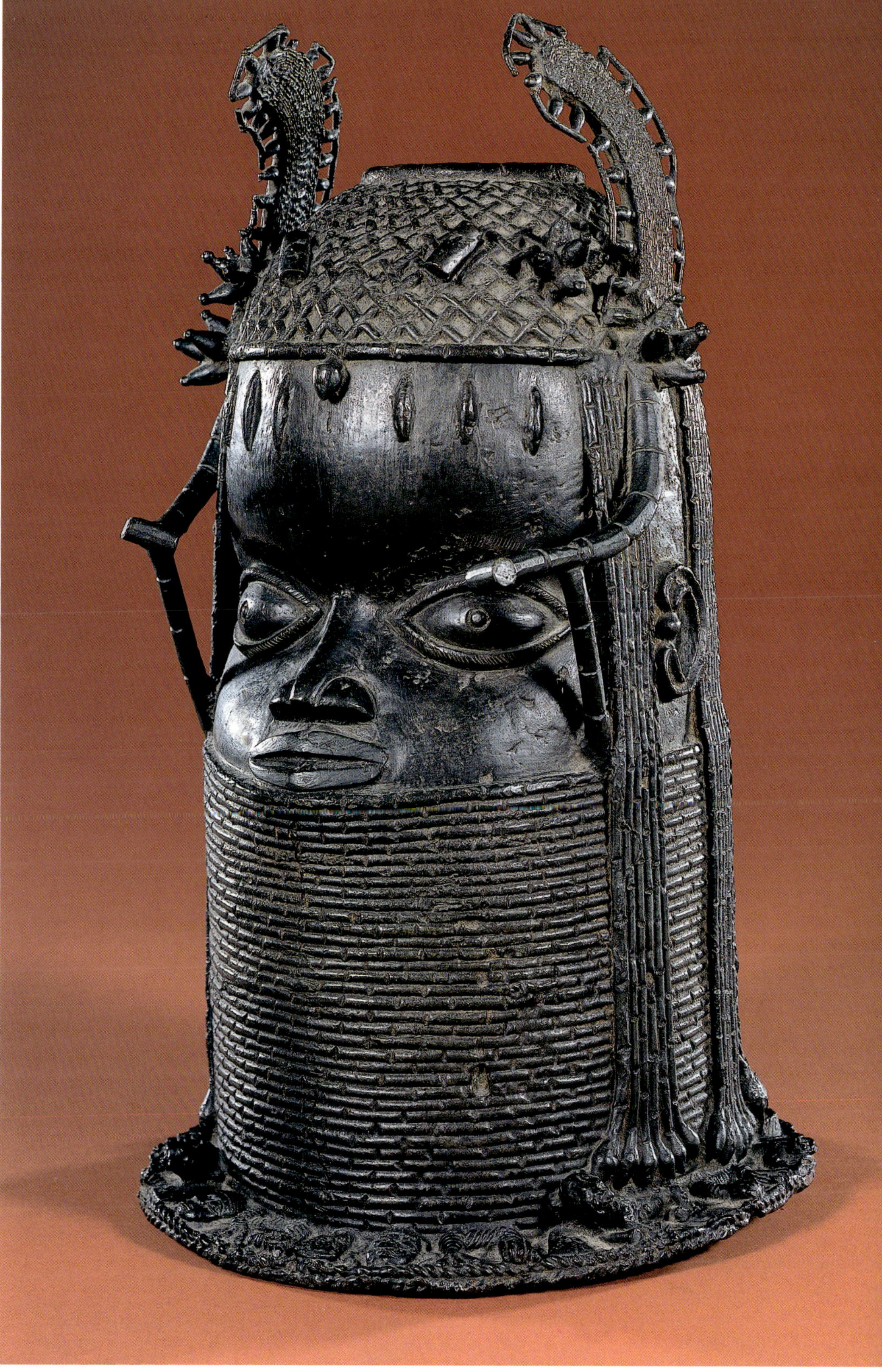

The purpose of these executions, according to Read and Dalton (1899:13) was "to keep the dead king informed of the condition of the kingdom and to reinforce the numbers of his retinue."

Girshick (1999:129–130; 1995:103–104) has documented the palace ritual (*Ugigun*) associated with the royal ancestral shrines which culminates in the three-day ceremony of *Ugie Erha Oba* in honor of the current king's immediate predecessor. On the first day is the "Greeting Ceremony," with the king seated before his father's altar, accepting homage from the chiefs, in order of their seniority, to whom he presents gifts of kola nuts and wine, confirming the hierarchical political structure. The second day brings the main ceremony in which the king, dressed in an elaborate beaded costume, offers sacrifices to honor his father and propitiate him, avert evil spirits, and appease the earth. The third day, the king's supporters stage a mock war against the seven highest-ranking chiefs (*Uzama*), vanquishing them and, symbolically, all other foes of the king. Girshick (1999:130, 134) sees this public display of acceptance and legitimacy as a mechanism for establishing the dominant, official social memory and subordinating and marginalizing any counter-histories. The ancestral altars are the site of the fashioning of memory; they "empower the winning version."

F. J. L.

Fruitfulness, Sensitivity, and the Vow: a Pende Mask (*Kipoko*)

Helmet Mask (*Kipoko*)
Eastern Pende, Congo (Kinshasa)
c. Late 19th–early 20th century
Wood; red, black, and white pigment, H. 31.3 cm
Gift of Robert Elkin, Bethesda, Maryland
BMA 1997.228

The bell-shaped Kipoko mask belongs to the Eastern Kasai Pende category of chief's insignia masks (*mbuya jia ufumu*) of which there are three: Kipoko, the principal mask, Pumbu, and Panya Ngombe. The mbuya jia ufumu masks are closely associated with the spiritual and secular authority and power of the chief, and with his principal role as intercessor between the living and the spirits of the dead ancestors. Pumbu and Kipoko represent the chief's dual nature; the former war-like, the latter benevolent. The three mbuya jia ufumu masks are the exclusive property of the chief, and, therefore, part of the treasure (*kifumu*) that is stored in the small inner room of his ritual house (*kibulu*) (Biebuyck 1985:243; Cornet 1978:136; de Sousberghe 1958:59, 64; Mudiji-Selnge 1981:229; Petridis 1992:16; 1993:72; Strother 1993:158–166, 168; 1998:193, 198, 216–217, 223; personal communication, 2003).

The Kipoko dancer's costume consists of an underlying crocheted raffia body suit draped with cloth and animal skins that flutter as he dances (Strother, personal communication, 2003). Attached to the mask's crown with a wooden hairpin, in imitation of ancient Pende headdresses, are pieces of ram's fur, monkey hide, or feathers. A very important part of the Kipoko's dance regalia are two fly whisks, one for each hand. On rare occasions, instead of the fly whisks, the dancer will carry an adze in his right hand (de Sousberghe 1958:65; Petridis 1992:17; 1993:72; Strother 1993: figs. 16 and 17, 167; 1998: fig. 75, 184, 193, fig. 81, 194, 198, 216–217).

Eastern Kasai Pende dance/masquerades take place out-of-doors in a dance area adjacent to the chief's ritual house. It is the task of women to clear this space in preparation for dance celebrations. On some occasions, Kipoko's dances begin in the early afternoon and end at sunset. When the dances occur during the late afternoon, the drummers sit on the western edge of the dance arena in order to avoid being blinded by the setting sun because it is essential that they have an unimpeded view of the dancers from whom the lead drummer, who plays the largest drum, takes his cues. The Kipoko dancer communicates with the lead drummer by varying the tempo of his constantly-moving fly whisks. For instance, by slowing down the rhythm of his sweeping gestures, he signifies a need to rest without leaving the dance arena. Since Kipoko often dances throughout the entire afternoon, these subtle slowing-down rest periods are essential for a dancer to conserve energy and maintain his stamina. However, sometimes, the role is reversed, and it is the dancer who must adjust his movements to the tempo set by the drummers (Biebuyck 1985:244; de Sousberghe 1958:63; Petridis 1992: 14–15; Strother 1993:167; 1998:14, 28–30, 193–194).

The Eastern Kasai Pende view Kipoko's dance, the *lukongo*, as an encyclopedia of dance, as well as a "type of danced prayer for the ancestors continued beneficience" (Strother 1998:195–196). It is of

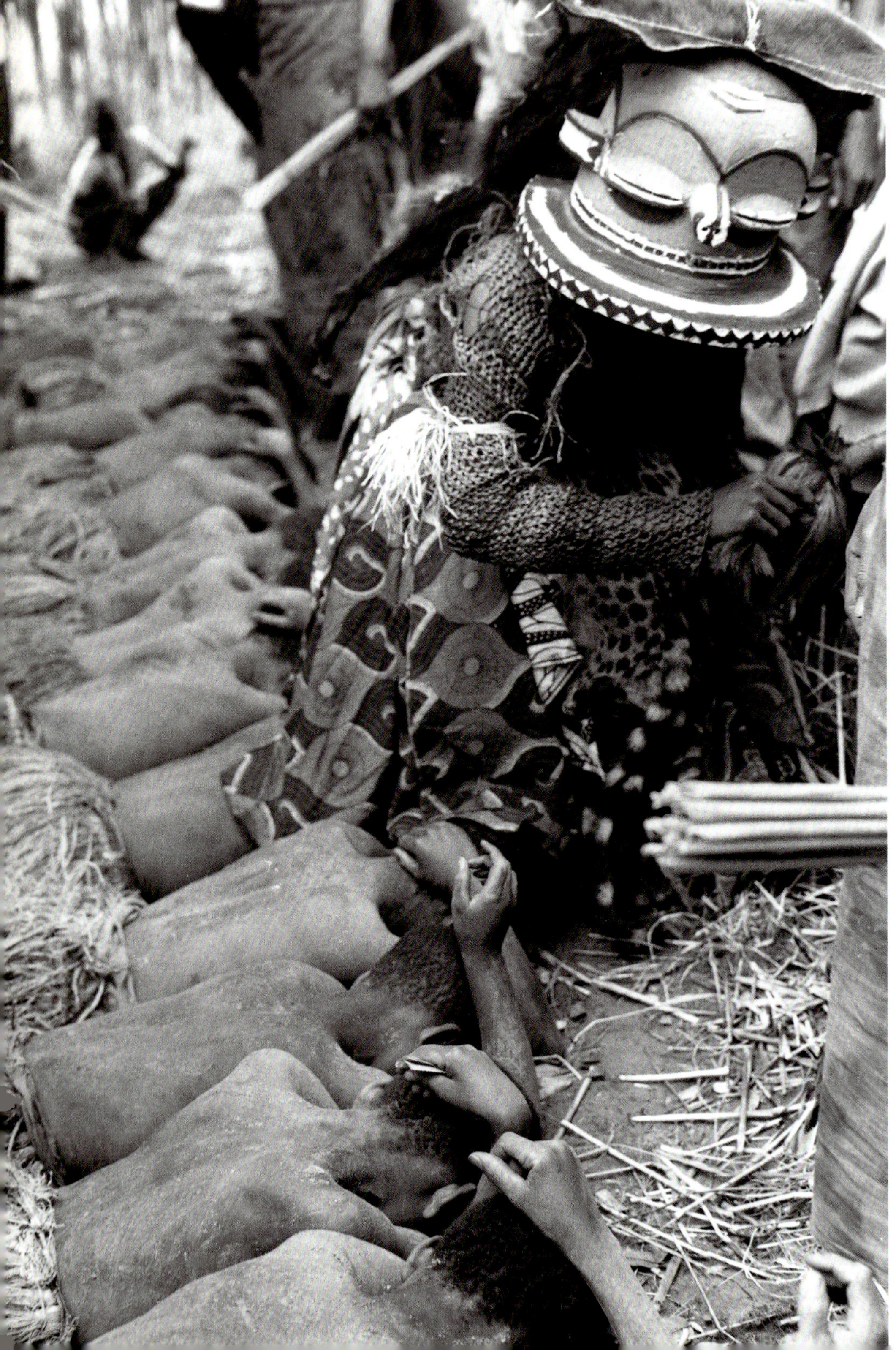

The Kipoko mask supervising a ritual concluding Chief Kende's boys' initiation into the men's fraternity. Pende, Ndjindji, Congo (Kinshasa). Photo: Z. S. Strother, 1987

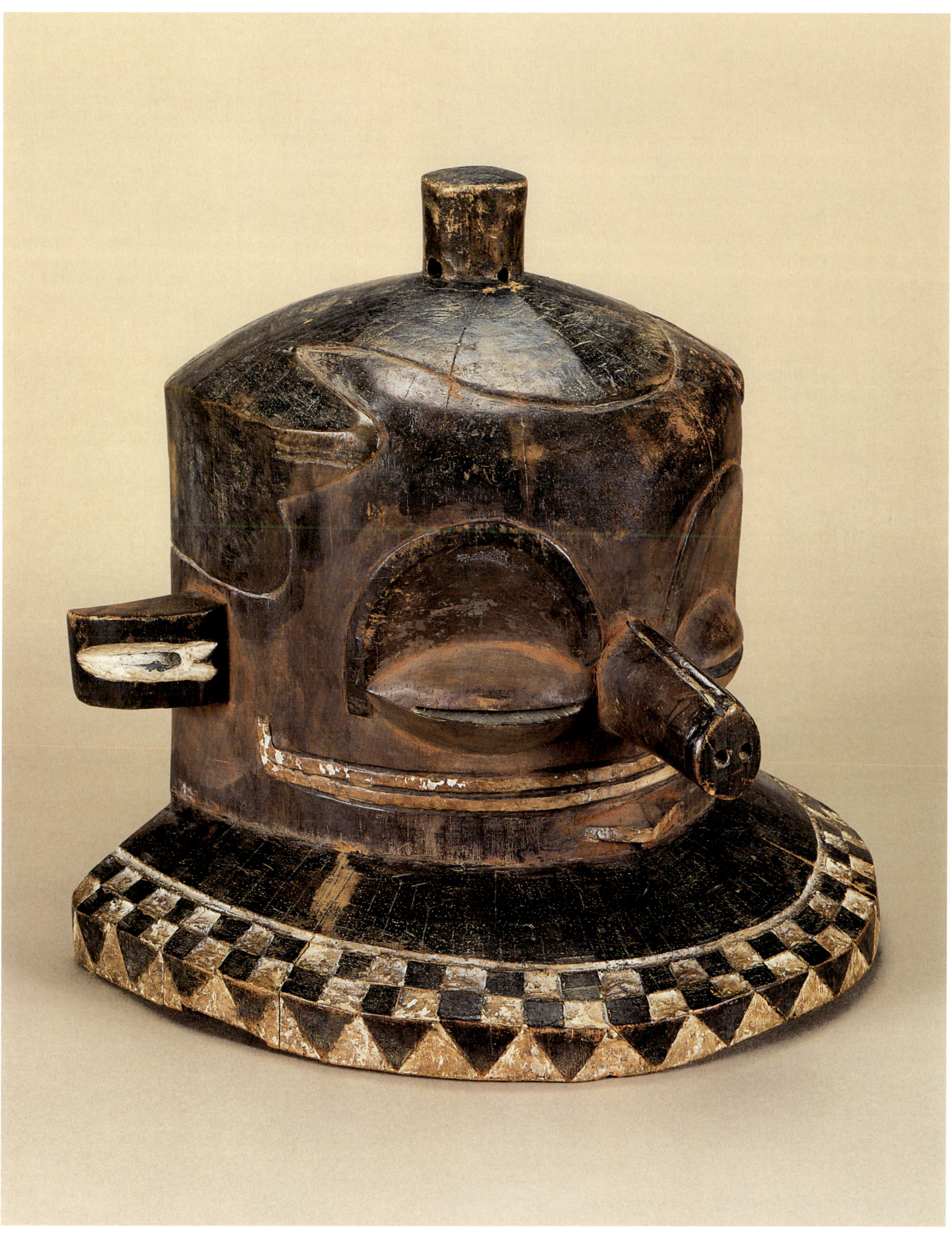

such significance that it is taught to all initiates. The most important part of the lukongo is associated with women's food production and preparation because "it reminds the audience of the purpose of the masquerade: to augment the production and health of the population" (Strother 1998:195). Kipoko dancers are encouraged to incorporate into their performances gestures and movements that mimic those of women going about their daily lives. Thus, they use the fly whisks or the adze to pantomine tasks such as sowing, harvesting, and the preparation of food. The continuous sweeping gestures made with the fly whisks also symbolize the clearing away of the malevolent forces that cause disease, infertility, and discord within the village (Strother 1998:107, 193, 196; personal communication, 2003).

Attendance at community dance/masquerades is mandatory, and spectators are encouraged to participate actively. In fact, audience participation is a determining factor when considering whether or not a dance/masquerade can be deemed successful. During 1987–1988, Strother observed that the active interaction between women and an important mask is more common among the eastern Kasai Pende than among other Pende groups. During the Kipoko dances, a few men and many women, eager to express their gratitude for the year's fruitfulness, would join the dancer on the dance arena. Sometimes men would approach the dancer with gifts of money and food; on other occasions, women carrying newborn infants would also join the dancer. (Strother 1998:196; personal communication, 2003). The spirits of the ancestors are said to join in the dances, thereby bringing the entire community of the living and the dead together (de Sousberghe 1958:65; Strother 1998:14–16, 200, 204–205).

The mask is so closely associated with healing that "it [Kipoko] is the one mask required by all chiefs" (Strother 1993:165). Kipoko's healing dance, witnessed by de Sousberghe in 1952 (1958:65, Fig. 67, 155), and by Strother in 1988 (1993:167; 1998:204–205) occurs on the last day of a masquerade, and takes place in front of the chief's ritual house. Wooden markers on the dance area indicate spots where medicinal material has been buried in the ground. In some Pende areas these medicines are intended to protect the dancers from the ill effects caused by the envy of others. Kipoko dances over these buried medicines for differing reasons: among some Pende groups, the purpose of the dance is to activate the medicine continuously, while among others, the dance is a prayer of supplication to the spirits of the ancestors asking for their protection for the entire village (Strother 1998:196–197; personal communication, 2003). When the final dance masquerade has come to an end, the ill or infertile, their heads and bodies covered with a cloth, kneel or lie down in front of the Kipoko dancer, who throws one leg, then the other in a high, horizontal, arching motion over their prostrate forms "to cover them with a shell of protection that will block the entry of the evil spirits or sorcerers who may be responsible for their afflictions" (Strother 1998:197) (de Sousberghe 1958:65; Strother 1993:167; 1998:196–197). Strother describes this vigorous dance motion as "the *shapi*, the signature dance step of the mask Kipoko, the kick he uses to activate medicine and to heal the infirm and the infertile" (Strother 1993:167; 1998:193). Another mask, Pota, sometimes joins Kipoko in the healing dance performing the same high arching kicks (de Sousberghe 1958:65; Strother 1998: 193, Fig. 81, 194, 196–197, 204–205; personal communication, 2003).

Kipoko also appears as part of an annual village ceremony of renewal that takes place during the planting season. Prior to the completion of the sowing of the millet, one of the village elders purifies the cleared dance area, and then the living and the spirits of the dead ancestors are summoned to the masquerades by a prelude of rhythms played on the appropriate big drums (Petridis 1992:15–16; Strother, personal communication 2003).

Finally, Kipoko plays an important role in a ceremony that takes place at the end of the *mukanda* (the initiation ritual held every ten years or so in any given location) to mark the reintegration of the newly initiated into the life of their village community. After the dances come to an end, the initiates eat a symbolic meal from the nose or forehead of the Kipoko mask. This meal consists significantly of a ball of manioc paste mixed with millet and a bit of chicken. The ability to swallow this viscous repast without regurgitating is taken to indicate the boys' potency, one of the principal objectives of intiation. It is a tense moment, as the boys know that they will receive a ritual thrashing after the meal. Following this final test, the initiates pledge to keep secret the teachings of the mukanda (Mudiji-Selnge 1981:229–230; Strother, personal communication 2003).

Why the initiates should eat off someone else's nose (albeit a mask) has to do with a characteristic of the chief, to whom the mask relates. Pende chiefs and Pende diviners are expected to have an extremely refined sense of smell, by which they can distinguish the odors of ritual and civil violations and the perpetrators. On the mask, the mouth is always tiny or completely absent, to symbolize the discretionary caution in the chief's speech, but the nose is large because, as consultants told Strother (in Pemberton 2000:103), the chief must be sensitive to the "smell of stolen meat":

> My host, chief Kende (Katshivi a Khoji), returned to the house one day in 1987, agitated because he had smelled goat meat cooking behind a closed kitchen door. Many Pende find cooking behind closed doors suspicious because it reveals a desire to hoard. In this case, the chief knew for a fact that the villager owned no livestock whatsoever.... Kende waited until the owner of the goat discovered his loss and then discreetly pointed the investigation in the right direction.
>
> Several oft-repeated proverbs emphasize that the chief should know all that is going on around him but should pretend not to know what he has heard, seen, or smelled.... Chief Nzambi explained that, in order to safeguard his people, the chief must be sensitive to the "odor of sorcery" (*vumba dia wanga*) and the "odor of the dead" (*vumba dia vumbi*). The hypertrophy of the sensory organs on Kipoko represents the chief's state of heightened consciousness.

This characteristic specifically connects the mask, and its referent, the chief, to the dead, whose natural medium is air, on which smells are carried and upon which the olfactory sense is exclusively dependent. The olfactory, based upon breathing, unlike any other sense, is acutely tied to life itself (Strother, in Pemberton 2000:104).

L. M. B. & F. J. L.

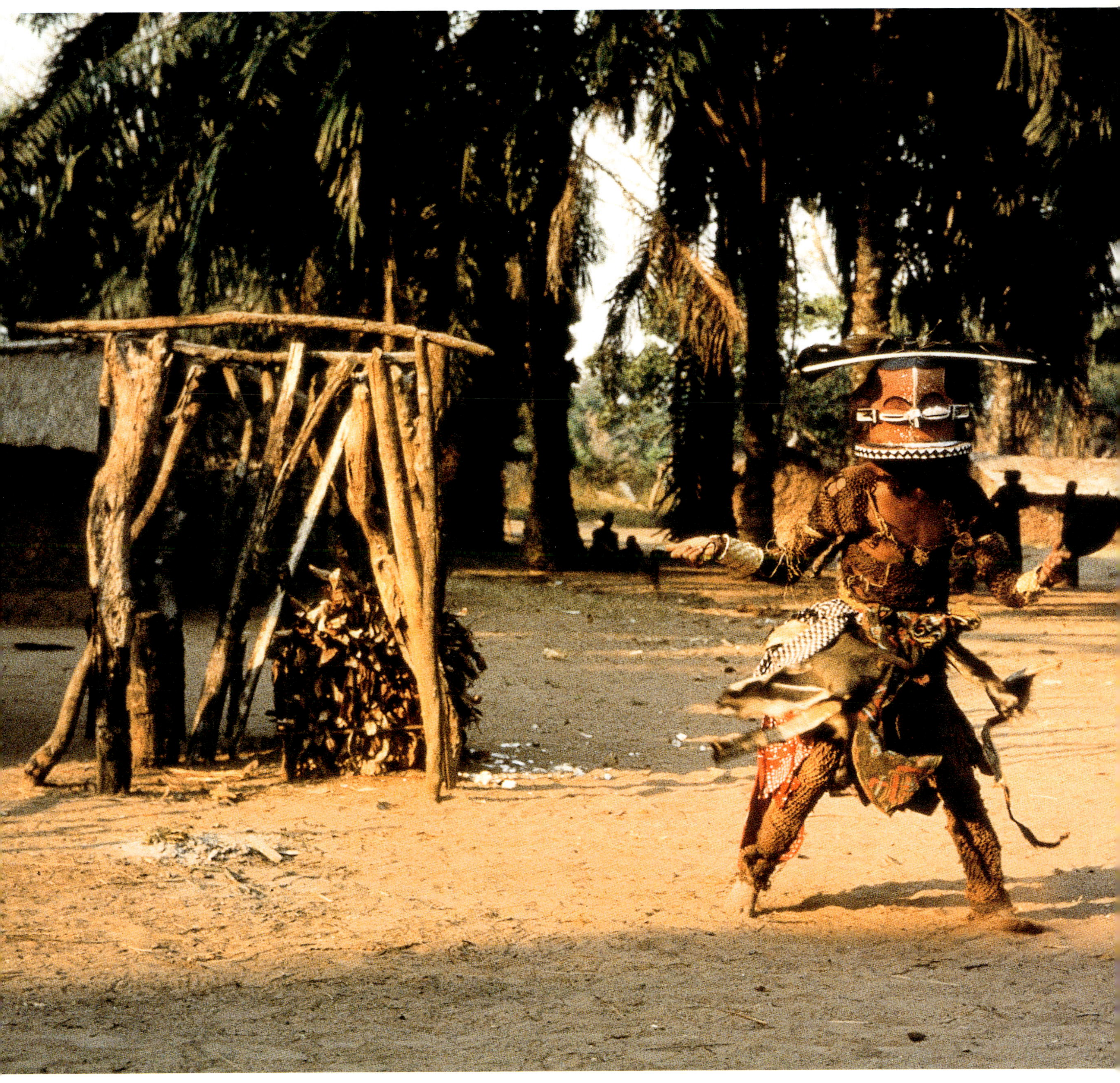

The dancer Sombola performing the mask Kipoko for Chief Kombo-Kiboto.
Pende, Ndjindji, Congo (Kinshasa). Photo: Z.S. Strother, 1987

61

The Aroma of Milk, the Container, and The Body: a Borana Milk Container (*Gorfa*)

One of the most elegant expressions of a woman's role in East African pastoral societies is the woven milk container. Among the Borana vessels like the BMA container are called gorfa, and among the Gabra, according to Labelle Prussin (1987:41), they are referred to as *xoda*. In this brief essay, we shall refer to the BMA vessel as a gorfa, from a Borana woman, though it is understood that it may have come from a closely-related people.[1] The gorfa and similar woven vessels are light and very durable—ideal storage vessels for people who periodically must relocate to accommodate the grazing needs of their cattle and camels.

A gorfa made by Jilo Holo held by her daughter who stands at the entrance to their home. Photo taken 23 May 1993 at Dololo Makala. Photo: Neal Sobania and Raymond Silverman

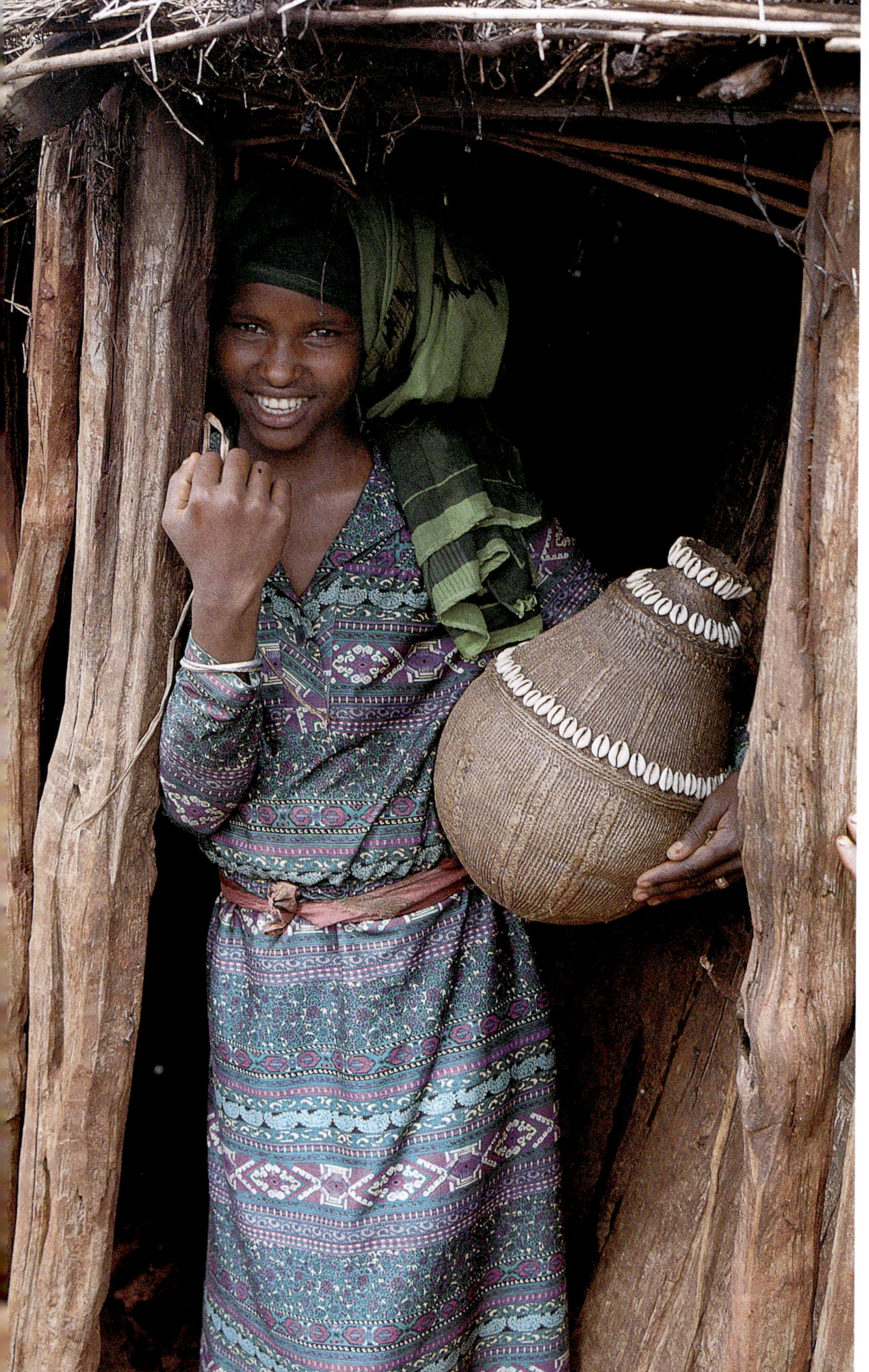

Milk Container (*Gorfa*)
Borana/Gabra, Kenya/Ethiopia
c. Mid-20th century
Fiber, leather, cowrie shells, giraffe hair, resin, H. 30 cm (w/o tail)
Gift of Carolyn Barnes, Alexandria, Virginia, in Memory of Murvil and Katherine Barnes
BMA 1998.587

A variety of containers used in various domestic and ritual contexts are made from different materials including, wood, gourd, animal horn, leather, and of course, plant fibers. In most pastoral societies in southern Ethiopia and northern Kenya the working of these materials follows gender lines. Wood and leather are the domain of men, whereas women make woven fiber containers as well as horn and gourd vessels. Marco Bassi (1999:73), an Italian anthropologist who has spent many years among the Borana, points out that this is an expression of the "differentiated but complementary roles of man and woman," in Borana society. Their interdependence is poignantly demonstrated in the production of certain vessels that incorporate two or more materials that require the work of both a man and woman, often a husband and wife.

The gorfa is an object intimately tied, both physically and symbolically, to the identity of women in Borana society. All women learn to weave these containers, usually from their mothers, as part of growing up in a Borana family. It takes considerable skill and many years of practice to attain the perfect symmetry and elegance that are a hallmark of these woven containers.

Several kinds of plant fiber are used in the production of the gorfa.[2] The container is built using a coil technique that begins at the base. Several strands of a fiber called *suta* are bunched together and wrapped at regular intervals with either one of two other fibers, *ergamsa* or *holota*. The weaver, using two types of awls, must be extremely careful when spacing the wrapping fibers, for these form the vertical ridges that are the fundamental surface design on the container. This is enhanced with a decorative cross-stitched pattern called *obrisa*, which consists of a number of more pronounced vertical lines. Most women know how to produce only one pattern, better weavers utilize several obrisa. The most common pattern, seen on the BMA gorfa, is called *obrisa loni* (gorfa of the cattle), because it resembles the hoof of cattle. This is painstaking work—Bassi (1999:84) estimates that it takes a woman, working several hours a day, several months to complete a container. A tightly defined set of formal and functional criteria govern the weaving of fiber containers, but Bassi (1999:70–71) suggests that there is room for creativity, for improvisation.[3]

Gudrun Dahl (1990:132) explains that the gorfa is one of many types of woven fiber vessels generically referred to as *kodda*, that are used for storing fresh milk and curds.[4] What distinguishes the gorfa from other woven milk containers are two horizontal bands, one called *laba* and another situated one or two centimeters above it, called *rifto*. These stitched lines visually divide the vessel in two sections, the lower section is roughly two-thirds the total length of the vessel. The laba and rifto provide a means for attaching a single band of cowrics (*clelani*) to the container—the application of these shells in this manner is another attribute that differentiates the gorfa from other woven containers.

In addition to serving as a mode of decoration, the cowries signify the concepts of prosperity, femininity, and fertility.[5] Cowries

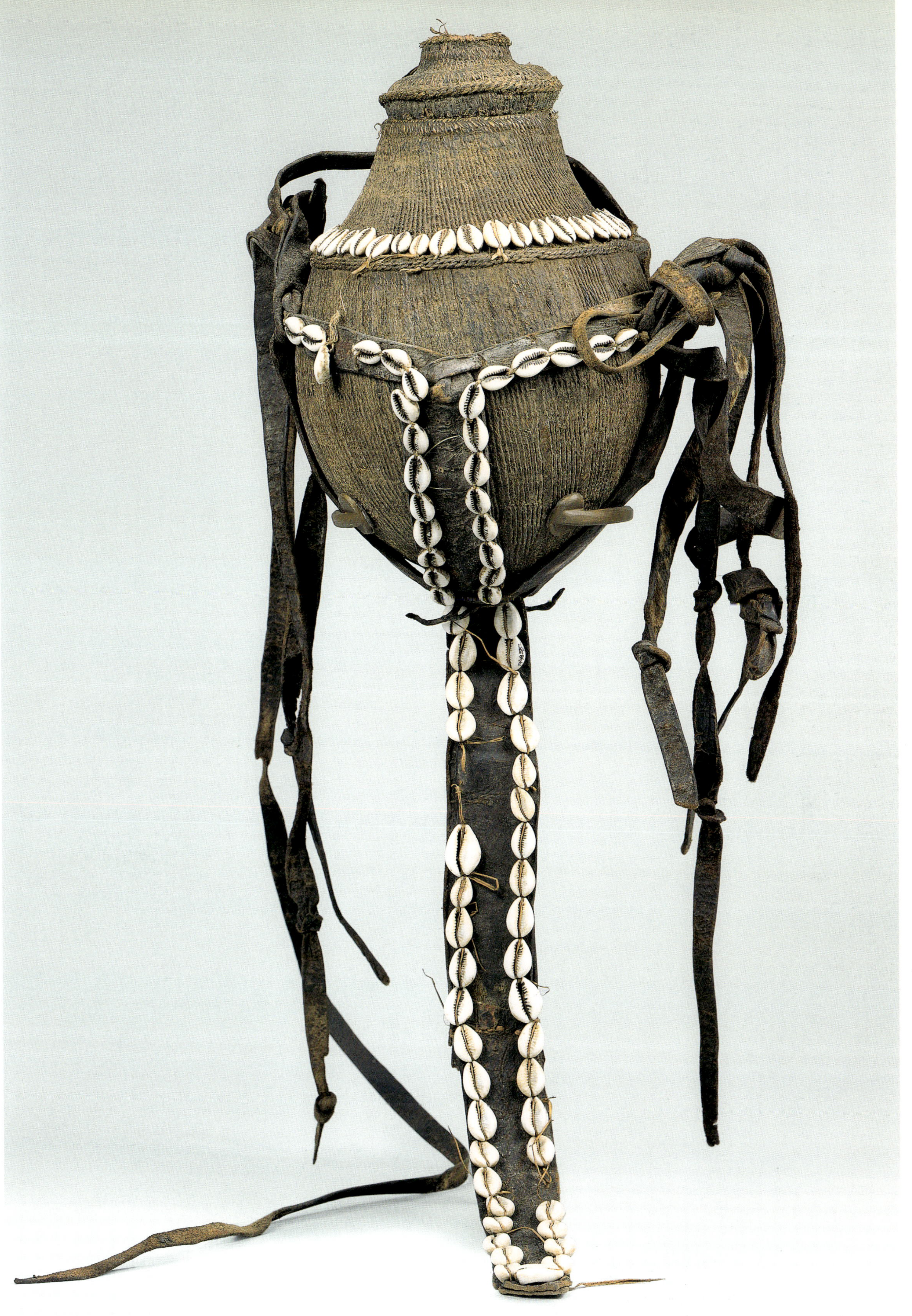

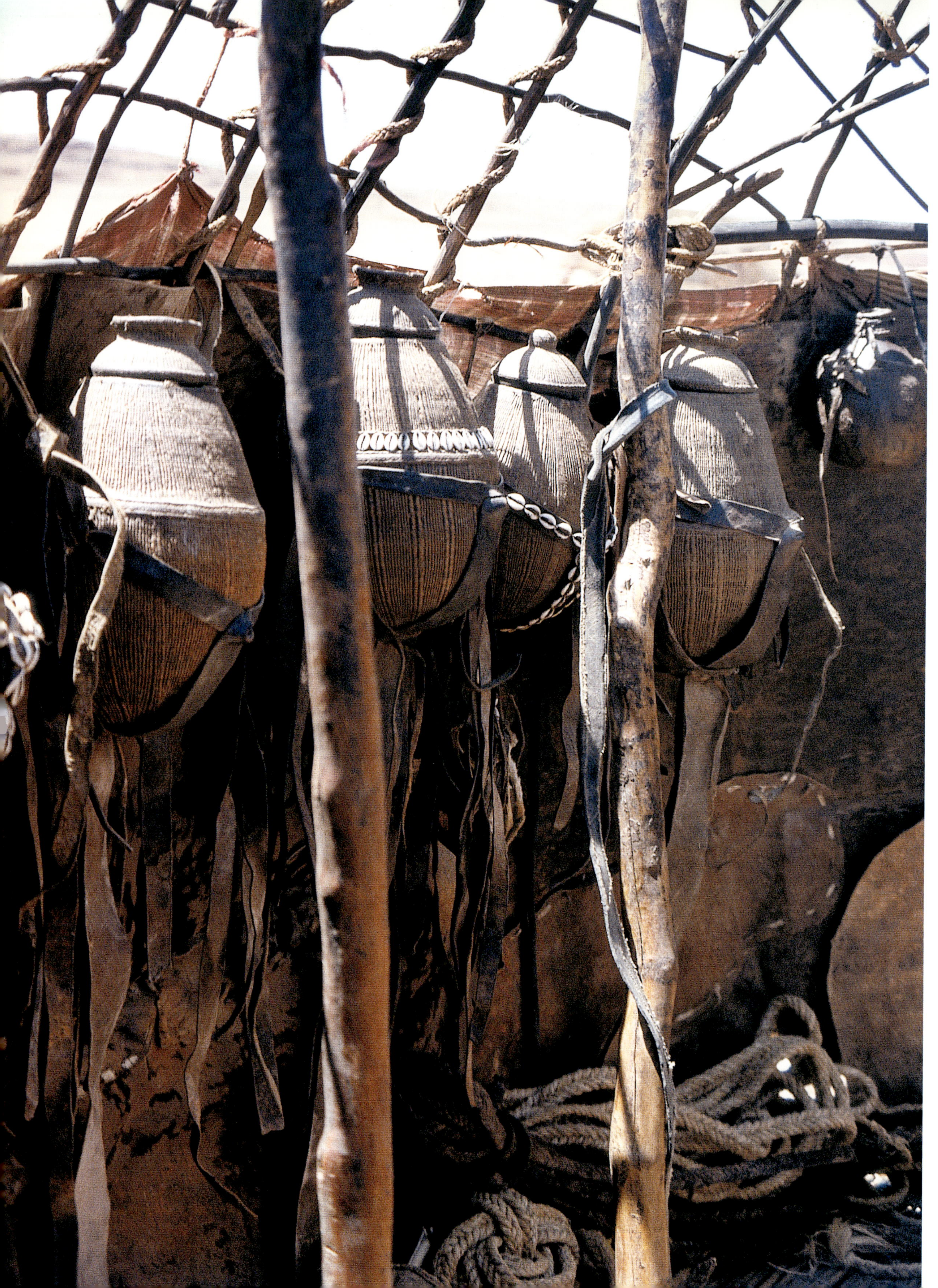

may also be sewn to the leather suspension straps (*seepani*), and to sheets of leather that are sometimes attached to the container and are part of the display aesthetic. The visual profile and function of the vessel also allude to ideas of femininity and fertility, especially to motherhood. The form of the gorfa and similar woven containers is likened to a womb, the milk contained within is nourishment that sustains the family. Milk and its by-products, like butter, also carry symbolic meaning. Dahl (1990:132–33) tells us that "Borana rituals of fertility frequently make use of lavish amounts of milk and butter. The association of milk with semen is underlined by an idea of the milk pot as a womb." Significantly, the containers used in such rituals are always the woven fiber vessels produced by women.[6] Even the technique used to fabricate these containers—the weaving of plant fibers—alludes to another important female activity, the plaiting of hair that occurs at critical times in a woman's life. When a girl marries, her hair is coifed in two plaits; when she is pregnant, all her hair is plaited (Bassi 1999:75).

The gorfa and another woven vessel called *chicho*, play important roles in marriage rites, and serve as an expression of the relationship between a husband and wife. When a girl marries, she must produce a chicho filled with milk, a chicho that was made by her mother when she thought it was time for her daughter to marry. And the groom's family must present at least one gorfa to the new couple. Bassi (1999:75) explains that the chicho, in effect, signifies the marriage itself. Losing or destroying the chicho is a portent of misfortune. When a husband dies, he is interred and his most important possessions are broken and put on top of the grave, including the chicho of his first wife. Bassi (1999:75–76) observes that "At death, the man's reproductive capacity ceases; his wife's *ciicoo* [chicho], which both stands for and promotes reproductive capacity, no longer has any reason to exist." Similarly, when a married woman dies, her gorfa is cut in half and put on top of her grave.

Still another dimension of the gender association of the gorfa is the context in which these vessels are stored and displayed. They may be seen hanging on the back wall of the house, a structure that is owned by a woman. The milk containers are suspended from the roof supports using seepani (the leather straps). There may be several types of vessels, including the *gorfa*, displayed in this fashion.

It may seem strange that a basketry container would be used for holding liquids. Indeed, the gorfa and similar woven vessels, are often mistakenly identified as gourds covered with plant fiber.[7] These containers are made watertight by placing a burning piece of aromatic wood or a piece of charcoal made from an aromatic wood inside the container, covering the container and then shaking it so that the ember comes in contact with the sides of the vessel. This process, repeated a number of times, pulls resins out of the wood and plant fiber that seal the inner surface. The interior is thus blackened and permeated with a distinctive smoky aroma. This process is repeated each time the gorfa is used as a means of sanitizing the vessel. Prior to filling an empty gorfa with milk, a small amount of water is put in the vessel along with a hot piece of aromatic wood. The vessel is covered and shaken, the steam that is produced cleanses the interior. Bassi (1999:84) reports that this process is usually repeated a least six times before the container is ready for use. A photograph cannot capture the distinctive smell—the melding of aromatic smoke and sour milk—that is a vital part of the aesthetic associated with these milk containers.

It is significant that like so many other qualities associated the woven milk container, the fumigation process has analogs in its owner's life. Both Dahl (1990:135) and Prussin (1987:41) note that Borana and Gabra houses contain a small depression covered by an openwork dome (*mano*) that functions as an incense burner, used by women to periodically fumigate (cleanse) the house as well as their own bodies. Dahl (1990:135) explains that a woman, "either expecting intercourse, or having had it ... may use the mano for a smoke bath to purify her private parts." As we have noted above, the sexual woman and the vessel are one.

Raymond A. Silverman

1 The cultural information presented in this entry has been gleaned from three sources, Prussin 1987, Dahl 1990, and Bassi 1999. Despite Bassi's (1999:65, 68, 70) assertion that the Borana consider themselves a "unique" people with an "autonomous ethnic identity" they do share many cultural characteristics with neighboring peoples, especially those who are members of other Oromo-speaking groups. In addition to the Borana and Gabra, similar vessels are found among the Somali, Rendille, and several Oromo groups.

2 Bassi (1999:78–83) offers a detailed account of the weaving as practiced by Borana women; Prussin (1987:42–43) describes a similar process employed by Gabra women.

3 Bassi (1999:69) has produced a table naming thirteen distinct container types used by the Borana that can be differentiated by the materials out of which they are made, their function, and physical profile.

4 Prussin (1987) uses an alternative spelling, *xoda*.

5 As is the case in many societies where cowries are used, these shells (that are harvested in the Maldive Islands and have long been an important trade commodity throughout Africa) are a visual metaphor for the human vagina.

6 See Bassi 1999:74 for a discussion of the use of gorfa and other woven vessels in ritual.

7 There are, in fact, certain types of gourd vessels that are completely or partially covered with woven fiber. See for example the two Guji (an Oromo people living near the Borana in Ethiopia) containers illustrated in Bassi 1999:67.

Milk containers hanging on the interior wall of a house. Gabra, Ethiopia
Photo: Labelle Prussin, 1987

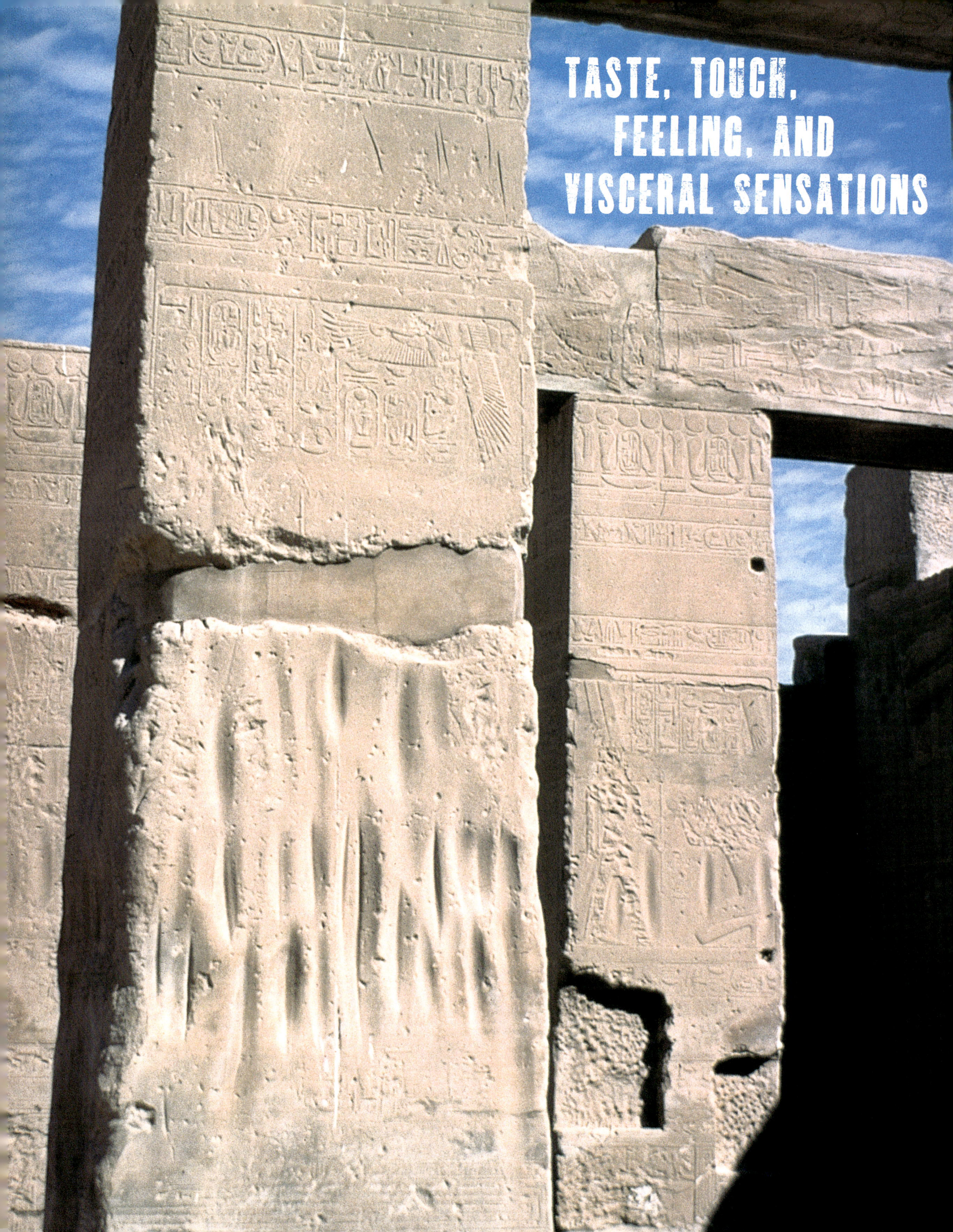

TASTE, TOUCH, FEELING, AND VISCERAL SENSATIONS

The Temne of Sierra Leone have two generic words to describe the five senses that European science identifies: *nànk* = see, and *tàl* = hear, feel, smell, and taste (although there are also distinct terms for each). These two divisions of the senses seem to correspond to spatial limitations. Ordinary human beings cannot see into spiritual space (except at night, an extraordinary time), but they can hear the sounds and they can feel the spirits touching them, as "just something behind my shoulder" (Butt-Thompson [1929] 1970:189). This is signified by a special word, *ninsnè* (Littlejohn 1963:13). A sudden gust of wind is said to be a spirit passing. A spiritual apparition is *a-yintàli*, "feeling a spirit." I mentioned above that the sense of smell is shown to give spiritual access to the Temne. Presumably they could also taste the spiritual world if the occasion arose though I have no data on this. This distinction between "seeing" and the other four senses is important in the ritual "closing" of space, as in the sanctifying of ritual arenas. Even though the space may still be seen after closing, for example, at a distance, it is said not to be perceived at all because it cannot be sensed in the other four ways. Understanding is more directly connected to hearing, feeling, smelling, and tasting, than it is to sight. In the West, one says "I see," to mean "I understand." The Temne say *i tàl*, "I hear/feel/smell/taste" (Lamp 1982:33–36; see also Stoller 1989).

The intimacy with which the African audience interacts with the performer and the art object in dance, in shrine ritual, and in utilitarian contexts, finds its ultimate expression in the sensory experiences of tasting and touching. "In taste, the experience of world and body is perhaps most closely interwoven; the act of perceiving involves the literal incorporation of the perceived" (Leder 1990:15). African performance sometimes involves not only participation in a feast, but also direct contact between mask or figure and the mouth, the lips, the teeth, the tongue, and the viscera, as we shall see in this section. The sense of touch is satisfied frequently in the physical contact that the audience has with the material art form. Robert Farris Thompson, in his essay here, shows how the power of sacred herbal substances can be absorbed into the body through touch.

Sacrificial foods are almost a ubiquitous element in the performance of ritual throughout Africa, involving feasts, especially of rice and yams, and of rather dramatically slaughtered cattle, goats, sheep, and fowl, with the consumption of beverages, especially alcoholic, such as palm wine or millet beer, inviting the participation of the entire community. Among the Baga, the bringing of the wine, itself, is an elaborate celebratory performance. Foods and beverages are often offered to shrines and shrine figures and placed on the site. Among the Igbo, "Many prestigious and powerful masked spirits may not dance without ritual preparations of mask, costume, wearer, and environment to ensure the success of their outing. First, certain forceful spirit-masks living in shrines must be awakened by sacrificial feeding before appearing in public.... Others need only small offerings (e.g., kola) ..." (Cole & Aniakor 1984:114). Yoruba twin figures (p. 261), described in this section, are offered plates of food which they are assumed to consume in order to mollify any penchant for malicious behavior. In the case of the Pende Kipoko mask (p. 247), the entire performance may be infused with the offerings of millet and other foods scattered about in the interaction of audience and mask performers.

Commonly, food, drink, herbs, and organic substances are applied to the object itself. In ceremonies with Moba figures (p. 185), accompanying the ritual invocation of "your sweet meal," a porridge is ladled onto the shrine and the wooden figure and the rest is distributed to the children to eat. Elaborate sacrificial preparations for several days precede the performance of the Numu Gbain mask, saturating its surface with powerful materials, as discussed below. Some figures, and their shrines, such as the Lobi figure (p. 159) or the Manding *Kòmò* Kun headdress (p. 233) are meant to grow with time and the application of substances chosen for their nutritional value.

Ritual scratching of inscriptions on a stone column for making sacred tea.
Temple of Seti I, New Kingdom, Dynasty XIX, West Bank, Luxor, Egypt
Photo: Frederick John Lamp, 2001

In some cases, the material art object comes in contact with the mouth of a ritual practitioner or participant, either in an active or passive way. Occasionally, the material object is actually tasted in a manipulation of the art form. Islamic tradition in Africa includes the drinking of sacred writing: when the ink used by a scholar is washed off the writing board, it can be drunk to absorb spiritual power (see imagery in the BMA example, p. 119). This follows closely a practice pursued for thousands of years in Egypt, from the dynastic era to the present, in which worshippers scratched off the surface of texts inscribed on stone temples. The collected stone dust was used to prepare a tea which the supplicants drank to absorb spiritual power inherent in the texts. In the use of the Pende Kipoko mask (p. 246) in initiation ritual, the young male initiates actually eat ritual foods off the nose of the mask, in which the art form literally enters the mouth of the participant in the performance. The initiates are in a state of anxiety as they eat the meal from the surface of the mask, and the critical response is in their ability, or disability, to digest the meal and not regurgitate. Male initiates of the Bamana Kòmò association may be forced to lick the *Kòmò* mask (p. 233), with all its accumulation of dreadful substances, in a metaphor for sexual violation, by which they are bound to the jurisdiction of Kòmò. These ingestions bring the sensory perception of the "art form" beyond the usual exteroception (of the five external senses), and even beyond proprioception (of the body structure: muscles, bones, joints, and the inner ear) experienced in shared movement and gesture, to the very recessive interoception, the sensations of the viscera (Leder 1990:39). In Kòmò initiation, the ability to ingest some fairly disgusting substances is concomitant with their vow of silence, i.e., their adherence to the exclusivity of Kòmò, and specifically their restraint in emitting prohibited sounds from the mouth, reinforced through symbolic violation of accepted cultural "taste."

In other cases, tasting may be literal or metaphoric. One often doesn't know because of the secrecy of African ritual. The men's Pòrò initiation among the Temne in Sierra Leone was described to me as sweet and alluring, and in Pòrò ritual the members sing: "Pòrò is tasty, More than Maggi [a commercial food seasoning]. Tasty—Ooh" (*am-Pòrò a nemnem-o, an-thas a magi-o. nemnem-o*—Lamp 1982:141). Whether this refers to the initiates actually eating something ritually, I wasn't told. But among the related Baga of Guinea, initiation into adulthood is called *kidi molom*, literally "to eat the sacred/secret," and the participants conceive of the process as one in which "knowledge is eaten and embodied, not only 'learned.' It is possible that the process of initiation among the Baga included a final stage in which the initiates would literally *eat* the objects (the masks), either smashed or burned to ashes. This is a common practice in other West African initiation rites; one in which objecthood literally feeds back onto individuals' subjectivity and personal growth ..." (Sarró 2002:227). When their sacred mask was confiscated by a Muslim missionary in the 1950s, the material manifestation of the spiritual was gone, but, as an elder ritual specialist told Sarro in 2001, "he could not open up our bellies," meaning that the most enduring manifestation of the spiritual form was not the wooden and fiber mask, but its ingestion.

The sense of touch is brought into play in masking, in the use of the shrine, and in body art. Wooden figures with rounded, voluptuous features, used by the Yoruba to commemorate twins (p. 261), or by the Baule to represent spirit lovers (similar to the BMA example on p. 139), are lovingly rubbed by the hands with oil and other substances as one would care for a baby's skin. When the Baga dance the D'mba headdress (p. 223) the men dancing around her will frequently pat her flat breasts dramatically and with great feeling in affirmation of her fecundity, creating a shiny dark patina that contrasts with the rest of the surface. Their act of boisterously coming in contact with the breasts emphasizes their firmness as well as the energy they engender, and recalls the closeness and familiarity between the child and the mother in an act of masquerade meant by the men to honor the mothers.

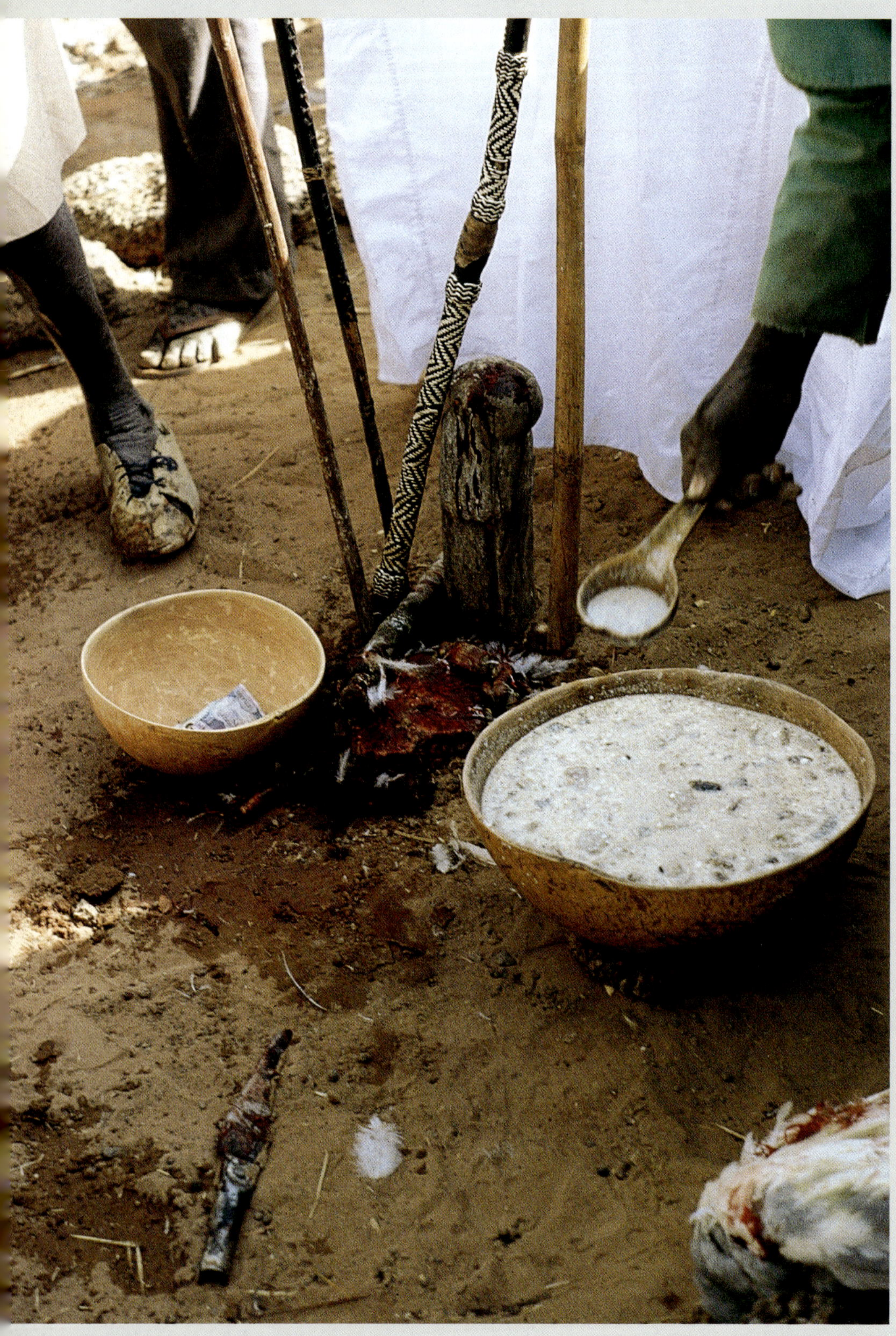

An offering of "porridge" is made to a shrine during the *saara* ceremony. Moba, village of Nasiet, Togo. Photo: Christine Mullen Kreamer, 1980

Aesthetic appreciation may involve the touch as much as sight. Decorative body scarification is appreciated by many Africans for its visual effect, but Henry Drewal (personal communication, 2003) has written, "While the sense of sight certainly is used to perceive and appreciate them initially, it is the sense of touch (whether actual or virtual) that provokes a deeper sensual pleasure and appreciation. As one Yoruba man confided to me, 'When we see a young woman with kolo, and try to touch the kolo with our hands, the weather changes to another thing [we become sexually aroused]!'" (see also H. Dread 1980:15). The tactile designs may act as an invitation to touch. Touching another's body, generally, in Africa, is less fraught with issues of personal space than it is for Westerners, and both women (in my experience) and men frequently touch persons of the same or opposite sex in ways Westerners would fear as threatening and invasive. There is no need to say "Excuse me."

Eberhard Fischer (1970:38–40) recorded the tactile evaluation of a new mask by its performer among the Dan of Liberia. An old mask had been illegally sold to a Malinke trader, so two carvers, Tame and Si, who had both had experience with this mask and its performance, were each asked to reproduce the mask. Through the sense of touch only, the performer evaluated and compared the masks:

> Then, during a family festival in the sacred grove, the performer of the mask, with his eyes blindfolded, made his choice of the mask that had been promised to him. It was the one by Tame. . . .

The sense of feeling, as the performer and the audience become one, and share physiological experiences through the medium of spiritual energy, is a common element in African ritual. The frequency of spiritual possession is testimony to this. Audience participants become so absorbed into music and the movement that they enter a transcendent state, from which they become inextricable from these elements of the art form. They become the art form. Strother, in her essay on the Pende (p. 88) in the previous section, shows that the masquerade has the power to effect kinesthetic change within the bodies of the viewers. In contrasting the heat of life to the coolness of death within the dance performance, the performer succeeds in "making rejoice the bodies that are shivering," i.e. freeing from their burdens the cold, the aging, and the ill. In contrast, prohibitions against touch may also protect the audience, especially women, as in the case of the Kuba Ishyeen Imaalu mask (p. 93), according to Torday & Joyce (1910).

Let us return for a moment to the account by Paul Stoller in the earlier section on Sound, in which the anthropologist's guide, the Songhay sorcerer, discovered a spirit "double" in a pile of millet husk. Can we really believe that, although Stoller heard nothing, felt nothing, and saw nothing of the spirit "double," the sorcerer did? Doesn't this rear up the head of "Negritude," or suggest some sort of primitivizing, a notion that somehow traditional Songhay have maintained heightened, primal senses that modern Westerners have lost? Or is it, rather, just the opposite: that African culture has developed in a way that Western culture intentionally has not? The sorcerer was shocked that the anthropologist could not sense these things. Rather than asking why he could hear, feel, and see, we ought to question why the anthropologist could not. To understand Western perception, we need to return to the philosophy of Descartes, on the division of mind and body, and further, to Saint Paul "denying the flesh," to Plato, who saw the body as a "prison," and the dialogues of Socrates. Socrates posed a question to his friend, Simmias, about the great truths of justice, beauty, goodness, greatness, health, and strength: "Now did you ever see any of these things with your eyes?" Simmias answered "No, never." "Or did you ever grasp them with any other of the bodily senses?" Socrates continued about acquiring true understanding:

> And the man who would do this most purely would be he who approaches each with thought alone, not adding the evidence of sight to thought, nor dragging in any of the other senses to join with reasoning; but who, in deploying pure thought, makes his attempt to track down each part—also pure—of what really is, separating himself to the greatest possible extent from his eyes and ears and, so to speak, from his body as a whole, in the conviction that whenever it participates the body disturbs and inhibits the acquisition of truth and thought by the soul (*Phaedo* in Ley 1999:5–6).

Western culture is not a single track, however, and has had many divergent periods and countercultures. The Middle Ages, for example, knew little of Plato, and seemed to care less, with great sensual appeal in its arts. Jean-Jacques Rousseau, in the 1760's, argued for the priority of feeling: "I feel my own heart, and I know human beings.... I felt before I thought.... I had no idea of things, at a time when all feelings were already known to me. I had conceived of nothing, I had felt everything" (*Confessions*, in Ley 1999:53). Although Western culture has not been immersed in 2000 continuous years of bodily denial, the influences of Paul, Socrates, and Plato, however, have been enduring and deep, even among those who have never read them.

Victor Turner (1986:73–74, 80) saw in modernist thought, concurrent with colonialism, an obsession with boundaries, polarization, restraint, and control, in which "cognition, idea, rationality, were paramount." Essentializing categories invited rigidity and compartmentalization. It is in this environment that the concept of negritude developed, separating reason (for the Europeans) from emotion (for Africans). Modernist art historians and artists frequently argued for the pure contemplation of art and the pristine production of art free from experience that would imprison the mind. Some used the term, "magic," to describe an untainted communication between mind and the art work on the walls—"pleasing to the eye, and enshrouded with an air of mystery," in the words of Duon Sadia quoted here in the introduction.

Drew Leder (1990) describes contemporary Western experience as "the absent body," in which self-understanding remains incomplete (p. 3):

> Western society is typified by a certain "disembodied" style of life. Our shelters protect us from direct corporeal engagement with the outer world, our relative prosperity alleviating, for many of us, immediate physical need and distress. Via machines we are disinvested of work that once belonged to the muscles. Technologies of rapid communication and transportation allow us to transcend what used to be the natural limits imposed by the body. Operations are mediated by the written word or the computer calculation, where once a living human presence was required. A rising interest in finding ways to "return to the body," whether via exercise, hatha yoga, body therapies, craftwork, or intimacy with nature, is but a reaction to this general trend toward a "decorporealized" existence.

To understand is to feel, for the Temne. Postmodern thought argues for understanding through bodily experience, through the somatic, without the separation of mind and body. This requires not just a new way of thinking, but a different kind of training. The difference between the traditional Western way of knowledge and that of much of Africa is in the privileging or non-privileging of literacy, and thus, of sight. This was expressed in a dialogue between the linguist, Charles Bird, and the renowned Manding jeli (musician/oral historian), Kele Monson Diabate (as recounted in Charry 2000:339):

> **Bird:** If you help us, if you help us, we will write down your words and they will live forever.
>
> **Diabate:** You and your dried words. What are they to me? The meaning of my words is in the moisture of the breath that carries them.

62

Idiom of Clairvoyance, Healing, and Shared Moral Inquiry: a Kongo Figure (*Nkisi Lumweno*)

Medicine Figure (*Nkisi Lumweno*)
Kongo, Mayombe District, Congo (Kinshasa)
c. Early 20th century
Wood, glass, metal, pitch, H. 27.5 cm
Gift of Alan Wurtzburger
BMA 1954.145.65

The mirror-medicine figure in Kongo takes us far and deep into the theatricalized performance of the healer [*nganga*] in action. Such images are the possession of visionaries, and they embody, as we shall see, idioms of clairvoyance and healing. They relate to the power to cross worlds.

Nkisi lumweno is one of the instruments nganga will use when he is working for society. When not in use, he keeps it hidden in his *ngumbu*, or secret cache. Here he keeps in readiness herbs and roots and the nkisi lumweno which he will use to detect [*mu landa*] mysterious sources of social dissension and 'to screen situations' [*mu séngumuna mambu*], that is, bringing them closer to sight and understanding.

Exorcism. Kongo, Loango region, Congo (Kinshasa). Drawing: Mme Paule Crampel, *c.* 1893, from Lehuard 1989

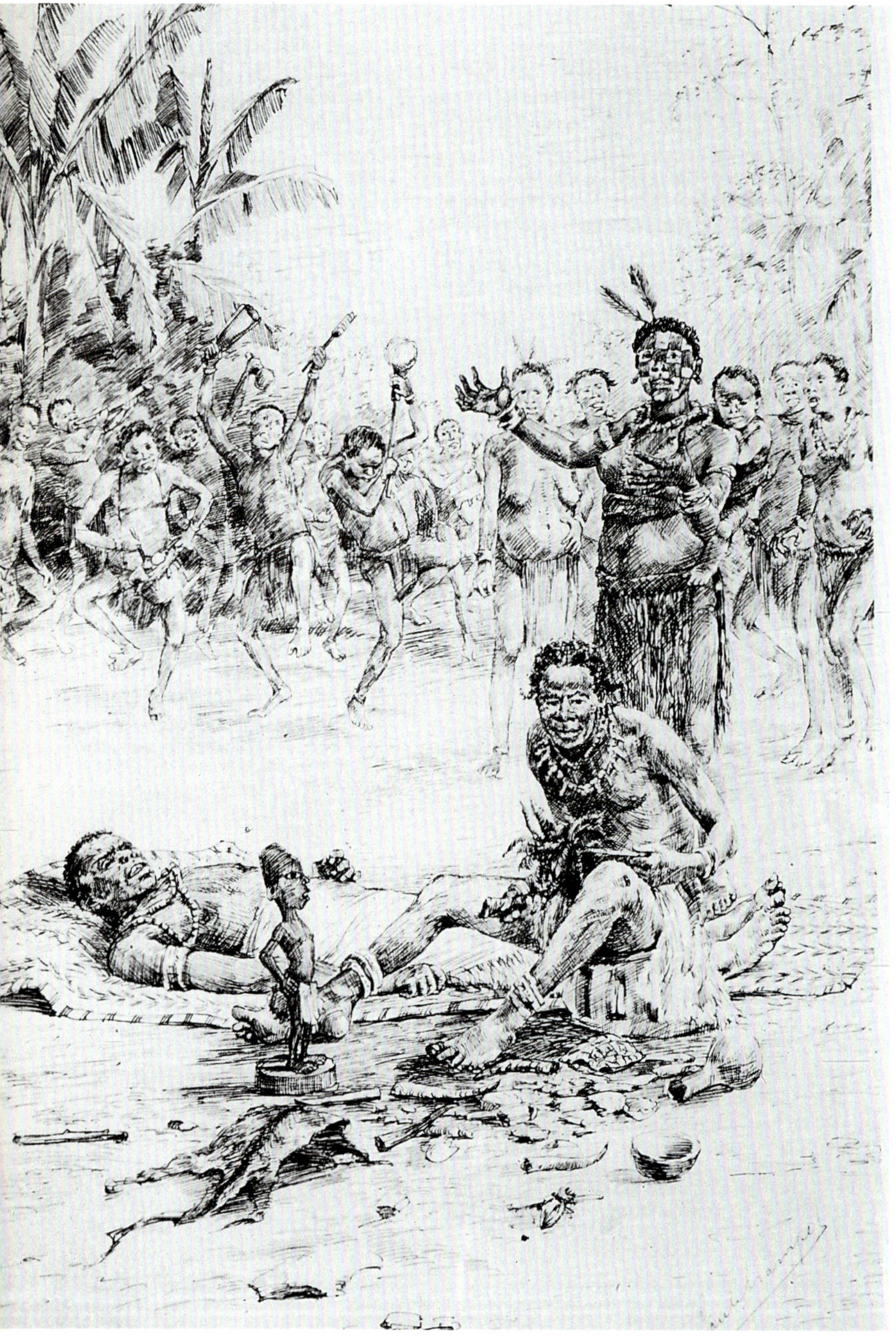

He will take the mirror-statuette out into the central court of a village or lineage compound when there is a healing process or ceremony [*nkungu*] to be performed. Often the nkungu relates to a situation when something has been lost in a village or to a problem with no comprehensible causes.

Nganga strides into the center of the circle and deposits nkisi lumweno [the mirror image] on a mat on the ground and places beside it a plate [*longa*]. In the plate he will build up the medicine to see [*ku mona*] into evil. This he will make with powerful herbs and roots. He may trace lines in white kaolin around both his eyes to emphasize clairvoyance. He may cause the villagers to wash their hands in this medicine of moral inquiry, binding the community to the process through common tactile experience. Instantly, the people absorb through their hands the power of that medicine. It is believed to cause any guilty person in the midst of the community to fall into possession [*mayembo*] and confess all his sins.

The nkisi figurine with an embedded mirror of vision, containing impacted medicines, functions like myriad volumes on the law, dripping erudition, which stud the walls of a lawyer's office and which are meant to impress all clients with his knowledge and his learning.

Nkisi lumweno's high-rise coiffure, according to informants in Mayombe, associates not only the crest of a rooster but the rooster's ability to herald the advance of the dawn. In other words, it intimates nganga's power to throw light on hard problems. This high-crested hairstyle, in Mayombe, announces the identity of a medium.

Towering crest, eyes of glass, mirror embedded in the chest, impacted and shared medicines—all these are stanzas in a poem promising expansion into pure mystic vision. The pieces of glass [*vela*] in the eyes and mirror [*nguya* or *matala-tala*] in the abdomen mean that nganga has the power to see wide and far.

The statuette is a device [*sadulu*] to anchor an unfolding positive divination, and detection of evil, in the middle of the circle, in the medicine-bearing dish set beside the statuette. In this heavily saturated atmosphere everything has its time and place: the nganga, his "statuette-diploma" (the latter a phrase coined by Fu-Kiau Bunscki) and the medicine itself on the plate. All three combine, delivering deep mastery for the good of a village under stress.

Robert Farris Thompson

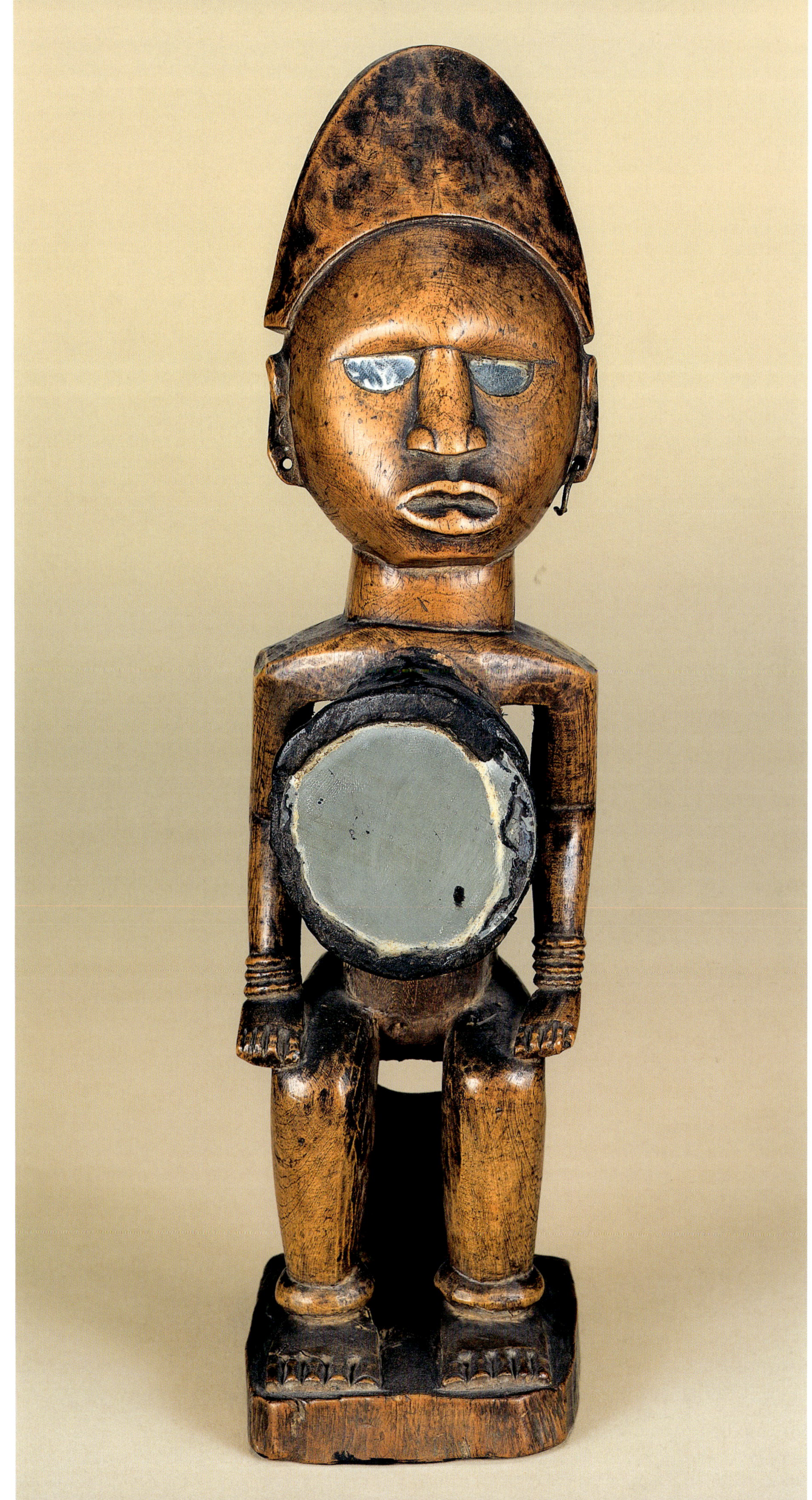

83 Cooling Double Trouble: Yoruba Twin Figures (*Ere Ibeji*)

Male and Female Twin Figures (*Ere Ibeji*)
Yoruba, Nigeria
c. Early 20th century
Wood, bluing, encrustation of camwood powder, H. 28.5 cm
Gift of Nance Asher, Denton, Maryland
BMA 1988.65.1 & .2

The Yoruba see the birth of twins as both auspicious and dangerous, requiring special ritual of propitiation. As late as the twentieth century, the death of a twin commonly prompted the parents to commission the carving of a small figure (*ere*—carving, *ibeji*—twin), the same sex as the deceased child. If the second twin died, a mate would be carved as well. The figure was cared for much as a real child is tended.

When a twin died, the mother would go to a diviner to determine the best person to carve the image. Before and during the carving, and upon completion of the sculpture, the mother would give food to the artist (Fagg, et al., 1980:80 and 162). A carver from Igbomina described what happened after the figure was complete (Houlberg 1973:91–92):

> "When my father would finish the ibeji he would wash it in a calabash of water with 'medicine' to make the spirit good. The leaves of a type of bean plant called *oweahun* where used.... He would then put a mixture of shea butter and palm-oil on the sculpture. By then it looked the color of butter"

The accumulations, he continued, were up to the owner:

> "He would not put *osun* (camwood) or beads on it. The mother did that."

The strings of beads were commonly wrapped around the figure's waist, neck, or arm. The colors are indicative of special relationship which a mother enjoys with one of the *orishas* (gods) in the Yoruba spiritual world. Blue beads and a lead bracelet are symbols of the Oshun, the goddess responsible for providing children; a red and white necklace is a sign of *Shangó* (Fagg, et al., 1980:140 and 162). Brass anklets were applied to the figure to prevent the living twin from becoming an *abiku*, or a child born to die. Beads made from palm nuts and tied around the waist protected against illness (Houlberg 1973:26). Some figures have a carved *tirah*, a leather pouch containing either quotes from the Koran or medicinal herbs.

The twin figures were clothed in real cloth clothing, just as a real child. If the family was wealthy, the clothes would be sumptuous, including heavily beaded vests, sometimes laden with cowrie shells, a traditional form of money in many West African communities, or even gold or silver jewelry (Thompson

Shrine for deceased twins, representing several generations of twins' deaths in a single-family, with offerings. Imosan, Ijebu, Nigeria. Photo: John Pemberton III, 1982

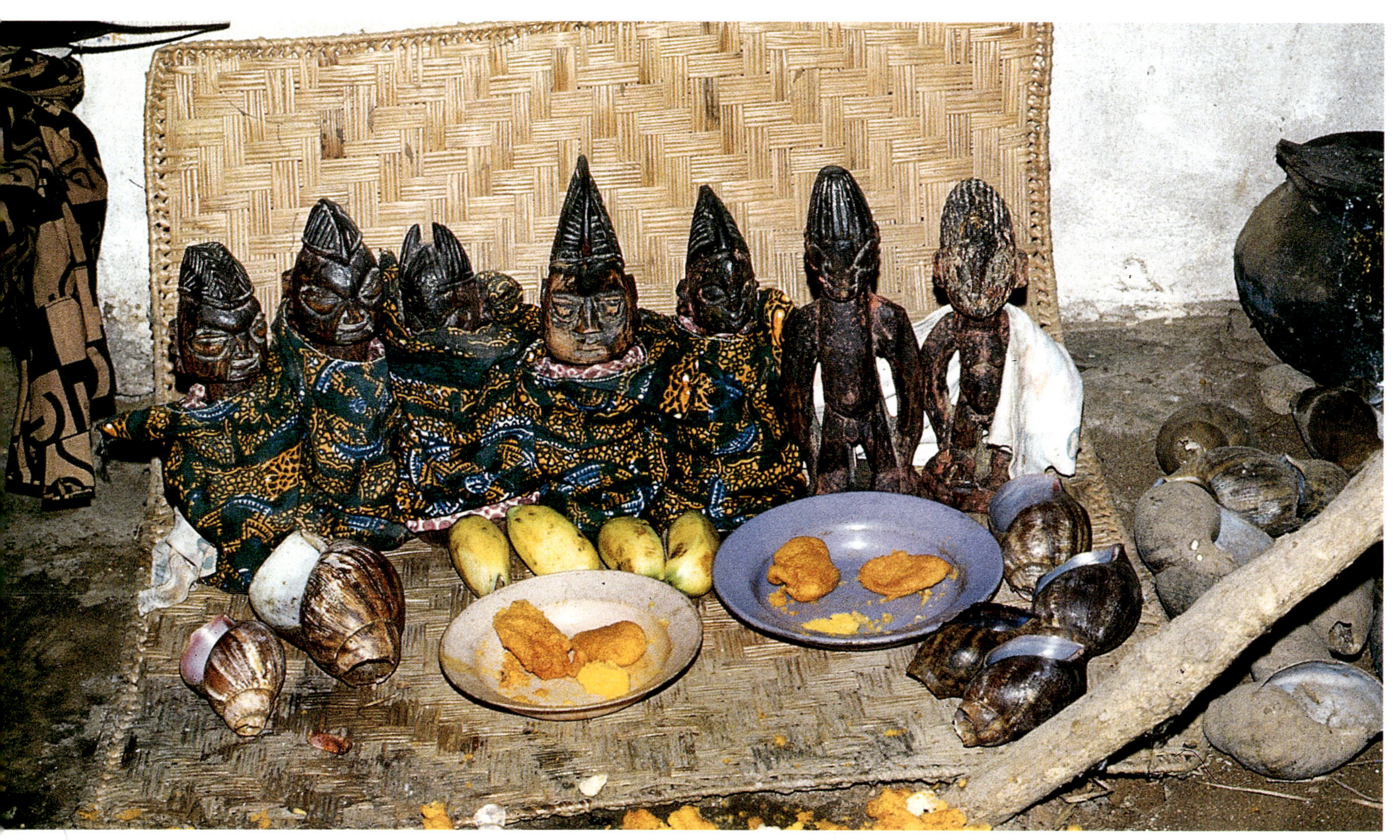

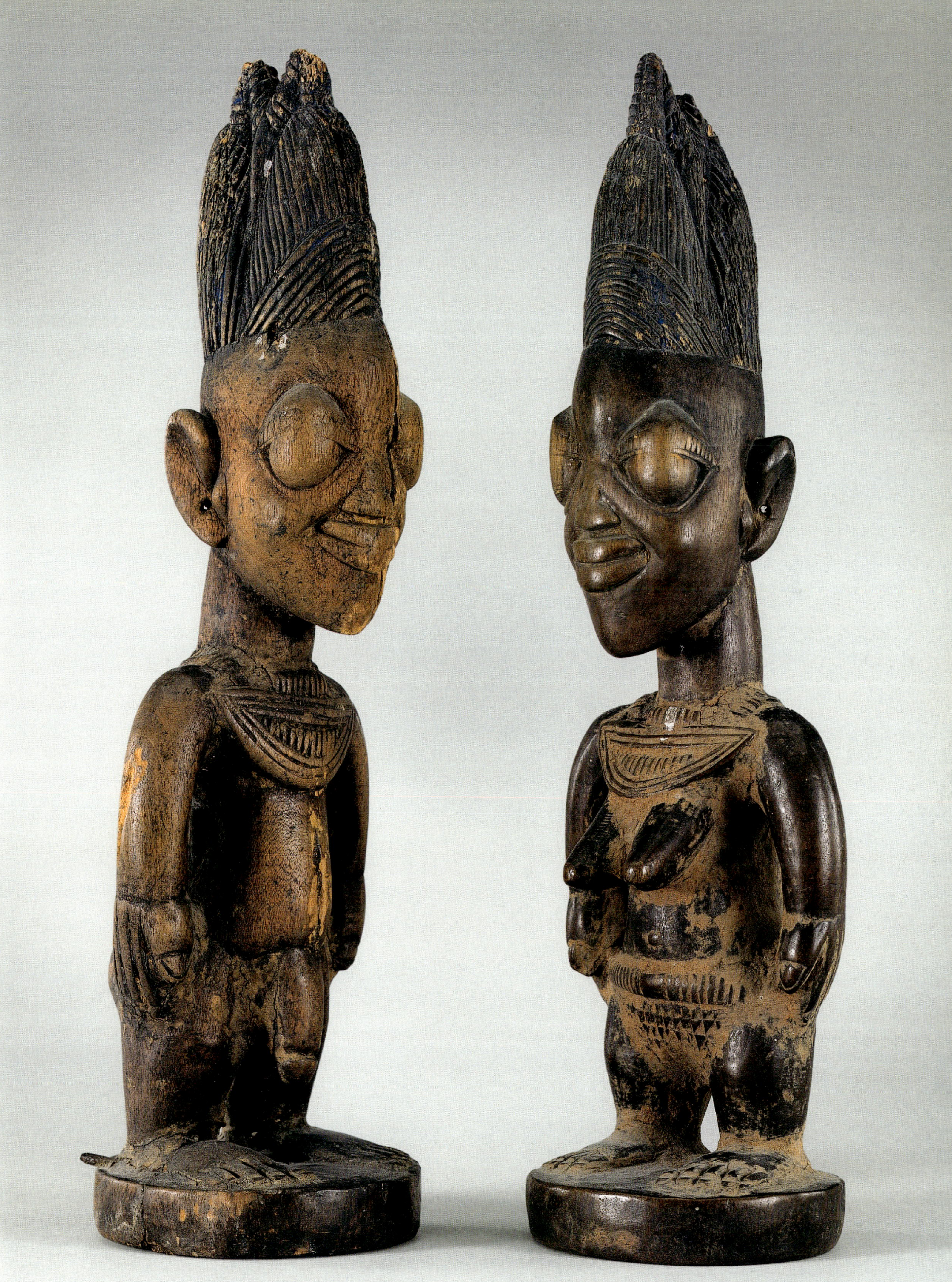

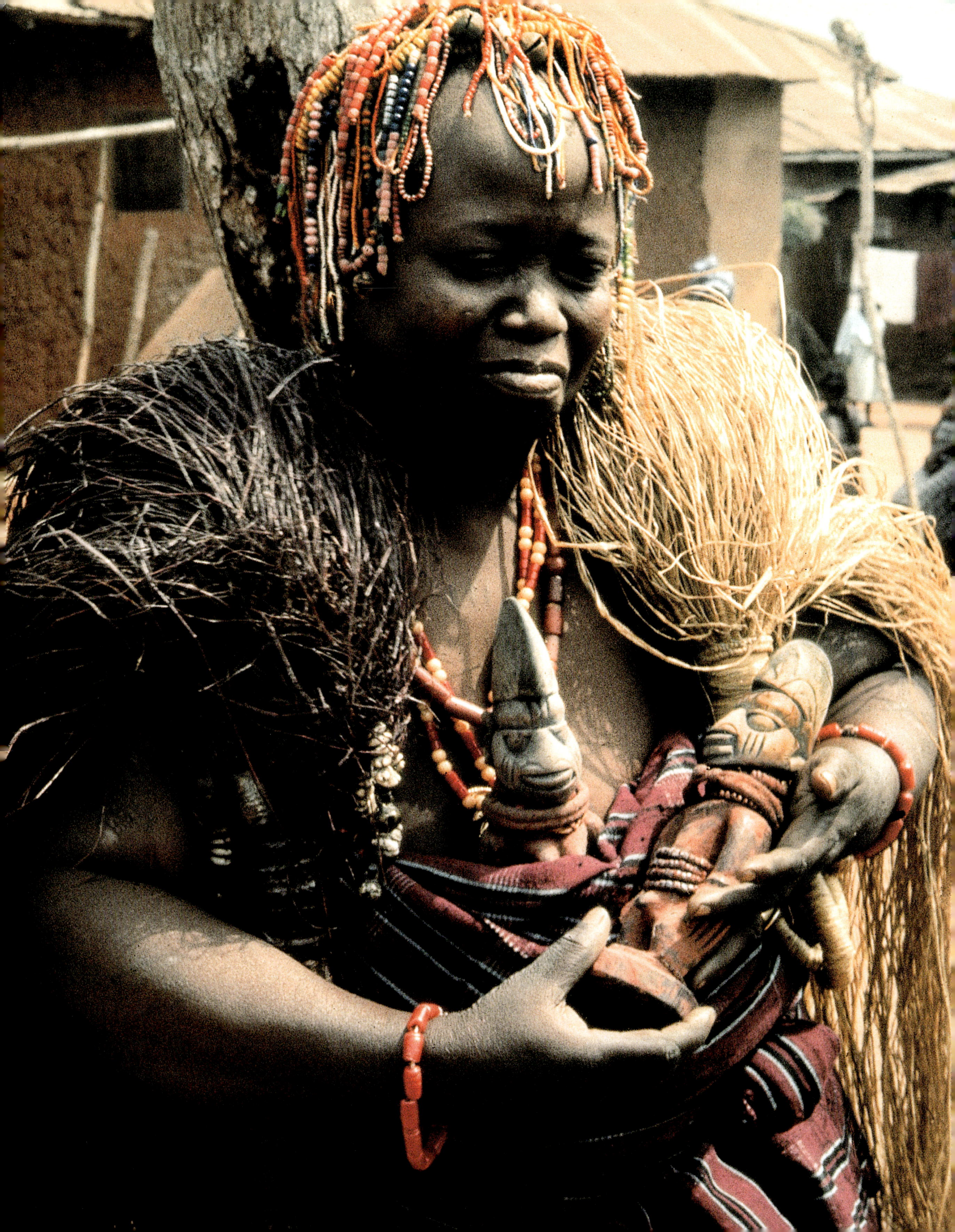

1971:11). The cowrie shells can be seen as both a display of parental wealth and as an indicator of the monetary potential associated with twins. As designations of wealth have changed in Nigeria, so have the attachments to the clothing. Currency, Virgin Mary medals, plastic measuring spoons and earrings with airplanes and other products of the West and modern technology are found on some ere ibeji clothing. In some cases, especially in the southwest, figures were carved with clothing (Houlberg 1973:22–25).

Twin figures were fed, as well. Mobolade (1971) lists the preferred foods: beans, red palm oil, vegetables, pumpkins, sugar cane, cake, and *ekuru*. While any food would do, the two most closely associated with twin figures are beans and palm oil (Houlberg 1973:23), as a song exemplifies: "There is palm-oil, there are beans. I am not therefore afraid—*oniye*. I am not therefore afraid of giving birth to twins. There is palm-oil, there are beans" (Mobolade 1971:15). A Lagos mother explains why:

> Beans are the special food of twins. Feeding beans to twins is like pouring oil on troubled waters. One eats beans to cool one's temper. So one serves beans to the twins to please them and to cool them down so they won't cause trouble. Whenever I quarrel with my husband, I cook beans and eat them quietly by myself to cool down my temper. That is what you must do. The beans are cooked with oil. Oil is to pacify trouble and so are beans. Therefore oil and beans cool double trouble. They are a double means of cooling double trouble (Houlberg 1973:25).

Houlberg notes that the "natural property of beans, its blandness which can offset the hottest of foods, is utilized in the metaphor. The Yoruba consider the stomach to be the seat of anger" (Houlberg 1973:25).

While feeding twin figures was a routine occurrence, there were occasions in which more ceremony was attached. On the third day of the Yoruba New Year celebration in late August, rituals were performed for the ere ibeji and women knelt before their shrines and offered food to them, a rooster for a male and a chicken for a female along with bean cakes and kola nuts (Fagg, et al., 1980:140).

After the ritual feeding, praise songs such as the following were sung.

> Taiwo [first-born] and Kehinde [second-born] are children of riches.
> They delight me as does a crown...
> It is good to see them in the morning.
> They attract attention
> They have beautiful eyes...
> They are to be honored with drum and carving.
> They sleep with the Ooni [king of Ife] without bothering to roll up their mats in the morning.
> They are taller than their comrades.
> They enter without greeting the Orangun [king of Ila]...
> "Puny in the eyes of the jealous-wife,"
> "Plump-twins-in-the-eyes-of-their-mother"
> Are the names we give them
> (Dorcas Opaleye P.C. 1981 in Fagg, et al., 1980:140).

Mobolade does not mention a specific time for a ritual feeding of twin figures, but he does discuss the feast prepared for them which is shared with small children in the neighborhood. Small amounts of food are given to the figures while the children, sitting in a circle around the mother, feast on the beans and other delicacies (Mobolade 1971:15).

These figures could be kept in a family shrine raised on a small clay pedestal, or in the mother's bedroom. They were also stored in calabashes wrapped in special clothes, or placed under blankets to protect them from the chill.

Far from static, the Yoruba imbued the twin figures with life and dynamism by incorporating them in dances in their honor. Special songs accompanied the dance.

> Taiyelolu,
> We worship you with dance
> Kehinde,
> We worship you with the dance.
> Panbotoroboto (twin nickname),
> Please help me to carry my twins to dance,
> Who asked you to give birth to twins
> When you don't even know how to dance!
> (Thompson 1971:80)

The first act of a mother after receiving the ere ibeji from the carver was to put it in her wrapper and dance with it (Drewal, Pemberton, and Abiodun 1989:173). If there was a live twin child, it was carried on the back, and the carved image of the deceased child was carried in the front. "The gist of twin cult dancing with sculpture at Ajilete in southern Egbado is calm flow enlivened with energetic cradling gestures and turnings entirely consistent with the blending of decorum and robustness characterizing the sculpture. A small household ceremony for twins at Ajilete in the summer of 1964 blended affection and honor in the dance. Mothers danced a cradling motion, images kept close to the breasts or to the abdomen" (Thompson 1971:77–78). At one point in the dance, "the mother broke the expected patterns of the dance and bent low, close to the earth, carrying the single image with her in one strong single sweep that brought the image parallel to the ground and then up." These motions resemble the homage which royal wives pay to the king indicating the degree of honor accorded the twins (Thompson 1971:77–78). The following song (attributed to Gboyinde P.C., in Fagg, et al., 1980:162) summarizes the reason for the elaborate dances, clothing, feeding, and songs associated with ere ibeji. "Abuse me and I shall follow you home. Praise me and I shall leave you alone."

F. J. L.

Olufunke Iye-Orisha holding Ibeji that represent her deceased twins. Yoruba, town of Ikenne, Ibejebu-Remo, Nigeria. Photo: Marilyn Houlberg, 1975

64 A Welcome to the Guest of God: a Gurage Basketry Table

Basketry Table on Pedestal with Lid
Gurage, Ethiopia
c. Mid-20th century
Grasses, hide, string, H. 45 cm
Gift of Alfred Peter Murphy, Colchester, Vermont
BMA 1997.119a–b
(Acquired *c.* 1971 on the road from Addis Ababa to Jimma, Ethiopia)

Basketry tables are used by a number of ethnic groups in Ethiopia, including the Gurage, who, like the Amhara and the Harari, are speakers of a South Ethio-Semitic language (Heldman 1993:34). They share the Christian religion with the Amhara, but, in 1959 (Murdock) were reported as one third Muslim and another third practicing an indigenous religion. Although villages are common, some Gurage live on dispersed homesteads (Murdock 1959:185).

The Gurage are agriculturalists, and their meal consists of what is raised and traded locally. The principal cultivation is *esset* (a perpetually green plant known also as "false banana") whose trunk and root is used to produce their principal dish, called *wussa*. This is eaten with dairy products and other vegetables: especially maize and sweet potatoes. Barley, wheat, eleusine, sorghum, and teff are important crops. Also on the menu are potatoes, cabbage, gourds, peppers, garlic, millet, sesame, oats, lentils, various types of peas and beans, and peanuts. Fruits raised include grapes, peaches, and bananas, and other crops are sugarcane and coffee. Among animals raised are cattle, sheep, goats, and chickens. Men engage in herding, while women do the milking, and both share the agricultural work. Ground meat is used in the production of the Gurage specialty called *kitfo* (Hailemariam 1991:1–2, 73; Fisseha 1990:213–215; Murdock 1959:185).

Banquet of Emperor Menelik II, 1889–1913. Ethiopia. *c.* 1907. Artist: Fre Heywat. Oil on canvas. H. 62 cm. Photo: M. Weidner-El Salamouny. Courtesy of the Staatl. Museum für Völkerkunde München. Inv. Nr. 80-301 188

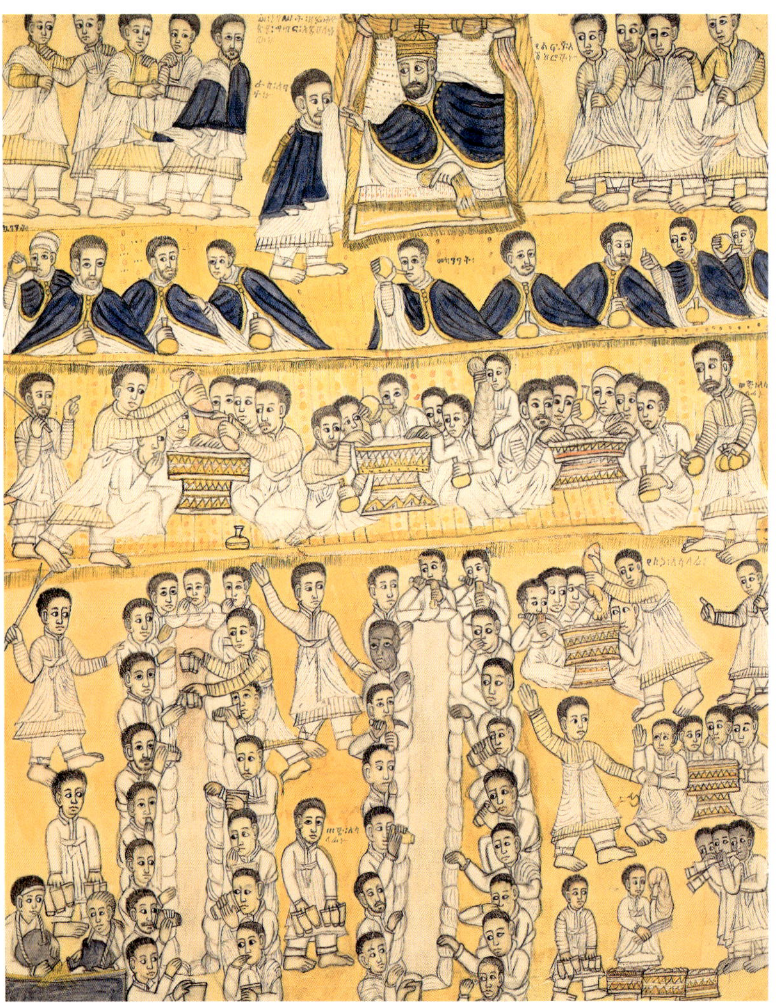

Skill in preparing the meal is a measure of the worth of the new bride. Once a marriage has been arranged, and before the bride cohabits with her husband, a ritual called *messaet* occurs in which the bride and her bridesmaids spend a night with the family of the groom. The bride takes her utensils with her, and prepares the meal. She is evaluated by the bridesmaids of messaet, and their satisfaction is marked by special song (Hailemariam 1991:109):

> We have witnessed of this super-woman
> We ate the best *wussa*
> We were fed and nourished with *Kitfwe*
> Even it was enough for our clothes to wash with butter
> No one would compete with you

Basketmaking is a women's art. A bride is expected to bring to her marriage a collection of baskets, many of which are used primarily in display, for the purposes of establishing social identity and economic status. Within the first year of marriage, the new wife is expected to produce a special basket for her mother-in-law. While Ethiopians remember a time when young women produced their own baskets, today most purchase them from basketmakers. Nevertheless, the imperative to enter a marriage with a set of baskets as a dowry is so strong even today that failure to do so can result in an annullment (Silverman 1994). Practicing such an art as basketmaking is an extremely demanding luxury in light of the fact that women's daily and seasonal work is extraordinarily heavy. While men's work in agriculture is seasonal, the women's is continuous, consisting of collecting water and fuel, fertilizing the *esset* crop, harvesting the vegetables and preparing all the food, washing, and cleaning, selling surplus produce in the market, buying and selling handicrafts (Hailemariam 1991:61).

Baskets of this type are made with an oversewn coil technique. Wild grasses (usually *sindedo*—Pennisetum Schimperi) are bound together by a spiral of more supple, thin grass (usually *gramt*—Cypera fischerianus—or *akirma*—Chloris), forming long coils that can be wound around on top of each other to form a vessel. As a vessel takes shape, the coil is lengthened with more bound grass. Using an iron awl, holes are bored on each successive layer, and the next coil is tied to it. Decorative patterns are formed with colored grasses, designed in advance, each with a special name and meaning (Fisseha 1988:38; Silverman 1994).

Among the Gurage, status is extremely important and is marked by a number of different criteria, among them bravery in battle, leadership status at birth, the ability to delegate authority in the home, modesty and reserve, age, tribal affiliation, clan affiliation, and generosity. To be generous, *wabi*, means to give to others,

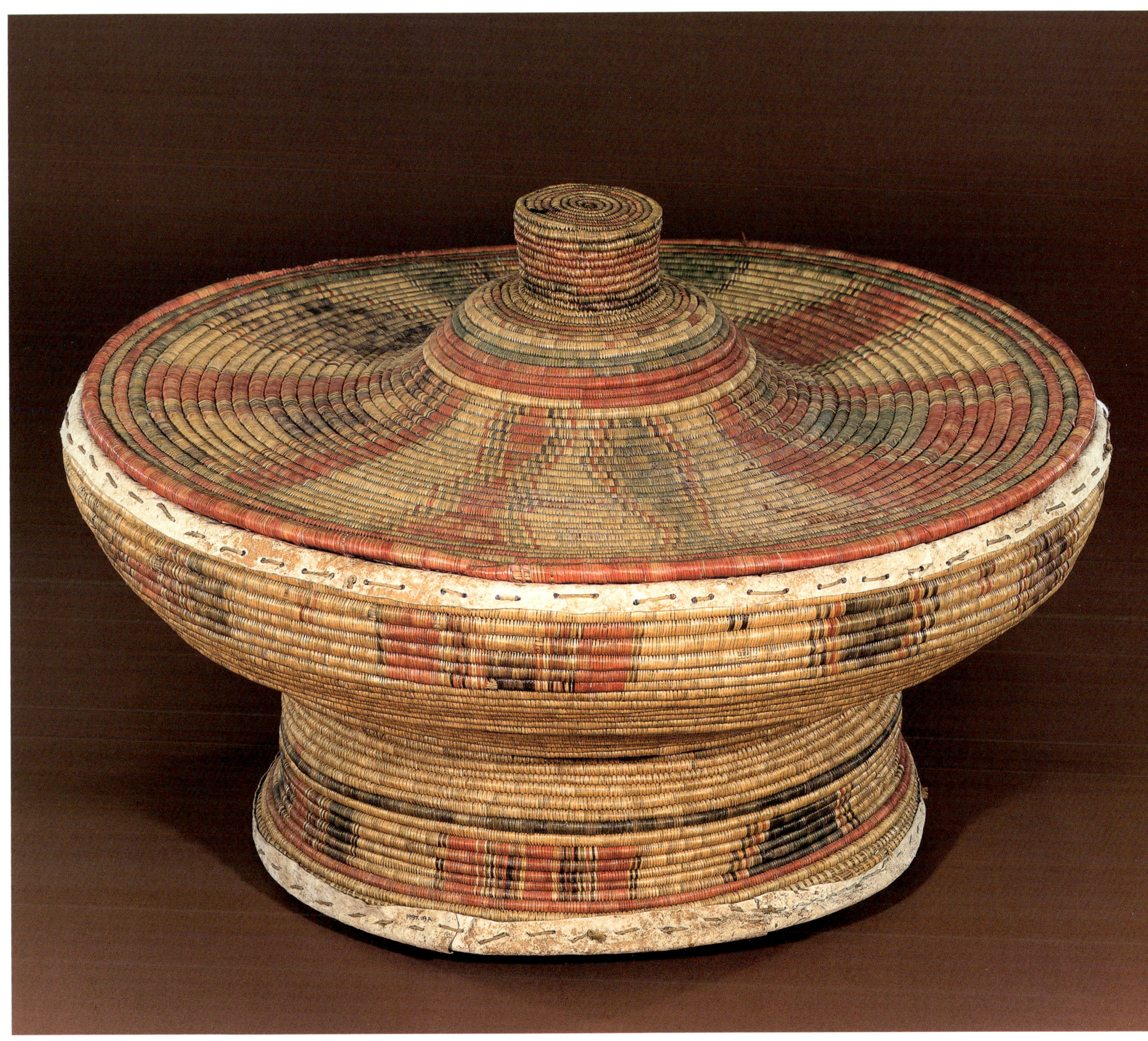

even beyond one's means. One does not close the door at mealtime, except at night. If a visitor, even a complete stranger, comes while one is eating, it is expected that the host will insist that the visitor join him for the meal. One who does not do so is labeled *nefung*, which negatively affects his status. The visitor enters saying "*Yighzer bazera*," meaning "Guest of God," to which the reply is "*Abshiru*," "Welcome." If the guest is of high status, an animal might be slaughtered, and the neighbors also invited to dinner (Hailemariam 1991:67–72, 98).

The centerpiece at any meal is the basket meant to hold the broad, flat, fermented bread (*injera*) on which the meal is served (Fisseha 1988:40; 1990:213). The occasion was described in 1907 (Lieberenz:45–46):

> One sits down on the ground on carpets and cushions in the Turkish way. First, warm water is brought for the hands, then huge baskets with flatbread. Between four and five people are set at a basket. Finally, clay pots are brought with finely ground meat sauce, chicken, eggs, and other things, all served in the middle of the flatbread. Everyone reaches with the right hand, tears off a piece of the flatbread, fishes around in the sauce with this piece of bread, and tries to grasp a piece of meat.... It is a special honor if the host rolls up an extra bit and, in a highly personal manner, shoves it into a guest's mouth.

F. J. L.

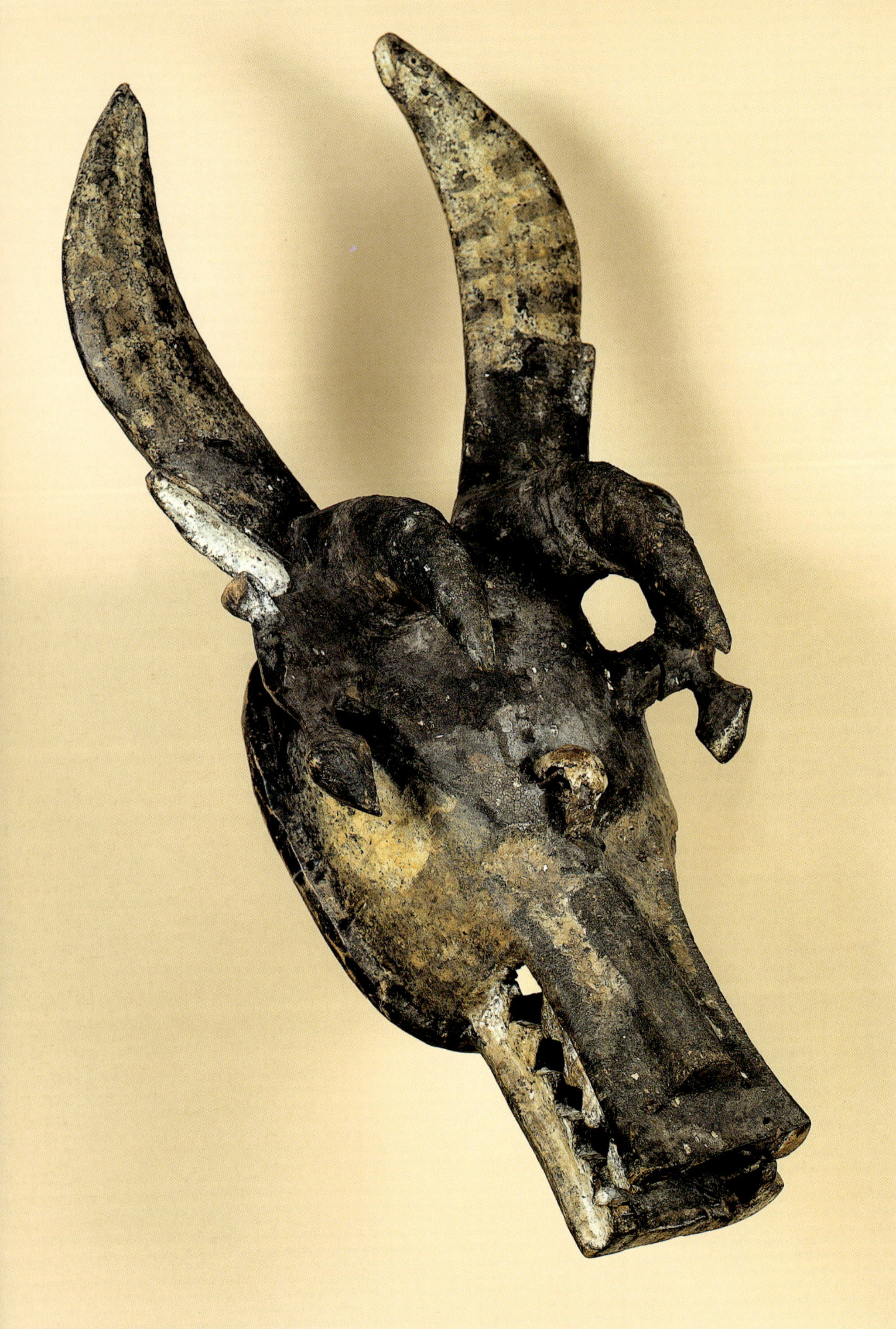

Mask (*Gbain*)
Numu, Ghana
c. Mid-20th century
Artist: possibly Kwado Gbyogoma
Wood, animal skull, fiber, pigment, encrustation (mud, blood, palm wine, egg shells), L. 79 cm
Friends of Art Fund
BMA 1966.34 (purchased for the BMA by the Director, Charles Parkhurst, in Dakar, April 1966)

65 Virtuous Meats Against Sorcery: a Numu Mask (*Gbain*)

Gbain associations are present in many Muslim and non-Muslim Mande societies on the central border of Ghana and the Ivory Coast. They are concerned with the presence of antisocial forces, generally referred to as witchcraft or sorcery in the literature (Bravmann 1974) and are responsible for controlling these forces, curbing their activity, and resolving accusations of anti-social behavior. To deal with this threat and presence and to maintain control, Gbain associations usually performed on a weekly basis when they were observed by Bravmann (1974) in the 1960s, and, when a particular force was suspected within a society, even more frequently. By the late 1980s this seemed to be no longer the case (Ray Silverman, personal communication, 2002). Annually there are purification rites for the associations and their mask. Gbain masks also perform at the funerals of the members of their associations (Bravmann 1974:120).

Typically, Gbain masks include the horizontal head and horns of the bush cow, with feathers and talismans attached to the snout of the mask, and a patina of eggshells, mud, traces of blood, and palm wine (Bravmann 1974:122, 125; Bravmann 1993:124). The materials applied to the mask are thought to strengthen its power to fight antisocial forces (Cole and Ross 1977:130; Bravmann 1993:124). The dancer wears the mask horizontally so that he is looking out the maw. When danced, a raffia or grass skirt is attached to the bottom of the mask, preserving the anonymity of the dancer (Bravmann 1974:120; Bravmann 1993:124).

The BMA mask may have been carved by Kwado Gbyogoma, a non-Muslim Numu man from Kwametintini trained by Muslim carvers (Bravmann 1974:130; Bravmann 1984). Bravmann (personal communication, 1984) writes that "the heaviness of the horns and their relationship to the massive head remind me of his work."

The annual purification ceremony of the Gbain mask and association, *san ielema seri*, takes place on the tenth day of the first month of the Muslim calendar, Muharram, known as Dyombende (or Dyomande) to the Mande (Bravmann 1974: 130–133). For Muslim Mande, the entire month of Dyombende, beginning the new year, is a time when both positive and negative forces can act more potently than during other times of the year, and the powers of various plants and animals are believed to be heightened. The tenth day, known as Asura, is the most potent day of the month, as it commemorates the end of the great flood when Noah and the animals in his ark were able to disembark to inhabit the earth and procreate (Bravmann 1974:130; Tauxier 1921, 1973:289). The ceremony of san ielema seri reaffirms and renews the strength of the Gbain mask and association to protect the community from malevolent activity. (Bravmann 1993:124).

The first nine days of the month of Dyombende are dedicated to the preparations for the tenth day. Women, who are prohibited from membership in the Gbain association, collect roots, herbs, and leaves, some of which will be used during the ceremony while the rest will be saved for the coming year. Special tasks are completed by the Dyotigui, the head of the spirit association, and the Dyologo, the carrier of the mask. The Dyotigui and the

Dyologo only work at night, remaining secret from the rest of the association. They carefully clean and fumigate the mask, mending and repainting it if necessary. They also sprinkle the entire mask including the raffia skirt and the accoutrements with water brought to them from the stream by the wife of the Dyotigui (Bravmann 1974:138–139). Flowing water is critical because it is understood to have greater healing power than stagnant water.

Other precautions are taken against the strong negative forces on san ielema seri, including the lighting of small fires. At some point during the day, small fires are lit around the Gbain-Lou (the small, sacred house in which the mask is stored), and the ceremonial area. Fire fights fire, as sorcerers are said to breathe fire, enabling them to harm ordinary human beings (Bravmann 1974:138–141).

A medicinal liquid is prepared consisting of leaves and medicines, to which is added *siliama gue* ("Muslim water"), a powerful liquid prepared by Muslim clerics by washing verses from the Koran off the writing boards. The Dyotigui sprinkles this liquid on the washing stones next to the bowls, on the perimeter around the clearing, on the Gbain-Lou and on the Gbain mask, which at this point is on the ground in front of the Gbain-Lou and is completely wrapped in raffia (Bravmann 1974:139). Finally, the Dyotigui and the Dyologo rinse their mouths and wash their bodies from the same clay pot that contained the water sprinkled on the Gbain mask (Bravmann 1974:139, 140).

Sometime in the middle of the morning, the members of the Gbain association assemble at the Gbain Lou, exchange greetings, and greet the mask. The young members bring the food that has been carefully prepared during the morning by the women and place it on the ground next to the raffia-covered mask. (Bravmann 1974: 139–141). The proper recipe includes a special combination of meats that have been boiled and stewed with peppers in the fresh water collected at the stream that morning. These meats are from animals that are considered to have virtuous qualities—especially cows, fowl, sheep, and goats—and are a source of strength for the Gbain (Bravmann 1974:141–143; Tauxier 1921, 1973:289–290).

When the food has been brought, the Dyotigui takes the siliama gue, offers it first as a libation to the Gbain spirits and its predecessors, and then sprinkles the raffia and ground around the mask. Then he ties the Koranic charms made the previous night to the forehead and muzzle of the mask. Since the mask must not be seen on this day by the rank-and-file, elders of the Gbain association surround the mask while the Dyotigui fixes the charms to it. He concludes the act with admonitions on the powers of the mask and the fight against sorcerers (Bravmann 1974:139–141). After several hours of bathing rituals involving the association members, the Dyotigui approaches the Gbain and offers it the first morsels of the food, saving some for himself.

Gbain musicians begin to play and sing songs that honor the mask. The hope is that the singing of the association's entire repertoire will "entertain the Gbain, ... publicize its strength and abilities to uproot (antisocial forces), and ... warn evil spirits that might attempt to do harm at this time (Bravmann 1974: 144)." The members of the Gbain association might also create a new song to add to their repertoire on san ielema seri, asserting their affection and regard for the Gbain and scaring away potential antisocial threats (Bravmann 1974:143–144).

Bravmann witnessed the performance of a new Gbain song created by Yaw Kra, the Dyotigui in the Hwela village of Namasa, in 1967. One verse in the song advises: "Whoever says that this stone is not heavy, pick it up and see" (*Sieleko sene magnole, ara korata kafre*) (Bravmann 1974:144–145). The Gbain is likened to a stone, and the tempted negative forces are likened to whoever says that the stone is not heavy. Yaw Kra explained that the song was meant to express that the Gbain is powerful, even on san ielema seri, when the Gbain mask is laid out and exposed on the ground.

Another song verse likens the antisocial being to an animal that causes destruction: "There are lions of the bush and of the compound" (*Eyia gyara bekumgu dobesu)* (Bravmann 1974: 144–145). In this verse, a distinction is being made between the lion of the bush that finds subsistence in the flesh of other animals and the lion of the compound—that is, the sorcerer—that finds subsistence in the flesh of humans (Bravmann 1974:144–145).

The wearing of the mask in performance takes place only at night, accessible only to the men, and occasionally postmenopausal women (Bravmann 1974:121). The event begins with a prelude of drumming by the youth. As the masked dancer enters the sacred area, the drumming is accompanied by sounds of blowing a cow's horn, striking a metal gong, and low-pitched songs sung by other young association members. The movements of the masked dancer include spectacular jumps, turns, and leaps, and other athletic acts "with controlled ferocity." He may jump onto the roofs of houses or to the top of trees, obtaining a better vantage point from which to see antisocial beings. The masked dancer also is said to breathe fire through its jaws, just as sorcerers do, critical to the association's function of fighting fire with fire (Bravmann 1993:124; Bravmann 1974:120, 122, 143; Cole and Ross 1977:130).

"The sight of *gbain* itself is both awesome and terrifying but it appears only when the order of things is threatened; its mission is to curb evil, and to calm and heal a village" (Bravmann 1993: 124). Through his virtuosity, through the richness of the mask, and through the power of virtuous meats, water, and sacrifices, evil is vanquished and the community is purified once again.

S. E. G.

Gbain masks carved by Sirikye awaiting purification. Degha, village of Zaghala, Ghana
Photo: Rene Bravmann, 1966

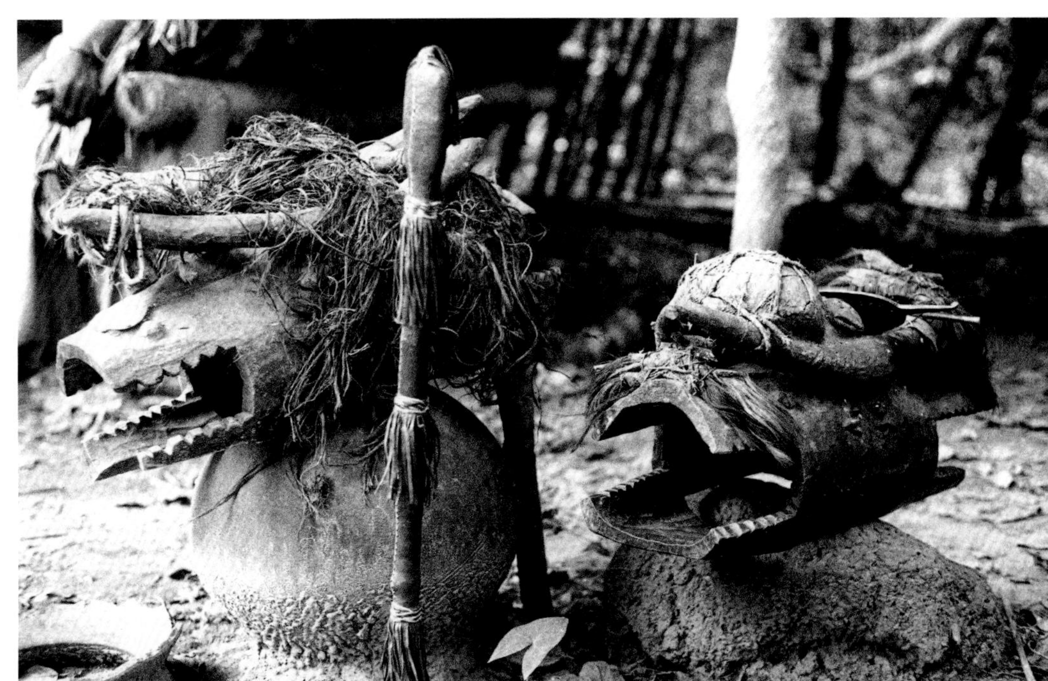

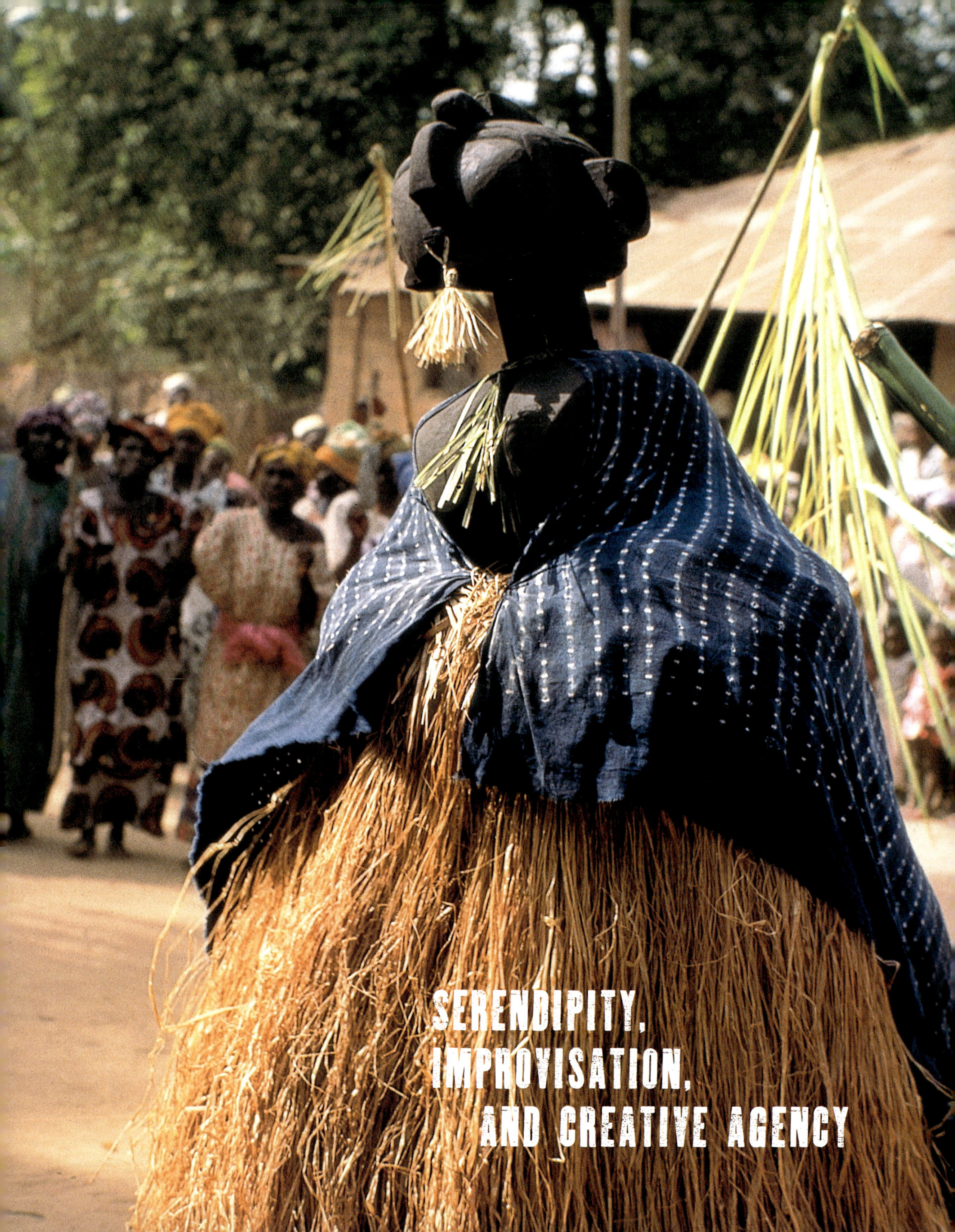

SERENDIPITY, IMPROVISATION, AND CREATIVE AGENCY

Improvisation probably reaches no more most pervasive and accomplished form anywhere than in African theater. The split-second judgment that is required in the introduction of personal contributions to an ensemble is mastered by the African artist at a young age and is an awesome phenomenon to watch.

Margaret Drewal (1992:7–8) suggests that improvisation and the play upon the actions of another constitute a critical pan-African aesthetic named by African Americans as "signifyin(g)." It involves a "multidimensional process of argumentation," a rhythmic negotiation which happens so poignantly in American jazz, distinguishing brilliance from mere competence:

> By improvisation I mean more specifically moment-to-moment maneuvering based on acquired in-body techniques to achieve a particular effect and/or style of performance. In improvisation, each move is contingent on a previous move and in some measure influences the one that follows. Improvisation requires a mastery of the logic of action and in-body codes....

In the work of art that incorporates sculpture as in any performance situation, the sensitivity to extraneous sound and movement plays an important part. The artistic event in Africa does not take place in a closed and silent theater, but exists often in the milieu of a deafening roar of the crowd and enormous billows of dust raised by stamping feet on dry earth. It is open to the interference of barking dogs, playful children, or wandering fowl; and these intrusions are incorporated by the performers into the artistic process frequently with serious ritual import, or with humor. Without these peripheral elements, the art form would simply not be the same.

I had the occasion to observe a Temne carver creating a wooden female figure. While he was carving, a white chicken entered the scene. Suddenly the fowl came from behind the carver, and with a great leap, jumped to the top of his head. The carver froze. For a fraction of the minute, he did not carve, he did not move any part of his body. He simply sat silently until the chicken flew off. At that point, he announced that it would be necessary to make a sacrifice of a white chicken and to make a feast. The message that he received through this happening was an auspicious one and required that he act accordingly to effect a good outcome.

In Benin, Nigeria, the contingencies of weather have created meaning and have contributed to the strategies of the performers. Initiates to the god, Ogun, in 1996, participated in a dance described by Charles Gore (1998:76):

> ... the two initiates were instructed to dance to the rhythms of the deity at the beginning and end of every day as a separate event, in order, in the words of the Ohen [priest], 'to catch the steps'. This is a cumulative and experiential acquisition of the conventions of possession. At a public afternoon ceremony these two initiates called out the Ogun names, Oguname, Ogun of water, and Oguneren, Ogun of fire, which were conceptualized by the presiding Ohen and other participants to describe the fluid and slow movements of the first initiate and the heated and more erratic movements of the second. Furthermore these identities were linked to the heavy cloud cover that had threatened rain during the first initiate's performance and was immediately succeeded by intense sunshine on the entry of the second initiate.

Performance has immediacy, even though it draws upon the timeless, often upon an oral "text" or ritual code. Creativity and tradition are both tremendously efficacious, but they move the viewer and participant in

D'mba mask created after a thirty-year hiatus of this ritual, designed in a more modern, sleek, non-traditional style. Baga Sitem, Guinea
Photo: Frederick John Lamp, 1987

different ways, as Edward Schieffelin (1998:198–199) has explained in his examination of "performance and text":

> Unlike text, performances are ephemeral. They create their effects and then are gone—leaving their reverberations (fresh insights, reconstituted selves, new statuses, altered realities) behind them. Performances are a living social activity, by necessity assertive, strategic, and not fully predictable. While they refer to the past and plunge towards the future, they exist only in the present. Texts are changeless and enduring. One may return to the same text for a new reading, but a performance which one goes to see again is not the same as yesterday's.

Art that is strictly material, as a product, can be regarded and assessed apart from the artist. But performance cannot, as it "is produced in *the self of the artist* and the entity thus produced each time is defined temporarily '*in vivo*', produced in and by the performer as both artist and art object.... and because of its immateriality outside of the performer, it is rendered *forever ephemeral*, existing only *for as long as the performer performs*" (Harding 2002:3, original emphasis). It can also be said that no two reproductions of the same work can ever be exactly the same because each dancer or actor interprets the choreography or script in a unique way. As soon as the performer undertakes a performance, the crucial components of intentionality and deliberateness are introduced, even though the performer is not the author of the act and not the founder of its identity (Hughes-Freeland 1998:6).

The art history of the Baga, with whom I worked from 1985 through 1992, has been driven throughout by individual innovation and virtuosity, always by the young, even though the Baga themselves may not acknowledge the innovators (Lamp 1996 *Art* & Lamp 1996 "Dancing"). Their perspectives, of course, had been shaped through several decades of enormous change, including an Islamic jihad in the 1950s. The older adults, who formed the largest bulk of my consultants, had been rebels in the era before and during the jihad, and their lives had been dedicated to change. Ironically, it was the young, university-educated Baga who were beginning to align themselves with the most aged elders who were nostalgic for tradition and desired a return to structure.

"Ritual is strictly programmed, expressing the individual's submission to forces 'larger' or at least 'other' then oneself" (Schechner 1988:14). In that sense it is not immediately a creative act, but always "handed down," even if imperfectly. However, the truly innovative person, the avant-garde, in the true sense of the word of an actor at the head of a following, can create and anticipate what will become accepted by enough people to modify culture. The example of the Dan female figure discussed below is one in which a rather rare instance of "celebrity" in Africa enabled one carver to establish a "tradition" of non-religious display. Created acts become ritual through cultural acceptance and repetition. In consideration of the departure, we seem to have come back to the beginning, "the invention of tradition" (Hobsbawm & Ranger 1992), or, at least, its "reinvention" (Lamp 1996).

That having been said, it should also be noted that there are societies, religions, and age grades in Africa that are, or were, more conservative than others, and some for whom individuality and change is negligible, or was, in certain periods of history, in the interior, especially prior to the 1950s. Verger-Fevre, in her essay here on the Wè (p. 43), refers to "the immutable discourse of the mask" learned by the dancer of the Gbona Gla. Among the Tallensi in northern Ghana, Harding (2002:22) found that although "new and eclectic elements in movement, costume and props are incorporated in the dances ..., people have also recognized that certain elements in the performance are not open to interpretation and innovation," for example, when "elders and some others depart from the central performance arena in order to fulfill specific ritual obligations in a more secluded location." Male and female initiations into adulthood, particularly, are often ruled by an insistance on adherence to culturally prescribed forms. In the Temne Bondo initiation for girls in Sierra Leone, the coming-out processions are marked by a consistancy from one village to another, and over time. One of their most important processional songs advises the girls, "step as your companions are stepping."

Failure to follow tradition faithfully can have negative consequences. In Guinea, I was told of and knew individuals who were killed because of their idiosyncrasies and their attempt to raise themselves above their peers. In Benin, Charles Gore (1998:78) has shown that the Ohens, charismatic practitioners of personal shrines, who are too idiosyncratic "are also constrained by the conventions of ideas and practice of the traditions that they utilize in its construction. The need to assert their unique and individual capabilities if unmediated by these traditions leaves them acutely vulnerable to accusations as quacks and fakes...."

On the other hand, much of Africa, especially today, freely welcomes innovation and celebrates individual agency. The Yoruba enjoy a rather free manipulation of tradition, as described by Margaret Drewal (1992). They are a people of thirty million souls, heterogeneous, urban, and with a history that has taken some to Brazil and back to Nigeria through the slave trade, and whose religion (with a reputed 402 gods to choose from, including Jesus Christ) is global, with contacts back and forth with Cuba, Brazil, and New York City. One of their most important figures in art and religion is Esu, the Yoruba god of disjunction and confusion.

Drewal proposes that the power of ritual to transform lies both in human agency within performance and in its structure, context, and symbols. She wisely advises the researcher: "Adopting a temporal perspective means following repeated performances of the same ritual by the same people and between different groups of people. It means focusing on individuals in specific performances as they use structure and process and then locating that performance within a larger body of performances and in history, society, and politics" (pp. xiv-xvi, 10). Ritual is time-based—it is historical, and its handed-down-ness is long-term—and its structure needs to be studied in terms of processes, evolution, and shifting shapes. One of the principal failures of the otherwise exhaustive work of Marcel Griaule, Germaine Dieterlen, and others in their team is that in seeking perfect connections, they generalized a timelessness and a convention out of the anecdotal and the individual view.

Current performance theory demands "a fundamental reorientation in the study of ritual" toward the consideration of individual creativity in performances, so that "rather than losing sight of structure, ... the performances illuminate structuring properties all the more brilliantly, indicating at the same time how performers handled them" (M. Drewal (1992:10). In the identification of change, underlying structure is revealed. The study of performance would ideally address the established standard and its negotiation by the artist at once: "... the dichotomization of structure and anti-structure breaks down in a performative approach to behavior.... Agency, creativity, structure, and constraint become simultaneous, rather than distinguished in time and space, whether real or metaphorical (Hughes-Freeland 1998:8).

In the essays that follow, Elisabeth Cameron describes the openness of masquerade procedure that allowed Lwena performers to respond to unforeseen contingencies (p. 279). A Dan figure is discussed as the product of a particular artist's innovation, the celebration of individual celebrity, and the departure from the norms of gender. In the first essay, Mary Jo Arnoldi, writing on puppets in Mali, shows that improvisation and innovation are inherent in the medium. Margaret Drewal (1992:23) posits that this is in the very nature of performance:

> When Yoruba people say that they perform ritual "just like" their ancestors did it in the past, improvisation is implicit in their re-creation or restoration. Innovations in ritual, then, do not break with tradition but rather are continuations of it in the spirit of improvisation. In practice, improvisation as a mode of operation *destabilizes* ritual—making it open, fluid, and malleable.
>
> Since what Yoruba performers "do" in ritual reflects their assessments of the moment, it would be naive and reductionist to think of their performances as a preformulated enactment or reenactment of some authoritative past ..., it suggests that more attention should be given to improvisation as praxis and to its potential to test propriety, to challenge convention, and even to commandeer and transform ritual structures."

The coming out procession of officials and initiates of the Bondo association, in which they sing, "Step as your companions are stepping." Temne, Sierra Leone
Photo: Frederick John Lamp, 1980

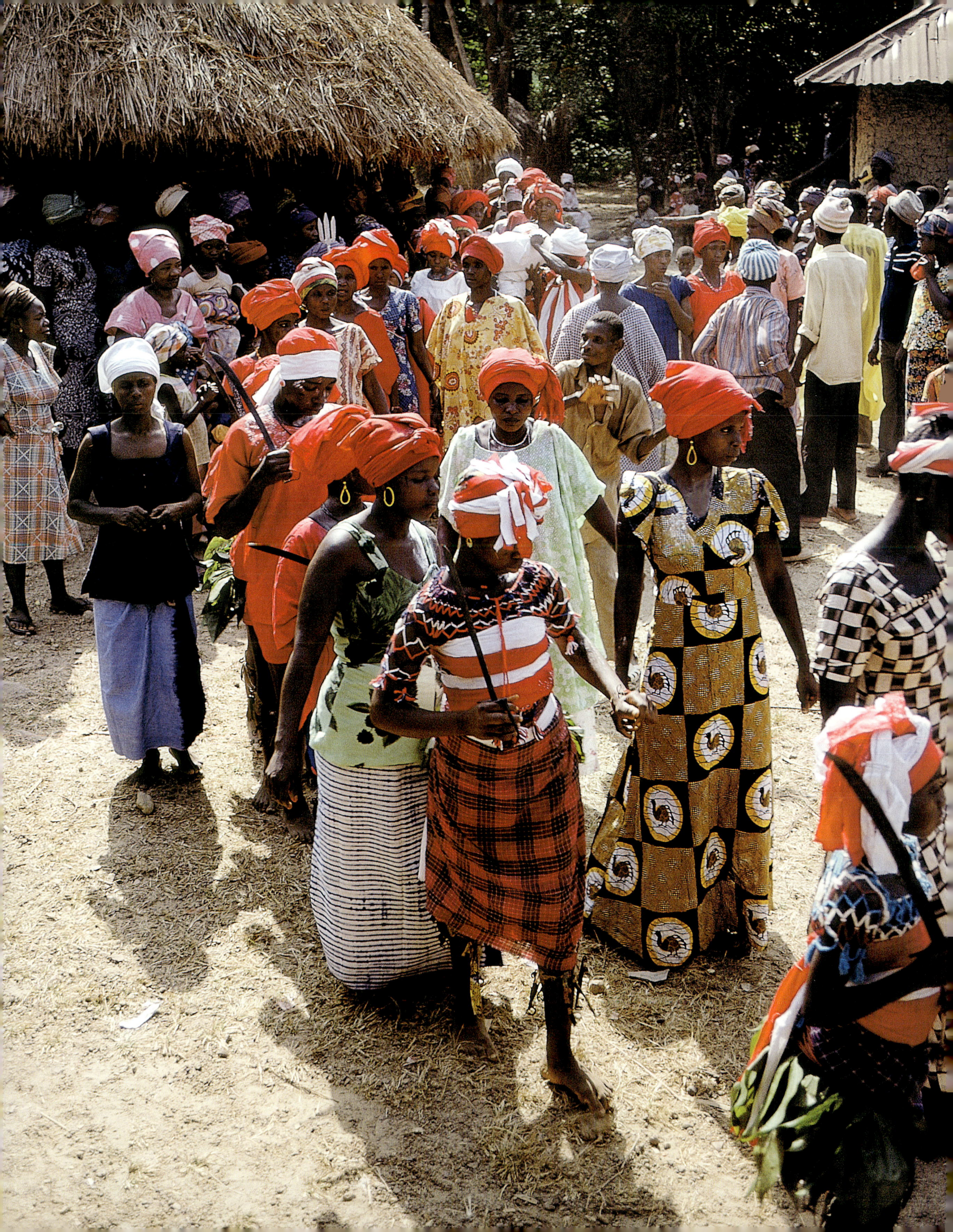

66

Commenting upon Critical Beliefs and Values: a Mali Puppet (*Jiné-Faro*)

Female Puppet (*Jiné-Faro*)
Bamana/Bozo/Somono/Maraka/Malinke, Mali/Guinea
***Sogo bò* theater**
20th century
Wood, cotton, fiber, polychrome, H. 93.4 cm
Gift of Barry and Toby T. Hecht, Bethesda, Maryland
BMA 1988.1407

Large rod and string puppets are the signature sculptures in the *Sogo bò*, a masquerade theater performed in communities along the Niger River and its tributaries from the Segou region in Mali, south into northern Guinea. The BMA puppet represents the character, Jiné Faro, a female water genie. Her long flowing hair identifies her as a genie, rather than a human being. Her bright eyes, long and straight nose, and perfectly white teeth conform to local definitions of female beauty. People often say that genies appear to men in the guise of beautiful women, and throughout the region there are countless stories of men having been placed in mortal danger by their encounter with these powerful water creatures.

In Sogo bò, theater communities in the region often assign specific local stories or legends to their water-spirit puppets. In a cluster of communities just north of Segou city along the Niger river, the Jiné Faro puppet recalls a popular legend, in which Jiné Faro's beauty was so awesome that it could entrap and kill men. Many a fishermen, who had the misfortune of passing her on the river, was struck down when she turned towards him and lowered her hands from her face to reveal her full beauty. One day a clever and brave hunter tricked the genie into keeping her hands in front of her face and thus he was able to kill her and free people from her wrath. During the puppet's performance this legend is alluded to in the puppet song and expressed by the puppet's gestures, when her arms are raised and lowered to cover and reveal her face to the audience.

Puppet masquerade is performed by five ethnic groups, the Boso and Somono who are fishermen, and the Bamana, Maraka, and Maninka who are farmers and traders. The history of the masquerade extends from the mid-nineteenth century or earlier to the present, from the Segou region in Mali southwards along the Niger River into northern Guinea. However, it must be emphasized that the masquerade was never unilaterally adopted by every ethnic group or community in this zone, nor did villages even in the same locale begin to play the theater during the same time period. (Arnoldi 1995:24–35).

Communities unilaterally define the masquerade as entertainment, *nyènajè,* which is part of a larger field of activities defined as play, *tulon*. The puppets and masks used in this theater are called play things, *tulon fenw*. These masquerades are performed under the auspices of the village youth association, the *kamalen ton,* which includes all young men from about the ages of fourteen to over thirty and young women from fourteen until their marriage. Young men in the association are the owners of the masquerades. They are responsible for the repertoire and for building the masquerade understructures and preparing the costumes. During the performance the masquerades are accompanied by drumming and singing. The drum teams are chosen from the ranks of the young men in the associations and young women act as the chorus for the performance. Each individual puppet masquerade has its own song and drum rhythm. The lead female singer or singers, who perform for the puppet theater, remain active in the theater for a longer period. They often start performing as young women, but some continue their careers well into middle age. Lead singers are chosen for their strong and melodious voices as well as for their knowledge of the entire body of songs associated with the characters in the drama. Drummers must have the necessary musical skills, great stamina to be able to perform over an entire evening, and knowledge of the appropriate drum rhythms associated with each of the characters. The puppeteer/dancers are chosen from the ranks of young men in the association and they must demonstrate both strength and agility because they are charged with bringing the character to life through a mimetic style of dancing.

While these five ethnic groups all speak Mande languages today, and share a number of social and cultural institutions, they do not in any sense see themselves as a single ethnic group. Rather they view their relationships with their neighbors through a historical lens recognizing points of similarity in ideology, social institutions, and practices while at the same time preserving different traditions of origin and family and village histories, and practicing diverse occupations which serve to draw distinctions among them. In the context of youth puppet masquerade theater, fishermen and farmers do share a sculptural style for their Sogo bò masks and puppets, and it is this shared sculptural style

Puppet performance. Bamana, Mali. Photo: Susan Vogel, 1986

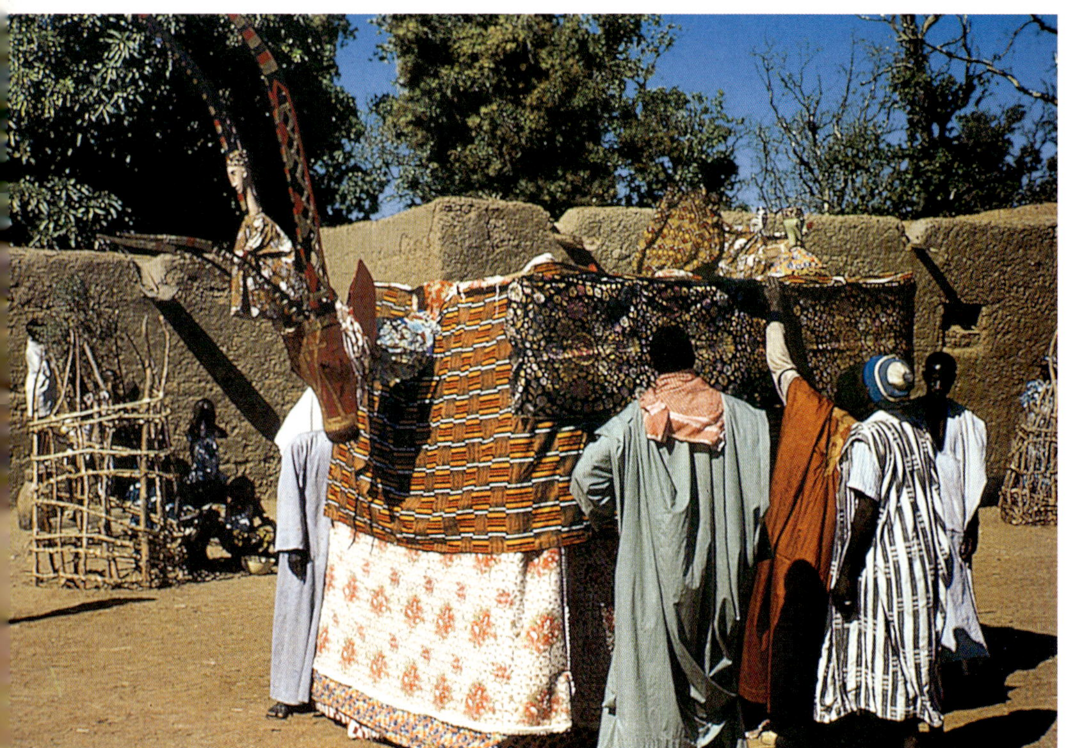

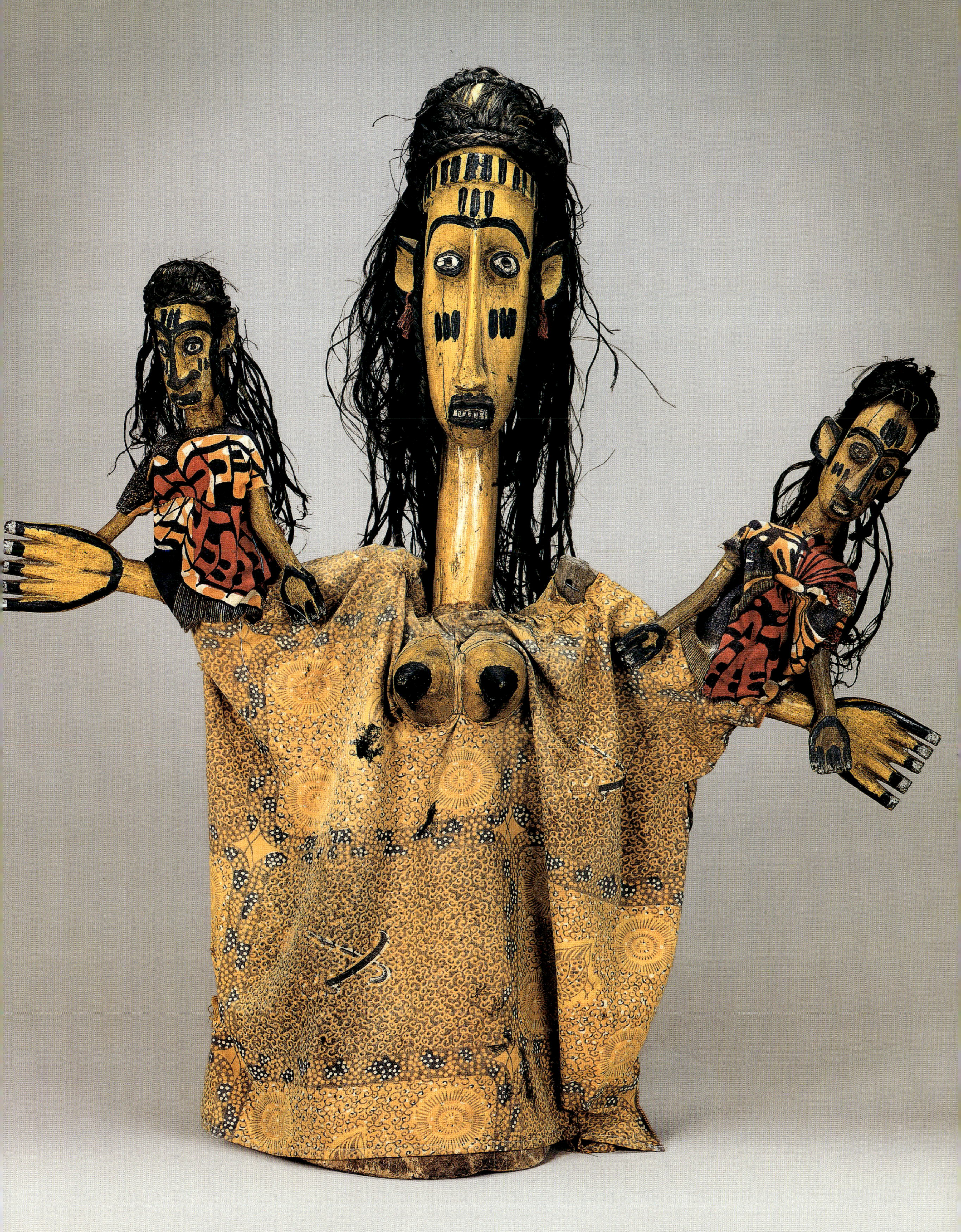

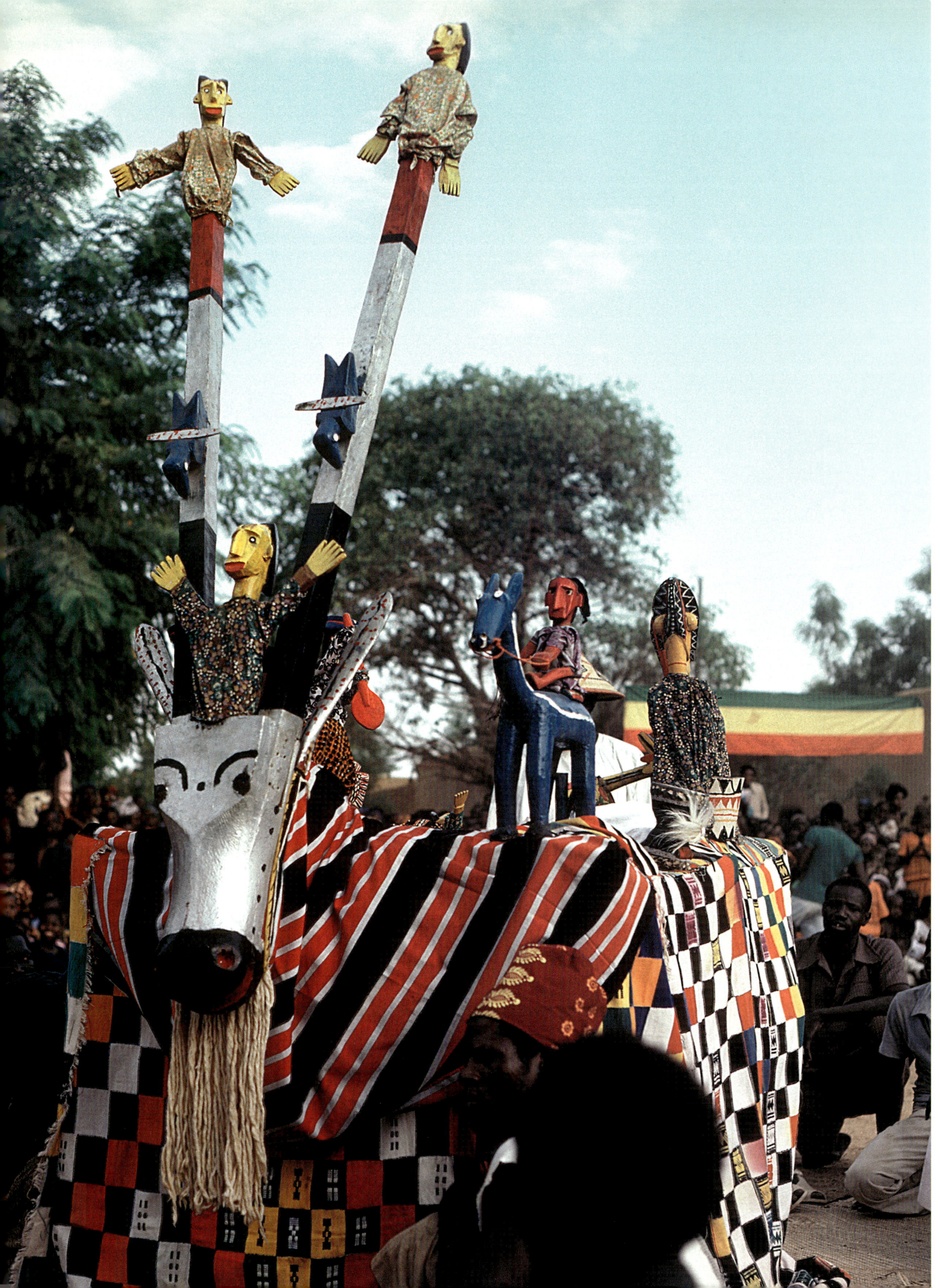

Performance of Sigi, the Buffalo. The Buffalo carries marionettes on its crown, horns, and back. Bamana, Segou region, Mali. Photo: Mary Jo Arnoldi, 1980

which contributes to people's sense of this genre's broad regional identity.

People in Mali define puppets and masks as belonging to a particular ethnic group by virtue of their inclusion in either a farmer's or fishermen's performance. In their worldview, it is not sculptural style (which all the groups' share), but performance style that distinguishes fishermen's and farmer's theaters from one another. Each of the different groups has a distinct style of singing, dance, and music and each claims certain signature characters, such as lions and bush buffaloes among the farmers, and hippos and manatees among the fishermen, as their own. (see Arnoldi 1988 and 1995).

Of all the masquerade traditions performed in this area, the Sogo bò enjoys the most extensive and varied repertoire of dramatic characters. Most troupes play up to twenty or more different characters during a single evening's performance. The repertoire includes a large number of wild animals, in fact one name for the theater, Sogo bò, means the animals come forth. It also includes sets of conventional social types or legendary persons, spirits, like the Jiné Faro puppet, as well as inanimate objects, such as automobiles and airplanes, and a handful of conceptual characters like *Mali kono,* a masquerade that celebrates Malian independence from the French in 1960 or *Furusa Tilè*, Divorce.

Communities see the *Sogo bò* as an activity that is appropriate to the *kamalen wati,* the time of youth, and puppet masquerade is *tonko*, the business of youth. Tonko stands in contrast to *ceko*, the business of elders. The division of activities into either *ceko* or *tonko* is consistent with the definition of elders and youth in these communities. It is commonly held that elders are knowledgeable and responsible, and are the guardians of history, tradition, and order. Young people are described as unpredictable and are identified with innovation and change. The ethos of young men is directed towards assertiveness, bravery, and courage through actions that will overcome their rivals and win them their *tògò*, reputation or name. But young men's rivals are not just their peers. In order to earn a reputation, young men must also challenge the accomplishments of their fathers and grandfathers. The high value people give to competition and innovation in the youth drama, is not merely innovation for its own sake, or for its novelty, but because innovation is at the very core of society's definition of youth and the expectations the community holds for young people.

The oldest Sogo bò characters are bush animals and they still enjoy a special place in the theater. During any performance it is not uncommon to see masquerades representing lions, bush buffalos, hippos, crocodiles, elephants, wild cats, antelopes, and powerful bush spirits. In these communities the bush is defined as the domain of men and it is the locus of power. The interpretation of the theater's bush animal characters are informed by beliefs and values associated with hunting and with hunters as men of action and society's heros. It is the world of the hunter and the association of hunting with heroic behavior that young men in the youth association, the owners of the masquerades, choose to identify with, and to celebrate through the performance of these bush animal masquerades.

The repertoire that a troupe plays in any year underscores a fundamental principle of youth theater which gives a positive value to innovation and change. The dramatic content of the youth theater is concerned with exploring the interplay between unity and rivalry, between the elders and youth, between the collective and the individual, and between tradition and change. Each season a troupe will choose to play many of the same characters popularized by their fathers and grandfathers before them. But each new generation of young men is also charged to create new characters to rival those of their elders. While the community invests a high value in unity through the maintenance of tradition, it also recognizes that creative rivalry energizes these performances, in the same way that people understand the necessity for innovation and change in order to move the society forward.

Troupes creatively exploit the full spectrum of arts—puppet masquerades, dances, drumming, and songs—to construct the dramatic characters in the fictional world of Sogo bò. These performances are important sites for the exploration of the moral universe. Like folktales and other theatrical forms, these masquerade performances throw cultural values and social relationships into high relief and open them up for public scrutiny. Even though they are defined as entertainment, young men and women proceed with a seriousness of purpose, often mediated by wit and humor, to examine the nature of their world and their lived experiences. For generations, this theater has constituted one important public avenue through which young men and women have gained access to knowledge, instruction, and experience by commenting upon the critical beliefs and values within their communities.

Mary Jo Arnoldi

61 Celebrating Virtuosity: A Dan Female Figure

Unlike many cases throughout Africa in which human figures were liberally owned by individuals and families to be used in ritual, Dan figures carved in wood were extremely rare, and were available only to chiefs and wealthy men, and to women only rarely. Furthermore, they had no spiritual, ritual function, but rather served to advance the social standing of the owner in the way that any work of art does. A man wanting one of these figures would first have to persuade a sculptor to carve it, as sculptors saw this as a particularly demanding task. In turn, the sculptor saw the commission as a test of, and a testimony to, his skill, as the figure generally would be a portrait of a living person, usually a woman esteemed by the patron. The patron would also have to sponsor a large feast, offering an animal sacrifice, usually a cow, to be shared by the community. This marked the "unveiling" of the figure, and the "transfer of title" to the patron (Fischer & Himmelheber 1984:117–118; Johnson 1986:36).

In some instances, the owner would build a small, separate structure to house the figure, as a miniature gallery, where it would be hidden from public view. He would show the figure by invitation only, on special occasions, to distinguished visitors, where it would enhance his prestige (Fischer & Himmelheber 1984:118).

Zlan (died *c.* 1955), one of the most well-known master carvers of the Dan, was born at Gangwebe, Ivory Coast, and worked most of his life, with his wife, Sonzlanwon, at Belewale, Liberia. Photo: Hans Himmelheber, *c.* 1950

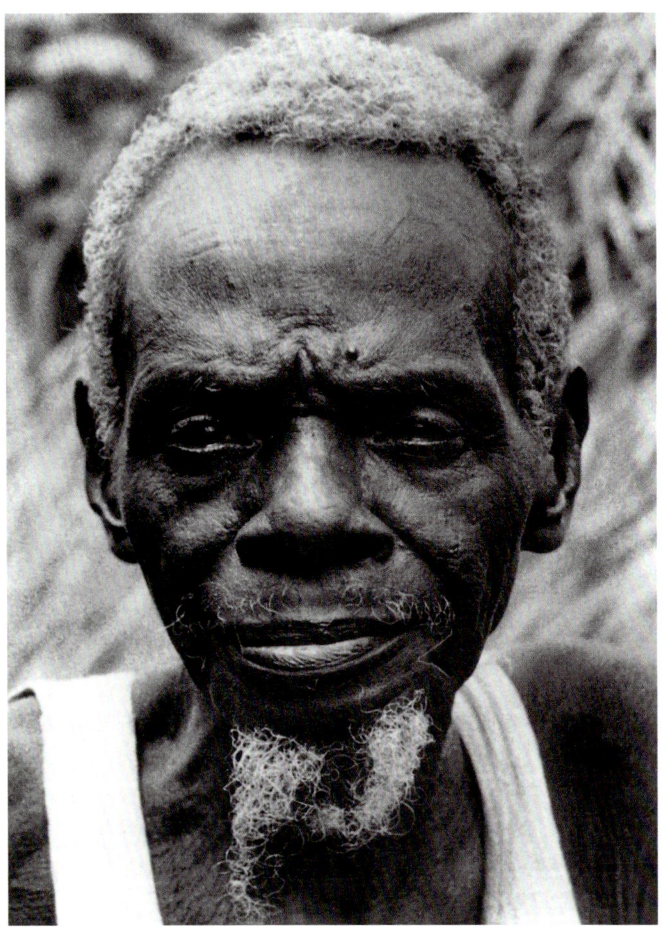

Female Figure
Dan, Liberia
Artists: Zlan & Sonzlanwon
c. Early 20th century
Wood, cloth, fiber, metal, black and white pigment, H. 35.5 cm
Gift of Catherine O'Carroll Bussell and Robert Bruce Bussell, Arlington, Virginia
BMA 1998.442 (collected in Liberia between 1923–1929 by the parents of donor [Bruce Bussell]: Pauline Bussell and Conrad Turner Bussell, Supervisor of Customs and Financial Advisor to President Charles Dunbar Burgess King of Liberia)

Zlan, one of the most well-known Dan carvers, was not a man of modesty. "I make everything especially well," he said. "Zlan [spelled 'Sra' in the original] means God. This name people have given me because, like God, I am able to create beautiful things with my hands" (Himmelheber 1960:171–173). It is a name sometimes given to a child expected to have supernatural abilities because of a premonition stimulated by unusual circumstances of pregnancy or delivery. One of Zlan's relatives dreamed, before his birth, that he would be a great carver of human figures. Zlan ultimately became well-known throughout the area of the Dan, Mano, and Wè, and he taught many proteges, spreading his influence widely (Johnson 1986:35–37).

Zlan attributed his special talent and innovation to spiritual sources. When he was a child, he received a sign: an adze fell from a palm tree his uncle was cutting, and his mother, mindful of earlier premonitions, saved the adze for him until he reached puberty. In initiation, he carved his first mask. Throughout his career he kept the special adze as an object of power, giving it to his younger brother just before he died, who gave it to his son, who still had it in 1986. Zlan attributed some of his creations to dreams, facilitated by special "medicine." His deceased father, for example, showed him a new mask form in a dream (Johnson 1986:35–36).

Although the figures in this particular style are always attributed to Zlan, Johnson (1986:36–37) reveals that the work was shared with his wife, Sonzlanwon, whose name means, "Snail, If God Agrees" (the significance of which she does not explain). Women carvers are extremely rare in West Africa, and among the Dan in particular. Sonzlanwon was credited by many elderly Dan consultants for carving the basic form of the figure, and often carving the figure to completion, especially after Zlan became incapacitated in old age. It is she also who completed the figures with plaited fiber tresses. If one elderly consultant is to be believed, more of these carvings might be attributed entirely to Sonzlanwon than to Zlan. In either case, it is an example of "celebrity" in the arts that is not often found by researchers in Africa, in which the emphasis is on individual virtuosity above the collective ritual function.

F. J. L.

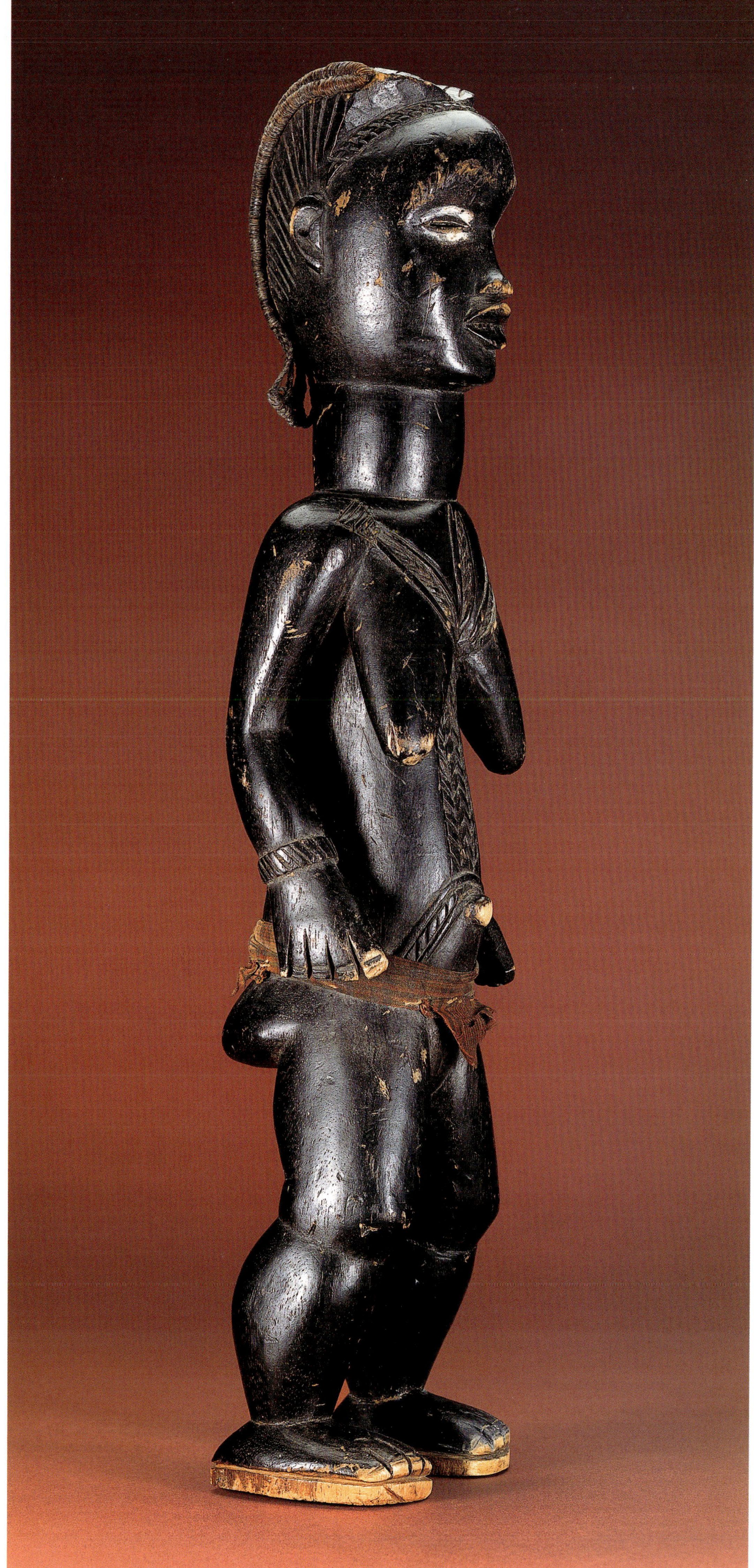

Each Performance is Unique: a Lwena Mask (*Mwana wa Pwevo*)

Female Mask (*Mwana wa Pwevo*)
Lwena, Angola
Makishi Association
c. Early 20th century
Wood, fiber, beads, H. 24.8 cm
Gift of Alan Wurtzburger, by exchange, through the cooperation of Murray and Barbara Frum, Toronto
BMA 1982.1

Bma Lwena Mwana wa Pwevo mask in use. Angola
Unknown photographer, *c.* 1925

Mwana wa Pwevo walked to the neighboring village surrounded by an entourage of young men. There should be an audience ready, but they might also have to round one up. During dry season afternoons, the women and children should be somewhere near home rather than in their fields or at the river. Besides, advance notice had been sent the day before to the men of Chitofu's family that she would arrive to play with and honor the Chitofu women. Every performance was different so there was some tension among the men who walked to Chitofu. Would everything go right today?

The fact that Mwana wa Pwevo was really an initiated man wearing a masquerade costume only added to the tension and excitement of the upcoming performance. Mwana wa Pwevo portrays an adult woman and mother and is dressed like the mother of one of the initiates. She was one of many *makishi* (sing. *Likishi*), masquerade characters that embody the ancestors of the Luvale peoples and their neighbors such as the Lwena in North-Western Province, Zambia. Initiated men bring her to life through masquerade performances that take place during *mukanda,* the men's initiation ceremonies.[1] Women say that all makishi come to honor and play with the mothers of the initiates but they differentiate between makishi that dance (*kuhangana*) and those that chase (*kuhanga*). Mwana wa Pwevo is a dancing likishi. The women, although they were not supposed to know that "she" was really a he, understood and could usually figure out who the he under the "she" really was. They jokingly called Mwana wa Pwevo the one "with breasts but no hole."

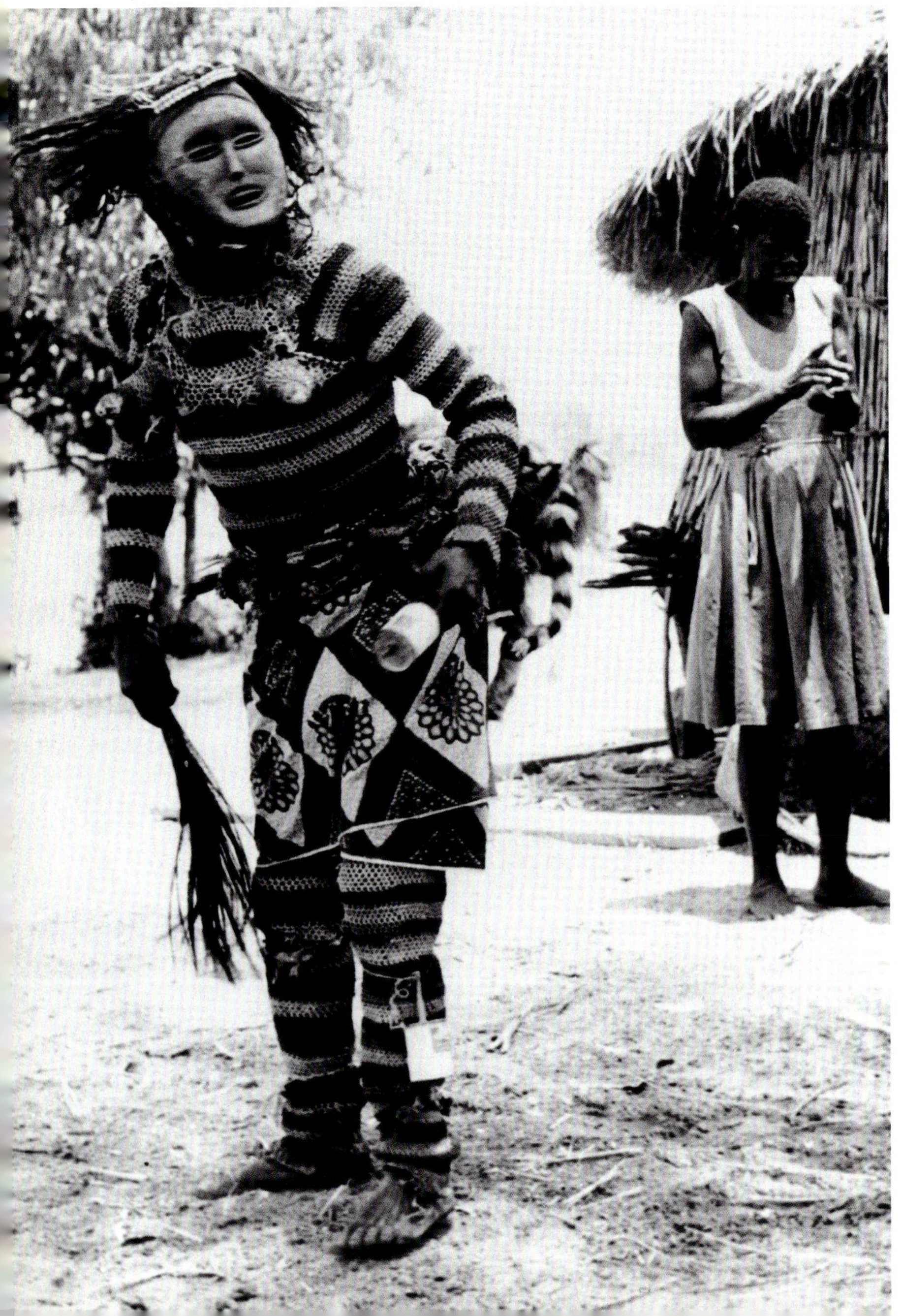

Mwana wa Pwevo walked to Chitofu's compound in the company of Ndeka likishi. They both had on similar mesh body suits, but from there they looked very different. Ndeka wore only natural materials like the thin bark strips tied like a skirt around his waist. He carried a switch in each hand. His head piece—an airplane painted blue—gave him his name. She, on the other hand, wore clothes borrowed from the mothers of the initiates in the men's initiation camp, tucked into a chord tied around her waist. The wood face mask that rested on the masquerader's forehead portrayed an adult woman, complete with facial scarifications of the past. When he looked down at his feet to dance, Mwana wa Pwevo's face looked straight at the audience.[2] Around her hips was tied a dance bustle with strings of hanging dried reeds that would rattle and rustle when she danced. The dance rattles tied around both ankles would also sound to the rhythm of her stamping feet. She had a whistle she would blow in time to the drums. She was, like any adult woman who was dressed to dance, a walking musical instrument.

Together—male and female, chaser and dancer, silent and musical—their performance that afternoon would acknowledge the connection between the two villages. The village they were visiting did not have any sons in mukanda—the men's initiation camp in Reserve Village where affiliated men made some of the masks and performed them—but there was a connection between the two families. Their sister Elizabeth had lived in this village for months while she was being treated for a malformed spine that caused her constant pain. They had a debt to Chitofu, the healer and headman of the village. The families were now tied together, honorary kin (see Jordan 1996, Wastiau 1998). Other villages they would visit on other days would be homes of the initiates' relatives who needed to know that the initiation was happening or to be invited to the final ceremonies and celebrations. Today, however, they would focus attention on the women of Chitofu's family, bringing them honor, and playing with them in the performance. They would also remind everyone in the community what a man and a woman, portrayed in the contrasting masquerade characters, should be like, how they should move, and what they should be doing.[3]

When Mwana wa Pwevo and Ndeka arrived at Chitofu's compound, there were very few people to be seen but Ndeka did not hesitate. He immediately charged several children who scurried out of his way with shrieks and giggles. They paused once they were out of reach and turned to see what Ndeka would do next. With all attention on Ndeka's antics, a man quietly brought out a chair and invited Mwana wa Pwevo to sit as an honored guest. People began to gather from different directions as they heard the unique combinations of screams and laughter that signaled a chasing masquerade. Word was passed that makishi were at Chitofu's compound. The message that the masqueraders were coming today had not been received so most of the women earlier had gone to visit a friend who lived across the river. They were not due back for quite some time so mainly excited children gathered for the unexpected entertainment.

While everyone's attention was riveted on Ndeka, several men quietly began to prepare for Mwana wa Pwevo's turn. The drums were brought out and set in place. Then all the men sat down with Mwana wa Pwevo to wait. Mwana wa Pwevo shifted restlessly on her chair. While wearing this costume, the dancer waiting to perform Mwana wa Pwevo was not particularly comfortable. Covered from head to foot, wood face mask sitting on his forehead, fiber mesh covering his face, he could not eat or drink without detaching the mesh neck from the body of the masquerade, something no woman should ever see.

Ndeka ran behind a house after about twenty minutes of a stop and start chase between a few women, many children, and Ndeka. The men, by busily setting the drums in order, indicated that he would not return. It was Mwana wa Pwevo's turn to play.

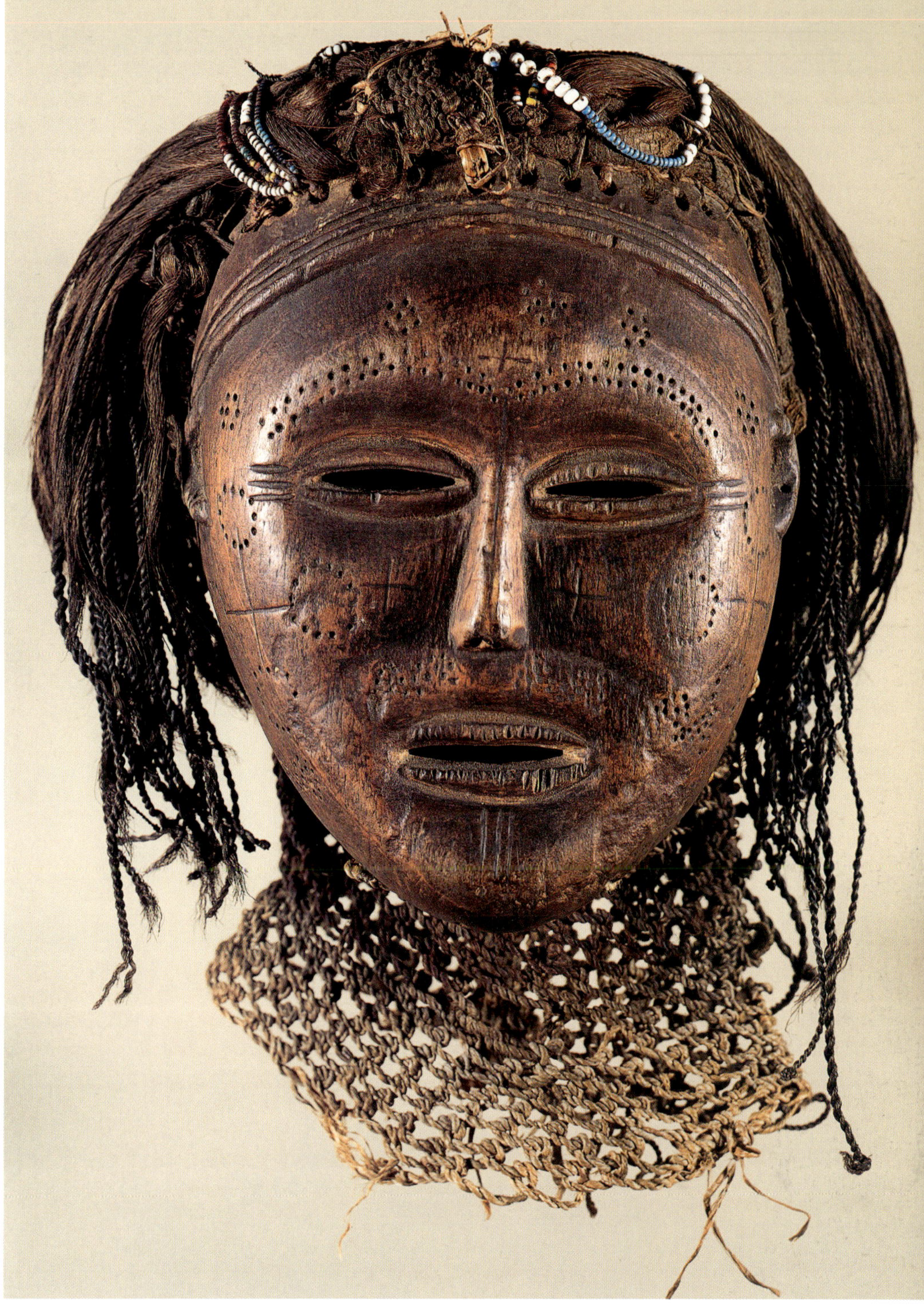

Mwana wa Pwevo stood up and beckoned for everyone to gather in a circle around her. The drummers began drumming and the few women present prepared to take on their role as song and dance leaders. Mwana wa Pwevo was not happy with how the circle was forming and sensed a lack in enthusiasm among the gathered women. She began to scold them, demanding that they close in and make the dance area smaller. She tried a few dance steps, her feet stomping and flying, her arms spread wide. She paused, stopping to encourage the women to sing and clap. This was not her role but no woman was stepping forward to lead.

Flora Chitofu ran into view and joined the circle. Everyone relaxed because they knew she was an excellent dancer and would lead the women and children, making sure Chitofu village would not disgrace itself by giving a lazy and unenthusiastic response to the visiting masquerader's performance. Excitement began to build when Flora began clapping in rhythm to the drums. The vibrating wail of the friction drum joined the orchestra. Flora sang the first line of a song and everyone joined in. Mwana wa Pwevo began to dance. Flora entered the dance area to dance beside her, encouraging her to dance well. After an intense but brief period, Mwana wa Pwevo slowed down and Flora moved back into the crowd. She turned to face her chorus and encouraged them to sing louder and more enthusiastically.

An older woman slipped into her house and returned with a colorful scarf. She approached Mwana wa Pwevo hesitantly, holding out the scarf. She wanted to give it to her but she did not want to touch the masquerader. To do so would cause the woman to become very ill and result in expensive healing treatments (Cameron 1998: 55). A man quickly moved from one of the drums, took the scarf and gave it to Mwana wa Pwevo who placed it over one shoulder and tied it under the opposite arm. After a bit another scarf appeared. Both scarves would be discretely returned to the donors at a later occasion.

After about thirty minutes of dancing that varied from short intense session to quieter dancing that was easier to maintain over longer periods of time, Mwana wa Pwevo retreated behind a house. The women and children continued to sing and clap for a moment but then began drifting away. Since the women did not call her back, Mwana wa Pwevo, Ndeka, and their entourage of initiated men returned, by back paths, to the initiation camp.

The women at Chitofu discussed the event, agreeing that the neighboring village had done them great honor in coming to their village, but criticizing both the masquerade dancer's skill and their own lack of eagerness. If there had been more enthusiasm among the chorus, Mwana wa Pwevo would have returned again and again until the dancer was totally exhausted. If the dancer performing the masquerade had been a more inspired performer, the women would have called him back. They also criticized the men for not giving them adequate warning so that most of the good dancers and leaders among the women were not present for the event. Flora was praised for her singing and dancing. One woman reminisced that when Flora publicly danced at her own initiation, men fell out of trees. Everyone agreed that for a good presentation that honored the men, the women, and the ancestors, that the male masquerade dancer, the male drummers, and the audience of women must perform well.

The afternoon performance had been very different from the evening one that had taken place a few days earlier in the village of the family whose sons were being initiated. The women had begun to suspect that the men were planning to bring a masquerader to the village that night when they saw them gathering large quantities of firewood for the fire that would light the performance. Women typically gathered firewood for their homes and cooking fires and it was rare to see men carrying wood. Several of the initiate's mothers scurried to help. Excitement began to build and word spread to neighboring compounds. People drifted towards the family's house and the pile of wood. A small pile would have indicated that they anticipated a short performance mainly for the family, but this large pile signaled a major performance. At dusk a few men brought out drums and set them near the pile of wood. Children, both boys and girls, began to play with the drums, experimenting with rhythms and combinations. The echoing sound acted as a call to those who might not have heard rumors of an evening performance.

As the early evening passed, men were conspicuously absent from firesides because they were gathered inside the initiation camp to dress the dancer. At last the men approached, with Mwana wa Pwevo at their center. Although the women knew that the likishi would be a dancing sort, they had thought it would be the more common Chiwigi. Mwana wa Pwevo's appearance engendered a buzz of excitement. The women began to whisper "have you guessed yet?" "Do you know yet?" From his height, the shape of his lean body, and his easy movements, the women knew the masquerade dancer was Charles, well known as the best dancer in the area. A glance around confirmed that Charles was not in the audience. He would not miss an event like this, although he would deny it in the morning, claiming to have spent his evening drinking with a hunter who lived on the other side of the river. The evening promised to be a treat for everyone and anticipation ran high.

The crowd quickly formed around the fire and drums, each person jostling the next to find a better spot. One boy climbed a nearby tree to get an improved view. The men cleared the center of the dance arena, scolding children and telling them to behave. Chairs for several important visitors were brought out and placed on the boundaries of the dance arena. The men began playing the drums and Mwana wa Pwevo took a few tentative steps, obviously warming up both limbs and the audience.

As the dancing intensified, Mwana wa Pwevo moved to Henry, one of the camp officials, and greeted him by kneeling and clapping. Henry responded by clapping and gave her a small gift of money. With the official recognition, the performance officially began. Alternating rapid dancing with slower steps, Mwana wa Pwevo soon wore multiple scarves. Men took gifts of money from the women as they approached the masquerader. It would be split up later between all the men involved in the performance with a large portion going to Charles since he had come as a paid performer.

Dance of Mwana wa Pwevo. Luvale, Chitofu village, Zambia
Photo: Elisabeth L. Cameron, 1992

In response to the enthusiasm of the crowd, Mwana wa Pwevo called for women's pounding sticks. Two young men placed two heavy poles on the ground parallel to each other, and rested a third pole across these perpendicularly, which they grasped at each end. They then began lifting the top pole and then pounding it down in rhythm to the drums. The audience cheered—this was a difficult dance for which Charles was especially known. Mwana wa Pwevo approached the pulsating pole and began dancing over it. His feet flashed from one side to the other, his steps perfectly timed with the pole so that he never tripped or fell. After a short session, he signaled for the young men to remove the poles. He never performed this dance for long periods because it was too exhausting.

Mwana wa Pwevo left the dance arena several times, going behind a house to catch his breath, grab a drink, and allow the other men to repair any damage to his costume. Each time he disappeared, the women danced and sang with greater vigor, pleading with him to return to the performance area. During one dance session, Mwana wa Pwevo sunk to the ground and began sculpting a woman of sand. He piled her breasts high while the crowd began to cheer and laugh. Then he began to simulate sexual intercourse with her—reminding the audience again that underneath the masquerade costume was indeed a virile man.

Finally, after dancing for over two hours, all the women's enthusiasm and pleading did not bring him back. Word quietly spread that the performance was over and everyone reluctantly went home, chatting and laughing in small groups as they walked away.

The next day, women in many different communities discussed the performance of Mwana wa Pwevo, complimenting the dancer's grace, style, and his mastery of many different dances. Rarely did you see such an excellent performance. They analyzed the initiates' mothers grace in leading the singing and encouraging the audience's participation. Some wondered how much money the men had earned during the evening. But most of all, they wished they could have recalled Mwana wa Pwevo to dance once more.

Elisabeth L. Cameron

1 While Mwana wa Pwevo appears mainly during men's initiations (*mukanda*), she might also appear at annual celebrations in support of a regional chief or in national political rallies. See Jordan 1996:107–114 and Jordan 1998b. For more information about women and masquerades in the ethically-mixed Kabompo District, see Cameron 1995, Cameron 1998, and Jordan 1996.

2 Manuel Jordan notes that the men consider the masquerade as a whole. If they have to refer to the mask itself, they call it "the head of the likishi" (Jordan 1998b:100).

3 The men's performance of Mwana wa Pwevo reminds the women of what men want in a woman. The women, on the other hand, critique each performance during and afterwards. Did the man inside the costume dance well? Did he dance properly like a woman? Occasionally adult women will coach aspiring young masquerade dancers. The most difficult skill is to make the dance bustle tied to a woman's back bounce. The women learn this during their own initiations. Mwana wa Pwevo also might arrive at a performance early and "assist" the women with their chores, helping while she encourages them to move towards the dance area. In performance, she might also pantomime a woman fishing with a basket. If the women, however, do not approve of the skill of the dancer, they will heckle him and even drive him from the dance arena. The men then must substitute another dancer and, gender roles are negotiated.

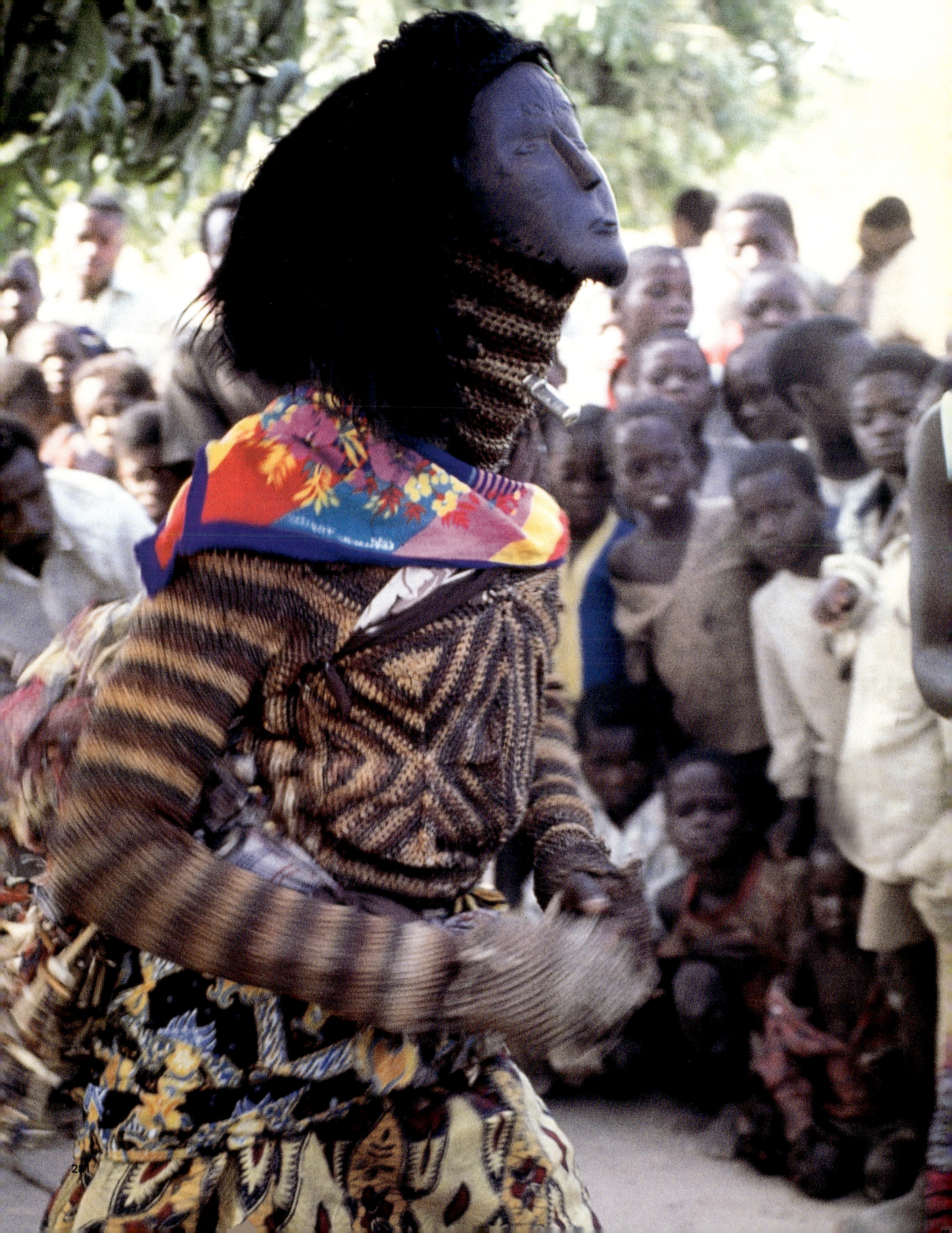

DENOUEMENT

On a visit to a museum with a collection of African art, we can enjoy observing the form of a mask or figure as it rests quietly on its pedestal or its glass case, still, isolated, pristine. But a vast amount of information is missing, the whole form isn't there, and we can only try to imagine the parts that are missing. Imagine the brass bells hanging from it. Imagine the plumes on top. Envision the masses of overlaid country cloth or brilliant lurex flowing from the mask to the ground. Think of the brass tacks as brilliantly shining in the sunlight. Visualize the dull color to its spectacular brightness or its deep blackness.

Try to hear the sounds of the crowd singing, shrieking, or chanting, of children laughing, of roosters crowing. Imagine the space a shrine figure or the mask requires to perform as it must. Fill in the untidy cluster of bottles or hide bags or seashells that surround the figure on its altar or the coterie of other masqueraders that intersect with the mask as it sweeps through the town plaza. Imagine joining the crowd waving palm branches or throwing rice at the mask as it moves. Imagine the mask swaying or being twirled into the air or seated quietly on the ground. Imagine the vertical figure on the gallery pedestal instead as horizontal, caressed by a mother, or manipulated by a ritual practitioner. Insert a dish of rice as a sacrifice to the figure that must be fed, that must be kept alive. Imagine a story of human heroism, spiritual benevolence, or treachery that provides the reason for being of the mask or the figure.

Placing ourselves together with an object of African art within the swirl of color, activity, space, and attitude, we can begin to appreciate the form as a vitally alive character. We can begin to imagine the work of art as it was conceived by its makers and performers in Africa.

What we know about the history of art in Africa has come to us primarily from art historians, anthropologists, historians, and folklorists. Art historians have focused on the sculptural form, even while acknowledging the importance of other artistic elements. Anthropologists have tended to emphasize the ethnographic, cultural, ritual, psychoanalytical, and symbolic contexts of the art form, but the study of an art form is seen by some social scientists as outside their purview. Folklore studies, a relatively new field, suffers less from the strictures of methodology and disciplinary identity, enabling a more encompassing approach.

Ideally, a study of any particular African performance art would address the issue of the integration of the arts through the collaboration of a team of five or ten scholars from a wide base of possible disciplines: music, dance, theater, performance, folklore, history, art history, architecture, ethnology, linguistics, philosophy, aesthetics, and possibly others. This mode of collaborative research, disdained in the past "'modern' climate of thought" as "boundary ambiguity ..., a form of pollution, ... an abomination" (Turner 1986:73), would break new ground in the humanities, where it is rare, as opposed to the sciences, where it is more common. It would be instructive also to include the viewpoint of practitioners of the arts: actor, director, sculptor, dancer, musician, or cook.

Collaboration would enable us to look at performance art from several vantage points with the expertise that each element requires. The dance historian may analyze the movements, the use of space, staging techniques, and duration, and may notate the choreography. This has never been done for African masked dance, although some other African movement has been notated. The musician or ethnomusicologist would analyze the meter, rhythm, melody, the use the musical instruments, vocalization, lyrics, body sounds, extraneous sound, and improvisation. An ethnohistorian would examine the narratives that underlie the performance or that take part in it, either explicitly or implicitly. A linguist might look at the way narratives are constructed and how speech is a function of cultural premises. An architect or architectural historian might examine the changing uses of space within an event. But most importantly, the interdisciplinary approach would bring distinct disciplinary vantage points to focus on all aspects of the performance and its cultural context. The way that an art historian looks at a movement sequence is markedly different from the way an ethnologist or a musician looks at the same movement, for example, and this would be expressed in the way of framing questions, in the weight given to particular aspects, or in the interpretation of empirical evidence. We would all attempt to understand the performance in our bodies as well as in our minds, employing each of the five senses. Again, as A. M. Ipoku, of the Ghana Dance Ensemble has said (Hampton 1982), we would want to "see the music and hear the dance."

We have attempted here to present African art in a form that would be recognizable to an African audience. We have not attempted to address African art and culture comprehensively, as any monograph on a particular art form should. A full study would include a history of style development, regional variations on form, the significance of iconography, the work of the carver, maintenance of the object, social and political context, ritual context, transition, and contemporary directions. It would also include preparations for the performance, which may be more elaborate, and involve more time, than the performance itself, a combination of ritual, economics, and a microcosm of social structure (Schechner 1988:121).

The evolving use of many African art forms in the momentum of the twenty-first century brings the discussion into the global marketplace: some objects have taken on new functions as black icons (such as the Baga D'mba, the Asante Akua'ba, or Akan strip-woven cloth), as promotional gimmicks, as monuments of modernism (the Kota reliquary figure, the Bamana Chi Wara), or as agents of the postmodern (Bamana mudcloth as Paris fashion) and international appropriation. The uses of imitation, and the impact of forgery is germane. The history of African art in the twentieth century, and into the twenty-first, is only partly situated in the original African context, and partly (if not mostly) in the context of the Western collection and the Western marketplace.

In its fullest artistic context, African performance art, though it appeals frequently to a notion of a spiritual world, and may act as ritual, still may function artistically in the most comprehensively postmodern way: as performance art, conceptual art, and installation art do in contemporary museums and public spaces, whether comfortable or incongruous. An attempt to re-situate a museum object back into the African context within the gallery would be contrived and would deny the historicity of the object, the trade in African art, and globalization in our time. To bring the original artistic whole into the museum (if that would be possible) would be to exoticize it within an alien context and to divorce it from the larger cultural and social milieu that makes it comprehensible intellectually. Perhaps those outside a particular culture do not have an inalienable right to experience all that is available to those within. But museums are now better situated to present some sense of the original art form as it was conceived by the African artists and viewed by its African audience.

Nòwo dancer of the women's Bondo association leading the final procession. Temne, Gbiri, Sierra Leone. Photo: Frederick John Lamp, 1976

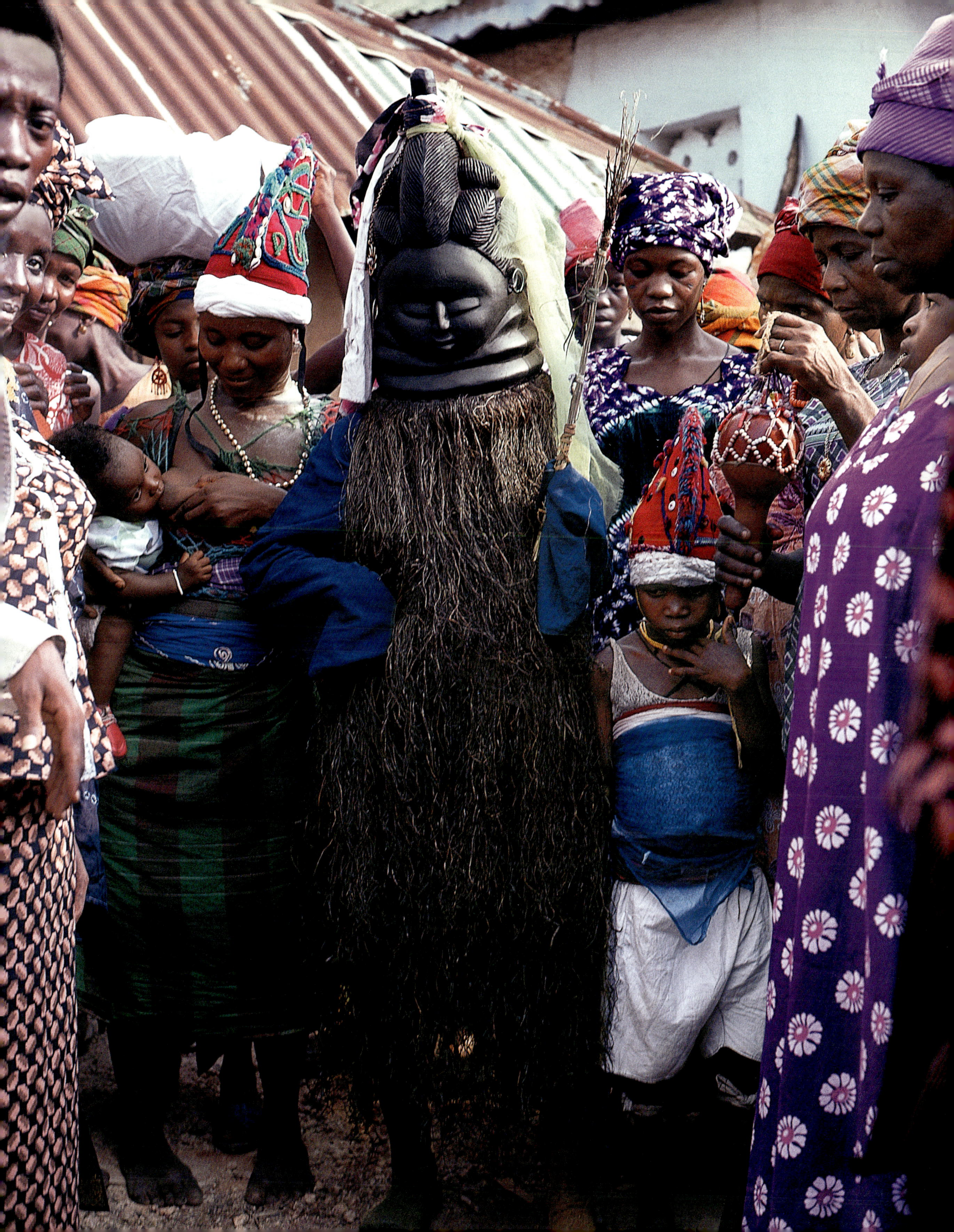

AFTERWORD

The tantalising and contradictory title of this book suggests its major theme: that of inserting life and movement into inanimate objects through a sensory immersion. This collection of essays and Frederick John Lamp's thoughtful essays introducing each section enables the reader-visitor to think further about the objects on display in The Baltimore Museum of Art and to consider them in a fuller context of art making in which originally they formed part of a performance. Although itself inanimate, and when not in performance, most often hidden, the object might nevertheless be perceived as being permanently imbued with spirituality, thus sustaining an invisible, often powerful, force. The performance brought that force into visibility. This book successfully brings that performative dimension of the objects in the museum to the fore.

Museums have played a key role in enabling people throughout the world to preserve objects of spiritual, social and, in some cases, material value in conditions which guarantee as far as is humanly possible, their permanent presence. That, the primary objective of museums, is one which has been admirably fulfilled at the BMA. It has enabled scholars, many from the originating contexts in Africa, to learn from, teach from, study, compare with, and add to the collections. Mute, glorious things, incomplete, perhaps, if viewed as collections, nevertheless the objects already provide texts of unending depth for the scholar and the public. The enhanced perspective can only increase that capacity.

However, for some time now, museums have been aware that in order for people, specialists and non-specialists alike, to more fully appreciate the individual object, it has become imperative to attempt to bridge the gap between the conditions of the 'object-in-use' and the 'object-on-display'. Context, rather than form alone, has become the watchword. The question that has followed is: What context to provide? How to provide something which adumbrates the original context without falling into the trap of essentializing and exoticising it? The museum inevitably re-contextualises the object. It can provide references and information about its original context but should avoid a sanitised, refined, and uniformly dressed version of the original, like the official dance troupes entertaining dignitaries and tourists around Africa. Because the original context has altered within the museum, so the original spectatorship has also altered.

In order to bring some understanding of the object in its original situation to these new spectators, new strategies of communication are needed—sound, light, written information, slides, video recording from the original field context. A new mise-en-scene can be provided, but one that is without the dust from dancing feet, without the scared but delighted cries of children running away from the chasing masquerader, and without the tension of the bravado of the young men performing to the crowd, seeking applause and dreading their approbation. Women visiting the museum and seeing the object will not be fearful of the power of the masquerade figure over their ability to bear children, nor will the changing rhythms of the drums indicate the progression of a performance through the day and into nightfall, for how long will the museum visitors stand and absorb the new show? Inevitably a hiatus persists between the lived experience and a mediated appreciation of it. How can the new mise-en-scene be sensory enough to hold them for the real time duration of an entire event?

This raises another issue. Should people outside a culture feel they have a right to experience *all* that is available to those within it? Within any given culture, individuals feel differently about selected aspects of it. This is as true of the many small ethnically defined cultures within Africa as it is of those more globally familiar. How to provide for the casual, but interested visitor at the museum, a sense of this individuality?

However much 'non-insiders' absorb intellectually and spiritually a particular belief system, it will never delineate the boundaries of choice available to them as it may for 'insiders'. Thus the perception and reception of the symbols and signs of the power inherent in the belief system will always be different from those of the 'insider'. This awareness of 'difference' is intrinsic to the museum visitor whose reasons for visiting the museum are likely to include the desire to see things which are strange and unlike their own everyday experience. Yet it is comprehension, appreciation, understanding, and enlightenment that the museum seeks to bring to the visitor. This text demonstrates the use of many of these objects in the context of performance, not on static display, and in making available this collection of essays as well as his splendid introductory texts to each section, Frederick John Lamp has addressed with restraint and imagination the contradictions and congruences of displaying performed art in a museum context.

Not all the answers are here, but many of the questions are.

Frances Harding

Mask (*Kifwebe*)
Luba, Congo (Kinshasa)
c. Early 20th century
Wood, wood fiber, synthetic fiber bag, feathers, hair, nut shell, polychrome
H. 33 cm
Gift of Barry and Toby T. Hecht, Bethesda, Maryland
BMA 1987.144

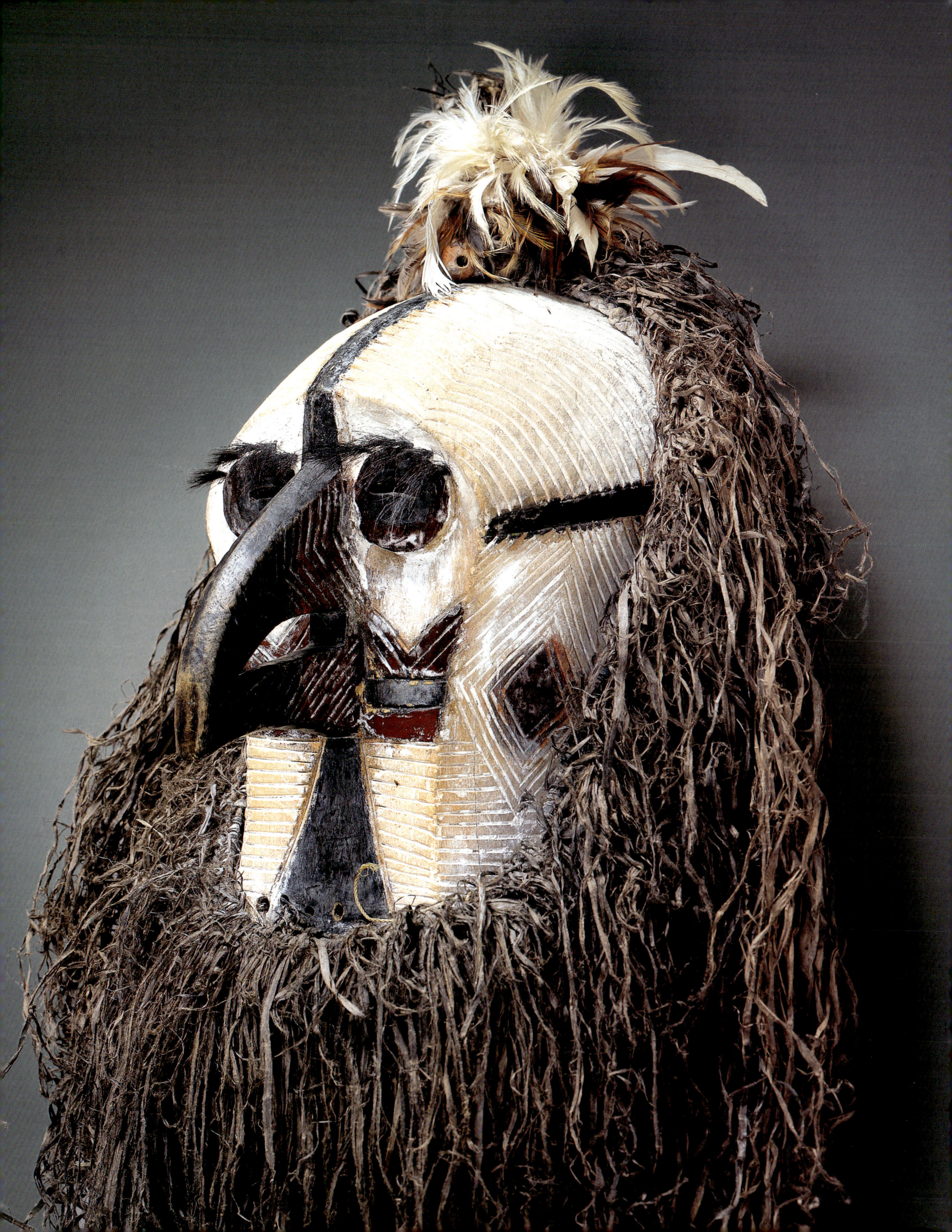

CONTRIBUTORS

(Essays written by scholars who have worked in the particular field are signed with the writer's full name. Essays written from research in the literature are signed with the writer's initials.)

Laurel Birch de Aguilar, of St. Salvator's College, University of St. Andrews, Scotland, has conducted field research in Malawi. She is the author of *Inscribing the Mask: Interpretation of Nyau Masks and Ritual Performance among the Chewa of Central Malawi* (1996). Her research has concerned such areas as oral history, "families" of masks and their social roles, stilt masquerades, and contemporary art.

Karel Arnaut is an art historian and Junior Lecturer at the Department of African Languages and Cultures, Ghent University (Belgium). He has done extensive field research in the Bondoukou region of the Ivory Coast. He is editor of *Re-Visions: New Perspectives on the African Collections of the Horniman Museum* (2000), and editor (with Elizabeth Dell) of *Bedu Is My Lover: Five Stories about Bondoukou and Masquerading* (1996). Arnaut has published widely on masquerading, parades, and demonstrations, and is currently finishing a doctoral thesis on identity and violence in public performances in Bondoukou and Abidjan.

Mary Jo Arnoldi is Curator of African Ethnology and Art in the Department of Anthropology, National Museum of Natural History, Smithsonian Institution, Washington, D.C. She is the author of *Playing with Time: Art and Performance in Central Mali* (1995). She curated and produced the catalogue for the exhibition (with Christine Mullen Kreamer), *Crowning Achievements: African Arts of Dressing the Head* (1995). She was the lead curator for "African Voices," the permanent exhibition of African history and cultures at the National Museum of Natural History, Smithsonian (1999), and she co-curated the section "Mali: From Timbuktu to Washington" at the 2003 Smithsonian Folklife Festival.

David A. Binkley is Deputy Director and Chief Curator, National Museum of African Art, Smithsonian Institution Washington, D.C. He has worked principally on initiations and funerary ritual among the southern Kuba of Congo (Kinshasa). His many articles have included subjects from royal masks to household objects and the interpretation of Kuba arts in the popular and scholary discourse of the nineteenth and twentieth centuries. He has edited (with Simon Ottenberg) *Playful Performers: African Children's Masquerades* (in preparation).

Carol Boram-Hays is a Lecturer at The Ohio State University, Newark and Marion Campuses, Ohio. Her dissertation, following research at the University of Natal in Durban, South Africa, is entitled *A History of Zulu Beadwork 1890–1997: Its Types, Forms, and Functions*, and she was awarded her Ph.D. in the History of African Art from The Ohio State University in 2002. She curated the exhibition "African Pathways: From Birth to Rebirth" at the Columbus Museum of Art, and has written several papers on Zulu beadwork and contemporary African art. Currently she preparing an exhibition of Ohio decorative arts for the Columbus Museum of Art.

Lillian Maria Burgunder is a research associate in the department of the Arts of Africa, Asia, the Americas & Oceania, at The Baltimore Museum of Art. She studied African art and received an M.L.A. in 1983 at The Johns Hopkins University, and is retired from the faculty of Gilman School, where she taught Art History and Criticism.

Alice Burmeister teaches in the Department of Art and Design at Winthrop University, Rock Hill, South Carolina. Her research for a dissertation at Indiana University is focused on the use of bird decoys by hunters and by ritual performers among the Hausa people.

Elisabeth L. Cameron is Assistant Professor of History of Art and Visual Culture Departement, at the University of California, Santa Cruz, and was previously Associate Curator at The Nelson-Atkins Museum of Art. She has curated and written catalogues for *The Art of the Lega* (2001) and *Isn't S/He a Doll? Play and Ritual in African Sculpture* (1996), among many others. And she has authored many articles and chapters, including "Potential & Fulfilled Mothers," In Manuel Jordan, ed., *Chokwe! Art and Initiation Among Chokwe and Related Peoples*, 1998. She has a Fulbright-Hayes Award for fieldwork in Zambia for 2003–2004.

Herbert M. Cole is Professor Emeritus at the University of California, Santa Barbara. He is the author of *Icons: Ideals and Power in the Art of Africa* (1989), *Igbo Arts: Community and Cosmos* (1984, with Chike Aniakor), *The Arts of Ghana* (1977, with Doran Ross), and he curated the exhibition and edited the oft-quoted catalogue, *I Am Not Myself: the Art of African Masquerade* (1985). In 2001 he was honored with the Leadership Award from the Arts Council of the African Studies Association (ACASA). He is currently editing *The Encyclopedia of African Art.*

Henry John Drewal is Evjue-Bascom Professor of Art History and Afro-American Studies at the University of Wisconsin-Madison and Adjunct Curator of African Art at the university's Elvehjem Museum of Art since 1991. He is author and curator (with John Mason) of *Beads, Body, and Soul: Art and Light in the Yoruba Universe* (1998–2000). He edited (with R. Abiodun and J. Pemberton III) *The Yoruba Artist: New Theoretical Perspectives on African Arts* (1994), and co-authored (with M.T. Drewal) *Gelede: Art and Female Power among the Yoruba* (1983). Recently, he has begun research on Africans in India, and he is preparing the book and exhibition, *Sacred Waters: Arts for Mami Wata and other Afro-Atlantic Water Spirits.*

Till Förster is an anthropologist with the Ethnologisches Seminar, University of Basel, Switzerland. Previously, he was director of the Iwalewa-Haus, The Africa Center at the University of Bayreuth. His fieldwork has included approximately six years in northern Ivory Coast, Burkina Faso, and Niger. He is the author of *African styles: Kleidung und Textilien aus Afrika: die Sammlung des Iwalewa-Hauses* (2001), *Zerrissene Entfaltung: Alltag, Ritual und künsterlische Ausdrucksformen im Norden der Côte d'Ivoire* (1997), *Die Kunst der Senufo* (1988), and *Divination bei den Kafibele-Senufo: zur Aushandlung und Bewältigung von Alltagskonflikten* (1985).

Susan Elizabeth Gagliardi is a doctoral student in African art history at the University of California, Los Angeles. With a grant from the Fulbright Program, she studied Lobi art and architecture in Ghana, resulting in her Master's thesis on the topic at the Sainsbury Research Unit, University of East Anglia. She has worked at the National Museum of Ghana in Accra, The Baltimore Museum of Art, and the UCLA Fowler Museum of Cultural History.

Frank Gunderson is Assistant Professor of Ethnomusicology at Florida State University. He received a Ph. D. in Ethnomusicology from Wesleyan University in 1999. He has taught at Ohio University, University of Michigan, and the University of Oklahoma. He has conducted extensive fieldwork in Tanzania, and has produced the CD *Tanzania: Farmer Composers of North West Tanzania* (1997, Multicultural Media), and has co-edited (with Gregory Barz) the book *Mashindano!: Competitive Music Performance in East Africa* (2000). He is currently writing a book about compositional processes and musical labor practices in northwestern Tanzania.

Emily G. Hanna is the Curator of the Arts of Africa and the Americas at the Birmingham Museum of Art. Her research interests include historic and contemporary African art, and African-American art. She is currently organizing an exhibition of contemporary African painting, entitled "Inside/Out: Painting Africa in the 21st Century," as well as an exhibition on the Bwa of Burkina Faso. Her recent exhibitions include "American Visions: Selections of African American art from 1960 to the Present," and "Symbols and Sayings: The Visual and Verbal Arts of the Akan."

Frances Harding is Lecturer in African Drama, The School of Oriental and African Studies (SOAS), University of London. She has conducted field research principally among the Tiv of Nigeria, concentrating on contemporary theater. She has recently produced an edited anthology, *The Performance Arts in Africa: A Reader* (2002), with an introduction on performance theory.

Christian Kordt Højbjerg is a Research Fellow at the Centre for African Studies, University of Copenhagen, Denmark. He has specialized in the religion and political culture of the Upper Guinea Forest region, especially among the Loma, and he has written on iconoclasm and on the construction of cultural identity. He is currently producing a book entitled *Violation of Tradition: Religion and Political Culture in Loma Society in Guinea and Liberia.*

Anita Jones is Associate Curator of Decorative Arts for Textiles at The Baltimore Museum of Art. She has curated thirty-five exhibitions on a wide variety of textiles, including French eighteenth- and nineteenth-century toiles, Chinese children's clothing, Japanese kesa, Chantilly lace, contemporary Inuit appliquéd hangings, and important designers such as Léon Bakst and William Morris. Her exhibition catalogs include *Patterns in a Revolution: French Printed Textiles, 1759–1821* (1990), and *Northern Lights: Inuit Textile Art from the Canadian Arctic* (1993, co-authored with Katherine Fernstrom).

Sidney Littlefield Kasfir is Associate Professor and Faculty Curator of African Art, Emory University, Atlanta, Georgia. She has conducted research in the Benue Valley, Nigeria, and in Kenya, Tanzania, and Uganda, in historic material culture as well as contemporary and popular arts. She is the author of *Contemporary African Art* (2000), and has edited and contributed to *West African Masks and Cultural Systems* (1988). Her many articles concern women and masquerading, artists, authenticity, and the trade in African art.

Thomas Kittredge earned his M.A. in Egyptology from The Johns Hopkins University, Baltimore in 2001. He specializes in the art and archeology of ancient Egypt, and he has participated in numerous field excavations, at sites such as Abydos, Giza, the Valley of the Kings, and at the Temple of Mut at Karnak.

Pawel Kozielski has been Director of Excavations in the Calabar region of Nigeria, the subject of his dissertation for the University of Maryland, College Park. He is on the faculty of the Pennsylvania College of Art & Design, Lancaster, Pennsylvania, and has taught at the University of Kentucky and other institutions.

Christine Mullen Kreamer is Curator, National Museum of African Art, Smithsonian Institution Washington, D.C. She is the co-author (with Martha Anderson) of *Wild Spirits, Strong Medicine: African Art and the Wilderness* (1989), and co-editor (with Ivan Karp and Steven D. Lavine) of *Museums and Communities: the Politics of Public Culture*, and co-editor (with Mary Jo Arnoldi) and co-author of *Crowning Achievements: African Arts of Dressing the Head* (1995). She was the Exhibit Developer/Content Coordinator for "African Voices," which opened at the National Museum of Natural History, Smithsonian, in 1999.

Frederick John Lamp is the Frances and Benjamin Benenson Foundation Curator of African Art at the Yale University Art Gallery, and through 2003 was the Curatorial Department Head of the Arts of Africa, Asia, the Americas & Oceania at The Baltimore Museum of Art. Lamp has conducted research in Sierra Leone and Guinea on male and female initiation, chieftaincy ritual, and ancestral ritual, with grants from the Fulbright Program, the Smithsonian Institution, The National Gallery of Art, Social Science Research Council, and the National Endowments of Art and the Humanities. He is the author of *Art of the Baga: A Drama of Cultural Reinvention* (1996), and *La Guinée et ses Heritages Culturels* (1992).

Babatunde Lawal is a professor in the Department of Art History at Virginia Commonwealth University, Richmond. He has conducted research in Nigeria, Ghana, Zimbabwe, and Brazil, among others. He has published extensively on different aspects of African and African diaspora art, contemporary art, archeology, aesthetics, and historical art in Nigeria. He is the author of *The Gèlèdé Spectacle: Art, Gender, and Social Harmony in an African Culture* (1996), and is currently completing a book on Sango sculpture among the Yoruba.

Wyatt MacGaffey is Professor Emeritus, Haverford College, Pennsylvania, where he taught from 1967 to 1998. He has conducted extensive anthropological research among the Kongo peoples, and his publications have covered politics, religion, medicine, and art, especially the construction of medicinal packets used in healing and divination. He is the author of *Kongo Political Culture: the Conceptual Challenge of the Particular* (2000), *Astonishment and Power* (1993), *Art and Healing of the BaKongo: Commented by Themselves: Minkisi from the Laman Collection* (1991), and *Custom and Government in the Lower Congo* (1970).

The late **Keith Nicklin** (1946–2002) began his career in 1970 with the Nigerian National Commission for Museums and Monuments, rebuilding the museum at Oron, and studying skin-covered masks of the Cross River, and Lower Niger bronzes. In 1982 he became Keeper of Ethnography at the Horniman Museum. Among his many publications is *Ekpu: The Oron Ancestor Figures of South Eastern Nigeria* (1999). Accompanying his essay here is a statement of concern for the Ogoni, who have suffered punishments for their demands for compensation from the Federal Government of Nigeria and Shell International for the oil taken from their land, and for the ensuing environmental and health problems: "It is to be hoped that this brave nation will soon be allowed to resume a life free from persecution and gross exploitation."

Tamara Northern is Senior Curator Emerita, Hood Museum of Art, Dartmouth College. She began her career as Associate Curator, working with Robert Goldwater, at The Museum of Primitive Art, New York, in 1962. Her fieldwork has covered the Cameroon Grasslands. She is the author and curator of numerous publications and exhibitions, including *The Sign of the Leopard: Beaded Art of Cameroon* (1975), *The Ornate Implement* (1981), *The Art of Cameroon* (1984), and *Focus on the Body: West African Body Ornaments of Brass* (1999).

Daniel B. Reed is Director of the Archives of Traditional Music and Assistant Professor in the Department of Folklore and Ethnomusicology at Indiana University. His primary research interests are music and mask performance in West Africa, and he has conducted field research in the Ivory Coast, Mali, and Guinea. His publications include *Dan Ge Performance: Masks and Music in Contemporary Cote d'Ivoire* (2003) and *Music and Culture of West Africa: The Straus Expedition* (CD-ROM, with Gloria Gibson, Indiana University, 2002).

Doran H. Ross served as Director of the UCLA Fowler Museum of Cultural History from 1996 to 2001. He is the author of *The Arts of Ghana* (with Herbert M. Cole, 1977) and of *Akan Gold from the Glassell Collection* (2002), and he edited *Akan Transformations: Problems in Ghanaian Art History* (with Timothy Garrard, 1983), *Elephant: The Animal and its Ivory in African Culture* (1992), and *Wrapped in Pride: Ghanaian Kente and African American Identity* (1998). He is a past president of the Arts Council of the African Studies Association. Currently he is co-editor of the journals *African Arts* and *Textile: The Journal of Cloth and Culture.*

Christopher Roy is Professor of Art History at the University of Iowa, where he is also Associate Dean of International Programs. He has published three catalogues of the Stanley Collection at the University of Iowa, and a CD-ROM titled *Art and Life in Africa.* He has also written Art of the Upper Volta Rivers (1987), *Kilengi: African Art from the Bareiss Collection*, (1997), and, most recently, *Forms and Functions in African Art* (*Fei-chou i shu* in Chinese), the catalogue of an exhibition in China. He is currently making documentary films of African art techniques.

Jill Salmons is Senior Lecturer in the School of Art & Design at the Worcester College of Technology, Worcester, England. She began her work in Africa as a Commonwealth Scholar attached to the University of Nsukka, Nigeria, 1973–76, during which she conducted fieldwork amongst the Annang and Ibibio, and she was Lecturer in West African History at the University of Uyo in S. E. Nigeria, 1976–78. Her many publications run from "Mammy Wata," *African Arts*, April, I977, to "The Arts of the Ogoni" (co-edited with S. Kpone-Tonwe) in *Ways of the River* (M. Anderson & P. Peek, eds.), 2002.

Raymond A. Silverman is Professor in the Department of the History of Art and the Center for Afroamerican and African Studies, and Director of the Museum Studies Program at the University of Michigan. He has conducted field research in Ghana and the Ivory Coast, and in Ethiopia, focusing on the interaction between Sub-Saharan West Africa and the cultures of the Islamic Middle East and the West. Silverman curated the exhibition and edited the catalogue for *Ethiopia: Traditions of Creativity* (1994), and recently curated *"Drinking the Word of God"—Expressions of Faith and the Search for Well-Being in Two West African Communities* (2001).

Z. S. Strother is Associate Professor of African Art History at the University of California, Los Angeles. During fieldwork in Zaire, 1987–89, masqueraders told her that she was wrong to concentrate on sculptors at the expense of dancers, resulting in her book, *Inventing Masks: Agency and History in the Art of the Central Pende* (1998), which won the Arnold Rubin Outstanding Publication Award, from the Arts Council of the African Studies Association in 2001. She has recently held fellowships from the John Simon Guggenheim Memorial Foundation (2002–03) and the National Gallery of Art, CASVA (2000–01).

Robert Farris Thompson is Master of Timothy Dwight College, and The Colonel John Trumbull Professor of the History of Art, Yale University. His early studies were grounded in the smoky jazz clubs and charismatic black churches of Harlem, where he developed proficiency in drumming and dance, and he went on to conduct field research among the Yoruba and the Kongo in Africa, African communities in the Western Hemisphere, and the global reaches of African culture. His numerous publications include *Black Gods and Kings: Yoruba Art at UCLA* (1971), *African Art in Motion: Icon and Act* (1974), *The Four Moments of the Sun: Kongo Art in Two Worlds* (1981), *Face of the Gods: Art and Altars of Africa and the African Americas* (1993).

Marie-Noël Verger-Fèvre is Research Associate, Muséum National d'Histoire Naturelle, Musée de l'Homme, Paris. She has taught African art at the Ecole du Louvre, Paris. Her publications include *Masques de l'ouest de la Côte d'Ivoire dans les collections publiques françaises* (1980), and *Présentation des objets de la Côte d'Ivoire dans les expositions universelles et coloniales, de 1878 à 1937* (1982). She has written extensively on the Dan and Wè and other groups of the western Ivory Coast.

Stephen Wooten Stephen Wooten is Assistant Professor of Anthropology and International Studies at the University of Oregon. He has been conducting ethnographic field research in rural Mali since 1992. His research explores the interconnections between economy and expressive culture in Bamana society. His publications include: "Antelope Headdresses and Champion Farmers: Negotiating Meaning and Identity Through the Bamana Ciwara Complex" (2000) in *African Arts* and "Women, Men and Market Gardens: Gender Relations and Income Generation in Rural Mali" (2003) in *Human Organization.*

REFERENCES

Abimbola, Wande

1971 "The Yoruba Concept of Human Personality." in *La Personne en Afrique Noire*. Colloques Internationaux du Centre National de la Recherche Scientifique. No. 544: 73–89. Paris: National Center of Scientific Research.

Abraham, Roy Clive

1967 *The Idoma Language*. London: University of London Press.

Adams, Marie-Jeanne (Monni)

1978 "Kuba Embroidered Cloth." African Arts XII, (1).

1981 "Skirt Wrapper." in *For Spirits and Kings: African Art from the Tishman Collection*. S. Vogel, ed. New York: The Metropolitan Museum of Art.

Adedeji, Joel A.

1972 "Folklore and Yoruba Drama: Obatala as a Case Study." in *African Folklore*. R.M. Dorson, ed. Bloomington: Indiana University Press.

Adediran, Abiodun A., and Samuel A. Arifalo

1992 "The Religious Festivals of Ife." in *The Cradle of a Race: Ife from the Beginning to 1980*. I.A. Akinjogbin, ed. Port Harcourt, Nigeria: Sunray.

Akpan, Joseph J.

1994 "*Ekpo* Society Masks of the Ibibio." *African Arts* XXVII, (4).

Ames, David W.

1989 "A Sociocultural View of Hausa Musical Activity." in *The Traditional Artist in African Societies*. Bloomington: Indiana University Press.

Amin, Mohamed, Duncan Willetts, and John Eames

1987 *The Last of the Maasai*. Nairobi: Publishers International.

Andersson, Efraim

1953 "Contribution à l'Ethnographie des Kuta I." in *Studia Ethnographica Upsaliensia VI*. Uppsala.

Andrews, Carol

1994 *Amulets of Ancient Egypt*. London: British Museum.

Antongini, Giovanna, and Tito Spini

1981 *Il cammino degli antenati. I Lobi dell'Alto Volta*. t.B.-t.-S.V.o.t.S. Institution, transl. Rome: Editori Laterza.

Appia, Beatrice

1943 "Masques de Guinée Français et de Casamance." *Journal de la Société des Africanistes* XIII.

Appiah, Peggy

1979 "Akan Symbolism." *African Arts* XIII, (1).

Arman

1980 *Fragments of the Sublime*. New York: J. Camp Associates, Ltd.

Arnoldi, Mary Jo

1988 "Playing the Puppets: Innovation and Rivalry in Bamana Youth Theatre in Mali." *TDR* 32, (2): 65–82.

1995 *Playing with Time, Art and Performance in Central Mali*. Bloomington: Indiana University Press.

Aufrèrè, Sydney

1991 *L'Univers Minéral dans la Pensée Égyptienne*. Cairo: L'Institut Français d'Archéologie Orientale.

Baginski, Alisa, and Amalia Tidhar

1980 *Textiles from Egypt 4th–13th Centuries C.E.* Jerusalem: L.A. Mayer Memorial Institute for Islamic Art.

Banes, Sally

2001 "Olfactory Performances." *The Drama Review*, Spring: 68–76.

Bangura, Seku Beka

1972 *Croyances et Pratiques Religieuses des Baga Sitemu*. (Memoire de Diplôme de Fin d'Etudes Superieures, Institut Polytechnique Julius Nyerere, Kankan, Guinea).

Barta, Winfried

1968 *Aufbau und Bedeutung der altägyptischen Opferformel*. Glückstadt: J.J. Augustin.

Bartenieff, Irmgard

1980 *Body Movement: Coping with the Environment*. New York: Gordon and Breach.

Bascom, W.

1969 *Ifa Divination Communication between Gods and Men in West Africa*. Bloomington: Indiana University Press.

Bassi, Marco

1999 "Every Woman an Artist: The Milk Containers of Elema Boru." in *Ethiopia: Traditions of Creativity*. R. Silverman, ed. Seattle: University of Washington Press.

Becker, Peter

1982 *Inland Tribes of Southern Africa*. London: Granada.

Bellman, B.L.

1980 "Masks, Societies, and Secrecy among the Fala Kpelle." *Ethnologische Zeitschrift Zürich* 1: 61–79.

Ben-Amos, Paula (Girshick)

1995 *The Art of Benin*. Washington: Smithsonian Institution Press.

1999 *Art, Innovation, and Politics in Eighteenth-Century Benin*. Bloomington: Indiana University Press.

Biebuyck, Daniel

1985 *The Arts of Zaire: Volume 1, Southwestern Zaire*. Berkeley: University of California Press.

Binkley, David A.

1987a "Avatar of Power: Southern Kuba Masquerade Figures in a Funerary Context." *Africa* 57, (1): 75–97.

1987b "A View from the Forest: the Power of Southern Kuba Initiation Masks." Ph.D. Dissertation. Indiana University.

1990 "Masks, Space, and Gender in Southern Kuba Initiation Ritual." in *Iowa Studies in African Art. Vol 3. Art and Initiation in Zaire*. C. Roy, ed. Iowa City: University of Iowa Press.

1996 "Bounce the Baby: Masks, Fertility, and the Authority of Esoteric Knowledge in Northern Kete Initiation Rituals." *Elvehjem Museum of Art Bulletin*: 45–56.

1996 "Figural palm wine cup/Cephalomorphic palm wine cup." in *Masterpieces from Central Africa*. G. Verswijver, E. de Palmenaer, V. Baeke, and A.-M. Bouttiaux-Ndiaye, eds. Tervuren: Musée royal de l'Afrique centrale.

Bittremieux, L.

1936 *La Société Secrète des Bakhimba au Mayombe*. Brussels: Institut Royal Colonial Belge.

Blackmun, Barbara, and Jacques Hautelet

1990 *Blades of Beauty and Death.* San Diego: Mesa College Art Gallery.

Blum, Odette

1973 *Dance in Ghana.* New York: Dance Perspectives, LVI.

Bognolo, Daniela

1993 "Art Lobi: lecture et connaissance." in *Images d'Afrique et Sciences sociales: Les pays Lobi, birifor et dagara.* Actes de Colloque de Ouagadougou, 10–15 December 1990. Michèle Fiéloux, Jacques Lombard and Jeanne-Marie Kambou-Ferrand, eds. Paris: Éditions Karthala and ORSTOM.

Boone, Sylvia A.

1986 *Radiance from the Waters: Ideals of Feminine Beauty in Mende Art.* New Haven: Yale University Press.

Boram-Hays, Carol S.

2000 "A History of Zulu Beadwork 1890–1997: Its Types, Forms, and Functions." Ph.D. Dissertation. The Ohio State University.

Borgatti, Jean

1983 *Cloth as Metaphor: Nigerian Textiles at the Museum of Cultural History.* Los Angeles: Museum of Cultural History.

Bowald, Frederick

1939 *In den Sümpfen des Rio Nunez.* Zurich: Büchergilde Gutenberg.

Boyer, Alain-Michel

1993 "Heddle Pulley." in *Art of Côte d'Ivoire from the Collections of the Barbier-Mueller Museum.* J.P. Barbier, ed. Geneva: Barbier-Mueller Museum.

Bradbury, R.E.

1973 *Benin Studies.* P. Morton-Williams, ed. London: Oxford University Press.

Bravmann, René A.

1974 *Islam and Tribal Art in West Africa.* Cambridge: Cambridge University Press.

1993 "Bondoukou: The Artistry of a City and Countryside." in *Art of Côte d'Ivoire from the Collections of the Barbier-Mueller Museum.* Vol. I. Geneva: The Barbier-Mueller Museum.

Brett-Smith, Sarah

1977 "The Mouth of the Komo." *Res,* (31).

Brincard, Marie-Thérèse

1989 *Sounding Forms: African Musical Instruments.* New York: The American Federation of Arts.

Brovarski, Edward

1978 *Corpus Antiquitatum Aegypticarum.* Mainz am Rhein: Philipp von Zabern.

Bunot, R.

1950 *Forêts du sud, brindilles de la forêt toma.* Mayenne.

Burmeister, Alice Ross

2000 *Demonstrating Iyawa: Hausa Hunters' Arts and Women's Wealth Display (Niger).* Ann Arbor, MI: UMI Dissertation Services.

Butt-Thompson, Frederick William

1929/1970 *West African Secret Societies.* Westport, CT: Negro Universities Press.

Cameron, Elisabeth

1994 "Palm Wine Cups." in *Visions of Africa: The Jerome L. Joss Collection at UCLA.* D. Ross, ed. Los Angeles: Fowler Museum of Cultural History, UCLA.

1995 "Negotiating Gender: Initiation Arts of *Mwadi* and *Mukanda* among the Lunda and Luvale, Kabompo District, North-Western Province, Zambia." Ph.D. Dissertation. University of California, Los Angeles.

1998 "Woman=Mask: Initiation Arts in North-Western Province, Zambia." *African Arts* XXXI, (2): 50–61.

Carroll, Diane Lee

1988 *Looms and Textiles of the Copts: First Millennium Egyptian Textiles in the Carl Austin Rietz Collection of the California Academy of Sciences.* Seattle: University of Washington Press.

Cauville, Sylvie

1997 *Le Temple de Dendara: Les Chapelles Osiriennes.* Cairo: Institut Français d'Archéologie Orientale.

Chaffin, Alain and Françoise

N/D *L'Art Kota: les figures de reliquaire.* Meudon: Alain & Françoise Chaffin.

Charry, Eric

2000 *Mande Music: Traditional and Modern Music of the Maninka and Mandinka of Western Africa.* Chicago: University of Chicago Press.

Chernoff, John Miller

1979 *African Rythm and Sensibility: Aesthetics and Social Action in African Musical Idioms.* Chicago: University of Chicago Press.

Clifford, James

1988 *The Predicament of Culture: Twentieth-Century Ethnography, Literature, and Art.* Cambridge, MA: Harvard University Press.

Cole, Herbert M.

1969 "Mbari is a Dance." *African Arts* II, (4).

1969 "Art As a Verb in the Igboland." *African Arts* III, (1).

1970 *African Arts of Transformation.* Santa Barbara: University of California Press.

1974 "Vital Arts in Northern Kenya." *African Arts* VII, (2).

1975 "The Art of Festival in Ghana." *African Arts* VIII, (3).

1985 "Introduction." in *I Am Not Myself: the Art of African Masquerade.* Los Angeles: Fowler Museum of Cultural History, UCLA.

2001 "Benin: Six Centuries of Royal Arts." in *A History of Art in Africa.* M. Visona, R. Poynor, H. Cole, and M. Harris, eds. New York: Harry N. Abrams.

Cole, Herbert M., and Chike Aniakor

1984 *Igbo Arts: Community and Cosmos.* Los Angeles: Fowler Museum of Cultural History, UCLA.

Cole, Herbert M., and Doran Ross

1977 *The Arts of Ghana.* Los Angeles: Fowler Museum of Cultural History, UCLA.

Colle, Pierre

1913 *Les Baluba.* Tomes I and II, A. Dewit, ed. Brussels: International Institute of Biography

Colleyn, Jean-Paul, and Catherine De Clippel

1998 *Bamanaya: Un art de vivre au Mali.* Milan: Centro Studi Archaeologia Africana di Milano.

Cornet, Joseph

1978 *A Survey of Zairian Art: The Bronson Collection.* Raleigh: North Carolina Museum of Art.

1980 "The Itul Celebration of the Kuba." *African Arts* XIII, (3).

1982 *Art Royal Kuba.* Milan: Edizioni Sipiel.

1993 "Masks Among the Kuba Peoples." in *Face of the Spirits: Masks from the Zaire Basin.* F. Herreman and C. Petridis, eds. Tervuren: Musée royal de l'Afrique centrale.

Courtney-Clarke, Margaret

1986 *Ndebele: The Art of an African Tribe.* Cape Town: C. Struik.

Crowley, Dan

1983 "Collecting in the Last Days of the Belgian Congo." *African Arts* XVI, (2): 70–73.

Dahl, Gudrun

1990 "Mats and Milk Pots: The Domain of Borana Women." in *The Creative Communion: African Folk Models of Fertility and the Regeneration of Life.* A. Jacobson-Widding and W. van Beek, eds. Uppsala: Acta Universitatis Upsaliensis.

Darish, Patricia

1989 "Dressing for the Next Life: Raffia Textile Production and Use Among the Kuba of Zaire." in *Cloth and Human Experience.* A.B. Weiner and J. Schneider, eds. Washington: Smithsonian Institution Press.

Dark, Philip C.

1973 *An Introduction to Benin Art and Technology.* London: Oxford University Press.

1981 "Head and Tusk." in *For Spirits and Kings: African Art from the Tishman Collection.* S. Vogel, ed. New York: The Metropolitan Museum of Art.

de Brazza, Savorgnan

1887 "Voyages dans l'ouest africaine." in *Le Tour du Monde.* Paris: Librairie Hachette et Cie.

de Faro, André

1945 "Peregrinação à terra dos gentios (1664). L. Silveira, ed. Lisbon: Officina da Tipographica Portugal-Brazil.

de Sousberghe, Léon

1953 "Cases cheffales du Kwango."

1955 "Cases cheffales sculptés des Ba-Pende." *Bulletin de la Société Royale Belge d'Anthropologie et de Préhistoire* LXV.

1958 *L'art pende*: Académie Royale de Belgique, Mémoires in-4°, 2d ser., vol.9, fasc. 2. Brussels.

1960 "De la signification de quelques masques pende: *Shave* des Shona et *Mbuya* des Pende." *Zaïre* (Brussels) 14, (5–6): 505–31.

de Surgy, Albert

1986 *La divination par les huit cordelettes chez les Mwaba-Gurma (Nord Togo).* Paris: L'Harmattan.

Desroches-Noblecourt, Christiane

1963 *Tutankhamen: Life and Death of a Pharaoh.* Boston: New York Graphic Society.

Devisch, René

1990 "The Human Body As a Vehicle for Emotions among the Yaka of Zaire." in *Personhood and Agency: The Experience of Self and Other in African Cultures.* M. Jackson and I. Karp, eds. Washington: Smithsonian Institution Press.

Diabate, M.

1985 *Les sociétés de chasseurs chez les Maouka de Côte d'Ivoire Région de Touba.* Paris: Mémoire de l'Ecole Pratique des Hautes Etudes, Sorbonne.

Dieterlen, Germaine, and Y. Cissé

1972 *Les Fondements de la Société d'Initiation du Komo.* Paris: Mouton & Co.

DjeDje, Jacqueline Cogdell

1999 *Turn up the Volume! A Celebration of African Music.* Los Angeles: Fowler Museum of Cultural History, UCLA.

Dmochowski, Z.R.

1990 *An Introduction to Nigeria and Traditional Architecture, Volume Two: Southwest and Central Nigeria.* London: Ethnographica.

Dodson, Aidan

1996 "A Canopic Jar for Rameses IV." *Göttinger Miszellen* 152: 11–26.

Drewal, Henry John

1977 *Traditional Art of the Nigerian Peoples: The Ratner Collection.* Washington: National Museum of African Art.

1992 "Image and Indeterminacy: The Significance of Elephants and Ivory among the Yoruba," in *Elephant: The Animal and its Ivory in African Culture.* D. Ross, ed. Los Angeles: Fowler Museum of Cultural History.

Drewal, Henry John, and Margaret Thompson Drewal

1983 *Gelede: Art and Female Power among the Yoruba.* Bloomington: Indiana University Press.

Drewal, Henry John, John Pemberton, and R. Abiodun

1989 *Yoruba: Nine Centuries of African Art and Thought.* New York: The Center for African Art.

Drewal, Margaret Thompson

1992 *Yoruba Ritual: Performers, Play, Agency.* Bloomington: Indiana University Press.

Drewal, Margaret Thompson, and Henry John Drewal

1978 "More Powerful than Each Other: An Egbado Classification of Egungun." *African Arts* XI, (3).

Dupre, Georges

1995 "The History and Adventures of a Monetary Object of the Kwélé of the Congo: Mezong, Mondjos, and Mandjong." in *Money Matters: Instability, Values, and Social Payments in the Modern History of West African Communities.* J. Currey, ed. Portsmouth, NH: Heinemann.

Eberl-Elber, R.

1936 *Westafrikas letztes Rätsel. Erlebnisbericht über die Forschungsreise 1935 durch Sierra Leone.* Salzburg: Verlag Das Berglandbuch.

Ehret, Christopher

1996 "Ancient Egyptian As an African Language, Egypt As an African Culture." in *Egypt in Africa.* Indianapolis: Indianapolis Museum of Art.

El Mahdy, Christine

1991 *Mummies, Myth and Magic in Ancient Egypt.* New York: Thames and Hudson.

Erikson, Marianne

1997 *Textiles in Egypt 200–1500 A.D. in Swedish Museum Collections.* Göteborg: Röhsska Museet.

Errington, Shelley

1998 *The Death of Authentic Primitive Art and Other Tales of Progress.* Berkeley: University of California Press.

Eyo, Ekpo

1996 "Carved Monolith." in *Africa: The Art of a Continent.* T. Phillips, ed. Munich: Prestel Verlag.

Farnell, Brenda

1999 "It Goes Without Saying—But Not Always." in *Dance in the Field: Theory, Methods and Issues in Dance Ethnography.* T. Buckland, ed. New York: St. Martin's Press.

Fernandes, Valenim

1506/1951 *Description de la Côte Occidentale d'Afrique (Sénégal au Cap de Monte, Archipels 1506–10).* T. Monod, A. Teixeira da Mota, and R. Mauny, eds. and transls. Bissau: Centro de Estudos da Guiné Portuguesa, Mem. 11.

Fernández, James W.

1992 "The Conditions of Appreciation Contemplating a Collection of Fang (and Kota) Mobiliary Art." in *Kings of Africa: Art and Authority in Central Africa.* E. Beumers and H.-J. Koloss, eds. Maastricht: Foundation Kings of Africa.

Fischer, Eberhard

1970 "Selbstbildnerisches, Porträt und Kopie bei Maskenschnitzern der Dan in Liberia." *Baessler-Archiv* XVIII, (40).

1978 "Dan Forest Spirits." *African Arts* XI, (2): 16–23, 94.

Fischer, Eberhard, and Hans Himmelheber

1984 *The Arts of the Dan in West Africa.* Zurich: Museum Rietberg.

Fisher, Angela

1984 *Africa Adorned.* New York: Harry N. Abrams.

Fisseha, Girma

1988 *Äthiopien—Kunst und Geschichte eines Landes.* Munich: Staatliches Museum für Völkerkunde.

1990 "Speisen und Tischsitten in Äthiopien." *Nubica* 1, (2): 213–232.

Förster, Till

1988 *Die Kunst der Senufo.* Zurich: Museum Rietberg.

Frobenius, Leo

1913 *Und Afrika sprach.* 3 vols. Berlin: Vita, Deutscher Verlag.

Gaisseau, Pierre Dominique

1954 *Forêt sacrée, magie et rites secrets des Toma.* Paris: Albin Michel.

Gamory-Dubourdeau, P. M.

1926 "Notes sur les coutumes des Tomas." *B. du Comitée d'Études Historiques et Scientifiques de l'Afrique Occidentale Française* (Paris), IX.

Gardi, René

1969 *African Crafts and Craftsmen.* New York: Van Nostrand Reinhold.

Garrard, Timothy

1979 "Akan Metal Arts." *African Arts* XIII, (1).

1980 *Akan Weights and the Gold Trade.* London: Longman.

Gba, Daouda

1982 "Les masques chez les Dan." Masters Thesis. Université National de Côte d'Ivoire.

Germer, Renate

1997 *Mummies: Life After Death in Ancient Egypt.* Munich: Prestel Verlag.

Glaze, Anita

1981 *Art and Death in a Senufo Village.* Bloomington: Indiana University Press.

Goépogui, M.

1975 *L'Art en Pays Loma*: Memoire (91 pp.) L'Universite de Kankan, Guinea.

Gonosová, Anna

1989 "Textiles." in *Beyond the Pharaohs.* F. D. Friedman, ed. Providence: Museum of Art, Rhode Island School of Design.

Goody, Jack

1967 *The Social Organisation of the LoWiili.* London: International African Institute, Oxford University.

Gore, Charles

1998 "Ritual, Performance and Media in Urban Contemporary Shrine Configurations in Benin City, Nigeria." in *Ritual, Performance, Media.* F. Hughes-Freeland, ed. New York: Routledge.

Gore, Georgiana

1994 "Traditional Dance in West Africa." in *Dance History: An Introduction.* J. Adshead-Lansdale and J. Layson, eds. New York: Routledge.

Griaule, Marcel

1972 *Conversations with Ogotemmeli.* London: Oxford University Press.

Grossert, J. W.

1968 *Art Education and Zulu Crafts.* Pietermaritzburg: Shuter and Shooter.

Gunderson, Frank

1999 "Musical Labor Associations in Sukumaland, Tanzania: History and Practice." Ph. D. Dissertation. Wesleyan University.

Gunderson, Frank, and Gregory Barz

2000 *Mashindano: Competitive Music Performance in East Africa.* Dar es Salaam: Mkuki na Nyota Press/African Books Collective L. T. D.

Hahner-Herzog, Iris, Maria Kecskési, and László Vajda

1997 *Afrikanische Masken.* Munich: Prestel Verlag. English Edition 1998

1997 *L'Autre Visage. Masques d'Afrique de la Collection Barbier-Mueller.* Paris: Sociéte Nouvelle Adam Brio.

Hailemariam, Gabreyesus

1991 *The Gurагué and their Culture.* New York: Vantage Press.

Hair, Paul E. H.

1969 "Some French Sources on Upper Guinea 1540–1575." *Bulletin de l'Institut Française de l'Afrique Noire* XXXI, (4).

1974 "Sources on Early Sierra Leone: 1) Beaulieu 1619." *Africana Research Bulletin* IV, (4): 41–50.

Hampton, Barbara L.

1982 "Music and Ritual Symbolism in the Ga Funeral." *Yearbook for Traditional Music,* (XIV): 75–105.

Hanna-Vergara, Emily

1996 "Masks of Leaves and Wood Among the Bwa of Burkina Faso." Ph. D. Dissertation. University of Iowa.

Harding, Frances

2002 *The Performance Arts in Africa: A Reader.* London: Routledge.

Harley

1941 "Notes on the Poro in Liberia." *Peabody Museum Papers* XIX, (2).

Harper, Peggy

1970 "Tsough: A Tiv Dance." *African Notes* VI, (1): 52–59.

Harter, Pierre

1993 "We Masks." in *Art of Côte d'Ivoire from the Collections of the Barbier-Mueller Museum*. Vol. 1. J.P. Barbier, ed. Geneva: Barbier-Mueller Museum.

Hastrup, Kirsten

1998 "Theater As a Site of Passage: Some Reflections on the Magic of Acting." in *Ritual, Performance, Media*. F. Hughes-Freeland, ed. New York: Routledge.

Heldman, Marilyn Eiseman, S.C. Munro-Hay, and Roderick Grierson

1993 *African Zion: The Sacred Art of Ethiopia*. New Haven and London: Yale University Press.

Henry, J.

1910 *L'Âme d'un Peuple Africain: les Bambara*. Paris.

Himmelheber, Hans

1960 *Negerkunst und Negerkünstler*. Braunschweig: Klinkhardt und Biermann.

Hobsbawm, Eric J., and Terence O. Ranger

1992 *The Invention of Tradition*. Cambridge: Cambridge University Press.

Højbjerg, C.K.

1995 "Staging the Invisible: Essays on Loma Ritual and Cultural Knowledge." Ph.D. Dissertation. University of Copenhagen.

Holas, Bohumil

1947 "Danses Masquées de la Basse-Côte." *Etudes Guinéennes (Conakry)* I: 61–67.

1952 *Les Masques Kono: Leur rôle dans la vie religieuse et politique*. Paris: Librairie Orientaliste Paul Geuthner S.A.

1969 *Animaux dans L'Art Ivorien*. Paris: Paul Geuther.

Houlberg, M.

1973 "Ibeji Images of the Yoruba." *African Arts* VI, (1).

Hughes-Freeland, Felicia

1998 *Ritual, Performance, Media*. New York: Routledge.

Hyde, Lewis

1998 *Trickster Makes His World: Mischief, Myth, and Art*. New York: Farrar, Straus and Giroux.

Idowu, E. Bolaji

1962 *Olódùmarè; God in Yoruba Belief*. London: Longman.

Jackson, Michael

1977 *The Kuranko: Dimensions of Social Reality in a West African Society*. New York: St. Martin's Press.

Jeffrey, David, and Peter Magubane

1986 "Pioneers in Their Own Land." *National Geographic* CLXIX, (2).

Jespers, Philippe

1995 "Mask and Utterance: the Analysis of an 'Auditory' in the Initiatory Society of the Komo (Minianka, Mali)." in *Objects, Signs of Africa*. Gent: Spoek-Ducaju & Zoon.

Johnson, Barbara C.

1986 *Four Dan Sculptors: Continuity and Change*. San Francisco: The Fine Arts Museum of San Francisco.

Jones, G.I.

1984 *The Art of Eastern Nigeria*. Cambridge: Cambridge University.

Jordán, Manuel

1996 "Tossing Life in a Basket: Art and Divination among Chokwe, Lunda, Luvale and Related Peoples of Northwestern Zambia." Ph.D. Dissertation. University of Iowa.

1998 *Chokwe! Art and Initiation among Chokwe and Related Peoples*. Munich: Prestel Verlag.

Kaeppler, Adrienne L.

1992 "*Ali'i* and *Maka'ainana*: The Representation of Hawaiians in Museums at Home and Abroad." in *Museums and Communities: the Politics of Public Culture*. I. Karp, ed. Washington: Smithsonian Institution Press.

Kasfir, Sidney

1988 *West African Masks and Cultural Systems*. Tervuren, Belgium: Musée royal de l'Afrique centrale.

1996 "African Art in a Suitcase." *Transition* VI, (1): 146–158.

Keita, S.O.Y., and A.J. Boyce

1996 "The Geographical Origins and Population Relationships of Early Ancient Egyptians." in *Egypt in Africa*. Indianapolis: Indianapolis Museum of Art.

Kendrick, A.F.

1921 *Catalogue of Textiles From Burying-Grounds in Egypt*. London: Victoria and Albert Museum.

Kjersmeier, Carl

1932 *Paa Fetishjagt i Afrika*. Copenhagen: Paul Branner.

Klopper, Sandra

1993 "Women's Work, or Engendering the Art of Beadwork in Southern Africa." in *Ezakwantu: Beadwork from the Eastern Cape*. E. Bedford, ed. Johannesburg: South African National Gallery.

Klumpp, Donna Rey

1987 "Maasai Art and Society: Age and Sex, Time and Space, Cash and Cattle (Kenya)." Ph.D. Dissertation. Columbia University.

Klumpp, Donna Rey, and Corinne Kratz

1993 "Aesthetics, Expertise, & Ethnicity: Okiek & Maasai Perspectives on Personal Ornament." in *Being Maasai: Ethnicity and Identity in East Africa*. T. Spear and R. Waller, eds. London: James Currey.

Knight, Natalie, and Suzanne Priebatsch

1983 *Ndebele Images*. South Africa.

Koloss, Hans-Joachim

1990 "Introduction." in *Art of Central Africa: Masterpieces from the Museum für Völkerkunde*. New York: The Metropolitan Museum of Art.

1990 *Art of Central Africa: Masterpieces from the Berlin Museum für Völkerkunde*. New York: The Metropolitan Museum of Art.

Krauss, Rosalind

1987 "Giacometti." in *"Primitivism" in 20th Century Art*. Vol. II. W. Rubin, ed. New York: The Museum of Modern Art

Kreamer, Christine Mullen

1986 "The Art and Ritual of the Moba of Northern Togo." Ph.D. Dissertation. Indiana University.

1987 "Moba Shrine Figures." *African Arts* XX, (2): 52–55, 82–83.

Laban, Rudolf

1975 *Laban's Principles of Dance and Movement Notation*. London: Macdonald & Evans.

Labi, Kwame A.

2003 "Fante Asafo Flags of Abandze and Kormantse: A Discourse between Rivals." *African Arts* XXXV, (40): 28–37, 92.

Lacan, Ph.

1942 *Grammaire et Dictionaire: Français-Soussou et Soussou-Français.* Bordeaux: Pères du Saint-Esprit.

Lamb, Alistair and Venice

1975 *West African Narrow Strip Weaving.* Washington: The Textile Museum.

Lamp, Frederick John

1978 "Frogs into Princes: the Temne Rabai Initiation." *African Arts* XI, (2): 34–49, 94.

1982 "Temne Rounds: the Arts as Spatial and Temporal Indicators in a West African Society." Ph.D. Dissertation. Yale University.

1983 "House of Stones: Memorial Art of Fifteenth-Century Sierra Leone." *The Art Bulletin* LXV, (2): 219–237.

1985 "Cosmos, Cosmetics, and the Spirit of Bondo." *African Arts* XIII, (3).

1992 *La Guinée et ses Heritages Culturels.* Conakry: United States Information Service (USIS), U.S. Embassy.

1996 "Dancing the Hare: Appropriation of the Imagery of Mande Power Among the Baga." in *The Younger Brother in Mande: Kinship and Politics in West Africa.* J. Jansen and C. Zobel, eds. Leiden: Leiden University.

1996 *Art of the Baga: A Drama of Cultural Reinvention.* New York: Museum for African Art.

2003 "Set of Four Viscera Jars with Stoppers." (Unpublished paper. Baltimore: The Baltimore Museum of Art)

Lan, David

1985 *Guns and Rain: Guerrillas and Spirit Mediums in Zimbabwe.* Berkeley: University of California Press.

Lawal, Babatunde

1974 "Some Aspects of Yoruba Belief." *British Journal of Aesthetics* 15, (3): 239–249.

1996 *The Gelede Spectacle: Art, Gender, and Social Harmony in an African Culture.* Seattle: University of Washington Press.

2001 "Àwòrán: Representing the Self and Its Metaphysical Other in Yoruba Art." *Art Bulletin* 83, (3): 498–526.

Leder, Drew

1990 *The Absent Body.* Chicago: University of Chicago Press.

Lehuard, Raoul

1989 *Art Bakongo: Les Centres de Style.* Arnouville-lès-Gonesse: Arts d'Afrique Noir.

Lexikon der Ägyptologie

1975–1992 Helck, Wolfgang, and Eberhard Otto, eds. Wiesbaden: Otto Harrassowitz. 7 vols. Volume 1 (1975): cs. 232–236, 610–614; Volume 3 (1980): 37–41, 316–319, 811–816; Volume 5 (1984): 1055–1074.

Ley, Graham

1999 *From Mimesis to Interculturalism: Readings of Theatrical Theory Before and After 'Modernism'.* Devon: University of Exeter Press.

Lieberenz, Paul

1907 *Das Rätsel Abessinien.* Leipzig.

Lifschitz, Edward

1988 "Hearing is Believing: Acoustic Masks and Spirit Manifestation." in *West African Masks and Cultural Systems.* S. Kasfir, ed. Tervuren: Musée royal de l'Afrique centrale.

Lise, Giorgio

1988 *Egyptian Amulets.* Milan: BE-MA editrice.

Little, Kenneth L.

1951 *The Mende of Sierra Leone.* London: Routledge & Kegan Paul.

Littlejohn, James

1963 "Temne Space." *Anthropological Quarterly* XXXVI, (1–17).

Lucas, Alfred

1989 *Ancient Egyptian Materials and Industries.* London: Histories & Mysteries of Man.

MacCormack, Carol P.

1979 "Sande: The Public Face of a Secret Society." in *The New Religions of Africa.* B. Jules-Rosette, ed. Norwood, NJ: Ablex.

MacGaffey, W.

1986 *Religion and Society in Central Africa: The BaKongo of Lower Zaire.* Chicago: University of Chicago Press.

1991 *Art and Healing of the BaKongo Commented by Themselves.* Bloomington: Indiana University Press.

2000 *Kongo Political Culture.* Bloomington: Indiana University Press.

Mack, John

1980 "Textiles of Africa. D. Idiens and K. Ponting, eds. Bath (Avon): Pasold Research Fund.

Macleod, T.M.

1925 "Report on the Western Areas of Okwoga." Kaduna, Nigeria: National Archives, Agency Mark K.2012, Vol. 1.

Maguire, Eunice Dauterman

1999 *Weavings from Roman, Byzantine, and Islamic Egypt: The Rich Life and the Dance.* Urbana-Champaigne: University of Illinois Press.

Mansfield, Alfred

1908 *Urwald-Dokumente.* Berlin: Dietrich Reimer.

Mariko, Kélétigui Abdourahmane

1981 *Le Monde mystérieux des chasseurs traditionnels.* Paris: Nouvelles Éditions Africaines.

Marion, Sheila

1997 "Toward a New Paradigm for Exploring Dance Notation." in *International Council of Kinetography Laban: Proceedings of the 20th Biennial Conference.* New York: ICKL.

McClusky, Pamela

2002 *Art from Africa: Long Steps Never Broke a Back.* Seattle: Seattle Art Museum in association with Lund Humphries.

McLeod, M.D.

1971 "Goldweights of Asante." *African Arts* V, (1).

1981 *The Asante.* London: Oxford University Press.

McNaughton, Patrick

1979 *Secret Sculptures of Komo: Art and Power in Bamana (Bambara) Initiation Associations.* Philadelphia: Institute for the Study of Human Issues.

1988 *The Mande Blacksmiths: Knowledge, Power, and Art in West Africa.* Bloomington: Indiana University Press.

2001 "The Power Associations: *Kòmò.*" in *Bamana: the Art of Existence in Mali.* J.-P. Colleyn, ed. New York, Zurich, Gent: Museum for African Art, Museum Rietberg, Spoek-Ducaju & Zoon.

Mengrelis, T.

1948 "La Voix des Niamou chez les Guerzé." *Notes Africaines* 38.

1952 "Le Sens des masques dans l'initiation des Guerzés." *Africa* 22: 257–264.

Messenger, John C.

1973 "The Role of the Carver in Anang Society." in *The Traditional Artist in African Societies.* W. d'Azevedo, ed. Bloomington: Indiana University Press.

Meyer, Piet

1981 *Kunst und Religion der Lobi.* Zurich: Museum Rietberg.

Mobolade, T.

1971 "Ibeji Custom in Yorubaland." *African Arts* IV, (3).

Monteil, C.

1924 *Les Bambara du Ségou et du Kaarta.* Paris.

Morris, David R. N. M.

2002 "Driekopseiland and 'the rain's magic powers': History and landscape in a new interpretation of a Northern Cape rock engraving site." Unpublished MA thesis. University of the

Western Cape.

Morris, Jean, and Eleanor Preston-Whyte

1994 *Speaking with Beads.* New York: Thames and Hudson.

Mudiji-Selnge, Malutshi

1981 "Mask (Kiphoko)." in *For Spirits and Kings. African Art from the Tishman Collection.* S. Vogel, ed. New York: The Metropolitan Museum of Art.

Murdock, George Peter

1959 *Africa: Its Peoples and Their Culture History.* New York: McGraw-Hill Book Company.

Ndiaye, Francine

1994 *Secrets d'Initiés. Masques d'Afrique Noire dans les Collections du Musée de l'Homme.* Paris: Éditions Sépia.

Neyt, François

1985 *The Arts of the Benue.* [S. I.]: Editions Hawaiian Agronomics.

1988 "36 Neckrest." in *Expressions of Belief: Masterpieces of African, Oceanic and Indonesian Art from the Museum voor Volkenkunde, Rotterdam.* S. Greub, ed. New York: Rizzoli.

1993 "South-East Zaire: Masks of the Luba, Hemba, and Tawa." in *Face of the Spirits: Masks from the Zaire Basin.* F. Herreman and C. Petridis, eds. Ghent: Snoeck-Ducaju & Zoon.

1994 *Luba: To the Sources of the Zaire.* Paris: Editions Dapper.

Niane, Djibril Tamsir

1982 "Nimba, Goddess of Fertility in Baga Land." *Afrique Histoire,* (1): 63–64.

Nicklin, Keith

1974 "Nigerian Skin-covered Masks." *African Arts* VII, (3): 8–15, 67–68, 92.

1979 "Skin-covered Masks of Cameroon." *African Arts* XII, (2): 54–59, 91.

Nicklin, Keith, and Jill Salmons

1984 "Cross River Art Styles." *African Arts* XVIII, (1): 28–43.

1988 "Ikem: The History of a Masquerade in Southeast Nigeria." in *West African Masks and Cultural Systems.* S. Kasfir, ed. Tervuren: Musée royal de l'Afrique centrale.

Nooter, Mary H. (Mary Nooter Roberts)

1992 "No. 171: Mask." in *Kings of Africa: Art and Authority in Central Africa.* E. Beumers and H.-J. Koloss, eds. Maastricht: Foundation Kings of Africa.

1992 "Keepers of Secrets: Rulers and Diviners in Central Africa." *FACES* 9, (3): 14–17.

Nooter Roberts, Mary

1996 "No. 94 Anthropomorphic Headrest." in *Masterpieces from Central Africa.* G. Verswijver, E. de Palmenaer, V. Baeke, and A.-M. Bouttiaux-Ndiaye, eds. Tervuren: Musée royal de l'Afrique centrale.

Northern, Tamara

1984 *The Art of Cameroon.* Washington: Smithsonian Institution Press.

Olbrechts, Frans M.

1959 *Les Arts Plastiques du Congo Belge.* Brussels: Editions Erasme, S.A.

Ottenberg, Simon

1975 *Masked Rituals of Afikpo: The Context of an African Art.* Seattle: University of Washington Press.

Parrinder, Geoffrey

1956 *The Story of Ketu.* Ibadan, Nigeria: University of Ibadan Press.

Parsons, Robert T.

1964 *Religion in an African Society.* Leiden: E. J. Brill.

Partridge, Charles

1905 *Cross River Natives.* London: Hutchinson and Co.

1906 "Honoring Ejagham Women." *African Arts* XXXI, (2): 38–49, 92–93.

Pemberton, John III, and Funso S. Afolayan

1996 *Yoruba Sacred Kingship: "A Power like that of the Gods".* Washington: Smithsonian Institution Press.

Pemberton, John III

2000 *Insight and Artistry in African Divination.* Washington: Smithsonian Institution Press.

Perrois, Louis

1968 *La Circoncision Bakota (Gabon).* Vol V, (1). Paris: ORSTOM

1970 *Chronique du Pays Gabon.* Vol. VII, (2). Paris: ORSTOM

1977 *Problèmes d'Analyse de la Sculpture Traditionelle du Gabon.* No. 32

1979 *Arts du Gabon.* Paris: ORSTOM

1981 "No. 118 Janus Reliquary Figure (Kota)." And "No. 119 Reliquary Figure (Kota)" in *For Spirits and Kings: African Art from the Tishman Collection.* S. Vogel, ed. New York: The Metropolitan Museum of Art.

Petridis, Constantijn

1992 *Wooden Masks of the Kasai Pende.* H. Burssens, E. Bruyninx, and R. Haeseryn, eds. Ghent: Department of Ethnic Art, University of Ghent.

1993 "Pende Mask Styles." in *Face of the Spirits: Masks from the Zaire Basin.* F. Herreman, ed. Ghent: Snoeck-Ducaju & Zoon.

Phillips, R. B.

1995 *Representing Woman: Sande Masquerades of the Mende of Sierra Leone.* Los Angeles: Fowler Museum of Cultural History, UCLA.

Phillips, T.

1996 *Africa: The Art of a Continent.* Munich: Prestel Verlag.

Picton, John
1990 "What's in a Mask." *African Languages and Cultures* III, (2): 181–202.

Pinch, Geraldine
1994 *Magic in Ancient Egypt.* London: British Museum.

Price, Sally
1989 *Primitive Art in Civilized Places.* Chicago: University of Chicago Press.

Prussin, Labelle
1986 *Hatumere: Islamic Design in West Africa.* Berkeley: University of California Press.

1987 "Gabra Containers." *African Arts* XX, (2): 36–45, 81–82.

Quintino, Fernando R. Rogado
1964 "A pintura e a escultura no Guiné Portuguesa." *Boletim Cultural da Guiné Portuguesa* XIX, (75) (July): 277–88.

Rattray, R.S..
1927 *Religion and Art in Ashanti.* London: Oxford University Press.

Read, Daniel B.
2001 "Pop Goes the Sacred: Dan mask Performance and popular Culture in Postcolonial Côte d'Ivoire." *Africa Today,* vol. 48 no. 4, pp. 67–87.

Read, Daniel B.
2003 *Dan Ge Performance: Masks and Music in Contemporary Côte d'Ivoire.* Bloomington: Indiana University Press.

Read, C.H., and O.M. Dalton
1899 *Antiquities of the City of Benin and from Other Parts of West Africa in the British Museum.* London: William Clowes & Sons.

Reisner, George
1899 "The Dated Canopic Jars of the Gizeh Museum." *ZAS,* (37): 61–72.

Roache, L.E.
1974 "Art of the Ifa Oracle." *African Arts* VIII, (1): 20–25, 87.

Roberts, Mary Nooter
1995 "Headrest." in *Africa: The Art of a Continent.* T. Phillips, ed. Munich: Prestel Verlag.

Roberts, Mary Nooter, and Allen F. Roberts
1996 *Memory: Luba Art and the Making of History.* New York: The Museum for African Art.

Robins, Gay
1997 *The Art of Ancient Egypt.* Cambridge: Harvard University Press.

Ross, Doran H.
1979 *Fighting with Art: Appliquéd Flags of the Fante Asafo.* Los Angeles: Fowler Museum of Cultural History, UCLA.

1994 *Visions of Africa: the Jerome L. Joss Collection of African Art at UCLA.* Los Angeles: Fowler Museum of Cultural History, UCLA.

1996 "Akan." in *The Dictionary of Art.* Vol. 1. Willard, OH: Macmillan.

Roy, Christopher
1999 *Kilengi: African Art from the Bareiss Collection.* Seattle: University of Washington Press.

Rubin, Arnold
1974 *African Accumulative Sculpture: Power and Display.* New York: Pace Gallery.

Rubin, William
1987 *"Primitivism" in 20th Century Art.* New York: The Museum of Modern Art

Rütimeyer, L.
1910 "Über westafrikanische Steinidole." *Internationales Archiv für Ethnographie* XIV.

Saitoti, Tepilit Ole
1980 *Maasai.* New York: Harry N. Abrams.

Salmons, Jill
1992 "The Arts of the Ogoni." in *Ways of the Rivers.* M. Anderson and P. Peek, eds. Los Angeles: Fowler Museum of Cultural History, UCLA.

Sankan, S.S. Ole
1970 *The Maasai.* Nairobi: East African Literature Bureau.

Sanogo, M.
1985 "Contribution à l'étude du Koma une société initiation masculine chez les Worodougou de Côte d'Ivoire (Région de Séguela)." Thèse de doctorat de 3ème cycle (Ethnologie). Ecole des Hautes Etudes en Sciences Sociales.

Sarró, Ramon
2002 "The Iconoclastic Meal: Destroying Objects and Eating Secrets among the Baga of Guinea." in *Iconoclash: Beyond the Image Wars in Science, Religion and Art.* B. Latour and P. Weibel, eds. Cambridge, MA: MIT Press.

Schaedler, Karl-Ferdinand
1987 *Weaving in Africa South of the Sahara.* Munich: Panterra-Verlag.

Schechner, Richard
1988 *Performance Theory.* New York: Routledge.

Scheel, Walter
1978 *Sahara.* Cologne: Rautenstrauch-Joest Museum für Völkerkunde.

Schieffelin, Edward L.
1998 "Problematizing Performance." in *Ritual, Performance, Media.* F. Hughes-Freeland, ed. New York: Routledge.

Schlenker, Christian F.
1851 "West African Mission." *Church Missionary Record* XXII, June: 121–133.

Schneider, E.
1986 "Paint, Pride and Politics: Aesthetics and Meaning in Transvaal Ndebele Wall-Art." Ph.D. Thesis. University of the Witwatersrand, Johannesburg.

Schoske, Sylvia, and Dietrich Wildung
1985 *Ägyptische Kunst München: Katalog-Handbuch zur Staatlichen Sammlung Ägyptischer Kunst München.* Munich: Karl M. Lipp Verlag.

Schwartz, Alfred
1971 *Traditions et changements dans la société guéré.* Paris: ORSTOM.

Scott, Gerry
1986 *Ancient Egyptian Art at Yale.* New Haven: Yale University Art Gallery.

Sethe, Kurt
1934 "Zur Geschichte der Einbalsamierung bei den Ägyptern und einiger damit verbundener Bräuche." *Sitzungsberichte der Preussischen Akademie der Wissenschaften, Philosophisch-Historische Klasse.* 13: 211–39.

Shaw, Ian

2000 *The Oxford History of Ancient Egypt.* Oxford: Oxford University Press.

Sieber, Roy

1972 *African Textiles and Decorative Arts.* New York: The Museum of Modern Art.

Sieber, Roy, and Michael Kan

1995 "Western Congo Basin and Ogowé River." in *African Masterworks in the Detroit Institute of Arts.* Washington: Smithsonian Institution Press.

Siegman, W.C., and J. Perani

1980 "Men's Masquerades of Sierra Leone and Liberia." *Ethnologische Zeitschrift Zürich* 1: 25–40.

Siegman, W.C., and C.E. Schmidt

1977 *Rock of the Ancestors: Liberian Art and Culture from the Collections of the Africana Museum.* Suakoko, Liberia: Cuttington University College.

Silverman, Raymond

1994 *Ethiopia: Traditions of Creativity.* East Lansing: Michigan State University Museum.

Siroto, Leon

1968 "The Face of the Bwiti." *African Arts* I, (3).

Sklar, Diedre

2001 *Dancing with the Virgin: Body and Faith in the Fiesta of Tortugas, New Mexico.* Berkeley: University of California Press.

Smith, J.N.

1919 "Okpoto Dances." Kaduna, Nigeria: National Archives, Agency Mark K.2012, Vol. 1

Smith, Robert

1988 *Kingdoms of the Yoruba.* Madison: University of Wisconsin Press.

Steiner, Christopher B.

1994 *African Art in Transit.* Cambridge: Cambridge University Press.

2002 "The Taste of Angels in the Art of Darkness." in *Art History and Its Institutions: Foundations of a Discipline.* E. Mansfield, ed. New York: Routledge.

Stevens, Phillips

1966 "Nupe Wood-carving." *Nigeria Magazine,* (88): 21–35.

Stoller, Paul

1989 *The Taste of Ethnographic Things: the Senses in Anthropology.* Philadelphia: University of Pennsylvania Press.

Stone, Ruth M.

1995 "African Music Performed." in *Africa.* P. Martin and P. O'Meara, eds. Bloomington: Indiana University Press.

1998 "African Music in a Constellation of Arts." in *Africa: The Garland Encyclopedia of World Music, Volume 1.* New York: Garland Publishing.

Strother, Z.S.

1993 "Eastern Pende Constructions of Secrecy." in *Secrecy: African Art that Conceals and Reveals.* M.H. Nooter, ed. Munich: Prestel Verlag.

1998 *Inventing Masks: Agency and History in the Art of the Central Pende.* Chicago: University of Chicago Press.

Sweeney, James Johnson

1935 *African Negro Art.* New York: The Museum of Modern Art.

Talbot, P. Amaury

1926 *Peoples of Southern Nigeria.* 4 vols. London: Oxford University Press.

Tambiah, S.J.

1981 *A Performative Approach to Ritual.* London: British Academy.

Tauxier, Louis

1921 *Le Noir de Bondoukou.* Paris: E. Leroux.

Thompson, Robert Farris

1971 "Sons of Thunder." *African Arts* IV, (3).

1973 "Aesthetic of the Cool." *African Arts* VII, (1).

1974 *African Art in Motion: Icon and Art in the Collection of Katherine Coryton White.* Berkeley: University of California Press.

1993 *Face of the Gods: Arts and Altars of Africa and the African Americas.* New York: The Museum for African Art.

Thompson, Robert Farris, and Joseph Cornet

1981 *The Four Moments of the Sun.* Washington: National Gallery of Art.

Tierou, A.

1975 *La vérité première du second visage africain.* Paris: Maisonneuve et Larose.

Torday, E.

1925 *On the Trail of the Bushongo.* London: Seeley.

Torday, E., and T.A. Joyce

1910 *Notes Ethnographiques sur les peuples communément appelés Bakuba, ainsi que sur les peuplades apparentées.* Tervuren: Musée royal de l'Afrique centrale.

Turner, Victor W.

1967 *The Forest of Symbols: Aspects of Ndembu Ritual.* Ithaca: Cornell University Press.

1986 *The Anthropology of Performance.* New York: Performing Arts Journal Publications.

Vandenhoute, P.J.

1948 "Classification du Masque Dan et Guéré de la Côte d'Ivoire Occidentale (A.O.F.)." Leiden: E.J. Brill.

Vansina, Jan

1954 "Les tribus Ba-Kuba et les peuplades apparentées." in *Ethnographic Monographs. No. 1.* Tervuren: Musée royal de l'Afrique centrale.

1955 "Initiation Rituals of the Bushong." *Africa* 25: 138–153.

1964 *Le Royaume Kuba.* Tervuren: Musée royal de l'Afrique centrale.

1973 "Initiation Rituals of the Bushong." in *Peoples and Cultures of Africa.* E. Skinner, ed. New York: American Museum of Natural History.

1978 *The Children of Woot: A History of the Kuba Peoples.* Madison: University of Wisconsin Press.

1984 *Art History in Africa.* London: Longman.

1985 *Oral Tradition as History.* Madison: University of Wisconsin Press.

1992 "Palm Wine Cup: Standing Female." in *Kings of Africa: Art and Authority in Central Africa.* E. Beumers and H.-J. Koloss, eds. Maastricht: Foundation Kings of Africa.

Verger-Fèvre, M.N.

1980 *Masques de l'Ouest de la Côte d'Ivoire dans les Collections Publiques Français.* 2 vols. Paris: Mémoire de l'Ecole du Louvre.

Vogel, Susan

1973 "People of Wood: Baule Figure Sculpture." *Art Journal* XXX: 23–26.

1977 "Baule Art as the Expression of a World View." Ph. D. Dissertation. New York University.

1980 *Beauty in the Eye of the Baule: Aesthetics and Cultural Values*: Working Papers in the Traditional Arts, No. 6, Institute for the Study of Human Issues, Philadelphia.

1981 *For Spirits and Kings: African Art from the Tishman Collection.* New York: The Metropolitan Museum of Art.

1986 "Baule Figure Sculpture." in *Arte Africa.* E. Bassani, ed: Edizioni Panini.

1989 *ART/artifact: African Art in Anthropology Collections.* New York: The Center for African Art.

1997 *Baule: African Art Western Eyes.* New Haven: Yale University Press.

La Voix de Notre-Dame

November 1926–May 1939 (Les Pères de Saint-Esprit, Conakry), I, I–XIV, 7

Wastiau, Boris

1998 "Art, God and Spirit Possession in the Interpretation of Illness among the Luvale and Related Peoples." in *Chokwe!* M. Jordán, ed. Munich: Prestel Verlag.

Welmers, W.

1949 "Secret Medicines, Magic, and Rites of the Kpelle Tribe in Liberia." *Southwestern Journal of Anthropology*, (5): 208–243.

Williams, Drid

1968 "The Dance of the Bedu Moon." *African Arts* II, (1): 18–21, 72.

1999 "Fieldwork." in *Dance in the Field: Theory, Methods and Issues in Dance Ethnography.* T. Buckland, ed. New York: St. Martin's Press.

2000 *Anthropology and Human Movement: Searching for Origins.* Lanham, MD: Scarecrow.

Wood, Marilee

1996 "Zulu Beadwork." in *Zulu Treasures: Of Kings and Commoners—A Celebration of the Material Culture of the Zulu People.* Durban: KwaZulu Cultural Museum and the Local History Museums.

The Wurtzburger Collection of African Sculpture

1958 Baltimore: The Baltimore Museum of Art.

Zahan, Dominique

1974 *The Bambara.* Leiden: E.J. Brill.

1980 *Antilopes du Soleil: Arts et Rites Agraires d'Afrique Noire.* Vienna: Edition A. Schendl.

Zemp, Hugo

1971 *Musique Dan: La musique dans la pensée et la vie sociale d'une société africaine.* Paris: Cahiers de l'Homme.

Zuckerkandl, V.

1956 *Sound and Symbol: Music and the External World.* W. Trask, transl. Princeton: Princeton University Press.

Zwernemann, Jürgen

1998 *Studien zur Kultur der Moba (Nord-Togo).* Cologne: Rüdiger Köppe Verlag.

INDEX OF ETHNIC GROUPS

Names of peoples to whom works illustrated in this volume are attributed. Countries are in italics. Numbers refer to pages.

A-Tshol dancer with musicians and followers. A-Tshol, the bird, is the companion of a-Bil-ña-Tshol, the canoe (p. 164). Baga Sitem, Guinea
Photo: Frederick John Lamp, 1987

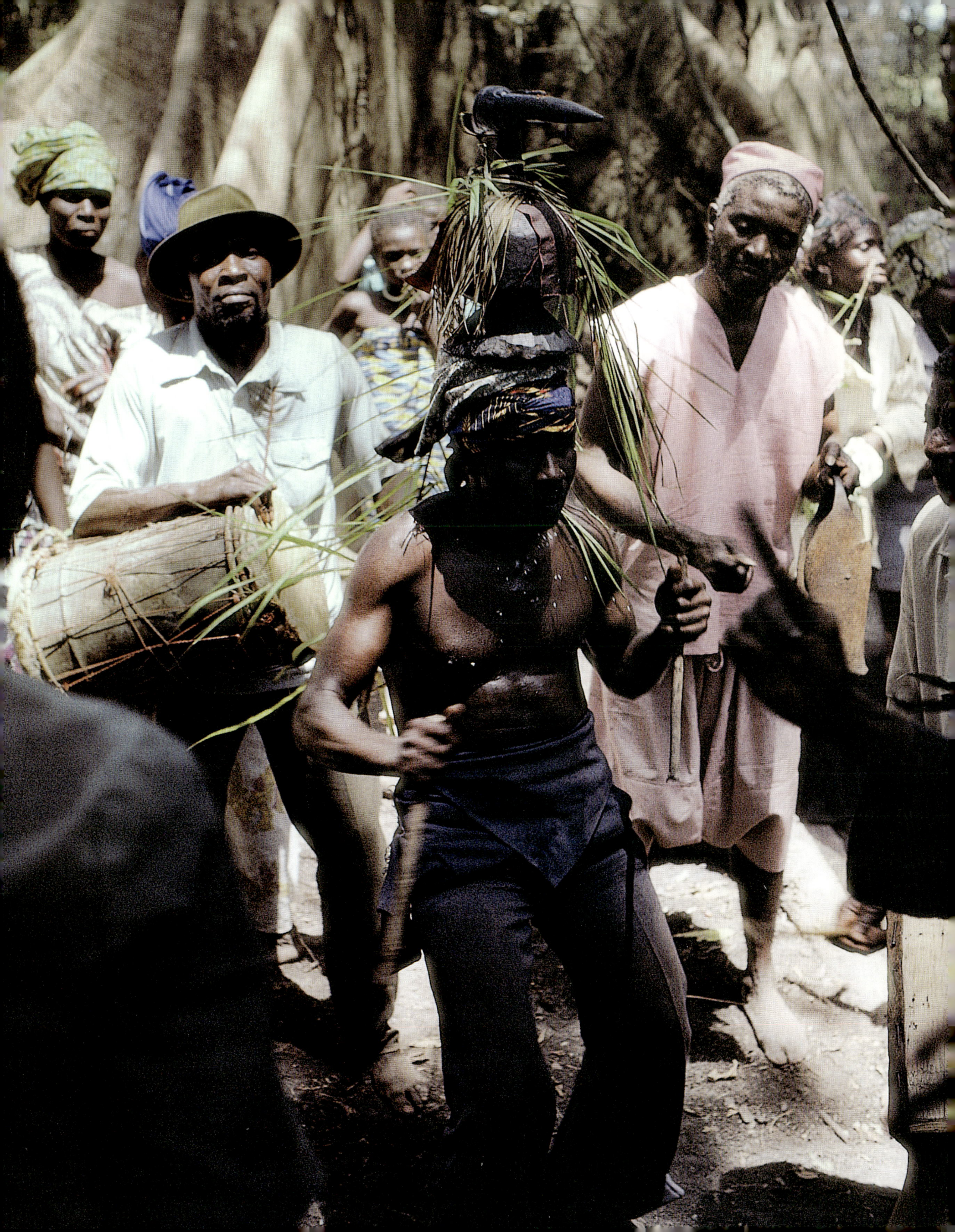

Published on the 90th anniversary of the founding of
The Baltimore Museum of Art, 2004.

This catalogue has been made possible through generous support from The St. Paul Companies, Inc. and the National Endowment for the Arts.

Additional support provided by The Baltimore Museum of Art's Andrew W. Mellon Foundation Publication Endowment Fund.

Front cover: Ngady Mwaash performs at a funeral for an initiated man. Southern Kuba, Community of Boganciala, Congo (Kinshasa). Photo: Patricia Darish and David A. Binkley, 1982, see p. 173.
p. 1: A Shangó possession priestess dancing with her Ose. Yoruba, Ohori subgroup, Nigeria. Photo: Henry John Drewal, 1975, see p. 112.
pp. 2/3: Dance of D'mba preceded by dancing male drummers and followed by women singers. Baga, Sitem subgroup, Guinea. Photo: Frederick John Lamp.
pp. 4/5: Zeu singers preparing to perform at the *kpaala*. Senufo, Nafoun, Ivory Coast. Photo: Till Förster, 1991, see pp. 104/05.

Library of Congress Control Number: 2003116557

British Library Cataloguing-in-Publication Data: a catalogue record for this book is available from the British Library

Deutsche Bibliothek holds a record of this publication in the Deutsche Nationalbibliografie; detailed bibliographical data can be found under: http://dnb.ddb.de

Prestel books are available worldwide. Please contact your nearest bookseller ore one of the following Prestel offices for information concerning your local distributor:

Prestel Verlag
Königinstraße 9, 80539 Munich
Tel. +49(89)38 17 09-0; Fax 49(89)38 17 09-35

Prestel Publishing Ltd.
4 Bloomsbury Place, London WC1A 2QA
Tel. +44(020)7323-5004; Fax +44(020)7636-8004

Prestel Publishing
900 Broadway, suite 603, New York, NY 10003
Tel. +1(212)995-2720; Fax +1(212)995-2733

www.prestel.com

The Baltimore Museum of Art
Project editor: Frederick John Lamp
Publications manager: Michelle Boardman

Prestel Publishing
Editorial direction: Peter Stepan
Copy-editing: Christopher Wynne
Designed and typeset by WIGEL, Munich
Originations by ReproLine Genceller, Munich
Printed and bound by Sellier-Druck, Freising

Printed in Germany on acid-free paper

ISBN 3-7913-3036-5